Educating Students with Severe and Multiple Disabilities

Educating Students with Severe and Multiple Disabilities

A Collaborative Approach

Fifth Edition

edited by

Fred P. Orelove, Ph.D.
Virginia Commonwealth University
Richmond

Dick Sobsey, Ed.D.
University of Alberta
Edmonton, Alberta, Canada

and

Donna L. Gilles, Ed.D.
Virginia Commonwealth University
Richmond

·P A U L·H·
BROOKES
PUBLISHING Cº ®

Baltimore • London • Sydney

Paul H. Brookes Publishing Co.
Post Office Box 10624
Baltimore, Maryland 21285-0624
USA

www.brookespublishing.com

Typeset by Absolute Service, Inc., Towson, Maryland.
Manufactured in the United States of America by Sheridan Books, Chelsea, Michigan.
Cover Art: Oil Painting by Jack M. Brandt

The information provided in this book is in no way meant to substitute for a medical or mental health practitioner's advice or expert opinion. Readers should consult a health or mental health professional if they are interested in more information.

Some case studies include real people, whereas others are composites based on the authors' experiences. Any real names and identifying details are used by permission.

Purchasers of *Educating Students with Severe and Multiple Disabilities: A Collaborative Approach, Fifth Edition* may download free of charge from the Brookes Publishing website various resources related to the book. Forms and PowerPoints are available at the following address: brookespublishing.com/orelove. Use of these materials is granted for educational purposes only; the duplication and distribution of these materials for a fee is prohibited.

All royalties earned on this publication will be donated to the MECP2 Duplication Syndrome Fund of the Rett Syndrome Research Trust.

Library of Congress Cataloging-in-Publication Data

The Library of Congress has cataloged the print edition as follows:

Names: Orelove, Fred P., 1951- editor. | Sobsey, Richard, editor. | Gilles, Donna L., editor
Title: Educating students with severe and multiple disabilities : a collaborative approach / edited by Fred P. Orelove, Dick Sobsey, Donna L. Gilles; with invited contributors.
Description: Fifth edition. | Baltimore, Maryland : Brookes Publishing, 2017. | Includes bibliographical references and index. Identifiers: LCCN 2016005307 (print) | LCCN 2016006504 (ebook) | ISBN 9781598576542 (paperback) | ISBN 9781598578164 (pdf) | ISBN 9781598578133 (epub)
Subjects: LCSH: Children with disabilities--Education. | Children with disabilities--Care. | BISAC: EDUCATION / Special Education / General. EDUCATION / Special Education / Mental Disabilities. | EDUCATION / Teaching Methods & Materials / General.
Classification: LCC LC4015 .O68 2016 (print) | LCC LC4015 (ebook) | DDC 371.9—dc23
LC record available at http://lccn.loc.gov/2016005307

British Library Cataloguing in Publication data are available from the British Library.

2020   2019   2018   2017   2016

10   9   8   7   6   5   4   3   2   1

Contents

About the Online Companion Materials

Purchasers of this book will find PowerPoints for Chapters 1–13 for course or professional development use at **brookespublishing.com/orelove**.

BLANK FORMS

Purchasers of this book may download, print, and/or photocopy the following blank forms for educational or professional use: Figure 3.2; Figure 5.2; Figure 6.1; Figure 7.3; Figure 8.2; Figure 10.2; Figure 11.4. These materials are included with the print book and are also available at **brookespublishing.com/orelove** for both print and e-book buyers.

About the Editors

Fred P. Orelove, Ph.D., Professor Emeritus, Special Education and Disability Policy, Virginia Commonwealth University, Richmond, Virginia

Dr. Orelove founded and served as director of the teacher preparation program in severe disabilities at Virginia Commonwealth University from 1981 to 2011. He also served for 20 years as Executive Director of the Partnership for People with Disabilities, Virginia's university center for excellence in developmental disabilities. Since the 1970s, Dr. Orelove has taught children and has directed numerous training and demonstration projects related to individuals with disabilities. In addition to this book, he has co-authored two books on teamwork and one on inclusive education. In his retirement, Dr. Orelove is engaged in nonprofit work in Richmond, Virginia, including working for an inclusive performing arts program and volunteering with children who have been traumatized.

Dick Sobsey, Ed.D., Professor Emeritus, Educational Psychology, University of Alberta, Edmonton, Alberta, Canada

Dr. Sobsey has worked with children and adults with severe and multiple disabilities since 1968 as a nurse, teacher, and researcher. He taught courses on teaching students with severe disabilities and inclusive education at the University of Alberta from 1982 to 2005. He also served as Director of the J.P. Das Centre on Developmental and Learning Disabilities from 1994–2008 and the John Dossetor Health Ethics Centre from 2006 to 2011. He is the father of an adult son with severe and multiple disabilities due to MECP2 (methyl CpG binding protein 2) duplication syndrome.

Donna L. Gilles, Ed.D., Associate Professor, Special Education and Disability Policy, Virginia Commonwealth University, Richmond, Virginia

Dr. Gilles is Executive Director of the Partnership for People with Disabilities (Virginia's UCEDD). She taught students with significant disabilities in Maryland public schools for 6 years while earning a master's degree in educating students with severe disabilities. After earning her doctorate, Dr. Gilles directed a variety of teacher preparation, professional development, and technical assistance projects at the University of Maryland and the University of Florida, focusing on students with severe and multiple disabilities, autism, and sensory disabilities. She served on the Executive Board of TASH for 7 years, including 3 years as board president. Dr. Gilles currently directs the severe disabilities teacher preparation program at Virginia Commonwealth University.

About the Contributors

Katherine Ahlgren Bouchard, Ph.D., is currently a Content Specialist in Special Education at the Madison Metropolitan School District. Dr. Bouchard received her Ph.D. from the University of Wisconsin-Madison in Special Education. In addition to facilitating professional development experiences for educators seeking to universally design instruction for all students, she also supports schools in developing infrastructure necessary to support inclusive environments.

Rachel Brady, PT, DPT, M.S., is a physical therapist and research assistant professor at the Georgetown University Center for Child and Human Development. She coordinates and provides professional development for early childhood intervention and special education providers around best practices for program planning and providing services.

Julie Causton, Ph.D., is Professor in the Inclusive and Special Education Program in the Department of Teaching and Leadership at Syracuse University. Her teaching, research, and consulting are guided by a passion for inclusive education. She teaches graduate and undergraduate courses focused on including students with disabilities, supporting behavior, differentiation, special education law, lesson design, and adaptation.

Deborah Chen, Ph.D., is a Professor of the Department of Special Education at California State University, Northridge, where she coordinates the early childhood special education program. Her research and publications focus on collaborating with families of diverse cultural and linguistic backgrounds, supporting the learning and development of young children with multiple disabilities and sensory impairments, and promoting caregiver–child interactions.

Chigee J. Cloninger, Ph.D., has been a teacher of children and adults with and without disabilities for many years. Even in leadership or research positions, teaching—in the sense of bringing about change—has been a key component of her work. Her interests in creative problem-solving approaches, communication, and learning processes are integral to her work in individualized education and leadership. Dr. Cloninger is Professor Emerita from The University of Vermont, having been a faculty member and executive director of The Center on Disability and Community Inclusion.

Julie A. Durando, Ed.D., directs the Virginia Project for Children and Young Adults with Deaf-Blindness at the Partnership for People with Disabilities at Virginia Commonwealth University. She served children with multiple disabilities and sensory impairments, including deafblindness, for 8 years as both a classroom and itinerant teacher in central Florida. She completed her doctorate in special education from the University of Northern Colorado as a National Center for Leadership in Visual Impairment Fellow. Dr. Durando's research and writing focus on early braille literacy experiences and instruction for children with sensory impairments and multiple disabilities.

June E. Downing, Ph.D. (1950-2011), was named Professor Emerita of Special Education at California State University, Northridge, and served as an Associate Professor in Special Education at the University of Arizona. Dr. Downing was a national leader in the field of special education, a model advocate for individuals with severe and multiple disabilities, and a champion of inclusive education. Having begun her special education career as a teacher of students with visual impairments and multiple disabilities, including deafblindness, she focused on ensuring that teachers could understand and implement best practice in the inclusive classroom, and that students with severe and multiple disabilities experienced positive outcomes from social, communication, and academic instruction. We made a conscious decision to carry her legacy forward by maintaining her presence in this edition, and we thank Dr. Pat Mirenda for supporting us in this endeavor.

Kathleen Gee, Ph.D., is a professor in the Departments of Teacher Credentialing and Graduate and Professional Studies in the College of Education at California State University, Sacramento. She has been a teacher and a teacher educator. Dr. Gee also has directed numerous demonstration and research projects in authentic school settings focused on the inclusion of students with the most intensive support needs. She is a frequent consultant and inservice training provider related to quality services for children and youth with the most intensive support needs.

Kiel Harell, Ph.D., is an instructor in elementary and secondary education at the University of Minnesota, Morris. He teaches classes on foundations of education and inclusive teaching practice. He is currently a doctoral candidate at the University of Wisconsin–Madison.

Kathryn Wolff Heller, Ph.D., RN, is Professor Emerita at Georgia State University. Dr. Heller currently draws from her nursing and special education careers to conduct research and provide instruction to teachers and nurses on children and adults with physical and health impairments. One of her primary interests is on providing effective educational instruction and health care for children with physical and health impairments.

Carole K. Ivey, Ph.D., OTR/L, is an assistant professor with the Department of Occupational Therapy, School of Allied Health Professions, and is the LEND faculty advisor for occupational therapy (OT) at Virginia Commonwealth University in Richmond, Virginia. She received her bachelor's and master's degree in OT and her Ph.D. in special education and disability policy at Virginia

Commonwealth University. She has worked as an occupational therapist in public and private schools, early intervention, outpatient therapy, and private practice. Recognizing the collaborative care needed to work with children with developmental disabilities, much of her teaching and research areas of interest centers on collaboration and teamwork.

Jacqueline F. Kearns, Ed.D., is Project Director/Principal Investigator at University of Kentucky. Dr. Kearns has worked in the area of moderate, severe, and multiple disabilities for over 33 years. First as a teacher of middle and high school age students and then as a technical consultant for inclusive education and neighborhood schools, she pioneered alternate assessments. Most recently, she led the professional development team on the National Centers and State Collaborative Alternate Assessment. Currently, she directs projects related to the implementation of communication for students with complex needs.

Harold L. Kleinert, Ed.D., is formerly Executive Director of the Human Development Institute—University Center for Excellence in Developmental Disabilities Education, Research, and Service at the University of Kentucky, and Professor Emeritus, Department of Rehabilitation Sciences, College of Health Sciences.

In his 45 years in the field of developmental disabilities, he has taught students with moderate and severe intellectual disabilities in settings ranging from state institutions to regular classrooms with typical peers. He was lead author of the first text published in alternate assessment for students with significant cognitive disabilities: *Alternate Assessment: Measuring Outcomes and Supports for Students with Disabilities,* as well as a second text on alternate assessment and access to the general curriculum: *Alternate Assessment for Students with Significant Cognitive Disabilities: An Educator's Guide.*

Dianne Koontz Lowman, Ed.D., is Director of Counseling and Advocacy at Safe Harbor, a center that serves survivors of sexual violence, domestic violence, and human trafficking. In addition to outpatient counseling, she facilitates support groups for female survivors who are incarcerated, and equine assisted groups for male and female survivors of sexual violence and groups for veterans with combat-related posttraumatic stress disorder.

Toby M. Long, Ph.D., PT, FAPTA, is Professor in the Department of Pediatrics, Georgetown University and Director of Professional Development for the Center for Child and Human Development, a University Center for Excellence in Developmental Disabilities. Dr. Long is Director of the Graduate Certificate Program in Early Intervention offered by Georgetown University and teaches *Children with Disabilities* within the undergraduate minor in education, inquiry and justice. Dr. Long is an internationally known speaker and consultant on service delivery to children with disabilities and special health care needs. The recipient of a variety of awards, Dr. Long was recently named a Catherine Worthingham Fellow from the American Physical Therapy Association.

Kate M. MacLeod, M.S.Ed., is a doctoral student in the special education and disability studies programs at Syracuse University and works as an instructor and graduate assistant within the teaching and leadership department. She is a former high school special education teacher and has focused her career on bringing inclusive opportunities to all. She works with districts and schools to create inclusive special education practices and serves as an educational consultant to families who wish to see their children included in general education settings. Her research and professional interests include inclusive education reform, inclusive teacher training, and best practices for the inclusion of students with extensive support needs.

Pat Mirenda, Ph.D., BCBA-D, is Professor in the Department of Educational and Counseling Psychology and Special Education, and Director of the Centre for Interdisciplinary Research and Collaboration in Autism (CIRCA) at the University of British Columbia. She teaches courses on augmentative and alternative communication, autism spectrum disorder, inclusive education, instructional techniques for students with significant learning challenges, and positive behavior support. The fourth edition of her co-authored book *Augmentative and Alternative Communication: Supporting Children and Adults and Complex Communication Needs* was published in 2013; and another co-edited book, *Autism Spectrum Disorders and AAC*, was published in December, 2009. She has published numerous research articles and chapters and presents frequently at international, national, and regional conferences.

Mary E. Morningstar, Ph.D., is Associate Professor in the Department of Education at the University of Kansas. She coordinates the teacher endorsement program for low incidence disabilities as well as the masters program in secondary/transition. Her interests lie in the intersection of inclusive education in secondary schools and the transition to inclusive adult lives for youth with severe disabilities.

Jerry G. Petroff, Ph.D., is Professor at The College of New Jersey (TCNJ) School of Education in the Department of Special Education, Language and Literacy. In addition, he is Executive Director of TCNJ's Center for Sensory & Complex Disabilities and the Faculty Director of the TCNJ Career and Community Studies Program. Dr. Petroff has over 35 years of experience working on behalf of students, youth and adults with developmental disabilities with a focus on those who are deafblind. Holding a doctorate in psychological studies in special education, he is an expert in inclusive education, assistive technology (augmentative and alternative communication), behavior support, and the transition of students with disabilities from school to adult life for youth with intellectual/developmental disabilities.

Alice Udvari-Solner, Ph.D., is a national consultant in education and holds a faculty appointment at the University of Wisconsin–Madison in the Department of Curriculum and Instruction. The graduate and undergraduate courses she teaches on the topic of accommodating diverse learners in inclusive settings are integral to the elementary, secondary, and special education teacher certification programs. Universal design, differentiation, active learning strategies, collaborative teamwork among educators and paraprofessionals, and systems change toward inclusive education are areas that are central to her research and teaching.

Foreword

~~~~~~

It is not often that a textbook in special education causes us to eschew the usual response – commentary tied closely to the text itself — and instead elicits a response that, while referencing the text, offers an entirely different understanding of the book. This is such a book, for, as we argue below, it asks you to think of your role in educating children with severe and multiple disabilities as a pursuit of three outcomes.

THE FIRST PURSUIT: JUSTICE IN EDUCATION

They are the minority of the minority. The least well understood, the least researched, the least well educated, the most likely to be denied access to effective education, and the least valued. They are the most restricted inside and outside of schools. Their quality of life is the most jeopardized among those with disabilities. They are the children with severe and multiple disabilities.

For these very reasons, they are the most deserving. Their claim arises out of a simple matter of justice. Call it distributive justice – the claim to a larger share of the nation's huge investment in education and disability service. Why is that so? The answer lies in an understanding of a theory of justice. Stay with us, dear reader, as we explain.

Now, close your eyes. Imagine yourself in your present adulthood. What do you most value now about your life? Imagine that you have no idea what lies ahead of you, no ability at all to conjure the future. You are in a stage of utterly not knowing your future.

Now, ask yourself another question: What as a child did I most want in my life? Then, you were more ignorant of your future than you are now. But you remember the "then" of your life. So, ask and answer the question.

Having considered yourself as you are now and were once, ask yourself: What do you most want for yourself in the future?

What one or more elements of your life do you most value at all of life's stages? What constitutes your quality of life?

For children and adults with severe and multiple disabilities? Try standing in their shoes. Exercise your empathetic imagination. How will they or their surrogates answer these three questions?

These are the questions that America's pre-eminent political philosopher, John Rawls, asks us to consider in his theory of justice (Rawls, 1971). They are especially appropriate for you to consider before reading this book, for this book may provide a satisfying answer.

Do your answers include education and access to effective schools? Good health and access to appropriate treatment? Being a person who is respected and valued – dignified – for who you are, not judged for what you are not?

If your answers – yours and those from millions upon millions of other Americans – are that you value an education and good health, and that you want to be valued, then these answers warrant a distribution of public and private resources to ensure that education, health, and dignity are available to you, indeed to all, especially to those who are the minority of a minority.

This is a book about the justice of educating children with severe and multiple disabilities, the children – later to become adults – whose most valued elements of life include their education, their health, their dignity – in short, their passports to quality of life while in school and thereafter.

THE SECOND PURSUIT: CORE CONCEPTS OF DISABILITY POLICY

It may be unseemly to reference one's self in a Foreword to a book by one's close friends and colleagues. But it is warranted to do so in order to still more fully explain what this book teaches and why it is so essential to you as an educator and, perhaps, as a member of a family or community in which a child or adult with a severe or multiple disability lives. So, please indulge us.

By way of its vignettes, its emphases on curriculum and instruction and on families and transition from school to adulthood, and its references to the seminal and current research on practice, this book surprisingly rests on the core concepts of disability policy (Turnbull, Beegle, & Stowe, 2001). These include

- individualized and appropriate education (chapters 3 through 9);
- capacity building and accountability for results (those chapters and also chapters 11 and 12);
- collaboration and cooperation within schools and across disciplines and sites (chapters 1, 10, and 13);
- inclusion and full participation in school and thereafter (chapters 10 and 13);
- liberty from physical restriction and the use of positive behavioral supports to secure that liberty (chapters 3 through 11);
- autonomy, self-determination, and supported decision-making (chapter 13); and
- parent and family participation (chapter 2).

More than that, this book responds to the findings of fact that Congress recited when it reauthorized the federal special education law – Individuals with Disabilities Education Act – in 2004: the impediments to children's appropriate education are, first, educators' low expectations for students and, second, their failure to apply replicable research on teaching and learning (IDEA, Sec. 1400 (c)).

Likewise, this book shows how highly qualified teachers can support children to attain the nation's policy goals and outcomes: equal opportunity, full participation, independent living, and economic self-sufficiency (IDEA, Sec. 1400 (c)).

THE THIRD PURSUIT: ETHICAL COMMUNITIES AND INDIVIDUAL DIGNITY

Let there be no doubt: by reason of their concern for their students' education, educators affect the quality of the lives of their students and their families. Quality of life is not an abstract; it is an element of justice; it is a desideratum of the core concepts; and it occurs in the communities where the students go to school and they and their families live.

Schools themselves can be ethical communities, places where children with severe and multiple disabilities are valued intrinsically, for who they are, not judged for what they are not. To be valued is to be dignified. The pursuit of dignity is a public policy (Turnbull & Stowe, 2001; Turnbull, 2013) and has been ever since President Kennedy launched the nation's first comprehensive effort to address the challenges facing those with severe and multiple disabilities, especially intellectual disability (Kennedy, 1961).

SUMMATION

What a book! It is about education, of course. But it is about justice, policy, ethical communities and dignity. Read it in those lights and you will appreciate it more deeply. It deserves that reading; you owe it to yourself to read it thusly.

Rud and Ann Turnbull
Distinguished Professors Emeriti
Co-founders, Beach Center on Disability
The University of Kansas

REFERENCES

Individuals with Disabilities Education Act (2004), 20 U.S.C. Sec. 1400 (c).

Kennedy, J.F. (1961). Accepting New York Liberal Party Nomination, September 14, 1960. Retrieved May 18, 2016 from www.pbs.org/wgbh/americanexperience/features/primary-resources/jfk-nyliberal

Rawls, J. (1971). A theory of justice. Cambridge: Belknap Press of Harvard University.

Turnbull, H.R., Beegle, G., & Stowe, M.J. (2001). Core concepts of disability affecting families who have children with disabilities. *Journal of Disability Policy Studies, (12),* 3, 133–143.

Turnbull, H.R. (2013). Quality of Life: Four under-considered intersections. In Brown, R.J. & Faraghar, R. M. (eds). Challenges for quality of life: Knowledge applications in other social and educational contexts. Haupaque, N.Y.: Nova Science Publishers.

Turnbull, H.R. & Stowe, M. J. (2001). A taxonomy for organizing the core concepts of disability policy. *Journal of Disability Policy Studies,* 12(3). 177–197.

Preface

The fifth edition of this book arrives nearly 30 years after it was first published in 1987. Children who received mandated early intervention services back then have long transitioned out of their secondary schools, and an entirely new generation has taken their place. We can safely say that there will be no shortage of children next year, or the year after, in need of highly skilled professionals who, working collaboratively, can assess, teach, and care for students with severe and multiple disabilities. The responsibilities of these professionals are great—they must design and adapt curriculum, create and adapt materials, provide instruction, and work hard to include all students in the general education classroom while attending to these students' unique physical, sensory, emotional, and health care needs. Will we have an educational workforce capable of understanding and responding to the complex educational and support needs of learners who think, communicate, and learn quite differently from typically developing children, and whose bodies often do not move in the same ways, or whose vision and hearing may be far less acute, or who may experience significant health care challenges?

This book has always been geared toward cultivating this competent and compassionate workforce, including teachers and other members of the educational team. For far too long, many school administrators have assigned the least skilled teachers to the learners with the most complex needs. In an era where standardized test scores often govern school accreditation and teacher retention decisions, children with the most severe disabilities may be viewed as a liability of sorts. It is our belief that children with severe and multiple disabilities require *and deserve* nothing short of the best educated, most creative, and most committed professionals a school can offer.

We continue to believe that the learners who are the focus of this book do need a *team* of professionals, working collaboratively, sharing information and skills across a range of disciplines. We are proponents of inclusive education, but we have seen evidence that many learners with the most severe disabilities often have failed to receive the kinds of interdisciplinary supports necessary to receive maximum educational benefits.

This book adheres to a core set of values, consistent with effective practice and a philosophy of inclusion and collaboration. These values include

- High expectations for *all* students

- Accountability for achievement based, in part, on each student's personal potential and educational experience

- Thorough analysis of each student's learning needs

- Emphasis on the importance of family involvement and home-school communication structures that are culturally responsive and which empower families

- Collaboration with school and nonschool personnel to plan and provide services

- Provision of a broad range of personal support services that are closely coordinated with the general education classroom's goals and activities, and that are only as specialized as necessary

- Instructional and assistive technologies that foster self-determination, participation, and choice

- The use of positive behavioral supports that are based on functional assessment of challenging behavior and that incorporate medical, educational, communicative, and environmental interventions

We also believe that it is important to blend research and theory into effective practices. In addition to citing the literature on current research and practice, chapters open with a vignette, designed to personalize and make real the information that follows. The vignettes are described in inclusive educational contexts, but also with an eye towards fully understanding the complexity of the child's educational, physical, sensory, health, and emotional needs.

As with the previous edition, the fifth edition was written in a climate of welcome change and openness to new possibilities. A glance at the short biographies of the contributors will reveal that we remain committed to including authors who represent a broad range of professional disciplines. We are happy to welcome Donna Gilles as a new editor. Her close association with many of the contributors and extensive collaboration in shaping the overall tone and direction of the book were invaluable. We also acknowledge and give thanks to Rosanne K. Silberman, our former co-editor on the fourth edition, for her previous contributions, which have continued to inform and support this new edition.

Although the book has retained its overall purpose and approach, the fifth edition is, in essence, almost entirely new. We have added new chapters and new contributors, incorporated the latest research and instructional strategies, and re-ordered the chapters to reflect our values of collaboration and family. We have also added a number of features designed to enhance this book's usefulness as both a textbook and professional resource. Each chapter begins with learning objectives, key terms, and an opening vignette introducing real challenges and successes that come from working with students with severe and multiple disabilities. At the end of each chapter are a set of reflection questions and an activity to promote critical thinking and enhance readers' understanding of their important work with students with severe and multiple disabilities. As a supplement to your course or professional development program, PowerPoints also accompany each chapter, downloadable at brookespublishing.com/orelove. This book is intended for both individuals studying to become professionals or those already employed as educational team members. May this fifth edition serve as one small resource in your quest to educate, support, and care for all children.

*To the many families, teachers, and team members
who have worked hard over the past generation to provide love, support,
and exemplary educational services to children who have deserved nothing
less. And especially to the children: past, present, and future.*

Designing Collaborative Educational Services

CHIGEE JAN CLONINGER

CHAPTER OBJECTIVES

1. Describe the collaborative approach to educational programming

2. Name the essential components of collaborative teaming

3. Understand the benefits of a variety of disciplines

4. Recognize the challenges in implementing the collaborative model and know the approaches to success

5. Describe the multidisciplinary, interdisciplinary, and transdisciplinary models and understand the progression to the collaborative team model

6. See an example of collaborative teaming in action for a student with severe and multiple disabilities

KEY TERMS

- Collaborative individualized education program (IEP)
- Collaborative team approach
- Discipline-free goals
- Valued life outcomes

Zach is 11 years old and rides to his neighborhood school on the bus with his brother and other children in his neighborhood to attend a fifth-grade class. Zach likes being in places where there is a lot of activity, and he enjoys music, books, and the outdoors. He presently does not have a formalized communication system—he communicates through facial expressions, vocalizing, crying, and laughing, and he seems to understand more than he is able to communicate. Zach does not have vision or hearing impairments; however, he does have physical disabilities that affect the use of his extremities. He is beginning to learn to use a power wheelchair for mobility and is beginning to use communication assistive technology (AT).

Zach's educational team uses the collaborative approach to plan, implement, and evaluate his IEP, which is supported by a special educator, classroom paraeducator, physical therapist (PT), occupational therapist (OT), and speech-language pathologist (SLP). These team members, including his parents, use a systematic process to determine Zach's learning outcomes for the year, who was going to teach or support these learning outcomes in the various school settings, and what skills needed to be taught to other team members so everyone could assist Zach in achieving his goals and objectives. Each member of the team shares the same vision—meeting Zach's educational needs and goals and providing for his successful future.

Putting the student with severe and/or multiple disabilities at the core of all planning is the key to truly making a difference in that student's life. The most successful IEPs are created through the dynamic, synergistic collaborations of team members who share a common focus and purpose and bring together diverse skills and knowledge (McDonnell & Hunt, 2014; Reiter, 1999). Together, professionals across a wide variety of disciplines, including special and general educators, SLPs, PTs and OTs, psychologists, and counselors, contribute to planning and implementing a successful educational program for students with severe and multiple disabilities. Although this chapter emphasizes supporting students with severe and multiple disabilities, all students can benefit from a collaborative approach to educational planning and supports (Idol, Nevin, & Paolucci-Whitcomb, 2000; Rose & Meyer, 2006).

WHY COLLABORATIVE TEAMS?

Students with severe and multiple disabilities are those "with concomitant impairments (e.g., cognitive impairments/blindness, cognitive impairments/ orthopedic impairments), the combination of which causes such severe educational needs that they cannot be accommodated in the special education programs solely for one of the impairments" (Code of Federal Regulations [C.F.R.] Chapter III, Section 300.8 [c][7], 1999). Students in this disability category include those with the most severe and/or combinations of disabilities. Most have some level of cognitive disability, but the nature and extent of cognitive impairments are often ambiguous and undetermined because of the interactional effects of the multiple disabilities and the difficulty in precise diagnoses. Because of their combination of physical, cognitive, medical, educational, and social-emotional challenges, these students require a collaborative and concerted effort so their IEPs result in learning outcomes that make a difference in their daily lives. Thus, they need the profound and foundational interconnectedness of a diverse group, including family members, to see that learning does happen

(Giangreco, Cloninger, Dennis, & Edelman, 2002; Selby, 2001). The many needs of students with intense, numerous educational challenges call for a collaborative approach in the educational environment to ensure the following:

- Services are coordinated rather than isolated and fragmented. Team members who work together to complement and support the student's goals and each other provide connected and integrated educational programming. Coordination of services takes place through the actions of team members who learn and implement the principles of educational collaboration, such as sharing expertise, agreeing on ways of working together, and putting the student first. Team members experience a sense of collegial belonging and satisfaction through collaboration (King-Sears, Janney, & Snell, 2015).

- All team members share a framework for team functioning and the assessment, implementation, and evaluation of the student's educational program. Team members define their roles in relation to direct and indirect supports that they provide to the student's educational plan and to other team members. Within a collaborative framework, the contributions of every team member are educationally relevant and necessary to the student's success. Gaps in services and overlapping functions (e.g., when the OT and SLP both work on eating skills with the student) are avoided. Involvement in the development of a student's total plan helps ensure commitment and ongoing learning (Giangreco, Cloninger, & Iverson, 2011).

- The student's goals belong to the student, and all team members collaborate to ensure that those goals are met. Goals, objectives, and general supports are developed based on valued life outcomes for the student, family, and team members. Valued life outcomes are those basic components that reflect quality-of-life issues, such as being safe and healthy, having a home now and in the future, having meaningful relationships and activities, having choice and control that matches one's age and culture, and participating in meaningful activities in various places. An individualized student plan, which includes goals and objectives, supports, accommodations, and specialized instructional strategies, is based on these valued life outcomes. These plans will be unique for each student and used as benchmarks for evaluating the success of the student's program (Giangreco et al., 2011).

- The student's needs are addressed through a coordinated and comprehensive approach. Students with severe and multiple disabilities face challenges in a number of areas, including 1) physical and medical conditions (e.g., movement restrictions; skeletal abnormalities; vision and hearing loss; seizure, breathing, and urinary disorders), susceptibility to infections and management of medications; 2) social-emotional needs, such as maintaining friendships, expressing feelings, showing affection, giving to others rather than always being passive recipients, and making decisions; and 3) educational challenges, such as how to appropriately position and handle students at school and how to promote best use of the student's vision, hearing, and movements for gaining access to materials and people. Appropriate communication methods and modes to match students' cognitive, visual, hearing, and motor functioning are essential to ensure that students can make choices, have some control over their lives, express basic needs, engage with others, and have access to preacademics and academics. Although students with severe and multiple disabilities may have physical, medical, and social-emotional challenges, any student's IEP should be based on individually identified educational needs, not on presumed disability characteristics (Giangreco et al., 2011).

THE COLLABORATIVE TEAM MODEL: EXEMPLARY PRACTICE

Collaborative teaming does not just happen; team members must practice skills in order to effectively work together. Although all members enter the team at different levels, new learning occurs for all. Being part of a team is a dynamic, ever-changing process, with most teams moving through stages of learning and ways of working together, then continuously recycling through these stages as new people join the team or as conflict or new situations arise.

The variety of people involved in the students' programs need to work well together in order to best serve children in educational environments. Each team member brings a unique set of professional and personal skills and experiences to the team relationship. The way teams are formed and how they operate influence both the process and outcomes of children's education. The collaborative team model has proven to be an exemplary model for people working together to bring about differences in the lives of students with severe and multiple disabilities.

Team models have progressed to best meet the unique needs of students with severe and multiple disabilities in educational environments by following the development of educational recommended practices, research, and legal mandates. They also are based on the realization that educational teaming requires an educational model for student assessment, program planning, and delivery—the collaborative approach rather than a medical (or single expertise) model.

The collaborative model is exemplary practice in service delivery models for the education of students with severe and multiple disabilities, incorporating the best qualities of other models (i.e., multidisciplinary, interdisciplinary, transdisciplinary) while adding features to address their limitations (Doyle & Millard, 2013; Giangreco, Cloninger, Dennis, & Edelman, 2000). These other models will be discussed later in this chapter. A significant difference between the collaborative model and others is that individuals bring their own perspectives to the team, but these are purposefully shaped and changed by working closely with other team members (Edelman, 1997) and by new learning, such as universal design for learning (UDL). The practice of role release (e.g., being able to share one's disciplinary expertise with others) used in the transdisciplinary model is essential. The transdisciplinary model provides a structure for interaction and communication among team members but does not go further.

The collaborative model goes beyond that concept to embrace influences on one's own practice. The collaborative model is multidirectional and dynamic. All team members acquire not only shared understanding and knowledge of each other's expertise, but also the ability to incorporate that expertise into collaborative evaluation, planning, and implementation. New ideas are generated through group interaction that would not be generated by working in isolation.

Another significant difference is that the collaborative model addresses the provision of services in meaningful or functional contexts as well as who provides the services and how multiple team members can provide the same service (Rainforth & York-Barr, 1997). The collaborative team model provides guidelines for who is on the team, how each team member's expertise will be used, and the contexts or situations in which team members will provide their expertise.

A collaborative team is a group of professionals working together on the four major areas of educational programming—assessment, development of instructional goals, intervention, and evaluation—with the shared goal of supporting student and family valued life outcomes. Collaboration on these four major areas of educational programming in the other models is an option rather than the basis of team expectations and operations.

Assessment

Determining relevant educational goals is the main purpose of assessment in the collaborative approach. Planned quality assessment of activities identified by the team (including the family and student) should be conducted in priority educational environments (York, Rainforth, & Giangreco, 1990). Once assessment is complete, the team establishes learning outcomes for the student across educational content areas, then writes educational goals and objectives based on those learning outcomes identified as priorities for the year.

Development of Instructional Goals and Objectives

Goals and objectives should be selected based on criteria such as whether performing the activity will make a real difference in the student's quality of life (i.e., whether the activity will support the student's valued life outcomes). Consider Taylor, a sixth-grade student with cognitive, motor, and hearing disabilities. This goal is listed on his IEP: "Taylor will reliably answer 'yes' or 'no' symbolically to a variety of questions to indicate wants and needs." These are the questions the team needs to address: Will teaching Taylor to use a communication device to indicate "yes" or "no" increase his quality of life? Will it provide him the capability to make choices or to participate in more meaningful activities?

The goals and objectives on students' IEPs dictate the supports and accommodations, schedule, instructional materials and strategies, and the required involvement of specific team members. Thus, it is critical to develop effective educational goals and objectives to successfully operate within a collaborative model. An IEP developed by a collaborative team is not simply goals and objectives written from individual disciplines compiled into a single document with the individual professionals responsible for implementing and evaluating progress on their individual goals. An option is not provided for members to write separate goals in the collaborative model, as they are allowed to do in other models. Rather, a collaborative IEP is based on goals and objectives that belong to the student and originate from priorities that the student and family select with input from other team members. It is the responsibility of the team to provide forward-looking planning strategies such as Choosing Outcomes and Accommodations for Children (COACH; Giangreco et al., 2011) and Making Action Plans (MAPs; Pearpoint, Forest, & O'Brien, 1996) so that the student and family are truly part of the team and involved in making educational decisions. The goals and objectives are based on what is best for the student educationally for a given year from a family-centered perspective.

The student's goals target educationally relevant learning outcomes that are not tied to any one discipline. "Isabella will improve postural stability and increase antigravity of head, trunk, and extremities" is an example of a discipline-specific and jargon-filled goal written by a PT (Giangreco et al., 2011). Another discipline-specific example might read, "Moira will extend her dominant hand to an augmentative device for expressive communication requesting salient items." Instead, a goal should be stated so that 1) everyone can understand clearly what is expected, 2) it can be carried out in natural environments, and 3) it provides an answer to the question, "What difference will this make in the student's life?" Restating a goal for Isabella in a discipline-free, jargon-free manner results in, "During lunch, Isabella will walk in line, get her lunch tray, reach for two food items, and carry her tray to the table," whereas Moira's goal might state, "Moira will point to pictures on her communication board to make requests for preferred people, toys, and food."

Delivery of Instruction, Intervention, and Related Services

The collaborative model incorporates integrated therapy and teaching in which team members provide at least some services by consulting and teaching other team members, but all team members have the capability for intervention. Skills and expertise of team members are integrated not only in the writing of the student's goals but also in deciding where and how the student's goals and objectives are taught. The team works together to support the student in all school and community environments and activities as indicated on the IEP, often through co-teaching (Villa & Thousand, 2009, 2011; Villa, Thousand, & Nevin, 2013).

For example, one of Linda's goals was to decrease transition time between activities in her sixth-grade class. Strategies included teaching her placement and organization of materials for easy access and storage, giving her pretransition signals, and providing points for decreasing transition time. Mr. Nawby, the sixth-grade teacher, was working with all the students on this same task as part of a positive behavior interventions and supports (PBIS) approach. He used ClassDojo (www.classdojo.com), a tracking and reward program application, for many appropriate class behaviors. Linda was added to the class roster so he and any team members could keep track of Linda's goal along with her peers' goals.

Team members share their personal and professional expertise and skills so the team can determine how best to address the student's goals and objectives without gaps or unnecessary overlaps in services. "Teams clarify the team's vision for the student's educational program" (Giangreco et al., 2011, p. 19) in the collaborative model. They must have a shared understanding of who will provide services and supports, how and where the IEP will be carried out, and ways team members will collaborate to meet the student's set of relevant, individually determined program components.

Evaluation of Program Effectiveness

Teams participate in ongoing evaluation processes by which they make necessary changes in response to the student's needs, priorities, and progress. Responsive evaluation addresses questions at various levels, including 1) student-focused questions concerning progress, satisfaction, and needs; 2) program-focused questions concerning methods, curriculum, and environments; and 3) team-focused questions concerning efficacy in implementing the educational program and in working together collaboratively. Team-focused evaluation can be addressed through two questions:

1. What was the effect of our collaboration on student outcomes? In other words, did team members work together in such a manner to enable the student to be successful in his or her educational program?

2. Did we maintain positive relationships throughout the process?

It is important to understand the essential components of collaborative teaming, which are discussed in the following section, to begin to answer these questions.

ESSENTIAL COMPONENTS OF COLLABORATIVE TEAMING

Collaborative teaming is defined as an approach to educational programming that exhibits all of the following five components:

1. Appropriate team membership

2. A shared framework of assumptions, beliefs, and values

3. Distribution and parity of functions and resources

4. Processes for working together

5. A set of shared student goals agreed to by the team (Giangreco et al., 2011; King-Sears et al., 2015; Thousand & Villa, 2000)

Component 1: Appropriate Team Membership

How is team membership defined? With the potential for a large number of people on a student's team, and the recognition that weekly or biweekly team meetings with all of the team members is neither possible nor necessary, a tiered team membership can be used that consists of core, extended, and situational levels. Giangreco explained that educational teams can

> Reduce the number of people involved in regular team meetings by designating a core team consisting of people who have the most ongoing involvement with the student, an extended team that includes the core team plus those team members who have less frequent involvement with the student, and situational teams consisting of individually determined combinations of team members to address specific issues or concerns. (2011, p. 18)

Membership at each level is related to the student's IEP and influenced by professional qualifications, regulations, personal skills, and experiences of each member. A thoughtful process for making decisions regarding who is to be involved at each level in each situation facilitates the best use of everyone's expertise and avoids unnecessary overlaps and gaps in delivery of services. Related services providers are involved at each level depending on their function (i.e., direct, indirect, consultation) and frequency of contact with the student. As Giangreco put it, "Everyone does not need to be involved in everything" (2011, p. 18). The levels of team membership are further described as follows:

- *Core level:* Team membership consists of those members who have daily contact and interaction with the child, usually the special and general education teachers, the paraeducator, the parents, and perhaps one or more of the related services personnel, such as the SLP, nurse, or PT, as appropriate.

- *Extended level:* Team membership includes those who have weekly, biweekly, or some other regular contact with the student, such as related services personnel and a school administrator.

- *Situational level:* It consists of those members such as a dietitian recruited for specific situations and questions and other teachers or related services providers (e.g., psychologist, counselor, bus driver). Information is shared and solicited from all, but attendance at meetings depends on function and relation to educational planning and implementation and is determined by the agenda (Giangreco et al., 2011).

Component 2: Shared Framework of Assumptions, Beliefs, and Values

Teams need to agree on their beliefs about the purpose of the team, best ways to educate students with severe and multiple disabilities, and involvement of families and professionals. Dialogue takes place in order for members to share perspectives and come to a consensus on various educational programming concepts such as valued life outcomes, collaborative relationships, integrated related services and instruction, inclusive education and UDL, professional development, and team communication strategies.

Component 3: Distribution and Parity of Functions and Resources

Team members value each member's input and alternately take on the roles of both teacher and learner and giver and receiver of expertise. Expertise, perspectives, experiences, and resources are equitably shared in meetings; in written communications; and in assessment, planning, and evaluation.

Component 4: Processes for Working Together

Team members develop processes for working together through attention to four critical factors: face-to-face interaction, positive interdependence, interpersonal skills, and accountability.

Face-to-Face Interactions Ongoing, regularly planned times for face-to-face interactions provide members with the opportunities to problem solve creatively, get to know each other, share and receive the expertise of others, and most important, plan for the implementation of the student's educational program. The core, extended, and situational tiers of team membership are used to designate who needs to be at specific meetings. When members are not at meetings, a system of sharing what happened and receiving input is set up for all to be informed.

Positive Interdependence Positive interdependence is "the perception that one is linked with others in a way so that one cannot succeed unless they do (and vice versa), and that their work benefits you and your work benefits them" (Johnson & Johnson, 1997, p. 399). Team members agree to provide educational services from a shared operational framework and set of values that not only greatly benefits the student but also benefits each member of the team. Positive interdependence can be fostered in a variety of ways:

- Stating group and individual goals publicly and in writing

- Sharing team functions, roles, and resources equitably by defining team roles and responsibilities (e.g., recording minutes, facilitating meetings, keeping time, communicating with absent members, using jargon-free language, completing paperwork) and taking turns fulfilling these roles

- Identifying norms or ways team members want to work together (e.g., take turns, listen respectfully, be nice, give compliments, celebrate successes)

- Sharing accomplishments and rewards by scheduling time at meetings to present positive achievements of the student and team members, attending workshops together, presenting at workshops together, having a team party, and participating in other wellness activities

Interpersonal Skills Interpersonal skills are essential to effective team functioning. Adults often need to learn, use, and reflect on the small-group interpersonal skills necessary for collaboration. These skills include trust-building, communication, leadership for managing and organizing team activities, creative problem solving, decision making, and conflict management. Improving interpersonal skills and relationships also includes learning about each other's cultural, personal, and professional backgrounds and experiences (Webb-Johnson, 2002). The team chooses interpersonal skills and values that are most reflective of how the team desires to behave and work together, which then become team norms that are ideally used and evaluated at each team meeting. Attention to these norms is enhanced when they are displayed and identified as part of the team agenda. These written norms and agendas also can be used as benchmarks for monitoring, discussion, and reflection as team members learn together and practice teaming skills.

Accountability   Individual and group accountability is necessary for members to inform each other of the need for assistance or encouragement, identify positive progress toward individual and group goals, and recognize fulfillment of individual responsibilities. The agenda at each meeting should include a brief time for processing (i.e., sharing observations, suggesting changes in team process as needed). The responsibility for processing is best rotated among members, as are other team roles. The content of the agenda also provides opportunities for accountability reporting (e.g., "Report from PT on co-teaching activity with physical education teacher—5 minutes"). A team may take more time one or two times per year to evaluate team operations, celebrate, and make adjustments for the next semester or year.

Component 5: Shared Student Goals Agreed to by the Team

The IEP goals and objectives are derived from the needs of the student and indicate what the student will be able to do as a result of instruction. Teams establish common student goals to avoid the problem of each member having his or her own separate, discipline-specific goals. All team members agree to collaboratively supply their expertise and resources so that the student can achieve his or her goals and objectives. All team members pull in the same direction for the student.

Reasons for a collaborative team approach to the education of students with severe and multiple disabilities stem from the educational difference this approach can make for students. Team members work in a collegial culture, within a community of caring and supportive adults, not in isolation. They share diverse perspectives and experiences integrated in creative ways to address the many ongoing learning challenges of students with severe and multiple disabilities. Team members provide context-specific, embedded instruction in meaningful activities that promote learning and generalization. They are able to address the learning characteristics of students with severe and multiple disabilities by designing and implementing coordinated, integrated services.

Team members must learn from and teach one another in order for collaborative teaming to occur. Team members must take the time to learn, practice, and evaluate teaming skills and take the time to work on challenges and celebrate successes. In doing so, they can provide effective, efficient, creative, and truly individualized programs for students.

Refer to works by Downey (2010), Thousand and Villa (2000), Villa and Thousand (2011), Villa et al. (2013), King-Sears et al. (2015), and Idol and colleagues (2000) for other helpful resources on collaborative teamwork.

IMPORTANCE OF A VARIETY OF PERSONNEL DISCIPLINES

"None of us is as smart as all of us" (Blanchard & Johnson, 2007, p. 22). To develop IEPs for students with severe and multiple disabilities, it is necessary to call on individuals from diverse disciplines such as special education, general education, nursing, social work, occupational therapy, physical therapy, and speech-language therapy, as well as from fields less traditionally associated with education, such as rehabilitation engineering, nutrition, and respiratory therapy. Whitehouse (1951) recognized that one or two people from different disciplines could not meet all of the needs or deliver all of the services for these students. Many others in the field of special education have stressed the importance of multiple services (Giangreco, Cloninger et al., 2000; King-Sears et al., 2015; Thousand & Villa, 2000). According to the Individuals with Disabilities Education Act Amendments (IDEA) of 1997 (PL 105-17), whether a professional's services and skills are deemed necessary for a student to benefit from his or her IEP is key to determining the involvement of any of these professionals in a particular student's IEP. The contributions of every team member are educationally relevant and necessary to the student's success within a collaborative framework, and gaps in services and unnecessary and contradictory overlapping functions are eliminated.

Although they are called on to work collaboratively, family members and professionals have distinct training backgrounds, philosophical and theoretical approaches, experiences, and/or specialized skills. The success of an educational team depends in part on the competence of the individual team members and on a mutual understanding and respect for the skills and knowledge of other team members.

Roles and Responsibilities of Various Team Members

All members of a student's collaborative team share in carrying out their roles so the team can function successfully and address goals intended to increase the student's quality of life. Some roles and responsibilities are generic and shared by all members; some are carried out individually or together; and some are specialized to a specific professional, although shared as necessary and appropriate. Team members include those who provide specialized education services as well as those who provide related services. *Related services* defined in IDEA include

> Transportation, and such developmental, corrective, and other supportive services (including speech-language pathology and audiology services, psychological services, physical and occupational therapy, recreation, including therapeutic recreation, social work, counseling services, including rehabilitation counseling, orientation and mobility services, and medical services, except that such medical services shall be for diagnostic and evaluation purposes only) as are required to

assist a child with a disability to benefit from special education, and includes the early identification and assessment of disabling conditions in children. (20 U.S.C. § 1401 [Sec. 602][22])

Team members provide specialized education services and/or related services to enable the student to reach his or her IEP goals and objectives. Special education can be provided without related services, but for the most part, related services cannot be provided without special education services. In a few states, speech-language pathology services can be provided as special education services if the only identified goals and objectives for the student relate to speech-language skills.

Related services providers, as well as other team members, engage in a variety of functions. Research by Giangreco and colleagues (Giangreco, 1990; Giangreco, Prelock, Reid, Dennis, & Edelman, 2000) found that the four most important functions of related services providers for serving students with severe and multiple disabilities were 1) developing adaptations, equipment, or both to allow for active participation or to prevent negative outcomes (e.g., regression, deformity, discomfort, pain); 2) transferring information and skills to others on the team; 3) serving as a resource, support, or both to the family; and 4) applying discipline-specific methods or techniques to promote active participation, to prevent negative outcomes, or both.

Team membership is configured differently for each student depending on the array of services required to support his or her educational program and can include the following people, whose discipline-specific roles are outlined in the following subsections.

Student   The student is the core of the team; the reason the team exists is to address his or her educational needs. The student should be present at all team functions, either in person or through representation by family members, peers or advocates, and other team members. Team members are responsible for educating the student to participate as a team member and teaching self-advocacy skills and ways to have choice and control over decisions affecting him or her.

Family Member or Legal Guardian   Although not always present in the school on a daily basis, a family member or legal guardian or caregiver is an important member of the educational team. Apart from the fact that parents have the right to participate in assessment and planning, it simply makes good sense for them to participate in all team meetings as the individuals with the most knowledge of their children and the greatest stake in their children's future (Gallagher, 1997; Giangreco et al., 2011). (See Chapter 2 for more on working with families.)

Special Educator   The special educator is primarily responsible for the development and implementation of the student's IEP (IDEA 1997). The special educator sees that the student with severe and multiple disabilities learns through direct instruction, through UDL, and by sharing expertise and skills with the student's peers and others (e.g., paraprofessional, general education teacher, OT, nurse, bus driver) who interact with the student. The special educator may also serve in roles shared by other team members, such as liaison between the parents and school personnel, supervisor of paraprofessionals, member and coordinator of the team, and advocate for the student.

General Educator   The general education teacher provides services for and represents students on his or her class roster, as well as those who spend time in a general education class most of the day. The general educator's role on the team is to contribute expertise and experience about the general education curriculum and standards; weekly, monthly, and yearly curricular plans; class schedule; class routines; class rules and expectations; the general culture of his or her class; and UDL. This professional also ensures that students with severe and multiple disabilities have opportunities to participate in class lessons and activities and to interact with other students. He or she shares responsibility for designing or delivering the general education components of the student's program, such as evaluating student progress. IDEA 1997 requires that at least one of the student's general education teachers be on the IEP team. In particular, the general educator contributes to discussions and decisions about the student's access to and participation in the general education curriculum.

Paraeducator   Paraeducators, also called paraprofessionals, classroom assistants, or aides, are vital to the daily operation of the classroom. Although their duties may vary from team to team, their core functions include

> Providing academic instruction; teaching functional life and vocational skills; collecting and managing data; supporting students with challenging behaviors; facilitating interactions with peers who do not have disabilities; providing personal care (e.g., feeding, bathroom assistance); and engaging in clerical tasks. (Giangreco, Edelman, Broer, & Doyle, 2001, p. 53)

Some paraeducators have specialized skills, such as serving as an intervener for students with deafblindness. Interveners usually receive specialized training and may be certified depending on the state (National Center on Deaf-Blindness, 2012).

Physical Therapist   The PT focuses on physical functions including gross motor skills; handling, positioning, and transfer techniques; range of motion; muscle strength and endurance; flexibility; mobility; relaxation and stimulation; postural drainage; and other physical manipulation and exercise procedures.

Occupational Therapist   The OT focuses on the development and maintenance of an individual's functional skills for participating in instruction and activities of daily living (ADL), which include using the upper extremities, fine motor skills, sensory perception, range of motion, muscle tone, sensorimotor skills, posture, and oral-motor skills.

Speech-Language Pathologist   The SLP focuses on all aspects of communication in all environments, including receptive and expressive levels, modes, and intent; articulation and fluency; voice quality and respiration; and the use of augmentative and alternative communication (AAC). He or she also may be trained in assessing and facilitating mealtime skills.

Assistive Technology Specialist   The AT specialist focuses on the use of high- and low-technology devices and adaptations to facilitate participation in instruction and ADL. Areas addressed through AT include communication, environmental management, instruction, social relationships, mobility, and recreation.

School Psychologist   The school psychologist focuses on social-emotional issues and is responsible for assessment and evaluation, interpretation of testing information, counseling of students and families, behavior and environmental analysis, and program planning.

Social Worker   The school social worker helps the student gain access to community and other services and resources; advocates for the child and family; and acts as a liaison among school, home, and community.

Administrator   Administrators may include the school principal, special education supervisor or coordinator, and program coordinator. One of these or another designated person acts as the local education agency (LEA) representative at the IEP meetings. All of these administrators work together to ensure compliance with local, state, and federal regulations in areas such as placement, transition, curriculum development, transportation, related services, equipment, scheduling, and time for planning as a team. The school and district administrators are important in promoting a school culture of success, openness, collaboration, ongoing professional development, and inclusion for all students (Causton & Theoharis, 2014).

Teacher of Students with Visual Impairments and Certified Orientation and Mobility Specialist   The teacher of students with visual impairments (TVI) provides instruction to meet the unique needs of students with vision impairments and other multiple disabilities. The TVI is responsible for providing direct instruction, adaptations, and accommodations. He or she assists with tactile communication, use of optical devices, and ADL skills and is responsible for adapting general education classroom materials and consulting with the general education teachers. The certified orientation and mobility specialist provides instruction in helping students with visual impairments learn how to maneuver safely and efficiently in the environment and may provide adapted equipment and strategies for those with significant challenges.

Audiologist   The audiologist identifies different types and degrees of hearing loss using traditional and alternative assessment techniques and equipment. The audiologist also provides consultation on equipment (e.g., hearing aids, FM devices) and their use, as well as environmental modifications.

School Nurse   The school nurse focuses on health-related issues and needs, and his or her responsibilities may include administration of medications and other treatments (e.g., catheterization, suctioning, tube feeding), development of safety and emergency procedures, and consultation with other medical personnel.

Nutritionist and Dietitian   The nutritionist and dietitian focus on students' diet and nutrition. Responsibilities include adjusting students' caloric intake, minimizing the side effects and maximizing the effectiveness of medications, designing special diets for individuals with specific food allergies or health care needs, and consulting with medical personnel.

Physician   The physician's focus is on the total health and well-being of the student. His or her responsibilities include screening for and treating common medical problems and those associated with a specific disability, prescribing and monitoring medications and other treatments, and consulting with other medical personnel. Physicians may include specialists such as a pediatrician, ophthalmologist, neurologist, otolaryngologist, orthopedist, and cardiologist. As related services providers, medical personnel provide services "for diagnostic and evaluation purposes only" (20 U.S.C. § 1401 [Sec. 602][22]).

Other Specialists   Other specialists may be needed to address specific needs and concerns. They function as consulting team members, usually providing time-limited services in response to a specific question by the educational team. Occupations in the field of severe and multiple disabilities may include dentist, optometrist, respiratory therapist, pharmacist, and rehabilitation engineer.

CHALLENGES TO IMPLEMENTING A COLLABORATIVE MODEL

Collaborative teams inevitably encounter a variety of challenges along the way regardless of how useful the collaborative approach is in meeting the educational needs of students with severe and multiple disabilities. Anticipation and team preparation can alleviate difficulties that often result from lack of understanding, lack of personal experience with the model, and logistics. As Casey Stengel said, "Getting good players is easy. Getting 'em to play together is the hard part" (Alvy & Robbins, 2010, p. 709). Challenges in implementing the model are discussed from three perspectives: 1) philosophical and professional, 2) personal and interpersonal, and 3) logistical.

Philosophical and Professional Challenges

Philosophical and professional challenges arise from differences in professional training and philosophy (Edelman, 1997). Team members from different disciplines often approach instruction and therapy differently. Many related services providers, such as OTs and PTs, psychologists, nutritionists, and SLPs, receive their professional preparation in a medical model in which one looks for the underlying cause of a behavior and then directs therapy toward fixing the presumed cause. Special educators, especially those who work with children with severe and multiple disabilities, receive their professional preparation in an educational model in which one administers functional or authentic assessment with the goal of teaching functional learning outcomes for the student, not to fix the student (Giangreco, Prelock, et al., 2000).

Preparation occurs in isolation from other disciplines in too many professions; thus, teachers and related services providers neither learn about each other's disciplines and jargon nor have opportunities to work together as members of an educational team. When serving as a member of an IEP team, they are unprepared for the change in roles necessary to be part of a collaborative team (King-Sears et al., 2015).

Releasing part of one's professional role may threaten some professionals' perceived status. Collaborative teams that operate smoothly, however, can actually enhance the status of team members by fostering greater respect and interdependence, providing opportunities to share expertise with others, and allowing for a creative team process (Edelman, 1997; Idol et al., 2000).

In an integrated related services and teaching approach, there may be a few highly specialized procedures for evaluation or intervention that only specifically designated, trained individuals should perform based on their professional judgment or as designated by a physician. For example, only nurses can perform catheterization or dispense medication at school in some states. In other instances, only a PT can appropriately deliver range of motion to a student returning to school after surgery. Other team members should learn and perform only those procedures appropriate for them, with the assurance that legally required supervision by licensed or certified professionals is planned for and regularly occurs.

Team members may have difficulty deciding who should provide what services, which is not as clear in the collaborative model as it is in other service delivery models. The paraeducator and special educator may be carrying out feeding techniques daily at snack time after being taught by the SLP, who provides his or her support to the student via indirect consultation and biweekly direct consultation. Parents or other team members may feel that the child is not receiving adequate related services when the process for integrating related services and instruction is not clear. To alleviate this concern, it can be helpful to track the number of professionals or peers beyond the related services providers who are providing a service and also track the number of opportunities the student has to use the skill.

An important step in enhancing team functioning is for all members to understand the collaborative model and the ways in which a specific array of instruction and related services can ensure the best educational results for the student (Rainforth, 2002). Team members recognize their numerous opportunities for involvement in educational planning, implementation, and evaluation when they understand their changing roles, and they can better appreciate how their expertise and resources benefit the student and other team members.

Personal and Interpersonal Challenges

Team members also encounter personal and interpersonal challenges when implementing a collaborative team model. One of the tenets of the collaborative model is that team members must share information and skills with others and accept advice and learn from other team members. Some may find this process threatening because it places a team member's skills under scrutiny, necessitates the release of expertise, and requires training on how to teach other adults. Thus, sharing one's expertise with others is a matter of trust and a challenge for some team members. Team members can use strategies such as modeling, practice, feedback, and coaching to share their expertise (Heron & Harris, 2001; Villa & Thousand, 2011; Villa et al. 2013). For example, the OT has expertise in designing a feeding program and shows other team members, especially the special educator and paraeducator, how to conduct the program. He or she may also make a recording of the feeding procedures for others to view, then provide feedback through direct observation or via a recording. Teaching others and being taught becomes easier, more effective, and enjoyable as team members learn new skills, practice sharing expertise, and develop trust.

A lack of clear differentiation of responsibilities among team members is another source of interpersonal problems. Functions within a collaborative approach are shared and purposefully melded, which makes it even more essential to clarify roles and responsibilities. Members identify who does what (e.g., contact parents, take minutes, repair equipment) at team meetings. As roles and responsibilities change over time, team members must be involved in and informed about these changes. The collaborative model advocates strategies to promote shared responsibilities; it does not advocate that related services or accommodations be reduced or that one person provides all of the services needed by the student.

Implementing a new service delivery model takes time and concerted effort as well as administrative support and technical assistance. It is important to understand that people respond to change in various ways, from total resistance to exuberance. Fostering dialogue, resolving conflicts, solving problems, and demonstrating the benefits to the student are strategies that can help address resistance to change and interpersonal challenges in implementing a collaborative service delivery model.

Logistical Challenges

Some of the most difficult challenges are ones that often seem out of the team's control, including finding the time for meetings and on-the-fly communication, running efficient meetings, and ensuring consistency in following the team norms and implementing the educational program. Addressing these challenges often requires the involvement of administrators and others in the school and may include strategies such as training and adapting the collaborative approach for everyone in a school or agency, such as providing an in-service on collaborative teaming; scheduling team planning time for everyone; training in and use of problem-solving processes for school or agency challenges; and providing e-mail access for all team members (Causton & Theoharis, 2014; King-Sears et al., 2015; Thousand & Villa, 2000).

PROGRESSION TO THE COLLABORATIVE TEAM MODEL AS EXEMPLARY

This section describes a progression of team models representing a hierarchy of increasingly more coordinated and connected approaches (Giangreco, York, & Rainforth, 1989), with the focus on three organizational structures—multidisciplinary, interdisciplinary, and transdisciplinary. Although each of these models may be appropriate in a given environment or situation, many of the models first adopted by special education originated in medical environments in which people may not have even thought of themselves as belonging to a team (Fox, Hanline, Woods, & Mickelson, 2014). The terms *transdisciplinary, integrated therapy,* and *collaborative teamwork* are often used interchangeably, but there are differences, first identified by Rainforth and others in the early 1990s. To emphasize the need for collaboration, Rainforth and colleagues noted, "'collaborative teamwork' is now used to refer to service provision that combines the essential elements of the transdisciplinary and integrated therapy models" (Rainforth, Giangreco, Smith, & York, 1995, p. 137).

Multidisciplinary Model

In the multidisciplinary model, professionals with expertise in different disciplines work with the child individually, in isolation from other professionals. Evaluation, planning, priority setting, and implementation are not formally coordinated with other professionals, although each discipline acknowledges the other disciplines, and information may be shared through reports or informally. They carry out isolated, separate assessment activities, write separate assessment reports, and generate and apply separate interventions specific to their area of expertise. The overlaps, gaps, inconsistencies, and conflicts in services are addressed only minimally, if at all. Parents, special educators, and case managers are left with the task of implementing different or incompatible strategies to address various goals. This model originated in the medical profession in which various disciplines coexist to meet the needs of patients whose problems are typically isolated within one particular domain (Heron & Harris, 2001).

Consider an example of how a student might be served under the multidisciplinary model. Lindsey, a fourth grader with motor (cerebral palsy) and cognitive disabilities, is served by an SLP who has skills in oral-motor eating issues and by an OT who also has skills in feeding issues. The SLP and OT separately evaluated Lindsey on her eating skills and are both working with her on intervention techniques. Although these techniques could be supportive and provide Lindsey more practice with her eating skills, these professionals' intervention techniques are not complementary and have not been taught to other team members who work with her daily.

Interdisciplinary Model

The interdisciplinary model is further along the continuum of how closely professionals work together and provides a structure for interaction and communication among team members that encourages them to share information and skills (Heron & Harris, 2001). Programming decisions are made by group consensus, usually under the guidance of a services coordinator, whereas assessment and implementation remain tied to each discipline. Team members are informed of and agree to the intervention goals of each discipline; however, team members do not participate in selecting a single set of goals that belong to the student (i.e., reflect the student's needs and supported by all team members).

Both the multidisciplinary and interdisciplinary models are discipline-referenced models, which means that decisions about assessment, program priorities, planning, intervention, evaluation, and team interactions are based on the orientations of each discipline. Such structures "are more likely to promote competitive and individualistic professional interactions resulting in disjointed programmatic outcomes" (Giangreco et al., 1989, p. 57). Consider if Lindsey, the fourth grader working on eating skills, was served under an interdisciplinary model. The separate disciplines of SLP and OT may refuse to acknowledge the other's expertise, promoting his or her approach as the right approach. Others serving Lindsey will be confused and eventually take sides. This is not collaboration!

Transdisciplinary Model

The transdisciplinary model was originally designed for the assessment of infants at high risk for disabilities (Hutchison, 1978; United Cerebral Palsy Association National Organized Collaborative Project to Provide Comprehensive Services for Atypical Infants and Their Families, 1976) and is next along the continuum of collaboration. The purpose of the transdisciplinary model is to minimize the number of people with whom the young child or family has to interact in an assessment situation, although each professional continues to write goals related to his or her discipline.

In contrast to the multidisciplinary and interdisciplinary approaches, the transdisciplinary model incorporates an indirect model of services whereby one or two people and parents are the primary facilitators of services, implementing goals written separately by each professional, and other team members act as consultants (Heron & Harris, 2001; Hutchison, 1978; King-Sears et al., 2015). Planned role release occurs when one team member releases some functions of his or her primary discipline to other team members and is open to being taught by other team members (Giangreco, Prelock et al., 2000; Lyon & Lyon, 1980; King-Sears et al., 2015; Woodruff & McGonigel, 1988). Confusion can occur with the transdisciplinary model, however. Let us return to Lindsey. In the transdisciplinary approach, the OT and SLP would both teach the special educator and paraeducator, the primary facilitators, their individual ways of implementing the feeding program. The educator and paraeducator then implement two different methods, thereby confusing the student as well as themselves.

Collaborative Model

The collaborative teaming model was developed from the other models of service delivery, with some subtle and not so subtle transformations along the way. The transdisciplinary model is the most similar model but differs in several ways. The collaborative model arose from an educational emphasis, whereas the transdisciplinary model has its roots in the medical approach, as do other models (i.e., interdisciplinary, multidisciplinary). The philosophy and practice of the collaborative model is that the team members not only will share their expertise and resources, but also will be purposefully changed by other members and will use their acquired skills to influence their own discipline. The collaborative approach offers benefits to the student by having not only a collection of people providing services, but also a team with a shared vision, a shared framework, and shared strategies that are more likely to ensure that the student will reach his or her IEP goals and objectives.

CASE EXAMPLE: ZACH'S COLLABORATIVE TEAM

Recall Zach, the fifth grader introduced at the beginning of this chapter. A look at the work of Zach's educational team provides insight into how professionals from a variety of disciplines, along with the family, develop an educational plan for a child using a collaborative approach. Zach's IEP was developed using COACH (Giangreco et al., 2011), which identified the priority learning outcomes through an interview process with Zach and his parents. Together, the team identified general supports and objectives to help Zach achieve his learning outcomes. Decisions about the specific roles and responsibilities of each team member for implementation of Zach's IEP were made using the Vermont Interdependent Services Team Approach (VISTA; Giangreco, 1996, 2000), a process for coordinating educational support services. Zach's IEP is supported by a special educator, classroom paraeducator, PT, OT, and SLP. Educational relevance and necessity determine how and where these professionals' expertise is used. Team members can eliminate overlaps and gaps in services because they know the expertise of each team member, and teaching of goals and objectives occurs more frequently throughout the day. Figure 1.1 presents Zach's educational program and support plan.

Not all team members will be involved in supporting all educational program components. The PT and OT on Zach's team have shared expertise in a number of motor areas, and thus both do not need to be involved on all of the goals (e.g., "doing classroom and school jobs with peers"). The SLP and OT have expertise in feeding, so the team decided that the OT would be involved with this general support, not the SLP.

Goal or general support	Support needed	Mode of service (indirect/direct)	Location of service
Making choices using eye gaze	SE GE PE SLP OT	D/I D D I/D I	Fifth-grade classes
Responding to yes/no questions using eye gaze and head movements	SE GE PE SLP OT	D D D I/D I	Fifth-grade classes
Making requests for food, people, places, and activities using a photo communication system and eye gaze	SE GE PE SLP OT	D D D I/D I	Fifth-grade classes, cafeteria
Doing classroom and school jobs with peers	GE PE PT P	D D/I I D	Fifth-grade classes, around school
Engaging in active leisure by activating devices (e.g., toys, iPod, page turner, computer, appliances) using an adaptive switch	SE GE PE P	D/I D D/I D	Fifth-grade classes, library, computer lab
Personal supports: Needs to be given food and drinks, dressed, assisted with personal hygiene	SE PE OT	D/I D I/D	Cafeteria, bathroom
Physical supports: Needs repositioning at regular intervals, environmental barriers modified to wheelchair access, equipment managed, moved from place to place	SE GE PE PT P	D/I D D I D	Fifth-grade classes
Teaching others: Staff and students need to learn about Zach's augmentative and alternative communication system, other communicative behaviors, and how to communicate with Zach	SE GE PE SLP	D D D I/D	Around school
Providing access and opportunities: Access to general education classrooms and activities, instructional and material accommodations prepared in advance for multilevel and curriculum overlap instruction in general education activities	SE GE PE SLP	D/I D/I D I/D	Fifth-grade classes, around school

Figure 1.1. Zach's individualized education program (IEP) and support plan reflecting a collaborative approach. (*Key:* SE = special educator; PE = paraeducator; SLP = speech-language pathologist; OT = occupational therapist; PT = physical therapist; GE = general educator; P = peers)

   As each team member is providing direct instruction to the student for
a particular goal, he or she is incorporating the released skills from other
team members into his or her teaching as well as teaching other adults (e.g.,
paraeducator). For example, each of the team members contributes his or her
expertise in a specific way as determined by the whole team for Zach's goal
of "making requests for food, people, places, and activities using a photo
communication system and eye gaze." All of the team members have the responsibility of assisting in instructional design, in teaching Zach, and in data
collection so that he may attain this goal:

- The special educator designs the specialized instructional program that
  includes the instructional strategies for teaching "making requests," such
  as directions Zach receives, prompting procedures, material and physical
  cues, consequence reinforcement and correction, and data collection procedures. She also co-teaches with the general educator and teaches Zach
  in small groups and in pregroup sessions.

- The general educator identifies class lessons and activities in which Zach
  can learn and practice "making requests," provides opportunities for Zach
  to make requests in these lessons and activities, teaches Zach's peers
  natural supporting and interaction strategies when he makes requests,
  and shares responsibility for designing and delivering instruction to Zach
  in general education group activities using UDL.

- The paraeducator teaches Zach in various school situations (e.g., small
  groups in the classroom), provides instructional support in large groups
  and one-to-one teaching in learning centers and computer labs, records
  data on Zach's learning outcomes, keeps Zach's equipment in working order, and supports Zach in his personal care activities, using these contexts
  for Zach to practice "making requests."

- The SLP takes the lead in identifying Zach's communication system,
  designing the sequence in his learning to "make requests," and teaching all team members how the communication system works and how to
  troubleshoot.

- The OT provides information on positioning of objects, the communication device, and Zach's body for optimal use of eye gaze. He also
  provides instruction to other team members and Zach's peers on placement of objects to teach "making requests." The OT's role in providing accommodations and adaptations for Zach's eating and drinking
  is related to this goal; he provides input on Zach's food preferences
  that could be incorporated in his "making requests" instructional
  program.

CONCLUSION

The success of students' educational programs and the quality of their lives depend on a highly connected and coordinated team of professionals. Students with severe and multiple disabilities need organized teams that can systematically plan, implement, and evaluate their educational programs and address their myriad educational, health, and social-emotional needs. Although other models for delivering services were explored in this chapter, the emphasis is on collaborative teaming for designing educational services for students with severe and multiple disabilities.

The inherent dynamism of teaching and learning, the ever-changing goals and needs of students with severe and multiple disabilities, and the variable nature of people mean there always will be questions without defined answers and new information to learn. There is an ongoing need for collaborative creativity and flexibility, open minds, and the willingness to share dreams and challenges. Educational programs can lead to meaningful, positive changes in the lives of children with severe and multiple disabilities and their families when team members let values and visions larger than their fears and doubts lead their work, when what they do is designed so that every child attains his or her valued life outcomes, and when they are committed to being a team together.

REFLECTION QUESTIONS

1. Arranging for team members to plan and evaluate together is one obstacle to collaborative teaming. What are some ways that schools can overcome this obstacle?

2. Explain how various team members (including parents) may share their expertise with other team members. Why is this practice necessary?

3. As a team, what questions need to be asked to determine if a goal/objective has truly made a difference in a student's life?

CHAPTER ACTIVITY

Choose one of Zach's goals (see Figure 1.1).

1. Indicate how each of the designated team members could support that goal in Zach's fifth-grade classroom using her or his expertise.

2. Designate the mode of service for each team member.

3. Explain how Zach's peers could help him reach his goal.

REFERENCES

Alvy, H., & Robbins, P. (2010). *Learning from Lincoln: Leadership practices for school success.* Alexandria VA: Association for Supervision and Curriculum Development.

Blanchard, K. (2007). *The heart of a leader.* Colorado Springs, CO: David C. Cook.

Causton, J., & Theoharis, G. (2014). *The principal's handbook for leading inclusive schools.* Baltimore, MD: Paul H. Brookes Publishing Co.

Code of Federal Regulations. (1999). C.F.R. Chapter III, Section 300.7 (c)(7).

Downey, E.J. (2010). *Academic instruction for students with moderate and severe intellectual disabilities in inclusive classrooms.* Thousand Oaks, CA: Corwin Press.

Doyle, M.B., & Millard, J.P. (2013). *Journey of novice teachers.* Retrieved from https://itunes.apple.com/us/artist/mary-beth-doyle-ph.d./id714918692?mt=11

Edelman, S.W. (1997). *The experiences of professional shift of school-based physical therapy leaders.* (Unpublished doctoral dissertation). University of Vermont, Burlington.

Fox, L., Hanline, M.F., Woods, J., & Mickelson, A. (2014). Early intervention and early education. In M. Agran, F. Brown, C. Hughes, C. Quirk, & D.L. Ryndak (Eds.), *Equity and full participation for individuals with severe disabilities: A vision for the future.* (pp. 133–153). Baltimore, MD: Paul H. Brookes Publishing Co.

Gallagher, J. (1997). *The million dollar question: Unmet service needs for young children with disabilities.* Chapel Hill, NC: Early Childhood Research Institute, Service Utilization, Frank Porter Graham Child Development Center, University of North Carolina at Chapel Hill.

Giangreco, M.F. (1990). Making related service decisions for students with severe disabilities: Roles, criteria, and authority. *Journal of The Association for Persons with Severe Handicaps, 15,* 22–31.

Giangreco, M.F. (1996). *Vermont interdependent services team approach (VISTA): A guide to coordinating educational support services.* Baltimore, MD: Paul H. Brookes Publishing Co.

Giangreco, M.F. (2000). *Guidelines for making decisions about IEP services.* Montpelier, VT: Vermont Department of Education.

Giangreco, M.F., Cloninger, C.J., Dennis, R.E., & Edelman, S.W. (2000). Problem-solving methods to facilitate inclusive education. In J.S. Thousand, R.A. Villa, & A.I. Nevin (Eds.), *Creativity and collaborative learning: The practical guide to empowering students and teachers* (2nd ed., pp. 111–134). Baltimore, MD: Paul H. Brookes Publishing Co.

Giangreco, M.F., Cloninger, C.J., Dennis, R.E., & Edelman, S.W. (2002). Problem-solving methods to facilitate inclusive education. In R.A. Villa & J.S. Thousand (Eds.), *Restructuring for caring and effective education: Piecing the puzzle together* (2nd ed., pp. 293–359). Baltimore, MD: Paul H. Brookes Publishing Co.

Giangreco, M.F., Cloninger, C.J., & Iverson, V.S. (2011). *Choosing outcomes and accommodations for children (COACH): A guide to educational planning for students with disabilities* (3rd ed.). Baltimore, MD: Paul H. Brookes Publishing Co.

Giangreco, M.F., Edelman, S.W., Broer, S.M., & Doyle, M.B. (2001). Paraprofessional support of students with disabilities: Literature from the past decade. *Exceptional Children, 68,* 45–63.

Giangreco, M.F., Prelock, P.A., Reid, R.R., Dennis, R.E., & Edelman, S.W. (2000). Role of related service personnel in inclusive schools. In R.A. Villa & J.S. Thousand (Eds.), *Restructuring for caring and effective education: Piecing the puzzle together* (2nd ed., pp. 360–388). Baltimore, MD: Paul H. Brookes Publishing Co.

Giangreco, M.F., York, J., & Rainforth, B. (1989). Providing related services to learners with severe handicaps in educational environments: Pursuing the least restrictive option. *Pediatric Physical Therapy, 1*(2), 55–63.

Heron, T.E., & Harris, K.C. (2001). *The educational consultant: Helping professionals, parents, and students in inclusive classrooms* (4th ed.). Austin, TX: PRO-ED.

Hutchison, D.J. (1978). The transdisciplinary approach. In J.B. Curry & K.K. Peppe (Eds.), *Mental retardation: Nursing approaches to care* (pp. 65–74). St. Louis, MO: Mosby.

Idol, L., Nevin, A., & Paolucci-Whitcomb, P. (2000). *Collaborative consultation* (3rd ed.). Austin, TX: PRO-ED.

Individuals with Disabilities Education Act Amendments (IDEA) of 1997, PL 105-17, 20 U.S.C. §§ 1400 *et seq.*

Johnson, D.W., & Johnson, F.W. (1997). *Joining together: Group theory and skills* (6th ed.). Upper Saddle River, NJ: Prentice Hall.

King-Sears, M.E., Janney, R., & Snell, M.E. (2015). *Collaborative teaming* (3rd ed.). Baltimore, MD: Paul H. Brookes Publishing Co.

Lyon, S., & Lyon, G. (1980). Team functioning and staff development: A role release approach to providing integrated educational services for severely handicapped students. *Journal of The Association for Persons with Severe Handicaps, 5,* 250–263.

McDonnell, J., & Hunt, P. (2014). Inclusive education and meaningful school outcomes. In M. Agran, F. Brown, C. Hughes, C. Quick, & D.L. Ryndak (Eds.), *Equity and full participation for individuals with severe disabilities: A vision for the future* (pp. 155–176). Baltimore, MD: Paul H. Brookes Publishing Co.

National Center on Deaf-Blindness. (2012). *NCDB library: Personnel > Intervener.* Monmouth, OR: Western Oregon University.

Pearpoint, J., Forest, M., & O'Brien, J. (1996). MAPs, Circles of Friends, and PATH: Powerful tools to help build caring communities. In S. Stainback & W. Stainback (Eds.), *Inclusion: A guide for educators* (pp. 67–86). Baltimore, MD: Paul H. Brookes Publishing Co.

Rainforth, B. (2002). The primary therapist model: Addressing challenges to practice in special education. *Physical and Occupational Therapy in Pediatrics, 22,* 29–51.

Rainforth, B., Giangreco, M., Smith, P.E., & York, J. (1995). Collaborative teamwork in training and technical assistance: Enhancing community supports for persons with developmental disabilities. In O. Karan & S. Greenspan (Eds.), *Community rehabilitation services for people with disabilities* (pp. 134–168). Newton, MA: Butterworth-Heinemann.

Rainforth, B., & York-Barr, J. (1997). *Collaborative teams for students with severe disabilities: Integrating therapy and educational services* (2nd ed.). Baltimore, MD: Paul H. Brookes Publishing Co.

Reiter, S. (1999). *Society and disability: An international perspective on social policy.* Haifa, Israel: AHVA Publishers and The Institute on Disabilities, Temple University.

Rose, D., & Meyer, A. (Eds.). (2006). *A practical reader in universal design for learning.* Cambridge, MA: Harvard University Press.

Selby, D. (2001). The signature of the whole: Radical interconnectedness and its implications for global and environmental education. *Encounter, 14,* 5–16.

Thousand, J.S., & Villa, R.A. (2000). Collaborative teams: A powerful tool in school restructuring. In R.A. Villa & J.S. Thousand (Eds.), *Restructuring for caring and effective education: Piecing the puzzle together* (2nd ed., pp. 254–291). Baltimore, MD: Paul H. Brookes Publishing Co.

United Cerebral Palsy Association National Organized Collaborative Project to Provide Comprehensive Services for Atypical Infants and Their Families. (1976). *Staff development handbook: A resource for the transdisciplinary process.* New York, NY: Author.

Villa, R.A., & Thousand, J.S. (2009). *Co-teaching at a glance.* Port Chester, NY: National Professional Resources.

Villa, R.A., & Thousand, J.S. (2011). *RTI: Co-teaching and differentiated instruction.* Port Chester, NY: National Professional Resources.

Villa, R.A., Thousand, J.S., & Nevin, A.I. (2013). *A guide to co-teaching: New lessons and strategies to facilitate student learning* (3rd ed.). Thousand Oaks, CA: Corwin Press.

Webb-Johnson, G.C. (2002). Congruence between roles and actions of secondary special educators in co-taught and special education settings. *Journal of Special Education, 36*(2), 56–68.

Whitehouse, F.A. (1951). Teamwork: A democracy of processions. *Exceptional Children, 18,* 45–52.

Woodruff, G., & McGonigel, M.J. (1988). Early intervention team approaches: The transdisciplinary model. In J.B. Jordan, J.J. Gallagher, P.L. Hutinger, & M.B. Karnes (Eds.), *Early childhood special education: Birth to three* (pp. 164–181). Arlington, VA: Council for Exceptional Children.

York, J., Rainforth, B., & Giangreco, M.F. (1990). Transdisciplinary teamwork and integrated therapy: Clarifying the misconceptions. *Pediatric Physical Therapy, 2*(2), 73–79.

Partnering with Parents and Families

DICK SOBSEY

CHAPTER OBJECTIVES

1. Understand the importance of the partnership between families and the educational team

2. Describe the diverse characteristics of families raising children with severe and multiple disabilities

3. Understand an overview of some common ways that parents and other family members respond to the presence of a child with severe and multiple disabilities

4. Describe some approaches and methods that school personnel can use to work in collaboration with families

KEY TERMS

- Child-centered approach
- Communication book
- Coping
- Family-centered approach

- Incidental communication
- Resilience
- Role balancing
- Transformation

ON A PERSONAL NOTE

I distinctly remember the time I spoke to a local group for parents of children with developmental disabilities, just shortly after my young son had been diagnosed with severe and multiple disabilities. I had given talks to this group as a professional on several other occasions. I was on good terms with these parents as a person who advocated on their behalf. Each time I had presented in the past, the president of the group thanked me with a warm handshake and a smile, but this time was different. She gave me a friendly hug and spoke to me quietly away from the microphone: "You're one of us now."

It was two decades ago that I became a member of a community of parents raising children with severe and multiple disabilities. Our son Dave, who was just an infant then, is a grown man now. The first edition of this book was published a few years before he was born. The second, third, and fourth editions were written as he moved through child care, then elementary and middle school. Since the fourth edition was published, he completed high school and then university in an inclusive postsecondary education program.

When Dave was younger, we had no name for his condition. He was finally diagnosed with MECP2 duplication syndrome, a condition that had only been discovered and described a few years earlier, when he was 18 years old. Typical features of this syndrome include severe to profound intellectual disability, autistic behaviors, hypotonia (low muscle tone), gastric reflux, immune compromise resulting in frequent and severe respiratory infections, osteoporosis, and a number of other challenges. In some ways, getting a diagnosis was very helpful. It relieved some of our concern that there might be something better we could do for him if we knew the cause of his condition. In fact, learning about his syndrome did lead to a few improvements in his care. It also put us in touch with other families with affected children for mutual support. In another way, however, we were glad that the diagnosis was delayed because we had the chance to get to know Dave for who he is as an individual without the inevitable influence of this kind of diagnosis.

I have no easy or earth-shattering wisdom to share as the father of a student with severe and multiple disabilities—even after participating in dozens of program planning meetings, joining the district inclusive education parent advisory group, struggling with the challenges, reveling in the successes, communicating on a daily basis with other families of children with severe and multiple disabilities, and going to five graduation events. I can tell you, however, that my experiences as a father have profoundly influenced my understanding of what is important for educators and other professionals to know about partnering with families.

As a parent, I have learned a few things that I did not fully understand and appreciate as a professional. Parenting is a unique and critical role in the life of every child. Sometimes, what is best for a child as a parent is different from what seems best as a teacher or therapist. Every parent, every child, and every family is different. There is no one-size-fits-all approach that will work for everyone.

Parenting a child with a severe disability is a challenge, but it does not have to be a tragedy. Professionals place too much emphasis on relieving stress in families and not enough emphasis on helping families find joy and satisfaction in their lives. Successful adaptation for the vast majority of families with children with severe and multiple disabilities is not about maintaining or restoring life as it previously existed; it is about constructing a new way of life. It is not about coping; it is about transforming.

PARENTS AND EDUCATORS AS PARTNERS

As discussed in the previous chapter, parents play critical roles in the education and care of their children. Law in many countries legally mandates a partnership between parents and educators. For example, the Individuals with Disabilities Education Improvement Act (IDEA) of 2004 (PL 108-446) mandates that parents have the right to gain access to their child's school records and participate in assessment and program planning. It also sets out due process procedures for resolving any disputes that may arise between educators and parents. Title 1 of the No Child Left Behind Act of 2001 (PL 107-110) also gives parents the right to play a role in school policy and reform. Parent groups played an important part in establishing the right of children with disabilities to educational services and in the development of these legal mandates (Kritikos, 2010). Many other countries, individual states, and provinces have similar mandates for parent involvement. In addition, professional standards stress the role of parents and families. For example, the American School Counselor Association's (ASCA) Ethical Standards call for "a collaborative relationship with parents/guardians to facilitate students' maximum development" (2010, p. 4). Similarly, the Council for Exceptional Children's Professional Ethical Standards require "developing relationships with families based on mutual respect and actively involving families and individuals with exceptionalities in educational decision making" (2010, p. 1).

Of course, meeting these legal and ethical requirements is important, but successful working relationships that contribute to the best educational outcomes for students with severe and multiple disabilities require more than minimal compliance (Turnbull, Turnbull, Kyzar, & Zuna, 2016). Effective family relationships should be tailored to each student and his or her family, and they require mutual respect and frequent communication. In their partnership with families, teachers typically play the lead role in education, and parents typically play the lead role in providing care. Most students with severe and multiple disabilities, however, have care requirements that must be met in school, and many educational goals benefit from follow-through by the family at home. For instance, teaching students signs or symbols in school will be more successful and functional if family members learn them and appropriately respond to them. Although the partnership between educators and parents is important for all students, children with severe and multiple disabilities have an increased need for successful collaboration between home and school for several reasons.

First, most students with severe and multiple disabilities have significantly increased care requirements that must be met during the school day in order to make education possible, including providing personal hygiene, feeding, positioning, assisting with mobility, administering medications, monitoring and managing seizures, and meeting other individual needs. Meeting these requirements requires good communication and coordination. For example, parents need to monitor fluid intake for many students with severe and multiple disabilities to avoid dehydration. A significant portion of their child's intake may occur at lunch and snack times at school, but if the student stops drinking at school, then the parents have no way of knowing unless it is communicated to them. Alternatively, the parent may be unnecessarily worried about the child's decreased fluid intake at home if he or she does not know that the student has increased fluid intake at school.

Second, many educational and behavioral objectives taught in school are unlikely to be achieved and maintained without support in the home environment. For example, school staff may work toward getting the student to point to or touch a cup when he or she wants a drink. Staff may work consistently to prompt and reinforce this behavior at lunch and snack time, so there are two natural learning opportunities each day. With weekends, holidays, vacations, and absences from school, this translates to about 380 learning opportunities at lunches and snacks on 190 days of attendance during a year. That same student has approximately 1400 additional meals and snacks at home during that year. In the best of possibilities, these also become opportunities to shape and reinforce the desired behavior and substantially increase the chances of attaining the skill. In the worst of possibilities, the target behavior may be misunderstood and discouraged outside of school, making successful attainment of the goal extremely difficult and maintenance almost impossible. It is essential to have collaboration and communication across home and school settings to help students maintain educational and behavioral goals.

Third, positive parenting styles and well-developed bonds between parents and children have been shown to contribute to better functional outcomes for children with developmental disabilities (e.g., Dyches, Smith, Korth, Roper, & Mandleco, 2012). A strong, positive relationship between the parent and child paves the way for a positive relationship between children and their educators.

Both educators and parents need all their energy and resources to fulfill the responsibilities of their respective roles. Difficult relationships between educators and parents divert energy and resources from care and education. Successful partnerships result in better educational and parenting outcomes. Unfortunately, many educators dread their interactions with parents of children with disabilities. As a group, these parents have often been stereotyped as angry, aggressive, demanding, and unrealistic about their children's abilities. Educators more frequently label parents of children with disabilities as problems rather than as partners (Marshak, Dandeneau, Prezant, & L'Amoreaux, 2010). This preconception can be a self-fulfilling prophecy because it can result in avoidance and defensiveness in parents. Educators should gain an informed understanding about family dynamics in order to cultivate an open and trusting relationship with parents.

UNDERSTANDING FAMILIES

It is important to consider some facts and beliefs about families, particularly about parents of children with disabilities, before addressing some of the practical information about parent–educator partnerships. Some information about families in general may be a good place to start.

There is no single, well-accepted definition of family. It is clear that our understanding of family changes over time and differs depending on the context and purpose. For example, a genetic definition of family can be useful in assessing health risks, but a legal or emotional definition of family may be more important in other contexts.

Educators need to consider at least two concepts of family. First, there is a legal definition that determines who has parental authority to make decisions on behalf of a child. Second, there is a social definition that may be much less precise but equally important. The social definition of family can involve a much wider group of people who have an ongoing relationship with the child, are emotionally bonded to the child, and participate in caregiving. Although knowing who has legal parental authority is essential for consent and some kinds of formal decision making, other members of the student's social family may be more important for coordination of home and school activities. Although these two kinds of relationships often coincide or overlap, they can be quite different for some students and particularly for children with disabilities who are less likely to live in traditional nuclear families. For example, many children with severe and multiple disabilities live in foster care homes. Foster parents often have strong emotional bonds with these children but lack the legal power to make major decisions for them or consent on their behalf. This legal authority may remain with the natural parents or a court-appointed guardian. Educators need to respect the relationship bond between the foster parent and child. At the same time, they must know who has legal authority to make decisions and ensure that consent is properly obtained when required.

As a group, families of children with disabilities differ in some ways from both families without children and families with only typically developing children. Great variability exists among families of children with disabilities, however—every individual family will not share characteristics common to this group. For example, as a group, families of children with disabilities have lower incomes than other families, but many families of children with disabilities have high incomes. Parents of children with disabilities typically report somewhat higher stress levels than other families, but most parents of children with disabilities report stress within the normal range, and some report very low levels of stress. It is therefore essential for educators to respond to the individual needs of families and not to stereotypes or group characteristics.

Children with intellectual or developmental disabilities, physical disabilities, or behavioral challenges live in many kinds of families, but, as a group, they are less likely than other children to live in traditional nuclear families and more likely to live in single-parent families or with nonrelated caregivers. According to the U.S. Centers for Disease Control and Prevention, slightly less than half (48.4%) of all children live in traditional nuclear families, which they define as living with two legally married biological parents (Blackwell, 2010). The percentage of children living in traditional nuclear families, however, drops to 43.5% for children with chronic health conditions, 40.4% for children with intellectual or developmental disabilities, 36.4% for children with physical disabilities, and 22.2% for children with diagnosed behavioral challenges.

Children with disabilities are much more likely to be placed in foster care than other children, and out of all children placed in out-of-home care, children with disabilities are less likely to be placed with relatives in kinship care. Various studies reported 30%–80% of children in foster care have disabilities. For example, Hill (2012) found that 60% of the foster care children in her sample had been identified as having disabilities by their schools.

In the research and professional literature on families of children with severe and multiple disabilities, most of the family literature focuses on parents, and most of the parent literature focuses on mothers. Fathers, siblings, and other family members have received less attention. This focus on the role of mothers likely reflects two facts. First, mothers of children with severe and multiple disabilities often take on caregiving roles that greatly exceed those of the typical parent in intensity, complexity, number of hours required for performance, and number of years of continued demand (e.g., Burkhard, 2013). Second, although fathers of children with disabilities may take on some of these roles, in many cases they become more focused on work or career as the family adapts to their child's needs and changes the division of labor within the family.

An increased division of labor within families often occurs in response to the presence of a child with a significant disability. Mothers of children with developmental disabilities are less likely to work outside the home, and of all mothers working outside the home, mothers of children with disabilities are more likely to work on a part-time basis. This results from a combination of the increased caregiving requirements of the child, a lack of adequate support services, and, in some cases, maternal needs and characteristics, such as the mother's own health challenges (Bourke-Taylor, Howie, & Law, 2011). In addition, although supports and services provided to families of children with disabilities are helpful, they frequently place additional demands on parents who are required to fill out forms, attend meetings, maintain records, and carry out other functions. Reduced participation of mothers in gainful employment typically results in reduced family income and, in many cases, fathers' increased focus on employment in an attempt to compensate for lost income. Of course, these parental roles of primary caregiver and wage earner are reversed in some families and shared more equally in others, but the most common pattern has been mothers assuming the primary caregiving role.

Stress and Challenges in Families of Children with Disabilities

As a group, families of children with disabilities experience somewhat more stress than other families, but stress levels are highly variable. Some of the variability is related to the specific nature of the child's condition. For example, behavioral challenges, such as aggressive outbursts or self-harm, or extreme medical fragility resulting in frequent health crises, can be significant sources of stress. Stress levels may also be influenced by family characteristics and available supports.

Single-Parent Families Some children with severe and multiple disabilities live in single-parent families. Although significant numbers of children with disabilities are raised by single fathers, most single parents raising children with intensive needs are mothers. Some single parents have expressed their plight like this:

> I am a single mother with four kids. My youngest has multiple disabilities. I need to work to support my family, but my job is taking me away from my family. I feel like I should be at home taking care of my daughter, who needs constant care. What should I do?

There are no easy answers to this mother's question. Maintaining a home, working to support the family, caring for siblings, and meeting the needs of a child with severe and multiple disabilities can be incredibly challenging. Of course, some single parents may have informal or formal supports from extended family, friends, or social services agencies that provide substantial help in meeting family needs to make life more manageable.

Family Conflict and Role Balancing The notion that two-parent families are better equipped to meet the challenges of raising a child with intensive needs is based on an assumption that parents share the responsibilities and mutually support each other. Unfortunately, this is not always the case. In some cases, all of the responsibilities may be placed on one parent who may have additional demands from a marriage partner. Marital conflict or even intimate partner violence can also be a major stressor in some families. As a result, having two parents in a home is not always an advantage for the parent who does most of the work.

Some popular and professional literature has asserted that having a child with a severe disability is a major factor causing marital discord and breaking up marriages. For example, newspaper stories have commonly published alarming statistics such as, "About 70 percent of U.S. couples with disabled children get divorced, therapists say" (Weiner, 1991, p. A16) and "Parents [of children with disabilities] have an 80% chance of divorce" (Griffen, 2000, p. G1). A study of 332 parents of children with trisomy 13 or trisomy 18, conditions that cause very severe and multiple disabilities, reported that health professionals had advised 23% of the parents that having a child with a disability would "ruin their marriage or ruin their family" (Janvier, Farlow, & Wilfond, 2012, p. 295).

Actual research studies that compare divorce rates are rare, but available research presents a much less negative picture. For example, the same parents who were told to expect that having a child with a disability would ruin their marriage or their family actually reported much different results. Although 3% of the marriages did break up sometime after their child with trisomy 13 or trisomy 18 was born, 98% of these parents reported that having a child with a disability enriched their lives, and 68% reported having this child had a positive effect on their marriage. In addition, 82% reported that having a child with a severe disability had a positive effect on their other children (Janvier et al., 2012). In a previous study, 22% of parents indicated that having a child with a disability neither strengthened nor harmed their marriage relationship, 26% indicated that the marriage relationship suffered, and 52% reported that the marriage relationship was strengthened as a result of having a child with a disability (Scorgie & Sobsey, 2000). These findings suggest that there is considerable variability in the way that families respond to the challenges of having a child with a disability, and catastrophic predictions about ruining marriages and families are unnecessarily pessimistic and potentially harmful.

Similarly, statements about extremely high divorce rates appear to be exaggerated if not entirely incorrect. Studies report no difference in divorce rates between families with and without children with disabilities, and others report slightly higher divorce rates among parents of children with disabilities (Sobsey, 2004). Risdall and Singer's (2004) meta-analysis of previous studies of divorce rates among parents of children with disabilities concluded the divorce rate of parents of children without disabilities was 13.22%, whereas the rate among parents of children with disabilities was 14.87%.

Even when slightly higher rates of divorce are reported, they do not control for other variables such as socioeconomic factors, substance abuse, and family violence that might better explain the results. For example, substance abuse problems increase the risk for family breakdown and for having a child with a disability. There is more evidence that having a child with a disability strengthens families than threatens them. The responses of families and individual parents can vary greatly, however, and there is some evidence of a significant correlation between divorce and certain childhood disabilities. For example, several studies reported increased rates of divorce among parents of children with autism and Rett syndrome, but not in Down syndrome (e.g., Hartley et al., 2010; Lederman et al., 2015). Nevertheless, the largest available study (Freedman, Kalb, Zablotsky, & Stuart, 2012), based on the U.S. National Study of Children's Health, found 64% of children with autism live in two-parent homes, about the same percent reported for children without disabilities. After controlling for other relevant variables, the authors concluded there was no evidence of increased divorce among parents of children with autism.

Milton Seligman, a major researcher on families of children with disabilities and father of a daughter with Down syndrome, voiced his conclusion that having a child with a disability does not lead to divorce, but that divorce is always painful for children and that children with disabilities are affected most severely:

> My suspicion is that the general public believes that a child with a disability creates enormous tensions within the family, eventually culminating in divorce. On the other hand, parents who speak and write about their experience with their child project the notion that a child with a disability marshals constructive forces within the family system and actually brings the family closer together. (Seligman, 1995, p. 179)

Parents with Disabilities or Other Life Challenges   Some parents have disabilities or other life challenges of their own. Estimates of the number of parents with disabilities vary widely from about 1 million to more than 8 million in the United States. In most cases, parents with disabilities are excellent parents, and many manage the demands of parenting a child with intensive needs very well. In some cases, a parent's disability makes it more difficult to meet a child's needs, and some parents with disabilities are reluctant to ask for help because they fear that their children might be taken away. Sadly, there is evidence that their fears may be well founded at two levels, particularly for parents with intellectual or psychiatric disabilities (e.g., Kay, 2009). First, there appears to be a greater tendency for these parents to be brought to the attention of child welfare. Second, there appears to be a greater tendency for child welfare agencies to apprehend these children. Some states still list parental disability as legal grounds for terminating parental rights (Lightfoot & LaLiberte, 2013). Biased assumptions about the abilities of parents with disabilities may contribute to this approach of terminating parental rights when this is not in the best interest of the child (Kay, 2009).

Educators need to carefully examine their own preconceptions regarding the abilities of parents with disabilities to care for a child with intensive needs. In addition, they need to exercise exceptional caution in asking these parents how they are managing or whether they need help. Establishing a trusting relationship is important to ensure that the parent does not feel his or her competence is being questioned or worry that asking for help may lead to termination of parental rights. Even when a trusting relationship is established, educators must exercise caution so that attempts to help families obtain needed supports do not inadvertently result in triggering a biased professional response that could result in terminating parental rights rather than assisting the family.

Siblings as Caregivers   Most of the focus on families of children with disabilities has centered on parents as caregivers of their children. Research, however, has also shed light on young caregivers, children who provide care to family members with disabilities, illnesses, or addictions. In some cases, siblings play major roles in the care of children with severe and multiple disabilities. The role of siblings in caregiving often remains somewhat hidden because this has not been a widely acknowledged role for children. Increased stress, anxiety, depression, social isolation, and diminished academic achievement can result when the demands placed on siblings is excessive (Earley & Cushway, 2002).

Young caregivers report positive outcomes such as increased life satisfaction and improved resilience, however, when the responsibilities are more manageable and the young caregiver's role is appropriately acknowledged (Cassidy, Giles, & McLaughlin, 2014). Including a child in the caregiving of a child with severe and multiple disabilities can also play a useful role in making the young caregiver feel included as a valued member of the family rather than feeling isolated as other family members' attention is taken up meeting the needs of the child with a disability. Families differ greatly in the extent to which siblings are involved in the care of a child with severe and multiple disabilities. It is important for educators to acknowledge the contribution of siblings who are involved in care. If there are indications that siblings are overburdened by caregiving responsibilities, then educators should recognize this as a need for family support and try to assist families in finding the supports they need.

Enduring Bonds and Intimate Connection   A secure, positive bond between a child and his or her parents promotes positive emotional, behavioral, social, and educational outcomes. This is equally true for children with and without developmental disabilities (e.g., Dyches et al., 2012). Numerous factors, however, can make the development of secure bonds more challenging when children have developmental disabilities, especially severe and multiple disabilities. As previously mentioned, children with developmental disabilities are more likely to live with foster parents and often are moved through a series of homes. Those who are medically fragile at birth may require medical interventions that interfere with or limit parental contact. For example, mothers may be sent home while their infants remain hospitalized, or the need for various monitors and medical equipment may make it difficult or impossible for parents to hold their infant.

Educators and other professionals can be a significant influence on the relationship between parents and children with disabilities. Sadly, professionals have often and sometimes intentionally undermined rather than supported attachment between parents and children with severe and multiple disabilities. For example, the negative impact of having a child with a disability has often been exaggerated and the positive impact on families ignored or dismissed as delusional. Children with developmental disabilities have been portrayed as causing their parents to divorce, their siblings to be neglected, and their entire families to suffer unbearable stress. Professionals have warned parents not to get too attached to these children because doing so will only increase their suffering.

In reality, parents report many positive effects of having children with disabilities on themselves and their families. In a survey of 538 parents, 71.5% agreed or strongly agreed that "our family has emerged stronger" (McConnell, Savage, Sobsey, & Uditsky, 2014) as a result of having a child with a disability. Most of these parents also agreed that they laugh more and are less bothered by trivial things (52.9%), wonderful people come into their lives (86.4%), and they learn what is really important in life (87.9%) as a result of having a child with a disability. These same parents reported significant challenges associated with their child's disability, but 63.0% reported that having a child with a disability had an overall positive effect on their families (McConnell et al., 2014).

Although it is important to support families by helping them identify and address the challenges they face, it can be of equal or greater importance to support the positive aspects of their relationships with their children and the bonds between the parents and their children. Educators should acknowledge and support the positive effect of children on families.

Family Adaptation

I was sitting in the audience in 1996 as the conference presenter was discussing her work with Chinese-Canadian mothers of children with disabilities. She recalled one mother who described her personal experience as being a wayward traveler who set out for Italy and somehow ended up in Holland. In the end, she concluded that it is better to enjoy the wonders of Holland than to regret not getting to Italy. I turned to someone beside me and said, "That's amazing. I heard exactly the same description from a mom in New Zealand, and I thought it was her own story." He replied, "Oh, really? I read that story in Dear Abby a few years ago." It turned out that *Welcome to Holland* was written by Emily Perl Kingsley in 1987. Kingsley, perhaps best known as an award-winning writer for *Sesame Street,* wrote it to describe her own emotional journey as the mother of a son with Down syndrome. *Welcome to Holland* has been translated into many different languages, circulated by numerous parents' groups, posted on hundreds of web sites, and, most important, embraced by hundreds of thousands of parents. Something in it clearly rings true for a lot of parents of children with disabilities, and knowing that can help us understand something important about parents' ability to adapt and view disability through a positive lens.

Models of Adaptation   Most parents are able to adjust to the reality of having a child with severe or multiple disabilities on their own or with the natural supports of their friends, family, and community. Some parents need the support of a professional counselor (Taylor, 2004). A few are never able to adjust to the new reality. The ability of parents and families to adapt to having a child with a disability is often described as resilience, and the changes required to accommodate a child with a disability are frequently described as coping. In psychology, *resilience* typically has been defined as the collection of characteristics, strategies, and behaviors that permit families to resist disruption in the face of stressors and challenges (e.g., Greeff & Nolting, 2013). This is consistent with the more general meaning of *resilience* as the property of springing back into shape. *Coping* is another term commonly used to refer to how parents and families successfully manage life amid the challenges of a child's disability while maintaining previous family relationships and patterns of interaction (e.g., Grant et al., 2013). Traditional models of family adaptation are based on the notion of balance and equilibrium. Challenges such as having a child with a disability are seen as disrupting the equilibrium, and families cope by taking action to restore it. Support for these families is typically conceptualized as providing additional resources (e.g., money, equipment, respite care, training) to assist families to cope and restore their previous balance.

A transformational model of parental or familial adjustment (Scorgie & Sobsey, 2000) can be viewed either as an alternative to resilience or a specific category within resilience, depending on how narrowly resilience is defined. Parents and families do not bounce back from the impact of a major challenge in a transformational model. They adapt by making substantial changes in their attitudes, beliefs, expectations, behavior, and relationships. Coping and transformation can be seen as two alternative styles of adjustment. In one, life goes on pretty much as before with a few changes required to make things work. In the other, pretty much everything changes. Each of these styles can be a successful approach to adjustment for some parents and families. In Kingsley's terms, some parents cope by attempting to find their way back to Italy, their original destination, whereas others abandon their plans for Italy and focus on a new life in Holland. Coping attempts to restore life to its previous state, but transformation attempts to create a new life.

Although it is important to understand the fundamental differences between these two styles of adjustment, parents can and usually do combine some elements of each style, and most families initially respond by attempting to maintain their former lives, transforming only if and when it becomes clear that their old lives are no longer manageable. The greater the impact of the challenges of disability to old patterns of behavior and old ways of thinking, the more likely transformation will be required. Because it is the impact on the parent and family, not the nature and severity of the disability, that determines the need for transformation, some parents and families may undergo transformations in response to the challenges associated with even minor disabilities. The challenges associated with parenting a child with severe and multiple disabilities, however, are usually very substantial. Maintaining life "pretty much as it used to be" can be extremely difficult and sometimes impossible. As a result, many parents of children with severe and multiple disabilities adopt a predominantly transformational style of adjustment.

Traditional approaches to supporting families of children with disabilities aim to help families cope, primarily by reducing demands on parents. Traditional approaches, however, may undermine transformational adjustment. For example, respite care has been a central focus of traditional support, and it certainly can be useful to families, but it is based on the notion that the child is primarily a source of demands and stress from which the parent needs relief.

Existential Choice   Japanese existentialist author Kenzaburō Ōe was faced with a difficult choice. His son was born with much of his brain outside his skull. Doctors told him that they could attempt a surgical repair, but his son might not survive the surgery and would almost certainly be severely disabled if he survived. Therefore, they suggested the alternative of simply keeping his son comfortable while he died. Colleagues suggested that having a child with severe disabilities would prove a burden for the young writer and would probably ruin his career. Ōe and his wife eventually decided to give their son a chance at life, but Ōe's career was not ruined as some predicted. Thirty years later, while accepting the Nobel Prize for Literature, Ōe acknowledged his son Hikari as the major influence on his writing over the three intervening decades. *A Personal Matter* is Ōe's (1964) fictionalized account of a father wrestling with the decision about whether to try to keep his son alive. *A Healing Family* is Ōe's

(1995) autobiographical account of how their son affected him and his family. Ōe described his son's role in transforming him:

> Indeed, I would have to admit that the very ideas that I hold about this society and the world at large—my thoughts, even about whatever there might be that transcends our limited reality— are based on and learned though living with him. (p. 44)

In choosing to give his son a chance to live, he also made the choice to be the father of a child with severe and multiple disabilities.

Some other parents of children with severe and multiple disabilities face similar decisions regarding lifesaving treatments. Some make decisions about whether to adopt a child with disabilities, whereas others make decisions about whether to give up their child or place the child out of the home. These kinds of decisions include explicit choices about whether to be the parent of a child with severe disabilities. Most parents of children with severe and multiple disabilities do not make this choice in such an obvious way. In a less explicit way, however, all parents of children with intensive needs that do not completely abandon these children need to make a choice: either to accept their role as the father or mother of this child as a major, if not the primary, part of their identity or reluctantly act in that role without accepting it.

Andrew Solomon (2012) explores this process of parents altering their identities in response to children who have significant differences from their parents in *Far from the Tree: Parents, Children, and the Search for Identity*. He identifies parallels among parents of children with a variety of significant differences from their parents (e.g., children with schizophrenia, deafness, sexual identity differences, and severe and multiple disabilities). He found that parents in each case must alter their own identities to accommodate these children. Solomon suggested that parents of children with severe disabilities feel ambivalence about adopting this new identity and must choose on which side of the ambivalence to act. Most parents choose to act on the side of doing whatever is necessary to care for their child, and in doing so, they have chosen to be the parents of children with severe and multiple disabilities.

INTERACTING WITH FAMILIES: IMPLICATIONS FOR EDUCATORS

Andrew's mother made it very clear that she was not satisfied with the program that the school offered her son, and his teacher felt that his mother's expectations were unrealistic. She explained to Andrew's mother that she had read in a special education textbook that parents of kids with disabilities were grieving the loss of the perfect children they expected and went through stages of denial, anger, and bargaining before reaching acceptance. Andrew's mother responded, "No! I am happy with Andrew just the way he is. I am grieving for the loss of the perfect teacher that I was expecting for him, but I do suddenly feel like I might be entering the anger stage." Of course, Andrew's mother was not serious, but it made the teacher think about her own comment dismissing the mother's concern as the product of a grief reaction.

Educators who work with the families of children with severe and multiple disabilities need to recognize that every family and every parent is different. Simplistic stereotypes that every parent of a child with a severe disability goes through a predictable sequence of adjustment, such as denial, anger, bargaining, depression, and acceptance, do not fit most parents (Blacher, 1984; Gallagher, Fialka, Rhodes, & Arceneaux, 2002). This stage model of grief was borrowed from Kübler-Ross's (1969) work on terminal illness, death, and dying. Applying this to parenting a child with a disability assumes that the experience of having a child with a disability is equivalent to the death of a child or being diagnosed with terminal cancer. In addition, an important element has typically been left out in applying Kübler-Ross's stage theory to parents of children with disabilities. Kübler-Ross also placed importance on hope as a theme running through all of her five stages.

Some parents may have expectations that seem unrealistic, but dismissing parental demands by attributing them to emotional states, such as anger or denial, is both unfair and unlikely to resolve the issue (Marshak et al., 2010). Some approaches to addressing differences in parental and professional expectations are explored in the following example.

Jayne was just starting school and was not speaking, but she communicated some of her needs through touching or pointing at things. The communication therapist assessed Jayne, and Jayne's teacher and the other professional team members agreed that they should focus on teaching Jayne to use sign language and symbols to communicate. Jayne's mother seemed upset by this. She said she wanted Jayne to learn to talk and did not want her daughter to learn sign language, and that was final. Jayne's mother was furious when Jayne's teacher told her that expecting Jayne to learn to talk was unrealistic because research shows that most children who are not talking by the time they start school never learn to speak. She told the teacher that this was probably true because most children's schools give up on them and stop trying to teach them to talk. In her view, her expectations for Jayne were not unrealistically high. Rather, the schools expectations were unrealistically low.

Later, Jayne's teacher met with the communication therapist, psychologist, and some other team members to discuss what to do next. The teacher felt that Jayne's mother was in denial about the severity of Jayne's disability and needed to accept the fact that Jayne would never learn to talk. The psychologist pointed out that no one actually knows the future with certainty, and considerable evidence shows that professionals' expectations are too low and too negative in a significant number of cases (e.g., Janvier et al., 2012; Miller, 2012). She also felt that trying to make Jayne's mother give up and accept that Jayne would not learn speech might just escalate the argument and poison the relationship between Jayne's mom and the team. She felt that they should find a way to resolve the issue without entering into a power struggle about who was right and who was wrong. This gave the communication therapist an idea. He pointed out that although it is true that it is rare for children who are not speaking by age 5 to develop speech after that time, it is also true that teaching children to use gestural language or symbols does not interfere with speech acquisition and sometimes promotes it (e.g., Millar, Light, & Schlosser, 2006).

The team met with Jayne's mother again and adopted a new approach. They did not try to tell Jayne's mother that she was unrealistic or in denial because she wanted her daughter to learn to talk. Yet, they did not try to pretend that they thought Jayne would learn to talk to humor her mother. They simply told her that they did not honestly know if Jayne would learn to talk, but that starting with gestures and picture symbols right now was the best option for expanding her communication. They made it clear that research has shown that this does not interfere with speech acquisition and sometimes is a helpful step toward developing speech. They were able to find some common ground, and Jayne's mother was satisfied that they had not given up on her daughter. They did not have to agree on everything; they just needed to focus on their areas of agreement rather than their differences.

Years later, Jayne's mother and her first teacher sat together at the grade school graduation event when Jayne was moving on to middle school. They had become good friends through the years, and neither one remembered that uncomfortable confrontation when Jayne was just starting school. It really did not matter who had been right and who had been wrong. As it turned out, they were both partly right. Jayne had developed a mixed-mode communication system that fit her needs and abilities. She occasionally used a few spoken words but primarily relied on gestures and pictures. Her mother and teacher were both very proud of her.

Although the terms are frequently used interchangeably, it may be useful to differentiate between hope and expectation. *Hope* often refers to a more general belief that things will be okay. *Expectation* typically refers to a belief that a specific outcome will or should occur. Hope may or may not express itself in specific expectations. Hopefulness has been shown to be extremely valuable in families of children with disabilities (Kauser, Jevne, & Sobsey, 2003; Miller, 2012). Specific expectations can be a double-edged sword. In some cases, they encourage meeting goals and objectives, but in other cases, both parents and professionals lose hope when their expectations are not met. Professionals should look for ways to cultivate and support hopefulness when interacting in families, but they need to individualize their approach to the specific needs of the families.

Encouraging Parental Involvement

Educators need to recognize that being a mother or a father of a child is a unique role that is critical in a child's life. The educational team often encourages

parents to take on additional roles as part of their children's educational program (e.g., behavior modifier, paraeducator, therapy assistant) to increase
parental involvement. Parents who take on these roles can make valuable contributions to their children's progress toward meeting goals and objectives, and
many parents are eager to assume these responsibilities. Educators, however,
must be careful about encouraging parents to take on these roles because these
sometimes can conflict with a parent's primary role as father or mother. Team
members should be sensitive to the parents' needs and preferences and ask
how involved parents want to be in extending their roles. For example, mealtimes can be important times for family bonding, but they can also be stressful
and difficult when children have significant challenges (Sullivan et al., 2000).
Parents can play critical roles in teaching their children new skills during mealtimes, but requiring parents to take on too much of a teaching role may actually
increase stress and discomfort for both parent and child. The team should consider how they can make meals more enjoyable for families as well as consider
how parents can help improve their children's mealtime skills. It is important
to ask parents what they feel comfortable with and what would make mealtimes more enjoyable.

Understanding the Family's Adaptation Style

Educators also need to consider the parents' or families' general adaptation
style. As previously discussed, some parents of children with severe and multiple disabilities cope by managing life with few changes in their beliefs, lifestyle,
or behavior, whereas most undergo profound transformations in almost every
aspect of their lives.

For example, Owen is a single father of a son who is medically fragile with
severe and multiple disabilities. At his son's program planning meeting, the
team asks Owen about following up with some of his son's programs at home,
but Owen says he does not feel like he can take on anything else. He tells the
team that he is very tired and stressed. He has a demanding job as an industrial
architect and is often taking work home with him. He can refuse these extra
last-minute work demands but feels like doing so will negatively affect his future career path. Owen's employer is understanding and willing to give him
less demanding and more flexible assignments, but Owen feels quite certain
that this would result in being passed over for potential future promotions. He
spent many years in school preparing for his career, has established himself
as a high performer, and has the potential to rise to the top of his career path.
Owen feels torn. On one hand, he wants to be a good father, and on the other
hand, he wants to continue to move forward in his career. He feels like he is
failing as a father and in his career. He does not think he can continue like this
indefinitely.

There is no simple solution for Owen's dilemma, but there are two primary
approaches. The first approach is to find additional supports for Owen and
his son so that he can better meet his work demands. The second is to reduce

the work demands so that he can better meet the needs of his son. There may be ways of combining these two approaches, and they should not always be viewed as mutually exclusive alternatives. For the purpose of simplifying this discussion, however, increasing supports so that Owen can continue his career can be viewed as coping, going on with life as much as possible as he would without his son. Altering his career path in order to better accommodate the needs of his son would be viewed as transformation.

Only Owen can decide what is best for him and his family. The traditional approach is to emphasize coping by helping Owen to find additional supports and reduce his caregiving demands so that he does not have to abandon his career goals. This, however, focuses on the rewards of careers and the burdens of caring for a child rather than acknowledging that both careers and child rearing have demands and rewards. It may also have a hidden implication that the demands of caregiving can be reduced without diminishing the rewards. Although having to choose between working and fathering roles may be unfair, it may be essential for Owen to determine his priorities before determining how to support him. If Owen is beginning to consider ramping back his career in favor of his fathering role, then it may be helpful to support his decision by letting him know that this is a legitimate option. Yet, if he is determined to maintain his career, then helping him cope by identifying sources of additional respite or in-home care support may be the best approach.

There is ample evidence that the vast majority of children with disabilities are best served in their families, but family care is only sustainable when there are adequate resources to maintain family function (e.g., McConnell, Savage, Breitkreuz, & Sobsey, 2015). Many factors play a role in influencing sustainable care, including child characteristics (e.g., the type and severity of disability) and family variables (e.g., parental health and work demands). Research suggests, however, that the family variables that influence the family's ability to maintain a daily routine play a greater role than the child's characteristics or needs (e.g., McConnell et al., 2015).

Interacting with Extended Families

Functionally, a child's family includes everyone who has a close, enduring bond with the child. At one extreme, a single parent and his or her child may be the only family members. At the other extreme, a large cohort of parents, grandparents, siblings, aunts and uncles, and close family friends may be important parts of the child's life (Taylor, 2004). Individuals in some cultures view child rearing more as a collective responsibility than others. This is generally a substantial asset for a child with intensive needs, but it can also create difficulties within some families if there are significant differences among family members in acceptance of the child or in how the child should be treated. This may also introduce complexity in home–school communication and program planning. For example, some parents may not feel that they can approve their child's goals or program plan until they have discussed it with a variety of extended family members.

In some cases, grandparents or other relatives may be functionally acting as the child's parents while the biological parents who are legal guardians are less directly involved. For example, the grandmother may be caring for the child while the parents are working or studying in another city or even another country. In such cases, it may be important to determine who has legal authority to make decisions on behalf of the child.

Respecting Cultural Diversity

We live in an increasingly culturally diverse world, and we need to acknowledge and respect linguistic, religious, and cultural differences in families (Taylor, 2004). About 40% of parents of children receiving special education services in American schools are members of cultural or linguistic minorities (Reiman, Beck, Coppola, & Engiles, 2010). It is essential for educators to know what language or languages are spoken in the home and whether translation services are required for parental participation in meetings. Although it seems obvious that the child's experience with language in the home and community is important for assessing the child's ability in schools, this issue is sometimes missed for children who are nonverbal, resulting in an overestimation of their impairments in receptive language.

It is important for all educators to acknowledge, respect, and celebrate the cultures of their students, but doing so can be especially challenging when students have severe disabilities that impair communication because these children may not be able to tell people at school about their family traditions. It is also important not to assume that all families of a specific nationality or culture practice their religion or traditions in the same way. For example, many religions and cultures have dietary restrictions (e.g., vegetarianism, no pork products, fast days), and various families within those cultures may observe them differently. Immigrant and minority families also differ greatly in their desire to maintain their culture or become part of the mainstream. Some believe that maintaining their former cultural identity is important, but others want to adapt to their new country and its culture as rapidly as possible. Therefore, it is important to find out what is important to each family. Once you have met and established a basic relationship with families, ask if there are any religious or cultural traditions of which the school should be aware, and tell the family to let you know if they have anything else to share any time during the school year. This topic should be addressed with all families, not just those with obvious indications of minority status.

Educators can do a lot to learn more about their students' cultural practices and how these can be addressed (e.g., Chen & Miles, 2004; Rogers-Adkinson, Ochoa, & Delgado, 2003). Although it is a good idea to specifically ask about cultural traditions, questions about many aspects of culture can be integrated into other discussions. For example, any special dietary practices can be addressed while discussing mealtimes. Discussions of whether the family would like a translator present for a meeting and, if so, if they would prefer to use a family friend, household member, or professional can occur as part of setting up that meeting. In some cases, siblings who attend the same school can be helpful as advisors on cultural matters. Educators who worked with the student in previous years can also provide valuable assistance.

Exercise some caution in using humor and being too informal when communicating with families from different cultures until you know the family well enough to feel confident about how they will respond. For example, an educator learning a single phrase to greet a family in their native language may be interpreted as disrespectful and condescending by some families. Refusing the offer of a small gift, food, or drink may be interpreted as an insult in some cultures. Keeping one's shoes on when entering a person's house is considered highly inappropriate in some cultures, whereas removing your shoes in someone else's house is considered an insult in other cultures. Educators must also be cognizant of their own cultural imprints. For example, many South Asians shake their heads from side to side when they are listening to you to indicate that they understand and agree. North Americans shake their heads in a similar way to indicate "no" or disagreement. As a result, a North American educator can be left with the feeling that a South Asian parent does not really accept what he or she is being told.

In addition, it is sometimes important to know how disability is portrayed and understood within the family's culture. Having a child with a disability is considered to be a punishment for parental sins in some cultures and something to be ashamed of in others. Having a child with an intellectual or developmental disability was considered to be shameful in mainstream North American culture prior to the end of World War II, and keeping such a child at home instead of institutionalizing the child was considered to be even more shameful. Although these concepts have substantially changed in the intervening years, some remnants remain, and similar attitudes persist in many other cultures. Although educators may not have the power to change deeply ingrained attitudes, they can play an important role in modeling, supporting, and encouraging positive attitudes among parents and families.

Forming collaborative relationships with parents is beneficial to all students, but it has been shown to have an even greater positive impact on educational outcomes for students from minority cultures (Kritikos, 2010). Although establishing a partnership with these families may require additional effort to overcome language or cultural differences, the educational benefits can be substantial. Although educators need to embrace cultural diversity and make every effort to work with a wide range of families, this does not override the educator's duty to act in the child's best interest. In most cases, what is best for the family is best for the child, and maintaining the best possible home–school relationship is always desirable. Practices that are abusive or grossly neglectful, however, cannot be overlooked in the name of respecting cultural diversity. If there is clear evidence that a child is endangered physically or emotionally, then educators must act to protect the child. In some cases, if treatment of a child appears to be less than optimal but does not appear to constitute abuse, then it may be more useful to try to encourage better parental practices or attitudes than to raise the issue of maltreatment.

Addressing Abuse

Most discussions about parents of children with disabilities focus on healthy families facing the challenge of caring for a child with exceptional needs. Child abuse and neglect are generally treated as separate topics. Nevertheless, child maltreatment is a risk for all children, regardless of the presence of disability, and children with disabilities experience greater risk. More information on the increased risk of abuse experienced by children with disabilities is included in Chapter 5.

Educators have a legal and ethical responsibility to file a report when there are reasons to believe that a child may be a victim of abuse. Specific procedures for reporting vary across school districts and sometimes across schools within a district, but the responsibility to report remains with the individual, regardless of the district policy or supervisory instructions. In some cases, a child may be immediately removed from parental care when it is clear that the child may be at immediate risk for significant harm. In many other situations, the child will remain with his or her family while an investigation takes place. In some cases, the child will remain in the family, possibly with some intervention or supports, even after abuse or neglect is confirmed. For example, the home may be monitored and parents may be required to undergo counseling or training.

Child welfare agencies play the major role in investigating possible maltreatment and determining what intervention might be needed. Schools may conduct their own inquiries into related matters, but they must be careful to work with child welfare agencies in order to avoid compromising the investigation. These inquiries should focus on whether the school should be taking additional actions of its own to protect the child. For example, if someone suspects that a child with a disability is being medically neglected because medication that should be administered in school is not being sent to school, then child welfare services should investigate whether this constitutes neglect and what action needs to be taken. The school may want to check its procedures, however, to determine how it should respond if the required medication is not provided. For example, should it require that medication be kept in the school for an extra week to ensure that it will always be available?

Educators must often interact with families after a report of suspected abuse or neglect has been made because reporting suspected maltreatment rarely results in immediate removal of the child from the family. This is often awkward and difficult. The parent is likely to be angry that a report has been made, and educators may be angry with the parent for what they believe to be mistreatment of the child. Educators should make an effort to maintain a respectful relationship with the family during these interactions. Blaming them or fighting with them is unlikely to be helpful for the child. If there is an ongoing investigation, then educators should not discuss it with the family, and if the family asks about it, then they should be referred to the investigating agency.

Although abuse of a student in the home is a difficult topic, some students with disabilities experience maltreatment by school personnel or other students. In some cases, a problem is identified in school that needs to be shared with parents. In other situations, parents note something that leads them to suspect that their child is being abused in school. Parents naturally find these circumstances alarming and may be extremely upset. All school personnel need to avoid taking a defensive position and minimizing parental concerns when these situations occur. They need to make it clear that the school will act to determine the facts and take any necessary action to protect the student.

FAMILY INVOLVEMENT IN EDUCATION

There is no single formula for parental involvement in education programs because every family is different, and team members need to find the best approach for each family. Some parents want to maximize their involvement in planning and program delivery. Others simply want the assurance that their child's education is in good hands, and once they are confident of that, they prefer minimal interaction with their child's school. Most parents fall someplace between these two extremes. It is essential for teachers and other professionals to understand the difference between the level of family involvement and the quality of parenting. Parents that seek intensive involvement with their children's programs and those who seek minimal involvement can be great parents, and both can be poor or even abusive parents.

The kind and amount of required interaction with families depend on a number of factors. Students with limited communication often require more home–school communication because they cannot share information about their experiences. This is especially true for children who have health challenges. For example, some parents need to closely monitor their child's fluid intake on a daily basis.

Child-Centered, Family-Centered, and Family-Friendly Approaches

Child-centered education is tailored to a student's unique set of needs and abilities and recognizes that children have individual rights independent of their families. A high degree of individualization is required, which is consistent with a child-centered approach, because students with severe and multiple disabilities differ greatly from one another and from other students.

Family-centered education shifts the primary intervention from the child to the parents or caregivers. Educators teach them skills that they use with their child. This approach is commonly employed in early intervention programs and home-based education. It assumes that the best interests of the child are also the best interests of the family as a whole. This is frequently but not always true. Sometimes the individual interests of the child are different than the interests of the parents, even in the best of families. Educators must remember that their first responsibility is to their students, but they also need to recognize that a happy and healthy family is in the student's best interest. A family-friendly approach is one that attempts to put the student's needs first while considering the needs of the family as a whole.

Getting Acquainted with Families

Although law and policy generally focus on formal requirements to include families in meetings and obtain consent, just getting to know families and becoming comfortable with each other is extremely important. This helps to open and maintain lines of communication, and it makes formal interactions more productive as well as more pleasant for everyone involved. Table 2.1 contains questions to consider asking parents and families while getting acquainted.

Although all of the questions can be helpful, it is important not to bombard parents with too many questions at once. In addition, some questions may be too probing to ask before a basic level of comfort is established. For example, asking parents how they discipline their child when first meeting them is likely to be perceived as intrusive and produce defensiveness. In addition, it is better to address many of these topics in context. For instance, asking parents how they discipline a child while discussing how to handle some challenging behavior in school may be perceived as acknowledging the parents' expertise, whereas asking the same question out of context may be seen as checking up on the parents.

It is also important for educators to share information about themselves in the process of getting acquainted. Asking too many questions about others while not sharing anything about oneself can make people uncomfortable. Finding some common interests is also helpful. There are often natural opportunities to identify common interests. For example, a family member may mention that he or she traveled over the summer to a destination where

Table 2.1.   Questions to ask parents and families to get acquainted

- What are your hopes and dreams for your child's future?
- Who are the members of the family?
- What works well with your child at home?
- What do you think are the most important things for us to know about your child?
- What is the best way for us to communicate with you?
- What were the best and worst aspects of your child's previous school experiences?
- Who are the family members that spend time with your child and participate in his or her care?
- What is considered respectful and disrespectful by the family?
- Who makes decisions affecting the children in the family?
- To whom does the family turn for support, assistance, and information?
- What are the family's values and customs?
- What are the family's child-rearing practices, forms of discipline, and expectations of children?
- What are the family's concerns and priorities related to their child with a disability?
- How can I learn more about the family's perspectives?
- What other health and community services does the family access for their child?

From Chen, D., Downing, J.E., & Peckham-Hardin, K.D. (2002). Working with families of diverse cultural and linguistic backgrounds: Considerations for culturally responsive positive behavior support. In J.M. Lucyshyn, G. Dunlap, & R.W. Albin (Eds.), *Families and positive behavior support: Addressing problem behaviors in family contexts* (p. 154). Baltimore, MD: Paul H. Brookes Publishing Co.; adapted by permission.

the teacher has also spent some time. Of course, the educator and parent always share a common interest in the student, and this is a great place to start. Educators can often engage parents by telling them about things they really like about the student or commenting on the student's possessions. For example, simple comments such as, "Sanjay has a beautiful smile" or "Where did you get that great lunchbox for Bonita?" can be great conversation starters.

Educators often find it difficult to acknowledge and address their own limitations to parents, but it is usually important to do so. Teachers and other professionals are sometimes expected to be experts and know exactly how to address the needs of every student. In reality, they are often unsure about their own abilities and their students' needs. This uncertainty is often at its zenith when educators face the prospect of meeting the needs of students with severe and multiple disabilities. Many educators respond by trying to mask their uncertainty with feigned confidence, which can be counterproductive. It may raise unrealistic expectations in parents, make communication more difficult, and encourage parents to adopt a similar pretense of absolute confidence in their abilities.

Program Planning

Although most educators and many parents have strong views on what makes a good educational program, few consciously consider this fundamental question: What is the purpose of education? We might also ask ourselves: Does education serve the same purpose for every student? Although these questions may seem abstract and more philosophical than practical, the answers to these questions are critical to placement and program planning decisions. It will be difficult to agree on placement and planning decisions unless educators and parents share common ideas about the answers to these questions. Although their wording may differ, most educational theorists and philosophers agree on a simple basic purpose—the purpose of education is to prepare individuals for their adult roles in society. John Dewey, often recognized as the father of modern education, put it like this many years ago: "The purpose of education has always been to every one, in essence, the same—to give the young the things they need in order to develop in an orderly sequential way into members of society" (1933, p. 441).

This purpose has not changed over the centuries, but education has changed because society and the roles available to individuals have changed. Literacy, numeracy, and other skills that are commonly the focus of today's schools are not the ultimate goal, but rather can be seen as tools that equip a child for a potential future role. The exclusion of students with severe disabilities from public schooling in the past was simply a step toward the planned exclusion from participation in society. Exclusion sent the message that these children did not need to be prepared for a role in society because they would not be a part of it. Similarly, segregated educational placements prepare students with disabilities for isolated futures. Of course, it might be argued that removing the student from the mainstream classroom of his or her same-aged peers would allow the teaching of some critical skills that will support enhanced reintegration into future environments, but this has not been well supported by outcomes from the last five decades of special education placements. For example, Myklebust (2013) found that students with similar levels of disability who were educated in regular classrooms with support services were more independent as adults than those educated in special education classes.

I can personally attest to the benefits of having a child with severe and multiple disabilities attend a general classroom. When my son Dave was 3 years old, he was enrolled in a special preschool for children with severe developmental impairments with a full complement of expert therapists. Parents attended along with their children, and no child in the class could walk yet. The first few classes were used to assess the students' skills, and then we were invited for a planning meeting, which did not go well for us. We were told that our son's impairments were too severe and that they would not be able to teach him to walk during that year, and therefore we were asked to leave the program. It was a shock, but we found an alternative within weeks. Dave was enrolled in regular child care with a support worker. Dave was walking independently within just a few weeks, lining up holding hands with a partner at child care. He learned to walk because that is what he needed to do to take part in activities with the other kids his age. I cannot tell you whether he would have learned to do that if he had not been expelled from the special preschool. I really do not know, but Dave never went back to a special classroom, and he walked across the stage at his high school and university graduations.

The essential point of this personal story is that we have to formulate a vision of what we hope a student's future can be rather than a limited view of the child's capabilities in order to plan a meaningful education for any student, but particularly for a student with severe and multiple disabilities. This vision may not always be accurate, and it is likely to undergo numerous revisions as the student progresses through the years, but it is an essential starting point.

Educators must work with parents as partners in developing programs for students with special needs. This partnership is required by law, but educators need to recognize that this is much more than a legal requirement. Parents are an extremely valuable resource. Karten pointed out, "Sometimes parents and guardians are not the ones in denial; it is the interventions of educators or experts that deny parents as being experts, the ones who are most knowledgeable about their own child's strengths and needs" (2010, p. 308).

Meetings with Parents

How parents are invited to program planning and other meetings to discuss their child's education is important (Browder & Spooner, 2011). A form letter notifying parents that the meeting will take place at a predetermined date may leave families with the impression that the school is doing the least possible to meet its legal obligations. Discussing upcoming meetings well ahead of actual scheduling and asking about the family's scheduling preferences are more likely to make parental attendance possible and also communicate a more welcoming attitude.

The student should be present at and participate in the meeting whenever possible, and this should be made clear to the parent. If for some reason the student will not be attending or if it is left to the parent to determine if the student will attend, then this should also be discussed in advance. If the student will not be included in the planning meeting, then determine how student preferences will be assessed and incorporated into the plan.

Be clear that parents are welcome to bring others to the meeting, and encourage them to bring those who are involved in the student's care or learning. Some parents may also want to bring their infants or young children to the meeting rather than leave them with another caregiver. This may be particularly important to accommodate in some cultures in which infants remain with their mothers continually for their first year or even longer.

Be certain parents have a clear idea of how long the meeting can be expected to last. Many parents have work commitments or child care requirements that they need to consider in scheduling. If the meeting runs longer than the parent expects, then this can create a problem, and if the parent is worried about whether the meeting will run late, then he or she will likely be anxious and distracted. Conversely, a parent who is expecting a 2-hour meeting and finds that the meeting only lasts 20 minutes may also be upset.

Be clear about the purpose of the meeting. If the meeting is designated as a time to discuss goals, objectives, activities, and instructional methods, then these topics should be open for discussion for all. Parents are often told that they are being invited to the meeting for their input and discover that they are being asked to sign a previously prepared plan with little or no opportunity to provide real input. This scenario may result in some parents passively accepting the plan while feeling resentful, and others demanding that the planning process starts over with their input.

Starting the meeting on time or as close to being on time as possible is also important. Delays that keep parents waiting increase anxiety and send a message that the parents' time is considered unimportant. It is important that team members who have a role in the meeting actually attend and arrive in a timely manner. There may be times when an absence or late arrival of a team member is unavoidable, but these should be rare exceptions. Having team members drop in for a few minutes also communicates a lack of involvement and interest. In addition, it is inconsistent with the fundamental concept of collaborative teaming, which requires sharing and discussion of input rather than a collection of separate ideas from various team members.

If parents cannot attend meetings despite efforts to include them, then educators must seek other ways to obtain input that suit the family. For example, some families may want to jot down some of their ideas in a communication book, others might e-mail, whereas others might be able to take part in the meeting by telephone or computer video link. In some cases, meeting at the family home can be considered an alternative to a school-based meeting. For example, it may be important for all the team members in an early intervention program with a significant home-based component to visit the home. Some families may find meeting in their home to be intrusive, whereas others may be much more comfortable meeting in their home.

When parents do attend, take time to introduce everyone at the meeting to help parents feel at ease. Having name cards for all who are in attendance may be useful to parents, especially to parents who have not had the opportunity to get to know all the team members. If there are more than two or three team members who are new to them, then most parents will forget some of the names and positions of the individuals present and may be reluctant to ask questions or address them if they are unsure of their names.

Offering food or beverages can be helpful in making some parents feel more comfortable, but it is optional. If food or beverages are not offered to family members in attendance, then team members should not bring them to the meeting. For example, team members should not arrive at the meeting with their coffee mug in hand if coffee is not served at the meeting. Table 2.2. provides additional tips for planning meetings.

Resolving Disputes with Families

Differences of opinion and disputes can sometimes occur, even in the best relationships between educators and parents. When they do, it is important to seek a resolution that addresses the specific issue and restores the relationship between school and family. In most cases, it is desirable to resolve the issue without involving others. In some cases, it may be necessary to bring others into the discussion. For example, a parent may want the classroom assistant to bring a student down the block to an after-school child care at the end of the school day, but this might conflict with school policy. As a result, the principal may need to be part of the discussion. Table 2.3 lists tips for effectively addressing conflicts.

Communicating with Families

Starting in preschool, a communication book traveled back and forth between home and school in our son's backpack every day. A single notebook never lasted a whole school year, and some years we filled three or more. We added dedicated cell phones for emergency calls by junior high school, one in his backpack and the other with myself or his mom. The paper notebooks are now gone and our face-to-face, cell phone, and e-mail communications are supplemented with an electronic activity journal, a blog that ties Dave's activities to his program goals.

Communication between educators and families can take place in various venues and utilize several different modes. Notebooks, commonly called communication books, that travel back and forth between home and school have been an essential part of communication for decades. They are still a very

Table 2.2. Tips for planning meetings

- If you are not well acquainted with the families, then take time to get to know them before the meeting.
- Find out who makes the decisions in the family regarding the child's education.
- Ask parents if they have any questions before the formal planning process begins.
- Let parents know that the most important role they have is parenting.
- Ask families whether they feel like they can take on an additional role in programming at home. Many families are delighted to take on an active role in programming, but many others are already stretched to their limits with work and caregiving responsibilities.
- Explain to families that their involvement in their child's educational program is invaluable and will result in learning experiences that benefit the child. Teachers need information about the child's strengths, interests, abilities, and needs and the family's preferences, goals, and concerns about the child. Because children spend more time with their families than with teachers, much of a child's learning will occur out of school, so parents need specific strategies and resources to promote the child's learning.
- Assist families in learning about the educational system by providing information about the services and programs in the school district, the families' rights, and the requirements of the individualized education program (IEP) process.
- Provide information in a format (e.g., individual discussion; print, video, or Internet resources) best suited to the individual family.
- Ask families what they would like to learn that is related to their child's education (e.g., assistive technology, augmentative and alternative communication devices or methods, positive behavior interventions and supports) or other topics of interest. Teachers may offer information on selected topics in a variety of formats (e.g., group meetings; video, print, or Internet resources) based on a family's needs and preferences.
- Prepare the family for the IEP meeting by discussing the agenda; explaining procedures; reviewing assessments; and asking about the family's goals, concerns, and questions about the child's education.
- Arrange for interpreters if needed, plan the meeting with the interpreter, and find out about culturally respectful ways of communicating with families and encouraging their participation in meetings. Ask parents if they want to help choose the interpreter. This can avoid the situation in which an interpreter may be linguistically qualified but culturally unacceptable to the family.
- Encourage a parent to bring a friend, relative, or representative to the meeting or event if he or she would be more comfortable.
- Create a welcoming atmosphere by providing a comfortable setting for the meeting, offering some refreshments, making introductions, having time for small talk, and having an open conversation about the issues being discussed.
- Recognize that some families may not be able to attend meetings despite your best efforts. Nevertheless, make sure that these families understand their legal rights and the educational options for their child. Let these parents know that they are missed and that you understand their particular situation. Continue to keep in touch through home–school journals, and call once in a while to find out how they are doing.

From Chen, D., & Miles, C. (2004). Working with families. In F.P. Orelove, D. Sobsey, & R.K. Silberman (Eds.), *Educating children with multiple disabilities: A collaborative approach* (pp. 31–66). Baltimore, MD: Paul H. Brookes Publishing Co.; Adapted with permission.

good option for many families. They allow parents to let the educators know about relevant events from home and educators to let family members know about relevant events from school. For example, a student's parent may want the school to know that his or her child had a rough night and little sleep, or the teacher may want the family to know that the student seemed uncomfortable and refused most of his or her lunch at school. Some days may require extensive entries, whereas others may be as simple as, "Sheena had a great day, lots of smiles. Send more flexistraws. –B.H." Other days may require much longer and more complex entries.

Daily notes back and forth in the communication book represent a simple and reliable way to report these events. Some basic rules to ensure that communication books are effective include the following:

- There should be at least one note from school and at least one from home each day, even if the note briefly states, "Good day, nothing unusual."

Table 2.3. Tips for effectively addressing conflicts between educators and parents

- Seek areas of agreement and focus on the child's needs and not on the school or the system.
- Find as much common ground as possible. For example, if you both can agree that you want what is best for the student, then you can start from there.
- Begin with the premise that most issues are negotiable and then problem-solve conflicts between family priorities and professional recommendations. Provide alternatives for suggestions.
- Remember that the ideal solution is the best interest of the student, not winning the dispute. Sometimes the family perspective may prevail because it is the best solution. Sometimes it may be better to allow families to prevail in order to preserve a positive relationship with the family.
- Although accommodating families is important, educators must place the student's best interests first.
- Make an effort to comment on positive aspects of the student and family, even when disagreement persists.
- Let the family know if there is a time limit for the discussion, and then do not watch the clock.
- Tailor your comments for the family's situation. For example, use the child's name and provide specific examples of the child's behaviors or activities.
- Explain acronyms and technical terms and use words that are easily understood, but do not talk down to families.
- Never dismiss the parents' concerns as denial or unrealistic expectations.
- Express a genuine interest in learning about the child (e.g., strengths, interests, needs, typical activities, home routine, social interactions) and understanding the family (e.g., composition, roles, responsibilities, activities).
- Invite the family to share their observations and concerns.
- Describe your understanding of the differences to be resolved.
- Communicate your concerns in a straightforward and nonjudgmental way, and ask the family for help.
- Admit that teachers do not have all of the answers. Share what you think, believe, and know, and identify what you do not know.
- Be prepared to genuinely consider the family's perspective.
- Evaluate the child's current performance and base recommendations on measurable outcomes.
- Look at the world from the family's perspective and accept the family's point of view.
- Discuss strategies to achieve objectives.
- Agree on and record who will do what, where, and when, and develop a written action plan.
- Identify a time for another discussion to obtain feedback from the family on what is working, what needs to be changed, and any results of the intervention strategies.

From Chen, D., & Miles, C. (2004). Working with families. In F.P. Orelove, D. Sobsey, & R.K. Silberman (Eds.), *Educating children with multiple disabilities: A collaborative approach* (pp. 31–66). Baltimore, MD: Paul H. Brookes Publishing Co.; Adapted by permission.

- One person from school and home should be responsible for reading the new entries each day.

- Entries should be legibly signed or initialed. If initials are used, then a list of names and initials should be provided so each reader knows who wrote each note.

- If abbreviations are used, then there needs to be a list of abbreviations someplace in the book to ensure that they are understood.

- Keep the book in a specified convenient place and make sure it goes back and forth with the student each day. For example, it might be kept in the student's school backpack or in a pouch on the back of the student's wheelchair.

The traditional communication books are sometimes being replaced with electronic alternatives because of the advent of smartphones and tablet computers. For example, some students with severe and multiple disabilities have tablet, notebook, or laptop computers that go back and forth between home and school each day that are used as part of their educational programs. Many teachers, students, and family members have smartphones available, and students who are medically fragile may have dedicated cell phones that go back and forth with them to facilitate immediate contact with families or medical assistance in case of any emergency. Home and school computers with Internet access are also frequently available.

In some cases, electronic devices have advantages over the traditional notebooks for home–school communication. In other cases, a simple notebook may be the better alternative. A number of things may make electronic alternatives worth considering. Table 2.4 lists some considerations for choosing electronic or paper alternatives.

There are sometimes advantages in blending the use of electronic communication with the traditional communication book. Many parents and educators may find a simple communication notebook easier to use but want to supplement occasional entries with photographs that are electronically recorded and transmitted. For example:

> Lenny has been staring off into space and moving his head to the left several times during the day. We do not know if this is a seizure or something else (see video on his iPad). Have you seen this? Do you know what this is?

Numerous free and low-cost journaling and diary apps are available from the Apple App Store, Google Play, Microsoft, and other software companies and can be easily adapted for use as a communication book. Several companies (e.g., WordPress, Blogspot) provide platforms for free, private blogs that also can be used for communication books.

Table 2.4. Paper communication notebook versus electronic alternatives

Traditional paper home–school communication book	Electronic alternatives: e-mail, instant messaging, blog, apps, and so forth
Simple	May require set up and, for some users, learning new skills
Inexpensive	Requires equipment, but may use equipment already available
Only requires basic literacy	Requires some computer literacy
Primarily text, but pictures or additional documents can be attached	Can easily incorporate pictures, videos, and attachments
Goes back and forth with student	Can go back and forth with student, or devices already in school, home, and elsewhere can be used
Only available to one author or reader at a time	Can be available at multiple times and places to various people
Works for one communication from home and one from school on each school day	Can be available at all times to both home and school
Durable and lasting	May be subject to computer crashes or service interruptions
May be lost or misplaced	Messages and entries may be intentionally or accidentally deleted

In many cases, there are frequent opportunities for informal communication between educators and family members. The frequency of these opportunities varies substantially across families. For example, some parents may personally bring their children to school each morning and pick them up at the end of the school day, whereas other children come and go by bus, and their parents only come to school for specific meetings. Opportunities for informal communication are good times to build a positive relationship with families and share general information about how things are going at home and school. Informal interactions, however, cannot take the place of a more formal system of communication for sharing important information. Returning to the example of a parent dropping off or picking up his or her child, both the parent and educator are likely to be juggling a number of tasks at this time. A teacher may be trying to make sure that all of his or her students remember their coats and backpacks, get several students out to their bus, greet other parents who are picking up their children, and determine why one student has been upset while this conversation with a specific parent is taking place. The parent may be putting on the child's coat, repositioning the child in his or her wheelchair, or checking to make sure his or her child's backpack has everything that should be there. These do not typically make good times for sharing important information, and it may be necessary to let parents know that they may need to remind you later of something with an e-mail or note so you will not forget.

SIBLINGS

Many children with severe and multiple disabilities have brothers or sisters. Two or more children in the same family may have severe disabilities in a significant minority of cases. This may occur by mere chance, as a result of common genetic risk factors, or other common risk factors such as extreme prematurity in multiple births. The family faces greater challenges and is likely to require greater support when more than one child has a disability. More frequently, however, children with severe and multiple disabilities have typically developing brothers and sisters.

Considerable research has demonstrated some positive, some negative, and some mixed effects on siblings of children with disabilities. Positive effects on siblings include personal growth, a more mature perspective on life, increased sensitivity, improved family dynamics, greater social-emotional maturity, more socially responsible attitudes as adults, and a variety of others (Findler & Vardi, 2009). Reported negative effects include increased stress, risk for depression, anxiety, and risk for behavior problems (Stoneman, 2005). Research results often conflict regarding whether siblings of children with disabilities differ from other children on measures of emotional and behavioral well-being. One reason for the conflicting results appears to be related to whether the studies control adequately for other factors that affect well-being. A study using a large sample and adequate controls for other variables known to influence well-being (Emerson & Giallo, 2014) found that siblings of children with disabilities fared slightly worse on measures of well-being than other children, without controlling for other variables. The difference was small, however, and most of the differences disappeared when other factors such as socioeconomic status and parental educational levels were controlled. This, as well as evidence from studies, indicates that the mere presence of a sibling with a disability does not harm children. Stoneman pointed out the following in her comprehensive review, "Many siblings thrive and benefit from having a sibling with a disability," but "it is also true that a few children seem to be harmed by the experience" (2005, p. 341). Why some siblings thrive while others experience difficulties is not entirely clear, but some factors have emerged.

Siblings also do better when parents are managing challenges well. The entire family is likely to suffer when parents are overwhelmed with challenges that they cannot manage. The parents and other adults may also act as models, and their children often display similar attitudes. So, if the parents and other adults express positive attitudes toward having a child with a disability in the family and how it affects their lives, then the sibling is likely to adopt similar attitudes. The level of a sibling's involvement in the life of the child with a disability also appears to be important. Placing too much responsibility on the sibling may be overwhelming and extremely stressful, but too little may also lead to difficulties. Because a large portion of parental activities are likely to be oriented around the child with a severe disability, leaving the sibling out of these activities can result in the sibling feeling isolated from the family. Siblings seem to do best when they are encouraged to take part at a level that is comfortable for them. Siblings also need to be acknowledged and respected for their contributions and need some time and attention of their own from their parents and others.

Educators can play a useful role by letting parents know that most siblings do fine, modeling positive attitudes, and acknowledging the contributions of siblings. If a sibling appears to be struggling emotionally, seems to be overwhelmed by stress or excessive responsibilities, or requests help, then he or she may require individual support. In many cases, if the sibling is experiencing difficulties, then it is a sign that the family as a whole needs more support.

CONCLUSION

Families of children with severe and multiple disabilities face exceptional challenges. Most handle these challenges well; some families are not strong enough to handle these challenges; and even the strongest families can be occasionally overwhelmed. Educators and other team members need to recognize that the most important role for fathers and mothers is to be a good parent, and they should acknowledge and support this role. Parents and sometimes siblings also play important roles in education. Thus, educators need to build rapport with families and individualize their involvement in educational programming based on what families can manage, maximizing input from and communication with families while minimizing demands on the family's time.

REFLECTION QUESTIONS

1. When meeting the parents of a new student with severe and multiple disabilities, what might be some good things to discuss to get to know the family?

2. What are some advantages and disadvantages of traditional communication notebooks and electronic alternatives?

3. What do you think parents would want to know about you as their child's teacher?

CHAPTER ACTIVITIES

1. Discuss some things that indicate that families are adapting or have adapted to their child's severe and multiple disabilities through coping, resilience, or transformation.

2. Imagine that a family tells you that they suspect that their child with severe and multiple disabilities is being physically abused by someone at school. How would you respond? What actions should you take?

REFERENCES

American School Counselor Association. (2010). *Ethical standards for school counselors.* Alexandria, VA: Author.

Blacher, J. (1984). Sequential stages of parental adjustment to the birth of a child with handicaps: Fact or artifact? *Mental Retardation, 22,* 55–68.

Blackwell, D.L. (2010). Family structure and children's health in the United States: Findings from the National Health Interview Survey, 2001–2007. *Vital Health Statistics, 10*(246), 1–166.

Bourke-Taylor, H., Howie, L., & Law, M. (2011). Barriers to maternal workforce participation and relationship between paid work and health. *Journal of Intellectual Disability Research, 55,* 511–520.

Browder, D.M., & Spooner, F. (2011). *Teaching students with moderate and severe disabilities.* New York, NY: Guilford Press.

Burkhard, A. (2013). A different life: Caring for an adolescent or young adult with severe cerebral palsy. *Journal of Pediatric Nursing, 28,* 357–363.

Cassidy, T., Giles, M., & McLaughlin, M. (2014). Benefit finding and resilience in child caregivers. *British Journal of Health Psychology, 19,* 606–618.

Chen, D., Downing, J.E., & Peckham-Hardin, K.D. (2002). Working with families of diverse cultural and linguistic backgrounds: Considerations for culturally responsive positive behavior support. In J.M. Lucyshyn, G. Dunlap, & R.W. Albin (Eds.), *Families and positive behavior support: Addressing problem behaviors in family contexts* (p. 154). Baltimore, MD: Paul H. Brookes Publishing Co.

Chen, D., & Miles, C. (2004). Working with families. In F.P. Orelove, D. Sobsey, & R.K. Silberman (Eds.), *Educating children with multiple disabilities: A collaborative approach* (4th ed., pp. 31–66). Baltimore, MD: Paul H. Brookes Publishing Co.

Council for Exceptional Children. (2010). *Special education professional ethical principles.* Reston, VA: Author.

Dewey, J. (1933). Why have progressive schools. *Current History, 38,* 441–448.

Dyches, T.T., Smith, T.B., Korth, B.B., Roper, S.O., & Mandleco, B. (2012). Positive parenting of children with developmental disabilities: A meta-analysis. *Research in Developmental Disabilities, 33,* 2213–2220.

Earley, L., & Cushway, D. (2002). The parentified child. *Clinical Child Psychology and Psychiatry, 7*(2), 163–178.

Emerson, E., & Giallo, R. (2014). The wellbeing of siblings of children with disabilities. *Research in Developmental Disabilities, 35,* 2085–2092.

Findler, L., & Vardi, A. (2009). Psychological growth among siblings of children with and without intellectual disabilities. *Intellectual and Developmental Disabilities, 47*(1), 1–12.

Freedman, B.H., Kalb, L.G., Zablotsky, B., & Stuart, E.A. (2012). Relationship status among parents of children with autism spectrum disorders: A population-based study. *Journal of Autism and Developmental Disorders, 42*(4), 539–548. doi:10.1177/1359104502007002005

Gallagher, P., Fialka, J., Rhodes, C., & Arceneaux, C. (2002). Working with families: Rethinking denial. *Young Exceptional Children 5*(2), 11–18.

Grant, S., Cross, E., Wraith, J.E., Jones, S., Mahon, L., Lomax, M., Bigger, B., & Hare, D. (2013). Parental social support, coping strategies, resilience factors, stress, anxiety and depression levels in parents of children with MPS III (Sanfilippo syndrome) or children with intellectual disabilities (ID). *Journal of Inherited Metabolic Disorders, 36*(2), 281–291.

Greeff, A.P., & Nolting, C. (2013). Resilience in families of children with developmental disabilities. *Families, Systems, and Health, 31*, 396–405.

Griffen, K.I. (2000, February 28). Parental break time. *The Milwaukee Journal Sentinel*, p. G1.

Hartley, S. L., Barker, E. T., Seltzer, M. M., Floyd, F., Greenberg, J., Orsmond, G., & Bolt, D. (2010). The relative risk and timing of divorce in families of children with an autism spectrum disorder. *Journal of Family Psychology, 24*(4), 449–457.

Hill, K.M. (2012). The prevalence of youth with disabilities among older youth in out-of-home placement: An analysis of state administrative data. *Child Welfare, 91*(4), 61–84.

Individuals with Disabilities Education Improvement Act (IDEA) of 2004, PL 108-446, 20 U.S.C. §§ 1400 *et seq.*

Janvier, A., Farlow, B., & Wilfond, B.S. (2012). The experience of families with children with trisomy 13 and 18 in social networks. *Pediatrics, 130*(2), 293–298.

Karten, T. (2010). *Inclusion strategies that work!* (2nd ed.). Thousand Oaks, CA: Corwin.

Kausar, S., Jevne, R., & Sobsey, D. (2003). Hope in families of children with developmental disabilities. *Journal on Developmental Disabilities, 10*(1), 35–46.

Kay, J. (2009). Representing parents with disabilities in child protection proceedings. *Michigan Child Welfare Law Journal, 13*(1), 27–36.

Kingsley, E. P. (1987). Welcome to Holland. Privately published.

Kritikos, E.P. (2010). *Special education assessment.* Upper Saddle River, NJ: Merrill.

Kübler-Ross, E. (1969) *On death and dying.* New York, NY: Scribner.

Lederman, V. R., Alves Bdos, S., Maria, J. N., Schwartzman, J. S., D'Antino, M. E., & Brunoni, D. (2015). Divorce in families of children with Down Syndrome or Rett Syndrome. *Ciência & Saúde Coletiva, 20*(5), 1363-1369.

Lightfoot, E., & LaLiberte, T.L. (2013, Fall). Parenting with disability: What do we know? *CW360 The Intersection of Child Welfare and Disability: Focus on Parents,* 4–5.

Marshak, L.E., Dandeneau, C.J., Prezant, F.P., & L'Amoreaux, N.A. (2010). The school counselor's guide to helping students with disabilities. San Francisco, CA: Jossey-Bass.

McConnell, D., Savage, A., Breitkreuz, R., & Sobsey, D. (2015). Sustainable family care for children with disabilities. *Journal of Child and Family Studies, 25*, 530-544. doi:10.1007/s10826-015-0245-0.

McConnell, D., Savage, A., Sobsey, D., & Uditsky, B. (2014). Benefit-finding or finding benefits? The positive impact of children with disabilities. *Disability and Society, 30*, 29-45. doi:10.1080/09687599.2014.984803

Millar, D.C., Light, J.C., & Schlosser, R.W. (2006). The impact of augmentative and alternative communication intervention on the speech production of individuals with developmental disabilities: A research review. *Journal of Speech, Language, and Hearing Research, 49*(2), 248–264.

Miller, G. (2012). Hope is a virtue. *Journal of Child Neurology, 27*(12), 1616–1617.

Myklebust, J.O. (2013). Disability and adult life: Dependence on social security among former students with special educational needs in their late twenties. *British Journal of Special Education, 40*, 5–13.

No Child Left Behind Act of 2001, PL 107–110, 115 Stat. 1425, 20 U.S.C. §§ 6301 *et seq.*.

Ōe, K. (1964). *A personal matter.* New York, NY: Grove Press.

Ōe, K. (1995). *A healing family.* Tokyo, Japan: Kodansha International.

Reiman, J.W., Beck, L., Coppola, T., & Engiles, A. (2010). *Parents' experiences with the IEP Process: Considerations for improving practice.* Eugene, OR: Center for Appropriate Dispute Resolution in Special Education.

Risdall, G., & Singer, D.H.S. (2004). Marital adjustment in parents of children with disabilities: A historical review and meta-analysis. *Research and Practice for Persons with Severe Disabilities, 29,* 95–103.

Rogers-Adkinson, D., Ochoa, T.A., & Delgado, B. (2003). Developing cross-cultural competence: Serving families of children with significant cultural needs. *Focus on Autism and Other Developmental Disabilities, 18,* 4–8.

Scorgie, K., & Sobsey, D. (2000). Transformational outcomes associated with parenting children who have disabilities. *Mental Retardation, 38*(3), 195–206.

Seligman, M. (1995). Confessions of a parent/professional. In D. Mayer (Ed.), *Uncommon fathers: Reflections on raising a child with a disability* (pp. 169–183). Bethesda, MD: Woodbine House.

Sobsey, D. (2004). Marital stability and marital satisfaction in families of children with disabilities. *Developmental Disabilities Bulletin, 32*(1), 62–83.

Solomon, A. (2012). *Far from the tree: Parents, children, and the search for identity.* New York, NY: Scribner.

Stoneman, Z. (2005). Siblings of children with disabilities: Research themes. *Mental Retardation, 43*(5), 339–350.

Sullivan, P.B., Lambert, B., Rose, M., Ford-Adams, M., Johnson, A., & Griffiths, P. (2000). Prevalence and severity of feeding and nutritional problems in children with neurological impairment: Oxford feeding study. *Developmental Medicine and Child Neurology, 42,* 674–680. doi:10.1111/j.1469-8749.2000.tb00678.x

Taylor, G.R. (2004). *Parenting skills and collaborative services for students with disabilities.* Lanham, MD: Scarecrow Education.

Turnbull, A.P., Turnbull, H.R., Kyzar, K., & Zuna, N. (2016). Fostering family-professional partnerships. In F.E Brown, M.E. Snell, & J.J. McDonnell (Eds.), *Instruction of students with severe disabilities* (8th ed., pp. 27–54). New York: Pearson.

Weiner, M.B. (1991, November 6). Stress or raising disabled children often leads to breakup of families. *The Orange County Register,* p. A16.

3

Educating Students with Physical Disabilities

TOBY M. LONG AND RACHEL BRADY

CHAPTER OBJECTIVES

1. Learn about the characteristics of students with physical disabilities

2. Understand important considerations for creating effective educational program plans for students with physical disabilities

3. Become familiar with classroom-based interventions to optimize learning and promote participation for students with physical disabilities

4. Understand the role of related services providers in educating students with physical disabilities

5. Learn how members of the educational team should collaborate and communicate in supporting the student with physical disabilities

KEY TERMS

- Arthrogryposis or arthrogryposis multiplex congenita (AMC)
- Assistive technology (AT) device
- AT services
- Cerebral palsy (CP)
- Consultation
- Handling
- International classification of function (ICF)
- Muscle strength
- Muscle tone
- Muscular dystrophy (MD)
- Osteogenesis imperfecta (OI)
- Sensory systems
- Spina bifida (myelomeningocele or myelodysplasia)
- Spinal muscular atrophy (SMA)
- Traumatic brain injury (TBI)

Randy Lewis was born at 25 weeks gestation, weighing 920 grams (a little more than 2 pounds). He was the third child of a two-parent family in which both parents worked full time outside of the home. Neonatal complications included respiratory distress syndrome and stage 1 retinopathy of prematurity. Randy was intubated for several months. He was eventually diagnosed with chronic lung disease that necessitated a long-term stay in the neonatal intensive care unit. He was irritable and tolerated only minimal handling because of his health complications.

Randy was discharged at 6 months of age, requiring 24-hour nursing care and 24-hour oxygen therapy. He began receiving early intervention services as soon as he was home. Collaborating with the family, the infant–toddler program developed a flexible individualized family service plan guided by the changing needs of Randy's health and his family's needs. The physical therapist (PT) served as the primary service provider and service coordinator because of Randy's significant motor delays. She helped the family discover efficient ways to comfort and console Randy, suggested oral feeding techniques, and encouraged play. The therapist consulted regularly with the family, a community health nurse, and the family's part-time child care provider.

Randy was diagnosed with CP at 16 months old. The PT consulted with the team's occupational therapist (OT) and AT specialist to introduce Randy to switches, buttons, or devices that cause an attached toy to make sounds or light up when pressed. This helped Randy play independently for short periods of time. The early intervention team began the transition process to a group child care setting when Randy was 25 months old. The early intervention service providers created a plan with the family and child care provider to prepare him for a full-time child care program. The team implemented the plan to help Randy increase time in sitting and standing with proper equipment, have regular play times with other children in the neighborhood 2 days per week, and be on a regular nap schedule.

Randy was attending a full-time child care program by the time he was 3 years old. He was able to stand in a stander, move with an adapted walker, pick up finger foods, and use a variety of switches to interact and play with other children. The intervention team helped the child care staff embed therapeutic strategies into inside and outside play activities, art, and center activities and adapted a variety of materials with switches that all the children could use.

Randy was using a power drive wheelchair and a simple computerized voice synthesizer communication device when he made the transition to kindergarten. His early childhood special education team consulted extensively with school staff prior to school because the kindergarten staff were hesitant to include him due to his special devices and significant physical disabilities, and they met regularly during the school year to support Randy's inclusion. A paraprofessional worked in the classroom to assist the teacher in adapting instruction for Randy. Randy successfully completed kindergarten and first grade with continuous consultation among his teachers and therapists.

Randy's AT was adapted throughout second and third grades as his academic demands increased, and his teachers were provided close consultation so they felt comfortable providing the necessary technology for the classroom. Consultation for Randy involved the service provider sharing her expertise and periodically collaborating with the classroom teacher and other team members to make decisions about what type of technology Randy could benefit from and how to effectively use it in the classroom to meet Randy's outcomes. It was clear that Randy needed individualized support, even with these additional adaptations and team support. He began receiving services in a resource room for 1 hour a day in the middle of third grade, where he learned to organize his assignments and projects and received help with his evergrowing AT. Randy's resource room teacher also had expertise in AT; thus, he was able to adapt the general education curriculum to meet Randy's individual strengths and needs, working daily with his third-grade teacher and paraprofessional. Although Randy is becoming increasingly independent, his physical disabilities will likely continue to present challenges for him. His team reports that they are committed to collaborating in order to provide Randy with the accommodations necessary for him to continue to succeed in an inclusion program. This strength-based approach, along with the unified support of Randy's family and all members of his team, including school building administrators and ancillary personnel (e.g., bus drivers, cafeteria workers), has helped Randy become a valued member of his school.

CHARACTERISTICS OF CHILDREN WITH PHYSICAL DISABILITIES

Physical disabilities are conditions that affect body function or structures; may limit physical activities such as sitting, walking, reaching, or activities of daily living; and restrict participation in self-care, classroom, and other school-related activities, including extracurricular social activities (World Health Organization, 2012). Physical disabilities may also limit a student's ability to verbally communicate if his or her mouth and jaw muscles and structures are affected. Students with severe physical disabilities often require intervention from personnel with highly specialized skills and knowledge. Low-incidence physical disabilities include cerebral palsy (CP), spina bifida, muscular dystrophy (MD), and traumatic brain injury (TBI). Students with physical disabilities often have co-occurring conditions such as visual impairment, cognitive delays or intellectual disabilities, and hearing loss. They also may have uneven muscle strength, stiffness and immobility of muscles or joints, laxity in muscles or joints, or difficulty coordinating movement.

Common Types of Physical Disability

This section describes several of the more common types of conditions experienced by children with severe and multiple disabilities. Table 3.1 provides a summary of these and less common conditions.

Table 3.1. Overview of low-incidence physical disabilities

Condition	Characteristics	Associated conditions	More information
Cerebral palsy: Injury to motor and other centers of the brain	Increased muscle tone Muscle weakness and imbalance Poor coordination and balance	Communication disorders Visual impairment Hearing impairment Contractures Learning or intellectual disabilities Seizures Challenging behavior Eating difficulties	United Cerebral Palsy http://www.ucp.org
Spina bifida: Incomplete spinal column formation	Muscle weakness or paralysis limiting function in the muscles of the legs and lower to mid body	Latex allergy Spinal cord restriction Obesity Skin breakdown Gastrointestinal disorders Learning, cognitive, and social-emotional delays or disabilities	Spina Bifida Association http://www.spinabifida association.org
Traumatic brain injury: Injury to the brain because of force that is not due to birth, disease, or infection	Injury to motor and other centers of the brain causing mild to severe movement and balance and coordination disorders; symptoms and recovery depend on severity of the injury	Seizures Increased muscle tone Memory and attention problems Behavioral challenges Cognitive and communication delays or disabilities	Brain Injury Association of America http://www.biausa.org/index.htm
Muscular dystrophy: Progressive disease that destroys muscles	Muscles progressively become weaker with loss of mobility and balance, fatigue	Hydrocephalus Cognitive delay	Muscular Dystrophy Family Foundation http://www.mdff.org/
Arthrogryposis: Connective tissue condition causing muscle and joint limitations	Joint contractures Muscle weakness	Heart and respiratory conditions	Avenues: A National Support Group for Arthrogryposis Multiplex Congenita http://www.avenues foramc.com
Spinal muscular atrophy: Progressive disease causing muscle wasting	Muscle weakness and paralysis in the legs and progressing up the body beginning in infancy through adolescence, depending on the type	Respiratory conditions Contractures Skin breakdown	Spinal Muscular Atrophy Foundation http://www.sma foundation.org/
Osteogenesis imperfecta: Disorder of collagen production	Easily broken bones and teeth causing muscle weakness, bone and joint deformities, and short stature	Bleeding Bruising Fractures Jaw and dental problems Hearing impairment Scoliosis Respiratory conditions Fragile skin	Osteogensis Imperfecta Foundation http://www.oif.org/site/PageServer

Sources: United Cerebral Palsy (2015); Spina Bifida Association (2015); Brain Injury Association of America (2015); Muscular Dystrophy Family Foundation (n.d.); Avenues: A National Support Group for Arthrogryposis Multiplex Congenita (n.d.); Spinal Muscular Atrophy Foundation (2015); Osteogensis Imperfecta (OI) Foundation (2015).

Cerebral Palsy   CP is the most common physical disability in childhood, affecting 1.5–4 infants per 1,000 live births (Arneson et al., 2009). CP is an umbrella term describing a nonprogressive condition characterized by varying degrees of movement disorder. CP is caused by damage to the motor control centers of the brain and often to other brain areas. Risk factors for the brain damage that results in CP include premature birth, disruption of oxygen or blood supply to the brain, infection to the mother during pregnancy, brain infection in an infant or young child, abnormal fetal brain development, or trauma. Students with CP may also have co-occurring conditions such as learning disabilities, intellectual disabilities, seizures, communication disorders, visual impairment, hearing loss, and challenging behavior (Hoon & Tolley, 2013). Classification systems have been created to help describe specific types of CP because CP is a broad term used to describe multiple motor impairments caused by damage to the brain. Classification systems range from descriptions of muscle tone abnormalities and types of movement disorders to limb or body distribution or motor function (Palisano et al., 1997; Rethlefsen, Ryan, & Kay, 2010). Table 3.2 describes these classification systems.

Table 3.2.   Classification systems for cerebral palsy

Classification system	Description
Muscle tone and movement disorders	
Spasticity	Increased muscle tone, decreased voluntary muscle control
Athetosis	Slow, writhing movements of the arms, legs, and facial/oral muscles
Ataxia	Decreased balance, lack of control around shoulders and hips and with reaching, standing, and walking
Hypotonic	Low muscle tone, especially in the neck and trunk, difficulty initiating movement, slumped posture, loose joints
Body distribution	
Hemiplegia	One side of the body affected
Diplegia	Legs affected but also some weakness or decreased coordination in the arms
Quadriplegia	Arms and legs affected; often includes weakness and poor coordination of the neck, trunk, and facial/oral muscles
Gross motor function classification system (GMFCS) *General function for school-age children*	
Level I	Walks without limitations in school and community; uses stairs; can jump and run but coordination limited
Level II	Walks with limitations; difficulty jumping, running, and walking long distances
Level III	Walks using a handheld mobility device; may require physical assistance for sit to stand
Level IV	Self-mobility with limitations; may use powered mobility, adapted seating
Level V	Transported by manual wheelchair; difficulty keeping head upright or sitting; complete physical assistance to move out of wheelchair

Sources: Palisano, Rosenbaum, Bartlett, & Livingston (2007); Wright & Wallman (2012).

Spina Bifida   Spina bifida, also called myelomeningocele or myelodysplasia, is a disorder of the formation of the spinal cord, surrounding structures, and sometimes the brain during fetal development. It affects approximately 3 per 10,000 children and youth under age 19 (Centers for Disease Control and Prevention, 2014b). Both genetic and environmental factors are believed to act together to cause the abnormal spinal development. Various layers and sections of the spinal column do not complete their closure at specific times during fetal nervous system development. The more layers and sections left open, the greater the motor disability. If the spinal coverings and nerve malformations are outside the spinal column or outside the body, it is called a myelomeningocele, causing a more severe disruption of the spinal nerves and function. Surgery is required to close the open structures but does not improve function. Associated motor disabilities range from muscle weakness in the lower leg affecting walking and balance to complete paralysis up to the middle or upper chest. Students with myelomeningocele also may have hydrocephalus. Hydrocephalus is a condition that is characterized by the abnormal accumulation of fluid in the brain, which leads to enlargement of the head and requires a shunt to manage the fluid in the brain. Other co-occurring conditions include spinal cord restrictions (tethering), obesity, skin breakdown, gastrointestinal disorders, tendonitis, and depression. Tethering is a condition in which the spinal cord becomes attached to the spinal column and may lead to further movement dysfunction. Students with spina bifida have a high incidence of latex allergies, and they may also have learning, cognitive, communication, and social-emotional disabilities.

Traumatic Brain Injury   TBI describes injury to the brain that disrupts brain function by physical force; TBI is not due to birth, disease, or infection. TBI is the leading cause of death and disability in children and youth ages birth to 19 years. An average of 62,000 children and youth sustain a brain injury requiring hospitalization each year (Brain Injury Association of America, 2013). TBI occurs because of falls, motor vehicle accidents, physical abuse, or recreation-related accidents. The brain is injured in more than one place because the initial forces to the head cause bleeding and swelling that damage brain tissue in many areas. Sometimes TBI is accompanied by spinal cord injuries because of the forces involved in the trauma. The severity varies greatly and is determined by the areas of the brain injured. Vision, hearing, and motor impairments may be present as well as difficulty with communication, memory, learning, planning, and behavior. Students with TBI may have seizures, loss of balance and coordination, increased muscle tone (spasticity) in some of the limbs, and attention problems. The degree of disability and function recovery varies greatly with each person and can range from full recovery to permanent disabilities.

Less Common Types of Physical Disability

Numerous other conditions result in physical disabilities. Most of the conditions listed here do not typically result in significant intellectual impairment, yet they require substantial attention of the educational team.

Muscular Dystrophy   MD is a group of genetic disorders that affects the neuromuscular system, causing progressive degeneration of muscles. Duchenne muscular dystrophy (DMD) is the most common form and affects mostly boys. Students with this form of MD are missing the protein dystrophin, which is critical to maintaining muscle function. About 1 out of every 3,500–5,000 boys is born with DMD (Centers for Disease Control and Prevention, 2014a). Symptoms develop in early childhood and are caused by the deterioration of the muscles. Early symptoms include leg muscle weakness, difficulty with balance, falling, and fatigue. Muscle weakness and deterioration progress through adolescence, with a loss of mobility and self-care in early adolescence and eventually compromised respiration and early death. There are other forms of MD that express symptoms later in adolescence and adulthood that may result in progressive disability but not death. Students with MD may also have hydrocephalus and global developmental delays. Monitoring of secondary conditions such as cardiopulmonary health, joint contractures, and scoliosis formation becomes increasingly important as the disease progresses.

Arthrogryposis   Arthrogryposis or AMC is a group of disorders that cause joint restrictions and malformations in the muscles and joints prior to birth, resulting in limited flexibility and movement (National Organization for Rare Disorders, 2013). It affects approximately 1 in 3,000 children. Students with AMC have at least two joints that are affected, but many joints typically are involved, including all joints of the limbs, spine, and frequently the jaw. Characteristics include atypical muscle development or absence of some muscles, joint contractures and rigidity, joint dislocation and fusions, and bone changes in the limbs and skull. Students also may have heart malformations and conditions affecting their urinary system, respiratory system, or skin.

Spinal Muscular Atrophy   SMA refers to a group of inherited diseases of the motor nerves that causes muscle weakness and atrophy (wasting) in all muscles of the body (National Institute of Neurological Disorders and Stroke, 2014). These motor nerves arise from the spinal cord and control the muscles that are used for breathing, swallowing, controlling the body and limbs, and walking. SMA is a rare disorder occurring in approximately 8 out of every 100,000 live births (National Institute of Neurological Disorders and Stroke, 2014). There are four types (I, II, III, IV) based on the level of motor function or ability. Type I, also known as Werdnig-Hoffmann disease, affects infants prior to birth. It is the most severe type, and children die usually within the first 2 years of life. Type II is usually identified in early childhood, and Types III and IV are identified in adolescence and adulthood with longer life expectancy and less weakness. With each type, the child or youth will have low muscle tone, progressive weakness with limited movement, poor feeding, and poor respiration. The child is at risk for breathing problems and joint stiffness or damage in later stages of the disease. Unlike some of the other disorders, cognitive function is not affected by the condition (D'Amico, Mercuri, Tiziano, & Bertini, 2011).

Osteogenesis Imperfecta   OI is a nonprogressive genetic disorder affecting collagen production that causes fragile bones and teeth that break easily during childhood. OI causes the skeleton to develop atypically, resulting in physical disabilities that range from mild to severe. Approximately 25,000–50,000 people in the United States have OI (National Institute of Arthritis and Musculoskeletal and Skin Disorders, 2012). There are many forms of OI, and the severity of symptoms such as bone fractures varies with the type of OI. Complications include muscle weakness, bone deformities and fractures, bleeding and bruising, jaw and dental problems, hearing loss, scoliosis, joint laxity, respiratory complications, fragile skin integrity, and short stature. Managing pain and monitoring the respiratory system are important for students with more severe forms. Although OI is rarely accompanied by an intellectual disability, learning disabilities and hearing loss are common. Many students with OI will experience fractures and will be out of school for periods of time, which may lead to poor academic performance requiring additional support. Also, the fragility of the student's skeletal system may require classroom adaptations and modifications in the early years.

The characteristics and associated conditions of students with physical disabilities require special considerations for the classroom environment and for education planning. Some considerations for students with physical disabilities are provided in Table 3.3.

Table 3.3.   Considerations for classroom environments and learning for students with physical disabilities

Student needs	Considerations during education planning
Universal design for learning	Modify and adapt lesson plans and learning materials to benefit all learning styles of all students. Create lesson plans in collaboration with related services providers.
Gaining access to the physical environment	Ensure access to transportation to and from the school building and outside activities. Arrange classroom for easy entry, exit, and within-classroom transitions. Have a plan for navigating hallways, stairs, elevator location, bathrooms, cafeteria, gym, and music/art rooms. Make appropriate positioning and seating systems available. Ensure access to learning materials. Individualize communication methods.
Assistive technology	Evaluate, develop, and secure appropriate • Communication systems • Seating and positioning systems • Mobility systems • Computer access
Time	Allow enough time within the schedule to ensure a child has time to • Gain access to learning materials • Complete learning activities • Change classes • Take bathroom breaks • Eat
Participation	Group learning activities Rest breaks Physical activities School events Extracurricular participation Emergency procedures

Common Motor Impairments

Several associated motor impairments are common to the physical disabilities previously described. Primary impairments in muscle strength, muscle tone, balance, and coordination may impede a student's mobility and participation in self-care, social activities, and academic lessons and may lead to secondary impairments that limit movement of the joints, lead to skeletal changes, and cause breathing difficulty, skin breakdown, and inactivity. These impairments may contribute to weight gain or obesity and sometimes mental health issues. Each child is unique, and each student may have some or all of these impairments to varying degrees.

Muscle strength is the force a muscle produces when it contracts. Single muscles must work together in groups around joints to produce force and control movement appropriate for the task. This force and control can range from gentle and slow while lifting an arm to assist with putting on a jacket to powerful and quick for jumping in gym class or from getting up from the floor. Students with physical disabilities have impairment in strength in groups of muscles around the joints of the limbs, body, and head and neck areas to varying degrees.

Muscle tone is the natural tension maintained by the brain and spinal nerves. Muscle tone allows the muscle to be ready to respond when signaled to move. Students with physical disabilities that affect the central nervous system, such as CP and TBI, have muscle tone that is disrupted and is either too high or too low for coordinated, smooth movement. Muscle tone that is too high is referred to as *hypertonicity* or *spasticity*. Spasticity is a resistance or catching of a muscle during the movement of limbs, sometimes described as stiffness (Malhorta & Pandyan, 2009; Pandyan et al., 2005). Spasticity interferes with the ability of a joint to move freely. If joints do not move freely, then secondary conditions such as muscle weakness or joint contractures can occur. These secondary conditions can further restrict movement. Muscle tone that is too low is called *hypotonicity* and causes movement to be difficult to initiate and maintain. Students with hypotonicity have muscle weakness and may fatigue quickly during physical activity. They may also have laxity around joints, making joints hypermobile and flexible and at risk for damage.

Sensory systems may also be affected in students with low-incidence physical disabilities. Impairments in hearing, vision, touch, taste, smell, and the systems responsible for balance and coordination can accompany physical disabilities. Students rarely have complete impairment of their sensory systems; rather, students often have partial visual, hearing, or other sensory impairments.

Impairments in the systems that control balance and coordination are most disruptive for students with physical disabilities. Movement is controlled by muscle tone, muscle strength, and by the person's ability to understand where his or her body is compared with other objects or people in the environment. This ability is called *proprioception* and is the complex feedback of the receptors found in joints and the brain (Blanche, Bodison, Chang, & Reinoso, 2012).

Students with proprioceptive impairments may have difficulty modulating their patterns of movement to avoid obstacles while moving. They may stand too close to or bump other students, which may impede social participation. Playing ball games may be difficult if the student cannot follow the trajectory of the ball because he or she cannot interpret where it is in relation to other objects or other players. The *vestibular system* is a second sensory system responsible for coordination and balance, which can also be impaired in students with physical disabilities. This system is in the inner ear and is connected to the hearing organs. The vestibular system gives feedback to the brain to help maintain balance and keep the head upright and the body in alignment against gravity during motor activity (De Kegel, Maes, Baetens, Dhooge, & Van Waelvelde, 2012). (See Chapter 4 for additional information on sensory impairments.)

General Effects of Physical Disabilities on Students

Muscle weakness, atypical muscle tone, and impairments in sensory systems may limit movement and physical activity for students with physical disabilities. Muscle weakness and immobility lead to secondary changes that have a negative impact on mobility, self-care, and health, and weakness and limited movement around joints can lead to joint contractures. Some conditions prevent the bones from growing optimally and maintaining their density. Changes or limitations in muscles, bones, and body posture caused by a physical disability, along with physical inactivity or limitations, can also affect breathing and respiratory endurance. Many students with physical disabilities are not able to shift their positions in sitting and have fragile skin, which leaves them vulnerable to skin breakdown and sores, most commonly in the areas of the heels, buttocks, elbows, and back.

Lack of physical activity is of growing concern for children with physical disabilities because it contributes to obesity (Slevin, Truesdale-Kennedy, McConkey, Livingstone, & Fleming, 2014). Participation in physical activity is essential for the health and well-being of all students and is particularly important for students with physical disabilities, who need support for participation. The recommended level of activity for students 6–17 years of age is 60 minutes per day through classroom-based physical activity, recess and social play, physical education, intramural physical activity, clubs, extracurricular athletics, or community physical activity programs (U.S. Department of Health and Human Services, 2008). Surveys find that one third of students with physical or chronic health problems in high school were overweight or obese, and the prevalence for obesity is higher than the general population for children with spina bifida, CP, and Down syndrome (Rimmer, Yamaki, Davis Lowry, Wang, & Vogel, 2010). Students with disabilities experience more restrictions to participation in physical activity, especially in adolescence, because of functional limitations, lack of accessible facilities, and the need for specialized equipment (Murphy & Carbone, 2008).

Although mental health conditions can be a primary disability (e.g., severe emotional disturbance) for school-age children, they can also be a secondary condition for students with physical disabilities. Children with physical disabilities may experience anxiety and depression at greater rates than their peers, especially in adolescence (Capone, Aidikoff, Taylor, & Rykiel, 2013; Flanagan, Kelly, & Vogel, 2013; Frish & Msall, 2013). These mental health conditions may affect a student's learning processes and participation in classroom, social, and extracurricular activities.

INTERVENTIONS AND SUPPORTS

Both the primary and secondary impairments associated with physical disability need to be considered when determining a student's appropriate school plan and intervening to provide supports. All educational team members need to be aware of possible problems that can affect a student's classroom attendance, participation in learning activities, availability for extracurricular activities, and specific classroom support needs. The following subsections discuss a framework for understanding students' functioning and emphasize important factors to consider in educating students with physical disabilities. Essential strategies for increasing participation in the classroom then follow.

International Classification of Function

Conditions and impairments influence functioning for students with physical disabilities, but they are not the only factors that are important for understanding how to support students in learning environments. In the ICF framework, the functioning of an individual with a disability is determined by complex interactions among the characteristics of a condition or diagnosis, environmental factors, and personal factors. The environmental factors comprise the physical environment and the macro system, including societal attitudes and expectations and policy and regulatory requirements that can influence the student's participation in and access to a variety of educational and extracurricular activities. Personal factors include the student's expectations, personality, strengths, skills, and desires.

Educational teams collect and analyze information related to the student, his or her environment, and the characteristics of the tasks he or she is expected to perform when devising supports based on the ICF framework (World Health Organization, 2002). Taken together, the information from this framework shifts the focus from providing services and supports to overcome impairments to taking advantage of personal characteristics, environmental demands, and activities to promote learning and participation. For example, a student with CP may have difficulty walking safely around tables, chairs, and classmates to participate in group activities in his or her elementary classroom. Services and supports focused on impairments would consider how to change the student's walking pattern and improve strength and balance as a means to improve participation in class. Using the broader information from the ICF framework, services and supports would also include rearranging the classroom environment to ease mobility around physical barriers and providing the student with a basket with a handle to easily carry materials such as books to reading group. These interventions build on the student's motivation to actively participate in all learning activities independently and bypass barriers by creating a physical environment that all students can negotiate.

Let us return to Randy, the student introduced at the beginning of the chapter. Construction of a map based on the ICF framework helps the team plan what Randy will need to participate in various school activities. The team will consider Randy's strengths, interests, and needs for participating; his impairments and limitations; and environmental barriers.

Randy's CP (spasticity, quadriplegia) can be classified as Level V on the Gross Motor Function Classification System. The condition affects his legs, arms, trunk, and oral-motor area. He has increased muscle tone in his arms and legs, making it difficult to move them for function, as well as trunk muscle weakness and difficulty coordinating his oral-motor area for sound making and eating. He has limited but not complete loss of vision and wears glasses. Randy uses a wheelchair to get around. He also uses braces on his legs to keep his ankles from getting too stiff and to help him stand when he needs to get up and change seats, use the toilet, or get into a standing device. A standing device is used when the classroom routine calls for children to be up and moving or doing activities at the group table or at the board. Randy's activity limitations include standing and moving freely in the classroom by himself, reading regular-sized print or the Smart Board, writing, eating by himself and independently completing other personal care tasks, being physically active, and communicating clearly with others. His understanding of language and his cognitive skills are within the low-average range for a child his age. Randy is learning to use a computerized communication device so other people will understand him. His strengths in the classroom include his persistence with academic tasks, his friendliness toward the other students, his ability to move his arms to point, and his ability to make choices when they are offered about his preferences for activities, books, or meals. Randy loves school and play practice, and these are very important to him.

Randy enjoys participating in all his classroom activities. The third-grade team has used a paraprofessional for part of the day to help move Randy to and from activities and in and out of his wheelchair to the stander; she also helps him use the bathroom and helps with eating at lunchtime. His teachers help him move around the latter half of the day. Randy's favorite activities are music class and visiting the playground to get out of his wheelchair so that he can wrestle and play with his friends. He has a friend, Bob, who is also his neighbor. Randy and Bob sit together during reading circle. They will be partners during the end of the school year musical. Randy's mother wants him to continue to participate with friends and be a part of activities both in and out of school.

In considering how the physical environment affects Randy's ability to participate in activities, the team notes that the classroom has doors directly to the playground, but there is one step down to get through the door. The doors at the front of the building have a ramp and a sidewalk to the playground for easier access, but they require Randy to travel all the way around the school. The stage in the multipurpose room, which will be used for the end-of-year musical, has stairs to enter from the front. There is one backstage door at the same level as the hallway that can be used to gain access to the stage from the back.

The team uses Randy's ICF map as a guide and designs interventions to support Randy's participation in the musical and his continued participation in music, gym, and recess. The services from the speech-language pathologist (SLP), PT, and OT will focus on his participation in recess and floor activities, tabletop and writing activities, clear communication, and participation in the class musical. The current music teacher and classroom teachers have staged the musical so that some students enter from the front of the stage and others, along with Randy, will enter from the back. Both groups will come together in the middle. See Figure 3.1 for a visual of the ICF map for Randy depicting the interplay between the impairments associated with a specific condition or diagnosis (CP), the factors that create barriers or are facilitators to participation and learning, the activities that students are expected to and want to perform, the student's strengths and abilities, and the environment.

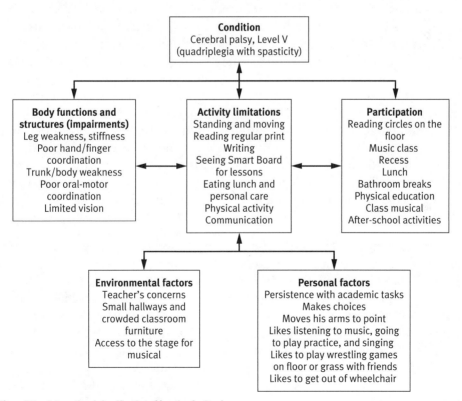

Figure 3.1.   International classification of function for Randy.

Considerations for Supporting Students with Physical Disabilities

Keep several key considerations in mind when supporting students with physical disabilities in their education. The educational team needs to understand the importance of movement, positioning and handling, collaboration, assessment, and developing educational outcomes and objectives when working with this population of children.

Movement The development and use of efficient motor skills are important prerequisites to cognitive, social, and communicative development in young children (Berenthal & Campos, 1987; Diamond, 2000). Environmental exploration through controlled movement forms the groundwork for later learning. Students with physical disabilities may have difficulty organizing their motor system for successful interaction with objects and people. They may have a range of physical impairments in body structure and function that limit their active participation in classroom and extracurricular activities. In addition, students with physical disabilities are often unable to interact with their immediate environment because they have difficulty controlling or activating simple mechanical devices commonly used in classrooms (e.g., computers, light switches, television monitors).

A lack of or decrease in movement abilities often gives the impression that the student is a passive participant in classroom activities or is reliant on others (Lancioni, Singh, O'Reilly, & Sigafoos, 2011). Sensory losses (e.g., vision, hearing) may also be present in students with physical disabilities, which, in conjunction with their motor and cognitive disabilities, create challenges for the team to determine successful learning strategies (see Chapter 4). Fostering independence and self-reliance in all students is one goal of education. Providing an environment that promotes these skills in students with multiple or physical disabilities is challenging and requires a comprehensive and collaborative team-based approach to program planning and intervention. Supporting a student to make choices between two activities he or she would like to do can help promote this independence. Letting students work at something until they indicate they need help or making sure they have a job in the classroom they need to complete on their own are all good ways to foster self-reliance. These strategies also foster independence and motor development.

Positioning and Handling The proper position of the body for classroom and school activities can maximize a student's ability to learn. Students with physical disabilities who have difficulty sitting, standing, or moving by themselves may need help and support to get into these or other positions to gain access to activities and learn. The position of a child's head, trunk, arms, and legs can make a difference in his or her ability to see, hear, touch, and interact with materials and participate with classmates. Help and support with positioning may include physical assistance, the use of specialized seating or mobility devices, environmental controls, or a combination. Most important, students should be positioned for learning so that the body is aligned in a way that promotes active movement and participation in the activity. The position should also be comfortable and should not lead to fatigue.

The team must consider several key elements when positioning students with significant physical disabilities—age appropriateness of the position, whether the position is functional for the task or activity, the length of time the student will be required to maintain the position, the student's ability to see and move in the position, the symmetry and alignment of the body in the position, and prevention of secondary impairments. The team must decide on the best positions for an individual student and how frequently to change positions. Table 3.4 describes common positions, what factors the team should consider, and the benefits for learning.

Table 3.4. Classroom positioning considerations

Position	Considerations	Benefits
Lying down on stomach or back	Appropriate for age and activity • Preschool/kindergarten nap • Floor activities when rest of class is on floor • Medical reasons for breathing or rest Line of vision Safety of position for breathing Support or devices needed to maintain position	Can improve breathing (reclining or lying down) Provides rest
Sidelying	Appropriate for age and activity • Preschool/kindergarten nap • Floor activities when rest of class is on floor • Medical reasons for breathing or rest Line of vision Safety of position for breathing Support or devices needed to maintain position	Can improve breathing (reclining or lying down) Provides rest Relaxes the body more easily than lying on back or stomach for some children
Sitting	Appropriate for age and activity • Reading, writing, math, and art activities • Assemblies or other school functions • Circle times or floor activities Body position • Head aligned in the middle of the body and upright • Trunk or body upright • Hands free to move • Pelvis and hips square with the back of the seat or supported • Feet resting on a stable surface (floor or foot rest) for sitting in chairs • Breathing relaxed Support or devices needed to maintain position	Easy to see Relaxes breathing Hands free to move and manipulate learning materials Trunk is supported
Standing	Appropriate for age and activity • Learning activities that require movement or exploration of learning materials • Board work • Alternative to sitting during tabletop or desk work Body position • Head aligned in the middle of the body and upright • Hands free to move • Pelvis and hips aligned with knees and ankles • Feet standing on a stable surface (floor or foot rest) • Breathing relaxed Support or devices needed to maintain position	Easy to see Relaxes breathing Increases alertness for learning For students who are not independently mobile • Reduces pressure on buttocks and back of the legs • Provides strengthening to legs

Handling is a term used to describe the physical assistance given to a student when needing to change a position. How to assist a student to move depends on the child's age, condition, and the amount of physical assistance a student needs. When teams decide what positions will benefit the student throughout the school day, they also need to consider how they will attain the position and what type of handling will be required to help the student assume and maintain the position. Sometimes teachers, paraprofessionals, or family members also offer physical assistance and guidance to help students move more effectively and efficiently by themselves. The amount of handling to facilitate movement should be minimal and provided in a way that encourages active movement as much as possible. There are many methods for properly supporting students' active efforts to move, so the team must specify these techniques and provide training to the team members. For example, facilitating how a student shifts his or her weight (e.g., making adjustments in sitting, moving from sitting to standing, turning the body to face another direction) requires the team to plan where the adult should stand, where to place the hands to encourage the correct movement, and how to provide support that ensures the student and teacher or paraprofessional are safe from falls or injury. Lifting should be done by two people to prevent injury to a teacher or paraprofessional or with assistive devices to safely lift a student for position changes. The education staff should do the following when it is necessary to lift a student:

- Stand with their feet shoulder width apart, which creates a stable base of support.

- Keep their back in a neutral position.

- Stabilize their trunk by contracting the stomach muscles.

- Bend from the knees and hips.

The PT on the team should instruct the educators on proper lifting for each student and monitor the procedure, ensuring that staff lift students appropriately and safely.

Positioning and handling were particularly important for Randy, with the goal of keeping him comfortable, engaged in learning, and as independently mobile as possible. Randy's team put together a positioning plan for floor, table, recess, and musical activities. Randy has a special classroom chair for tabletop activities and a stander for activities at the high science table and when at the board. He also has a gait trainer he can propel short distances for gym and recess. The team decided that the wheelchair and the special chair with the headrest and hip strap continue to be appropriate for table and desk activities. These chairs provide him with the best line of sight to the teacher, the Smart Board, and desktop materials. Use of the equipment also positions his arms for activities and to use his communication device.

The team recommends that he not be kept in a sitting position for more than 2 hours at a time. It was determined that Randy should lean forward, slide himself to the edge of his wheelchair, and, with an adult sitting in front of him and providing support at his waist, push himself into standing with his hands on the shoulders of the teacher or paraprofessional for balance. With some assistance, he would then turn his body to get out of his wheelchair into the special chair or onto a commode. The stander also continues to be appropriate when the class is up on its feet and exploring materials in math or other lessons at the board. Randy, like all children in the class, has the option of using the computer that is mounted on a high table. This table requires all children to stand to use this computer. He also has the option to use the stander during music class, which the teacher gives him the choice of using at the beginning of the class. Randy is able to stay in the stander up to 30 minutes before he gets tired and needs to sit.

The PT and OT provided written guidelines for the use of this equipment and directions for handling to maximize Randy's ability to push into standing on his own and use the least amount of help to turn his body. The teacher, special education teacher, music teacher, and paraprofessional were all instructed in the proper use of equipment as well as these positioning and handling techniques.

Collaboration Among Team Members   Students with physical disabilities often receive services from a wide variety of education and rehabilitation personnel (see Chapter 1). Although students with physical disabilities may have impairments, delays, or atypical behaviors in a variety of developmental domains, it is recommended that students receive services in an integrated format, limiting the number of individual providers focusing on only one skill area. The interdisciplinary or transdisciplinary models of service delivery are most often used. The general education teacher or special educator in whose classroom the student is placed is considered the team leader because he or she is the person who provides ongoing instruction and is responsible for implementing the individualized education program. The role of the team described in Table 3.5 is particularly relevant for students with physical disabilities (Giangreco, Suter, & Graf, 2011). A synergistic and integrated set of strategies consistently delivered by readily available skilled personnel is needed to ensure that students with severe physical disabilities receive the intensity, frequency, and duration of instruction and practice needed to learn functional tasks and standards-based academic knowledge. Disjointed approaches based on individual domain or discipline-specific goals may result in the teaching of separate splinter skills that fail to prepare the student for independent living and community participation.

PTs and OTs who have specific expertise in movement-related disabilities collaborate with classroom teachers of students with physical and multiple disabilities to design instruction, and they support the instructional staff in implementing positioning or handling strategies that allow the student full access to the classroom activities and participation in all school-based activities.

Table 3.5.   Team member roles

Roles of team members should	Roles of team members should not
Be grounded in collaborative teamwork based on shared purpose and goals	Be based on disjointed approaches based on individual purposes or separate goals
Be consistent with their respective skills, knowledge, training, and certification/licensure to engage in tasks they are qualified to undertake	Include engaging in tasks for which they are inadequately qualified
Be complementary, synergistic, and based on evidence-based practices	Be contradictory, working at cross-purposes, or lack an evidence base
Result in equitable opportunities for students with disabilities (e.g., participation in class/school activities and environments, access to instruction from highly qualified teachers and special educators, access to the general education curriculum and instruction, access to necessary supports)	Result in inequitable, though unintended, double standards (e.g., restricted involvement in class/school activities and environments, separation from classmates, inadequate access to instruction from highly qualified teachers and special educators, inadequately modified/adapted curriculum and instruction, inadequate or unnecessary supports)
Contribute to positive outcomes for students with disabilities (e.g., classroom membership, achievement of individually appropriate learning outcomes, positive peer relationships, access to increasing opportunities)	Interfere with positive outcomes by inadvertently creating barriers to membership, access to inclusive setting, achievement, peer relationships, or other opportunities available to students without disabilities

From Giangreco, M.F., Suter, J.C., & Graf, V. [2011]. Roles of team members supporting students with disabilities in inclusive classrooms. In M.F. Giangreco, C.J. Cloninger, & V.S. Iverson, *Choosing outcomes and accommodations for children (COACH): A guide to educational planning for students with disabilities* (3rd ed., pp. 197–204). Baltimore, MD: Paul H. Brookes Publishing Company; reprinted by permission.

Therapists also collaborate with the AT specialist to ensure that the student's equipment is appropriate to meet the educational demands and context. Equipment should promote independence and active environmental control.

Randy's team consists of his parents, general education teacher, special education teacher, resource room teacher, special teachers (music and art), paraprofessional, PT, OT, SLP, and adapted physical education teacher. The school's vice principal and bus driver are also consulted about field trips, after-school activities, and transportation. All team members work collectively on Randy's educational goals and communicate about supports and strategies in person and through documentation. For example, the PT and OT collaborated with the classroom teacher and bus driver, devising a strategy that promotes Randy getting to the bus independently. The team created a method for Randy to 1) gather his homework and place it in his backpack, 2) get himself to the bus, and 3) position himself at the wheelchair lift. The OT and PT provided strategies to help Randy manage the physical activities of this task, whereas the teacher and bus driver provided strategies to make sure Randy had the time needed to safely get to the bus and onto the lift.

Assessment for Education Planning   A comprehensive assessment of students with physical disabilities is required to effectively create an outcome-driven, functional education program. The complex characteristics of a student with physical disabilities require a team approach to conducting this comprehensive assessment. The assessment team includes the classroom teacher, a special educator, related services providers, the student's family, and other caregivers and providers. If the student is being followed by a community-based health care team because of his or her medical condition, then the educational team may need to communicate with the health care team to ensure that all of the student's strengths, limitations, and needs are being addressed (McEwen & Hansen, 2006). Ongoing communication with all team members may prevent duplication of service recommendations and/or conflicting recommendations, which may confuse the family or education team (Rainforth & York-Barr, 1997). In addition, assessing a student requires the use of assessment tools that inform the team on how best to integrate the student into general classroom activities or develop an appropriate education program. This approach is consistent with the transdisciplinary approach, which supports a discipline-free, domain-free, integrated education program (see Chapter 1).

School-based intervention plans for students with physical disabilities stress functional and standards-based academic skills rather than developmental milestones (Ayres, Lowrey, Douglas, & Sievers, 2011). Instructional and curriculum priorities guide the assessment process. Assessment tools should be chosen that help team members develop outcomes that assist students to gain access to the general curriculum. Table 3.6 describes a variety of tools that are useful in creating outcome-driven education plans, with special relevance for students with significant motor or physical disabilities. Emphasizing function rather than developmental skill acquisition is the common thread to all these tools. This emphasis helps teams develop age-appropriate, functional outcomes that are educationally relevant and future oriented.

In addition to using a tool to gather skill performance information, it is important to assess how a student's musculoskeletal impairments may be affecting classroom performance as well as participation in nonacademic classes and activities, extracurricular activities, and, as students age, career development plans. An ecological approach can be used to determine how the student's musculoskeletal impairments are affecting classroom performance (see Chapter 9). Students with severe physical disabilities may require the use of AT devices and services. Assessing the student with a tool such as the Student, Environment, Task, and Tool (SETT; Zabala, n.d.) will assist teams in creating student-centered, environmentally useful, and task-focused outcomes using technology/tools that foster participation and achievement.

Developing education using information derived from the functional tools described here helps teams 1) determine how a student's skills and physical impairments influence functional abilities; 2) develop outcomes that are meaningful to students, parents, caregivers, and educators; and 3) create activities and intervention strategies that are practical, take little time, and do not disrupt classroom activities. Contemporary special education practices stress the importance of collaboration among team members. Because students with physical disabilities may use a variety of alternative strategies to solve problems and

Table 3.6. Assessment tools

Tool	Purpose	Content	Age range	Comments
Choosing Outcomes and Accommodations for Children (COACH; Giangreco, Cloninger, & Iverson, 2011)	To assist teams in creating functional outcomes for students with severe disabilities within the typical classroom	Process of identifying family and classroom priorities for student; determining services, supports, and strategies to meet outcomes; and creating a system to determine accomplishment of outcomes	3–21 years	Organized process requiring team-based input and decision making Can be lengthy Particularly relevant for students with severe disabilities as it requires creative problem solving to determine outcomes that are based on family/students' own valued life outcomes
Pediatric Evaluation of Disability Inventory-Computer Adaptive Test (PEDI-CAT; Haley, Coster Dumas, Fragala-Pinkham, Moed, 2012)	To determine the functional skill level in broad skill areas; influenced but not dependent on developmental milestones	Daily activities Mobility Social/cognitive Responsibility	Birth to 20 years	Normed on typically developing peer group Computer program that adjusts questions and tasks in relation to answers provided Revision of original PEDI
School Function Assessment (SFA; Coster, Deeney, Haltiwanger, & Haley, 1998)	To determine students' ability to perform nonacademic tasks required in early elementary school and level of independent participation in various school environments	Participation in classroom, playground, transportation, bathroom activities, transitions to and between classes, meal or snack time; task supports including assistance and modifications; activity performance in mobility tasks and classroom-based nonacademic tasks	Kindergarten through sixth grade	Useful to create nonacademic outcomes that meet classroom expectations Team-based process Assesses functional skills and activities relevant for educational environments Assesses modifications and assistance required Lengthy, and requires all team members to contribute to information gathering
Student, Environment, Task, and Tool (SETT; Zabala, n.d.)	Assesses the environment and tasks of student learning	Framework with questions about the student, the environment, and specific learning tasks expected and a series of forms called scaffolds to help teams make decisions on assistive technology, tools, implementation, and evaluation	School-age children and youth	Available online on author's web site (http://www.joyzabala.com) Meant to be used for collaborative discussions and planning
Support Intensity Scale(s) (SIS; Thompson et. al., 2004)	Assesses the amount, type, and frequency of support needed to perform a variety of functional, home, and school-oriented tasks	Forty-nine tasks in six subscales • Home living • Community living • Health and safety • Lifelong learning • Employment • Social activities Supplemental protection and advocacy scale Exceptional medical and behavioral support needs	16–72 years	Interview people who know the student well to determine status (student, family, teacher) Determines support that may be more changeable than skill performance Focuses on age-appropriate experiences and expectations Standard scores for comparison Lengthy—can take up to 2 hours

interact with their environment, team assessments provide a comprehensive picture of the student that no one service provider could do alone. Regardless of the tools used, the assessment process must provide a detailed description of a child's strengths and needs in order to develop appropriate interventions (Long & Sippel, 2000).

Developing Outcomes and Learning Objectives

Appropriate interventions are based on the development of outcomes delineated in the educational program and derived from the information gathered during the interdisciplinary evaluation and assessment process. Information is gathered from the student, family members, the classroom staff, and the student support personnel team during a comprehensive interdisciplinary team assessment. Effgen (2006) recommended that teams first develop broad-based outcomes and from those determine more specific goals and objectives. Outcomes are participation-oriented statements and are not necessarily measurable. For example, an outcome could be that the student will enter the school building independently. The goals and objectives will then describe what components are needed to result in that outcome and how progress toward that outcome will be measured. Learning outcomes, goals, and objectives can include academic and nonacademic achievements based on the student's present levels of development, academic performance, and classroom expectations.

The elementary school Randy attends expects all fourth-grade students to play a musical instrument. Randy, his family, and education team would like Randy to accomplish this outcome. The team agreed that learning to use a musical keyboard would be appropriate for Randy because he has learned to control a computer keyboard and has upper extremity and oral-motor control difficulties. Randy's goals and objectives spell out how he is to accomplish this task. While sitting in his wheelchair controlling the keyboard with his right two fingers, the sequence of steps to accomplish include: 1) playing three notes on the electronic keyboard at the beginning of the musical piece with the rest of the class, 2) playing half of the musical piece, keeping time with his classmates, and 3) playing the full musical piece with his class on stage at the end of the year.

Students with physical disabilities who want to accomplish education-related goals and objectives as described for Randy may require further delineation of objectives that are oriented toward remediating impairments. These objectives would not be part of the team-based education plan but rather part of the therapist's intervention plan. For example, Randy may need to increase strength in his trunk muscles to sit upright at the keyboard. The PT may need to create specific trunk-strengthening exercises for Randy. Teams that create educationally relevant education plans for students with physical disabilities consider the expectations for all students at the classroom and school levels. These expectations can focus on skills in academics, mobility, self-help, community, or social interactions. Education plans for students with physical disabilities often include using the bathroom independently, moving from classroom to classroom in a timely manner, or carrying a cafeteria tray independently. Related services providers, including PTs, OTs, and SLPs, are helpful as teams develop functional, meaningful, and integrated education plans.

The social participation expected of the student also needs to be considered when creating learning objectives. Physical disabilities, and sometimes accompanying AT or adult supports such as teaching assistants, often act as a barrier to more naturally occurring social participation. Specific learning objectives may need to be created so that students with physical disabilities develop social skills expected for their age. This becomes particularly relevant as students make the transition into middle and high school and are preparing to exit the education system. Students with physical disabilities should be expected to participate in age-appropriate activities with their peers. For example, a student with significant physical disabilities may not be able to move around easily but should be expected to actively participate in after-school activities such as the school play if it is one of his or her identified interests or if it is required of all other students. Exemplary program planning requires the team to assess all school-related activities and expectations, including extracurricular activities and social events, to determine the type and levels of support students require to participate in these activities.

Daily routines at the beginning, during, and at the end of the school day, as well as after-school routines, play an important role in learning and should be addressed in the student's education plan. Learning objectives that address access and time to complete daily routines can be constructed to promote independence, self-help, and social participation for children with physical disabilities. Getting into and out of vehicles (e.g., bus, car) when transported to and from school, school entry, start-of-the-day routines (e.g., Pledge of Allegiance, announcements), classroom transitions or class changes, snacks and meals, bathroom access, recess or open class periods, study hall, and end-of-the-day routines (e.g., exit school, transportation) all must be considered. Table 3.7 provides an overview of daily school routines and what team members might consider to promote students' independence and participation.

Students also participate in many extracurricular activities such as field trips, school events, clubs, student government, volunteer work, and athletics, which should be considered in education planning but often are not. These activities not only may be an expectation for all students graduating high school and for students entering postsecondary education, but also are opportunities to build friendships, leadership skills, and team building skills—all expected behaviors of young adults. The education and related services team should consider extra planning to determine the needs and supports required to include a student with a physical disability in these activities. For example, field trips and school events may require considering a permission slip, type

Table 3.7. Considerations for daily school routines for education planning

Routine	Considerations
Transportation to and from school	Mode of transportation and requirements (walker/wheelchair, car, bus) Social interactions and friendship opportunities
Start-of-the-day routines	Environment—entry to school and class (ramps, elevators, clear doorways) Physical requirements and supports for participation Attention to announcements or video (visual, auditory) Assistive technology requirements
Classroom transitions/change classes	Environment—in class and hallways Getting in and out of seating Carrying materials Time needed to get from place to place Participation in group activities and level of support needed
Snacks or meals	Environment—tables, chairs, entry to and exit from cafeteria, height of counters, access to vending machines Ability to carry items Eating time and need for support Social exchange and friendship opportunities Ability to handle money or meal cards
Bathroom access	Access to and ability to use with or without assistance (management of clothing, level of self-care) Time needed to complete routine Number of times during the day
Recess or physical education	Environment—outdoors (playground, blacktop), gym or multipurpose room Access to outdoor or indoor spaces and equipment Participation in group games Rest breaks and endurance for physical activity
End-of-the-day and exit routines	Environment—egress path from school and class (ramps, elevators, clear doorways) Time required for standing and walking Attention to announcements or video (visual, auditory) and dismissal procedures Extracurricular participation
Homework	Environment—varies Organizing materials and homework Carrying materials Access to materials (books, online management) Level of support needed to complete Time to complete Mechanism for turning in (carry to class, online)

of transportation, access to buildings or outdoor spaces, and mobility requirements across long distances. Similarly, emergency procedures such as fire and lock-down drills or evacuations will need modifications or special procedures for students with physical disabilities. Participation in clubs and activities (e.g., student government) requires consideration of a student's interests; access to and removal of barriers in the physical environment; transportation when the activity is off school grounds; and level of support needed for the specific club, activity, or volunteer role. Athletic participation is particularly important for social participation, postsecondary education admission, and regular physical activity. Based on the interests of the student, the education team would consider the options for inclusive or adapted sports in the district or community; the supports needed by the coaching staff; transportation availability; physical access to indoor or outdoor spaces for the sport; and individual skill, endurance, equipment, or support needs for the activity.

Strategies to Promote Classroom Participation

Because of the complexity of physical disabilities, a variety of strategies and supports are needed to help students move more efficiently or functionally, to optimize student learning, and to help students fully participate in educational activities, including extracurricular activities.

Positioning   Students with physical disabilities often need to be positioned and repositioned to promote function and symmetrical body alignment, preventing further disability. Therapists show classroom personnel how to position students in ways that encourage social interactions with others and promote learning. For example, students should always sit at eye level with other students. Sometimes this means a chair must be adapted or modified. The creative use of pads or rolls when a child is placed in prone (stomach lying), supine (back lying), or sidelying positions can help a student maintain a position while playing with toys or other children. Nonsitting or standing positions, however, should be used judiciously only when age and task appropriate and when other students are also standing or on the floor. For example, it is common for younger students to sit on the floor during circle or reading. Older students may be standing at the board doing math problems or will stand during group presentations or during a spelling bee. Older students may also sit on high stools during science lab activities. During these types of lessons, it would be appropriate for the younger student with a physical disability to be lying on the floor or the older student to be standing in a stander, respectively. If students are in classrooms where it is not usual to be on the floor for learning activities, then it would be inappropriate to use floor positioning as an alternative for students with multiple or severe physical disabilities.

Although a student may be placed in a position to help relax tight muscles, positioning is most often used to promote independent, functional skills. Sitting is the preferred position in the classroom. The student must maintain postural control, or the ability to balance and maintain sitting upright, while sitting upright in a chair to look at the teacher; to listen; or to use a communication device, computer, or other similar devices. Because sitting is the most common classroom posture, a variety of chairs or other seating systems may need to be available to help the student maintain a correct posture. The ideal posture for most classroom activities is sitting in a chair with hips, knees, and ankles all positioned at 90 degrees. The PT or OT on the team should collaborate with classroom staff to determine if the student is positioned adequately or if adjustments need to be made. Figure 3.2 provides a checklist to help verify if the student is optimally positioned for learning.

A number of commercially available chairs can be used as alternatives to the traditional classroom chair to help a student maintain an upright, symmetrical posture. It may not be feasible to have a variety of seating systems available as

PELVIS AND HIPS

_____ Hips flexed to 90 degrees

_____ Pelvis tilted slightly forward

_____ Pelvis centered on the back edge of seat

_____ Pelvis not rotated forward on one side

THIGHS AND LEGS

_____ Thighs equal in length

_____ Thighs slightly abducted (apart)

_____ Knees flexed to 90 degrees

FEET AND ANKLES

_____ Aligned directly below or slightly posterior to knees

_____ Ankles flexed to 90 degrees

_____ Feet supported on footrest

_____ Heel and ball of feet bearing weight

_____ Feet and toes facing forward

TRUNK

_____ Symmetrical, not curved to the side

_____ Slight curve at low back

_____ Erect upper back, slight extension

SHOULDERS, ARMS, AND HANDS

_____ Shoulders in flexed, neutral position (not hunched up or hanging low)

_____ Upper arm flexed slightly forward

_____ Elbows flexed in midrange (about 90 degrees)

_____ Forearms resting on tray to support arms and shoulders if necessary to maintain alignment

_____ Forearms neutral or rotated slightly downward

_____ Wrists neutral or slightly extended

_____ Hand relaxed, fingers and thumb opened

HEAD AND NECK

_____ Midline orientation

_____ Slight chin tuck (back of neck elongated)

Figure 3.2. Checklist for seating positioning. (From York, J., & Weimann, G. [1991]. Accommodating severe physical disabilities. In J. Reichle, J. York, & J. Sigafoos [Eds.], _Implementing augmentative and alternative communication: Strategies for learners with severe disabilities_ [p. 247]. Baltimore, MD: Paul H. Brookes Publishing Co; Adapted by permission.)

students enter middle and high school and are required to change classes. If the student is required to have a certain amount of continuous support, then a wheelchair, scooter, or other type of individualized seating system may be more practical.

Increasing Physical Access to Learning Materials   Students with physical disabilities may need to have learning materials adapted to make manipulating them easier or even possible. Materials may need to be stabilized, enlarged, or made more textured for easy grasping. Changing the switch mechanism that controls a learning device such as a computer or attaching a switch to a device may allow the student to operate the device independently. For example, a teacher can build up a toggle switch with masking tape so a student with limited dexterity can easily move it or change a toggle switch to a large button for a student who uses the full hand to hit the switch. Learning materials may need to be made less distracting by removing extraneous parts or cues. Taping sections of the material not being used or making the material more inviting by adding colors to a worksheet may make the material more engaging and appropriate for a student, especially a preschooler or someone with a visual impairment (see Chapter 4).

Finally, learning materials need to be made physically and mechanically accessible, a special concern for students with physical disabilities. Physical accessibility may entail changing the position of the material in relationship to the student to allow the student better access. Putting a piece of nonslip material on a student's desk so his or her materials do not slide around is a simple modification for children whose arm movements are not smooth or controlled. Access to science experiment materials and a lab table may require a lower surface to accommodate a student who is not able to sit on a high, unsupported stool or who is using a wheelchair. A student with significant physical disabilities may need to be placed in a supported position to promote accessibility, or a student may require a mechanical adaptation. *Mechanical adaptation* refers to making changes to the switches of mechanical devices to promote independent use. A mechanical adaptation can be changing out a small switch to a bigger switch or one that needs only a light touch to activate if it is too difficult to use. Switches are easy to change, and a large variety of switches are available that increase a student's independence in controlling his or her environment. See Chapter 11 for more information on adaptations.

Using Play as a Context for Movement and Learning   Play is an ideal context for movement exploration and improvement, especially for young students and preschoolers (Menear & Davis, 2007). Creative movement can be designed to meet therapeutic goals and be incorporated into lesson plans, especially those focusing on language development. Creative movement and games should be designed so that all children are involved in a way that is beneficial to everyone. Activity-based, play-oriented activities increase the pleasure, engagement, and motivation of all students and can be creatively integrated into all subjects.

For example, in teaching math concepts to first- and second-grade students, a game of hopscotch in which the students need to move to the answer of the problem that has been laid out on the floor is fun for all students but also allows the student who is learning to walk or is increasing endurance or speed to practice those skills while participating in the lesson plan.

Promoting Gross and Fine Motor Skills   The development of gross motor skills is the foundation for many games and sports-related activities for young children. Students who have difficulty smoothly and efficiently executing gross motor skills are often frustrated by motor games and may shy away from participation. They may hesitate to play with their classmates during recess and prefer more solitary or passive activities that limit social interaction and friendship building. Education teams can structure activities that promote foundational motor skills, however, regardless of a student's abilities (Menear & Davis, 2007). Motor skills can be easily incorporated into activities involving communication, cognitive development, or preliteracy/literacy learning. For example, a child who has difficulty controlling his or her upper body and hands can learn to count by sliding pennies off his or her desk into a bucket taped on the edge of his or her desk. For a child who uses a standing frame, the child can do a similar activity while standing. These children can count out loud as they hear the penny hit the bottom of the can. This learning strategy uses movement of the arms, can involve standing, and develops language and early math skills. The development of skilled hand use requires young children to bear weight on their arms and explore their environment by touching and manipulating a variety of materials with one or both hands.

A few early childhood special education curricula have been specifically developed to promote motor skills. The most common are *Fit for Me: Activities for Building Motor Skills in Young Children* (Karnes, 1992), *The Carolina Curriculum for Infants and Toddlers with Special Needs* (Johnson-Martin, Attermeier, & Hacker, 2004) and *Play and Learn: A Motor-Based Preschool Curriculum for Children with All Abilities* (Sullivan, Coleman, & Krueger, 2002). In addition, several books describe motor activities appropriate for young children with motor delays and disabilities. *Fine Motor Dysfunction: Therapeutic Strategies in the Classroom* (Levine, 1991), *PT Activities for Pediatric Groups* (Kane & Anderson, 1999), and *Hands at Work and Play: Developing Fine Motor Skills at School and Home* (Knight & Decker, 1994) are all useful resources for early childhood special educators. It becomes more difficult to find specific commercially available curricula as students age. The *Mobility Opportunities via Education (MOVE) Curriculum* (Bidabe, Barnes, & Whinnery, 2001) is an activity-based program for children and adolescents with severe physical disabilities that teaches functional skills in the context of the school environment. The program focuses on basic movement skills.

Adapting Educational Activities   For a student with a physical disability to benefit from the general curriculum, therapists collaborate with other professionals on the team to adapt educational activities to better meet the individualized needs of a student. There are several ways to adapt the environment or activities for students with physical disabilities:

- Use proper handling prior to an activity to diminish detrimental effects of atypical posturing and tone.

- Use positioning to help a student maintain an appropriate, functional posture.

- Arrange activities in a way that minimizes movements required by the student to accomplish the tasks.

- Offer choices to the students to allow them to explore their interests.

- Allow students to work together, encouraging peer-to-peer support.

- Anticipate difficulties and plan to prevent atypical movements and to promote functional, efficient skills.

- Modify activities as needed to adapt to a student's needs.

Promoting Adaptive Skill Development In addition to promoting the acquisition of gross and fine motor skills, PTs and OTs often assist teachers and other team members to help students learn adaptive skills necessary for daily living, such as feeding, dressing, and completing personal hygiene tasks. Children gradually develop independence in self-care activities. Basic self-care skills are established by the time a typically developing child enters kindergarten. Children with disabilities often have more difficulty developing these skills and may need instruction in alternative procedures or direct assistance to accomplish the task. Therapists may advise family members, caregivers, and professionals in ways to adapt or modify tasks to assist a young student. Modifications may need to be made to a task or to the child's environment, depending on a student's needs. This is particularly important for older students who use the mainstream hallway restrooms. The education team may need to assess the restrooms and recommend adaptations and modifications so that all students can use them as independently as possible for their developmental and functional skill level. Adaptive skill development is crucial as students age. If the ultimate goal of education is to foster independent living and community participation, then it is important to initiate teaching functional or adaptive skill development in preschool and early elementary grades.

Feeding Students with physical disabilities frequently have oral-motor problems that lead to feeding difficulties. Atypical control of the lips, tongue, and facial musculature may also make feeding difficult. Feeding problems may be due to problems with the oral-motor processes, problems with the sensory processes, or problems with the feeding processes. Many students with physical disabilities such as CP have a combination of these problems. Educational team members must work together to address feeding challenges and help improve mealtime for students with physical and other severe and multiple disabilities. Chapter 8 provides more detailed information on this critical topic.

Dressing   Dressing is another important area of self-care. In school, this may mean donning and removing coats, hats, and mittens to go outside or changing clothes for physical education or to participate in extracurricular activities that require uniforms or costumes. Dressing skills typically include putting on and taking off clothes and manipulating fasteners such as snaps, buttons, and zippers. Children may acquire dressing skills at different rates, depending on a family's routine and cultural views on the importance of these skills. A child is generally expected to dress alone, except for difficult tasks such as tying shoes, around the age of 5 years (Werner, 1999). Students who have difficulty using their muscles may find skills related to dressing challenging (Werner, 1999). If a student has attended preschool, then dressing skills may have been initiated and perhaps accomplished. If not, then the education team should consider the needs of the student in this area periodically throughout his or her school years to ensure he or she is as independent as possible (Ayres et al., 2011). The following general strategies help encourage the development of dressing skills (Orelove & Sobsey, 1987):

- Be patient. Supporting a student to learn to dress him/herself takes time. Resist the urge to simply do it for the student. Allow the student ample opportunities and ample time to put on and take off clothes.

- Encourage the use of loose-fitting clothing without fasteners such as elastic waistbands, which are easier for the student to put on independently.

- Encourage the use of clothes with fasteners that are easy to manipulate, such as snaps, large buttons, and Velcro.

- If the student has a disability that affects one side of the body more than the other, then put clothes on the affected side first.

- Students with poor balance may need to sit while dressing.

- If dressing is challenging or tiring for a student, especially when preparing to leave for the day, then provide a bit of extra time or only require certain items to be donned by the student until endurance improves.

- Students with perceptual or spatial difficulties may find dressing particularly difficult. They may need additional help and creative cuing to differentiate back from front, left from right, or outside from inside. For example, color coding the insides of the backs and fronts of garments may help a student avoid putting clothes on backward.

- The use of Velcro, elasticized shoelaces, or slip-on shoes may be helpful for students who are unable to tie their shoes.

Personal Hygiene   Personal hygiene skills such as toileting, hand washing, and oral care may need to be taught or at the very least supported, especially in the younger grades. Therapists such as PTs or OTs commonly suggest ways the team can compensate for a lack of skills or intervene when a student has difficulty performing activities because of muscular concerns such as muscle tightness or decreased flexibility. Evaluating the bathroom environment can be an important first step. Bathrooms should be assessed to determine if any modifications would be helpful. Grab bars, lower sink heights, special commode seats, and so forth are available to improve a student's independence in the restroom. Special commode seats may improve the student's ability to transfer onto the toilet and remain stable while seated. Seats with armrests or seats that can be raised to ease transfer are also commercially available, as are safety straps. An upright sitting posture with feet placed firmly on the floor, or on a sturdy stool if the child's feet do not touch the floor, will assist the child with bowel movements (Shepherd, 2001). Simple clothing with few fasteners is also helpful, especially for students with fine motor dexterity concerns.

The bathroom environment may also need to be changed to ease physical access to the sink and commode. Simple suggestions such as providing a step stool so students can reach the sink may be helpful. Students with poor balance or those who feel insecure may need to have a step stool with arm supports.

As students age, they will need to open and close stall doors and secure the lock. Students who are independent wheelchair users or use walkers may need assistance or training in how to manage doorways and doors. Students with weak grasps or wrist and forearm movement limitations may need built up handles on doors or toothbrushes and hairbrushes. A battery-operated toothbrush is more efficient for students with joint limitations, tight muscles, or weakness. Many commercial devices are designed to assist with grooming. OTs and PTs can assist with the selection of appropriate tools. Most children learn which devices are helpful through trial and error.

Randy is becoming aware that his need for assistance in the bathroom makes him different than his classmates. Ms. Lewis wants him to learn at least some part of the bathroom routine by himself this coming school year. The assessment information gathered by the team indicated that a paraprofessional helps Randy with his hand washing (getting soap, rubbing hands, rinsing hands and drying) after using the bathroom or before lunch. The barriers to his independence in this routine, which is expected of all the students, were the size of the sink and the distance the soap dispenser was placed in proximity to the sink. The team determined that an inexpensive new soap dispenser mounted closer to the edge of the sink and a simple, commercially available faucet extension in the bathroom would be feasible and would allow Randy to reach these items and complete the task by himself as his classmates do.

Utilizing Assistive Technology   The field of AT has grown significantly since the 1990s. AT can assist students with physical disabilities to be more fully included in school and community activities (Long, 2005). AT encompasses both the devices and the services needed to ensure successful use of devices. An AT device is any item or piece of equipment, either customized or commercially available, that will help a child increase, maintain, or improve function. Devices such as switches, computer access devices, augmentative and alternative communication systems, or mobility devices are examples. AT services as defined in the Technology-Related Assistance for Individuals with Disabilities Act of 1988 (PL 100-407) include assisting a child and the family with the selection, acquisition, or use of a device; training the user and caregiver in the appropriate selection and use of the device; maintaining the device in working order; and supporting any other activities that will ensure that the device continues to meet the needs of the child.

There is a wide range of AT used in the classroom, from low- to high-tech devices. Low-tech devices are generally inexpensive, readily available, and may already exist in the educational setting. They do not require training to use and are often not seen as different from items or devices that children typically use or play. For example, large diameter crayons and a slant board with a large binder clip to hold paper for a writing activity in a preschool classroom are examples of low-tech AT. Other examples of low-tech AT include large button calculators that can support a student in math activities or letter or word stamps that can be used to put a name on homework or other papers if a student does not have the fine motor skill and dexterity to use a pencil. High-tech items, although costly, are also increasingly available. Tablet and laptop computers offer many options for communication, writing, and math activities and are socially acceptable for students. High-tech devices also include mobility and positioning devices, environmental controls such as switches, and sophisticated communication devices. Table 3.8 lists common low- and high-tech assistive devices that can be used successfully in classrooms.

Contemporary education programming stresses the importance of AT for students with all disabilities, including those with physical disabilities. Consideration of AT to meet educational goals is a team process. Teams that are charged with developing education programs must discuss the need for AT in meeting the needs of a student and must document that the consideration was

Table 3.8. Low- and high-tech assistive technology

Low tech	High tech
Velcro closures	Computerized communication devices
Suction cups	Powered mobility
Adapted utensils	Speech synthesizer
Picture communication boards	Environmental control systems such as universal remote controls to turn on lights, open doors, turn on electronic devices, and appliances
Simple switches that turn on toys, computers, electronic devices, and appliances	Braille reader to transfer written words into braille

discussed. Many school systems have specific AT teams or AT specialists who assist teachers with correct selection of technology and train professionals and students in appropriate AT use. Once the team selects a device, it is imperative that the team offer training and support to the student, the family, and all professionals serving the student. Reassessment of AT is necessary as the needs of a student change over time.

There is more than one decision-making framework for determining the best AT solutions to meet educational goals for students, but all of them have some steps in common, including collecting information on the student, activity, and environment; identifying possible devices and funding sources; conducting a trial period; planning for obtaining the device; and reassessing the usefulness of the device. It is a cycle that is important to successful use of the AT. Table 3.9 illustrates the decision-making and implementation cycle for AT for students.

AT such as a wheelchair, adaptive equipment such as cushions and pencil grips, and orthotics (braces) such as ankle/foot orthoses and splints are frequently used and implemented in the classroom for students with physical disabilities. For example, children with spina bifida tend to be

Table 3.9. Team decision making for considering assistive technology

Step of process	Important information to consider	Involved team members
1. Evaluation of needs	Expectations Student strengths and needs Preferences (student, family, teacher)	Student Family Teacher/classroom staff Service provider
2. Assessment and identification of assistive technology (AT) and AT services	Function or activity Environment(s)	Student Family Teacher Service provider AT supplier or program Administrator
3. Consider AT options	Low- to high-tech options Training needs	AT supplier or program Service provider
4. Trial and identification of AT	Length of trial Data on each device or option	Service provider Teacher Family Student
5. Plan for AT	Supplier Funding source Training Maintenance Data gathering	Student Family Teacher Service provider Administrator
6. Implementation	Student and family feedback Teacher/staff feedback Data on use	Student Family Teacher/classroom staff Service provider
7. Reassessment	Expectations Student strengths and needs Preferences (student, family, teacher)	Student Family Teacher/classroom staff Service provider

fitted with appropriate orthotics around 8–12 months of age when they are beginning to stand and attempting to walk. These students may enter elementary school having mastered the use of the orthotics and may not need further instruction or consideration for AT. Other students with significant physical disabilities may be provided with AT only when they enter school. Intensive consultation with staff and instruction for the student on the correct use of AT may be needed when a student first receives the AT or equipment.

Short-term increases in certain AT related services may also take place following a student's medical intervention. For example, students with CP may receive medications such as Botox and Baclofen, undergo neurosurgery to reduce spasticity or rigidity, or undergo orthopedic surgeries to lengthen muscle tendons. Surgery is often scheduled during the summer months or during school vacations to avoid disruptions in the student's education, but if it is necessary for a student to have surgery during the academic year, then the education staff should be provided with guidelines on when the student will be able to resume his or her typical physical activities, such as standing, and should be prepared for some students to return to school using a wheelchair or in casts. Because surgery is frequently individualized, the physician will often provide instructions to the school team on what to expect. In addition, the PT on the school team should closely monitor the student as well as be available to the classroom staff to answer any questions or provide guidance, especially if the student is included in a typical classroom. Students returning to school may require a temporary increase in direct services or a change in classroom procedures. The classroom teacher and paraprofessional may also need increased support to be confident and competent in any changes needing to be implemented. Today, many professionals and families are able to select a variety of services due to expanding resources. Therapists play an important role in helping team members examine the effectiveness of available treatments that require various levels of AT.

CONCLUSION

Therapeutic intervention for students with physical disabilities promotes active movement, functional skills, and community integration and prevents further impairment. Contemporary intervention practices for students with physical disabilities can be integrated and embedded into a student's educational setting and routines. Ideally, specialists in the area of physical disabilities, such as PTs and OTs, use a collaborative model of service delivery within the education system. Education planning requires therapists, in collaboration with other team members, to collect information using a variety of authentic methods and tools about a student's abilities, strengths, and interests. PTs and OTs can provide direct service to the student as well as consult with teachers and other team members, as needed, to help the student meet his or her goals and realize desired outcomes. PTs and OTs have the principal goal of promoting independence and participation in all aspects of educational life and assume the responsibility of training education personnel in ways that promote participation in learning activities, regardless of which model of teamwork or service delivery is used. For instance, to optimize a student's participation in school, the educational team needs to be aware that students with severe physical disabilities may need to be positioned and repositioned to promote function and symmetrical body alignment and prevent further disability. Depending on an individual student's needs, modifications may need to be made to the task or environment to assist a student in learning standards-based academic tasks and functional skills such as personal self-care. The use of low- and high-tech AT should also be considered for every student. Such strategies can be essential to success in the classroom and help improve overall life functioning.

REFLECTION QUESTIONS

1. Using Randy's case study, discuss the following:

    *   Randy's team consisted of specific individuals who contributed to his overall participation in his education. Who were these individuals, what were their roles, and how did they collaborate to ensure Randy's success, particularly in the classroom setting?

    *   What were some of the methods and approaches used to support Randy's participation in the classroom and to become more independent?

2. Miley is 5 years old and is preparing to attend school for the first time. She was diagnosed with OI. Outline a general intervention plan for her integration into the classroom setting to promote optimal participation. What are some of the critical considerations you would focus on and service provision approaches you would utilize for her case?

3. How can you maintain effective, open lines of communication among health providers, educational and related services provider teams, and families for children in school?

CHAPTER ACTIVITY

Divide into groups of three or four people and select one low-incidence physical disability from Table 3.1, excluding CP or OI. Create a fictional case study and outline the considerations for an effective educational program plan and specific classroom-based intervention. Considerations should take into account classroom environments and learning, classroom positioning, and daily school routines for education planning. It should also apply the models of service delivery, promotion of adaptive skill development, and the use of AT. Report your case study to the entire class.

REFERENCES

Arneson, C.L., Durkin, M.S., Benedict, R.E., Kirby, R.S., Yeargin-Allsopp, M., Van Naarden Braun, K., & Doernberg, N.S. (2009). Prevalence of cerebral palsy: Autism and developmental disabilities monitoring network, three sites, United States, 2004. *Disability and Health Journal, 2*(1), 45–48.

Ayres, K.M., Lowrey, A., Douglas, K., & Sievers, C. (2011). I can identify Saturn but I can't brush my teeth: What happens when the curricular focus for students with severe disabilities shifts. *Education and Training in Autism and Developmental Disabilities, 45,* 11–21.

Berenthal, B.I., & Campos, J.J. (1987). New directions in the study of early experience. *Child Development, 58,* 560–567.

Bidabe, D., Barnes, S., & Whinnery, K. (2001). MOVE: Raising expectations for individuals with severe disabilities. *Physical Disabilities: Education and Related Services, 19,* 31–48.

Blanche, E.I., Bodison, S., Chang, M.C., & Reinoso, G. (2012). Development of the Comprehensive Observations of Proprioception (COP): Validity, reliability, and factor analysis. *American Journal of Occupational Therapy, 66*(6), 691–698.

Brain Injury Association of America. (2013). *Brain injury in children.* Retrieved from http://www.biausa.org/brain-injury-children.htm

Capone, G.T., Aidikoff, J.M., Taylor, K., & Rykiel, N. (2013). Adolescents and young adults with Down syndrome presenting to a medical clinic with depression: Comorbid obstructive sleep apnea. *American Journal of Medical Genetics Part A, 161*(9), 2188–2196.

Centers for Disease Control and Prevention. (2014a). *Muscular dystrophy.* Retrieved from http://www.cdc.gov/ncbddd/muscular dystrophy

Centers for Disease Control and Prevention. (2014b). *Spina bifida.* Retrieved from http://www.cdc.gov/ncbddd/spinabifida

Coster, W., Deeney, T., Haltiwanger, J., & Haley, S. (1998). *School function assessment.* San Antonio, TX: Pearson.

D'Amico, A., Mercuri, E., Tiziano, F.D., & Bertini, E. (2011). Spinal muscular atrophy. *Orphanet Journal of Rare Diseases, 6*(71), 1–10.

De Kegel, A., Maes, L., Baetens, T., Dhooge, I., & Van Waelvelde, H. (2012). The influence of a vestibular dysfunction on the motor development of hearing-impaired children. *The Laryngoscope, 122*(12), 2837–2843.

Diamond, A. (2000). Close interrelation of motor development and cognitive development and of the cerebellum and prefrontal cortex. *Child Development, 71*(1), 44–56.

Effgen, S. (2006). The educational environment. In S.K. Campbell, D.W. Vander Linden, & R.J. Palisano (Eds.), *Physical therapy for children* (3rd ed., pp. 955–982). St. Louis, MO: Saunders.

Flanagan, A., Kelly, E.H., & Vogel, L.C. (2013). Psychosocial outcomes of children and adolescents with early-onset spinal cord injury and those with spina bifida. *Pediatric Physical Therapy, 25*(4), 452–459.

Frish, D., & Msall, M.E. (2013). Health, functioning, and participation of adolescents and adults with cerebral palsy: A review of outcomes research. *Developmental Disabilities Research Reviews, 18,* 84–94.

Giangreco, M.F., Cloninger, C.J., & Iverson, V.S. (2011). *Choosing outcomes and accommodations for children (COACH): A guide to educational planning for students with disabilities* (3rd ed.). Baltimore, MD: Paul H. Brookes Publishing Co.

Giangreco, M.F., Suter, J.C., & Graf, V. (2011). Roles of team members supporting students with disabilities in inclusive classrooms. In M.F. Giangreco, C.J. Cloninger, & V.S. Iverson (Eds.), *Choosing outcomes and accommodations for children (COACH): A guide to educational planning for students with disabilities* (3rd ed., pp. 197–204). Baltimore, MD: Paul H. Brookes Publishing Co.

Haley, S., Coster, W., Dumas, H., Fragala-Pinkham, M., & Moe, P. (2012). *Pediatric Evaluation of Disability Inventory-Computer Adaptive Test.* Retrieved from http://pedicat.com/category/home

Hoon, Jr., A.H. & Tolley, F. (2013). Cerebral palsy. In M.L. Batshaw, N.J. Roizen, & G.R. Lotrecchiano (Eds.), *Children with disabilities* (7th ed., pp. 423–450). Baltimore, MD: Paul H. Brookes Publishing Co.

Johnson-Martin, N.M., Attermeier, S.M., & Hacker, B.J. (2004). *The Carolina curriculum for infants and toddlers with special needs (CCITSN)* (3rd ed.). Baltimore, MD: Paul H. Brookes Publishing Co.

Kane, K.L., & Anderson, M.M. (1999). *PT activities for pediatric groups.* San Diego, CA: Academic Press.

Karnes, M.B. (1992). *Fit for me teacher's guide: Activities for building motor skills in young children.* Circle Pines, MN: American Guidance Service.

Knight, J.M., & Decker, M.J. (1994). *Hands at work and play: Developing fine motor skills at school and home.* Tucson, AZ: Communication Skills Builders.

Lancioni, G.E., Singh, N.N., O'Reilly, M.F., & Sigafoos, J. (2011). Assistive technology for behavioral interventions for persons with severe/profound multiple disabilities: A selective overview. *European Journal of Behavior Analysis, 12,* 7–26.

Levine, K.J. (1991). *Fine motor dysfunction: Therapeutic strategies in the classroom.* San Antonio, TX: Therapy Skill Builders.

Long, T. (2005). Assessment of human performance across the lifespan. In A. Cronin & M.B. Mandich (Eds.), *Human development and performance across the lifespan* (pp. 390–406). Clifton Park, NY: Delmar.

Long, T., & Sippel, K. (2000). Screening, evaluating, and assessing children with sensorimotor concerns and linking findings to intervention planning: Strategies for pediatric occupational and physical therapists. In The Interdisciplinary Council on Developmental and Learning Disorders (Eds.), *Clinical practice guidelines: Redefining the standards of care for infants, children, and families with special needs* (pp. 185–213). Bethesda, MD: Interdisciplinary Council on Developmental and Learning Disorders Press.

Malhorta, S., & Pandyan, A.D. (2009). Spasticity: An impairment that is poorly defined and poorly measured. *Clinical Rehabilitation, 23,* 651–658.

McEwen, I., & Hansen, L. (2006). Children with motor and cognitive impairments. In S.K. Campbell, D.W. Vander Linden, & R.J. Palisano (Eds.), *Physical therapy for children* (3rd ed., pp. 591–624). St. Louis, MO: Saunders.

McWilliam, R.A. (1996). *Rethinking pull-out services in early intervention: A professional resource.* Baltimore, MD: Paul H. Brookes Publishing Co.

Menear, K.S., & Davis, L. (2007). Adapting physical activities to promote overall health and development: Suggestions for interventionists and families. *Young Exceptional Children, 10,* 11–16.

Murphy, N.A., & Carbone, P.S. (2008). Promoting the participation of children with disabilities in sports, recreation, and physical activities. *Pediatrics, 121*(5), 1057–1061.

National Institute of Arthritis and Musculo-skeletal and Skin Diseases. (2012). *Osteogenesis imperfecta overview.* Retrieved from http://www.niams.nih.gov/Health_Info/Bone/Osteogenesis_Imperfecta/overview.asp

National Institute of Neurological Disorders and Stroke. (2014). *Spinal muscular atrophy information.* Retrieved from http://www.ninds.nih.gov/disorders/sma/sma.htm

National Organization for Rare Disorders. (2013). *Arthrogryposis multiplex congenita.* Retrieved from http://www.rarediseases.org/rare-disease-information/rare-diseases/byID/211/view

Nochajski, S.M. (2002). Collaboration between team members in inclusive educational settings. *Occupational Therapy in Health Care, 15*(3/4), 101–112.

Orelove, F.P., & Sobsey, D. (1987). *Educating children with multiple disabilities: A transdisciplinary approach.* Baltimore, MD: Paul H. Brookes Publishing Co.

Palisano, R., Rosenbaum, P., Bartlett, D., & Livingston, M. (2007). *Gross motor function classification system expanded and revised.* Hamilton, Ontario, Canada: CanChild Centre for Childhood Disability Research, McMaster University.

Palisano, R., Rosenbaum, P., Walter, S., Russell, D., Wood, E., & Galuppi, B. (1997). Development and reliability of a system to classify gross motor function in children with cerebral palsy. *Developmental Medicine and Child Neurology, 39*(4), 214–223.

Pandyan, A.D., Gregoric, M., Wood, D., Van Wijck, F., Burridge, J., Hermens, H., & Johnson, G.R. (2005). Spasticity: Clinical perceptions, neurologic realities and meaningful measurement. *Disability and Rehabilitation, 27* (1/2), 2–6.

Rainforth, B., & York-Barr, J. (1997). *Collaborative teams for students with severe disabilities: Integrating therapy and educational services.* Baltimore, MD: Paul H. Brookes Publishing Co.

Rethlefsen, S.A., Ryan, D.D., & Kay, R.M. (2010). Classification systems in cerebral palsy. *Orthopedic Clinics of North America, 41*(4), 457–467.

Rimmer, J., Yamaki, K., Davis Lowry, B.M., Wang, E., & Vogel, L.C. (2010). Obesity and obesity-related secondary conditions in adolescents with intellectual/developmental disabilities. *Journal of Intellectual Disability Research, 54*(9), 787–794.

Shepherd, J. (2001). Self-care and adaptations for independent living. In J. Case

Smith (Ed.), *Occupational therapy for children* (4th ed., pp. 489–527). St. Louis, MO: Mosby.

Slevin, E., Truesdale-Kennedy, M., McConkey, R., Livingstone, B., & Fleming, P. (2014). Obesity and overweight in intellectual and non-intellectually disabled children. *Journal of Intellectual Disability Research, 58*(3), 211–220.

Sullivan Coleman, M.J., & Krueger, L. (2002). *Play and learn: A motor-based preschool curriculum for children of all abilities.* Roseville, MN: Ablenet.

Technology-Related Assistance for Individuals with Disabilities Act of 1988, PL 100-407, 29 U.S.C. §§ 2201 *et seq.*

Thompson, J.R., Bryant, B.R., Campbell, E.M., Craig, E.M., Hughes, C., Rotholz, D.A.,...Wehmeyer, M.L. (2004). *Support intensity scale(s).* Washington, DC: American Association on Intellectual and Developmental Disabilities.

U.S. Department of Health and Human Services. (2008). *Physical activity guidelines for Americans.* Retrieved from http://www.health.gov/paguidelines/pdf/paguide.pdf

Werner, D. (1999). *Disabled village children: A guide for community health workers, rehabilitation workers, and families* (2nd ed.). Berkeley, CA: Hesperian Foundation.

World Health Organization. (2002). *Towards a common language for functioning, disability and health: ICF.* Retrieved from http://www.who.int/classifications/icf/training/icfbeginnersguide.pdf

World Health Organization. (2012). *Early childhood development and disability.* Retrieved from http://www.who.int/disabilities/media/news/2012/13_09/en

Wright, M., & Wallman, L. (2012). Cerebral palsy. In S.K. Campbell, R.J. Palisano, & M.N. Orlin (Eds.), *Physical therapy for children* (4th ed., pp. 577–627). New York, NY: Elsevier.

Zabala, J. (n.d.). *SETT scaffold for consideration of AT needs.* Retrieved from http://www.joyzabala.com

4

Educating Students with Sensory Disabilities

JULIE A. DURANDO, DEBORAH CHEN, AND JERRY G. PETROFF

CHAPTER OBJECTIVES

1. Understand different types and degrees of visual impairment and hearing loss

2. Learn the impact of sensory disabilities on learning and development from early childhood to young adulthood

3. Learn to recognize behaviors that may indicate that a referral for an audiological and/or visual examination is warranted

4. Learn basic and specific strategies to guide instructional practices for learners with sensory disabilities

5. Learn selected strategies to support communication with learners who have sensory disabilities

6. Understand strategies to adapt instructional materials and activities for learners with sensory disabilities

7. Understand the roles and responsibilities of specialists in sensory loss

KEY TERMS

- Acuity
- Auditory neuropathy spectrum disorder (ANSD)
- Blindness
- Cochlear implant
- Conductive hearing loss
- Cortical visual impairment (CVI)
- Deafblindness

- Deafness
- Field restrictions
- Hand-over-hand guidance
- Hand-under-hand guidance
- Hearing loss/hearing impairment
- Incidental learning
- Interactive signing
- Intervener

- Mixed hearing loss
- Object calendar
- Routines
- Sensorineural hearing loss
- Sensory input

- Tangible symbols
- Touch cues
- Visual loss/visual impairment
- Universal design for learning (UDL)

Joey is an 8-year-old second-grade student with multiple disabilities as a result of cerebral palsy (CP). He uses a combination of expressive communication strategies that include one- or two-word utterances, a simple voice output communication device with eight choices and several overlays, and tangible symbols used primarily for his schedule. He has a demonstrated sight word vocabulary of approximately 10 words in very large print and recognizes simple representations that are not complex, such as a line drawing of a spoon, cup, or another single picture. Joey has been identified as having vision loss involving a combination of ocular motor and visual processing difficulties (cortical visual impairment). Unfortunately, Joey's vision loss was not identified until he was 5 years old. He uses a wheelchair and is mobile in the classroom with limitations due to strength, endurance, and visual functioning. He has limited use of his hands, however, and he is able to skillfully explore objects presented to him by an adult familiar with strategies to enable him to attend to the important features. For example, Ms. Lenk helped him explore a three-dimensional triangle and pentagon during math class. She first held the triangle about 14 inches from his right eye, as suggested by his teacher for students with visual impairments. After he looked at it for about a minute, she moved it to his desk and held it on her open palm. Keeping her hand under the object helped to prevent Joey from accidentally knocking it off of his desk while still allowing him to freely explore the object. Ms. Lenk then repeated this procedure with the pentagon. Finally, both objects were presented together so that they could compare the two shapes. Joey used his communication device to answer questions about the number of sides on each object.

Teachers, parents, and others who influence the growth and development of children with multiple disabilities benefit from a basic understanding of the human sensory systems to support ongoing developmental gains in areas such as communication, movement, social-emotional status, and cognition. Sensory loss occurs at higher rates in individuals with severe and multiple disabilities than the general population (Beange, Lennox, & Parmenter, 1999). Furthermore, research found that more than half of sensory losses remain unidentified in individuals with multiple and intellectual disabilities (Fellinger, Holzinger, Dirmhirn, van Dijk, & Goldberg, 2009; Hild et al., 2008). Fellinger et al. (2009) conducted a study using screeners experienced in working with individuals with intellectual disabilities and found that 38.4% of a sample of individuals with intellectual disabilities in a residential facility had vision loss, 46% had hearing loss, and 21.4% of the individuals had a combined sensory loss. It is worth noting that 55.8% of the visual losses, 72.8% of the hearing losses, and 83.3% of the combined vision and hearing losses had not been previously identified. Similar identification shortcomings were noted in a study of hearing screenings conducted at the Special Olympics by the Healthy Hearing Program. They found that 23.5% of those tested had a hearing loss, and only 5.7% of the hearing losses had been previously identified (Hild et al., 2008). Accurate identification of sensory loss enables teams to provide the individual with better access to the information needed for developing concepts, communication, and emotional security. In addition, when teachers and other team members have a clear understanding of the child's sensory loss, their efforts to implement instruction and support overall development can be more clearly tailored to the individual. Those students with sensory loss and intellectual disabilities may be in greater jeopardy for developmental delays if team members do not have accurate information on sensory functioning of the child (Beange et al., 1999).

This chapter provides information and guidance about the current knowledge, considerations, and approaches to educating children with severe and multiple disabilities who present difficulties in sensory functioning, with a specific focus on hearing and vision. Beginning with an overview of the sensory system and its influence on learning and development, the chapter then discusses considerations for designing an appropriate educational program and implementing accessible instructional strategies within the context of the general education curriculum for individuals in early childhood, who are school age, and who are making the transition to adulthood.

OVERVIEW OF THE HUMAN SENSORY SYSTEMS

The human sensory systems are a component of the central nervous system and consist of vision, hearing, touch, taste, smell, movement, and body position (Dunn, Saiter, & Rinner, 2002). Information from the environment is received through the sense organs (i.e., eyes, ears, skin) and then transmitted across a network of internal neural pathways to the brain. Vision and hearing are recognized as the primary avenues for receiving information critical to human growth and learning (Dutton & Bax, 2010; Hild et al., 2008). Each system has distinct functions and attributes that provide the brain with data, enabling an individual to perceive and understand the world. As a result, the human brain receives an undetermined amount of information that must be recognized, analyzed, and stored. The way that the human brain integrates and prioritizes information from the array of sensory systems is recognized as fundamental to learning but is not well understood (Molholm et al., 2002). Many students with sensory loss compensate well, causing teachers and family members to underestimate the extent to which learners miss critical information. As a result, students with multiple disabilities who have sensory impairments remain in jeopardy of not receiving information essential to the development of concepts and skills.

Visual Sensory System

The visual sensory system consists of the sense organ of the eye, the associated cranial nerves (I–Optic Nerve; III–Oculomotor Nerve; and IV–Trochlear Nerve), and the brain (Riordan-Eva, 2011). Figure 4.1 illustrates the anatomy of the eye. Each structure of the eye plays a part in the process of seeing. The images we see consist of light that is reflected off the objects in our field of vision. Light travels through the cornea, the clear front of the eye, and then through the pupil, which is adjusted by the iris (colored part of the eye) to allow the amount of light needed. The image passes through the lens, which ensures that the image is focused. The lens automatically focuses as a reflex response through the use of a network of muscles, then projects a picture (upside down due to the curved nature of the cornea) onto the back of the eyeball, called the retina. The image on the retina stimulates photosensitive cells (cones and rods) contained within and is then transmitted through the cones and rods to the optic nerve, which is attached to a small section in the back of the retina. Finally, the image travels to the brain to be interpreted.

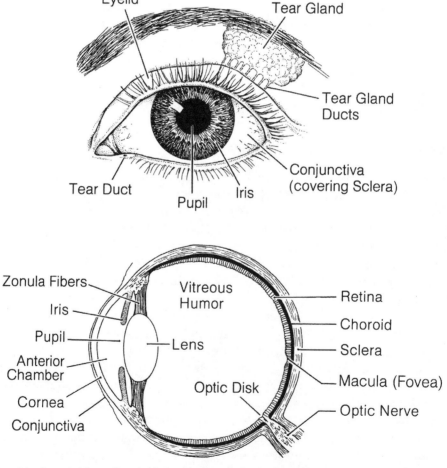

Figure 4.1. Anatomy of the eye. (From Geddie, B.E., Bina, M.J., & Miller, M.M. [2013]. Vision and Visual Impairment. In M.L. Batshaw, N.J. Roizen, & G.R. Lotrecchiano (Eds.), *Children with disabilities* [7th ed., p. 170]. Baltimore, MD: Paul H. Brookes Publishing Co; Reprinted by permission.)

Visual Loss and Blindness   Specific, well-accepted guidelines are used to determine when an individual is blind or has a visual loss. The Individuals with Disabilities Education Improvement Act (IDEA) of 2004 (PL 108-446) defined visual impairment, including blindness, as "an impairment in vision that, even with correction, adversely affects a child's educational performance. The term includes both partial sight and blindness (§300.8[c][13])." This definition focuses on the educational impact of the visual impairment and includes many children who are not considered blind. A person in the United States is legally blind if he or she presents with vision acuity (how clearly one sees) in the better eye with correction (contact lenses or glasses) of 20/200 or worse, or a field of vision of 20 degrees or less in the better eye (typical field of vision is 135 degrees). The 20/200 ratio compares the number of feet a person needs to be from a symbol or picture to identify it compared with a person with perfect sight; he or she sees from 20 feet what a person with normal sight sees from 200 feet. *Blindness* refers to having no sight or merely light perception, meaning a person can distinguish between the presence of light and darkness.

In addition to the measures of acuity and field restrictions, it is important to consider *functional vision,* defined as an individual's current use of residual vision and the extent to which the vision loss still allows for visual functioning. For example, a student with 20/200 acuity who wears glasses may use his or her vision in ways that vary from another student with the same acuity. One child may be comfortable and able to move around the classroom without much difficulty, whereas another child with the same acuity will be unable to even find his or her desk. This is a result of the manner in which each child uses his or her vision, which should be assessed by a vision teacher. A teacher with specialized training in vision loss should conduct a functional vision evaluation to determine the extent to which the student uses his or her existing vision and to determine the accommodations and supports necessary for each student to maximize his or her access to the environment and instruction. For instance, the child that cannot find his or her desk may need the classroom environment modified, such as placing a brightly colored and contrasting top on the desk or tactile cues around the classroom to assist in his or her orientation.

Many children with multiple disabilities sustain visual loss due to damage to the visual sensory system at birth, which sometimes results from lifesaving medical interventions provided to a premature child; the presence of infectious diseases; or a component of a genetic or chromosomal condition or a degenerative disease. A variety of known syndromes include visual loss. Visual loss can also result from damage to the brain, which may or may not occur in conjunction with ocular dysfunction. As sensory systems yield information from the environment, this information is ultimately received, interpreted, and cross-analyzed in the brain to complete the process of perception. If the components of the brain involved in vision are damaged, then visual images are not seen effectively, regardless of the integrity of the eye itself. These circumstances often result in what is referred to as either cerebral or cortical visual impairment; both are abbreviated with the acronym CVI.

CVI is considered the leading cause of bilateral visual loss in children in developed countries (Soul & Matsuba, 2010). Unfortunately, the challenges children with CVI have with processing visual information may go unrecognized because they may have no medical conditions associated with the eyes themselves (Dutton & Bax, 2010). Most children improve their use of vision when they are given appropriate accommodations and interventions (Lantzy & Lantzy, 2010). Children diagnosed with CVI have varying degrees of fluctuating visual functioning, have difficulty in figure-ground skills (seeing something in context), often see things more accurately when they are moving, and have most success in viewing familiar stimuli. Children with CVI can experience improved or resolved vision if provided the appropriate intervention started at an early age. The following are some general suggestions in addressing CVI:

- Provide visually uncluttered instructional settings with minimal complexity and glare.

- Use objects familiar to the child because novel objects require more processing.

- Be cognizant of the fact that the child with CVI will more likely see objects when they are in motion.

- Give the child with CVI extended wait time, which is necessary for the child to process the visual information. If the child looks away from an object presented, then do not move it to where the child looks. Instead, hold the object in the same place it was presented so that it is in the same location when the child looks back after processing.

- Use whole objects instead of pictures until a child has demonstrated the ability to discriminate details in a two-dimensional format.

- Use single-colored objects in highly saturated colors such as red, blue, purple, or yellow.

Children who have undiagnosed visual conditions may exhibit behaviors that suggest the need for further evaluation. These behaviors include holding objects or materials close to the eyes, tilting the head when walking, tilting the head when viewing objects or materials, staring at bright lights, eye pressing, eye poking, clumsiness or frequent tripping, light sensitivity, or inconsistent visual responses. Table 4.1 describes the medical and educational professionals who specialize in blindness and visual loss. These individuals can be valuable in determining the medical and educational implications of a student's vision. Accurate diagnosis and functional vision evaluations are sometimes difficult to obtain when a student has additional disabilities, but they are necessary to ensure that a child can meaningfully receive instruction.

Impact of Visual Loss on Learning and Development Although estimates vary, sighted children receive about 80% of what they learn in the classroom

Table 4.1. Specialized professionals in vision loss in the United States

Specialists in blindness and visual loss	Description and role
Ophthalmologist	A medical doctor specializing in the diagnosis and treatment of eye problems, including performing surgery and prescribing medication and corrective lenses.
Optometrist	A doctor of optometry is able to diagnose and treat diseases of the eye. An optometrist can prescribe lenses and medication to manage certain conditions.
Optician	A technician trained to grind lenses and fit and adjust eyeglasses and other low-vision devices that have been prescribed by an ophthalmologist or an optometrist. An optician does not diagnose conditions or prescribe treatment.
Teacher of students with visual impairments (TVI)	A teacher with certification in educational implications of visual loss and strategies for instruction, including the expanded core curriculum. A TVI may provide direct instruction to the student or consult with the classroom teacher and other team members to ensure the student has access to materials and instruction. A TVI also conducts a functional vision assessment and a learning media assessment. A TVI also coordinates the provision of adapted materials, such as large-print or braille textbooks, worksheets, and testing materials.
Orientation and mobility specialist (O&M; if certified, COMS)	O&M specialists are certified to work with students to help them know where they are in their environment and travel safely and effectively. O&M specialists also provide instruction in the use of devices such as a cane.

through their vision, and as much as 40% of our brains are devoted to the vision process (American Optometric Association, 2014; Titiro, 2008). This primary sense plays a critical role in every child's development and learning process. A person whose vision is compromised or not available must rely on the other senses in order to benefit from using strategies and tools to accommodate. The environment should be evaluated to ensure that it provides the child who is blind or visually impaired optimal access to information using hearing, touch, and movement. The child with multiple disabilities who is blind or visually impaired must be given the same access to learning as their peers without disabilities through methods such as braille, auditory description, orientation and mobility instruction, and tactile representations of learning concepts. Utilizing the strategies and interventions outlined in this chapter can help reduce the impact of visual impairments on the development of cognition, motor skills, social skills and networks, communication, and concept development critical to language.

Auditory Sensory System

The auditory sensory system consists of the sense organ of the ear that is divided into three parts—the outer ear, the middle ear, and the inner ear (see Figure 4.2). The outer, or external ear, consists of the visible structure on each side of a person's head, called the *pinna*, and the canal that funnels into the ear. The pinna is structured to attract sound waves and determine their direction.

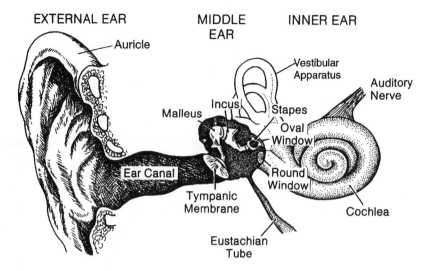

Figure 4.2. Structure of the ear. (From Buethe, P., Vohr, B.R., & Herer, G.R. [2013]. Hearing and deafness. In M.L. Batshaw, N.J. Roizen, & G.R. Lotrecchiano (Eds.), *Children with disabilities* [7th ed., p. 143]. Baltimore, MD: Paul H. Brookes Publishing Co.; reprinted by permission.)

The sound waves are collected by the pinna and directed into the canal, where they fall onto the eardrum, also called the *tympanic membrane,* which is kept so taut by a muscle that even the slightest sound will vibrate the drum. The eardrum marks the beginning of the middle ear, which contains three tiny bones called the *malleus, incus,* and *stapes.* They are sometimes referred to as the *hammer, anvil,* and *stirrup,* respectively, and compose the ossicular chain. The eustachian tube connects between the middle ear and the inside of the mouth to ensure that the tiny bones are free from increased air pressure and thus able to do their job.

Because the malleus is connected behind the eardrum, it receives the sound wave vibrations, translates them to the incus, and then to the stapes, which sits in the window of the inner ear, called the *oval window.* The structure between the eardrum and the oval window is considered the middle ear.

The oval window lies against the inner ear and translates sound waves to vibrating fluid within its larger structure, called the *cochlea.* The cochlea is a shell-like, coiled structure filled with fluid and has tiny hair cells attached, called *cilia.* Sound waves are amplified by vibration moving across the ossicular chain to provide the appropriate amount of pressure to move the fluid within the cochlea. As the stapes vibrates in the oval window, it produces ripples in the fluid of the cochlea, moving the tiny hair cells, which in turn produce electrical impulses (signals) through the cochlear structure that travel up through the VIIIth cranial nerve to the brain. The brain then interprets the quality and direction of the sound, and hearing is the result (Yost, 2006).

Hearing Loss and Deafness   The definitions for hearing loss and deafness provided in the federal regulations for IDEA 2004 are appropriately rooted in their effects on learning and development. *Hearing impairment* is defined by IDEA 2004 as "an impairment in hearing, whether permanent or fluctuating, that adversely affects a child's educational performance" (34 C.F.R. §300.8[c][5]). *Deafness* is defined as "a hearing impairment that is so severe that the child is impaired in processing linguistic information through hearing, with or without amplification" (34 C.F.R. §300.8[c][3]). Hearing loss within the science of audiology is typically categorized as mild, moderate, severe, or profound, depending on the degree of loss (Clark, 1981). Behaviors that suggest further hearing evaluation is needed include children holding noise-making toys and electronics to their ear, ignoring or frequently misunderstanding spoken words and/or directions, listening to the television at a high volume, relying on imitation rather than following directions, misarticulating words, or demonstrating reduced response within loud or noisy environments. See Table 4.2 for a list and description of specialists in deafness and hearing loss.

Damage to the auditory sensory system can be present at birth or may result from lifesaving medical interventions provided to a premature child, the presence of infectious diseases, a genetic or chromosomal condition, or a degenerative disease. Many other syndromes and other prenatal conditions share

Table 4.2. Specialized professionals in hearing loss in the United States

Specialists for individuals who are deaf or hard of hearing	Description and role
Teacher of the deaf or hard of hearing	A teacher with certification in educational implications of deafness and hearing loss and strategies for instruction. He or she may provide direct instruction to the student or consult with the classroom teacher and other team members to ensure the student has access to instruction and communication. This professional may also provide training and coordinate routines for the care and use of devices such as hearing aids, FM systems, and cochlear implants.
Otolaryngologist	A physician specializing in the diagnosis and treatment of problems in the ears, nose, and throat. They are commonly referred to as ENTs.
Otologist	An otolaryngologist with additional specialized training in the treatment and surgery of disorders in the ears. These physicians can perform cochlear implant surgery.
Audiologist	A health care professional certified to diagnose, assess, and treat hearing and balance disorders. Audiologists with specialized training can map a cochlear implant.
Speech-language pathologist (SLP)	An SLP is certified to work on a range of communication disorders, addressing language, articulation, fluency, voice/resonance, and swallowing. Based on a learner's communication needs, SLPs should also participate in the development, selection, and use of augmentative and alternative communication strategies and devices (American Speech-Language-Hearing Association, 2007).
Sign language interpreter	Sign language interpreters are certified to convey spoken and signed information to support communication between deaf and hearing individuals. In addition to fluency in sign language, they should have specialized training in interpreting and specific skills depending on the student's needs.

etiologies with hearing loss and other disabilities; therefore, it is not unusual for children with multiple disabilities to present with a hearing loss. The auditory sensory system can be affected in the outer or middle ear, the inner ear (cochlear), or as a result of damage to the brain. The most common hearing difficulty occurs when the middle ear chamber is filled with fluid that restricts vibration of the tiny bones. This problem often occurs in children under the age of 5 and often resolves as they age. This type of hearing loss is referred to as a *conductive loss*. Children with multiple disabilities, particularly those who do not have independent movement and/or are less often sitting upright than their peers, are at higher risk for this type of conductive hearing loss because a reclined position makes it difficult for the eustachian tube to rely on gravity to maintain appropriate ventilation and drain fluid that may build up in the middle ear. Conductive hearing losses are measured in decibels, which indicate the extent to which a person hears. The decibel is a mathematical logarithmic unit which correlates to a number; the louder the sound, the higher the number of decibels reported.

Damage to the inner ear or structures of the cochlea result in a sensorineural hearing loss and cannot be reversed. Although children with sensorineural hearing losses wear hearing aids (amplification), the quality of what they hear is not the same as children with typical hearing. Damage to the cochlea often will affect both the loudness of sound a child can hear as well as the frequencies (pitch) they can hear, as measured in hertz. Different phonemes or speech sounds are heard at different frequencies. For example, the /f/ sound is heard at a high frequency, and the /n/ sound is heard at a lower frequency. The occurrence of a conductive hearing loss in combination with a sensorineural loss is called a *mixed loss* (i.e., due to problems in both the middle and inner ear.)

Auditory neuropathy or auditory neuropathy spectrum disorder (ANSD) is an additional category of hearing impairment that has become increasingly more prevalent. ANSD occurs when the inner ear or cochlea appears to receive sounds, but the neural signals proceeding through the nerve pathways are disorganized, resulting in poor auditory perception (Abdala & Winter, 2014). In some cases, individuals with ANSD may also have mild to severe hearing loss due to an additional conductive or sensorineural loss.

Impact of Deafness and Hearing Loss on Learning and Development   An inability or diminished ability to hear can have a significant impact on a child's development and learning. The development of speech and language is dependent on consistent, reliable, and accurate auditory information. In fact, even a unilateral hearing loss (only in one ear) can negatively affect the language development of a young child. Children who are deaf need special considerations to develop appropriate literacy skills and often demonstrate reading/writing abilities below their peers (Traxler, 2000). Hearing loss will further affect communication, literacy, and social success when combined with the presence of additional challenges such as intellectual and motor disabilities.

Deafblindness

IDEA 2004 defined *deafblindness* as "concomitant hearing and visual impairments, the combination of which causes such severe communication and other developmental and educational needs that they cannot be accommodated in special education programs solely for children with deafness or children with blindness" (34 C.F.R. 300.8[c][2]). This definition may be broadened by state regulations that include the need to substantiate both existence and degree of the hearing and vision loss. It is critical to understand that the resulting disability of deafblindness is a separate disability from having either a vision or a hearing loss alone. Deafblindness is not merely the simple combination of two single disabilities, deafness and blindness, but rather represents effects greater than the sum of these two component disabilities (Arnold, 1998; Miles, 2008). Children who are deafblind require more specialized educational interventions, services, and support compared with children who are solely deaf or hard of hearing or have only a visual disability (34 C.F.R. 300.8[c][2]). Children who are deafblind are an extremely heterogeneous group representing the lowest incidence of disabilities among the 13 disability categories of IDEA 2004 (Killoran, 2007). Extreme prematurity, infectious diseases, and genetics are the leading causes of deafblindness (Killoran, 2007). Children who are deafblind have varying degrees of vision and hearing loss, although very few experience the total absence of any vision or hearing (Chen, 2004; Fredricks & Baldwin, 1987). The majority of children who are identified as deafblind present with additional developmental disabilities and, therefore, only a small percentage of individuals have combined visual and hearing disabilities without an additional significant disability. This results in the variability within this group and adds to the complexity of providing appropriate educational supports.

Impact of Deafblindness on Learning and Development   The combined effects of vision and hearing loss are so significant to learning and development that children who are deafblind require intensive and individualized support from professionals who have specialized knowledge and skills. Table 4.3 provides a list of professionals specializing in deafblindness. Children who do not see and hear well require structured opportunities to gain access to and interact with their environment in order to develop an understanding of the physical world and people around them. The significant impact of multiple sensory loss on the development of communication, social interaction, and overall learning requires that a child who is deafblind receive ongoing individualized support. Specialized support is critical if a child who is deafblind is to learn within the general education setting and have access to the core curriculum content. This individualized support in inclusive settings is more often being provided by trained paraeducators called *interveners* (see Table 4.3). Interveners (spelled *intervenor* in Canada) are specially trained professionals who provide clear and consistent sensory information to bridge the gap between the information presented by the teacher and the information received by the student who is deafblind (Bourquin, 1996; Bruce, 2002). The role of an intervener is broader than that of a sign language

Table 4.3.   Specialized professionals in deafblindness in the United States

Specialists for individuals with deafblindness	Description and role
Intervener	An individual with specialized training to provide access to information and communication and facilitate the development of social-emotional well-being for individuals who are deafblind. An intervener provides consistent one-to-one support to a student who is deafblind (age 3–21) throughout the instructional day (National Center on Deaf-Blindness, 2013).
Support service provider	Service providers with specialized training to facilitate communication, provide sighted guide, and provide environmental information to individuals who are deafblind in home and community settings.
Teacher of students with deafblindness	A teacher with certification in educational implications of dual sensory loss and strategies for instruction. The teacher may provide direct instruction to the student or consult with the classroom teacher and other team members to ensure the student has access to materials, communication, and instruction.
Deafblind technical assistance projects	The U.S. Department of Education's Office of Special Education Programs and part of the Technical Assistance and Dissemination Network fund deafblind projects to provide information and training to the families and educational teams of individuals who are deafblind from birth through 22 years of age across all states and territories.

interpreter because interveners assist students during educational and daily living activities in addition to providing access to communication.

The intervener provides information as well as assistance throughout the day to the student when he or she is unable to complete a task independently. A well-trained intervener is sensitive to the student's abilities and fosters independence and learning not only by encouraging the student to do much of the task independently but also by providing assistance in an instructional way so that the student actively engages in the completion of the task (Giangreco & Edelman, 1997; Marks, 1998).

Interveners specialize in providing access to communication and information. They are not intended to take the place of a trained, certified teacher because they are not trained in instructional strategies. Instead, they must work under the direction of the teacher and work collaboratively with the entire educational team (Alsop, Durkel, Killoran, Prouty, & Robinson, 2004). The intervener serves as the primary avenue to open channels of communication with others, provides equal access to information, and facilitates opportunities for learning and development.

Vestibular Sensory System

The vestibular sensory system controls the sense of balance or position in space as well as appropriate movement. In fact, the vestibular apparatus is considered a component of the inner ear. The anatomy of this structure consists of three semicircular canals filled with liquid that provide information to the brain on the position and movement of one's head (see Figure 4.2). In addition, the vestibular sensory system is closely aligned with the visual sensory system in that it sends messages to the neurological structures that control eye movements and influence the manner in which images are presented on the retina. It is not surprising that we often experience balance and movement issues resulting from events such as ear infections or instances in which vision is distorted.

The vestibular sensory system plays a critical role in our everyday lives by providing a vehicle to self-regulate; it is the system that mediates movement with the incoming information provided by the key senses such as hearing and vision (Ayres, 1974). Due to limited sensation or stimulation, many children with complex and multiple disabilities rely on the vestibular system to mediate the loss of the other senses. These children seek vestibular stimulation through swinging or rocking. These compensatory behaviors should be noticed and either replaced if not appropriate or understood as necessary. Some children who are deafblind have missing vestibular systems that result in making everyday activities extremely difficult and stressful (Brown, 2007). A child with a missing vestibular system (semicircular canals) experiences extreme difficulty in organizing movement and/or realizing a healthy sense of equilibrium. Therefore, these children do not want to engage in movement. It is important to recognize the vital role of the vestibular system and address the needs of children that either rely on increased stimulation due to sensory loss (e.g., hearing, vision) or experience an absence or lack of vestibular function. It is also important to recognize and respect actions and positions used by a child to compensate for compromised vestibular input as a behavior with an important function. For example, a child may need to use a chair with support under the feet and arms to feel stable enough to focus on table work. Collaborate with a physical therapist and/or an occupational therapist to determine the best strategies to meet the student's needs.

Relationship Between the Sensory and Motor Systems

The relationship between the sensory and motor systems is interdependent (Zull, 2006). The motor system is highly dependent on sight and hearing, which provide information and enhance motivation to move and learn. Joey's visual impairment was not diagnosed until he was 5 years old. He made few attempts to reach out for people or objects, much less to scoot or crawl, when he was a toddler. The assumption was made that he did not explore his environment because of his physical limitations. Joey's kindergarten teacher, Ms. Taylor, noticed he kept leaning so that his head would touch the books she showed him during storytime and referred him for a vision screening. His mother took him to an ophthalmologist, who diagnosed Joey with CVI as well as acuity loss. His new prescription glasses correct his acuity to nearly normal; however, he still has difficulties due to his cortical vision loss that require adaptations such as reducing clutter in the environment and using familiar objects.

The use of vision, hearing, and movement together enhance a child's access to the world, its people, and objects. The information derived from the sights and sounds of the world around children with sensory impairments may be incomplete. Attempting to process incomplete information may result in fear rather than curiosity, especially if they have had negative experiences in previous attempts to explore beyond their immediate reach. Teachers and parents must provide opportunities for children to coordinate the use of the two systems successfully. For example, teachers may encourage independent mobility through the coordination of sight, hearing, balance, and movement for the purposes of obtaining an object or satisfying the need to interact with another person. The teacher can consider the child's sensory needs and preferences by placing objects that make sound, vibrate, or light up just outside the child's reach. Joey's kindergarten teacher found that he explored most when lying on a mat in a dark corner of the room. He would work especially hard to knock over big, red blocks that were stacked on a light box, laughing with delight when they landed loudly on the box. It is important that these opportunities for the child to explore occur in areas free from obstacles between the child and objects of interest that could discourage movement. Finally, familiarizing the child with objects that catch his or her attention, such as a vacuum cleaner, water fountain, or a copy machine, can help the child begin to make sense of noises that otherwise may seem like random and meaningless sensory information. The first time Joey heard another student make the blocks fall, they actually startled him. It was when Ms. Taylor helped him explore the blocks for the first time, discussing the noise they made, that he realized how much fun they could be to knock down.

STRATEGIES FOR SUCCESS FROM EARLY INTERVENTION TO TRANSITION

Effective instruction for learners who have sensory and additional disabilities requires specialized strategies to address their complex learning needs. This section highlights a variety of basic and specialized strategies to guide instructional practices for students with hearing and/or vision loss. Sensory loss influences a learner's social interactions and access to everyday information at home, school, and in the community, potentially delaying development of the interdependent areas of social, communication, and language skills. The strategies identified and implemented should provide access to information, promote social interactions, and address learning needs.

Basic Strategies to Consider Across the Age Span

The literature in special education identifies basic instructional strategies that should be considered for all learners with disabilities. This section identifies several of these strategies, with particular emphasis on the learner with dual sensory impairments.

Universal Design for Learning   The principles of UDL should be applied to curriculum design of instructional activities, supports, and materials to provide functional and cognitive access to instruction and meet the variability among learners. UDL comprises three principles—multiple means of representation, multiple means of action and expression, and multiple means of engagement (Center for Applied Special Technology, 2011). Multiple means of representation require different and multiple modalities (e.g., visual, auditory, tactile, kinesthetic) for presenting information and addressing the student's learning needs (e.g., selecting vocabulary that is easily understood, changing the volume and rate of sound to facilitate auditory processing, choosing a background color to promote high contrast for visual discrimination). If a learner is totally blind, then multiple means of representation should include auditory (e.g., spoken descriptions) and tactile input (e.g., objects, tangible symbols, braille). If a learner has a visual impairment and has functional vision, then multiple means of representation should also address visual displays, pictures, high-contrast colors, font size, and spacing of letters for ease of visual access and discrimination, along with auditory and tactile input. Similarly, if a learner is deaf, then multiple means of representation should address visual access to information, including sign language. This strategy ensures that information and materials used will be accessible to learners with sensory, perceptual, and cognitive disabilities and easily understood by all.

Multiple means of action and expression encourage a learner to respond; to demonstrate understanding; and to express ideas, feelings, and preferences in a variety of ways. Responses can include facial expressions, gestures, and speech, as well as augmentative and alternative communication means to answer questions, to make a choice, or to make a comment. For example, a learner who is nonverbal and has CP and a visual impairment may require time to process and understand the question (represented through speech and use of a picture or object) before expressing a response by pointing at a picture, object, tangible symbol, or touching a voice output device. Multiple means of action and expression may also require providing alternative requirements for the rate, speed, and range of motion with which learners interact with materials, complete a task, or communicate.

Multiple means of engagement include flexible and varied learning opportunities that facilitate a learner's attention, curiosity, and motivation. Teachers should take students' interests and preferences into account when designing instructional activities. For example, a learner with functional vision enjoys playing with cars, but rejects other classroom academic activities, such as looking at books or tracing lines. The teacher could create an interactive book about cars so the learner can match and attach (with Velcro) the wheels, doors, and other parts of cars to an easy-to-see picture of a car on each page. This learner may be motivated to draw and make lines by creating a parking lot on a large piece of butcher paper and drawing the road that cars need to follow. When shared by another child, this activity may also facilitate social interaction between peers. See Chapter 10 for more information on UDL.

Accessibility of Visual Information   The visual characteristics of the environment should be organized and monitored to enhance the learner's access to targeted visual information. The use of lighting and the learner's position in relationship to the light source and target materials must be considered. Practical considerations include reducing glare and visual clutter and using high-contrast colors to accentuate the visual target. Just as the impact of different types of visual impairments differs, so do individual accommodations. For example, a child with low acuity may need large print. Using large print, however, would likely reduce access for a child with a field loss because less information would be visible at one time. Similarly, a brightly lit window may optimize some children's ability to see, make it more difficult for a child with CVI to look at anything other than the light, and cause great discomfort for a child with albinism, who may have sensitivity to light due to a lack of pigment in the eyes.

Accessibility of Auditory Information   To increase access to auditory information, the acoustics of the environment should also be tailored and monitored to enhance the ease of hearing the teacher's voice or other auditory sounds critical to instruction. Practical considerations include reducing competing ambient sounds (e.g., air conditioners or heaters, other speakers, background music) and using rugs and window coverings to dampen background sounds. Access to auditory information may also be increased by the listener's proximity to the sound source.

Embedded Instruction within Routines   Embedded instruction within routines is an evidence-based practice that has been implemented in early childhood special education and in the education of school-age learners with severe disabilities (Chen, Klein, & Haney, 2007; Snell, 2007; Trief, Cascella, & Bruce, 2013). Embedded instruction involves targeting specific learning opportunities during the learner's daily routines and activities. For example, lunchtime is a natural learning opportunity for a learner to practice communication (e.g., making choices or requests, commenting on likes and dislikes), social (e.g., following the lunch routine, interacting with peers and adults), and self-help (e.g., using a fork, cleaning up) skills. Embedding instruction into daily routines first requires ecological assessment of environments at home, at school, and in the community. An ecological assessment involves observing the learner's interaction, participation, and behaviors in different situations and activities. These observations provide information about the learner's abilities and learning needs that may be addressed by the educational team. This process also promotes collaboration with families and cross-disciplinary teaming of service providers. In addition, embedded instruction within daily routines allows for a predictable sequence of activities, provides repeated opportunities for learning, and supports learner participation and generalization of skills to everyday contexts.

The sequence of daily activities may be made more concrete and obvious to a learner through the development and use of visual and tangible (e.g., pictures, objects, print) schedules that include multiple means of representation (e.g., pictures of reading, recess, lunch, music), objects to represent each activity (e.g., book, ball, fork, bell), and printed labels for each classroom activity. These symbols can be used receptively to help the child anticipate activities and expressively so that the child can make requests or express refusal. Results from one study that highlighted the importance of teaching symbols within the context of daily routines found that even though the students on average correctly identified 46% of their tangible symbols within their daily routines, only 16% of the students identified any of the items from their schedule when they were presented outside of the context of the routines (Trief et al., 2013). These representations (i.e., whole or parts of objects) of daily and preferred activities and objects become the words that make up the child's vocabulary (e.g., tangible symbols, speech, signs) and are the foundation for literacy and language development.

Use of Peer Models   Educating students with and without disabilities together is a desirable goal and recommended practice. A particular advantage of inclusive education is that learners with disabilities are likely to imitate and learn from peers without disabilities (Hanline & Correa-Torres, 2012; Locke, Rotheram-Fuller, & Kasari, 2012), and peers may be asked to model a skill or activity for a learner with a disability. Peer-mediated interventions are considered an effective practice in social skills training with learners who have autism spectrum disorders (Bellini, Peters, Benner, & Hopf, 2007; White, Keonig, & Scahill, 2007). Applying this practice with students with sensory disabilities may involve helping peer models understand the unique communication needs and techniques of the individual with sensory disabilities, such as sign language or hand-under-hand guidance.

Specialized Strategies for Learners with Sensory Disabilities

This section outlines specific strategies derived from the literature and from practice with learners who have sensory and additional disabilities. Strategies should be carefully selected to fit the learner's learning style and needs and help the learner accomplish the targeted instructional goal. Professionals who specialize in sensory loss on the IEP team can help determine the most appropriate strategies to embed throughout the educational program (see Table 4.1).

Corrective Lenses and/or Magnification   Most learners with certain types of visual loss (i.e., refractive errors) benefit from corrective lenses. If corrective lenses have been prescribed, then the family should be supported in obtaining them and the learner should be encouraged to wear them (Topor, 2014). Service providers should find out whether the learner's corrective lenses are prescribed for near or distance vision. For example, some learners may try to take their eyeglasses off when looking at things up close if they have functional near vision without correction. Visual images (including pictures and print) should be easier to discriminate, recognize, and understand when a learner wears prescribed corrective lenses.

Amplification   Most learners with a hearing loss may benefit from use of an amplification device, such as a hearing aid, to improve their discrimination, recognition, or comprehension of auditory information. Similar to the use of corrective lenses, if amplification has been recommended, then the family should be supported in obtaining the device and the learner should be encouraged to wear it. An FM (frequency-modulated) system may be used to block background noise and help the student to discriminate the teacher's voice (Abdala & Winter, 2014). Many learners who are deaf and have additional disabilities are now receiving cochlear implants. Service providers will need to learn about the care and maintenance of the learner's amplification device(s) and assist the learner in developing responsibility for checking and caring for the device(s). Sounds including speech should become more meaningful and comprehensible when a learner uses prescribed amplification.

Cochlear Implants   A cochlear implant is a surgical procedure in which an electronic device is implanted under the child's skin above the ear and directly attached to the auditory nerve. Although used in conjunction with a receiver that is worn similarly to a hearing aid, the child is not immediately able to hear and receive sounds. Unlike a hearing aid that simply amplifies sounds, the cochlear implant converts acoustic sounds into electrical pulses that directly stimulate the nerve. The resulting sound is different; some describe it as having a robotic quality. The child will require frequent, extensive, and ongoing training to learn to interpret environmental sound and speech. Children with multiple disabilities and hearing loss are seen as candidates for cochlear implants more often than in prior years (Bashinski, Durando, & Thomas, 2009). It should be noted that the child cannot hear when the receiver is turned off or disconnected. This may happen because a child pulls the magnet and intentionally disconnects the device, or the child's head movement accidentally disconnects the device (e.g., by rubbing against the headrest on a wheelchair). Teachers should work closely with the professionals monitoring and providing rehabilitation (Black, Hickson, Black, & Perry, 2011; Chute & Nevins, 2011).

Acoustic Highlighting   Some learners with hearing loss may benefit from accentuating or highlighting a target sound to make it easier to discriminate within a word or phrase (Easterbrooks & Estes, 2007; Nussbaum, Waddy-Smith, & Doyle, 2012). For example, stress on a sound (e.g., "piZZa") or word (e.g., "Get your JACKET") will focus a learner's auditory attention to the emphasized part. Acoustic highlighting may increase a learner's speech discrimination and improve his or her articulation and speech production.

Hand-over-Hand Guidance   This full physical prompt involves placing an adult's hand over a learner's hand to show the learner an object or how to do something by guiding his or her hands through an action (Chen & Downing, 2006). Hand-over-hand guidance used to physically guide the learner's hand(s) to produce a sign or a sequence of signs is called *coactive signing*. Some learners, particularly those who have a significant vision loss, may dislike having their hands manipulated and are threatened by the lack of control. Others may become passive or prompt dependent, waiting for the adult to place a hand on theirs as a signal to initiate an action. This approach is commonly used, but it may interfere with a learner's development of independent skills. It should be used judiciously and limited to when it is the most effective and efficient way to demonstrate a new action or unfamiliar task to a learner. It may also be used when there is a strong connection between the action and a reinforcing result (e.g., pressing a switch to hear a favorite song) that is likely to motivate the learner's independent efforts. The use of this intrusive prompt, however, should be faded as soon as possible by decreasing the level of physical support (e.g., to tapping the learner's wrist and then the elbow) to promote the learner's motivation and independence.

Hand-Under-Hand Guidance   This prompt involves placing an adult's hand under a learner's hand to encourage action or exploration of materials (Chen & Downing, 2006). Children with significant vision loss do not have access to the natural cues in the environment that can promote independent behavior. For this reason, the hand-under-hand strategy, which is less intrusive than hand-over-hand guidance, allows the learner to follow the adult's hands to gain access to the action being demonstrated. Although this method may easily be used with children who have experience with this strategy, it may be more challenging to use with young children or children who may not keep their hands on top of the adult's hands. In these cases, the adult may use a finger or some other physical prompt to help keep the learner's hand in place. The adult may also need to execute the activity more slowly or even pause between steps in the activity to allow the child's hands to explore in greater detail. Sometimes resistance to this strategy occurs if the child has yet to develop trust with the adult. In this case, attracting the child's interest by holding highly preferred objects and inviting the child to explore can encourage the concept that following the adult's hands will lead to interesting, positive experiences. Hand-under-hand guidance provides the learner not only with a safe opportunity to experience the targeted action or explore an unfamiliar material, but also with the option of how much to participate in a learning activity. The use of hand-under-hand guidance or tactile modeling by placing the learner's hands on the adult's to feel the movements of the sign being produced is called *interactive signing*.

Mutual Tactile Attention   An adult may follow the learner's tactile explorations or actions by gently placing his or her hand beside the child's, without interrupting the child's focus, in an effort to share in the focus of attention. Using mutual tactile attention with individuals who are blind or visually impaired is the tactile analogy to joint visual attention (Chen & Downing, 2006), a key developmental target for children with autism. Over time, the child may follow the adult's hands to share the adult's focus of attention. Mutual tactile attention promotes social interaction, shared attention, and communication skills in learners with severe visual loss.

Tangible Symbols   Three-dimensional (e.g., objects) and two-dimensional (e.g., photographs) symbols that can be manipulated by the learner as a means of expressive communication have been called *tangible symbols* (Rowland & Schweigert, 1989). This term refers to concrete items (e.g., object, picture, textured form) that are initially used to 1) promote the learner's understanding of the daily routine, activity sequences, or options or to refer to people, places, events, or things (receptive communication); and 2) provide a means by which the learner can make requests, refusals, or choices (expressive communication). The use of tangible symbols has been found to increase the communication of learners with sensory and additional disabilities (Rowland & Schweigert, 2000).

The use of selected basic and specialized strategies may be demonstrated in the case of 8-year-old Joey. The principles of UDL are implemented as the teacher provides multiple means of representation of information through speech, enlarged print, and simple line drawings. Joey conveys what he knows through multiple means of action and expression, including one- to two-word utterances, a voice output device, and tangible symbols for his daily schedule. Embedded instruction occurs when Joey is encouraged by peer models to drive his wheelchair to move from the classroom to different areas (e.g., cafeteria, playground). He manipulates the tangible symbols on his daily schedule to identify where he needs to go. Adults and peers also use hand-under-hand guidance to support Joey's exploration of unfamiliar materials (e.g., in art class) when he is hesitant.

EDUCATIONAL CONSIDERATIONS IN EARLY CHILDHOOD, SCHOOL AGE, AND TRANSITION TO ADULTHOOD

The impact of sensory loss is broad and stretches across the lifespan. This section is organized to focus on the main areas of development, particularly social-emotional development, communication, and approaches to problem-solving and concept development. Each of these developmental areas, as well as other relevant educational considerations, will be addressed for children with multiple disabilities who are blind or visually impaired, deaf and hard of hearing, and deafblind across the age range of birth to 22 years. The age range will be divided into three stages—early intervention to prekindergarten, primary through middle school, and high school through transition to adult life.

Early Intervention to Prekindergarten

Carlota Torres wonders how to teach a new child with an individualized education program (IEP) in her general education preschool class of 16 children. Three-year-old Lakeisha has a moderate hearing loss, severe CVI, and developmental delays. She communicates mainly through body movements, gestures, and facial expressions and has definite preferences, such as

putting her hands in water, patting surfaces, and shaking materials. Carlota
believes that Lakeisha will benefit from being with other preschoolers in her
play-based classroom but realizes that she will also require some specialized
supports. Carlota is depending on the special education consultants from the
school district and on the state deafblind technical assistance project to train
her and the paraprofessional who will support Lakeisha.

A young child's social interactions and early relationships have a profound
influence on early social-emotional development, communication/language development, and cognitive development. The natural course for developing social
relationships and engaging in experiences may be disrupted when a child has a
visual disability and/or hearing loss alongside additional disabilities. In such circumstances, specific consideration must be given to interventions that promote
the child's healthy social-emotional, communication, and concept development.
Although recognizing that these areas of early development are intertwined, it
is important to review relevant research and recommended practices related to
each of these selected areas.

Social-Emotional Development   Research with young children without
disabilities demonstrates that responsive caregiving promotes children's attachment to caregivers, a sense of trust, and the development of autonomy and
further influences communication and other areas of development (Center on
the Developing Child, 2007). Similarly, studies with children with disabilities indicate that a caregiver's responsiveness to a child's signals is associated
with the child's security of attachment and early social, communicative, and
cognitive development; and it promotes the caregiver's sense of confidence
and competence (Chen et al., 2007; Dote-Kwan, 1995; Dunst & Kassow, 2008;
Mahoney, 2009). Every effort should be made by significant caregivers, family
members, and teachers to identify, interpret, and respond to subtle, nonverbal,
and sometimes idiosyncratic signals from young children with sensory and
additional disabilities. Familiar adults recognize the child's communicative efforts through this process, and the child learns he or she has the ability to influence caregiver responses and develops a sense of competence. In addition,
caregivers and teachers should identify ways to help the child recognize and
discriminate them from other people by using a special greeting (e.g., visual,
tactile, auditory) or identification cue (e.g., watch, ring). Furthermore, the es-
tablishment of predictable routines for everyday activities and use of objects
or pictures to represent these activities are likely to facilitate the child's feelings of security though anticipation and participation in these activities.

"Learning through play" is a common adage in early childhood education, and it is essential that young children with sensory and multiple disabilities have many opportunities to engage in a variety of play activities,
particularly with typically developing peers. Young children with vision loss
(Celeste, 2006) and multiple disabilities (DiCarlo, Reid, & Stricklin, 2003) may

have restricted play skills. Based on a child's interests and preferences, parents, teachers, and other service providers may create and structure activities that motivate the child's interest and participation in play. Parten (1932) described six different stages of play that children may demonstrate depending on their age, abilities, interests, and the setting. Table 4.4 provides a description of each stage of play, the possible influence of multiple disabilities, and suggestions for intervention.

Table 4.4.   Stages of play and intervention suggestions for young children

Stages of play	Impact of disability	Intervention suggestions
Unoccupied behavior: The child seems to be making random actions without a specific goal; this type of behavior is common in infants.	Children with multiple disabilities may engage in repetitive or self-stimulatory behaviors such as tapping surfaces with their hands or waving paper.	Identify and use the child's preferred toys, materials, and actions to redirect or shape repetitive behaviors and engage the child in more acceptable play behaviors (e.g., provide a drum and encourage the child to pat the surface, shake maracas).
Solitary play: The child plays alone and learns how to entertain him- or herself; solitary play is common in 2- and 3-year-old children.	Children with multiple disabilities may have a limited repertoire of solitary play behaviors, such as patting drums or shaking tambourines or maracas.	Imitate the child's play actions to promote the child's awareness of another person's play. Extend the child's preferred play actions by adding another movement or element (e.g., pat the drum three times, then clap three times; pat the drum three times, then drop three blocks in a can).
Onlooker play: The child watches other children play; onlooker play is common in children who are developing language.	A child with severe sensory and additional disabilities may not be able to observe or communicate with others.	Identify the child's interests in other children and materials and create opportunities for the child to be close to these activities so he or she can see, touch, or hear them, as appropriate. Promote the child's access to these children and their play by communicating what the other children are doing in a way that the child can understand.
Parallel play: The child plays alongside another child; this type of play is an important transition to later stages of play.	A child with severe sensory and additional disabilities may not be able to observe or communicate with others.	Structure opportunities for parallel play with the child and a preferred peer (e.g., standing beside each other at the water table, pouring water with cups, squeezing sponges).
Associative play: Children play separately but are involved with each other by sharing materials, solving problems, and cooperating.	A child with severe sensory and additional disabilities may not have the language or social skills to initiate play with other children.	Support the child's interactions with peers by prompting children to request and share materials with each other (e.g., ask a friend for the sponge, suggest that a friend hold the funnel while the child pours water in it).
Cooperative play: Children play together; common in older preschoolers and may involve physical (e.g., riding tricycles around the track), constructive (e.g., building a tower with blocks), and dramatic/fantasy (e.g., preparing a meal) play; and games with rules (e.g., simple board or physical games).	A child with severe sensory and additional disabilities may not be able to observe the skills learned incidentally by their peers.	Make sure that the child develops appropriate skills (e.g., ride a tricycle with adapted pedals and seat, if needed) to take turns building with blocks, to learn a simple script for dramatic play (e.g., making a sandwich and serving it to a friend), or to play "buddy" Duck, duck, goose.

Communication and Language Development   Sensory and multiple disabilities have a significant impact on a child's language development, interfering
with the usual means of receptive (input) and expressive (output) communication. Interventions to support the child's communication development should
be derived from gathering information through observations of familiar and
structured activities, conversations with the family and service providers, and
consideration of the child's individual characteristics, strengths, and needs
(Rowland, 2009). Multiple modes of symbolic representation may be considered to determine the method(s) of receptive communication that a child is most
likely to understand, and multiple modes of expression may be identified to determine the expressive communication means that is easiest for an individual
child to produce (Chen, 2014) and most likely for the listener to understand.
Table 4.5 outlines various means of receptive and expressive communication

Table 4.5.   Means of receptive and expressive communication

Receptive communication (input)	Expressive communication (output)
Touch cues: Specific tactile signals made by another on a child's body that are used to prepare the child for an upcoming activity (e.g., patting the child's back to indicate "let's put your backpack on").	General body movements: Movements that are elicited by the child's emotional responses (e.g., waving arms or moving side to side when excited or to convey feelings, preferences, and dislikes).
Object cues: Selected objects that are used to represent particular activities (e.g., a paintbrush that is used to indicate art time).	Object cues: Use of objects to indicate a need or preference by touching, picking up, pointing to, looking at, looking away from, or pushing away an object used in an activity.
Tangible symbols: Three-dimensional (objects, or parts of objects) or two-dimensional (pictures) representations that are used to represent a person, place, or activity (e.g., a photograph of a child's mother to indicate home, Lego blocks to indicate *playtime*).	Tangible symbols: Use of an object, parts of objects, pictures, or other representations to indicate need or preference or to refer to a person, place, or activity by touching, picking up, pointing to, or looking at the representation.
Gestures: Conventional actions made by the hand, head, or body to convey a message (e.g., nodding the head for "yes").	Gestures: Movements of the hand, head, or body that may be conventional gestures (e.g., shaking head to indicate refusal) or idiosyncratic movements (e.g., rocking the body to request the outdoor swing).
Vocalizations: Sounds produced by the voice that have meaning (e.g., saying "Uh oh" to indicate a small accident or mistake).	Vocalizations: Imitation of sounds that are heard (e.g., "dada" to call *father*) or production of own particular sounds that are recognized by familiar adults (e.g., "ka" means *cracker*).
Manual signs: Use of the symbolic system of manual communication (e.g., manual sign that represents DADDY AT WORK).	Manual signs: Use of manual signs to communicate, make requests, comment, answer questions, and engage in conversation.
Speech: Spoken words (e.g., "Let's find mama").	Speech: Use of spoken words to make requests, comment, and answer questions and engage in conversation. May also involve use of a voice output switch or device that is programmed to say what the child needs to express.

that may be considered in designing a communication program for a young child with multiple disabilities.

Selected communication means should then be used systematically and consistently in everyday interactions to support a child's communication development. The literature has identified evidence-based input strategies for supporting receptive communication and output strategies for supporting expressive communication in young children with disabilities (see Tables 4.6 and 4.7; Chen, 2014; Coogle, Floyd, Hanline, & Kellner-Hiczewski, 2013).

Strategies that support communication and language development also promote early literacy development; these include using finger plays or action songs, interacting with print-rich materials, telling stories, recognizing letters, and having conversations (Chen, 2014). Children with sensory impairments and additional disabilities benefit from multiple opportunities to engage in accessible early literacy activities that build on their interests, including books with tactile and auditory components (Erickson, Hatton, Roy, Fox, & Renne, 2007; Hatton, Erickson, & Lee, 2010; Johnston, McDonnell, & Hawken, 2008; Murphy, Hatton, & Erickson, 2008).

Concept Development   Young children develop concepts of ways of organizing and understanding experiences through everyday interactions. Young

Table 4.6.   Selected strategies to promote receptive communication in young children

Input strategies	Examples
Use child-directed speech (e.g., exaggerated intonation, repetition, slower rate of speech, and short simple phrases; current topics) to obtain the child's attention (Segal & Kishon-Rabin, 2011).	Adult uses characteristics of child-directed speech to sign and read the story *The Very Hungry Caterpillar* (Carle, 1994); facial expressions, gestures, and props for items in the story also can be used.
Comment on the child's focus and interest (McDuffie & Yoder, 2010; Perryman et al., 2013).	Child moves to the water table and puts hand in water. Adult says, "Oh, the water is warm."
Use parallel talk to describe the child's actions (Ingersoll, Lewis, & Kroman, 2007).	Child splashes hands in water. Adult says, "Splash, splash, splash the water."
Use self-talk to describe one's own actions (Ingersoll et al., 2007).	Adult squeezes a big wet sponge and says, "Squeeze the sponge."
Repeat and emphasize key words (Easterbrooks & Estes, 2007).	Reading a tactile book about dogs, adult says, "Find the doggy. Pat the doggy." Signs DOG SOFT and says, "Soft doggy! Woof, woof."
Use a variety of verbal or object cues to increase child's understanding of words (Chen, Klein, & Haney, 2007).	Adult says, "Time to clean up," signs CLEAN UP, and places a tub close to the child to put the toy cars away. Child does not respond. Adult moves tub to touch child's hand, drops a car in tub, and says, "Listen! Let's put the cars in the tub. Bye, bye, cars."
Expand or modify one's own utterance (Thiermann & Warren, 2010).	Adult says, "Snack time. Wash hands. Get hands clean."
Expand or modify the child's utterance with syntactic and semantic expansions (Thiermann & Warren, 2010).	Child pats the family's dog and signs dog. Adult says "Yes, Snoopy dog. He's a brown dog. Good Snoopy," and signs SNOOPY DOG, BROWN DOG, GOOD SNOOPY.

Table 4.7.   Selected strategies to promote expressive communication

Output strategies	Examples
Interpret and respond to the child's gestures and vocalizations (McDuffie & Yoder, 2010).	At the table, child reaches toward cup and says, "mm." Adult says, "You want milk? Want a drink?" while signing MILK, DRINK.
Imitate the child's vocalizations or actions to promote turn-taking (Ingersoll & Dvortcsak, 2009).	Child bangs on table, pauses, and adult imitates child's action, then pauses for child to take a turn.
Provide language and communication models for child's expressive use (Ingersoll & Dvortcsak, 2009).	At snack, child claps hands together. Adult says and signs MORE COOKIE.
Use the interrupted routine or pause-and-wait procedure to interrupt familiar and preferred movement activities or action songs (Chen, Klein, & Haney, 2007).	Adult gives the child three times on the swing, then stops and waits for the child to request "more push" through a vocalization or body movement. The child moves his or her legs, and the adult responds, "You want MORE SWING" while signing more swing and pushing the swing.
Use wait time or time delay to motivate the child's initiation of a request for a favorite activity (Chen et al., 2007).	Once the child consistently responds to the interrupted swing routine, the adult may wait for the child to initiate the request to be pushed on the swing. The child sits on the swing and moves his or her legs. The adult responds, "You want to swing" and immediately pushes the swing.
Offer choices in daily activities (Clark & McDonnell, 2008).	On the playground, the adult uses two representative objects of play equipment to offer a choice. The adult shows or places one object at a time in the child's palm (waits for the child to handle the item) and asks, "Want to swing?" (piece of chain and sign SWING) or "Want to ride a trike?" (plastic handlebar grip and sign TRICYCLE). Child holds on to the piece of chain. Adult responds, "You want to swing" and helps the child sign SWING.
Provide natural reinforcers for child's communication efforts (Ingersoll, Lewis, & Kroman, 2007).	Child points to a picture of a light-up musical toy, and adult immediately offers the toy to the child and turns it on.
Create a need for the child to ask for help (Chen, 2014).	Wait for child to request assistance to obtain item that is out of reach or difficult to activate. Say and sign HELP ME before responding to the child's request.
Establish joint attention with the child and an object that is of interest to the child (Whalen, Schreibman, & Ingersoll, 2006).	Child is tapping the keys of a toy piano. An adult places his or her hands on the piano keys, touching the child's hands and imitating the child's actions (mutual tactile attention).
Encourage back-and-forth interactions and two-way conversations (Mahoney & Perales, 2005).	Adult points to a peer, shakes the funnel, says "Jason's turn," and waits for Jason to pour a cup of water in the funnel. Adult points to the other child, shakes the funnel, and says, "Carina's turn," then helps Carina pour a cup of water in the funnel. Adult asks, "Whose turn?" and waits for Jason or Carina to respond.
Use completion prompts to encourage the child to complete familiar rhymes, chants, or refrains (Chen, 2014).	Counting the number of children in the circle, the adult touches each child's shoulder and says, "1, 2, 3, 4," then pauses and waits for the children to say "5."
Make planned "mistakes" (Chen, 2014).	Adult deliberately makes a mistake when reciting a familiar rhyme (e.g., says and signs, TWINKLE, TWINKLE, LITTLE BUS) and waits for child to correct the mistake (i.e., STAR).

Table 4.8. Selected early concepts and suggested interventions

Concepts	Suggested interventions
Object permanence: Recognition that an object or person exists even when the object or person cannot be seen or touched	Encourage games to motivate a child to seek and find favorite objects and people (e.g., Peekaboo, seek and find a preferred adult, search for a favorite toy). If appropriate, use sound cues to help the child search for the object or person that is out of sight (e.g., activate a musical toy in the next room, ask the parent to call the child's name).
Use of symbols to identify and label: Discrimination of objects and people and recognition that everything has a name	Help children identify and label common objects and people that are in the immediate environment through multiple opportunities for interactions. Use multiple modes of representation (e.g., speech, signs, pictures, objects) to identify and refer to objects and people.
Identification of defining features of objects and people: Discrimination and recognition of differences such as big, little; rough, smooth; soft, hard; long, short; and wet, dry	Provide opportunities for children to play with and manipulate objects with a variety of textures. Emphasize the defining features that distinguish a particular object from others. Similarly, encourage interactions with familiar people and point out defining characteristics (e.g., long, soft hair).
Identification of spatial concepts (e.g., in, out; on, off; over, under)	Provide opportunities for children to engage in physical activities that build spatial concepts (e.g., going under a table, getting in a box, sitting on a bench, putting a hat on and taking it off). Next, provide objects for the child to manipulate in relationship to another item (e.g., putting a ball in a box, putting a book on the table).

children with sensory and additional disabilities benefit from repeated opportunities to interact with real objects in meaningful situations (e.g., learning about the characteristics of a banana by peeling and eating a banana for a snack). Predictable daily routines provide learning opportunities about many concepts, including 1) language or symbols associated with activities (e.g., labels and explanations through speech, signs, gestures, objects, or pictures); 2) the sequence of activities (e.g., first, second, and so forth; first do this, then do this; go home after lunch); and 3) a sense of time (e.g., five more minutes to play, then clean up the toys). Table 4.8 outlines selected early concepts and provides suggestions for promoting them.

Primary and Middle School (Ages 5–13)

Tina is fully included in a fourth-grade class at the elementary school near her home. She has a severe visual acuity loss that is estimated at 20/1600. She seems to notice objects within 2 feet, yet must tactually explore them to identify them. Tina has a moderate hearing loss and responds to familiar voices when wearing her hearing aids. Tina has very low muscle tone and uses a wheelchair for mobility. She enjoys music and movement.

Ms. Pat, Tina's intervener, greets Tina as she arrives at school and exits the lift on the school bus. Ms. Pat says good morning and rests her wrist at Tina's fingertips so that Tina can feel the unique bracelet she wears each day. Tina's fingers pause a moment before relaxing against the bracelet. Then her smile lets Ms. Pat know she recognizes the cue. Ms. Pat takes Tina to her classroom, where she greets her teacher and two classmates using the same

process. Her teacher has already set up her object calendar with the scheduled activities for the day. Ms. Pat invites Tina to follow her hands as she
reaches into each section of the calendar, takes the object, and places it on
the tray of Tina's wheelchair. Ms. Pat names the activity and allows her to feel
it for 45–90 seconds, depending on the object. Some objects she recognizes
right away, and others she will think about for at least a minute. Ms. Pat re-
calls when Tina started kindergarten and was reluctant to touch any objects.
She now relaxes her hand around familiar objects. She needs to be cued
with a warning when something new is about to be touched. She prefers to
explore new objects with her hand resting on Ms. Pat's hand, with just the tip
of her thumb in contact with the object.

Social-Emotional Development The school environment brings with it
new people, sights, sounds, smells, routines, and expectations. This new environment can be emotionally unsettling for a child with limited access to the
distance senses of vision or hearing, which can potentially lead to anxiety and
withdrawal. When entering a new environment, such as a new classroom on
the first day of school, time must be spent orienting the child to the classroom.
Students with visual loss may need to tactilely explore the perimeter and activity centers of the room with an adult who can point out the important details
in a communication mode each student understands best. An orientation and
mobility specialist may also be necessary to help a student identify landmarks
and learn routes in the school to be able to travel safely and independently.
Even for students who are not yet able to travel independently, familiarity
with the immediate environment can add to a sense of security and ready the
student for learning.

Just as toddlers and preschool children with sensory loss may have restricted play skills, research with children between 3–10 years old who are deaf-
blind and have multiple disabilities and visual loss also identified impairments
in play skills for symbolic or pretend play, such as playing with dolls (Pizzo
& Bruce, 2010). Additional supports and many opportunities are required for
children with sensory loss to be aware of the dialogue and actions of their peers
during playtime because they are unable to gain this information incidentally
(Silberman, 2000). It is also important to teach peers how to communicate in the
student's receptive mode and how to understand the modes, including behaviors, the student uses to communicate.

Greetings are especially important for children who do not have sufficient
functional vision and hearing to determine who is approaching them. Greetings serve as more than a polite communication, providing the students with
knowledge of who is about to interact and work with them. It is important to
greet the student in a consistent way to help increase predictability and reduce
the student's stress. The person greeting the student can use a consistent cue or
gesture. Finally, students should be informed when a person is about to leave
their social milieu so they can visually and auditorily perceive the departure.

The simple act of saying hello to students who are deafblind may take 2 or 3 minutes if proper care is taken to ensure the student has time to determine the identity of the person initiating the greeting and has the opportunity to respond. The amount of time needed will also depend on the familiarity of the person and the context of the greeting. For example, saying hello to the art teacher in the routine context of the doorway to the art classroom when entering art class may not require as much time as in a less familiar situation (e.g., one in which the art teacher stopped by to say hello during lunch in the cafeteria, a context in which the student and the art teacher do not typically interact). Teachers may need to prevent the well-meaning passerby from offering brief and confusing greetings, such as simply patting the student who is deafblind on the head and walking away. Making others aware of the confusion this type of interaction can cause and the importance of quality interactions will increase the probability that the connections the student does engage in are meaningful and reinforcing.

Communication   The topic of communication most often is interpreted to mean the receptive and expressive communication skills of the student. For students with sensory loss, it is also necessary to address the receptive and expressive skills of the teacher. Teachers must be acutely aware of the mode of communication, rate of speech or sign, and the use of familiar vocabulary. The optimal mode, rate, and vocabulary will differ for each student. The following additional considerations must be addressed for students with sensory loss:

- Does the student have equal access to instruction provided to other students?

- When a teacher responds to a student's communication effort with a gaze or vocal response, does the student have sufficient access to realize these forms of acknowledgement are occurring?

- Does the student have a way to confirm that the teacher understands the message the student communicated?

Bruce (2003) and Stillman and Battle (1986) investigated access to communication in classrooms with students with sensory loss who were unable to hear speech well enough to understand verbal communication. Both studies found that even in classrooms where teachers reported using a variety of accessible communication methods when interacting with students who could not hear speech, more than half of the time that teachers were communicating to their students, they were talking without any added communication forms such as sign language or gestures.

Janssen, Riksen-Walraven, and van Dijk (2003) found that missed communication attempts can increase a student's feelings of insecurity and incompetence. If a student continually experiences failed attempts at communicating in the school setting, then the possible result is that the student loses motivation to try to communicate or escalates to undesirable behaviors. Acknowledgement and validation of a student's communication attempts need to be clear and immediate; moreover, responsiveness by the teacher can increase the student's motivation to communicate. Some strategies include providing a tactile cue to let a student know the teacher is listening, asking the child to repeat a message that was not understood, or giving a choice of objects to clarify an unclear message (Bruce, 2005).

Approaches to Problem Solving and Concept Development   The qualities of effective instruction for students with sensory disabilities are not much different from effective teaching strategies for students without sensory disabilities. Instructional activities should be enjoyable and delivered in contexts related to personal experiences, and they should provide the student with an active role (Lawhon & Cobb, 2002), allowing the student to feel a sense of control and motivation while likely increasing the amount of time he or she remains engaged in the activity (Erickson & Koppenhaver, 1995; Koppenhaver et al., 2001; Marks, 1998).

Students with sensory loss may be reluctant to engage with a new activity. They may need many repeated experiences to understand the activity and learn to enjoy participating in it. Because students with sensory loss may have had limited prior knowledge of a new concept being presented, measuring a student's time engaged in the task, anticipating the next step in a routine, or realizing and correcting his or her own errors during a task can promote more active learning than measuring accuracy.

Teaching Problem Solving   Teachers of students with sensory disabilities must provide multiple opportunities to develop strategies for problem solving in the context of meaningful activities (Rowland & Schweigert, 2001). It is important that the support given helps the student systematically explore and process the problem or the big picture. This may require the teacher to point out information a student with vision loss is having difficulty discovering independently (e.g., materials have fallen on the floor). At the same time, the teacher should avoid providing the solution to the student and should give the student plenty of time to process the information and solve the problem independently. Some sensory processing behaviors such as directing the gaze away from the activity or pausing in the middle of a task can be mistaken for off-task behavior. Knowing the difference is critical because all forms of prompts, including touch, verbal communication, signs, and gestures, interrupt information processing and should be used only at times when the student has truly disengaged or is requesting assistance.

Independence and Autonomy   Educational plans should ensure that ample time and supports are in place to maximize the student's independence. Unnecessary assistance given to the student can lead to learned helplessness or the student becoming more dependent on someone else's help. Yet, training those working with the student to use appropriate distancing, have high expectations, and understand the impact of sensory loss can provide them with the perspective and skills needed to help the student develop a much greater level of independence (Giangreco & Edelman, 1997; Marks, 1998). The pace of instruction may need to be considerably slower to ensure the student has time to gain access to communication from the teacher and interact with the educational materials.

Consider a vocabulary lesson with a 10-year-old student named Timothy, who is deaf, has intellectual disabilities, and relies on sign language for communication. Timothy's teacher uses objects related to an adapted text she is reading to the class that connect with target vocabulary words printed on index cards. As she reads to the class, a teaching assistant sits next to Timothy to direct his attention to the correct object and word when necessary. The teaching assistant carefully observes him as he switches his attention between the teacher and his materials. If he misses information or directions given by the teacher while he is focused on matching his objects and index cards, then the assistant allows him to complete his task and then signs the information to him. It is important that the teaching assistant give Timothy several seconds to process the signed instructions before he engages in the task. Such wait time could be greater if a student also has a visual impairment and relies on tactile exploration to locate the objects and the index cards, which would need to have braille. In both cases, frequent prompting would interrupt not only the student's independence but also his learning.

Literacy   The strategies for literacy instruction for students with sensory loss are the same as many of those discussed in Chapter 10. Students with sensory disabilities, however, may need additional accommodations to ensure they are able to gain access to those strategies. Students without sufficient vision to see print will need to have the same access to braille as their peers have to print. Braille can be written in many ways, including the Perkins Brailler, the Mountbatten Brailler, a slate and stylus, or using various computerized devices. Working with the teacher of students with visual loss, an IEP team can determine how to ensure a student will have appropriate access to reading and writing. Students who are deaf or hard of hearing may need accommodations such as the use of an FM system during storytime or positioning to ensure they can clearly see the teacher's face and the sign language used during literacy instruction and throughout the school day. The teacher may need to pause after signing the words of the story to allow children time to shift their visual attention to the words and pictures on the page. It is also important to consider if the students have had meaningful experience with the topic of the literature. For example, the moon and stars will be difficult for a child who is blind to understand. Stories that relate to the student's own experiences can make it easier for the student to understand the concepts and vocabulary in the text (Koenig & Farrenkopf, 1997; Zago, 1996).

Helping a student to create a book or story based on an activity or event incorporates meaningful text with a student's experiences. Teachers can ask the child probing questions such as, "When we made pesto, which herb was your favorite?" The student can then indicate his or her choice using his or her own mode of communication, and the teacher can write the sentence in print, braille, or on a computer or tablet using authoring software. Rather than using photographs, whole objects can be used for students with visual loss by attaching them to the book with Velcro or in a resealable bag (Lewis & Tolla, 2003). Print, braille, or even a picture of the signs can be included on the pages as appropriate. Experience stories can be based on special occasions, such as a birthday party, or simple daily activities, such as playing on the school playground. Rereading experience stories before and after the activity can help the student connect the meaning of the text to the objects in the activity.

Object Calendar or Schedule Boxes   Object calendars, also referred to as *schedule boxes*, combine the strategies of using tangible symbols and embedding instruction within routines. Although they vary in how they are designed to meet a student's needs, they are used similarly to a personal visual schedule. Using whole objects can provide a static, concrete base of communication when it is difficult to determine with certainty what a student can clearly see or hear. Unlike a signed or spoken word, the permanence of an object allows for extensive exploration (Blaha, 2001). Just as a child needs to hear a word many times before understanding its meaning, a student may need multiple, meaningful exposures to an object in a systematic way to develop the concept that the object has a representational meaning.

Teachers and other school personnel must select objects that represent the student's daily activities and are systematically presented to the student prior to beginning the activity. These objects should have a direct relationship with what they represent in order to be as iconic as possible. Calendars constructed of truly representational objects can help students who have not yet developed formal communication or concepts of symbolic representation begin to anticipate what is going to happen (Blaha, 2001). Students can anticipate upcoming activities with the use of objects that represent these events. For example, when Tina is provided with a spoon at her calendar, she can anticipate that it is snack time. The spoon symbolizes the snack time. A teacher may expand the use of objects, thereby expanding the student's vocabulary.

It is important to recognize that the learning objectives that can be addressed by an object calendar go far beyond simply anticipating activities. Object calendars can be used to teach sequencing, time skills, and concepts such as before, after, finished, and next (Blaha, 2001). Using more objects within the context of the student's day can then expand the student's vocabulary. Discontinuing the use of an object calendar once a student demonstrates anticipation of the next activity is a common mistake teachers make. Just as many adults continue to use calendars or check the clock throughout the day, students should continue to have access to their calendars. Once the student demonstrates understanding of the objects, the teacher can continue to build on these understandings by adding more objects, pairing the known objects with print or braille, and slowly making the transition to more symbolic forms of representation. Therefore, once mastered, the usage of objects should not be discontinued but expanded to include more symbolic forms to increase communication and literacy.

Using Tactile Materials and Modifications   Instructional staff must be sensitive to concept development and the preferences of the student when selecting and modifying materials for students who will be relying on touch. Making every effort to use textures that are pleasant to the touch is a critical step because most individuals do not enjoy running their hands over sand paper for any length of time. That said, it is important to remember that raised line drawings and miniatures do not provide meaningful representations to a child with vision loss because they are based on visual features of the objects and are not to scale. In other words, the features of a representative object, such as a toy school bus, will not resemble the parts of the actual school bus that a child comes in contact with on the way to school. Instead, a harness worn on the bus or piece of a seatbelt could represent the bus ride home.

Regulation and Learning   Sensory regulation is a final consideration for learning for students with sensory loss. Homeostasis, or a balance of one's internal sensory needs, is a natural tendency for all people, regardless of the presence or absence of disabilities. It is natural to seek to increase sensory input when bored. A look around any auditorium or lecture hall reveals people drawing, looking at their smartphones, or shaking their foot. Decreasing sensory input when overwhelmed is illustrated by turning down the car radio when driving in a severe storm or heavy traffic. Each person has his or her own optimal level of sensory input for homeostasis.

Individuals with sensory loss can experience a state of sensory deprivation or sensory overload. Difficulty understanding or organizing external stimuli can also lead a person to engage in repetitive behaviors as a form of regulation (van Dijk, Klomberg, & Nelson, 1997). Teachers should be aware of the levels of sensory input students receive during the school day, taking care that students' individual needs are met within and between activities. A teacher's first reaction to a student's use of regulating behaviors should be to consider if the sensory environment needs to be adjusted. Then, consider if the student has the concepts and physical skills needed to meaningfully engage in the task without additional accommodations.

Transition from School to Adult Life

Larry is an 18-year-old young man with intellectual and global developmental disabilities, including visual loss. His vision is assessed at 20/300 with refraction (glasses). Larry communicates effectively using single words and short

phrases to express his thoughts, needs, and ideas. He has a sight word vocabulary of approximately 250 words, and he uses the texting feature with an
enlarged font on his smartphone to communicate with his family and friends.
Larry consistently expressed his desire to become an airplane pilot during the
initial stages of transition planning. As expected, there was the tendency to
immediately dismiss his career choice as unrealistic by stating the obvious—
pilots need to have good vision, or his lack of literacy skills would prevent
him from applying to flight school or the military. The transition planning
team did not discourage Larry, however, but rather listened to him. They identified all of his strengths and abilities, which included a strong work ethic, an
ability to learn a routine, an interest in always being presentable, a capacity
to do physical labor, and an overall friendly and pleasant personality.

Larry's community-based instructor consulted with his teacher of
students with visual impairments and identified four job sampling experiences within a regional airport near their community. Each of these jobs was
customized for the purpose of reducing any visual tasks that Larry would not
be able to accomplish or would present a danger. In addition, accommodations were provided, such as placing colored tape on the steps leading to the
employees' entrance.

Because it is difficult to identify the numbers of students with multiple
disabilities that present with sensory disabilities, little is known about their
postschool success. Some evidence, however, shows that youth with disabilities do not achieve the outcomes of independent living, community participation, and productive employment as experienced by their peers without
disabilities (Newman, Wagner, Cameto, & Knokey, 2009). Students without
disabilities typically move from high school to postsecondary educational
programs, vocational/technical training programs, or competitive employment. The status of postschool outcomes for students with disabilities in
the United States indicates low employment rates, underemployment, low
attendance at postsecondary educational programs, high incidence of drop
out from postsecondary education programs, and overall poor adjustment to
adult life (Carter, Austin, & Trainor, 2012). Efforts supported by federal legislation, however, have identified fundamental practices that are necessary
to promote the transition of all youth with disabilities from school to successful adult life within their communities. These effective practices of transition planning and associated programming include person-centered planning
during the early years in secondary education, the use of community-based
vocational experiences, direct instruction in social skills to promote meaningful relationships, opportunities to demonstrate age-appropriate levels of
independent living, and skill building in self-determination and advocacy.
Although these areas are central to realizing a successful transition to adulthood for all youth with and without disabilities, youth with sensory loss require special considerations.

Transition Assessment and Planning for Youth with Sensory Disabilities It is critical to take a personalized approach that considers the individual's strengths, abilities, and preferences when assessing a youth in transition who presents with sensory loss for the purpose of planning his or her path toward adult life. Approaching assessment from this vantage will minimize the tendency to assume that a person with hearing and/or vision loss would not be successful, thus eliminating a variety of experiences and opportunities. Disregarding Larry's aspirations to become an airplane pilot would have eliminated him from consideration for many other jobs in the airline industry that can be carved out or accommodated. Larry graduated high school at the age of 21 and went to work part time as an assistant baggage handler. His employer has provided accommodations of additional lighting in the baggage areas that allow Larry to be safe, and he is assigned to a senior employee.

Transition assessment for youth with sensory loss is an ongoing process that begins with and must be rooted in person-centered thinking. Because these youth represent a highly diverse group with varying needs, individualized approaches to planning are much more effective in producing positive and sustainable outcomes. The term *person-centered planning* is used to describe an array of approaches to planning that are derived from the perspective of the individual and their families (Turnbull, Turnbull, Erwin, Soodak, & Shogren, 2011). It is recommended that facilitators of person-centered planning processes have a familiarity with the nature and implications of sensory loss, which will result in a comprehensive and cohesive transition plan.

Vocational Preparation and Employment for Youth with Sensory Disabilities Youth with sensory loss face challenges in obtaining information incidentally, which limits opportunities to be introduced to new knowledge and skills. Therefore, when approaching vocational instruction, new knowledge and skills are best taught in a systematic and sequential manner within a community or real-life setting. In other words, these students learn best by direct instruction involving actual work experiences and settings. Experiences working in community-based settings can amplify a student's vocational success and more likely result in postschool competitive employment (Carter, Trainor, Ditchman, Swedeen, & Owens, 2009). As with Larry, youth with sensory loss require well-planned and robust opportunities to experience work in the community. Transition to work begins with an ecological assessment of the working or community environment and its demands (see Chapter 13). In addition, students with sensory loss will require considerations of how to provide incidental information that supports their conceptual understanding and awareness of the environment. Youth with sensory loss typically do not have the same experiential backgrounds as their peers without sensory loss. For example, a student with vision loss may not observe peers greeting each other in the hallway and would require direct instruction to become familiar with social norms such as a high five instead of a handshake. These youth benefit from involvement and consultation with professionals trained in approaches to accommodations and modifications that are unique to students with sensory loss.

Self-Determination for Youth with Sensory Disabilities   Youth with sensory loss often are marginalized by limitations imposed by a loss of vision and/or hearing. These youth experience limited interactions with their peers and the environment and miss many opportunities for incidental learning. Vision and/or hearing loss may also influence a youth's opportunity to self-direct activities due to the need for scheduling that allows adequate time for moving through all of the components of a routine. For example, Larry arrives at work 15 minutes early to ensure there is enough time for him to complete his work arrival routine. This routine begins as he goes to his locker, puts his coat and lunch away, and gets into his uniform. Although it takes Larry more time to do this himself, he benefits from experiencing the sense of independence. Therefore, it is critical that direct and deliberate efforts are made to assist youth in developing self-direction and self-determination.

> The term 'self-determination' can be described as the capacity of individuals to exercise the degree of control over their lives they desire in areas they value and over which they wish to exert personal control. The amount of personal control will vary as the young person gains more knowledge and develops more skills. It does not mean total independence and autonomy. (Southeast Regional Transition Institute Team, 2013, p. 24)

As a result, teachers and parents must provide youth with sensory disabilities with frequent and planned opportunities to exercise choice and self-direction in their lives so the young person can acquire interdependence and independence as appropriate for the individual. Youth with multiple disabilities and vision and/or hearing loss benefit from planned interactions with peers, strategic instruction addressing missed incidental information, and extended time to allow for independence in everyday activities. Additional skills that support self-determination involve direct instruction in activities of daily living and independent living. Learning these skills may be maximized by the use of assistive technology to remediate for the loss of hearing or vision. For example, Larry may use a talking GPS device to navigate with independence around the job site.

Developing a Social Network for Youth with Sensory Disabilities   Friendships and positive social relationships are considered a critical component of overall human development, specifically for social competence and functioning. The experiences of developing and maintaining relationships, receiving and providing social support, and maintaining a social network are essential to a successful adult life. The isolating nature of a sensory loss, especially when combined with additional disabilities, can result in diminished opportunities for social interaction and serve as a barrier to developing social relationships and friendships. Youth with multiple disabilities that include sensory loss are at serious risk of underdeveloped social networks because of difficulties in communication and the need for adult support to successfully participate in activities or simply to address issues of mobility. Considering the importance of a social network and its interrelationship with participation in community and vocational activities, it is critical to ensure that youth with multiple disabilities and sensory loss are effectively connected to others.

Youth with sensory loss require ongoing and consistent support to facilitate critical social connections to other people and the environment. This is unfortunately often left to the responsibility of family members who either do not know how to make connections outside the family or cannot provide the level of support necessary for success. It is essential that teachers, parents, and others plan together and implement deliberate and systematic interventions that foster friendships and social relationships for children and youth with sensory loss. Although schools are designed to promote interaction among students within similar chronological ages, youth with sensory loss require ongoing support to socially engage in school and community environments. Specialized supports for youth with sensory loss may include a well-designed system of communication, the use of interveners, development of age-appropriate circles of friends/support, and ongoing, solution-oriented team initiatives that focus on social network development. For example, Larry's team could identify a small group of same age-peers, possibly from his high school or a local college, that would routinely meet to create opportunities for him to engage in social activities. In addition, a community intervener may be able to support Larry to participate in activities that he enjoys and connect him to others within the community (e.g., attending the local gym, participating in a yoga class).

CONCLUSION

The eyes, ears, and brain make up the visual and auditory systems, which play a critical role in overall human development and learning. The incidence of sensory loss in students with severe and multiple disabilities is higher than that of students without disabilities (Fellinger et al., 2009; van den Broek, Janssen, van Ramshorst, & Deen, 2006). Basic educational considerations for students with sensory loss include addressing movement and mobility so that the student is able to reach information that would not be perceivable from a distance and utilizing specialized strategies and efforts to facilitate incidental learning and concept development. Teachers and others must be aware of the need to build trust through responding to a child's unique and sometimes difficult-to-understand communication and behavior. Specialized approaches to communication development are needed for students with sensory loss, such as creating predictable daily routines to support learning and reduce anxiety. Teachers must stay vigilant of students' sensory needs and demands through careful planning of instructional activities. Collaboration with vision, hearing, and deafblindness specialists can contribute critical information to educational team planning and aid in the implementation of specialized instructional strategies throughout the age span.

REFLECTION QUESTIONS

1. How does the combination of a vision and hearing loss affect a child's learning and development?

2. What are specific UDL strategies for students who have multiple disabilities and a visual impairment or hearing loss?

3. Identify how a student's learning objectives might be embedded within the daily routine.

CHAPTER ACTIVITY

1. Pair up with a classmate.

2. One person is the teacher (do not talk or sign) and the other person is the student who is deafblind (close eyes).

3. The teacher shows the student how to use an object using hand-under-hand guidance and hand-over-hand guidance.

4. Switch roles and use a different object.

5. Debrief to discuss the differences between the hand-over-hand and hand-under-hand experiences.

REFERENCES

Abdala, C., & Winter, M. (2014). Pediatric audiology: Evaluating and managing hearing loss in young children. In D. Chen (Ed.), *Essential elements in early intervention: Visual impairments and multiple disabilities* (2nd ed., pp. 341–391). New York, NY: AFB Press.

Alsop, L., Durkel, J., Killoran, J., Prouty, S., & Robinson, C. (2004). *Recommendations on the training of interveners for students who are deafblind.* Logan, UT: SKI-HI Institute and The National Technical Assistance Consortium for Children and Youth who are Deaf-Blind.

American Optometric Association. (2014). *School-aged vision: 6 to 18 years of age.* Retrieved from http://www.aoa.org/patients-and-public/good-vision-throughout-life/childrens-vision/school-aged-vision-6-to-18-years-of-age?sso=y

American Speech-Language-Hearing Association. (2007). *Scope of practice in speech-language pathology.* Retrieved from http://www.asha.org/policy/SP2007-00283. htmhttp://www.asha.org/policy/SP2007-00283.htm

Arnold, K.D. (1998). Deaf-blindness. In L. Phelps (Ed.), *Health-related disorders in children and adolescents: A guidebook for understanding and educating* (pp. 224–232). Washington, DC: American Psychological Association. doi:10.1037/10300-032

Ayres, A.J. (1974). *The development of sensory integrative theory and practice: A collection of the works of A. Jean Ayres.* Dubuque, IA: Kendall/Hunt Publishing.

Bashinski, S.M., Durando, J., & Thomas, K.S. (2009). Family survey results: Children with deaf-blindness who have cochlear implants. *AER Journal: Research and Practice in Visual Impairment and Blindness, 3*(3), 31–90.

Beange, H., Lennox, N., & Parmenter, T.R. (1999). Health targets for people with an intellectual disability. *Journal of Intellectual and Developmental Disability, 24,* 283–297.

Bellini, S., Peters, J.K., Benner, L., & Hopf, A. (2007). A meta-analysis of school-based social skills interventions for children with autism spectrum disorders. *Remedial and Special Education, 28,* 153–162.

Black, J., Hickson, L., Black, B., & Perry, C. (2011). Prognostic indicators in pediatric cochlear implant surgery: A systematic literature review. *Cochlear Implants International: An Interdisciplinary Journal, 12*(2), 67–93.

Blaha, R. (2001). *Calendars for students with multiple impairments including deafblindness.* Austin, TX: Texas School for the Blind and Visually Impaired.

Bourquin, E.A. (1996). Using interpreters with deaf-blind clients: What professional service providers should know. *Re:View, 27*(4), 149–154.

Brown, D. (2007, January–June). The vestibular sense. *Deafblind International Review,* 17–22.

Bruce, S.M. (2002). Impact of a communication intervention model on teachers' practice with children who are congenitally deaf-blind. *Journal of Visual Impairment and Blindness, 96*(3), 154–168.

Bruce, S.M. (2003). The importance of shared communication forms. *Journal of Visual Impairment and Blindness, 97*(2), 106–109.

Bruce, S.M. (2005). The impact of congenital deafblindness on the struggle to symbolism. *International Journal of Disability, Development and Education, 52*(3), 233–251. doi:10.1080/10349120500252882

Carter, E.W., Austin, D., & Trainor, A.A. (2012). Predictors of postschool employment outcomes for young adults with severe disabilities. *Journal of Disability Policy Studies, 23*(1), 50–63. doi:10.1177/1044207311414680

Carter, E., Trainor, A.A., Ditchman, N., Swedeen, B., & Owens, L. (2009). Evaluation of a multicomponent intervention package to increase summer work experiences for transition-age youth with severe disabilities. *Research and Practice for Persons with Severe Disabilities, 34*(2), 1–12.

Carle, E. (1994). *The very hungry caterpillar.* New York, NY: Philomel Books.

Celeste, M. (2006). Play behaviors and social interactions of a child who is blind: In theory and practice. *Journal of Visual Impairments and Blindness, 100,* 75–90.

Center for Applied Special Technology. (2011). *Universal design for learning guidelines version 2.0.* Wakefield, MA: Author.

Center on the Developing Child. (2007). *InBrief: Early childhood mental health.* Retrieved from http://www.developingchild.harvard.edu

Chen, D. (2004). Young children who are deaf-blind: Implications for professionals in deaf and hard of hearing services. *Volta Review, 104*(4), 273–284.

Chen, D. (2014). Promoting early communication and language development. In D. Chen (Ed.), *Essential elements in early intervention: Visual impairments and multiple disabilities* (2nd ed., pp. 395–462). New York, NY: AFB Press.

Chen, D., & Downing, J.E. (2006). *Tactile strategies for children with visual impairments and multiple disabilities: Promoting communication and learning skills.* New York, NY: AFB Press.

Chen, D., Klein, M.D., & Haney, M. (2007). Promoting interactions with infants who have complex multiple disabilities: Development and field-testing of the PLAI curriculum. *Infants and Young Children, 20,* 149–162.

Chute, P.M., & Nevins, M.E. (2011). Providing services in educational contexts: Defining the role of the pediatric audiologist. In R. Seewald & A.M. Tharpe (Eds.), *Comprehensive handbook of audiology* (pp. 799–810). San Diego, CA: Plural Publishing.

Clark, C., & McDonnell, A.P. (2008). Teaching choice making to children with visual impairments and multiple disabilities in preschool and kindergarten classrooms. *Journal of Visual Impairments and Blindness, 102,* 397–409.

Clark, J.G. (1981). Uses and abuses of hearing loss classification. *Asha, 23,* 493–500.

Coogle, C.G., Floyd, K., Hanline, M.F., & Kellner-Hiczewski, J. (2013). Strategies used in natural environments to promote communication development in young children at risk for autism spectrum disorder. *Young Exceptional Children, 16*(3), 11–23. doi:10.1177/1096250612473126

DiCarlo, C.F., Reid, D.H., & Stricklin, S.B. (2003). Increasing toy play among toddlers with multiple disabilities in an inclusive classroom: A more-to-less, child-directed intervention continuum. *Research in Developmental Disabilities, 24,* 195–209. doi:10.1016/S0891-4222(03)00025-8

Dote-Kwan, J. (1995). Impact of mothers' interactions on the development of their young visually impaired children. *Journal of Visual Impairment and Blindness, 89,* 47–58.

Dunn, W., Saiter, J., & Rinner, L. (2002). Asperger syndrome and sensory processing: A conceptual model and guidance for intervention planning. *Focus on Autism and Other Developmental Disabilities, 17*(3), 172–185.

Dunst, C.J., & Kassow, D. (2008). Caregiver sensitivity, contingent social responsiveness and secure infant attachment. *Journal of Early and Intensive Behavioral Intervention, 5*(1), 40–56.

Dutton, G.N., & Bax, M. (2010). Introduction. In G.N. Dutton & M. Bax (Eds.), *Visual impairment in children due to damage to the brain* (pp. 1–4). London, England: MacKeith Press.

Easterbrooks, S.R., & Estes, E. (2007). *Helping deaf and hard of hearing children to use spoken language.* Thousand Oaks, CA: Corwin Press.

Erickson, K.A., Hatton, D., Roy, V., Fox, D., & Renne, D. (2007). Literacy in early intervention for children with visual impairments: Insights from individual cases. *Journal of Visual Impairment and Blindness, 101,* 80–95.

Erickson, K.A., & Koppenhaver, D.A. (1995). Developing a literacy program for children with severe disabilities, *The Reading Teacher, 48,* 676–684.

Fellinger, J., Holzinger, D., Dirmhirn, A., van Dijk, J., & Goldberg, D. (2009). Failure to detect deaf-blindness in a population of people with intellectual disability. *Journal of Intellectual Disability Research, 53*(10), 874–881. doi:10.1111/j.1365-2788 .2009.01205.x

Fredricks, H.D., & Baldwin, V.L. (1987). Individuals with sensory impairments: Who are they? How are they educated? In L. Goetz, D. Guess, & K. Stremel-Campbell (Eds.), *Innovative program design for individuals with dual sensory impairment* (pp. 3–12). Baltimore, MD: Paul H. Brookes Publishing Co.

Giangreco, M.F., & Edelman, S.W. (1997). Helping or hovering? Effects of instructional assistant proximity on students with disabilities. *Exceptional Children, 64*(1), 7–18.

Hanline, M.F., & Correa-Torres, S.M. (2012). Experiences of preschoolers with severe disabilities in an inclusive early childhood setting: A qualitative study. *Education and Training in Autism and Developmental Disabilities, 47,* 102–121.

Hatton, D.D., Erickson, K.A., & Lee, D.B. (2010). Phonological awareness of young children with visual impairments. *Journal of Visual Impairments and Blindness, 104,* 743–752.

Hild, U., Hey, C., Baumann, U., Montgomery, J., Euler, H.A., & Neumann, K. (2008). High prevalence of hearing disorders at the Special Olympics indicate need to screen persons with intellectual disability. *Journal of Intellectual Disability Research, 52*(6), 520–528. doi:10.1111/j.1365-2788.2008.01059.x

Individuals with Disabilities Education Improvement Act (IDEA) of 2004, PL 108-446, 20 U.S.C. §§ 1400 *et seq.*

Ingersoll, B., & Dvortcsak, A. (2009). *Teaching social communication to children with autism: A practitioner's guide to parent training and a manual for parents.* New York, NY: Guilford Press.

Ingersoll, B., Lewis, E., & Kroman, E. (2007). Teaching the imitation and spontaneous use of descriptive gestures in young children with autism using a naturalistic behavioral intervention. *Journal of Autism and Developmental Disorders, 37,* 1446–1456.

Janssen, M.J., Riksen-Walraven, J.M., & van Dijk, J.P.M. (2003). Toward a diagnostic intervention model for fostering harmonious interactions between deaf-blind children and their educators. *Journal of Visual Impairment and Blindness, 97*(4), 197–214.

Johnston, S.S., McDonnell, A.P., & Hawken, L.S. (2008). Enhancing outcomes in early literacy for young children with disabilities: Strategies for success. *Intervention in School and Clinic, 43*(4), 210–217.

Killoran, J. (2007). *The national deaf-blind child count: 1998–2005 in review.* Monmouth, OR: National Technical Assistance Consortium for Children and Young Adults who are DeafBlind (NTAC), Teaching Research Institute, Western Oregon University.

Koenig, A.J., & Farrenkopf, C. (1997). Essential experiences to undergird the early development of literacy. *Journal of Visual Impairment and Blindness, 91*(1), 14-24.

Koppenhaver, D.A., Erickson, K.A., Harris, B., McLellan, J., Skotko, B.G., & Newton, R.A. (2001). Storybook-based communication intervention for girls with Rett syndrome and their mothers. *Disability and Rehabilitation, 23*(3/4), 149–159.

Lantzy, C., & Lantzy, A. (2010). Outcomes and opportunities: A study of children with cortical visual impairment. *Journal of Visual Impairment and Blindness, 104*(10), 649–653.

Lawhon, T., & Cobb, J.B. (2002). Routines that build emergent literacy skills in infants, toddlers, and preschoolers. *Early Childhood Education Journal, 30*(2), 113–118.

Lewis, S., & Tolla, J. (2003). Creating and using tactile experience books for young children with visual impairments. *Teaching Exceptional Children, 35*(3), 22–28.

Locke, J., Rotheram-Fuller, E., & Kasari, C. (2012). Exploring the social impact of being a typical peer model for included children with autism spectrum disorder. *Journal of Autism and Developmental Disorders, 42,* 1895–1905.

Mahoney, G. (2009). Relationship focused intervention (RFI): Enhancing the role of parents in children's developmental intervention. *International Journal of Early Childhood Special Education, 1*(1), 79–94.

Mahoney, G., & Perales, F. (2005). A comparison of the impact of relationship-focused intervention on young children with pervasive developmental disorders and other disabilities. *Journal of Developmental and Behavioral Pediatrics, 26,* 77–85.

Marks, S.B. (1998). Understanding and preventing learned helplessness in children who are congenitally deaf-blind. *Journal of Visual Impairment and Blindness, 92*(3), 200–211.

McDuffie, A., & Yoder, P. (2010). Types of parent verbal responsiveness that predict language in young children with autism spectrum disorder. *Journal of Speech, Language, and Hearing Research, 53,* 1026–1039.

Miles, B. (2008). *Overview of deaf-blindness.* Monmouth, OR: National Information Clearinghouse on Children Who Are Deaf-Blind.

Molholm, S., Ritter, W., Murray, M.M., Javitt, D.C., Schroeder, C.E., & Foxe, J.J. (2002). Multisensory auditory–visual interactions during early sensory processing in humans: A high-density electrical mapping study. *Cognitive Brain Research, 14*(1), 115–128.

Murphy, J.L., Hatton, D., & Erickson, K. (2008). Exploring the early literacy practices of teachers of infants, toddlers, and preschoolers with visual impairments. *Journal of Visual Impairment and Blindness, 102*(3), 133–146.

National Center on Deaf-Blindness. (2013). *Definition of intervener services and interveners in educational settings: Technical report.* Retrieved from http://documents.nationaldb.org/Intervener%20Services%20Definition%20Technical%20Report.pdf

Newman, L., Wagner, M., Cameto, R., & Knokey, A. (2009). *The post-high school outcomes of youth with disabilities up to 4 years after high school: A report from the National Longitudinal Transition Study-2 (NLTS2).* Menlo Park, CA: SRI International.

Nussbaum, D., Waddy-Smith, B., & Doyle, J. (2012). Students who are deaf and hard of hearing and use sign language: Considerations and strategies for developing spoken language and literacy skills. *Seminars in Speech and Language, 33,* 310–321.

Parten, M.B. (1932). Social participation among preschool children. *Journal of Abnormal and Social Psychology, 28*(3), 136–147. doi:10.1037/h0074524

Perryman, T.Y., Carter, A.S., Messinger, D.S., Stone, W.L., Ivanescu, A.E., & Yoder, P.J. (2013). Brief report: Parental child-directed speech as a predictor of receptive language in children with autism symptomatology. *Journal of Autism and Developmental Disorders, 43,* 1983–1987. doi:10.1007/s10803-012-1725-3

Pizzo, L., & Bruce, S.M. (2010). Language and play in students with multiple disabilities and visual impairments or deafblindness. *Journal of Visual Impairment and Blindness, 104*(5), 287–297.

Prickett, J., & Welch, T. (1995) Module 3 deaf-blindness: Implications for learning. In K.M. Huebner, J.G. Prickett, T.R. Welch, & E. Joffee (Eds.), *Hand in hand: Essentials of communication and orientation and mobility for your students who are deaf-blind* (pp. 25–60). New York, NY: AFB Press.

Riordan-Eva, P. (2011). Anatomy and embryology of the eye. In P. Riordan-Eva & T. Asbury (Eds.), *Vaughan and Asbury's general ophthalmology* (pp. 1–26). New York, NY: McGraw-Hill.

Rowland, C. (Ed.). (2009). *Assessing communication and learning in young children who are deafblind or who have multiple disabilities.* Retrieved from http://www.designtolearn.com/uploaded/pdf/DeafBlindAssessment Guide.pdf

Rowland, C., & Schweigert, P. (1989). Tangible symbols: Symbolic communication for individuals with sensory impairments. *Augmentative and Alternative Communication, 5,* 226–234.

Rowland, C., & Schweigert, P. (2000). Tangible symbols, tangible outcomes. *Augmentative and Alternative Communication, 16*(2), 61–78.

Rowland, C., & Schweigert, P. (2001). Problem solving for deaf-blind kids: the approach is "hands-on." In G. Leslie (Ed.), *Research to real life: Innovations in deafblindness* (pp. 8–10). Retrieved from http://www.eric.ed.gov/PDFS/ED461953.pdf

Segal, O., & Kishon-Rabin, L. (2011). Listening preference for child-directed speech versus nonspeech stimuli in normal-hearing and hearing-impaired infants after cochlear implantation. *Ear and Hearing, 32,* 358–372. doi:10.1097/AUD.0b013e3182008afc

Silberman, R.K. (2000). Children and youth with visual impairments and other exceptionalities. In M.C. Holbrook & A.J. Koenig (Eds.), *Foundations of education: History and theory of teaching children and youth with visual impairments* (Vol. 1, pp. 186–190). New York, NY: AFB Press.

Snell, M. (2007). Effective instructional practices. *TASH Connections, 33,* 8–12.

Soul, J., & Matsuba, C. (2010). Causes of damage to the visual brain: Common aetiologies of cerebral vision impairment. In G.N. Dutton & M. Bax (Eds.), *Visual impairment in children due to damage to the brain* (pp. 20–26). London, England: MacKeith Press.

Southeast Regional Transition Institute Team. (2013). *Transition toolkit: Enhancing self-determination for young adults who are deaf-blind.* Retrieved from http://documents.nationaldb.org/transitiontoolkit/TransitionToolkit_Final.pdf

Stillman, R.D., & Battle, C.W. (1986). Developmental assessment of communicative abilities in the deaf-blind. In D. Ellis (Ed.), *Sensory impairments in mentally handicapped people* (pp. 319–335). Beckenham, England: Croom Helm.

Thiermann, K., & Warren, S.F. (2010). Programs supporting young children's language development. In R.E. Tremblay, M. Boivin, & R.D.V. Peters (Eds.), *Encyclopedia on early childhood development* (pp. 1–8). Montreal, Quebec, Canada: Centre of Excellence for Early Childhood Development and Strategic Knowledge Cluster on Early Child Development.

Titiro, A. (2008). *Improving services to children with mild and moderate vision impairment in New Zealand.* Wellington, New Zealand: JR McKenzie Trust.

Topor, I. (2014). Functional vision assessment and early intervention practices. In D. Chen (Ed.), *Essential elements in early intervention: Visual impairments and multiple disabilities* (2nd ed., pp. 214–293). New York, NY: AFB Press.

Traxler, C.B. (2000). Measuring up to performance standards in reading and mathematics: Achievement of selected deaf and hard-of-hearing students in the national norming of the 9th Edition Stanford Achievement Test. *Journal of Deaf Studies and Deaf Education, 5,* 337–348.

Trief, E., Cascella, P.W., & Bruce, S.M. (2013). A field study of a standardized tangible symbol system for learners who are visually impaired and have multiple disabilities. *Journal of Visual Impairment and Blindness, 107*(3), 180–191.

Turnbull, A., Turnbull, H.R., Erwin, E.R., Soodak, L.C., & Shogren, K.A. (2011). *Families, professionals, and exceptionality: Positive outcomes through partnerships and trust* (6th ed.). Boston, MA: Pearson.

van den Broek, E.C., Janssen, C.C., van Ramshorst, T.T., & Deen, L.L. (2006). Visual impairments in people with severe and profound multiple disabilities: An inventory of visual functioning. *Journal of Intellectual Disability Research, 50*(6), 470–475. doi:10.1111/j.1365-2788.2006.00804

van Dijk, J.P.M., Klomberg, M.J.M., & Nelson, C. (1997). Strategies in deafbind education based on neurological principles. Retrieved from http://www.acfos.org/publication/ourarticles/pdf/acfos1/intro_vandijk.pdf

Whalen, C., Schreibman, L., & Ingersoll, B. (2006). Collateral effects of joint attention training on social interaction and positive affect, imitation, and spontaneous speech for young children with autism. *Journal of Autism and Developmental Disorders, 36,* 655–664.

White, S.W., Keonig, K., & Scahill, L. (2007). Social skills development in children with autism spectrum disorders: A review of the intervention research. *Journal of Autism and Developmental Disorders, 37,* 1858–1868.

Yost, W.A. (2006). *Fundamentals of hearing: An introduction* (5th ed.). Bingley, United Kingdom: Emerald Group Publishing Limited.

Zago, P.A. (1996). Weaving the cloth of literacy: The relationship between braille and reading. *Journal of Visual Impairment and Blindness, 90*(3), 274–276.

Zull, J.E. (2006). Key aspects of how the brain learns. *New Directions for Adult and Continuing Education, 110,* 3–9. doi:10.1002/ace.213

5

Educating Children with Special Health Care Needs

DICK SOBSEY

CHAPTER OBJECTIVES

1. Obtain an overview of some of the common health care needs of students with severe and multiple disabilities at school

2. Learn how to recognize and prevent abuse of students with severe and multiple disabilities

3. Understand how to respond to and plan for classroom emergencies

4. Learn how seizures are diagnosed and treated and understand seizure management in the classroom

5. Understand dual diagnosis in children with severe and multiple disabilities, particularly intellectual and developmental disabilities coexisting with emotional and behavior disorders

KEY TERMS

- Advanced care planning
- Airway obstruction
- Anaphylaxis
- Cerebral palsy (CP)
- Child maltreatment
- Communicable disease
- Defibrillator
- Dignity of risk
- Do not resuscitate (DNR) order/ do not intubate (DNI) order
- Dual diagnosis
- Electroencephalogram (EEG)

- Emergency care plan (ECP)
- Generalized seizure
- Goals of care designation (GCD)
- Immune compromise
- Medical emergency response plan (MERP)
- Partial seizure
- Seizure
- Self-injurious behavior
- Subdiaphragmatic thrust
- Violence-induced disabilities

Hannah taught second grade last year, and she was looking forward to teaching third grade this year. She remembered how worried she was about Jenny last year at this time. Jenny had severe and multiple disabilities. She needed special positioning and assistance with feeding and using the bathroom. She had frequent seizures, and it was difficult to tell how much she understood when anyone spoke to her. Hannah wanted to do a good job teaching Jenny, but she worried because the situation was new to her. Because Jenny had no specific diagnosis, information was not readily available on teaching students with Jenny's challenges.

Hannah's concerns were diminished, however, during the year that she taught Jenny in second grade. She got to know Jenny, understand her needs, and feel comfortable with her. There were still challenges, but Hannah actually enjoyed having Jenny in her class and was now looking forward to teaching her again in third grade.

Jenny's mom told Hannah that she had some exciting news when she brought Jenny to school on the first day of third grade. Jenny's doctor had ordered a newly available genetic test over the summer, and Jenny now had a specific diagnosis—CDKL5 disorder. Hannah told Jenny's mom that she would find out everything she could about teaching students with CDKL5 disorder, but she felt a little worried again. She worried that she would find out that she had been doing everything wrong with Jenny or that the new diagnosis would lead to many more classroom demands.

Hannah looked up CDKL5 disorder, but she found very little information on teaching students with the disorder or accommodating their needs in the classroom. She thought to herself, "Why didn't they have a class on teaching children with CDKL5 disorder in my teacher training program?" She asked the school nurse if she had any helpful information. The nurse said she could probably get a couple articles for her. She went on to say that getting information about the syndrome was a good idea, and it might occasionally be helpful, but it would not make much difference. After all, students with the same syndrome can differ from each other about as much as other students differ. She told Hannah, "Knowing your student is much more important than knowing your student's diagnosis, and next to Jenny's mom, you know Jenny better than anyone."

Learning about the many physical challenges shared by significant numbers of students with severe and multiple disabilities can be helpful, particularly when encountering new challenges. This knowledge can provide useful starting points for developing approaches to teaching and caring for individual students. It is important, however, to remember that applying this knowledge effectively depends on getting to know the individual needs of each student.

ALL CHILDREN HAVE HEALTH CARE NEEDS

Schools play a vital role in ensuring the health of all students—good health promotes learning, and poor health interferes with the learning process (e.g., Basch, 2010). Every child has individual health care needs, but students with severe and multiple disabilities typically experience health challenges that are often more frequent, severe, and complex than those experienced by most other students. Approximately 20%–33% of all school children have some special health care needs or long-term health conditions that require medical treatment or result in functional limitations (Forrest, Bevans, Riley, Crespo, & Louis, 2011).

This chapter describes some special health care needs that are commonly found among children with severe and multiple disabilities. It suggests strategies to prevent some problems and address some of the challenges that cannot be prevented. It includes some practical suggestions for responding to emergencies, with two important cautions. First, this chapter is not intended to provide first aid training. All teachers, especially those working with students with severe and multiple disabilities, should take practical courses in first aid and emergency procedures, including cardiopulmonary resuscitation (CPR) and airway obstruction rescue procedures. Schools should keep appropriate emergency supplies and equipment on hand in places where they can be quickly located and used by school staff in case of an emergency.

Second, individualization is an essential principle to ensure quality in both health care and education. General strategies and approaches discussed here will not always apply to every individual or every situation. When the health care team has made individual plans based on a particular student's needs, those plans, rather than more general rules, should be carried out for that individual. Although it can be useful to know something about some of the most common diagnoses and syndromes found in school children, and particularly those found among students with severe and multiple disabilities, the list of specific conditions and syndromes is far too long to address each one, and individuals with the same diagnoses often have very different needs.

COMMON HEALTH ISSUES IN CHILDREN
WITH SEVERE AND MULTIPLE DISABILITIES

Food allergies, asthma, seizure disorders, and child maltreatment are among the most common health challenges faced by school children that affect their education. Food allergies and asthma are prevalent among all school children, but asthma is about twice as common—and frequently more severe—among children with intellectual and developmental disabilities. Food allergies, however, are equally prevalent among both groups (Schieve et al., 2012). A study conducted in Ohio schools found that more than 10% of students had physician-diagnosed asthma, and many others exhibited symptoms but had not been diagnosed (Clark, Burkett, Andridge, & Buckley, 2013). About 5% of students have food allergies, and about one sixth of those with allergies have had an allergic reaction to something they ate at school (Centers for Disease

Control and Prevention, 2013). Some allergic reactions can become life threatening within minutes and require an immediate response once symptoms appear. Although many students understand their allergies and play an important role in protecting themselves from allergic reactions, students with severe disabilities usually depend more heavily on caregivers for their protection.

A little more than 1% of school-age children have seizure disorders (Russ, Larson, & Halfon, 2012), but approximately 22% of children with intellectual disabilities have seizure disorders (Oeseburg, Dijkstra, Groothoff, Reijneveld, & Jansen, 2011). Approximately 5 in 1000 children are reported to have at least one seizure in a given year, whereas approximately 151 in 1000 children with intellectual disabilities are reported to have at least one seizure in that same 1-year period (Schieve et al., 2012). Seizures can also be linked to CP. About 3.3 out of 1000 children have CP, but about 198 out of 1000 children with intellectual disabilities have CP (Oeseburg et al., 2011), and approximately half of all children with both intellectual disability and CP also have a seizure disorder.

Child maltreatment is also a serious health issue for children. There are confirmed child maltreatment reports each year in the United States involving about 1% of all children (U.S. Department of Health and Human Services, 2012), and this is believed to be only a fraction of unreported or unconfirmed cases that actually occur. The rate of victimization for children with intellectual or behavioral disabilities is approximately four times higher than the rate for children without disabilities (Jones et al., 2012).

Visual impairments, hearing impairments, congenital malformations, endocrine disorders, and digestive tract problems are other health problems frequently reported among children with intellectual disabilities (Oeseburg et al., 2011). Although the prevalence of chronic health conditions is greatly increased for all children with intellectual disabilities, the increase in prevalence is even greater among students with severe intellectual disabilities. As a result, in most cases, children with severe disabilities are also children with multiple disabilities.

Addressing these health challenges may be different when they occur in students with severe and multiple disabilities. For example, as most students with food allergies mature, they can learn to take a major role in avoiding foods that present problems, but students with severe disabilities may continue to rely on others to protect them. In addition, common problems such as pain sometimes go untreated because many children with severe and multiple disabilities have limited formal communication. Careful interpretation of behavior patterns can play a critical role in identifying health concerns (Oberlander & Symons, 2006). Identifying and providing proper treatment for such problems can greatly improve the student's quality of life, facilitate learning, and prevent or reduce challenging behavior. In addition, recognizing and responding to symptoms such as pain at an early stage may prevent more serious problems from developing. For example, identifying and helping a child who has abdominal discomfort receive treatment for constipation (if that is the cause) may prevent the development of a life-threatening bowel obstruction that requires surgery. Careful attention should be given to children with limited communication skills to rule out medical problems before inferring the cause of behavioral challenges as solely environmental or as stemming from the child's diagnosis. For example, some students may become aggressive or disruptive to avoid taking part in instructional activities, but this resistance and inappropriate behavior may disappear after a previously undiagnosed sinus infection or dental problem is appropriately treated.

SOME GENERAL HEALTH CARE CONSIDERATIONS

This section addresses a few health-related issues that educators of children with severe and multiple disabilities should consider. Each of these considerations has always been important, but our understanding of them has deepened since 2000.

Genetic Disorders and Syndromes

Ms. Jones got word in October that a new student who had MECP2 duplication syndrome would be coming to her school and placed in her third-grade classroom. She had never heard of this syndrome and decided to search for some information about it. She found an article that described some of the most common symptoms—severe/profound intellectual disability, autistic behavior, frequent and uncontrolled seizures, immune compromise resulting in recurrent life-threatening respiratory infections, hypotonia, gastric reflux, intestinal pseudoobstruction, neurogenic bladder, osteoporosis resulting in frequent fractures, and bruxism (teeth grinding). Ms. Jones wanted to welcome the new student into her class, but she also felt anxious and overwhelmed. She was nervous about meeting with the new student's mother. She had a million questions but finally settled on just two for their first meeting. First, she asked, "What do you think I need to know about Jordon?" Much later in their meeting, she asked, "Is there anything that I need to know about Jordon's syndrome?" These questions turned out to be a good place to start.

A rapid increase in scientific knowledge about genetics since the 1990s has led to the recognition that genetics play a much larger role in children with severe and multiple disabilities. The ability to identify deletions and duplications of single genes and improved understanding of gene interactions have led to the diagnosis of new syndromes among many individuals who previously had no specific diagnosis and have provided a clearer understanding of the role that genetics may play in conditions such as CP and autism.

Although it may seem like an oxymoron, rare disorders are actually very common. Although the individual conditions identified as rare disorders occur infrequently, the list of rare disorders is a very long one. For example, approximately 7,000 known rare diseases affect 25–30 million individuals in the United States (Field & Boat, 2010). Approximately 50% of these are children, and about 80% of rare disorders have genetic causes.

General information about rare disorders is available from many organizations, such as Unique and the National Organization for Rare Disorders, as well as various disorder-specific organizations. The best information about individual students with any of these conditions, however, generally comes from families, educators, and caregivers who know the student well, so Ms. Jones did well to ask questions and solicit feedback from Jordon's mother, an individual very close to the child.

Pain in Children with Severe and Multiple Disabilities

Historically, individuals with severe intellectual disabilities were commonly described as being insensitive to pain (Oberlander & Symons, 2006). This belief was often derived from observations that children and adults with severe and multiple disabilities allowed others to inflict apparently painful stimuli on them with little obvious reaction. For example, allowing doctors to suture their lacerations without anesthesia was presented as proof of the patients' insensitivity to pain rather than the doctor's indifference to their suffering. Advances in measuring physiological and behavioral responses to pain, however, have made it clear that the vast majority of individuals with severe and multiple disabilities experience pain, it is often unrecognized and untreated or undertreated, and it results in a variety of secondary problems. Among other things, pain interferes with learning, increases behavioral challenges, disturbs sleep, and generally disrupts health and behavior.

Fortunately, better awareness of these problems, better assessment, and better management of pain are becoming more frequent realities (e.g., Shinde et al., 2014). Educators should learn how to recognize signs of pain in students with limited communication, and when they suspect a student is experiencing problems with pain, they should take action to ensure that it is properly assessed and treated.

Advanced Care Planning

Sue suddenly became unconscious while having her lunch in the cafeteria. Her assistant realized that she was choking and could not breathe and prepared to do back blows and subdiaphragmatic thrusts to clear her airway. Sue's panicked teacher intervened, exclaiming, "Wait, she has a DNR order! I do not think we can do anything." The teacher and assistant froze and were not sure how to proceed as a crowd gathered. Time was quickly running out.

Some students attending schools may have DNR orders, but these typically refer only to CPR. They do not mean that nothing can or should be done to save the child's life. There is rarely time in an emergency situation to find out if there is an order and exactly what it means, so it is important to have a clear understanding before an emergency arises. Some students with severe and multiple disabilities may have advanced directives or DNRs. An advanced directive is a document issued by an individual indicating his or her preferences for what kind of treatments may or may not be given in the future if he or she is unable to make or communicate a decision at that time. A DNR or DNI order is a doctor's order indicating what treatments shall be withheld.

There are ethical concerns and controversy about whether an advanced directive is ever appropriate for a child (e.g., Beringer & Heckford, 2014). The ethical rationale for this practice is based on an individual being competent now to make a decision that he or she may be incompetent of making later—the individual communicates preferences for care in advance for when someone else has to make decisions on his or her behalf. An adult will need to make these medical choices because a child is not assumed to be legally competent to make these kinds of health care decisions, so there is little benefit to determining preferred care in advance when the exact circumstances are unknown, except for instances when a parent or guardian cannot be contacted in an emergency situation.

Significant ethical issues exist about the use of DNR or DNI orders with students with severe and multiple disabilities. These should not be issued simply because a child with a disability is presumed to have a poor potential quality of life; children with disabilities have a right to treatment. They may be appropriate on a time-limited basis, however, for a child who is terminally ill. Some states or school districts have specific policies on whether DNR or DNI orders can be followed and how they are handled in schools. The American Academy of Pediatrics Council on School Health and Committee on Bioethics suggests that they may be appropriate for some students with chronic complex conditions who are expected to die within the next 6 months (American Academy of Pediatrics, 2010). When there are orders to limit treatment, it is important that school staff discuss them with the child's parent or guardian to ensure that there is a common understanding, and areas of concern or disagreement should be sorted out before an emergency occurs.

DNR and DNI orders are being replaced in many places by the GCD document because of the ethical issues related to their use (Ells, 2010). The GCD is generally signed by the individual and physician and more specifically states what treatments may and may not be provided. In the absence of any other designation, it is often advisable to have a GCD specifying all emergency measures for students with severe disabilities because it can save time and confusion in emergencies.

School personnel will not have to address these issues under ordinary circumstances, but they can be critical in an emergency. A lack of information or understanding can result in a potentially life-threatening delay in providing treatment in some cases or in legal action against staff and the school in other cases. If a GCD, DNR, or DNI is in place, then it should be discussed with the family, attached to the child's individual ECP, and provided to any emergency medical responders if an emergency occurs. Every effort, however, should be made to contact parents or guardians and the physician who issued the order because these documents will direct care only if a decision is needed and they are unavailable.

Managing Risks

Everyone must balance risks and benefits in life, and no one can completely eliminate all sources of risk. In fact, our attempts to limit our exposure to one source of risk often increase our exposure to another. For example, a sedentary lifestyle may reduce risk for sports injuries, but it also increases risk for obesity and chronic illness.

Adults typically make most of their decisions on balancing risks and benefits for themselves. These kinds of decisions are usually made for young children by their parents or other caregivers, and children frequently make more of their own decisions as they mature and approach adulthood. Although it may be tempting for parents to always make the safest decisions, their children are more likely to advocate for increasing freedom. In addition, community norms tend to influence parents to loosen the reins on their children. Unfortunately, children with severe and multiple disabilities usually have difficulty advocating for themselves, and it is difficult to apply community norms to this group of individuals. Children with severe and multiple disabilities face most of the same risks as others, but they may also face additional risks. Moreover, as they reach the age in which most other children are considered able to make or at least participate in their own decisions, adults often continue to make risk–benefit decisions for children with disabilities.

Although parents, teachers, and other caregivers strive to keep these children safe, well-motivated attempts to protect them may lower their quality of life and, in some cases, may expose them to other less obvious risks. For example, preventing a child from walking because he or she falls frequently may prevent some injuries, but it also restricts the child's freedom and may lead to loss of bone and muscle mass that increases risk of future injuries. Perske's (1972) classic article on the dignity of risk raised issues about the negative effects of overprotectiveness on the quality of life of people with disabilities and posed questions that still need careful consideration today. No scientific formula can be applied to identify the perfect balance between risk and benefit. There are a few guidelines to follow, however, in considering risk decisions, which should be made in consultation with parents to ensure a common perspective:

- Avoid excessive and unnecessary risks. A risk is excessive if the probability and extent of potential harm are unacceptably high. An unnecessary risk may have a lower probability of occurrence and potential for lesser harm, but it can easily be avoided by a less risky, alternative means of achieving the same benefit.

- Consider potential benefits and personal preferences. For example, although swimming or other water-based activities can pose a significant risk to individuals with multiple disabilities, participating in swimming can also provide important physical and social benefits. In addition, many individuals with severe and multiple disabilities enjoy water-based activities, but others may not. Every reasonable effort should be made to honor the preference of an individual who demonstrates the desire to take part in an activity.

- Look for ways to manage risks without restricting activities. For example, wearing a personal flotation device and ensuring hands-on, one-to-one supervision in the pool can greatly reduce risk without eliminating the opportunity to participate.

ABUSE OF STUDENTS WITH SEVERE AND MULTIPLE DISABILITIES

Child maltreatment is a terrible global reality that transcends ethnicity, religion, socioeconomic status, and place of residence (Cyr, Michel, & Dumais, 2013). Significant proportions of children from all segments of society are subjected to physical, sexual, or emotional abuse or serious neglect. The U.S. National Survey of Children's Exposure to Violence found 13.8% of all children (ages 1 month–17 years) experienced maltreatment by a known adult in the previous 1-year period, and 25.6% had experienced maltreatment by a known adult at some point during their lifetime (Finkelhor, Turner, Shattuck, & Hamby, 2013). Children with disabilities, however, are even more likely to experience abuse (Jones et al., 2012).

Since the 1960s, studies have repeatedly linked increased risk for abuse with childhood disability, and recent studies have confirmed this association. Although more research is needed to clarify the nature of the link, the consistent findings of substantial, well-controlled studies leave no room for doubt that abuse and disability are connected. Sullivan and Knutson's (2000) study of a cohort of more than 50,000 children in a Midwest American city was among the first and remains one of the best studies of the relative risk of abuse for children with disabilities. This study started with all children registered in school and preschool programs and then determined which children had been identified as having special needs in school and which children had a history of reported abuse. A history of abuse was 3.4 times more common among children identified as having special learning needs as among other children. Almost one quarter (22%) of children with a history of maltreatment had been identified as needing special education, and almost one third (31%) of children in special education had a confirmed history of child maltreatment. Children with intellectual disabilities were even more at risk. They were 4.0 times as likely to have experienced at least one form of maltreatment, 4.0 times as likely to be sexually abused, 3.8 times as likely to experience physical abuse, 3.8 times as likely to experience emotional abuse, and 3.7 times as likely to experience neglect.

Jones and colleagues (2012) published a large-scale meta-analysis of well-designed studies that measured the prevalence of child maltreatment among children with and without disabilities, and the results were similar to Sullivan and Knutson's (2000) data. Table 5.1 shows the odds of experiencing reported abuse are more than three times higher for a child with any type of disability than for a child without a disability and more than four times higher for a child with an intellectual or mental disability than for a child without a disability.

These prevalence estimates and odds ratios indicate the best estimate relative risk of reported maltreatment. Whether unreported maltreatment is more common for children with disabilities than for other children remains unknown

Table 5.1. Prevalence of maltreatment of children with disabilities with odds ratios

Type of reported abuse	Prevalence among children with any disability % (95% CI)	Odds ratio for children with disabilities	Prevalence among children with intellectual or mental disabilities % (95% CI)	Odds ratio for children with intellectual or mental disabilities
Any abuse	26.7% (13.8%–42.1%)	3.7	21.2% (5.8%–42.8%)	4.3
Physical violence	20.4% (13.4%–28.5%)	3.6	26.8% (11.4%–45.8%)	3.1
Sexual abuse	13.7% (9.2%–18.9%)	2.9	14.5% (7.1%–24.0%)	4.6
Emotional abuse	18.1% (11.5%–25.8%)	4.4	26.7% (11.1%–46.0%)	4.3
Neglect	9.5% (2.6%–20.1%)	4.6	7.8% (3.6%–13.4%)	Not computed

(CI = Confidence intervals)

Source: Jones, Bellis, Wood, Hughes, McCoy, Eckley, et al. (2012).

and the subject of speculation, but it is clear that the prevalence rates would be even higher if unreported cases could be included. Considerable focus has been on the responsibility of teachers and other professionals to report suspected abuse. Law generally mandates educators to report suspected abuse, but details of laws differ across jurisdictions. Preservice and in-service training typically places emphasis on educators' responsibility for detecting and reporting possible abuse that occurs within students' families. This is an important responsibility, but it is also important to recognize the reality that school staff and other students are sometimes abusers. For example, according to a U.S. Department of Education Report, approximately 6.7% of American students are victims of sexual misconduct involving contact in school. The perpetrators were school employees in 21% of cases and other students in 79% (Shakeshaft, 2004). A survey on the sexual abuse of students with disabilities in American schools reported that school staff were responsible for about half the cases, and students were responsible for the other half. Students perpetrated the abuse in 48.3% of cases (Caldas & Bensy, 2014). Teaching personnel (including teachers, teaching assistants, and substitute teachers) were perpetrators of the abuse in 30.3% of cases. Other perpetrators included related services providers, such as physical therapists (PTs) or speech-language pathologists (8.3%), nonprofessional school personnel, such as janitors (6.1%), transportation providers (5.1%), and school administrators (21.1%). Bullying is also a significant problem for many students with disabilities. About a quarter of elementary students with disabilities and about one third of middle school students with disabilities experience bullying, and students with disabilities are more likely to experience chronic bullying than other students (Blake, Lund, Zhou, Kwok, & Benz, 2012).

The association between disability and maltreatment appears to be a complex one. Three major pathways, each with distinct subdivisions, appear to link disability and maltreatment. First, abuse and neglect are significant causes of disabilities, sometimes described as violence-induced disabilities. Second, other events and conditions that increase the risk for disability also increase the risk for child abuse. These can be described as confounding variables because they make it difficult to determine whether a causal relationship exists. Finally, the presence of a disability acts in some ways to increase the risk for victimization. Although this final possibility is the most commonly discussed pathway, it is difficult to determine how much of the association between violence and disability can be attributed to each of the three pathways.

Violence-Induced Disabilities

Violence is a significant cause of childhood disability. It is the sole or primary cause in some cases, and it contributes to the severity of the disability in other cases. For example, improved brain neuroimaging techniques have helped to identify many cases of shaken baby syndrome, which likely would have been diagnosed only as brain damage of undetermined origin in previous years (Sobsey, 2002). In addition, many children released from hospitals with normal neurological exams after being admitted for shaking injuries develop significant developmental and neurological anomalies as long as 2 years after being released. Although the direct effects of traumatic injuries due to child abuse can be devastating, the psychological trauma caused by more subtle mechanisms can be equally tragic. For example, posttraumatic stress disorder (PTSD) has been frequently observed in children and adults with intellectual and developmental disabilities who have been abused (e.g., Hall, Jobson, & Langdon, 2014; Razza & Sobsey, 2011). Although once conceptualized as a purely psychological construct, PTSD is now known to produce physiological and anatomical changes that can be particularly significant in children.

Research has made it clear that physical, sexual, or emotional abuse or severe neglect (De Bellis, 2005) also affects the development of children's nervous systems by producing biochemical changes related to extreme stress or psychological trauma, even in the absence of a physical injury (e.g., De Bellis, Woolley, & Hooper, 2013; Doom, Cicchetti, Rogosch, & Dackis, 2013). These biochemical changes can increase the complexity and severity of existing disabilities. For example, they can add emotional and behavioral challenges to preexisting physical and intellectual disabilities. Although any one form of abuse or severe neglect can produce this effect, it is typically more extreme as the number and types of emotional trauma accumulate. Although these neurological changes occur whether or not any direct physical injury results from abuse, physical injuries that do occur can compound this effect.

Although these effects have not been specifically studied in children with severe and multiple disabilities, research on children in the general population suggests that emotional abuse, physical abuse, sexual abuse, and severe neglect all result in extreme anxiety and stress in the developing child that significantly harm intellectual ability, academic achievement, learning, language development, social-emotional adjustment, and behavior. These effects of extreme anxiety and stress during the developmental period are persistent and continue into adulthood. Maltreated children with severe and multiple disabilities appear to experience these same consequences. Unfortunately, these effects may be misattributed to the child's primary disability.

Evidence also suggests that exposure to family violence may have similar effects, even if a child is not a direct target of violence. In addition to experiencing or witnessing violence, children from abusive families typically grow up in a home that fails to provide appropriate developmental opportunities.

Confounding Variables

Confounding variables are factors that tend to associate child maltreatment with disability but not as a result of a direct causal relationship. Other factors can contribute to both abuse and disability. For example, parental substance abuse increases risk for physical abuse, sexual abuse, and neglect of children and also directly (e.g., fetal alcohol syndrome) and indirectly (e.g., poor prenatal care and nutrition) increases risk for childhood disabilities. Socioeconomic factors such as poverty and immigration status have also been linked both to increased risk for child abuse and neglect and increased risk for disability.

Disability Increases Risk for Abuse

Traditional explanations for the increased prevalence of abuse of children with disabilities focused on increased parental stress associated with the exceptional needs of the child. This dependency-stress model, however, has not been supported by research and tends to place blame on the victims of abuse rather than the offenders. Severity of disability and level of dependency are poor predictors of abuse, whereas personality profiles of caregivers have proven to be much better predictors. In addition, some findings are difficult to explain in this model. For example, although physical and emotional abuse might be easier to rationalize as a result of the caregiver's frustration with increased caregiving demands, it is more difficult to imagine how this frustration manifests as increased odds of sexual abuse.

Although all infants and young children are extremely vulnerable, this vulnerability typically diminishes as children grow older and may be able to avoid danger, escape, recruit help, or even defend themselves. Children with disabilities, particularly those with severe or multiple disabilities, usually remain more vulnerable at later ages. This may result directly from the child's disability—for example, a child who cannot stand or walk also cannot run away, and a child who has limited communication may not be able to tell someone what is happening to him or her to recruit help. Rather than providing supports to diminish this power disadvantage, however, the social response to disability is often to teach students greater compliance, which increases their power disadvantage (Sobsey & Mansell, 2007).

A multifactorial model of abuse of individuals with disabilities (Sobsey & Calder, 1999) considers numerous factors influencing the interactions

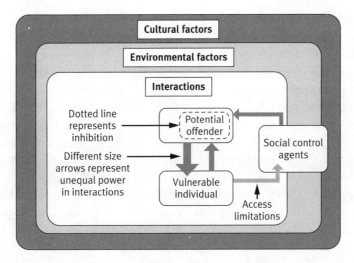

Figure 5.1.   Multifactorial model of abuse of individuals with disabilities. (*Source*: Sobsey & Calder (1999)).

between the potential victims and the offenders, the environment, and the social and cultural milieu (see Figure 5.1; Petersilia, 2001; Sobsey, 2002). Although this model was developed specifically to integrate factors that contribute to abuse of children and adults with disabilities, the same general factors can be applied to other instances of abuse. This model incorporates elements of several other models, including Skinner's (1953) counter-control model, Belsky's (1980) ecological model, and Cohen and Felson's (1979) routine activities model. The counter-control model looks at two interacting individuals and their relative influence and power. Increased inequality in the relative power of the two individuals increases the potential for abuse. The ecological model considers the influences of the immediate environment, other individuals or agencies, and the culture on the interacting individuals. The routine activities model and the closely related lifestyle-exposure model (Hindelang, Gottfredson, & Garofalo, 1978) consider potential offenders, potential targets, and potential protectors, along with the routine activities that bring them together.

Abuse always involves a potential offender who uses a power advantage to harm or violate the rights of a vulnerable person. The unequal size of the arrows between the potential offender and vulnerable individual in Figure 5.1 represents the unequal power between these two individuals. Power advantages may be physical, emotional, or social. For example, adults are usually physically stronger than children. Caregivers also may have emotional power over those who depend on them for care. Teachers and parents also have a social advantage over children because children are normally expected to respect them and recognize their authority. In this sense, everyone who is in a position of authority or has responsibility for others is a potential offender. Although it may be disconcerting to think of all of us who regularly interact with children with disabilities as potential offenders, it is important to understand that most abusers are not different from nonabusive individuals. Inappropriate thoughts or impulses do occur in most, if not all, people from time to time, but nonabusers do not act on these abusive thoughts and impulses. As a result, understanding abuse and managing risks are less about what motivates some individuals to abuse and more about what prevents others from committing abuse.

Inhibition, represented in Figure 5.1 by the dotted line around the potential offender, is an internal psychological control that discourages individuals from committing abusive or other inappropriate acts. It plays an important role in preventing abuse, and it can be strengthened by a sense of conscience (reluctance to do wrong), a sense of attachment with the potential victim (sharing distress or suffering with the victim), or simple fear of consequences (worrying about job loss, jail, or social rejection if caught). It can also be weakened by factors such as substance abuse or beliefs that undermine the inhibiting factors. For example, people with severe intellectual disabilities have often been portrayed as nonpersons (e.g., Singer, 2000) or as insensitive (Oberlander & Symons, 2006). These ideas about people with severe disabilities undermine inhibition and increase the likelihood of abuse.

Social control agents are individuals, social units, or formal organizations that are external to the primary interaction between the vulnerable individual and the potential abuser but that potentially exert influence on them. For example, the police and child protection services are formal organizations that can exert influence to prevent or terminate abuse. Informal agents may include friends, family members, co-workers, or members of the general public that exert a potential protective influence. The fact that most abusers hide their offenses demonstrates the power of these social control agents to discourage abuse, but social control agents cannot respond to what is hidden from them. Children are more able to recruit the help of these social control agents as they grow older, develop more communication skills, and become more independent. Children with severe and multiple disabilities, however, often have impairments that make it more difficult to recruit help from social control agents. The arrow connecting the vulnerable individual to the social control agents in Figure 5.1 represents the recruitment of help, but it is striped, indicating that access to these agents may be limited or nonexistent for children with severe and multiple disabilities. These limits are often a product of limited communication and mobility skills and may be compounded by the social isolation often experienced by children with severe disabilities and their families.

Interactions always occur within an environment (see Figure 5.1). Both physical and social environments are important (e.g., home, school, playground, after-school care, any other place where interactions occur). Environments influence the number and types of interactions. For example, some classrooms that cluster together students with severe disabilities sometimes group students who are aggressive with those who are extremely vulnerable, increasing the risk of abusive interactions among students. Family homes that become isolated from extended family and former friends also have increased risk.

Finally, interactions and environments exist within a culture, and cultural attitudes and beliefs influence both environments and interactions. For example, attitudes and beliefs that devalue individuals with disabilities or justify maltreatment by caregivers as an understandable response to the stress generated by the excessive demands of caregiving increase risk in two ways. First, they reduce inhibition in potential offenders, and second, they diminish responsiveness from social control agents.

Abuse Prevention and Intervention

Protecting children with severe and multiple disabilities requires a multipronged approach because risk factors for abuse operate in various ways at interpersonal, environmental, and cultural levels. The following subsections discuss how to prevent, detect, and report abuse and intervene in cases of maltreatment.

Detecting and Reporting Abuse   Most states require educational and health care professionals to report suspected abuse to police or child protection agencies, and some states require any individual to report suspected abuse. Nevertheless, abuse frequently goes undetected, and it often goes unreported when it is detected. Several reasons contribute to poor detection and reporting of abuse.

First, offenders usually hide their abusive behavior well. They select times and places that provide privacy, and they often choose individuals who cannot or will not tell what has happened to them. Offenders also may go to great lengths to construct alternative explanations for unexplained injuries or other signs of abuse.

Second, many children with severe and multiple disabilities cannot clearly communicate about their mistreatment and may not know that they have a right to better treatment. They may also view the treatment as normal or think that others know about it and are just not saying anything. For example, when one mother asked her 5-year-old daughter why she never told about the frequent sexual assaults she had endured, her daughter simply replied, "I thought you knew." Even when they understand that they are being mistreated and are capable of telling about the abuse, many individuals are intimidated by the offenders or disbelieved by others.

Bill's teacher was alarmed when she saw the bruise on his upper arm. It formed the clear outline of a handprint and looked like someone must have grabbed him with great force. She eventually decided to discuss it with his mother, who said she had not noticed it, but this bruising had happened before. She said Bill's drop seizures meant that he often went crashing to the ground, so catching him to break his fall sometimes left bruises. This jogged the teacher's memory, and she recalled catching Bill when he had a seizure in the hall 2 days ago. She suddenly realized the handprint on Bill's arm was her own.

It is important to keep an open mind and not jump to conclusions. Assuming maltreatment has occurred each time there is a possible indicator is problematic; however, dismissing the possibility of maltreatment too easily can have worse implications. Some children with disabilities do have conditions that increase risk for injuries that may be difficult to differentiate from signs of abuse and thus may mask genuine signs of abuse. Symptom masking or diagnostic overshadowing, the attribution of a particular symptom to a known preexisting condition rather than its real cause, often occurs when the person who has been abused has a disability. Behavior changes, withdrawal, fearfulness, and frequent bruises or even fractures that result from abuse may be attributed to a child's disability rather than mistreatment. Abuse may also go undetected because team members may be reluctant to accept evidence that their colleagues and co-workers are abusing the children they serve.

In spite of these problems, knowing the signs of abuse can be useful in detecting it (see Table 5.2). Many of these signs are ambiguous, and it is often an overall pattern or impression that is more powerful than any single sign. Each school or agency should have a protocol in place for reporting suspected abuse. Because there is rarely direct or overwhelming evidence at the time of the initial

Table 5.2.   Common signs of child abuse

All forms of abuse	Physical abuse	Sexual abuse	Neglect	Abusive caregiver traits
Direct observation (tangible acts)	Frequent injury	Genital irritation	Low affect	Authoritarian behavior
Withdrawal	Unexplained coma	Aggression	Dehydration	Seeks isolated contact
Resistance to touch	Noncompliance	Resistance to touch	Indifference to other people	History of violence or coercion
Fear of specific caregivers	Unexplained injury	Noncompliance	Unusual need for attention	Dehumanizing attitudes
Poor self-esteem	Threats	Gender-specific fear	Poor nutritional status	Difficulty relating to authority
Victimization of others	Grab marks	Promiscuity	Stoical responses to discomfort	Hostility toward reporters
Disclosure	Atypical injury	Threats	Untreated illness or injuries	Abusive counterculture in environment
Escape behavior	Aggression	Sexual precocity		Fearful of victim
Hypervigilance	Unreported fractures	Extreme withdrawal		Grooming behavior
Sleep disturbances	Patterned injury	Inappropriate sexual behavior		Competition with child
Passivity	Temporarily dispersed injuries	Unexplained pregnancy		Rationalization and euphemism
Reenactment		Sexually transmitted disease		Unusual concern for privacy
Fear of specific environments				Use of alcohol or disinhibiting drugs
Self-abuse				Problems of self-control
Stoical responses to discomfort				Negative evaluation of child
Inappropriate behavior				Failure to support abuse control measures
Behavior regression				Expression of myths of devaluation
				Subverts investigation
				Blames victim
				Tests limits and boundaries
				Self-reports of stress

report, it is important that staff understand that they must report suspected abuse and that many of these reports will prove unfounded or lack sufficient evidence for confirmation. Provisions should mandate external reporting in schools and agencies that have protocols requiring internal reporting. No report should be arbitrarily dismissed; thorough investigation is essential.

A Multipronged Approach to Abuse Prevention   Abuse prevention efforts cannot eliminate all risk of abuse, but they can significantly reduce those risks. Effective prevention methods may involve efforts directed toward the child, potential offenders, other program staff and family members, administrative reform, legislative reform, and cultural attitude change.

Education is a powerful intervention against abuse. Teaching children that they have a right to be treated decently and instructing students on how to assert those rights help to reduce children's risk for abuse. Communication skill training is vital to abuse prevention (see Chapter 7). Children who can express their feelings and indicate when they believe that they are being mistreated are less likely to be abused or exploited. Teaching students to make choices and allowing them real choices in their life are also essential steps. When students are expected to be fully compliant with every adult caregiver making legitimate demands in their daily lives, they become powerless to resist inappropriate demands, such as those made by abusive adults. Appropriate social and sex education also is important to preventing sexual abuse and exploitation. Children who do not receive appropriate sex education from parents and teachers are likely to accept inappropriate sex education from an abuser.

Program staff, parents, and advocates also need education on recognizing and reporting abuse. Early recognition and response to problems are essential elements of abuse prevention because most abuse begins in milder forms and escalates to more severe forms. Reducing isolation of students with severe and multiple disabilities can be preventative as well. Inclusive education that keeps children with severe and multiple disabilities in mainstream school activities does not eliminate all risk of abuse within the school environment, but it does help normalize the level of risk. Modeling respect and positive regard for students with disabilities also reduces the risk of abusive behavior by students or fellow staff members. In contrast, negative attitudes or demeaning perceptions of students with disabilities that are present in the classroom send a message that abuse may be acceptable.

Although caregiver stress has been largely rejected as a significant cause of abuse of children with disabilities, displaced anger and frustration are thought to play a role in some cases. People who have unresolved anger toward individuals exercising power in their lives may redirect it toward those who are more vulnerable (Sobsey, 1994). Adding to the problem, others tend to avoid discussing these unresolved anger problems with colleagues who are often seen as difficult. It is important to create a dialogue and provide support and assistance to those individuals whenever possible before more serious problems occur. Maintaining positive relationships and open communication among staff members and between staff members and families also helps protect students. Although it is better to prevent anger and frustration, providing or allowing for appropriate outlets for pent-up feelings can also help.

Administrative reform can be especially useful in preventing abuse. Careful screening of staff is essential. Individuals with known histories of perpetrating physical or sexual abuse or other violent crimes should not be hired to provide care to children with disabilities. Administrative reform includes demonstrating an unequivocal commitment to protecting the children served by a school or agency. Criminal behavior must be treated as such and not as an employee relations problem or, perhaps worse, as a public relations problem. Agency administration must ensure that employees place a high priority on protecting the children whom they serve. Staff should be periodically trained on the nature of child abuse and its prevention. They also should be trained to provide adequate safeguards in the classroom in order to protect children from each other. Clustering children with disabilities who are vulnerable with children who are aggressive can be considered another form of abuse.

Finally, attitude change can be critical to preventing abuse. The powerful role of attitudes in facilitating abusive behavior cannot be ignored (Sobsey, 2002). Perceptions that people with disabilities are less than fully human, damaged merchandise, incapable of suffering, dangerous, or helpless have all been identified as factors in abuse. These myths become full blown in the abuser and provide the rationale that he or she may use in disinhibiting aggressive and sexual drives. Thus, promoting more enlightened and positive perceptions of individuals with severe and multiple disabilities helps protect them from maltreatment.

Intervention for Individuals Who Experience Abuse and Their Families   The best general intervention for the child with severe or multiple disabilities who is being abused is ending the abuse and ensuring a supportive environment that can begin to nurture some positive growth in the child. Medical treatment is required for some children. Teaching self-protection skills may reduce the chances for repeated occurrences.

Counseling is typically an important component of the intervention that children receive to minimize or reverse the effects of abuse (Razza & Sobsey, 2011). Counseling will often require significant modification to be appropriate for children with severe communication impairments. Nevertheless, individualized programs developed through consultation between generic abuse counselors and specialists in areas related to the child's disability are probably the most effective approach to providing services to an abused child with severe or multiple disabilities.

Child welfare agencies need to be called when maltreatment occurs or is suspected within a student's family, and they will take the lead role in investigation and intervention. This often leads to difficult relations between the school and family. The child may be removed from the family in some cases, but the child will remain in the family in many cases. Even when the child is eventually removed from the family, he or she may remain in the family until a determination is made, unless there is substantial reason to believe he or she is at immediate risk. This means that school personnel often need to continue to interact with families after abuse or neglect is suspected and reported. Every effort should be made to maintain a dialogue with the family while being clear that the child's best interest is the primary goal. See Chapter 2 for additional information on working with troubled families.

Child welfare agencies and the police may both investigate when maltreatment occurs or is suspected by someone outside the family. One of these agencies will be designated as the lead and coordinate investigative activities. If abuse is suspected within the school, then the school may conduct its own investigation. It is important to remember that each of these investigations has a different purpose. Child welfare investigates to determine if the child is in need of protective services. Police investigate to determine if a crime has been committed and gather evidence that might result in prosecution. The school investigates to determine what can be done to reduce the risk of future incidents. It is essential that schools follow the lead agency in conducting their own investigation. For example, school personnel should not interview possible victims, abusers, or witnesses until given clearance by the lead agency because this can compromise the other investigations.

Families of students who have been abused or who are suspected of being abused often need additional support. Members of the educational team should strive to determine how they can support families going through a difficult time. The kind of supports that are needed will differ from family to family. Some may need professional counseling, whereas others may not need or want it. If it has not already been offered through child welfare or police services, then school personnel can assist families in gaining access to this service. It is important to be as open and honest as possible with families, especially if a problem has occurred or may have occurred in the school. It is still possible to let families know that you share their concern, even if it is not possible to share details of an ongoing investigation. If the school is waiting for clearance from the lead investigative agency before conducting its own investigation, then let the family know that so they understand why no action is being taken. School social workers and psychologists can play an important role in counseling staff and families. School administrators will also play an important role in investigating potential risks in the school.

PHYSICAL ACTIVITY AND FITNESS

The harmful health effects of inactive lifestyles are major concerns in modern society. Individuals with significant disabilities have generally been shown to be more likely to have health issues related to inactivity and have more extreme effects. For example, Srikanth, Cassidy, Joiner, and Teeluckdharry (2011) found a high rate of osteoporosis among their sample of individuals with intellectual disabilities. They reported a lack of activity was among the important contributing factors. Rimmer, Schiller, and Chen (2012) described many harmful health effects of inactivity that impede quality of life, reduce life expectancy, and interfere with learning. In addition to loss of bone mass, a lack of activity results in metabolic disturbances, diminished cardiorespiratory fitness, fatigue, pain, lethargy, and diminished alertness. The low levels of cardiorespiratory fitness in many students with severe and multiple disabilities result in much more severe illness from respiratory infections that prolong absences from school and sometimes become life threatening.

Although Rimmer and colleagues (2012) acknowledged that some of the factors contributing to inactivity are the direct result of impairments, they also identified social and environmental factors that compound the problem. These factors include overly negative assumptions about the individual's ability to participate in activities, overprotective restrictions, excessive medications, lack of accessible environments and equipment, and the tendency for caregivers to do things for people with disabilities because it is often easier than providing them with the supports they require to do things for themselves.

Most students with severe and multiple disabilities will benefit from increased physical activity. Integrating more physical activity in functional activities and daily routines is usually the best approach. Interventions such as episodic range-of-motion exercises are unlikely to be effective unless they are provided with functional use of the same muscles in similar movement patterns. For example, plantar flexion, pointing the foot downward due to excess muscle tone, is often treated though range-of-motion exercises by firmly pushing the foot upward and stretching the leg muscles. The same stretching effect, however, can be accomplished for some students by walking. The program planning team should carefully assess the student and his or her opportunities to participate more actively in activities. The team should then set appropriate goals for increased activity as part of the student's program plan. Physical education teachers, PTs, and occupational therapists can work together to find appropriate activities for students with severe and multiple disabilities.

CLASSROOM EMERGENCIES

Efforts to prevent classroom emergencies can greatly reduce the frequency and severity of these events. Emergencies sometimes occur, despite even the best prevention efforts, and all staff working with children with severe and multiple disabilities must be prepared to respond to them.

General Strategies

A practical course in safety and first aid with periodic refresher classes should be included in the training of all staff. Most professionals who work with children are required to be periodically certified in basic life support and CPR. It is important that staff understand how and when to use defibrillators as they become available in more schools. Staff working with students with severe and multiple disabilities also need specific training related to the special needs of these children. For example, unless there is a possibility of brain injury, first aid procedures dictate that children who have lost a considerable amount of blood be positioned on their backs with their feet raised to reduce shock and ensure a better supply of blood to the brain. Children who do not understand the reason for being asked to assume this position, however, may resist. Forcing a child to assume the shock position can be counterproductive. The physical demands and emotional stress of confrontation typically increase blood loss. Therefore, allowing a child to sit and relax is generally better than forcing an unwilling child to lie down.

The educational team needs to be familiar with any modifications to the rescue procedures that may be required for some children with special health care needs in emergencies (Best, Heller, & Bigge, 2010). For example, children with tracheostomy require modification to the rescue breathing procedures. Similarly, teachers who work with students who are in wheelchairs need to know how resuscitation and procedures to clear the airway can be modified to apply to these children, if necessary.

One of the difficult decisions often encountered by educators facing medical emergencies is when to call for help. Some individuals will make such rapid recoveries in the few minutes between a 911 call and emergency medical assistance arriving on the scene that it seems like the call was unnecessary. The condition of others will deteriorate in those same few minutes, however, so seconds separate recovery from death. These decisions often become easier as the educator becomes more familiar with the student and his or her health condition. Sometimes a more knowledgeable individual, such as a school nurse, may be readily available to handle the emergency or determine a need to call for help. Calling 911 as soon as possible is the better option in situations in which it remains unclear whether it is necessary to call for emergency medical assistance. Although the call may prove to have been unnecessary, the consequences of delaying when immediate help was required can be dire.

Some Specific Emergencies

The following are descriptions of specific emergencies that team members may encounter when working with students with severe and multiple disabilities. School nurses can be helpful in providing first aid measures and helping to train staff. Nevertheless, it is important to ensure that all staff are prepared to respond to emergencies and have first aid training.

Choking/Foreign Body Airway Obstruction   Airway obstruction is the fourth leading cause of accidental deaths in children 14 years and younger (Protecting Kids from Choking, Suffocation, Strangulation, 2009). Whereas foreign body airway obstruction, sometimes called *mechanical airway obstruction*, is an emergency that occurs when food or a small object blocks the airway, shutting off airflow into the lungs (Sidell, Kim, Coker, Moreno, & Shapiro, 2013), it differs from anatomical airway obstruction, a blockage of the airway caused by swelling due to infection or allergic reaction. Preventing and treating foreign body airway obstruction are probably the most important emergency health care skills for teachers of students with severe and multiple disabilities. These skills are essential for four important reasons:

1. Airway obstruction is a major cause of accidental death of children.

2. The risk of airway obstruction is greater for children with disabilities.

3. If complete obstruction of the airway occurs, then treatment must be provided immediately; there is rarely enough time to obtain outside help to save a child.

4. Simple prevention and treatment methods can save almost every choking victim.

Although the exact extent of the increased risk for children with severe and multiple disabilities is unknown, several risk factors have been identified in the general public that suggest substantially increased risk for children with disabilities: 1) decreased gag reflex, 2) incomplete chewing, 3) use of medication, 4) missing teeth, and 5) altered level of consciousness.

Signs and Symptoms   Choking incidents will continue to occur from time to time, despite the best prevention efforts. Parents, teachers, and other mealtime caregivers must be adequately trained to recognize and treat airway obstruction. Early symptoms of complete airway obstruction are nonspecific. The child is likely to remain conscious in the first 1–3 minutes but indicate distress through agitated movement and possible clutching of the throat or tears in the eyes. The child attempts to breathe, but no air can be felt entering or leaving the nose or mouth. Because no air can enter or leave, the child cannot vocalize. Pulse and blood pressure increase rapidly. Color gradually begins to change to a deep red or purple, the beginning of cyanosis. The child loses consciousness during the next phase, which lasts approximately 3 minutes. Cyanosis deepens to a mottled blue or purple. Pulse and blood pressure drop rapidly. Attempts at respiration weaken. Convulsions usually occur about 5 minutes (often less) after the initial obstruction, and the child enters a third phase, deep coma. Blood pressure, pulse, and attempts at respiration are absent. Pupils become dilated. Brain damage and death will ensue rapidly unless the airway is cleared and pulse and respiration restarted.

Treatment   The rapidity of these events demands immediate action. Available time is often further restricted by failure to notice a problem until the second stage or by the mistaken belief that an epileptic seizure or other problem is the cause. Attempting mouth-to-mouth resuscitation and finding that air will not go in or come out confirm airway obstruction.

Recommended first aid procedures for clearing an airway obstruction have evolved over time, may vary across international boundaries, may differ for children and adults, and may differ depending on whether the choking victim is conscious or unconscious. For example, the American Red Cross changed its recommended procedures in 2006 and generally recommends a series of five back blows as the first method attempted for a conscious child followed by five abdominal thrusts (Katz, 2006). Chest thrusts are recommended once a victim is unconscious. Everyone working with children with severe and multiple disabilities should be fully trained in choking rescue procedures.

Proper training requires direct instructor-to-student contact, which can be provided in first aid courses or specialized training programs, but there are some important considerations. First, it is important to properly distinguish the cause of the child's distress. Airway obstruction can be partial or complete. Complete airway obstruction is always a life-threatening emergency that requires immediate action, but the type of action required depends on the cause of the obstruction. Upper airway obstruction can be caused by a foreign body, usually food, or can be the result of swelling following an injury, severe allergic reaction, or other medical condition. Foreign body airway obstruction can often be corrected with rescue procedures such as back blows or abdominal thrusts, but these procedures will not be effective in treating obstruction caused by allergic reactions or other medical conditions that produce swelling. These require other kinds of intervention, such as the administration of medication with an epinephrine autoinjector (e.g., EpiPen). It is important to seek assistance quickly because complete airway obstruction can be fatal in a few minutes, but it is also important to take immediate action. Therefore, as one staff member is providing rescue procedures, a second staff member or reliable student should contact emergency services.

A finger sweep of the mouth and upper throat also may remove obstructions when the airway is completely obstructed. This method is sometimes effective after other methods fail but should be used as an initial measure only if the choking victim is unconscious and the obstruction is visible in the back of the mouth because of the danger of pushing obstructions farther into the airway or compacting the obstruction. These difficulties are especially likely to occur with a young child with a small oropharyngeal space in which to work. Performance of a finger sweep involves the rescuer positioning the victim supine (on a sloping surface with head lower than feet if possible) with the head extended back. The rescuer carefully inserts an index finger into the side of the mouth and hooks it around the obstruction, then pulls it out. If part of the obstruction is removed, then the procedure is repeated only after a check reveals that the airway remains obstructed.

Brain Injury   Any child can sustain a brain injury. They are the most common causes of death and disability among children. Acquired brain injuries are most frequently the result of a traumatic injury but can also occur as a result of a blockage or rupture to part of the brain's blood supply. Brain injury is frequently classified as a concussion (i.e., a temporary disturbance in brain function as a result of an impact) or compression (i.e., pressure on some part of the brain caused by a fracture of the skull, swelling, or the collection of fluid in an area of the brain). Table 5.3 lists some of the common signs of concussion and compression, some special considerations for children with severe and multiple disabilities, and basic first aid measures. Signs of concussion and compression

Table 5.3.   Concussion and compression: Signs, symptoms, and suggested treatments

Concussion signs/ symptoms[a]	Compression signs/ symptoms[b]	Special considerations for severe and multiple disabilities	First aid treatment and response
Partial loss of consciousness	Partial loss of consciousness	Many of these signs can be masked if they are present prior to injury.	Assess consciousness, observe for breathing difficulties, and keep under constant observation.
Shallow breathing	Seizures (mild to severe)		
Weak pulse	Slowing of pulse		
Pale appearance	Raised body temperature	Seizures are more common in concussion among people with preexisting seizure disorders.	Maintain open airway and provide assisted breathing, if required.
Headache	Dilated pupils		
Confusion	Coordination problems		Call for medical assistance.
Complete loss of consciousness	Confusion		Do not give food or fluids.
Rapid pulse	Complete loss of consciousness	Seizures sometimes produce many of the same signs as brain injury.	Protect area of injury from any further trauma (and from contamination, if open wound).
Cool skin	Irregular breathing		
Vomiting	Flushed face		
Loss of memory (especially for recent events)	Unequal pupils	Medications (e.g., anticonvulsants, tranquilizers) may mask symptoms.	Do not move person, if possible, to avoid further injury.
Potentially injurious event (may have been seen)	Weakness (may affect one side more than the other)		Keep injured person calm and inactive if possible. (Do not use excessive restraint.)
	External injury may or may not be present	Some individuals may not be able to communicate how they feel.	Prevent nose blowing, if possible.
	Potentially injurious event (may have been seen)		Avoid pressure to area of injury.
			Do not use direct pressure to skull injuries unless bleeding is so severe that it must be stopped.

[a]Usually these signs and symptoms begin immediately or shortly after injury.

[b]These signs and symptoms may begin immediately or shortly after injury but may be delayed significantly.

overlap, and the distinction between the two is more difficult to make if the individual sustaining the injury has a seizure disorder, a movement disorder, or communication impairment. Many medications used by people with disabilities can also mask symptoms. Because the rapid diagnosis and treatment of brain injury are essential for the best outcomes, and accurate diagnosis may be impossible without careful evaluation by a physician using sophisticated tests and equipment, it is better to err on the side of safety and have the child evaluated if signs of injury are ambiguous.

First aid measures often consist only of keeping the child safe and calm until help arrives. No food or fluids should be given because intake may increase swelling in the brain. Eating and drinking also may cause aspiration because swallowing may be difficult and the typical reflexes to close the airway during swallowing may be impaired. The danger of vomiting is also increased, which is particularly problematic because vomiting is likely to increase pressure on the brain and create further risk of aspiration.

Because children sustaining brain injury are likely to lose consciousness or have a seizure, they should be protected against falling. If bleeding from a head wound is not too severe, then it is better to allow bleeding than to apply pressure. One should keep the child calm and comfortable, observing continuously for changes, particularly any difficulty with breathing. If the child will lie down quietly, then he or she should be encouraged to do so, but it is important that the child avoid restraint or struggling, both of which may aggravate the injury. Do not use shock position or elevate feet above the head in the case of suspected brain injury because this may increase pressure on the brain.

Poisoning   Schools can be the source for a surprising array of toxic materials. Pesticides and herbicides are frequently used in schools. Science classes often use highly toxic and sometimes attractive substances such as mercury, whereas art classes frequently use toxic materials such as ceramic glazes and paints. Cleaning supplies can also be toxic if ingested. Medications kept in schools may also be toxic when consumed in large amounts or by the wrong students, and common plants such as mistletoe used in holiday decorating can be toxic if eaten. Many children are allergic to foods such as peanuts, which can be highly toxic and even fatal if ingested even in very small amounts. Schools must be careful to check for hidden peanut products, such as peanut oil, when distributing snacks to children and ensure that students' peers do not share food with them. Many children are also severely allergic to insect stings. Certain materials such as latex can cause a serious allergic reaction in some children, so nonlatex gloves and other products should be used in school.

Children with severe and multiple disabilities may not understand the danger associated with ingestion of these substances and therefore are at greater risk than most other students. Problems often can be prevented, and everyone who works with children who have severe and multiple disabilities should practice vigilance, including 1) keeping all cleaners, pesticides, drugs, and other dangerous substances safely locked away; 2) being certain that no poisonous plants are kept in areas frequented by children; 3) discarding old or excess medication, pesticides, cleaners, and so forth in a safe manner; 4) keeping all dangerous substances in childproof containers; 5) helping children learn to communicate that they have come in contact with a toxin; and 6) making plans of action in the event that a child is exposed. Rescue medications, such as EpiPens for anaphylaxis or Diastat for seizures, need special consideration to ensure that they are kept safely away but readily available in an emergency. In some tragic cases, children have died while their rescue medications were safely locked away someplace in the school but unavailable to save their lives.

Fortunately, the development of a network of poison control centers across North America has greatly simplified the basic first aid protocol for ingestion of toxic substances. One should contact the poison control center immediately, be prepared to give information about the situation, and follow the instructions provided. Staff of the poison control center will need to know what substance was ingested, how much, and how long ago. They should also be told the child's age, approximate weight, any available information regarding special medical conditions, and what medications, if any, the child normally takes. Poison control staff may recommend immediate first aid measures and will often suggest that the child be brought in for examination.

The container that held the substance, any labeling material available, and any remaining sample of the substance should be brought when the child goes for an examination. If the toxic substance was a plant, then one should bring it or part of it for identification. If the child vomited, then one should try to bring the vomitus or at least a sample of it for examination. It is essential to note the time of the ingestion and bring along any records available regarding health conditions, allergies, and medications. In the rare case that contacting the poison control center is not possible, one should check the label of the substance for directions on how to treat ingestion.

Providing fluids or inducing vomiting is not normally recommended unless instructed by qualified medical personnel or the poison control center because vomiting can make things worse in some cases. For example, many cleaning products and paints contain petroleum products that could cause much more harm if aspirated during vomiting than in the stomach. The few seconds or minutes required to check with the appropriate experts can help avoid such situations. In case appropriate medical authorities do instruct the induction of vomiting, however, syrup of ipecac is commonly used for that purpose and should be kept on hand. Inducing vomiting may be difficult in some children with severe and multiple disabilities because of medications that they are receiving or depressed reflexes.

Bleeding   External bleeding is easily recognized and usually easily treated. Almost all bleeding, including bleeding resulting from severe injuries, can be controlled by direct pressure. If available, a sterile bandage or clean cloth can be pressed over a wound. When those items are unavailable, pressure applied with the bare hand works quite well. Whenever possible, and particularly if the individual applying pressure has any broken skin, it is recommended that he or she wear gloves to minimize the risk of transmission of communicable disease. Immediate emergency medical intervention should be sought in all instances of severe bleeding to avoid shock or even death from blood loss.

The child who is injured should be encouraged to rest and stay calm and, if possible, the injured body part should be elevated in relation to the rest of the body. If the injury appears to be severe, then medical advice and assistance must be sought. If internal bleeding is suspected, then the child who is injured should be at rest. If possible, and especially if there are signs of lightheadedness or shock, the child should lie down with the legs slightly elevated. The child who is injured should be kept warm, and medical advice and assistance should be sought as quickly as possible.

Emergency Planning   Students with severe and multiple disabilities need special consideration when planning for both individual and mass emergencies in schools. Individual medical emergencies occur with some frequency in schools. One study found that 68% of school nurses had reported at least one life-threatening emergency in their school in the previous school year (Olympia, Wan, & Avner, 2005). An immediate and appropriate response is essential in some emergencies, such as anaphylaxis (a sudden, life-threatening allergic reaction), airway obstruction, cardiac arrest, drug overdose, or severe bleeding. It is imperative in these kinds of life-threatening emergencies that those already present are prepared to provide assistance because even a quick response from responding emergency medical technicians is likely to be too late. Although many ambulance services strive to keep the response time for ambulances under 8 minutes, 90% of the time this goal is difficult to meet reliably in urban settings and impossible to meet reliably in many rural settings. More important, 8 minutes is too long in many emergencies to prevent death or serious harm.

An ECP for an individual, also known as a MERP, that school personnel know well can save critical seconds and often lives. These plans should indicate who has the responsibility to make critical decisions; what actions should be taken; and how access to essential supplies, equipment, medications, and assistance is managed. Although most schools do have ECPs, some do not, and some that have them have not followed them because staff were not adequately familiar with the plans (Olympia et al., 2005). Although it is important for all schools to engage in emergency planning, it is even more critical for schools serving students with severe and multiple disabilities. All school personnel working with students with severe and multiple disabilities should be well acquainted with the individual ECPs relevant to their students.

The American College of Emergency Physicians and American Academy of Pediatrics (1999) established standard forms for briefly summarizing the emergency preparedness information for children with special health care needs. This form or an equivalent document should be updated regularly, and copies should be kept at home and in school. If an emergency occurs, then such information can prove valuable and may help those who provide medical assistance to save lives. Blank copies and samples can be found on the American Academy of Pediatrics web site (http://www.aap.org/advocacy/emergprep.htm).

In addition to preparing for individual emergencies, schools also need to be properly prepared for mass emergencies, such as storms, earthquakes, fires, gas leaks, and even school shootings or other violence. The shootings of students with disabilities at Columbine High School and Sandy Hook Elementary School serve as a sad reminder that these students are not immune from mass violence. Although emergencies are difficult to predict, plans should consider the risks most relevant to the geographic location of the school. For example, one area may be at greater risk than others for tornadoes, whereas other areas may be at greater risk for forest fires, earthquakes, floods, or blizzards. All schools should have and practice evacuation plans and plans to shelter in place, when appropriate. It is important that these plans accommodate the needs of students with disabilities. For example, school shelter areas must be accessible to students with disabilities, and emergency evacuation plans must include plans for students with limited mobility to be rapidly evacuated from all areas of the school when power is off. The U.S. Federal Emergency Management Agency established its Ready campaign to assist schools and other agencies in developing plans, and the U.S. Department of Education, Office of Safe and Healthy Students also provides useful information for school emergency plans.

INFECTIOUS DISEASE AND IMMUNE COMPROMISE

An infectious disease results when disease-producing organisms, such as bacteria or viruses, invade a host. A communicable disease is an infectious disease that may be transmitted from one person to another either directly or indirectly. Exposure to communicable disease may occur by direct person-to-person contact or through contaminated food or objects.

Schools often play a role in the transmission of communicable disease because they bring together large numbers of children. Schools can also play an important role in preventing the spread of communicable diseases. Although all children are susceptible to infection, many children with severe and multiple disabilities are particularly vulnerable to communicable diseases.

Susceptibility and Effects

Increased vulnerability to infectious diseases among children with severe and multiple disabilities appears to result from a combination of interacting factors. Some children with severe and multiple disabilities have genetic or metabolic conditions that reduce their resistance to infection. For example, students with Down syndrome typically have reduced immune response to infection (Ram & Chinen, 2011). Nutritional deficiencies and reduced levels of physical activity can reduce immunity and result in more severe illnesses. In addition, many of the medications that are commonly used by children with disabilities can produce side effects that inhibit the body's natural defenses against infection. For example, anticonvulsant drugs can result in reduced immune response (e.g., Smith, Fernando, McGrath, & Ameratunga, 2004).

Some students with severe and multiple disabilities typically lack the self-care skills that help protect against communicable disease. A few behaviors that add to children's risk include handling potentially contaminated objects, drinking from cups left by others, or frequently putting their hands and a variety of other objects in their mouths. Teaching children with severe and multiple disabilities the best attainable sanitary skills can have important health benefits in addition to enhancing their social relationships.

Children with severe and multiple disabilities are also more likely than children without disabilities to experience severe symptoms when they are infectious because diagnosis is often delayed. Caregivers may not recognize early signs of illness such as changes in behavior, lethargy, or irritability. Even when caregivers recognize that a child is not feeling well, a precise diagnosis may be difficult to make in the absence of more specific signs because of the child's inability to communicate the nature of the distress.

Controlling Communicable Diseases

Educators and other team members working with children with severe and multiple disabilities have a responsibility to do their part both in protecting the children they serve and in protecting themselves from the spread of communicable diseases. Additional precautions are sometimes appropriate because some children with severe and multiple disabilities experience increased risk. All schools should have information available on protecting children from communicable disease. Rapid access to appropriate health care professionals who are knowledgeable about public health measures is essential in some situations. According to the U.S. Centers for Disease Control and Prevention (CDC, 2011), approximately two thirds of school districts offer general staff development on infectious disease prevention, and three quarters of districts offer special training for school nurses. According to the CDC, schools can be instrumental in preventing the spread of infections through six areas of influence:

1.   Encouraging students to stay home from school when they are infected

2.   Promoting staff and student hygiene, particularly hand washing

3.   Cleaning and sanitizing materials and surfaces vigilantly

4.   Adopting proper practices for handling foods and managing bodily excretions

5.   Encouraging staff and students to get appropriate vaccinations

6.   Sharing information regarding precautions with students and families

Internet resources can serve as valuable sources on sanitation and communicable disease prevention. There is one caution: Although a lot of excellent information is available through Internet resources, anyone using the Internet must exercise careful judgment to select reliable sources and avoid sources that provide outdated, useless, and sometimes even dangerous ideas. For example, lowering the temperature of water heaters serving environments with young children was briefly recommended as a means to protect children from scalding, but it was soon discovered that these water heaters became breeding grounds for bacteria and spread diseases to people with weakened immune systems. Unfortunately, many Internet sources never revised their information to reflect this risk.

Sanitation and Hygiene   Arguably, advances made in sanitizing, sanitary sewers, and modern cooking and hygiene practices have done more to extend the lives of people in contemporary society than all other developments in science and medicine (e.g., Kennamer, 2002). All children need to be taught personal hygiene and sanitation skills to protect them and those around them. These skills should be reflected in the goals of students with severe and multiple disabilities and should be given the highest priorities for training. Normalizing personal hygiene and sanitation behavior is often easier in inclusive environments in which other students provide typical examples, and informal feedback from peers can be a useful supplement to formal training. School nurses can play an important role in advising on classroom sanitation.

Immunizations

Alice is a third grader with a genetic syndrome that weakens her resistance to infections. She is particularly vulnerable to respiratory infections and has had several extended hospitalizations for life-threatening pneumonia in previous years. This has been a bad year for influenza in her school, and although she has had the flu vaccine, her doctor thought it might not be effective because of her weakened immune system. Another student in her class was not immunized and is now coming to school with a bad cough and other flu symptoms. His mother tells his teacher, "I can't afford to miss work. He isn't that sick, he's tough, and he'll get through this okay without staying home." Should the mother be told that her son will not be allowed to come to school until he is well? Should Alice be kept at home to avoid exposure? Should the teacher just hope for the best?

There are no easy answers to these questions. Schools do have a right to exclude students or staff with communicable diseases if they pose a threat to other students, but students with mild cases of flu are rarely excluded because there are often too many students carrying the virus to exclude, and some students with no obvious symptoms may carry and spread the virus. Keeping Alice home when she is well because other families are sending sick children to school seems unfair, but school staff members have a responsibility to let her family know that there may be an infectious disease risk in school so that her parents can make an informed decision about what to do.

Vaccines can provide complete immunity against some infections and partial immunity against others. Many schools require proof of vaccination against some diseases (e.g., polio, measles, mumps, chickenpox) for all students as a method of preventing the spread of disease, but other vaccinations are strictly voluntary (e.g., influenza). Some students cannot be effectively immunized against infectious diseases because of conditions that compromise their immune responses or because vaccines may cause allergic or other adverse reactions. Other students with compromised immune systems may require more frequent booster shots to maintain immunity. These students, however, can receive some protection if other students and school staff are fully immunized.

Some families have refused to immunize their children because of their fears about the risk of adverse reactions. Of course, there are real risks associated with vaccinations, but the risk of serious adverse reactions are extremely small, particularly when compared with the risks of refusing immunization. A *Lancet* article published in 1998 claiming that vaccines caused autism in children created a new wave of public resistance to immunizations. Although the publishers retracted this paper, pointing out that some of its content was "incorrect" and "proven to be false" (The Editors, 2010, p. 445), and immunization rates have rebounded after this research was discredited, there continues to be significant public resistance to immunization. Although vaccinations involve some risk and discomfort, the benefits of being inoculated outweigh the risks for the vast majority of students. Individual families and their physicians are the most qualified to make decisions regarding specific immunizations, but is important for school personnel to encourage all families to consider immunization and avoid spreading irrational fears about vaccines. Teachers should also encourage families to inform them when students have been vaccinated and should let families know about any signs of possible adverse reactions (e.g., fever, pain, swelling, rashes) if they occur.

It is important to recognize that there are many categories of immune compromise and many degrees of severity. As a result, appropriate measures need to be individualized. Because immunizations depend on the immune system response, some children with immune compromise cannot be protected or cannot be fully protected by immunizations. Others require more frequent boosters for adequate protection. Some cannot be given attenuated live-virus vaccines. For example, vaccines typically used for injectable influenza immunizations do not contain live attenuated virus, but the nasal spray influenza vaccines typically do and are not recommended for anyone with a weak immune system. In fact, healthy individuals who receive the nasal mist have been known to infect individuals with severely weakened immune systems.

Schools typically provide general recommendations to families regarding immunizations, and all states and some provinces require certain vaccinations for school entry. Almost all states, however, allow religious or personal belief exemptions, as well as exemptions for medical reasons. The school nurse and other health professionals should carefully review the immunization history of each child with multiple disabilities and work with families and other health care professionals to ensure that each child receives appropriate protection.

Diagnosis and Treatment of Communicable Diseases   The primary responsibility for the diagnosis and treatment of communicable diseases rests with the family and their physician. Nevertheless, teachers and other program staff can and should play an important role in the detection and treatment of communicable diseases.

The symptoms of a communicable disease may be first noticed in the classroom for at least two reasons. First, many infectious diseases are cyclical. This means that the symptoms may be more apparent at certain times of day, and in some cases, they may be more obvious during school hours. Second, the collaborative team has the opportunity to observe many students over the course of days or weeks. This can provide additional information unavailable to parents. For example, a particular child may be predisposed to allergic rashes, but if several children in close contact with this child begin developing similar rashes, then more careful evaluation is required. When communicable diseases are discovered among students, efforts to treat those infected and to protect other students and teachers from exposure should be coordinated among the school, the family, and health professionals. In most cases, treating the individuals who have the illness as soon as possible is essential not only for that child's own recovery but also for protecting other children from being infected.

Classrooms may occasionally experience epidemics of parasites or other infectious diseases. The term *epidemic* simply refers to the occurrence of more than the usual or expected number of cases among a particular group of individuals. The control of epidemics in the school often requires careful coordination of home- and school-based efforts to eliminate the problem. Concurrent disinfection is typically a key element in controlling these outbreaks. Concurrent disinfection requires simultaneous treatment of all members of the group and simultaneous eradication of other sources of infection from the environment. For example, head lice (*pediculus capitis*) are a fairly common problem among school children and are transmitted directly from child to child through direct, typically prolonged contact. Although medicated shampoo is generally effective in treating the problem, failure to eliminate sources of reinfection often leads to recurrence. If several children in a classroom have head lice, then it may be important to coordinate the treatment of all of them in order to prevent a recurrence.

Children with Increased Vulnerability and Classroom Placement   As previously mentioned, individual students with immune compromise or immunosuppression vary greatly in their symptoms and needs. Most students, including the majority of those with some degree of immune compromise, build immunity to infection through normal social contact. Attempting to isolate an individual may result in greater susceptibility and more severe illness when that person is exposed to a pathogen. In some rare, extreme cases, it may be impossible for a student to attend school because of his or her extreme vulnerability to common pathogens. It is important to remember, however, that in addition to the social and educational disadvantages of isolation, it may actually increase vulnerability to communicable disease. A balanced approach is best in most cases, taking reasonable precautions to avoid exposure to active and severe illness but encouraging normal social participation.

SEIZURE DISORDERS

Seizures are sudden and unpredictable changes in consciousness, behavior, sensation, or motor function caused by rapid and disorderly electrochemical discharges in the brain (Hauser & Bannerjee, 2008). They can be caused by a wide variety of factors that interfere with normal brain activity, such as brain injury, inadequate oxygen, very low levels of blood glucose, toxic substances, or very high fevers. The term *epilepsy* has been used to refer to a pattern of recurrent, unprovoked seizures in an individual, but there is considerable disagreement and controversy regarding any exact definition for this term (e.g., Hauser & Bannerjee, 2008). The term *seizure disorder* has become more common as a result of the difficulty in precisely defining epilepsy. Generally, neither *epilepsy* nor *seizure disorders* refers to a specific diagnosis or condition but rather to a group of conditions that result in a predisposition to seizures. Statistics on incidence and prevalence vary greatly depending on the diagnostic criteria used, but estimates of the cumulative incidence of convulsive disorders in American children usually range from 1% to 4% (Hauser & Bannerjee, 2008).

Seizure disorders occur more frequently in boys than girls. They are also much more common among children with developmental disabilities.

In a cohort of 818 children and young adults with developmental disabilities, Bandino, Garfinkle, Zickefoose, and Hsieh (2014) reported that 32.3% had a seizure disorder. Although most of them had seizures infrequently, 27% had seizures ranging from about once a month to several every day. Schieve and colleagues (2012) conducted a large-scale study of more than 35,000 children and reported that children with intellectual disabilities were 46.7 times as likely to have had a seizure in the last 12 months as children without developmental disabilities. Seizures occur even more frequently among children with severe and multiple disabilities than among children with milder developmental disabilities.

Etiology

Although there have been many new discoveries about the causes of seizure disorders, particularly in genetic causes, more than half of known cases have no specifically identifiable cause (Hauser & Bannerjee, 2008). Many of the known causes of seizure disorders also are causes of CP and intellectual disabilities. As a result, it is not surprising that many children with severe and multiple disabilities have seizures. Causal factors are typically divided into three major categories: 1) prenatal (occurring before the child's birth), 2) perinatal (occurring during or very close to birth), and 3) postnatal (occurring later in life) (Hauser & Bannerjee, 2008). In many cases, there appears to be an interaction between causal factors in more than one of these major categories. For example, a child may have a genetic (prenatal) predisposition to seizures that may or may not result in seizures. A later infection or head injury (postnatal) might result in a seizure disorder, although it might have been insufficient to produce it in a child without the predisposition.

A variety of events before a child's birth can result in a seizure disorder. Exposure to radiation, toxic substances (e.g., alcohol, cocaine), or infectious diseases (e.g., toxoplasmosis, herpes simplex, German measles) during pregnancy can damage the developing nervous system of the fetus. Fetal anoxia (i.e., lack of sufficient oxygen) can occur for several reasons (e.g., improperly attached placenta, compression of the umbilical cord) and can damage the child's brain. Despite the excellent natural protection provided in utero, trauma can occur as a result of an accident or violence before birth. Siblings and children of individuals with seizure disorders appear to be approximately twice as likely to be affected as other people. Studies have revealed a larger role for genetic causes both as a primary cause and a contributing factor (e.g., Sánchez-Carpintero Abad, Sanmartí Vilaplana, & Serratosa Fernandez, 2007).

Seizure disorders may also result from trauma or oxygen deficit during the birth process or any time during the individual's life. Brain injuries and childhood infections that cause encephalitis or meningitis (e.g., measles, tuberculosis, viral infections) also can cause seizure disorders. Trauma from both accidents and violence are major causes of brain injury in children.

Seizures may be first observed at any age, regardless of the cause. As a result, some students may already have a history of seizures and a diagnosis of seizure disorder when they first enter the classroom, and others may begin to exhibit seizures sometime during the school year. In most cases, the cause of a seizure disorder does not matter for determining appropriate treatment, but there are some exceptions, such as when the cause is related to an active and progressive disease process.

Seizure Mechanisms

Seizures can be described as electrochemical events. Nerves are activated through the exchange of ions (e.g., sodium, potassium, calcium, chloride) across the cell membrane. These discharges take place in an orderly fashion during normal function, and the firing of one neuron selectively activates associated neurons and inhibits others. During seizures, however, neurons in the central nervous system fire in an excessive and disorganized chain reaction, which can cause convulsions, changes in muscle tone, disturbances in consciousness, altered sensations, or some combination of these possibilities.

Seizures can add further insult to the damaged brain in people with severe and multiple disabilities. The onset of seizures or periods of uncontrolled and intense seizure activity are observed in some individuals along or at about the same time as a progressive loss of skills, but it remains unclear whether the seizures cause regression or whether the regression and seizure activity are both the result of other processes in the central nervous system. Although it remains controversial whether seizure activity in itself can do further damage to the nervous system, there is no doubt that anoxia and frequent falls associated with poorly controlled seizures can result in more damage. Adding additional seizure medications or increasing doses of those already in use, however, can result in side effects that threaten health and impair function.

Diagnostic Procedures

Some other medical, neurological, and psychiatric conditions may mimic seizures. A thorough clinical examination, detailed laboratory investigations, and an inpatient observation may be necessary to confirm the diagnosis and start appropriate treatment. In some cases, response to trial treatment may be considered in arriving at a diagnosis. For example, a physician may suspect that the frequent, sudden changes in a child's behavior result from seizures, but inadequate data may be available to confirm this diagnosis. If episodes of atypical behavior clearly decrease during a trial period of antiepileptic medication, then a diagnosis of seizure disorder is more likely to be correct. Fainting spells, breath-holding spells, panic attacks, restless leg syndrome, transient ischemic attacks, and hysterical convulsions are some conditions that may be mistaken for epileptic seizures (Freeman, Vining, & Pillas, 2003). Because many conditions mimic seizure disorders, they tend to be overdiagnosed, especially in children. Getting the right diagnosis is important. If the student has a seizure disorder, then treatment may be required, but if he or she does not have the condition, then anticonvulsants usually will do more harm than good. If the observed event is not the result of a seizure, then it may be the result of another condition that requires medical attention.

Electroencephalogram   An EEG is the most common diagnostic test for seizure disorder. The shape, voltage, and frequency of waves from specific areas of the brain help determine whether a child has a seizure disorder and, if so, which type of seizure disorder. This test can provide valuable clues to finding the best treatment. Many children with seizure disorders have abnormal brainwave patterns between seizures, but these are evident on fewer than half of brief EEGs taken on a single occasion. Extended EEGs with telemetry can last for 90 hours or longer while a video camera records the child's behavior and a computer identifies spike waves for closer examination.

Neuroimaging of the Brain   Computed tomography (CT) scans and magnetic resonance imaging (MRI) of the head are used frequently to get pictures of the brain. Positron emission tomography (PET) scans are also used in some cases (Duncan, 2010). CT can give good images of the skull and the cavities within the brain called *ventricles*. MRI scans produce images of the brain with much higher resolution. The gray and white matter of the brain can be differentiated in greater detail in an MRI. PET scans can provide even more detail. These procedures can help rule out that seizures are a result of a tumor or other circulatory problem in some part of the brain. In some cases, they can also help identify a specific focal area of the brain where an individual's seizure begins. If identified, the focal area may be removed surgically.

Not all individuals with seizure disorders have abnormalities in their brains that can be detected with neuroimaging, and not all abnormalities that can be visualized can be treated surgically. For example, some individuals have many foci in their brains that could be the source of seizures, and surgical intervention is not normally recommended in these cases. In many children with severe and multiple disabilities, these neuroimaging procedures reveal other information about brain development that can prove helpful in assessing the child, even if it does not provide information useful in treating seizures. For example, an underdeveloped corpus callosum, which connects the two sides of the brain, may help to explain why a student has difficulty working across his or her midline.

Teachers' Role in Diagnosis   Teachers and other team members can play a vital role in helping physicians arrive at the correct diagnosis of their students' seizure disorders. Doctors rarely have an opportunity to observe their patient's seizures because these episodes occur at unpredictable times. They depend on family members and school staff to provide them with accurate descriptions. School staff who carefully observe and record what they see can play a critical part in the process. The seizure observation form shown in Figure 5.2 is intended to guide that observation. The proliferation of tablets and cell phone video cameras, however, provides a better alternative. A video recording of a seizure will provide an ideal record of the event.

Seizure Record

Student's name: _____ Date: _____

Time (of occurrence): _____ Location: _____

How did the seizure begin?

_____

_____

What was the student doing before the seizure?

_____

_____

What was happening in the area when the seizure occurred?

_____

_____

Warning signs: ❒ No   ❒ Yes

If Yes, describe:

_____

_____

What was the first indication of seizure activity?

_____

_____

What happened during the seizure?

Duration (if approximate, state it): _____

Did student's body stiffen?   ❒ No   ❒ Yes

Parts of body involved: _____

Did student's body shake?   ❒ No   ❒ Yes   Arms: ❒ Left   ❒ Right

Did the student fall?   ❒ No   ❒ Yes   Legs: ❒ Left   ❒ Right

(continued)

Figure 5.2.   A blank seizure observation report form. Source: Sobsey (1982).

Figure 5.2. *(continued)*

Any apparent injury? ❏ No   ❏ Yes   Other: _____

Describe:

_____

_____

Did the student appear to become unaware of the environment? ❏ No   ❏ Yes

Was there a change in color of the student's lips, nail beds, etc.? ❏ No   ❏ Yes

Describe:

_____

_____

Did student wet or soil?   Urine: ❏ No   ❏ Yes   Feces: ❏ No   ❏ Yes

Did student have difficulty breathing?

Before: ❏ No   ❏ Yes   During: ❏ No   ❏ Yes   After: ❏ No   ❏ Yes

Other/Describe:

_____

_____

How did the seizure end?

Describe first aid given:

_____

_____

Describe student's activity after seizure:

_____

_____

Notifications: ❏ None required   ❏ Parents   ❏ Physician

Other (Specify):

_____

_____

Reported by: _____   Filed: _____

                                                                (Date/Time)

Source: Sobsey (1982).

Types of Seizures

There is no precise, reliable, and universally accepted system of classifying seizures. Seizures can be classified on the basis of their cause or etiology, on the location of the responsible lesion, or on presumed mechanisms. Traditional terms, such as *grand mal* (generalized convulsive seizures) and *petit mal* (brief disturbances in consciousness), were based largely on observed behavior. The International League Against Epilepsy introduced a classification based on clinical seizure type and EEG findings in 1969 and revised it slightly over the years, subsequently revising it more substantially in 2010 (Berg & Scheffer, 2011). As a result, a wide variety of labels are used to categorize seizures. Although it is generally better to avoid using these labels because they may be misleading, it may be helpful to be familiar with some of the terms that are commonly used to describe seizures. Table 5.4 summarizes one frequently used system of classifying seizures.

Table 5.4.   Classification of seizures

Partial-onset seizures	Generalized-onset seizures
Simple partial seizure: Individual remains conscious Individual may engage in repeated or stereotyped behavior Typically lasts a few seconds to a few minutes May include blinking	*Absence seizure:* Impairment of consciousness Typically lasts 2–20 seconds Previously called *petit mal seizure*
	Tonic seizure: Sudden onset Impairment of consciousness Rigid extension or flexion of the head, trunk, and/or extremities Typically lasts several seconds, occasionally longer
Complex partial seizure: Consciousness is impaired Aura or prodrome is common Often includes staring, automatisms (e.g., chewing, lip smacking, mumbling, fumbling with the hands), and posturing (e.g., turning to one side, unusual position of one arm) Typically lasts about 60–90 seconds and is followed by brief period of confusion Sometimes previously called *temporal lobe epilepsy*	*Clonic seizure:* Impairment of consciousness Rhythmic, motor, jerking movements of arms, legs, and body Typically lasts more than a few seconds
Secondary generalized seizure: Begins as simple partial or complex partial seizure May sometimes generalize to tonic-clonic or other type of generalized seizure	*Myoclonic seizure:* Impairment of consciousness may be hard to identify due to brevity Jerking, motor movements that last less than a second
	Primary generalized tonic-clonic seizure: Impairment of consciousness Generalized tonic extension of the extremities lasting a few seconds Clonic rhythmic movements may last from 10 seconds to several minutes Previously called *grand mal seizures*
	Atonic seizure: Impairment of consciousness Brief loss of postural tone, often results in falls and sometimes in injuries
Unclassified seizures: Do not fall in the existing categories	

Although some seizures share enough similarity to be categorized based on behavioral observation, areas of the brain affected, EEG patterns, etiology, or various other dimensions, seizures are incredibly diverse, and many do not fit neatly into any category. Nevertheless, various labels or types of seizures are identified in an attempt to determine how to best treat them or simply to communicate about them for general purposes. Seizures are typically described by their symptoms. The specific manifestations seen in any child depend on the area of the brain from which the seizure originates (i.e., focus) and how the abnormal activity spreads through the brain.

Partial Seizures Partial seizures involve a group of neurons in some part of one cerebral hemisphere.

Simple Partial Seizures Consciousness is not impaired when the epileptic activity remains localized and does not spread to the reticular activating system (i.e., an area of the brain that regulates arousal level). These are called *simple partial seizures*. The clinical manifestations depend on the area of abnormal electrical activity. If the epileptic activity is localized to the motor area of the cerebral cortex, then the muscles on the opposite side of the body contract in a rhythmic fashion. For example, if there is an epileptic focus in the area of the left-brain that controls the hand and the focus slowly spreads toward the area of the brain supplying nerves to the forearm, upper arm, and shoulder, then there will be initial rhythmic contractions of the right hand that spread to the right forearm, upper arm, and shoulder. Simple partial seizures can also produce sensory symptoms (e.g., pain, tingling, numbness), special sensory symptoms (e.g., strange visual or auditory perceptions, atypical taste, strange smell), autonomic symptoms (e.g., palpitation, sweating, flushing of face, discomfort in abdomen), or psychic symptoms (e.g., loss of speech, dreamy states, distortion of time sense, illusions, hallucinations). Simple partial seizures often go unnoticed and undiagnosed in children with severe and multiple disabilities because they are typically brief and sometimes have few observable symptoms.

Complex Partial Seizures Complex partial seizures are associated with additional symptoms and usually produce loss of consciousness and automatisms (i.e., complex, involuntary movements that occur during loss or impairment of awareness). These can take the form of sucking movements, lip smacking, looking around, searching, grimacing, fumbling with clothes or sheets, or scratching movements. Some children may hum or vocalize (verbal automatisms). Automatisms can also include apparent goal-directed motor behavior.

Secondary Generalized Seizures In some cases, seizures that begin as simple or complex partial seizures can become generalized seizures. Although the generalized phases of these seizures are identical to other generalized (typically tonic-clonic) seizures, the best medication to control these seizures may be different. Therefore, it is important to identify if there is a partial seizure phase that precedes the generalized phase.

Generalized Seizures   Generalized seizures spread throughout the brain and may be convulsive or nonconvulsive. Convulsive seizures may be tonic (i.e., muscles become rigid), clonic (i.e., rhythmic, jerky movements of the limbs), tonic-clonic (i.e., rigidity followed by jerky movements), or myoclonic (i.e., sudden and sometimes repeated twitching or jerking movements). Generalized tonic-clonic seizures (formerly called *grand mal seizures*) are the most common epileptic convulsions (approximately 60% of cases). Generalized seizures occasionally occur repeatedly without the individual regaining consciousness between seizures and result in almost continuous seizures. Such a condition is called *status epilepticus* (continuous seizures) and requires immediate medical attention.

Generalized seizures may be primary or secondary. If they are primary, referred to as *generalized onset seizures*, then the epileptic discharge starts suddenly throughout the cerebral cortex. Then, the child immediately loses consciousness, becomes rigid, and often falls over. Breathing does not occur during this tonic (rigid) phase, and the person may begin to experience cyanosis (i.e., turn blue). The following clonic (shaking) phase is characterized by rapidly alternating, involuntary contraction and relaxation of muscles, which produces undirected movement throughout the body. This movement is usually most noticeable in the arms and legs. The child remains unconscious during this phase, and breathing is very inefficient, which may lead to additional cyanosis. Individuals frequently urinate or defecate involuntarily while unconscious. They sometimes injure themselves while falling or unconsciously flailing their arms and legs. They sometimes bite their tongue. An entire seizure rarely lasts more than 5 minutes. During the postictal (i.e., after-seizure) phase, the individual has no recollection of the seizure and may be confused or irritable. People are typically drowsy at this stage and usually require rest. The individual may sometimes remain unconscious after the seizure and require positioning to maintain an open airway. Secondary generalized seizures begin as focal seizures in one area of the brain, but the focal seizure spreads to become a generalized seizure. Once the seizure generalizes, it proceeds just like any other generalized seizure. Differentiating between primary and secondary generalized seizures, however, can be useful.

Whereas tonic, clonic, and tonic-clonic seizures are closely related and commonly overlapping categories, myoclonic and atonic seizures form a separate group of generalized seizures that involve sudden, brief changes in muscle tone. Myoclonic seizures are characterized by sudden, jerky movements of the muscles that may be symmetrical, asymmetrical, unilateral, bilateral, confined to a group of muscles, and so forth. Different syndromes (e.g., infantile spasms, Lennox-Gastaut syndrome, juvenile myoclonic epilepsy) may be diagnosed based on the clinical type and age of onset. Sudden jerky movements of muscles cause the individual to collapse in all of these syndromes, and he or she may sustain injury. Myoclonic seizures also are encountered frequently in children with Down syndrome, tuberous sclerosis, Tay-Sachs disease, and phenylketonuria. Atonic seizures, also called *akinetic* or *drop seizures*, are sudden losses of muscle tone. Some atonic seizures may only involve the head dropping, but others involve the entire body. They can be very brief (less than a second) or last as long as 15 seconds or more. They may occur many times a day in some students. Although they are brief, the sudden and complete loss of all muscle tone often results in injuries. Drops can occur with enough force to do significant harm, even for a child who is sitting at a desk or table. Some students have myoclonic-atonic seizures, which are characterized by a sudden increase in muscle tone immediately followed by a sudden loss of muscle tone or vice-versa. This combination can be particularly challenging because it can result in accelerated falls with a high potential for injury.

Absence seizures (previously known as *petit mal seizures*) are generalized seizures without convulsions. They occur most frequently in childhood between the ages of 4 and 10. They occur as a series of isolated absence spells. The child suddenly loses consciousness for a brief period (usually 5–30 seconds), typically staring into space without moving. The child looks momentarily dazed, stops speaking, becomes immobile, appears pale, and assumes a fixed, glazed appearance with dilated pupils. Posture and balance are maintained, and the child may have minor, brief muscular contractions around the eyes. The child is unaware of having had an absence attack but sometimes perceives a change in the environment. Some absence seizures produce clonic movements of the eyelids, head, or (in rare cases) arms. Others may produce repeated chewing, swallowing, or lip-smacking movements. When the seizure is over, the child typically resumes previous activities and is unaware of any interruption (Appleton, Baker, Chadwick, & Smith, 2001). These seizures may be frequent and, if so, disruptive to learning and other activities. Absence seizures that occur infrequently generally cause few problems and may go unnoticed much of the time. Nevertheless, if changes in frequency or duration occur, then these should be reported to the family and health care team.

Some individuals experience symptoms for varying periods of time before a seizure begins. These are called a *prodrome*, and if they occur primarily as feelings or sensations, then they are commonly called an *aura*. Although many children with severe and multiple disabilities cannot describe an aura if they experience one, other prodromal symptoms can be observed by teachers or caregivers. In some cases, students who cannot tell others that they are experiencing an aura will change their behavior by seeking a safe place or refusing to stand. When these actions occur with some regularity before seizures, they may provide valuable warnings before impending seizures, including changes in behavior such as unusual hyperactivity, hyperventilation, irritability, or a variety of other behaviors unique to the individual.

Provoked and Reflex Seizures   Some individuals with seizure disorders are said to have provoked or reflex seizures (Kasteleijn-Nolst Trenité, 2012). The line between precipitating conditions and seizure triggers is not firm, but precipitating conditions involve general situations or events that increase seizure activity, whereas *seizure triggers* refer to specific stimuli that can immediately trigger seizures. Many individuals report that conditions such as stress, sleep deprivation, fever, constipation, or extreme physical exertion can precipitate seizures.

Some individuals have reported being startled, seeing flashing lights, hearing specific sounds, being immersed in cool bath water, or participating in events such as tooth brushing as seizure triggers. Although this phenomenon has been given considerable attention, it is important to note that only a small proportion of people with seizure disorders report that sensory stimulation triggers or exacerbates seizure activity. Therefore, people with seizure disorders do not need to be generally restricted from any stimulus (e.g., fluorescent lights, television, cold water) unless their personal histories indicate that a specific stimulus affects them. Restrictions on exposure to stimulation should occur only if justified by demonstrable benefits to the specific student.

Pseudoseizures   In some cases, there are questions about whether apparent seizure behavior is the result of abnormal discharges in the brain or may be intentional behavior that functions to gain attention, escape demands, or serve some other social or psychological need. Although these are rare in children with multiple disabilities, they have been reported in some cases. These pseudoseizures may occur in individuals with no genuine epileptic activity or in those who also have genuine seizures at times. Differentiating between epileptic seizures and these pseudoseizures is difficult in some cases. Although some pseudoseizures may appear genuine, some genuine seizures may appear to be intentional. Children who have atypical seizures—for example, those who are conscious and respond to others while having significant seizure activity—may have real seizure activity ignored by caregivers who are convinced they are faking it. Usually the best approach is to treat all seizures routinely without excessive attention but with appropriate consideration for health and safety concerns. This reduces the chance that the behavior will be reinforced or imitated while ensuring that health and safety needs are given proper attention. Nonaversive behavior management or counseling may be employed in rare cases when seizures can be clearly identified as pseudoseizures.

Treatment of Seizure Disorders

Administering anticonvulsant drugs is the most common treatment for seizure disorders. Research continues to produce many new anticonvulsant medications. Most anticonvulsant medications are long-acting drugs that do not require frequent administration. In most cases, a medication schedule can be established that does not require administration in school, but if these medications are given in school, then it is essential that any missed doses be reported to the family. It is also critical that those who administer medication in schools are properly trained and follow legal and policy requirements.

Most physicians will assume total medication compliance unless presented with evidence to the contrary. Many factors can influence the amount of medication that reaches the bloodstream. Failure to take prescribed medication can be a major cause of difficulty in controlling a seizure disorder. Some children with severe and multiple disabilities may refuse medication because they do not like the taste or may not swallow the capsules. Some may conceal the medications in their mouths for later disposal. Others may spit them out. These practices may result in an insufficient dosage. The resulting low blood levels of medication may influence the physician to increase the dosage prescribed; subsequently, if the child begins to accept the medication more consistently, then an overdose may result. When administering medications, it is essential to be certain that the child accepts them.

The manner in which drugs are given also affects blood levels. A number of anticonvulsants are available in different forms such as sprinkles, syrup, chewable tablets, and long-acting forms. For example, some anticonvulsants are given in suspension form. Unless the suspension is thoroughly shaken just before the dose is measured out and administered, dosage will be unreliable because the medication may sink to the bottom of the bottle. Doses poured from the top of the full bottle will be too weak. Those poured from the sediment at the bottom of the bottle will be much too strong. Mixing medications in food can also affect dosage, especially if not all of the food is eaten. Some drugs will be absorbed differently if tablets are crushed or chewed or capsules are opened before swallowing. Enteric-coated capsules need to be swallowed whole because they are designed to remain whole until they enter the intestine. When these or other factors influence dose maintenance, careful consultation among pharmacist, physician, and individuals administering the medication can help these professionals develop suitable strategies for ensuring accurate and consistent dosage. The benefits of taking any particular type and amount of medication must be carefully balanced with the negative effects and risks of taking the medication.

In addition to medication, some individuals have found relief in surgery, behavioral intervention, implanted nerve stimulators, and dietary control. Surgical procedures mainly consist of removing a lesion that acts as an epileptic focus (if one can be identified) or preventing spread of epileptic discharges by cutting some pathways in the brain. Sometimes pressure on the brain can be relieved either by taking out bone fragments or removing excess cerebrospinal fluid. Although surgery remains an infrequent option, it is becoming more common as better diagnostic imaging and surgical techniques are developed.

Vagus nerve stimulation (VNS) is a treatment that is being used increasingly to treat people with intractable seizures. The vagus nerve is the 10th cranial nerve that emerges at the base of the brain and passes through the neck to the abdomen. A programmable signal generator powered by a lithium battery is implanted in the patient's chest. Stimulating electrodes are connected to the vagus nerve. Terra and colleagues (2014) reported that VNS is a safe procedure for children with intractable seizures. Furthermore, VNS does not have the side effects of multiple medications, is reversible unlike some other surgical procedures, and permits involuntary treatment compliance. An external magnet is sometimes used to turn on VNS stimulation when a prodrome occurs. Teachers can be trained to use this appropriately for students who have observable prodromes. Teachers should avoid providing toys with powerful magnets to a child who has a VNS implant. External magnets may interfere with the programmed stimulation from the implant. Similar devices that stimulate the trigeminal nerve and do not require surgical implantation are being prescribed in some countries and may become more widely available.

Behavioral intervention can be useful in treating some children with seizure disorders (e.g., Polak, Privitera, Lipton, & Haut, 2012). If a trigger for a seizure is identified, then systematic desensitization (gradual exposure) to triggering stimuli may help control seizures. The motivating factors for self-induced seizures should be studied, and the child should be rewarded for not inducing a seizure. Seizures can also be reduced when prodromal behavior chains are interrupted. Each of these approaches has enormous potential for some children. They provide alternatives or supplements to medications, which often have deleterious side effects. Children with seizure disorders should be considered good candidates for behavioral intervention if they have one or more of the following: 1) self-induced seizure activity, 2) identifiable preseizure behavior patterns, or 3) identifiable environmental seizure triggers. Careful evaluation and planning by the entire collaborative team are required to determine the appropriateness of behavioral intervention and to evaluate its success.

Dietary treatment is also used to treat seizure disorders in some individuals. The ketogenic diet accumulates byproducts of fat metabolism in the blood and was developed in 1921 to control seizures, primarily in children (Cervenka & Kossoff, 2013). Ketogenic diets were used less frequently as awareness of problems related to high fat intake increased and better drug therapy became available. The medium-chain triglyceride ketogenic diet, however, came into use in the 1970s and reduced some concern over high intake of saturated fats. Dietary intervention should be considered when drugs are ineffective or have serious side effects and when decreased seizure activity can be demonstrated during a trial period. A dietitian or nutritionist should be part of the collaborative team considering and monitoring dietary intervention.

Seizure Management

Donna had seizures almost every day when she was in the fifth and sixth grade. School staff and her classmates were accustomed to them, and they caused little disruption. She had another seizure on her first day in seventh grade in a new school. Her teacher and classroom assistant evacuated the classroom and called 911 for an ambulance. Her parents, who were called at work to meet their daughter at the hospital, thought that school personnel overreacted.

Whether the school staff overreacted in a case such as Donna's is a matter of opinion. As they got to know Donna and obtained a better understanding of her seizures, school personnel learned that they could manage them with much less drastic measures and got a better sense of how to respond. Perhaps staff could have been better prepared on the first day if they had been given more information or training. Without knowing exactly how to respond, however, they chose what they believed to be the safest option.

Seizure management refers to prevention, protection, and first aid measures applied by the collaborative team in the case of seizures. Because every child is an individual, seizure management must be tailored to the specific needs of the child, and none of the management provisions discussed here will be appropriate for every student. Rather, these provisions should be thought of as general recommendations to be considered for each individual.

Prevention   Although complete control over seizures is not always possible, a reduction in the frequency and severity of seizures can be accomplished for most children through a program of prevention and treatment. Avoiding factors that may precipitate seizures is an important component of seizure prevention for some children with seizure disorders. Specific environmental stimuli that trigger seizures may be identified for some individuals through careful observation. Identified triggers may be eliminated or controlled in the child's environment. Other more general factors can lower the threshold for seizures, including stress, fatigue, missed meals leading to low blood sugar, and electrolyte imbalances (e.g., inappropriate fluid or salt intake). Carefully recording events that precede seizures can help identify contributing factors for a specific child. Once identified, these factors can often be eliminated or controlled.

Intervention during the prodrome can also help prevent seizures in some individuals. For example, careful observation may reveal that a child frequently stares out the window and hums prior to having a seizure. Interrupting this behavior may prevent the child from having a seizure in some cases (e.g., Lee & No, 2005; Zlutnick, Mayville, & Moffat, 1975).

Protection   Protection against injury is important when seizures do occur. Atonic and myoclonic seizures are associated with the greatest risk for injuries from falls (Bellon, Walker, & Peterson, 2013). Protective measures need to be individualized to meet the needs of the specific child. For example, absence seizures typically do not require special risk-reduction procedures, but some activities (e.g., swimming, riding a bicycle, using scissors, working on machinery) can be hazardous if periods of unconsciousness are long or frequent. It is important to employ measures that do not overprotect the child (Epilepsy Foundation, 2009) because overprotection is often an issue for students who experience seizures. There is no simple formula for maintaining safety for these students. Some students wear helmets to protect their heads, and some are not allowed to take part in swimming or other activities. Some students who are able to stand and walk remain in wheelchairs throughout the school day to reduce the risk of injuries from falls. Although these kinds of measures do reduce risks, they also can result in physical, mental, and social harm. They can isolate students from their peers, deprive them of badly needed physical exercise, and deny them opportunities to participate in enjoyable activities. The team must carefully consider the nature and extent of the risk, the extent of risk reduction, and the intrusiveness of the risk-reduction measure before working with the family on seizure management.

Many methods are available for reducing risks associated with seizures. One method is environmental modification. Architectural decisions made during building design stages may greatly influence environmental hazards. For example, long, steep, straight staircases present much greater hazards than stairs interrupted by large landings. Many simple modifications can be made in existing buildings. Padded carpeting will greatly reduce the risk of brain injury for some children with seizure disorders. Furniture with rounded corners also reduces the risk of injury during a fall. These and other modifications can be achieved, when needed, within the standards of typical classrooms or school environments. On a smaller scale, little things can make big differences. For example, regular plastic drinking straws can cause serious injuries to the mouth, face, or eyes of students who have drop seizures. Flexible straws eliminate almost all of this risk.

Using helmets is another common risk-reduction measure most often used with children with myoclonic or atonic seizures who have frequent falls. The potential benefit to the wearer, however, must be weighed against the intrusiveness of the intervention. Wearing a helmet may contribute to the perception that the child is unusual, may restrict the child's movements, and/or may be uncomfortable (especially in warm weather) and thus poorly tolerated by the child. If protective headgear is required, then it should be lightweight, well fitting, and as appropriate in the social environment as possible. For example, a bicycle helmet is much lighter than a football helmet and is not necessarily unusual apparel for a school-age child at play. A knit hat or other common type of thick hat will provide considerable protection and is more common in many environments than a helmet. The thick hair typically found on the human scalp provides significant natural protection as well, so it may be helpful for a child to adopt a hairstyle that maximizes protection.

Restricting hazardous activities is another strategy for risk reduction. Again, weighing the potential for risk reduction against the restriction of the activity requires careful judgment on the part of the team, and the child's input should be included in the decision-making process, regardless of the child's communication and cognitive skill level. Restricting a child from a favorite or highly prized activity should occur only if great risk is present and restriction substantially reduces the risk. Swimming is a common example of an activity that many children with severe and multiple disabilities (including seizure disorders) enjoy. For example, children with CP who participate in aquatic activities have been reported to benefit in flexibility, respiratory function, muscle strength, gait, gross motor function, and confidence (Gorter & Currie, 2011). It can be dangerous if the individual has a seizure while in the water, however. Most children with uncontrolled seizures can enjoy time in a swimming pool or hot tub without excessive risk with the support and assistance of a caregiver who remains in constant contact and who can keep the child's head above water if a seizure occurs. Students with poorly controlled seizures should have constant one-to-one supervision during swimming from someone in physical contact and remain in water shallow enough for the supervisor to stand and support the individual in case of a seizure to ensure the student's head remains above water (e.g., Besag, 2001).

First Aid Measures   Simple first aid measures may be required when seizures occur (see Table 5.5). Little intervention is required in most cases, and misguided efforts are potentially harmful. First aid measures are aimed at preventing injury caused by the seizure and generally involve using common sense. Generalized tonic-clonic and other major motor convulsions often cause injury as a result of the child falling or experiencing powerful involuntary movements. The onset is often too sudden for the child to be eased to the floor, but sometimes (usually when the child is sitting in a chair) he or she does not fall immediately. Easing the child to the ground can prevent serious injury. Furniture with hard or sharp edges and other hazardous objects should be removed from the area, if possible. The child should be moved away only if a hazard cannot be moved (e.g., stairwell, swimming pool). Placing a soft object (e.g., cushion, sweater) under the head or other vulnerable body parts can also prevent injury.

Never attempt to put anything in a person's mouth during a seizure. Although people can bite their tongues, which may be injurious during seizures, such injuries are not as frequent or severe as those caused by items placed in the mouth. Items placed in the mouth may force jaws out of joint due to unequal pressure, break teeth, obstruct the airway, or injure oral structures if the child flips over on his or her face. Anything given by mouth may enter the airway because the child is unconscious, so it is essential to refrain from giving food or fluid until the child has fully recovered. It is usually not useful to attempt to open or clear the airway during the seizure, but this may be necessary after the seizure is over. If the child remains unconscious, then it is desirable to position him or her on the right or left side, with the neck in slight extension and the

Table 5.5.   General first aid measures for seizures

Type of seizure	Do	Do not
Generalized tonic-clonic (grand mal)	*During* Ease to floor Remove hazards Cushion vulnerable body parts *After* Position for clear airway, if required Check for injuries Allow for rest	*During* Put anything in the person's mouth Move the person, unless absolutely necessary Restrain the person's movements *After* Give food or fluids until fully conscious
Generalized absence (petit mal)	Protect from environmental hazards	Give food or fluids until fully conscious
Partial complex with automatisms (psychomotor)	Remove hazards from area or pathway Supervise until fully conscious	Restrain movements Approach, if agitated, unless necessary Give food or fluids until fully conscious

Note: Seizures are highly individual and frequently do not fit these general categories. The best first aid measures are individualized to the student. Each student with a history of seizures should have his or her own first aid instructions. These first aid measures are intended as general guidelines when individual instructions are not available.

head slightly lower than the midline of the body to encourage saliva or any other secretions to run out of the mouth and not back into the throat. The child should then be examined for signs of injury. Observation should continue until the child is fully conscious, but it is not generally necessary to call for medical help unless one or more of the following occurs:

- Breathing does not resume (in which case mouth-to-mouth resuscitation should be started)

- One seizure follows another

- The child sustains a significant injury

- The seizure lasts more than 5 minutes

- The child has no history of seizures

- The seizure appears substantially different from previously known seizures

Other types of seizures typically require no first aid procedures. Only general precautions, such as removing dangerous objects, are necessary to protect the child from hazards with which he or she might come into contact. For example, a child experiencing a complex partial seizure might walk off a step or ledge, or a child having an absence seizure might not be conscious of an approaching car. Prolonged or repeated seizures usually require immediate medical attention. Some individuals routinely have two or more generalized tonic-clonic seizures in a day or have seizures that last as long as 7 or 8 minutes, but immediate medical assistance should be requested unless the observer is certain that this represents typical behavior for the child. In cases of uncertainty, it is better to request assistance when it is not required than to fail to request it when it is needed. Whether a seizure is reported immediately, it should be carefully observed and recorded for the planning of care and treatment.

Some students with seizure disorders have emergency medications, such as rectal diazepam or buccal midazolam, in case of prolonged or repeated seizures. These must be easily available in the school, and staff members need to be trained on when and how to use them. See Chapter 6 for more information on emergency medications.

Educational Implications of Seizures

Many of the topics already discussed greatly affect the provision of education for children with seizure disorders (e.g., observing and reporting seizures in the classroom, behavioral intervention), but a few specific educational concerns are addressed here as well: 1) the effects of seizure disorders on learning and behavior, 2) the social implications of seizure disorders, and 3) some specific roles of the collaborative team.

Learning and Behavior   Although seizure disorders are only weakly correlated with intelligence, they may influence learning in several ways. Drugs, intense and frequent seizures, brain damage, related behavior problems, and attention deficits are impediments to learning for some children with seizure disorders. Symptoms of confusion, mental impairment, headache, or fatigue following a seizure may interfere with learning. It is important to remember, however, that not all children who experience seizures are affected equally by these factors, and some are not significantly affected by any of these factors. Team decisions must be reached through careful consideration of the effects on specific children. For example, impulsive behaviors, irritability, and attention deficit may be reported and found to be the result of subclinical seizure activity. Although these deficits may be controlled by medication, the medications may result in sluggishness, lethargy, depression, irritability, or behavior problems that also interfere with learning. Careful evaluation of both liabilities and benefits of treatment must be undertaken by the team based on clear and complete records of the child's social, learning, and seizure behavior.

The role of seizure disorders in lack of impulse control, aggression, and violence remains controversial. Studies of this role are difficult to interpret because there are numerous intervening variables. The majority of children with seizure disorders exhibit no special behavior problems. Therefore, behavior problems should not be anticipated simply because a child has a seizure disorder. Behavior problems in children with seizure disorders should be treated exactly like behavior problems in any other child. Medical treatment with anticonvulsants may be considered in the rare instances in which behavior problems appear to be the direct result of seizure activity. Teachers should take note of any children who become aggressive during the immediate period following seizures and should provide appropriate supervision to ensure safety.

Social Implications and Peers   Epilepsy has a long history of social stigma. Public opinion and attitudes toward seizure disorders have improved over time, but stigma remains among some individuals and cultural groups (Fiest, Birbeck, Jacoby, & Jette, 2014). Attitude changes occur with improved education. The presence of seizures may add to stigma or negative appraisals that some people hold toward students with severe and multiple disabilities, but it probably plays a small role for these students because seizures are only one of many characteristics that might become the focus of social stigma.

Because seizures typically occur at unpredictable times, they often happen in the presence of other students and may elicit a variety of reactions from them. Some students may be upset by the event. They may be worried about the student who has the seizure or worried that the same thing could happen to them. It is important for school staff to model calm but supportive responses during the seizure. It may be helpful to discuss seizure disorders with the other students once the seizure is over, providing factual information and promoting positive attitudes. Numerous excellent resources provide information about seizure disorders to teachers, and some include suggestions on teaching students about seizures. For example, materials from the Epilepsy Foundation include "Key points to help children understand" (2009, pp. 9–10). The exact nature and extent of information shared with other students need to be tailored to their ages and specific circumstances, but it is important to listen to their questions and concerns and respond accordingly. This general approach to teaching students about seizures can also be applied to other medical emergencies, procedures, and events that occur in the classroom.

Parents and other family members will be accustomed to their children's seizure activity in many and probably most cases and will have developed a reasonable level of acceptance. Family members may require assistance to gain access to more information or support in some cases, however.

Collaborative Team Roles   Because seizures are unpredictable, all team members who work directly with students with severe and multiple disabilities must be prepared to provide appropriate first aid measures for individual students, observe seizures accurately, and record their observations. Although all team members need to be prepared to manage, observe, and record seizures, it is important to designate primary responsibility to a specific staff member who will ensure that this is completed. For example, a student may have a seizure in the classroom when several staff members are present, and each staff member might assume someone else has recorded it. As a result, the seizure may go unrecorded. One team member also needs to be responsible to make sure relevant information about seizure activity is reported to the student's family. For some students, any seizure may need to be reported immediately to the family. For others, only unusual or severe seizure activity needs to be reported. The teacher is typically the person with primary responsibility for making sure seizures are recorded and reported to parents, but this primary responsibility may be assigned to another individual, such as the school nurse, in some cases.

It is also critical that the student's family communicate relevant information about seizure activity at home. For example, if a student has had multiple or severe seizures at home before coming to school, then the student may be drowsy later that day. The school team can make better decisions about how to respond to the student's drowsiness if they know the likely cause.

DUAL DIAGNOSIS

The term *dual diagnosis* generally refers to the diagnosis of two conditions in the same person. Dual diagnosis in the area of intellectual and developmental disabilities typically refers to coexisting emotional or behavior disorders and intellectual disabilities. Children with severe and multiple disabilities can manifest the full range of psychopathological conditions and behavior problems seen in other children. Although anyone can have emotional or behavior disorders, research suggests that they are found in children and adults with intellectual disabilities more frequently than in the general population (e.g., Bielska, Ouellette-Kuntz, & Hunter, 2012). Disruptive behaviors are three to four times more common in children with intellectual disabilities as compared with other children.

Children with intellectual disabilities are a high-risk group for emotional and behavior difficulties for various reasons, including 1) the greater likelihood of experiencing violence or neglect, 2) organic brain damage, 3) inadequate coping strategies, 4) social-emotional stress, and 5) poorly developed defense mechanisms (Fletcher, 2011). Prevalence figures for children having a dual diagnosis vary widely because of differences in diagnostic criteria, diagnostic instruments, sample size, type of study, and location of residence; however, a conservative estimate would be 20%–30% (Sheehan et al., 2015). Having characteristics such as physical or sensory disabilities and limited communication skills often impair children's performance on tests and contribute to the difficulties of diagnosing mental health problems in children with intellectual disabilities.

The lack of standard diagnostic criteria appropriate for children with intellectual disabilities is one of the major problems noted by researchers in this field. Standard classification systems, such as the *Diagnostic and Statistical Manual of Mental Disorders, Fifth Edition, Text Revision (DSM-V-TR*; American Psychiatric Association, 2013), have been used to classify mental illness among children with intellectual disabilities, but they can result in inappropriate diagnoses. For example, a child without a disability whose speech is disorganized and out of control and who uses many gestures could be diagnosed with a psychotic disorder, but that diagnosis may not be appropriate for a child with severe intellectual disabilities who uses adaptive communication. Furthermore, psychiatric diagnoses are often based on a child's reporting of his or her subjective experiences and feelings, which may be difficult or impossible for children with severe communication impairments. Therefore, a separate or modified diagnostic and classification system may be needed for children with severe and multiple disabilities. Groups such as NADD (previously known as the National Association for the Dually Diagnosed) have developed assessment tools and treatment protocols for this population. Although some of the same psychological diagnostic tools that are used with the general population can also be used with children with severe and multiple disabilities, they need to be carefully adapted and individualized when used with individuals with intellectual or developmental disabilities (Beail, Mitchell, Vlissides, & Jackson, 2013).

Rapid growth has been occurring in clinical and scientific interest in and knowledge regarding recognition and response to mental health challenges in individuals with intellectual disabilities since the 1980s. It would be impossible to review the entire body of knowledge here, so the following discussion is limited to some aspects most relevant to educational team members.

Reiss, Levitan, and Szyszko (1982) introduced the concept of *diagnostic overshadowing*, which refers to instances in which the presence of an intellectual disability makes it more difficult to interpret mental health symptoms. In other words, atypical behavior may be attributed to an intellectual disability rather than to a mental health problem. For example, self-harm is often a symptom of PTSD, but this possibility may be ignored if self-injurious behavior is attributed to the presence of intellectual disability. Of course, this does not mean that every instance of self-injurious behavior exhibited by an individual with an intellectual disability is the result of PTSD. It simply means that this possibility should not be dismissed, and all the possibilities considered for someone without a disability exhibiting self-harm must also be considered. Diagnostic overshadowing is not limited to behavioral or emotional symptoms. It can also extend to the tendency to attribute all physical health difficulties to an individual's disability, masking other causal factors and thereby reducing access to appropriate treatment. The essential implication for team members is simply to ask what can cause any observed symptom and not simply limit the question to whether the symptom could be explained by the individual's disability.

Several approaches address potential behavioral and mental health challenges in students with severe and multiple disabilities, including positive behavior interventions and supports (PBIS), communication training, social intervention, play therapy, psychotherapy, and drug therapy. They are often used in various combinations. Each of these is described very briefly here, but more comprehensive descriptions and instructions are available from many resources (e.g., Davis & Dixon, 2010; Fletcher, 2011; Koegel, Koegel, & Dunlap, 1996).

Positive Behavior Interventions and Supports

PBIS are based on a functional analysis of behavior, which uses careful observation to describe the behavior, the conditions under which the behavior occurs, and the consequences of the behavior. The conditions or consequences (or both) are then systematically altered in order to change the behavior (Rapp & Arndt, 2012). For example, disruptive behavior may function to get attention for some individuals or to escape demands for others. Providing more appropriate ways for individuals to achieve these ends may reduce or eliminate the disruption.

Communication Training

Communication training is one critical area of PBIS. Many individuals with severe and multiple disabilities have very limited communication skills. As a result, they have limited social control and often experience frustration. They may exhibit problem behaviors simply because they lack more appropriate ways of making their needs known. Teaching them more acceptable means of communicating their needs can result in substantial improvements in behavior (see Chapter 7).

Individual, Group, and Play Therapies

Individual and group psychotherapy, including play therapy and other related forms of intervention, are increasingly being used with individuals with intellectual disabilities, including those with severe disabilities (e.g., Fletcher, 2011). These appear to be particularly useful with individuals with specific diagnoses, such as traumatic stress disorders.

Social Intervention

Social intervention, such as parent training or family supports, may also be appropriate in some cases as a primary intervention and in combination with other methods in other cases (e.g., Reichow, Servili, Yasamy, Barbui, & Saxena, 2013).

These interventions may teach parents effective strategies for interacting with their child or may be focused on helping parents address specific behavioral challenges. In some instances, these strategies may be implemented to address specific issues with parenting style, but in most cases, these interventions are provided to support the efforts of parents who are already functioning well.

Drug Therapy

Treating challenging behavior with medications is a controversial issue. Between the 1950s and mid-1980s, children and adults with severe and multiple disabilities and challenging behavior often were given massive doses of tranquilizers to calm them (Gadow & Poling, 1988). The consequence was inhibition of the person's total functioning, not just a decrease in the target behavior. In addition, these individuals often experienced severe long-term side effects such as tardive dyskinesia, which is characterized by involuntary movements of the limbs and face, and other conditions that interfere with day-to-day activities. Although there is much less reliance on major tranquilizers to control challenging behavior today, drugs continue to be used with both adults and children with multiple disabilities and challenging behavior. Medical treatment is appropriate and helpful in some cases, but it is inappropriate and harmful in other cases (Tsiouris, 2010).

Decisions regarding the use of medications must be based on the individual needs of the student after carefully weighing the potential for harm and benefit to the individual. Medications should never be prescribed primarily for the benefit of others, and they should not be used in place of PBIS or other appropriate programs. A proper program may make drugs unnecessary, and even when drugs are necessary and appropriate, they should be used concurrently with an appropriate behavior program.

Although the prescription of medication is a medical responsibility, members of the educational team often play important roles in assessing the need for medical intervention and evaluating the positive and negative effects of medication on the student. It is important to note more than just the frequency of challenging behavior when considering the effects of medication. For example, if a medication makes a student so drowsy that he or she sleeps much of the school day, then the frequency of challenging behavior will probably decrease, but learning opportunities and participation in activities will almost certainly suffer.

SELF-INJURIOUS BEHAVIOR

Self-injurious behavior is one category of challenging behavior exhibited by some students with severe or multiple disabilities. These students harm themselves through their own repetitive, stereotypic, or intense episodic behavior. They may bang their heads, poke their eyes, scratch or tear their skin, bite their arms or fingers, or engage in other self-damaging behavior. It can be occasional and mild or frequent and severe. The effects of this behavior range from mild irritation to severe and permanent injury. In addition, self-injurious behavior is often very disruptive to activities and demoralizing to parents, staff, classmates, and others. Self-injury is not restricted to people with intellectual disabilities or autism. Deliberate self-injury can occur in people with typical intelligence, may serve multiple functions within a given individual, and may be the result of an underlying neurochemical or environmental condition or both.

No single cause appears to explain all self-injurious behavior among children with disabilities (Oliver & Richards, 2010). Self-injurious behavior has a social function in some individuals, such as gaining attention or escaping from demands, but this behavior occurs regardless of social context or response in other individuals. A few specific organic conditions, such as Lesch-Nyhan syndrome and Prader-Willi syndrome, appear to predispose individuals to self-injurious behavior. Some theories suggest that self-inflicted pain helps block other more aversive sensations such as untreated physical or emotional suffering (e.g., Symons et al., 2009). Self-harm has been reported in survivors of physical and sexual abuse with and without disabilities.

The educational team should ensure that a careful medical and physical assessment has been completed and that any source of pain is managed to the greatest possible degree. PBIS, including functional communication training, has been shown to help in many cases of self-injurious behavior, particularly with children. Because self-harm can be a symptom of child abuse or other severe trauma, this possibility should be carefully evaluated. If there is evidence of psychological trauma, then intervention should be directed, at least in part, toward resolving traumatic effects (e.g., Razza & Sobsey, 2011). If medical treatment is required, then various opiate antagonists, beta-blockers, stimulants, antidepressants, and anticonvulsants have been shown to be helpful in some individuals. The educational team can play a critical role in monitoring the frequency and severity of self-injurious behavior. Medication should be discontinued after a trial period if it is not working.

Restraints

Using restraints is another common approach to managing severe self-injurious behavior and sometimes to control other challenging behavior. Restraint devices have been applied in the form of elbow or knee splints, camisoles (straightjackets), restraint nets, support belts, or other appliances. Restraint has also been used in the form of an adult holding the child and restricting movements.

Every possible effort should be used to avoid the use of restraints. Although restraints continue to be frequently used in some environments, several serious problems must be considered. First, restraints are dangerous and must be considered high-risk procedures. Serious injuries and significant numbers of deaths have resulted from attempts to use restraints. Although many of these cases involve poorly trained staff and misapplication of procedures, injuries and deaths frequently occur even when model restraint procedures are used.

Second, the use of restraint has been shown to reinforce the self-injurious behavior in some individuals. Even though the immediate effect of restraint may be to make it more difficult for the child to cause an injury, the frequency and intensity of self-injury may increase as soon as the child is released. This can lead to a vicious cycle in which the use of restraint becomes more and more frequent while self-injurious behavior intensifies (e.g., Rooker & Roscoe, 2005).

Third, restraints are socially stigmatizing and make inclusion and normal interaction much more difficult. This increases social isolation and often results in fewer opportunities to take part in desired activities that might help develop more desirable behavioral alternatives.

Fourth, the application of restraint is governed by a long list of professional policies, agency procedures, laws, and court decisions that are rarely considered in the use of these procedures in school environments. Unfortunately, the failure to consider the appropriate regulatory law and policy is commonly identified after restraint results in injury. As a result, schools and individual personnel who employ these procedures may find themselves civilly or even criminally liable for any harm resulting from their use.

Finally, restraints always interfere with a much broader class of behavior than the ones they are intended to suppress (e.g., restraints that are intended to stop a child from biting his or her fingers may also make self-feeding impossible). The goal of educators is to enable children, not incapacitate them. Restraint is never a desirable procedure for all of these reasons. Its use should be avoided if there is any reasonable alternative and used as briefly, infrequently, and humanely as possible only to prevent clear and present danger (e.g., stopping a child from running out into traffic).

CONCLUSION

Health and education are inseparable for all children, but children with severe and multiple disabilities have more frequent and more severe health challenges than most other students. Recognizing and addressing these health challenges is crucial to good educational practice. The following chapter discusses how to recognize and respond to specific medical conditions that can develop in the classroom, aid in necessary medical procedures, and integrate health care into the student's educational programs.

REFLECTION QUESTIONS

1. If a student had a seizure in your classroom and other students seemed upset, then what might you do to address their concerns?

2. What policies are in place in your local schools regarding mandatory vaccinations? Why do you agree or disagree with this policy?

3. The multifactorial model suggests that cultural attitudes and beliefs may increase the risk of abuse of individuals with disabilities. What common attitudes or beliefs do you think may contribute to this risk?

4. If a student with severe and multiple disabilities is disrupting the classroom to get attention, then what might be a positive approach to addressing this behavior?

CHAPTER ACTIVITY

1. Select one emergency situation schools in your area might face.

2. Develop a set of emergency response procedures.

3. Identify how students with physical and mental disabilities would be accom-
    modated in your plan.

REFERENCES

American Academy of Pediatrics. (1999). Emergency preparedness for children with special health care needs. *Pediatrics, 104,* e53. 1-6.

American Academy of Pediatrics. (2010). Policy statement: Honoring do-not-attempt resuscitation requests in school. *Pediatrics, 25,* 1073–1077.

American Psychiatric Association. (2013). *Diagnostic and statistical manual of mental disorders, fifth edition, text revision (DSM-V-TR).* Washington, DC: Author.

Appleton, R., Baker, G., Chadwick, D., & Smith, D. (2001). *Epilepsy* (4th ed.). London, England: Martin Dunitz.

Bandino, M.L., Garfinkle, R.A., Zickefoose, B.A., & Hsieh, D.T. (2014). Epilepsy at a summer camp for children and young adults with developmental disabilities: A 3-year experience. *Military Medicine, 179,* 105–110.

Basch, C.E. (2010). *Healthier students are better learners: A missing link in school reforms to close the achievement gap.* New York, NY: Teachers College Press.

Beail, N., Mitchell, K., Vlissides, N., & Jackson, T. (2015). Concordance of the mini-psychiatric assessment schedule for adults who have developmental disabilities (PASADD) and the brief symptom inventory. *Journal of Intellectual Disability Research, 59,* 170-175. doi:10.1111/jir.12073

Bellon, M., Walker, C., & Peterson, C. (2013). Seizure-related injuries and hospitalizations: Self-report data from the 2010 Australian Epilepsy Longitudinal Survey. *Epilepsy and Behavior, 26,* 7–10.

Belsky, J. (1980). Child maltreatment: An ecological integration. *American Psychologist, 35*(4), 320–325.

Berg, A.T., & Scheffer, I.E. (2011). New concepts in classification of the epilepsies: Entering the 21st century. *Epilepsia, 52,* 1058–1062.

Beringer, A.J., & Heckford, E.J. (2014). Was there a plan? End-of-life care for children with life-limiting conditions: A review of multi-service healthcare records. *Child Care, Health, and Development, 40,* 176–183.

Besag, F.M. (2001). Lesson of the week: Tonic seizures are a particular risk factor for drowning in people with epilepsy. *British Medical Journal, 322,* 975–976.

Best, S., Heller, K.W., & Bigge, J.L. (2010). *Teaching individuals with physical or multiple disabilities* (6th ed.). Boston, MA: Pearson.

Bielska, I.A., Ouellette-Kuntz, H., & Hunter, D. (2012). Using national surveys for mental health surveillance of individuals with intellectual disabilities in Canada. *Chronic Diseases and Injuries in Canada, 32,* 194–199.

Blake, J.J., Lund, E.M., Zhou, Q., Kwok, O.M., & Benz, M.R. (2012). National prevalence rates of bully victimization among students with disabilities in the United States. *School Psychology Quarterly, 27,* 210–222.

Caldas, S.J., & Bensy, M.L. (2014). The sexual maltreatment of students with disabilities in American school settings. *Journal of Child Sexual Abuse, 23*(4), 345–366.

Centers for Disease Control and Prevention. (2011, November 17). *Infectious diseases in school.* Retrieved from http://www.cdc.gov/healthyyouth/infectious/#2

Centers for Disease Control and Prevention. (2013). *Voluntary guidelines for managing food allergies in schools and early care and education programs.* Washington, DC: U.S. Department of Health and Human Services.

Cervenka, M.C., & Kossoff, E.H. (2013). Dietary treatment of intractable epilepsy. *Continuum, 19,* 756–766.

Clark, B.R., Burkett, S.A., Andridge, R.R., & Buckley, T.J. (2013). Evidence of high rates of undiagnosed asthma in central Ohio elementary schoolchildren. *Journal of School Health, 83,* 896–906.

Cohen, L., & Felson, M. (1979). Social change and crime rate trends: A routine activity approach. *American Sociological Review, 44*(4), 588–608.

Cyr, C., Michel, G., & Dumais, M. (2013). Child maltreatment as a global phenomenon: From trauma to prevention. *International Journal of Psychology, 48*, 141–148.

Davis, K., & Dixon, S. D. (2010). *When actions speak louder than words: Understanding the challenging behaviors of young children and students with disabilities*. Bloomington, IN.: Solution Tree Press.

De Bellis, M.D. (2005). The psychobiology of neglect. *Child Maltreatment, 10*, 150–172.

De Bellis, M.D., Woolley, D.P., & Hooper, S.R. (2013). Neuropsychological findings in pediatric maltreatment: relationship of PTSD, dissociative symptoms, and abuse/neglect indices to neurocognitive outcomes. *Child Maltreatment, 18*, 171–183.

DePaepe, P., Garrison-Kane, L., & Doelling, J. (2002). Supporting students with health needs in schools: An overview of selected health conditions. *Focus on Exceptional Children, 35*, 1–24.

Doom, J.R., Cicchetti, D., Rogosch, F.A., & Dackis, M.N. (2013). Child maltreatment and gender interactions as predictors of differential neuroendocrine profiles. *Psychoneuroendocrinology, 38*, 1442–1454.

Duncan, J.S. (2010). Imaging in the surgical treatment of epilepsy. *Nature Reviews Neurology, 6*(10), 537–550.

The Editors. (2010). Retraction: Ileal-lymphoid-nodular hyperplasia, non-specific colitis, and pervasive developmental disorder in children. *The Lancet, 375*, 445. doi:10.1016/S0140-6736(10)60175-4

Ells, C. (2010). Levels of intervention: Communicating with more precision about planned use of critical interventions. *American Journal of Bioethics, 10*(1), 78–79.

Epilepsy Foundation. (2009). *Epilepsy in children: The teacher's role*. Washington, DC: Author.

Field, M.J., & Boat, T.F. (2010). *Rare diseases and orphan products: Accelerating research and development*. Washington, DC: National Academies Press.

Fiest, K.M., Birbeck, G.L., Jacoby, A., & Jette, N. (2014). Stigma in epilepsy. *Current Neurology and Neurosciences Report, 14*(5), 444.

Finkelhor, D., Turner, H.A., Shattuck, A., & Hamby, S.L. (2013). Violence, crime, and abuse exposure in a national sample of children and youth: An update. *JAMA Pediatrics, 167*(7), 614–621.

Fletcher, J. (1972). Indicators of humanhood: A tentative profile of man. *Hastings Center Report, 2*(11), 1–4.

Fletcher, R.J. (Ed.). (2011). *Psychotherapy for individuals with intellectual disability*. Kingston, NY: NADD.

Forrest, C.B., Bevans, K.B., Riley, A.W., Crespo, R., & Louis, T.A. (2011). School outcomes of children with special health care needs. *Pediatrics, 128*, 303–312.

Freeman, J.M., Vining, E.P.G., & Pillas, D.J. (2003). *Seizures and epilepsy in childhood: A guide for parents* (3rd ed.). Baltimore, MD: Johns Hopkins University Press.

Gadow, K.D., & Poling, A.G. (1988). *Pharmacotherapy and mental retardation*. New York, NY: Little, Brown.

Gorter, J.W., & Currie, S.J. (2011). Aquatic exercise programs for children and adolescents with cerebral palsy: What do we know and where do we go? *International Journal of Pediatrics*, Article ID 712165. doi:10.1155/2011/712165

Hall, J.C., Jobson, L., & Langdon, P.E. (2014). Measuring symptoms of post-traumatic stress disorder in people with intellectual disabilities: The development and psychometric properties of the impact of event scale-intellectual disabilities (IES-IDs). *British Journal of Clinical Psychology, 53*(3), 315–332.

Hauser, W.A., & Bannerjee, P.N. (2008). Epidemiology of epilepsy in children. In J.M. Pellock, B.F.D. Bourgeois, & W.E. Dodson (Eds.), *Pediatric epilepsy: Diagnosis and therapy* (3rd ed., pp. 147–164). New York, NY: Demos Medical Publishing.

Hindelang, M., Gottfredson, M., & Garofalo, J. (1978). *Victims of personal crime: An empirical foundation for a theory of personal victimization*. Cambridge, MA: Ballinger.

Jones, L., Bellis, M.A., Wood, S., Hughes, K., McCoy, E., Eckley, L., Bates, G., Mikton, C., Shakespeare, T., & Officer, A. (2012). Prevalence and risk of violence against children with disabilities: A systematic review and meta-analysis of observational studies. *Lancet, 380*, 899–907.

Kasteleijn-Nolst Trenite, D.G. (2012). Provoked and reflex seizures: Surprising or common? *Epilepsia, 53* (Supplement 4), 105–113.

Katz, A. (2006, October 23). Red Cross reverses policy on choking aid. *New Haven Register*, A1.

Kennamer, M. (2002). *Basic infection control for health care providers*. Albany, NY: Delmar Thomson Learning.

Koegel, L.K., Koegel, R.L., & Dunlap, G. (1996). *Positive behavioral supports.* Baltimore, MD: Paul H. Brookes Publishing Co.

Lee, S.A., & No, Y.J. (2005). Perceived self-control of seizures in patients with uncontrolled partial epilepsy. *Seizure, 14*(2), 100–105.

Oberlander, T.F., & Symons, F.J. (Eds.). (2006). *Pain in children and adults with developmental disabilities.* Baltimore, MD: Paul H. Brookes Publishing Co.

Oeseburg, B., Dijkstra, G.J., Groothoff, J.W., Reijneveld, S.A., & Jansen, D.E. (2011). Prevalence of chronic health conditions in children with intellectual disability: A systematic literature review. *Intellectual and Developmental Disabilities, 49,* 59–85.

Oliver, C., & Richards, C. (2010). Self-injurious behaviour in people with intellectual disability. *Current Opinion in Psychiatry, 23,* 412–416.

Olympia, R.P., Wan, E., & Avner, J.R. (2005). The preparedness of schools to respond to emergencies in children: A national survey of school nurses. *Pediatrics, 116,* e738–e745. doi:10.1542/peds.2005-1474

Perske, R. (1972). The dignity of risk and the mentally retarded. *Mental Retardation, 10,* 24–27.

Petersilia, J. (2001). Crime victims with developmental disabilities: A review essay. *Criminal Justice and Behavior, 28,* 655–694.

Polak, E.L., Privitera, M.D., Lipton, R.B., & Haut, S.R. (2012). Behavioral intervention as an add-on therapy in epilepsy: Designing a clinical trial. *Epilepsy and Behavior, 25,* 505–510.

Protecting kids from choking, suffocation, strangulation. (2009, November 2). Retrieved from http://www.kdheks.gov/news/web_archives/2009/11022009.htm

Ram, G., & Chinen, J. (2011). Infections and immunodeficiency in Down syndrome [Review]. *Clinical and Experimental Immunology, 164,* 9–16.

Rapp, W.H., & Arndt, K.L. (2012). *Teaching everyone: An introduction to inclusive education.* Baltimore, MD: Paul H. Brookes Publishing Co.

Razza, N., & Sobsey, D. (2011). Treating survivors of sexual and interpersonal abuse. In R.J. Fletcher (Ed.), *Psychotherapy for people with intellectual disabilities* (pp. 131–144). Kingston, NY: NADD.

Reichow, B., Servili, C., Yasamy, M.T., Barbui, C., & Saxena, S. (2013). Non-specialist psychosocial interventions for children and adolescents with intellectual disability or lower-functioning autism spectrum disorders: A systematic review. *PLoS Medicine, 10*(12). doi:10.1371/journal.pmed.1001572

Reiss, S., Levitan, G.W., & Szyszko, J. (1982). Emotional disturbance and mental retardation: Diagnostic overshadowing. *American Journal on Mental Deficiency, 86,* 567–574.

Rimmer, J.H., Schiller, W., & Chen, M.D. (2012). Effects of disability-associated low energy expenditure deconditioning syndrome. *Exercise and Sport Sciences Review, 40,* 22–29.

Rooker, G.W., & Roscoe, E.M. (2005). Functional analysis of self-injurious behavior and its relation to self-restraint. *Journal of Applied Behavior Analysis, 38*(4), 537–542.

Russ, S.A., Larson, K., & Halfon, N. (2012). A national profile of childhood epilepsy and seizure disorder. *Pediatrics, 129,* 256–264.

Sánchez-Carpintero Abad, R., Sanmartí Vilaplana, F., & Serratosa Fernandez, J. (2007). Genetic causes of epilepsy. *The Neurologist, 13,* S47–S51. doi:10.1097/NRL.0b013e31815bb07d

Schieve, L.A., Gonzalez, V., Boulet, S.L., Visser, S.N., Rice, C.E., Van Naarden Braun, K., & Boyle, C.A. (2012). Concurrent medical conditions and health care use and needs among children with learning and behavioral developmental disabilities: National Health Interview Survey, 2006–2010. *Research in Developmental Disabilities, 33,* 467–476.

Shakeshaft, C. (2004). *Educator sexual misconduct: A synthesis of existing literature.* Washington, DC: U.S. Department of Education, Office of the Under Secretary, Policy and Program Studies Service.

Sheehan, R., Hassiotis, A., Walters, K., Osborn, D., Strydom, A., & Horsfall, L. (2015). Mental illness, challenging behaviour, and psychotropic drug prescribing in people with intellectual disability: UK population based cohort study. *British Medical Journal, 351,* h4326.

Shinde, S.K., Danov, S., Chen, C.C., Clary, J., Harper, V., Bodfish, J.W., & Symons, F. J. (2014). Convergent validity evidence for the pain and discomfort scale (PADS) for pain assessment among adults with intellectual disability. *Clinical Journal of Pain, 30,* 536–543.

Sidell, D.R., Kim, I.A., Coker, T.R., Moreno, C., & Shapiro, N.L. (2013). Food choking hazards and multiple disabilities in children. *International Journal of Pediatric Otorhinolaryngology, 77*(12), 1940–1946.

Singer, P. (1979). *Practical ethics.* Cambridge, UK: Cambridge University Press.

Singer, P. (2000). *Writings on an ethical life.* New York, NY: HarperCollins.

Skinner, B.F. (1953). *Science and human behavior.* New York, NY: Free Press.

Smith, J., Fernando, T., McGrath, N., & Ameratunga, R. (2004). Lamotrigine-induced common variable immune deficiency. *Neurology, 62,* 833–834.

Sobsey, D. (1982). Behavioral observation and recording of seizures. *DPH Journal, 1,* 14–19.

Sobsey, D. (1994). *Violence and abuse in the lives of people with disabilities.* Baltimore, MD: Paul H. Brookes Publishing Co.

Sobsey, D. (2002). Exceptionality, education, and maltreatment. *Exceptionality, 10*(1), 29–46.

Sobsey, D., & Calder, P. (1999, October). *A conceptual analysis of increased risk for people with disabilities.* Paper presented at the U.S. National Research Council, Commission on Behavioral and Social Sciences and Education Committee on Crime and Justice Symposium on Victims with Disabilities, Irvine, CA.

Sobsey, D., & Mansell, S. (1997). Teaching people with disabilities to be abused and exploited: The special educator as accomplice. *Developmental Disabilities Bulletin, 25,* 77–93.

Srikanth, R., Cassidy, G., Joiner, C., & Teeluckdharry, S. (2011). Osteoporosis in people with intellectual disabilities: A review and a brief study of risk factors for osteoporosis in a community sample of people with intellectual disabilities. *Journal of Intellectual Disability Research, 55,* 53–62.

Sullivan, P.M., & Knutson, J.F. (2000). Maltreatment and disabilities: A population-based epidemiological study. *Child Abuse and Neglect, 24,* 1257–1273.

Symons, F.J., Harper, V.N., McGrath, P.J., Breau, L.M., & Bodfish, J.W. (2009). Evidence of increased non-verbal behavioral signs of pain in adults with neurodevelopmental disorders and chronic self-injury. *Research in Developmental Disabilities, 30*(3), 521–528.

Terra, V.C., Furlanetti, L.L., Nunes, A.A., Thome, U., Nisyiama, M.A., Sakamoto, A.C., & Machado, H.R. (2014). Vagus nerve stimulation in pediatric patients: Is it really worthwhile? *Epilepsy and Behavior, 31,* 329–333.

Tsiouris, J.A. (2010). Pharmacotherapy for aggressive behaviors in persons with intellectual disabilities: Treatment or mistreatment? *Journal of Intellectual Disability Research, 54*(1), 1–16.

U.S. Department of Health and Human Services. (2012). *Child maltreatment: 2012.* Washington, DC: Author.

Zlutnick, S., Mayville, W.J., & Moffat, S. (1975). Modification of seizure disorders: The interruption of behavioral chains. *Journal of Applied Behavior Analysis, 8*(1), 1–12.

6

Integrating Health Care in Education Programs

KATHRYN WOLFF HELLER

CHAPTER OBJECTIVES

1. Increase knowledge on how to maintain a safe, healthy environment

2. Learn to recognize and respond to common medical conditions of students with severe and multiple disabilities

3. Understand medication and treatment management for students with severe and multiple disabilities

4. Learn how to assist in common health care procedures, such as tube feeding and clean intermittent catheterization

5. Increase knowledge and skills in the construction and utilization of individual- ized health care plans (IHPs) and emergency care plans (ECPs)

6. Understand the impact of disability on health and school performance with the Physical and Health Disability Performance Model

KEY TERMS

- Asthma
- Clean intermittent catheterization
- Contractures
- Dehydration
- Diastat
- Disability-specific monitoring
- ECP
- EpiPen

- Experiential deficits
- IHP
- Otitis media
- Pressure ulcers
- Rescue Inhaler
- Self-Advocacy
- Tube feeding
- Vagus nerve stimulation

Andy is a 15-year-old student who has cerebral palsy (CP), a vision impairment, and asthma. He has difficulty swallowing because of his CP and is
only able to take a small amount of food by mouth, so he receives liquid
nutrition through a gastrostomy tube (tube that goes into his stomach). The
school nurse constructed an IHP, in conjunction with the educational team,
to address problems and issues that could arise with Andy's asthma and
tube feeding. The teacher and paraprofessional have both been taught to
recognize an asthma attack and steps to take should one occur. They also
know how to work his nebulizer, through which Andy receives medication. An
ECP is in place so everyone is clear on what to do if Andy has a severe asthma
attack that cannot be averted with his medication. In addition, the nurse has
taught Andy's teacher and paraprofessional how to give Andy his tube feeding. The team has decided that Andy is to learn to perform part of his tube
feeding himself as an educational goal in order to promote more independence. The teacher is providing systematic instruction to Andy to reach this
goal, including using several adaptations to accommodate Andy's motor and
visual impairments. Andy is making good progress in learning to be more
self-sufficient during mealtime.

As discussed in the previous chapter, teachers who have students with severe
and multiple disabilities often need specialized knowledge and skills to address
specific health issues. In some instances, teachers will need to know how their
students' health can affect educational performance, and, in others, they will
need to know what to do if a student experiences a health problem. Understanding these students' special health care needs can make a significant difference in
managing their health and providing appropriate educational adaptations.

Students with severe and multiple disabilities have a wide range of medical problems that teachers need to understand so that they can effectively monitor students and intervene should a problem occur. Some of these common
medical problems include dehydration, skin irritation and pressure ulcers,
respiratory infections, asthma, ear infections, and contractures. Teachers need
to monitor for those problems in addition to any specific health concerns the
student may have as a result of his or her disability (e.g., conditions with degenerative muscles, seizures). Teachers should also have an understanding of
the treatments and medications used to manage common medical problems
and disability-specific problems.

Some students with severe and multiple disabilities have conditions that
require specialized health care procedures, including tube feeding, clean intermittent catheterization, colostomy care, and tracheostomy suctioning. Due
to advances in medical technology and educational policies supporting the
education of all students, students who require health care procedures are often found in the school environment, and their procedures frequently need to
be performed during school hours. Teachers not only need to be familiar with

these procedures, but they also must consider if a student should be taught to assist with the performance of his or her own procedure.

This chapter provides information on creating a safe, healthy environment for all students in order to assist teachers and school staff in addressing students' health needs and integrating health care and educational programs. This section is followed by information on common medical conditions for students with severe and multiple disabilities and information about administering medications. Because some conditions are managed by health care procedures, a special section on those procedures is included. The chapter concludes with a discussion of the impact of severe and multiple disabilities on health and school performance and the importance of the educational team.

MAINTAINING A SAFE, HEALTHY ENVIRONMENT

School personnel should maintain a safe, healthy environment for all students by arranging the environment to prevent injury and the spread of infection and having accessible evacuation procedures. School personnel should also be knowledgeable regarding students' disabilities and related health issues and should be able to make appropriate accommodations to address students' health needs in the school environment (Division for Physical, Health, and Multiple Disabilities [DPHMD], 2008). In addition, they should put clear plans of action in place for responding to specific problems and emergencies through the development of IHPs and ECPs, which are constructed to address a student's health needs, problems, and emergencies.

Teachers should carefully inspect their classrooms for any hazards that could result in an accident or aggravate an existing disorder. For example, paths should be kept clear to avoid the possibilities of falls for students who use mobility devices such as walkers and canes. Students who have a tracheostomy (i.e., surgically made hole in the neck through which to breathe) should not use plastic bibs because of the possibility of suffocation. Teachers might need to avoid having pets such as hamsters in their classrooms if they precipitate a student's asthma attacks. Use of flashing lights in a classroom display should be avoided if students in the class have seizures that are triggered by such lights. Understanding each student's specific health condition or disability and discussing needed cautionary measures with the team will help ensure a safe classroom environment.

Teachers also need to maintain standard precautions to prevent the spread of infection. *Standard precautions* refer to a basic set of practices that school personnel should perform as part of the daily routine, regardless of whether a known infection is present. Standard precautions consist of five major areas: 1) proper hand washing, 2) use of personal protective equipment when indicated (e.g., gloves), 3) proper cleaning of environmental surfaces and handling of contaminated equipment, 4) cough etiquette, and 5) safe injection practices (e.g., Centers for Disease Control and Prevention, 2011). These procedures have been adopted by schools and are used routinely with all students.

Students should also be taught the standard precautions, especially proper hand washing. Hand washing, like other multistep skills, can be broken down into a series of steps referred to as a *task analysis.* The task analysis will need to be modified to meet a student's specific disability. For example, if the student has the use of only one hand, then the task analysis will need to be modified to allow for changes in the hand-washing procedure as well as any needed adaptations to the soap dispenser. Children with other types of disabilities may require such adaptations as the use of handle extensions or scrubbing brushes. In some cases, the student will be able to do only some of the steps and will require assistance with others. Part of the teaching process should include instruction on when hand washing should occur. Hand washing is commonly performed before preparing food, before eating, after using the restroom, before taking medications, and when hands are dirty. In addition to hand washing, students should be taught proper hygiene to reduce the risk of infection. Proper hygiene includes such skills as brushing teeth and hair and washing one's face. Students should learn to use their personal hygiene items and not share them with others. Students should also be taught to cover any open cuts with a Band-Aid to help protect the wound from infection and prevent the leakage of blood into the environment.

Being certain that the classroom emergency evacuation procedures (e.g., in the case of a fire alarm or bomb threat) can be carried out for students who use mobility devices is another important aspect of maintaining a safe, healthy environment. The plan for assisting students with severe and multiple disabilities to move from a classroom to a safe area can often be accomplished, but sometimes little thought is given to how students would evacuate the building if they are in a cafeteria, gymnasium, or other location at the time of an emergency. Several adults are often needed to help evacuate these students. School personnel need a thoughtful plan, with teachers trying out the various evacuation routes to determine whether the route will accommodate a mobility device (e.g., wheelchair, walker) and will safely take students away from the school to the designated area.

School personnel should be prepared for a wide range of emergencies, including basic first aid and cardiopulmonary resuscitation (CPR). Because of the possibility of choking accidents, personnel should be trained on how to assist a person who is choking (e.g., Red Cross's procedure of using back blows and abdominal thrusts). School staff also need to be aware of each student's IHP and ECP. A well-prepared school staff can make a significant difference in the outcome resulting from an emergency.

Finally, information and adequate knowledge can be critical for educators looking to promote a safe, healthy environment for students with severe and multiple disabilities. Teachers specifically need to be knowledgeable about 1) common medical conditions, 2) medications and treatments, 3) health care procedures (including IHPs and ECPs), 4) impact of disabilities on health and school performance and 5) working as a team. These five areas will be described across major sections of this chapter.

COMMON MEDICAL CONDITIONS

Teachers may encounter several common medical conditions in students with severe and multiple disabilities. It is important to know what to look for to detect problems early. Any suspicions should be reported to the parents and school nurse so that the student's physician can be contacted. Dehydration, skin irritation and pressure ulcers, respiratory infections, asthma, ear infections, and contractures are some of the most common medical problems.

Dehydration

Dehydration occurs when the amount of fluids leaving the body (from respiration, urination, defecation, vomiting and/or sweating) exceeds the amount of fluids taken into the body (from drinking and eating). All students are at risk of dehydration from diarrhea or vomiting; however, students with severe and multiple disabilities are at higher risk. This may be due to the student's inability to communicate that he or she is thirsty or the child's lack of mobility skills to obtain a drink of water. In other cases, the higher risk may be due to associated swallowing difficulties that put the student at risk not only for dehydration but also for poor nutrition and possible aspiration (Chadwick, Jolliffe, & Goldbart, 2002). Changes in environmental temperature and humidity can make substantial differences in requirements for fluids, and students with severe and multiple disabilities may be unable to adjust their fluid intake to accommodate these changes. Changes in medications or diet can also alter fluid intake requirements. Even students receiving tube feeding may need their hydration monitored (McGowan, Fenton, Wade, Branton, & Robertson, 2012).

Treatment and Prevention   It is important to be alert for warning signs of dehydration and report any observed symptoms of dehydration to the nurse and parents. An individual who is mildly dehydrated may become restless, thirsty, have decreased urinary output, and have dark yellow urine. Skin turgor (skin elasticity) also becomes reduced (Diggins, 2008). Skin elasticity can be easily evaluated by gently pinching the skin on the back of the hand, abdomen, or thigh. Normally, the skin should immediately retract back into position. The skin retracts into position slowly when an individual is dehydrated (Clynes & O'Connor, 2010).

The individual becomes lethargic, tears are decreased or absent, the mouth is dry, and sunken eyes may be present as dehydration worsens. Signs of shock may occur if dehydration becomes severe, including rapid breathing, rapid heart rate, and low blood pressure. Signs of confusion can be present because the brain is sensitive to dehydration, and unconsciousness eventually ensues (Porter & Kaplan, 2011). Severe dehydration can result in death if not treated.

The treatment of dehydration will depend on its severity. Mild to moderate dehydration may be treated by increasing oral fluid intake. Severe dehydration requires IV fluids (Diggins, 2008). Prevention of dehydration is the best course. Fluids should be given regularly with meals and at regularly scheduled times throughout the day. Students should be taught to request a drink, either verbally or through augmentative and alternative communication (AAC). They also should be taught to use a cup and water fountain to drink independently whenever possible. Communication between home and school is essential to prevent, identify, and manage dehydration.

Skin Irritation and Pressure Ulcers

All students can get scrapes and skin irritation from participating in everyday activities, but students with severe and multiple disabilities are especially prone to developing skin irritations that may lead to infection. This can occur from prolonged contact with sweat, urine, or feces. Many of these students may not be fully toilet trained and thus use diapers. Some students may use external urinary catheters (condom catheters) that collect urine in a leg bag. Other students may have colostomies (i.e., part of the large intestine is brought through a surgical opening in the abdominal area to allow feces to exit the body, often into a colostomy bag). These situations result in an increased likelihood that urine or feces will come in contact with the skin and result in skin irritation.

Personnel should promptly and thoroughly clean the area to prevent skin irritation from occurring. Students also should be taught to perform this skill, either independently or partially, depending on their physical ability. If the student does an inadequate job of cleaning, however, then the adult needs to assist the student to ensure skin health and hygiene.

Students with severe and multiple disabilities may also develop pressure ulcers (i.e., bed sores). Students with physical disabilities (e.g., CP, spina bifida) and developmental delays with neurologic impairments are at higher risk for developing pressure ulcers. This condition is due to decreased mobility, altered nutrition, decreased sensation, urinary incontinence, difficulty communicating, and feeding problems. Pressure ulcers may also develop due to poorly fitting orthoses (e.g., leg brace) or wheelchairs (Coha, 2012).

Treatment and Prevention   Teachers need to be alert for signs of skin irritation and pressure ulcers and report any symptoms they may observe to the nurse and parents. Skin irritation typically appears as skin redness that may be accompanied by swelling or a rash. Treatment will depend on the cause and severity.

The appearance of pressure ulcers will vary depending on how long they have been developing and their severity. Nonblanchable redness in a localized area is all that will be present to indicate the beginning of a pressure ulcer (Pieper, 2012). Keeping weight off of the area may be all that is needed at this point. The condition will worsen without proper treatment, resulting in cell death and skin breakdown. An opening or ulceration on the skin occurs when this happens. The ulceration can extend to the bone without proper treatment. A systemic infection can result in extreme cases, which can be life threatening. Pressure ulcers are always preventable (except at the end of life). Students who use wheelchairs attain pressure relief by standing, performing pressure relief push-ups, having the wheelchair tilted back 65%, and/or leaning forward or shifting weight from side to side every 15 minutes to 1 hour (Bryant & Nix, 2012; Wound, Ostomy and Continence Nurses, 2012). Students who have impaired lower body movement should not sit continuously in their wheelchairs for more than 2 hours. They can be repositioned in other equipment or take short breaks from their wheelchairs and often are taught to request assistance in repositioning themselves. Care should be taken when moving a student to avoid sliding the student's skin against any surface to decrease the risk of tearing the skin.

It is important that students maintain good skin health. For example, the skin should be kept clean and dry because skin that is wet or sweaty has been linked to pressure ulcer formation. Harsh soaps or preparations should be avoided; skin softeners may be helpful. Also, maintaining range of motion and good body alignment and posture can help with decreasing the incidence of skin breakdown. Many types of pressure-minimizing devices, such as special cushions, can help reduce pressure ulcer formation when these devices are carefully selected to address the needs of the child (Bryant & Nix, 2012; Coha, 2012).

The skin should be checked for any signs of skin irritation or pressure ulcers on a regular basis. This includes skin that is under pressure as well as skin that could be irritated from being in contact with equipment such as an orthosis or wheelchair support. Students with impaired sensation may not sense that they are getting a pressure ulcer, or they may be unable to effectively communicate with others. Teachers need to check for redness, irritation, or ulceration (in a way that respects the student's privacy) and report any skin problem to the parent, school nurse, or other designated individual. Whenever possible, students should be taught to inspect their skin for problems and to inform an adult. If a student or teacher detects any signs of skin breakdown, then the student needs to be positioned so that there is no further pressure on the skin where the breakdown is occurring. For example, if a pressure ulcer is detected on a student's buttocks, then the student may be positioned on his or her side.

Respiratory Infections

Many individuals with severe and multiple disabilities have an increased risk of acquiring respiratory infections. Some individuals have physical impairments such as CP that can result in a weak cough and difficulty clearing the airway due to muscular weakness. Secretions then accumulate in the lungs, resulting in bacterial growth that could possibly be followed by serious infection. Many individuals with developmental disabilities also have weak immune systems (Markova & Chuvirov, 2007). It has been found that people with moderate to profound intellectual disabilities are more likely than the general population to die from respiratory infections (Tyrer & McGrother, 2009).

Treatment and Prevention   Prevention is the best course in decreasing the occurrence of respiratory infections. Having good infection control procedures in place will be important (e.g., cover cough). Students receiving tube feeding or who are at risk for aspiration (food going into lungs) will need to eat in an upright position and follow feeding recommendations to decrease the possibility of aspiration. Children who have conditions that result in excess respiratory secretions may use aerosol therapy, postural draining (assuming certain prescribed positions to help in the removal of secretions by gravity), percussion or vibration over the lungs to loosen secretions, suctioning to decrease secretion accumulation and improve respiratory functioning, and other techniques (Heller, Schwartzman, & Fowler, 2009). Teachers may need to adjust a student's activities to include these procedures. It will also be important to provide opportunities for students to engage in regular exercise that may help improve respiratory functioning.

Proper infection control also decreases the risk of transmission of a respiratory infection. Students should be taught to cover their mouths and turn their heads when they cough or sneeze and should be instructed in proper hand washing and toothbrushing techniques. School staff should also engage in hand washing and regularly clean environmental surfaces. Sick students should be sent home to reduce the spread of infection. If a respiratory infection is detected, then school personnel should inform the parents so that they may take their child to the doctor to determine the course of treatment (e.g., medication). Influenza and pneumonia vaccines can play a critical role in preventing respiratory infections in students with increased vulnerability. Although vaccines may be less effective in children with weakened immune systems, ensuring immunization of family members and caregivers provides considerable protection for these students. Although individuals and their health care professionals make the decisions about whether to immunize, school staff can play an important role in helping families understand the role of immunization.

Asthma

Asthma is a chronic respiratory disorder, and a greater percentage of children under age 17 have this disorder compared with adults. Children also experience a higher rate of visits to the emergency department due to asthma as compared with adults. Asthma can result in frequent school absences. The occurrence of this condition in children is high, with an average of nearly three children in a classroom of 30 having asthma (Hester et al., 2013). Students with developmental disabilities have a higher prevalence of concurrent medical conditions, including asthma (see Chapter 5; Schieve et al., 2012).

Asthma is described as a lung disease with reversible airway obstruction and airway inflammation. An increased responsiveness (or hyperreactivity) to a variety of stimuli is also present. Students who have asthma usually have no difficulty breathing unless they are exposed to a trigger that results in an acute episode known as an asthma attack. Students will vary as to what triggers an asthma attack. Some common triggers include allergens (i.e., substances the person is allergic to such as animal dander, dust mites, molds), infection (e.g., sinusitis), exercise, change in weather, air pollution, certain foods, certain medications (e.g., aspirin), reflux (i.e., stomach contents flowing back up the esophagus) and intense emotions (Centers for Disease Control and Prevention, 2006; Heller et al., 2009).

Treatment and Prevention   School-based asthma education programs may help increase awareness of asthma management and result in improved outcomes for children with asthma (Hester et al., 2013; Toole, 2013). Teachers need to maintain a healthy school environment, even if there is not a formal program, by trying to minimize the student's exposure to the triggers of an asthma attack. If a student is allergic to a pet in the classroom, then the animal should be moved to a different location. Students with exercise-induced asthma may need medication prior to exercising and require close monitoring during physical activity. There may be exercise restrictions in some instances. Students who are sensitive to pollution may need to stay indoors on days with high levels of pollution.

Teachers also need to know the signs indicating when a student is having an asthma attack and what to do should one occur. An asthma attack typically consists of episodes of shortness of breath, wheezing, and difficulty breathing due to the narrowing of the airway from inflammation and secretion obstruction. Wheezing may be absent, however, when extreme respiratory distress is present. Shortness of breath may be so severe that the student is unable to walk or talk.

In most cases, medication such as a rescue inhaler will need to be given near the onset of an attack. A plan must be in place if the inhaler does not relieve the symptoms, however. An ambulance should be called if a student is having severe difficulty breathing and medication is not working. Although rare, deaths have occurred from asthma. Students should be taught what to do when an attack occurs, including communicating on an AAC device that they are having trouble breathing and learning how to administer the inhaler themselves (Heller et al., 2009).

Otitis Media

Children often acquire otitis media, an infection of the middle ear. It is often associated with upper respiratory tract infection, such as a cold (Waterson, Helms, & Ward-Platt, 2005). The infection travels along the eustachian tube into the middle ear, causing the middle ear infection. Risk factors for developing otitis media include lying supine on one's back during feeding, not being fully immunized, exposure to second-hand smoke, and the occurrence of developmental disorders and other inherited conditions. Children who have specific disabilities that can result in eustachian tube dysfunction are at higher risk, including children with Down syndrome, Williams syndrome, Apert syndrome, fragile X syndrome, Turner syndrome, and autism (Zeisel & Roberts, 2003).

Treatment and Prevention   The first sign of an ear infection is typically a persistent earache, which may be accompanied by fever, nausea, vomiting, and diarrhea in young children (Porter & Kaplan, 2011). Children may experience a mild to moderate conductive hearing loss in some instances, although some children may have a more severe hearing loss (50 dB or greater) (Zeisel & Roberts, 2003). Students with severe and multiple disabilities may rub their ears, head bang, or engage in other self-injurious behaviors when otitis media is present (O'Reilly, 1997). When these types of behaviors occur, it is always important to rule out a medical basis for the behavior. Also, it is important that students are taught to communicate pain or discomfort. The school should notify the parents when a student communicates that his or her ear hurts, and they should take the student to a physician for examination because serious complications can occur (e.g., meningitis). Medical treatment may include antibiotics (for those at high risk), analgesics (e.g., acetaminophen), and decongestants. Tympanostomy tubes (ear tubes) may be placed in the ear when the child has had multiple recurrent infections of otitis media or a persistent ear infection. The tubes allow fluid to drain from the ear, improving hearing (Harmes et al., 2013). The teacher will need to make appropriate modifications when otitis media is present and hearing is affected (see Chapter 4).

Contractures

A contracture is a permanent shortening of a muscle or joint that limits the mobility of joints and can restrict activity (Farmer & James, 2001). Contractures occur when students have conditions resulting in limited movement, immobilization, muscle weakness, paralysis, or spasticity (e.g., CP, stroke, Duchenne muscular dystrophy). There is an imbalance between opposing muscles in muscle weakness and spasticity, resulting in the stronger or spastic muscles continuously contracting and pulling the limb into a deformed position that results in a contracture. Fibro-fatty connective tissue moves into the joint space when joint mobility is present, resulting in adhesions that affect the mobility of the joint and can result in a contracture (Farmer & James, 2001). Contractures result in a decrease in range of motion. For example, a contracture of the elbow will result in the inability to straighten the arm. A contracture can interfere with everyday tasks, such as sitting, walking, and eating, depending on its location and severity.

Treatment and Prevention   The physician may order physical therapy and/or occupational therapy to help prevent contractures or their progression. The therapists may have the student go through range-of-motion stretching exercises that often can be integrated into functional activities. Several studies, however (e.g., Katalinic, Harvey, & Herbert, 2011), have found that stretching does not result in clinically important changes in joint mobility, pain, or spasticity in individuals with neurological conditions. Bracing equipment (e.g., orthoses) may help maintain alignment and decrease the development of contractures, or a variety of medications and treatments may be given to try to relax or inhibit spastic muscles. Contractions will often still develop and require surgery to correct, despite the best treatment and practices (Smith, Chambers, Subramaniam, & Lieber, 2012; Tilton, 2006). The factors that predispose an individual to the development and worsening of contractions, however, are still present even after treatment, so it is important that long-term management programs be developed and followed (Farmer & James, 2001).

It is important to encourage students to be active and to use their arms and legs as much as possible in the classroom. For example, most students with hemiplegic CP will have a tendency to use the arm unaffected by CP and not the affected side. Doing so typically results in the formation of contractures on the affected side. The teacher should encourage the student to use the affected arm in order to help prevent or lessen contractures. Teachers can prompt students to participate in activities that require both arms (e.g., picking up a ball) or position desirable materials near the affected arm to promote its use.

MEDICATIONS AND TREATMENTS

Students with severe and multiple disabilities often take medications for a wide range of disorders. Teachers should be familiar with their students' medications to help determine their effectiveness and be able to recognize and report any side effects. Ideally, teachers may teach some of their students with severe and multiple disabilities to participate in certain aspects of medication management (e.g., remembering when to take their medications, positioning themselves for medication administration). Teachers also may need to know certain types of treatments aimed at addressing emergency situations (e.g., rescue inhaler for asthma).

Medication Guidelines

School personnel who are involved in administering medication need to be familiar with proper medication guidelines related to storing and administering medications. In addition, students should also be encouraged to assist in taking their medications whenever possible.

Receiving and Storing Medications Schools should accept prescription and over-the-counter (nonprescription) medications only when accompanied with a permission form. The medication should be in its original container and have the student's name, dosage, and frequency of administration. The pharmacy's and physician's telephone numbers should also accompany the medication in case they need to be contacted.

The expiration date should be checked upon receiving medication. The month displayed indicates that the medication will expire at the end of that month. The person receiving the medication should also check how the medication is to be stored. Some medications cannot be exposed to light, whereas others need to be stored in the refrigerator. For medications requiring refrigeration, it is important that the medication never be placed in the refrigerator door because that portion of the refrigerator may not be cold enough when the door is frequently opened. All medications should be kept in a secure, locked storage container. The only exceptions to this are medications taken on an as-needed basis that must be close at hand for emergencies, such as an inhaler for asthma or medication for severe insect sting allergy.

Administration of Medications Schools should have policies in place regarding who can administer medications. If nonnursing personnel are allowed to administer such medication, then it is important that they be given proper training, typically by the school nurse. Although directions for administering oral medications may seem obvious, situations can arise that necessitate giving the medication to the student when he or she is unwilling to take it, making administration difficult. Also, nonoral routes of administration, such as nebulizer use, may not be as familiar to nonnursing personnel.

Several practices should be put in place to prevent errors in medication administration. First, the person who is administering the medication should check the five Rs: 1) right student, 2) right drug, 3) right dose, 4) right route, and 5) right time (Lippincott, Williams, & Wilkins, 2012). Second, any precautions should be noted, such as whether the medication should be taken with food. Third, the person administering the medication should then check it for contamination or spoilage by looking for a change in the medication's color, consistency, or odor. Fourth, the medication label should be read three times: 1) when taking it out of storage, 2) before giving it, and 3) before returning it to storage. Finally, a form should be used to document when the medication was administered. A sample form that can be used to report medications and health care procedures is provided in Figure 6.1.

The form of a medication is also important. For example, some oral medications can be crushed and mixed with food, but others must be swallowed whole. Medications for students with severe and multiple disabilities are often provided as liquid suspensions that must be shaken well before use. Some doses will be much too weak to be effective without adequate shaking, whereas others may be massive overdoses.

Many possible problems can occur during medication administration, including side effects, allergic reactions, intolerance, missed dosage, overmedication, incomplete administration, wrong medication or dose, and choking. It is important that the person administering the medication and the school staff know what to do if such problems arise. A plan should be made for each separate medication that specifies what to do if one of these problems should occur. It is essential to prepare before a problem happens.

Teaching Students to Be Involved in Medication Administration Some students with severe and multiple disabilities can be taught to take their medication with assistance or supervision. These students are taught the times they take each of their medications. Some may learn this schedule through a picture or object schedule. Others may be taught to use a compartmentalized dispenser that separates the pills into the different times of the day they are to be administered.

Learning the purposes of the medications is also important for students. Some students may be able to learn what each medication is for or have

Monthly Medication/Procedure Report

Student's name: <u>Joe Smith</u>   Month: <u>February</u>

Direction: Write the medications/procedures, dates and times for each week. At the beginning of each day, write in the times for that day. When procedure is performed, cross out times and initial. If not done, circle time. If done at different time, circle time and record new time.

Meds/procedure	Dates	Time(s)	Mon.	Tues.	Wed.	Thurs.	Fri.
Dilantin 5 mg oral	2/1–2/5	10	~~10~~^{KH}	~~10~~^{KH}			
Tube feed	2/1–2/5	9 12	~~9~~^{KH} ~~12~~^{KH}	~~9~~^{KH} (12)$^{1:30\ KH}$			
Suction	2/1–2/5	p.r.n.	~~10~~^{KH} ~~2:30~~^{KH}	~~9~~^{KH} ~~12:45~~^{KH}			

Meds/procedure	Dates	Time(s)	Mon.	Tues.	Wed.	Thurs.	Fri.

Meds/procedure	Dates	Time(s)	Mon.	Tues.	Wed.	Thurs.	Fri.

Meds/procedure	Dates	Time(s)	Mon.	Tues.	Wed.	Thurs.	Fri.

Figure 6.1. Sample monthly medication/procedure report. (Republished with permission of South-Western College Publishing, a division of Cengage Learning, from Heller, K.W., Forney, P.E., Alberto, P.A., Schwartzman, M.N., & Goeckel, T. (2000). *Meeting physical and health needs of children with disabilities: Teaching student participation and management.* Permission conveyed through Copyright Clearance Center, Inc.)

information programmed on their AAC device (e.g., THAT IS MY SEIZURE PILL, THAT IS TO HELP ME BREATHE). Errors are decreased and independence is promoted when students are able to identify their medications.

Medications for Emergencies

In addition to becoming familiar with their students' regular medications and observing for effectiveness and any side effects, teachers may also need to administer medications used in emergencies. Examples of these include a rescue inhaler, Diastat, and EpiPen. There may also be emergency treatments required, such as vagus nerve stimulation. When students require these types of emergency medications or treatments, teachers should receive proper training from the school nurse or their administration and have ECPs in place (or emergency plans as part of the IHP).

Rescue Inhaler   Students with asthma may have an asthma attack at school and need to use their rescue inhaler (short-acting bronchodilator for emergencies). First, the rescue inhaler needs to be kept where the student can easily access it, which is usually with the student. Instances have occurred in which students have died when no one could get the inhaler in time. In one situation, a 12-year-old boy had an asthma attack during recess at school and died trying to get to the office where the rescue inhaler was locked. In this instance, the parent reported that the school would continually confiscate spare inhalers from the student because the school wanted to keep it locked in an office (Canadian Press, 2013).

School personnel also need to be sure they can recognize signs of an asthma attack, and they need to believe the student if he or she says the inhaler is needed. As previously discussed, an asthma attack usually consists of shortness of breath, wheezing, and difficulty breathing. It will be important to discuss with the parents how the student looks or behaves when having an asthma attack, especially for children who cannot communicate that they are having an attack. In some instances, students with severe or multiple disabilities may be unable to use a rescue inhaler correctly, and a nebulizer may be used instead. A nebulizer is a device that uses compressed air to turn liquid medication into a mist that is inhaled into the lungs. When a nebulizer is used, teachers will need to be familiar with the device (e.g., how to add the medication into the device, how to hold it, how to determine when all the medication is administered).

Teachers need to understand the student's procedure for rescue inhaler use, including the use of a spacer. A spacer is a tube or container that attaches to the rescue inhaler, adding a space between the rescue inhaler and the child's mouth so as to provide better delivery of the medication. Physicians often order a spacer to be used with the rescue inhaler. One typical procedure of using a rescue inhaler with a spacer is as follows: 1) insert rescue inhaler mouthpiece into spacer, 2) remove mouthpiece cover from spacer, 3) hold upright and shake the rescue inhaler to mix the medication, 4) have student exhale slowly through pursed lips, 5) press down on rescue inhaler canister that dispenses the medication, 6) after activation, have the child inhale slowly and deeply through the mouth for about 10 seconds, 7) have the student then exhale and relax, 8) follow directions on the student's medical emergency response plan (or IHP) of what should happen if the asthma attack is not relieved (e.g., repeat use, call 911), 9) if rescue inhaler use was successful, rinse mouth with water, and 10) clean equipment (Smith, Duell, & Martin, 2011). Even students who self-administer their rescue inhaler may not be doing it correctly and might need to have their rescue inhaler use monitored for accuracy.

Diastat   Although seizures are typically brief and self-limiting, some individuals may go into a continuous convulsive seizure or acute repetitive seizures and require medication to stop the seizure activity (see Chapter 5). In these instances, a student may have a physician's order for Diastat. Medication given shortly after a seizure begins is more effective (Sem, 2013).

Diastat (or Diastat AcuDial) is also known as Diazepam or Valium. It is a fast-acting rectal gel that is administered through a prefilled, dose delivery system for seizures. The procedure of administering Diastat is as follows: 1) place the student on his or her side and lower clothing, 2) remove cap of Diastat syringe and lubricate tip (pharmacist should have adjusted Diastat to appropriate dose, which is visible in the dose display window), 3) bend upper leg forward and separate buttocks to expose rectum, 4) gently insert tip of syringe into rectum and push plunger over 3 seconds until it stops, 5) slowly count to three before removing syringe from rectum, 6) remove plunger from rectum and hold buttocks together for a count of three to promote retention, 7) keep student on side, observe student, and follow his or her ECP (of what steps to take next or what to do if the seizure does not stop) (Coffey & Obringer, 2009; Lexicomp, 2013).

There has been debate regarding who can give Diastat. Emergency medications, like all medications, are regulated by state laws, school district policies, and state nurse practice acts. Students who have lifesaving medications should have a nursing assessment, and an ECP should be developed (Zacharski, Kain, Fleming, & Pontius, 2012). Training should be required when unlicensed school employees are authorized to give Diastat when a nurse is not available (e.g., Chapter 560 in California) (Sem, 2013). The use of Diastat should be included in the student's ECP (or IHP), which provides information on what the student's specific seizure looks like and the step-by-step directions of what to do when a seizure occurs. This would also include when an ambulance should be called (e.g., after 5 minutes of seizure activity, when a seizure stops and immediately restarts) and any specific directions pertaining to Diastat use (e.g., stay with student and monitor reactions).

Vagus Nerve Stimulation   Some students' seizures will be well controlled with medication, whereas other students may continue to have seizures or require surgery or vagus nerve stimulation (VNS). A VNS is a device that is implanted under the skin in the chest and has a wire that wraps around the vagus nerve in the neck (see Chapter 5). The VNS produces mild, regular electrical

impulses to the vagus nerve that travel to the brain to prevent or reduce seizures (Schachter, 2006). Vagus nerve stimulation has been found to be effective
in reducing seizures in children with seizure disorders that are difficult to treat
(Colicchio et al., 2012; Murphy, Torkelson, Dowler, Simon, & Hudson, 2003).
When a student with a VNS has a seizure or detects the onset of a seizure, there
is usually a doctor's order to use a magnet to cause the device to deliver an immediate, on-demand electrical stimulation in addition to the regular, intermittent stimulation that the device delivers. Using a magnet has been reported in
stopping the seizure, shortening the seizure, or decreasing its severity (Tatum
& Helmers, 2009).

Teachers should receive training on magnet use when they have students
who have VNS and orders to use the magnet. This should become part of
the student's ECP (or IHP). Typically, the steps of magnet use are as follows:
1) retrieve the magnet that comes with the device (which should always be near
the student) at the earliest sign of an aura or seizure, 2) swipe the magnet across
the pulse generator, and 3) if the seizure continues, then follow physician directions as to how often this should be repeated (e.g., three times at 1-minute
intervals) and when 911 should be called. It is important that the teacher does
not stop and hold the magnet over the pulse generator because that turns the
device off. Clear step-by-step written directions should be provided as part
of the training to be sure magnet-induced stimulation is properly performed
(Tatum & Helmers, 2009).

EpiPen Students with life-threatening allergies may need to use an epinephrine auto-injector (e.g., EpiPen) in the school setting when anaphylaxis
occurs and should have an ECP with step-by-step directions of what to do in
case of a dangerous allergic reaction. Anaphylaxis is a severe, possibly fatal,
systemic allergic reaction that can suddenly occur when the student is in contact with an allergy-causing substance, including food (e.g., peanuts), medication (e.g., sulfa drugs, latex), and insect venom (e.g., bee sting). Signs and
symptoms of anaphylaxis vary across individuals and can look different with
the same individual on different occasions. Some signs and symptoms include
headache, dizziness, confusion, hives, itching, swelling of lips/tongue, shortness of breath, chest tightness, wheezing, low blood pressure, chest pain, fast
heart rate, cramping, abdominal pain, and vomiting (Gupta, 2014). School
personnel need to know how to recognize anaphylaxis and appropriately administer an epinephrine auto-inject device, such as an EpiPen, because a delay
in its administration increases the risk for fatality (Bock, Munoz-Furlong, &
Sampson, 2007; Luu et al., 2012; Pumphrey, 2000). Fast and correct administration of an epinephrine auto-inject device is critical because about 10% of fatal
food-associated anaphylactic reactions occur in the school setting (Bock et al.,
2007; Luu et al., 2012).

Students with known allergies leading to anaphylaxis are encouraged
to have two EpiPens available. Due to the possibility of students having unknown allergies leading to anaphylaxis, the School Access to Emergency

Epinephrine Act of 2013 (PL 113-48) encourages states to require schools to stock undesignated epinephrine auto-injectors, and several states have enacted laws that require public schools to keep auto-injectors in the school with regular training on anaphylaxis emergency management plans (Cicutto et al., 2012; Gupta, 2014).

Teachers and school personnel will need to receive training from the school nurse on the use of the student's epinephrine auto-injector. There are four steps for administering an EpiPen: 1) remove grey safety cap, 2) place the black tip against the mid-outer thigh, 3) apply firm pressure against the end of the device until a click is heard (this activates the device), 4) hold device in place for 10 seconds, then remove (Luu et al., 2012). Training EpiPens are available to assist with proper instruction.

HEALTH CARE PROCEDURES

Many students with severe and multiple disabilities require various health care procedures, which often need to be performed during school hours. Procedures such as tube feeding, clean intermittent catheterization, suctioning, colostomy care, oxygen delivery, and ventilator management are encountered in the school environment (Heller & Avant, 2011). Teachers need to be familiar with these procedures to effectively monitor for problems, assist with implementation, and help determine if students can learn to self-perform all or part of their own health care procedure as educational goals. This section begins by discussing policy and procedures regarding students' health care, then proceeds with an overview of two common health care procedures (tube feeding and clean intermittent catheterization), followed by descriptions of IHPs, ECPs, individualized education programs (IEPs), and instructional considerations.

Policy Guidelines and Role Responsibilities for Health Care Procedures

Although the question of who is responsible for providing health care procedures for students has generated controversy, Supreme Court decisions have made it clear that it is the school's responsibility to provide these services. *Irving Independent School District v. Tatro* (1984) was a landmark case that involved a boy with spina bifida who required clean intermittent catheterization. The Supreme Court's decision obligated the schools to provide health care services as related services if three criteria were met: 1) the child required special education, 2) the child was unable to participate in an educational program without the necessary service being performed during the school day, and 3) the procedure did not require a physician but could be performed by a nurse or other qualified person (Rapport, 1996). Similarly, *Cedar Rapids Community School District v. Garret F.* (1999) involved a student with a spinal cord injury who required several health care procedures, including ventilator management, tracheostomy suctioning, urinary catheterization, and blood pressure monitoring. The Supreme Court supported its previous ruling in the Tatro case that obligated the school system to provide the necessary health care services, thus enabling students with complex health care needs to be provided with necessary supports in the school environment.

Public schools are abiding by these legal rulings, and nurses, teachers, paraprofessionals, and other school personnel are performing health care procedures in the school setting when they are required during school hours. The decision as to who will provide the health care service is based on health laws, state regulations, education law, and local regulations. Health care laws, such as state nurse practice acts, provide the legal parameters of nursing practice. Due to the nursing shortage, most states' nurse practice acts authorize registered nurses to delegate nursing tasks under certain circumstances. If delegation is determined to be appropriate, then nurses will provide training and supervision to the unlicensed personnel. This practice has often resulted in teachers and paraprofessionals being trained to perform health care procedures under the nurse's supervision, with the nurse retaining accountability for the appropriateness of delegating the health care procedure (American Nurses Association, 2006). Some health care procedures may not be delegated because of the health status of the student, the complexity of the health care procedure, or the inability of the unlicensed personnel to master the skills needed to perform the procedure.

Registered nurses do more than perform procedures; they assess students' health and make professional clinical judgments regarding interventions and plan of care. School administrators may erroneously delegate health care procedures without understanding the regulations that guide delegation (Heller & Avant, 2011; Resha, 2010) or the changes that are necessary in implementing a procedure in a school setting (which may result in a different or more rigorous protocol). Legal rulings have supported the role of the school nurse in determining delegation (e.g., *Mitts v. Hillsboro Union High School District* [1990], *Moye by Moye v. Special School District No. 6* [1995]). Having nurses determine when delegation is appropriate protects school children by ensuring the circumstances are right for delegating the procedure, thus avoiding possible injury or harm that can occur. Also, teachers should keep in mind that even if the procedure is not delegated, it is important that those school personnel who are in contact with the student understand the procedure and know what to do if a problem occurs.

Training Issues

Appropriate training must be in place if a procedure is going to be delegated to unlicensed personnel (e.g., teacher, paraprofessional). Although other teachers and parents may be familiar with the procedure, training should be provided by a registered nurse or other qualified medical personnel who can also provide appropriate supervision (Gursky & Ryser, 2007; Heller & Avant, 2011). More than one person typically receives the training so that back-up personnel are available should the primary person be absent from school. It is also important to remember that the procedure may be performed differently in the school setting (e.g., a procedure such as suctioning a tracheostomy may use a sterile technique in the school setting [with sterile gloves, sterile catheter and sterile procedure] for better infection control, whereas a clean technique may be satisfactory in the home environment).

Training usually consists of 1) the rationale for and correct implementation of each step of the procedure; 2) the ability to identify early subtle signs of side effects, problems, or complications; 3) knowledge of appropriate interventions when side effects, problems, or complications occur; 4) knowledge of emergency procedures; 5) knowledge of how to document giving medications or performing procedures; and 6) documentation of training (Heller & Avant, 2011; Heller, Fredrick, Dykes, Best, & Cohen, 2000). Training should occur with the actual student over several guided sessions. The steps of the procedure should also be provided in written format. Information should be provided on what should be monitored, what problems to look for, and what to do if problems occur. Knowledge of emergency procedures must also be in place.

The person performing the procedures should be shown how to maintain documentation each time the procedure is performed. A simple form with the times checked to indicate that the procedure was performed can easily be maintained. If it is determined that the teacher (or other designated person) is not comfortable performing the procedure when training is finished, then further training should be given until the person is comfortable, or someone else should be selected. A health care procedure should not be delegated to someone who is unable to perform the procedure.

After the teacher or adult has been trained on the procedure and on associated problems and interventions, a form may be used to document that the training took place and the nurse has verified the trainee's competence performing the procedure with a particular student. It is important to note that health care procedures are considered nongeneralizable across students. For example, if a teacher has demonstrated knowledge and skill in performing tube feeding with Susan, then the teacher will need to be taught to tube feed Joe because subtle differences may exist between the two students, or the procedure may be slightly different. Training and documentation of the training are student specific, not procedure specific.

Once someone has successfully completed training, he or she should receive periodic supervision. Several areas may be evaluated through a series of questions:

1. Is the procedure still being performed as trained?

2. Is the procedure being performed in a safe and effective manner?

3. Is the record-keeping system sufficient and not cumbersome?

4. Are staffing needs adequate?

5. Are the parents comfortable with how the procedure is being performed?

6. Is communication between the school and home ongoing and effective?

7. Is the process supportive of the student's educational program?

8. Is there ready access to the student's ECP and IHP (Heller, 2004)?

If any problems are identified, then additional training may be needed or adaptations may need to be put in place. Ongoing supervision ensures that the procedures are being performed correctly and that the necessary supports are in place so that the procedure goes smoothly. As mentioned previously, two of the most common procedures that teachers may encounter are tube feeding and clean intermittent catheterization.

Tube Feeding (Enteral Feeding)

Some students with severe and multiple disabilities are unable to obtain proper fluids and nutrition orally due to conditions resulting in problems such as impaired swallowing (e.g., severe CP with oral-motor difficulties, stroke); obstruction along the throat, esophagus, and stomach (e.g., tumors, congenital abnormalities); altered level of consciousness affecting ability to eat; and inadequate oral intake (e.g., cystic fibrosis, human immunodeficiency virus wasting, facial injury) (Wireko, 2010). A tube may be placed into the student's stomach or intestines when these conditions are present and interfere with eating, and a liquid nutritional formula is delivered through the tube to provide proper nutritional support. This is referred to as *tube feeding* or *enteral feeding*.

Tube feeding is most commonly delivered as nasogastric feeding or gastric feeding. Nasogastric feeding is performed with a polyvinyl or polyurethane nasogastric tube (NG tube) that is passed through the nose (naso) and into the stomach (gastric). In some cases, the tube may be placed through the mouth to the stomach (orogastric) or placed through the nose to the small intestine (nasojejunal). This type of route is typically temporary and used on a short-term basis. The NG tube may be inserted prior to each feeding or remain in place. In either case, when this type of route is used, the tube must be checked for proper placement every time before the feeding is given. It is possible that the tube can became dislodged and go into the trachea (windpipe). If this occurs and placement is not checked prior to feeding, the food will go directly into the lungs and result in an emergency situation.

Gastric feeding occurs through a gastrostomy, in which an artificial opening is made through the stomach wall and a tube is inserted for feeding. In some cases, the tube will be placed into the small intestine (jejunal or duodenal feedings) to decrease the risk of food aspiration (caused by formula that is inhaled into the lungs due to conditions such as reflux and vomiting) (Lippincott et al., 2012). There are different types of gastrostomy tubes. They are often used on a long-term basis, but they are not necessarily permanent because some children may be able to take sufficient food orally at a future time and can have the gastrostomy tube taken out and the opening closed. When a student has a PEG tube (or balloon type gastrostomy tube that was placed surgically), a tube can be seen coming through the skin and is usually coiled and taped against the skin when not in use. When a student has a low-profile gastrostomy tube, all that can be seen is a small opening and a small cap that closes off the opening of the gastrostomy button. When feeding occurs with a low-profile device, an extension tube is attached to the device through which liquid nourishment can be delivered.

Tube feedings may be delivered in a variety of ways. Some students are fed using a bolus method in which a syringe barrel is attached to the end of the tube (or the connecting tube of a low-profile gastrostomy tube). The formula is poured into the syringe barrel and is delivered by gravity over a short period of time several times during the day (e.g., every 4 hours). The girl in Figure 6.2 has a low-profile gastrostomy tube and is participating in performing her own

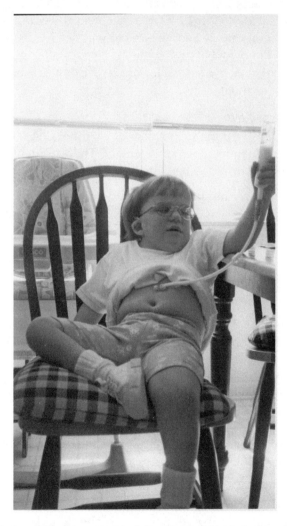

Figure 6.2.   A girl feeding herself through her gastrostomy button using the bolus tube-feeding method. (Republished with permission of South-Western College Publishing, a division of Cengage Learning, from Heller, K.W., Forney, P.E., Alberto, P.A., Schwartzman, M.N., & Goeckel, T. (2000). *Meeting physical and health needs of children with disabilities: Teaching student participation and management.* Permission conveyed through Copyright Clearance Center, Inc.)

feeding using the bolus method. Another method uses an intermittent gravity drip method in which the formula is usually in a bag and drips more slowly over a longer period of time. A third method is a continuous method in which the formula is given continuously throughout the day. Feeding may only be cyclic in some cases, in which the formula is given only at certain times, such as while the student sleeps at night.

The physician will determine the type of delivery based on what the student can tolerate. If the student cannot tolerate bolus feedings (e.g., cramping, nausea, significant amount food still in the stomach when it is time for next feeding), then the physician may order a much slower method that delivers small amounts of food over a longer period of time, such as with the intermittent gravity drip method or the continuous method. When a slower delivery method is used, the student may have a mechanical feeding pump to deliver the food at a constant rate. School personnel will need to be familiar with the feeding pump and know what to do if an alarm goes off (e.g., tubing is kinked and formula cannot be delivered so alarm goes off; device is not plugged in and low-battery alarm sounds).

Tube-Feeding Guidelines   Several basic guidelines pertain to all methods of tube feeding. It is important that school personnel be familiar with them for safe and correct tube-feeding management. These guidelines are as follows (Heller, 2004; Heller, Forney, Alberto, Schwartzman, & Goeckel, 2000):

1. School personnel should know if the student can take any food or drink by mouth.

2. Tubing should be checked for placement (if an NG tube) and patency (openness).

3. Students should never be fed flat on their backs; they should be elevated at least 30 degrees. Students may be tube fed sitting upright or on their side.

4. Tube feeding should be given at an appropriate rate because feeding too fast can result in cramping, diarrhea, nausea, vomiting, and reflux with a risk of aspiration. The higher the syringe barrel or feeding bag is placed, the faster the rate of delivery when using gravity.

5. Correct tube-feeding procedure involves preventing air from entering the stomach because this can cause cramping, diarrhea, nausea, and vomiting.

6. Usually, the liquid should be given at room temperature. Storage of unused feeding should follow the package insert or physician's orders. Refrigeration is often necessary.

7. Equipment should be properly cleaned. Cleaning with soap and water is usually all that is needed, but personnel should follow the procedure given by the physician or nurse.

8. Personnel should know what they should do for the common problems associated with this health care procedure—aspiration, tube displacement,

nausea, vomiting, cramping, diarrhea, site infection, leaking of stomach contents, and clogged tube.

9. Appropriate training and supervision should occur for school personnel involved with the student.

10. The educational team should determine if the student can or will learn to perform or partially participate in the performance of the health care procedure.

Clean Intermittent Catheterization

Some students with severe and multiple disabilities are unable to empty their bladder normally and will require clean intermittent catheterization in which a catheter (tube) is inserted into the urethra and up into the bladder. The catheter stays in place only long enough for all of the urine to be expelled from the bladder and then is removed. This is often repeated several times during the day. The procedure typically is used to treat students who have neurogenic bladders resulting from conditions such as spinal cord injury or spina bifida. A *neurogenic bladder* refers to an abnormality of the nerves that control the bladder and the sphincter (muscle that allows urine to be released from the bladder). Children with neurogenic bladders cannot feel when their bladders are full and are unable to control their sphincters. The damaged nerves will result in the sphincter muscle being too loose in some children, so urine will dribble continually, which increases the risk of pressure ulcers and skin irritation. Other children with neurogenic bladders may have sphincters that are too tight and that require a lot of pressure in the bladder to allow the sphincter to open, which can result in complications by the urine being forced backward toward the kidney (reflux) (Shaer, 1997). Kidney infections and kidney damage can occur over time. An abnormally tight sphincter may also result in the bladder not completely emptying the urine, which increases the risk of infection.

The clean intermittent catheterization procedure is a clean procedure, meaning that the procedure is not sterile (e.g., no sterile gloves, no sterile technique). When a physician orders clean intermittent catheterization, he or she may decide that the catheter can be reused multiple times as long as it is thoroughly cleaned between uses. In some instances, the physician may decide that a sterile catheter should be used and discarded after a one-time use. In both of these instances, the procedure uses a clean technique in which only clean (not sterile) gloves are worn. Studies have shown no differences between using sterile or clean technique in regard to incidence of urinary tract infection (Moore, Fader, & Getliffe, 2007; Wyndaele et al., 2012). A urinary tract infection, however, is the most frequent complication of catheterization. Instead of the classic symptoms of a urinary tract infection, such as frequent and urgent urination and discomfort urinating, symptoms of a urinary tract infection may present differently in children with neurogenic bladders. They may also have fever, pain in the area of the bladder, new onset of incontinence, blood in the urine, impaired general well-being, decreased bladder capacity, and increase in general spasticity (Pannek, 2011; Wyndaele et al., 2012). Teachers need to be alert for signs of urinary tract infection and alert the nurse and parents should one be suspected.

Some students cannot be catheterized through the urethra due to difficultly gaining access to the urethral opening, discomfort on catheterization, or structural abnormalities. The student in these cases may have a catheterisable urinary stoma. A urinary stoma is an opening on the abdomen (or through the umbilicus) that is surgically created, and a channel is made from the opening on the abdomen to the bladder for urine to pass through. No differences are found in the level of acceptance between children using urethral catheterization or those catheterized through the urinary stoma (Mitrofanoff catheterization), although fewer episodes of urinary tract infection and greater adherence to the procedure have been found in children who had a catheterisable urinary stoma (Kari et al., 2013).

Clean Intermittent Catheterization Guidelines   Several basic guidelines pertain to clean intermittent catheterization. It is important that school personnel be familiar with these guidelines for the safety and correct management of students receiving this procedure:

1. Be sure catheterization occurs at the times specified. It is typically ordered every 3–4 hours.

2. When assisting a student to catheterize, the student should be treated with dignity and respect at all times.

3. Catheterization should occur in a private location.

4. Adults assisting the student should always wear gloves. Plastic gloves will need to be used rather than latex gloves if a latex allergy is present or if the student has a disability in which there is a high incidence of latex allergies (e.g., spina bifida).

5. Personnel should know what to do to address the common problems associated with this health care procedure—infection, inability to pass the catheter, omission of catheterization, no urine on catheterizations, urine between catheterizations, bleeding, swelling, and discharge.

6. Appropriate training and supervision should occur for school personnel involved with the student.

7. The educational team should determine if the student should be taught to perform or partially participate in the performance of the health care procedure.

8. If a girl is being taught to perform the procedure, then she should be taught not to rely on a mirror to view the area of catheter insertion because problems can occur should a mirror be unavailable.

Individualized Health Care Plan and Emergency Care Plan

The ECP and IHP are two important plans that may be created for students with special health care needs. These documents should align with the student's physician's orders and should be regularly updated through communication with the physician. The school nurse is responsible for the management of the IHP and ECP and should collaborate with school personnel and parents (or caregivers) on plan development and communicate the plan to all appropriate personnel (Council on School Health, 2008).

Students who have chronic conditions or require health care procedures should have an IHP. An IHP is designed to provide vital information regarding a student's medical condition and contains a plan to address the student's health needs. IHPs vary as to the information contained in them. Some students will have IHPs that cover an array of areas such as medical history, current medical condition, type of health care procedures being performed, feeding and diet considerations, special equipment and devices, and transportation needs (Heller & Avant, 2011). If a student has one or more health care procedures, then an IHP should contain each of these procedures as well.

IHPs addressing health care procedures contain general and specialized information. The IHP will typically include student information, emergency contacts, medical history, and the nursing plan of care (which contains the nursing assessment, diagnosis, goals of care, intervention, and expected outcomes) that the nurse has created in collaboration with the educational team. It provides important information on training staff and/or the student in the performance of a procedure as well as important health information (e.g., asthma triggers, type of epilepsy, whether a student can take food by mouth in addition to having tube feeding). In addition, many IHPs will include a section that contains an action plan for school personnel that consists of three parts: 1) conditions requiring monitoring and interventions, 2) specialized information regarding the health care procedure, and 3) common health care problems and actions (Heller & Avant, 2011). IHPs should be written for students with a range of medical conditions and for students who require health care procedures.

Susie Jones is an 8-year-old girl with CP who is fed through a gastrostomy tube. Her IHP contains information about why she needs tube feedings and addresses whether she can take food orally, which she cannot do because of risk for aspiration (see Figure 6.3). The IHP contains goals, interventions, and outcomes, one of which is for her to learn to partially or fully participate in tube feeding herself. The IHP also has specialized information specific to Susie's tube feeding, such as the tube feeding route, type of delivery, type of formula used, preparation of formula, and tube feeding schedule. This IHP also indicates that a written procedure is attached and lists the typical feeding problems and emergencies, detailing the appropriate responses for each. Susie's mother, the school nurse, and the teacher collaborated on this section to determine what would be the appropriate actions to take for Susie. For example, for tube displacement, Susie's school nurse has the appropriate skills to replace the tube, and mom agrees with this plan. (For other children, the parent may come in to replace the tube, or the student may go to the emergency room or doctor's office).

Name: <u>Susie Jones</u>   Date: <u>3/1/02</u>

School: <u>Banks Elementary School</u>   Grade: <u>3rd</u>

Contact person regarding this IHP: <u>Miss Long, R.N. or Mrs. Warnick</u>

Student's Information and History

Susie is an 8-year old girl with moderate spastic quadriplegia cerebral palsy. She had a gastrostomy inserted when she was 4 years old due to a severe gag reflex and an inability to take in enough nutrition. Her doctor ordered no oral feeding due to aspiration.

Diagnosis and Assessment Data

Susie has appropriate weight for her height. She is currently tolerating her feedings well and has appropriate bowel elimination. Her diagnosis consists of impaired swallowing resulting in an inability to eat independently. This has resulted in the need for tube feedings.

Goal of Care

Administer tube feedings (via gastrostomy tube) as primary form of nutrition.

Interventions

1. The nurse (Miss Long) will instruct Susie's special education teacher (Mrs. Warnick), paraprofessional (Mrs. Thomson), and one other teacher (Mr. Lennox) on Susie's tube feeding procedure. Included in the instruction is information on how to monitor for common tube feeding problems and what to do should they occur.

2. The nurse will supervise staff administering feedings on a regular basis.

3. The nurse and teacher will collaboratively teach Susie to self-administer tube feedings.

Expected Outcomes

1. Susie will receive adequate nutrition through tube feeding.

2. Staff will demonstrate competence in tube feeding and the actions to take should a problem occur.

3. Susie will learn to partially or fully participate in tube feeding herself.

Emergency information and contacts

Dr. Bove: (678) 651-2222,

Mrs. Jones: work number: (404) 555-1234; home number: (404) 555-9876; cell phone number: (404) 555-5678

(continued)

Figure 6.3.   Sample individualized health care plan for tube feeding. (Republished with permission of South-Western College Publishing, a division of Cengage Learning, from Heller, K.W., Forney, P.E., Alberto, P.A., Schwartzman, M.N., & Goeckel, T. (2000). *Meeting physical and health needs of children with disabilities: Teaching student participation and management.* Permission conveyed through Copyright Clearance Center, Inc.)

Figure 6.3.   *(continued)*

Specialized information

1. Tube feeding route: gastrotomy tube

2. Type of tube feeding: Bolus method

3. Formula: 1 can Ensure, 1 can dry baby food with water, extra water as needed for flushing tube and providing hydration

4. Preparation of formula: add amount of water specified on baby food box

5. Schedule of feeding: every four hours (9:00 a.m., 1:00 p.m.)

6. Child specific procedure attached: _X_ yes   ___ no

7. Directions for feeding problems and emergencies specifically for *Susie Jones:*

   a) Aspiration: Immediately stop feeding at any signs of aspiration and page nurse. Call 911 if any difficulty in breathing is present.

   b) Tube displacement: Immediately stop tube feeding. Call the nurse to come replace the tube. If she can not be reached, contact school administrator to arrange transportation to hospital for replacement. (Important to note that the opening will close within a few hours unless a new tube is inserted.)

   c) Nausea, vomiting, and cramping: Stop tube feeding immediately. Check for the following: spoiled formula, tube feeding being delivered too rapidly, excess air entering the stomach, & formula is at room temperature. Check for signs of illness. Contract school nurse to determine illness and to check your procedure of administering food.

   d) Diarrhea: Follow directions for nausea, vomiting, and cramping.

   e) Infection: If site is red, swollen, or has suspicious discharge, fill out a health report and send to school nurse and parents. Nurse will follow up regarding appropriate treatment.

   f) Leaking of stomach contents: Check to be sure clamp is securely fastened. If stomach contents are leaking from opening, around the tube, call the nurse.

   g) Clogged tube: Follow proper procedure of first "milking" the tube. If this does not work, introduce small amounts of water with the plunger, slowly pulling forward and back with the plunger until clog is cleared (as demonstrated in initial training). If still clogged, call the school nurse.

This last section on the IHP on feeding problems and emergencies could be invaluable to a student such as Susie. By including this information on an IHP, everyone is prepared if a problem should arise instead of wasting time determining what to do once something has happened.

Children who are at risk of having an emergency event in the school setting (e.g., uncontrolled seizure, asthma attack, ventilator stops working) may have a separate ECP that is developed based on the IHP. Although the IHP contains several common problems that may occur with a health care procedure, many of them are not emergencies (e.g., nausea). The ECP provides school staff with clear steps on how to respond to a health emergency. The ECP may be included as part of the IHP or be provided as a separate document.

Health Care Procedures and the Individualized Education Program

Health care procedures such as tube feeding and clean intermittent catheterization are often viewed as self-care skills or independent living skills. A position paper from the DPHMD (2008) of the Council for Exceptional Children urged teachers to consider teaching students to perform these procedures in order to increase independence. Just as students with severe and multiple disabilities may receive instruction on how to use a spoon or the restroom, students may receive instruction on how to tube feed or catheterize themselves.

Tony is a 16-year-old student with CP, moderate intellectual disability, and deafness who requires tube feeding. Tony is preparing for supported employment and participates in community-based vocational training. A teacher and nurse taught Tony to tube feed himself, thus increasing his possibility of gaining supported employment because he can take care of his own nutritional needs.

Demetria is a 10-year-old student with congenital toxoplasmosis and severe intellectual disability who has never participated in her tube-feeding procedure. Her teacher is going to begin teaching her to assist with her tube-feeding procedure by shaking the can of formula before it is opened, helping to pour the formula into the syringe barrel, and cleaning her equipment when she is finished.

The students in both of these examples were taught to independently perform or partially participate in the functional skill of tube feeding. Teaching these students to participate in tube feeding decreases learned helplessness, increases independence and attention to the task, and makes it easier for someone to assist with the procedure. Many students have been taught to self-perform their health care procedure, including students with intellectual disabilities and learning problems (Cobussen-Boekhorst et al., 2009; Katrancha, 2008). As with other self-help or independent living skills, the team will need to decide if teaching the student to self-perform his or her health care procedure is an appropriate goal to address at this time.

A student may be taught a health care procedure on four different levels, which can be incorporated into the student's IEP in terms of objectives: 1) independent performance of the task, 2) partial performance of the task (also referred to as *partial participation in task performance*), 3) directing the task, and 4) knowledge of the task (Heller, Forney et al., 2000). The goal of the first level is for the student to learn to do the entire procedure. The student may be unable to perform the entire health care procedure in some cases, due to physical or cognitive impairments, but he or she can do a part of it. Objectives are written with the intent that the student will complete partial performance of the task, thus promoting some independence. For example, the student may assist with tube feeding by mixing the formula, holding the syringe barrel,

Table 6.1.   Sample individualized education program (IEP) objectives

Type of IEP objective	Example of objective
Independent performance of task	The student will self-perform the tube-feeding procedure according to the task analysis with 100% accuracy for 1 week.
Partial performance of task	The student will add more food to the syringe barrel during the tube-feeding procedure with 100% accuracy for four consecutive sessions.
Directing the task	The student will use his or her augmentative and alternative communication device to direct another person in performing each step of the tube-feeding procedure with 100% accuracy for 2 weeks.
Knowledge of the task	The student will tell the teacher when it is time for his or her tube feeding to occur.

or cleaning the equipment (see Table 6.1 for sample IEP objectives related to performance in tube feeding).

A student who has a severe physical disability and is unable to physically participate in the task may be taught to direct another person in its performance after the student has learned the steps.

> Fernando is a 12-year-old student with multiple disabilities who requires tube feeding, but he is unable to perform or partially perform the procedure himself because of his severe physical disabilities. He has been taught the steps of how to perform the procedure, however, and he directs the person performing the tube feeding by telling him or her each step.

Students may communicate the steps of the procedure through speech or an AAC device. An advantage of having the student communicate the procedure is that he or she may be able to inform the person who is doing the procedure if he or she is doing it incorrectly. The ability to communicate the steps of the procedure is also empowering for the student.

The last type of objective is one in which the student is taught something about the task. For example, the student may be taught the times that tube feeding occurs and communicate to another person when it is time to be fed. In another example, a student who is experiencing nausea or abdominal cramping may be taught to signal another person.

It is important that the performance criteria for IEP objectives on health care procedures be set high, typically 100%, because there is usually no room for performing these procedures incorrectly. If the student cannot reach high criteria on all parts of the procedure, then only those steps in which the student is likely to achieve a high percentage of correct responses should be targeted. Other parts of the procedure may be taught once those steps are achieved with a high level of success.

Teaching Students to Perform Health Care Procedures

Teaching a student to perform his or her own health care procedure requires a team approach. The nurse provides expertise on the procedure, and the teacher provides expertise on instruction. Other team members may have valuable input. A physical therapist (PT) may need to provide input on positioning, and an occupational therapist may need to provide information on manipulating materials. A speech-language pathologist may provide information on AAC use pertaining to the health care procedure. The parent's or caregiver's input is particularly important because he or she can provide specific information about the child and current health care procedure practices. For example, the parents of a child who undergoes clean intermittent catheterization could provide information about the child and the procedure (e.g., familiar vocabulary surrounding the procedure, student's emotional response to the procedure) as well as information related to the current clean intermittent catheterization program, frequency of catheterization, type of catheter and its reuse, position the student uses during clean intermittent catheterization, cleaning and storage of equipment, cleaning agents used, and the current level of student participation (Katrancha, 2008).

An instructional plan needs to be designed once vital information is communicated among the team members. First, a task analysis is performed in which the health care procedure is broken into small steps. A sample task analysis for a student with a gastrostomy tube is provided in Figure 6.4. The steps may initially be taken from the written steps of the procedure that are attached to the IHP. After the initial task analysis is written, the next step is to closely examine each step of the procedure and identify any caution steps or time limited steps (Heller, Forney et al., 2000). A caution step is any step of a procedure in which the student could injure him- or herself by making a quick, jerking, or incorrect movement. The caution step in the tube-feeding task analysis is connecting and disconnecting the syringe barrel as well as removing and reinserting the plug at the end of the tube because the student may pull on the gastrostomy tube when doing these steps, which could lead to him or her inadvertently pulling out the gastrostomy tube. A time-limited step is a step that must be completed within a certain time frame to avoid injury. A time-limited step for tube feeding occurs when more formula (or water) needs to be added to the syringe barrel before all of the formula (or water) empties. Doing this incorrectly could introduce air in the stomach and result in abdominal cramping.

Once the caution and time-limited steps are identified, the team needs to decide if they will teach these steps along with the others or teach them at a later time. If these steps are going to be taught, then the teacher must use the instructional procedure of shadowing with these steps in order to prevent injury. Shadowing is a procedure in which the teacher keeps his or her hands within 1 inch of the student's hands. The teacher may use any other instructional strategies with the other steps, but the teacher must provide either shadowing or a more intrusive prompt (i.e., full physical guidance) on caution and time-limited steps to avoid injury.

Steps of Task Analysis

	1. Wash hands
	2. Prepare formula
	3. Kink the G-tube
CS	4. Remove plug at the end of G-tube
CS	5. Attach syringe barrel to end of G-tube
	6. Pour prepared formula into barrel
	7. Hold barrel 6 inches above stomach
	8. Unclamp or unkink tube
	9. Wait while food goes through G-tube into the stomach
TLS	10. Add more formula before it completely empties the syringe barrel
	11. Wait while food goes through G-tube
TLS	12. Continue adding food until completed (repeating steps 6, 9 and 10)
TLS	13. Add water before food is completely emptied from syringe barrel
TLS	14. Add more water when formula nears bottom of syringe barrel to flush tube
	15. Kink G-tube before water completely empties from barrel
CS	16. Take off syringe barrel
CS	17. Put plug in tube

Figure 6.4. Sample task analysis for gastrostomy (G-tube) feeding, bolus method, with caution steps (CS) and time-limited steps (TLS) indicated.

After an initial task analysis is constructed and the caution and time-limited steps are identified, the student needs to be assessed on his or her ability to perform the steps of the procedure. The aim of this assessment phase (also referred to as a *discrepancy analysis*) is to determine what changes need to occur in regard to adaptations, instructional strategies, or task analysis steps. As the student is guided through each step of the task analysis, the types of errors the student makes on each step are examined to ascertain if the errors are due to physical, sensory, learning, health (e.g., endurance), motivational, or communication problems (Heller & Avant, 2011). For example, the assessment may reveal that the student has a learning problem that necessitates breaking down the step of preparing the formula into several smaller steps. The assessment of another step may reveal that the student has difficulty pouring the formula due to a physical impairment. A funnel may be used to address this problem. Perhaps the student has difficulty knowing when to pour more formula, so a red line is placed on the syringe barrel as an antecedent prompt to indicate when more formula needs to be added. When it is determined that adaptations are needed, the teacher and nurse should work together to be sure the adaptations do not compromise the procedure (see Chapter 11).

Instruction is ready to begin after the student is assessed on the task analysis and adaptations and adjustments are made to the task analysis based on the results. A variety of instructional strategies may be used to teach health care procedures, such as prompting strategies, antecedent prompts, learning strategies (e.g., mnemonics, jingle), time delay, picture prompting systems, simulation practice on a doll (e.g., with doll oriented in same direction as the student for initial teaching of suctioning a tracheostomy), and others. The teacher will select the instructional strategy based on which strategies have been most effective with the student in the past and the student's present performance on the targeted task (see Chapter 10). The task analysis should be put on a data sheet once the instructional strategy is selected. The caution and time-limited steps are highlighted to remind the teacher to shadow the student during those steps. The needed adaptations (e.g., funnel on syringe barrel, red line on syringe barrel) determined during the discrepancy analysis (assessment phase) should also be written on the data sheet. Data should be taken regularly to document the student's progress and determine if further adaptations are needed.

IMPACT OF DISABILITIES ON HEALTH AND SCHOOL PERFORMANCE

Health is not only the absence of disease or infirmity, but also a state of optimal mental, social, and physical well-being (World Health Organization, 1946). Given this broader definition of health, not only do teachers need to monitor students for common health problems and problems involving health care procedures, but they also need to have a broader understanding of the student's disability and its impact on health and school performance.

Disability-Specific Monitoring

Although countless conditions compose the category of severe and multiple disabilities, teachers need to be familiar with each of their student's specific medical conditions. By knowing about the student's specific disability, the teacher will have a greater understanding of what health issues can arise and how educational functioning can be affected. Depending on the disability, students may also need to be taught certain activities that will address some of their health issues.

Students with severe and multiple disabilities will typically have conditions that require monitoring during the school day. For example, teachers will often need to monitor for common problems such as dehydration, pressure ulcers, and infections. Students often will need to be monitored for specific problems depending on their disability. For example, students with seizure disorders will need to be monitored for seizures, and students with asthma will need to be monitored for asthma attacks. The nurse, family, and teacher will need to work together to be sure they are accurately monitoring each student's specific condition and have a plan in place if problems arise.

General Impact of Severe and Multiple Disabilities

Students with severe and multiple disabilities may have difficulty learning due to their specific type of disability as well as a wide range of factors that can affect learning and the student's well-being. The Physical and Health Disability Performance Model (Heller, 2009) explains how these factors can affect performance, which helps the teacher and school personnel determine the best interventions to improve performance. The model identifies several major factors that can affect performance: 1) atypical movements and motor ability, 2) sensory loss, 3) communication impairments, 4) fatigue and lack of endurance, 5) health factors, 6) experiential deficits, 7) cognitive impairments and processing issues, 8) motivation, 9) self-concept and self-advocacy, 10) behavioral and emotional functioning, and 11) social, physical, technological, learning, and attitudinal environments (Heller, 2009). The following subsections describe how school personnel should address each area of the Physical and Health Disability Performance Model to improve students' learning and performance and provide for their health and well-being.

Atypical Movements, Motor Abilities, and Sensory Loss Many students with severe and multiple disabilities have impairments in motor movements, vision, or hearing that affect their ability to participate in the classroom. It is important that teachers closely monitor the students' motoric, visual, and auditory functioning because changes can occur over time. These physical and sensory impairments should be addressed with appropriate adaptations in order to promote optimal functioning and performance in school.

Proper positioning is needed when physical disabilities are present to allow for stability and improved movement of the extremities (i.e., arms and legs; see Chapter 3). Also, adaptive equipment and assistive technology (AT) is needed to allow these students to independently or partially perform a variety of school tasks (e.g., adapted spoons, adapted toothbrush, stabilized paper, alternate computer access). Students with limited mobility will need specialized equipment such as wheelchairs, walkers, or canes to navigate the classroom environment. In addition to learning how to use the equipment, some students will need to learn how to care for the equipment, such as learning how to check their wheelchair for proper functioning. Because of the potential for frequent changes in a student's condition, the teacher should monitor for any changes and report any worsening or improvement of his or her motor abilities. It is equally important for the teacher to examine the effectiveness of the adaptations, AT, and equipment over time to determine if further changes are needed (e.g., different type of switch to use a device due to worsening of contractures, a new wheelchair because a student has outgrown the old one).

Students with vision loss, deafness or hearing impairment, or deafblindness will have difficulty receiving information, which can significantly affect performance. Teachers will need to closely monitor these students because some of these conditions can be progressive. Many adaptations, AT devices, and instructional approaches are available to help meet these students' needs. For example, adaptations can vary for a student with a vision loss from using high-contrasting materials to using low-vision devices to using tactile graphics. Students with hearing loss may also use any number of ATs, such as amplification devices to assist with auditory input and AAC to assist with communicating with others (see Chapter 4).

Communication Impairment   Students with communication impairments may lack the ability to communicate simple wants or interact with others using more complex communicative messages. Students will need to be taught to communicate through multiple forms of AAC (e.g., gestures, communication boards, electronic devices). Students who do not have an effective form of communication will be severely restricted in their ability to interact across various environments. In some cases, students who lack an effective communication system may withdraw or display severe behavior problems (e.g., self-injurious behavior) that can jeopardize their health. Students who are nonverbal or who have restricted communication abilities will need to be systematically taught communication skills (see Chapter 7).

It is important to consider vocabulary related to health needs when determining the content of the communication system. Whenever possible, students should be taught to communicate that they do not feel well. Some students will be able to learn to communicate about a variety of health problems, indicating that they are sick or signaling the presence of nausea and pain. Some communication systems will have a picture of a person so that the child can point to where the pain is located, whereas others will have symbols for different parts of the body. For example, a picture of an ear may be used because otitis media occurs more frequently in individuals with severe and multiple disabilities. Having a way to indicate what hurts is especially important when students have physical disabilities that prevent them from reaching for their ear or other body part to indicate pain. Because of increased hospitalizations for many students with severe and multiple disabilities, it can be helpful to teach some students vocabulary specifically addressing needs that they may have when in the hospital. Teaching students simple messages can ease the anxiety, fear, and confusion that can occur with hospital stays.

Some students will have information about their health needs on their communication systems, whereas others will be taught the time that medications or health care procedures occur. They may have a message on their communication system that states IT IS TIME FOR MY MEDICATION or I NEED A RESTROOM BREAK (for students requiring clean intermittent catheterization who do not want everyone to hear an explicit message about needing this procedure). Students who are physically unable to perform their health care procedures sometimes have the steps of the procedure on their communication device to direct someone else in performing the procedure (Heller, Forney et al., 2000). The communication device may also have additional messages such as YOU ARE DOING IT WRONG so that students can correct those who are assisting in performing their health care procedure if necessary. Being able to direct another person can increase student independence as well as minimize errors.

Fatigue and Lack of Endurance Many students with severe and multiple disabilities have fatigue and endurance problems. Repeated motor movement may tire an individual who has a physical disability. For example, a student with CP may experience fatigue from using AAC or hitting a switch if a great deal of effort is needed. Other students may experience fatigue from the type of disability they have, such as those with sickle cell anemia. In other cases, the medication the student is taking may result in fatigue. Teachers need to monitor for fatigue and endurance problems and make appropriate modifications so these students can perform best. Adjusting students' schedules so that more demanding activities take place when the students are the most alert is one possible modification. A change of activities or a short break will help decrease fatigue in some instances. Students may also be taught to indicate when they are tired and need a short break.

Physical exercise also plays an important role in promoting health and increasing endurance. Although some limitations on physical activities are unavoidable for many individuals with severe and multiple disabilities, most benefit from physical exercise. Team members should evaluate each student and determine how best to integrate appropriate physical activities into the student's program using functional activities (e.g., use of a manual wheelchair), play, fitness exercises, or a combination of these options.

Health Factors Students who have health issues may be at risk for not performing optimally. Some students may not feel well because of health problems, or they may experience discomfort. In these instances, the student's attention will be drawn away from educational tasks. Teachers need to monitor for health problems and make appropriate accommodations (e.g., alleviate discomfort as indicated, provide breaks). Teachers also need to remember that classroom performance may be erratic when the student is feeling poorly. Most students will need more repetition of the classroom material when feeling ill or having discomfort than they would when feeling healthy.

In addition, students with severe and multiple disabilities often have increased absenteeism because of illness or surgeries. Some students also miss classroom time because they need to leave classes early due to slower mobility or to perform a health care procedure. Teachers need to be prepared to accommodate student absences, whether they are for a few months or a few minutes. They may need to reteach skills because of prolonged absences, modify the length of a student's lesson, or build in more repetition when time is available. When students miss more than a few days of school, they may require homebound services and receive instruction in the home from a teacher from the student's school.

Experiential Deficits Students may have experiential deficits in which they lack critical information about the world around them and may miss out

on life experiences because of their impairment, which can affect school performance and health. A student with a physical or sensory impairment may also
acquire incomplete or inaccurate information. For example, a student who has
never felt a cotton ball because he or she has limited arm movement may think
the cotton ball will be hard, or a student who is blind may not realize that the
tube-feeding formula is mixed and poured into the syringe barrel. Teachers
must give students meaningful experiences and not make assumptions about
what they already know. For example, students with physical limitations need
items brought to them to touch and manipulate with assistance (e.g., a tree leaf
on a discussion about maple trees).

Students with physical or health impairments who are learning to independently perform or partially participate in the performance of their health
care procedures should be systematically introduced to the materials. It is important that assumptions are not made regarding what the student already
knows about the materials or equipment when he or she has never participated
in performing a procedure. Although a student may have repeated exposure to
the health care procedure, the child is often inadvertently taught a passive role
in which the procedures are "done to" the student (Heller, Forney et al., 2000;
Tarnowski & Drabman, 1987).

A lack of experience may also create false assumptions on the part of
school personnel. Some students minimize the amount of pain they are feeling because they lack experience with pain or comparison of different levels of
pain. Teachers should take any communication or indication of pain seriously
and notify the nurse or take appropriate action (e.g., pain medication). Some
students with communication difficulties also will be unable to report feeling
pain but will nonverbally indicate that they are hurting. Teachers should be
alert for nonverbal signs of pain, such as a lack of movement, grasping an area,
crying, or even behaviors such as head banging. If pain is suspected, then the
appropriate person should be notified (e.g., parent, nurse, physician) so that the
student can receive proper treatment (Oberlander & Symons, 2006).

Cognitive Impairments Most students with severe and multiple disabilities have some level of cognitive disability, although some students may have a
multiple disability that does not affect intellectual functioning (see Chapter 1).
Many students with a cognitive impairment may have an intellectual disability,
whereas others may have specific learning disabilities, distractibility, disorga-
nization, visual-motor impairments, or other cognitive difficulties affecting
their ability to learn and provide for their own health care needs. The type and
extent of cognitive impairment will influence how well the student will be able
to take care of his or her own health care needs. The educational team will need
to examine the student's cognitive functioning to determine the student's level
of participation in his or her own health care. The student's abilities are often
underestimated when physical disabilities are involved along with restricted
speech. The educational team will need to be sure that decisions regarding the
student's educational goals and participation in health care procedures are

based on the student's demonstrated abilities with proper adaptations in place, rather than on false assumptions about the student's capabilities (e.g., mistakenly believing a student with severe CP will always have an intellectual disability) or inaccurate assessments (e.g., mistakenly using assessments that are not designed for students with severe motor and communication impairments).

Motivation   Students with physical and multiple disabilities are at risk of having decreased motivation to fully engage in school tasks. If students are experiencing pain, discomfort, or fatigue because of their condition, then their motivation can be decreased and affect school performance. These underlying problems will need to be addressed through adaptations, treatments, and/or medication (e.g., repositioning a student, giving pain medication when indicated) to effectively increase motivation. If there are no apparent physical or health reasons affecting motivation, then reinforcement may be used to increase performance.

Some students with severe and multiple disabilities develop learned helplessness, a condition in which a student either does not attempt a task that he or she could perform, applies reduced effort toward a task, or expects failure (Hamill & Everington, 2002; Seligman, 1975). This outcome typically results from adults doing tasks for the student instead of assisting or teaching the student to perform the task. For example, if an adult feeds the student, then the student often does not learn to eat independently and might passively wait for someone to feed him or her, increasing the risk of malnutrition and dehydration. A student who does not learn how to self-catheterize is more vulnerable to being sexually abused. It is important that teachers help students learn to do as much as possible for themselves to increase independence.

Self-Advocacy   *Self-advocacy* in the classroom can refer to communicating about specific needs, which requires the student to be able to initiate communication. Some students' communication may depend on others, and they may not initiate communication when they need something (e.g., rescue inhaler, suctioning, repositioning, assistance with an item). A lack of self-advocacy skills not only can affect educational performance but also a student's well-being when the necessary communication pertains to health. Teachers should systematically instruct students to communicate their needs and promote self-advocacy skills related to their students' health needs.

Behavioral and Emotional Functioning   Students with severe and multiple disabilities may have emotional or behavioral issues that interfere with learning and health. For example, students can be at risk for lower self-concept and self-esteem, especially those with mobility impairments who experience pain or have an acquired condition (Jemta, Fugl-Meyer, Oberg, & Dahl, 2009), and this can affect school performance and negatively affect emotional health. Severe behaviors can also be present, such as aggressive or self-injurious behaviors (Richards, Oliver, Nelson, & Moss, 2012). To effectively address these severe behaviors, health reasons need to be ruled out as a causal factor first because the behavior may be due to pain, infection, or other medical problem (e.g., head banging due to otitis media). Once ruled out, teachers should perform a functional behavioral assessment and determine an appropriate course of action (e.g., behavior management plan, more appropriate ways to communicate). This is critical because self-injurious behaviors are deleterious to the student's health (e.g., eye gouging resulting in loss of vision, head banging resulting in concussions).

Environmental Factors   Teachers need to closely examine the learning environment to be sure it is appropriately meeting their students' needs. An ineffective social environment in which the other students are not accepting of students with disabilities affects students' ability to make friends and socialize with others, which is important for development and emotional well-being. Teachers need to promote positive social interaction through a variety of strategies (e.g., educating students about disabilities, promoting activities that everyone can participate in, establishing a helper program, modeling). The environment also needs to address physical and health needs of students to promote learning, health, and safety (e.g., widened aisles, appropriate desk height, wheelchair accessible sinks, appropriate evacuation plans for students using wheelchairs). Appropriate technological environments are also needed in which students have access to the necessary AT to allow them to gain access to activities and environments (e.g., AAC, alternate access device for the computer, weighted spoon). Finally, the learning and attitudinal environments need to encourage learning and acceptance and promote an attitude that all students can learn with the proper teaching strategies and adaptations in place.

WORKING AS A TEAM

It is important that school, home, and medical personnel work closely together to successfully integrate health care and educational programs. Each has a vital role to help promote a student's health and education. The well-being of the student is at risk without a collaborative process.

Sharing of Information and Problem Solving

Students with health care needs require clear communication among parents, school nurses, physicians, teachers (e.g., general education teacher, special education teacher), and other school personnel. It is important that everyone understands how to recognize a student's medical problems (e.g., asthma) and what to do when a medical issue arises. In the example of asthma, one child may wheeze and be short of breath during an attack, whereas another child may be unable to talk due to severe airway constriction and remain motionless (with wheezing audible only with a stethoscope or on movement). Parents can provide helpful information about their child's signs and symptoms, which should be communicated to the child's teachers, school nurse, and other relevant school personnel (e.g., PT). Parents have much more experience with their own children than professionals, and they often have developed great expertise regarding their child's medical procedures, so it is often helpful to involve parents or other caregivers in staff training on nursing procedures. This can help to ensure consistency between how procedures are provided at home and in school. Whereas the nurse provides expertise on the procedure, the parent provides expertise on the child. For example, although the nurse may know an acceptable rate for gastrostomy feedings, the parent may know that this rate is too fast for his or her child.

The school nurse and parents need to communicate to teachers and other school personnel about the student's specific condition and the course of treatment that has been prescribed by the physician. For example, an inhaler or nebulizer is often prescribed for an asthma attack. The school nurse will need to teach school personnel how to administer medication using an inhaler or nebulizer. Should medication not stop an asthma attack (or other emergency or problem), it will be important that a plan of action be put in place that the entire educational team is aware of and knows how to implement (as written in the IHP or ECP).

Discussing written guidelines for the student's treatments can promote good communication among team members. For example, if the physician prescribes tube feeding, then it is important that those performing the procedure have a clear understanding of how the physician wants that to be carried out. Some school systems have the school nurse send a written tube-feeding procedure to the physician's office for the physician to approve or make changes to be sure that it is being correctly implemented. The written procedure is then shared and discussed with the team and becomes part of the IHP.

It is important to utilize each team member's unique knowledge and skills when planning health-related goals for students. When decisions need to be made regarding whether a student can participate in his or her own health care procedures, the team needs to carefully determine these decisions together. The nurse, teacher, parent, and related services staff all have important roles in teaching the student these health care procedures and determining the most appropriate strategies and adaptations to use. In addition, the IHP requires input from each team member, especially for the actions to take when a problem occurs for a particular child (e.g., the parents would come to school and reinsert a gastrostomy tube that has been pulled out, whereas another student may be transported to the hospital).

For a team to be effective, team members should support each other and problem-solve together for accomplishing common goals, which includes developing individualized academic, behavioral, and health interventions in the school setting (Lytle & Bordin, 2001; McNamara, Rasheed, & Delamatre, 2008). Several attributes contribute to effective teaming. First, roles should be clearly defined, which can result in different perspectives and add to the team's effectiveness. Team members need to respect and value varying perspectives, however, and use effective communication (Lytle & Bordin, 2001). Ineffective teaming has occurred when various perspectives are not vocalized, discussed, or considered relevant, which has not benefited the student (Hjorne & Saljo, 2014). Providing social support to the parents and making them feel that they are part of the team are other elements for effective teaming. The team should also have a sense of unity with the focus being on the student, and all team members should feel that they have a fair and equitable role in creating the best possible plan for the student (Lytle & Bordin, 2001).

Nursing Roles and Collaborative Teaming

Nurses are an important component of the educational team, especially for students with a health care team. As described earlier in this chapter, some roles traditionally performed by the nurse, such as tube feeding, may be delegated to a teacher or paraprofessional. The nurse still retains accountability in this role-sharing situation and is an important resource to the person performing the procedure. This type of role sharing found in collaborative teaming may not be possible or desirable in certain situations, however. In some instances, a nurse may determine that it is unsafe to delegate a procedure. Nurses may also be prohibited in delegating certain procedures based on their state's nurse practice act. Noncompliance with their nurse practice act can jeopardize their nursing license. Each team member, whether he or she is the nurse, teacher, parent, or other school personnel, has important information and skills that require close collaboration so successful health care will be integrated within the student's educational programs.

CONCLUSION

Every child should experience mental, social, and physical well-being in schools and be able to learn in a safe and healthy environment. School personnel maintain this healthy environment and support their students' optimal health in a variety of ways, including arranging the environment to prevent injury, maintaining standard precautions, ensuring that evacuation procedures are accessible, and knowing how to respond to an emergency. Teachers of students with severe and multiple disabilities should be familiar with common medical problems such as dehydration, skin irritation and pressure ulcers, respiratory infections, asthma, otitis media, and contractures. Because students with severe and multiple disabilities often take a range of medications, teachers should also understand these medications, their side effects, and the proper procedures for administration. Teachers also need to be familiar with students' health care procedures so that they know what to do if something should go wrong. Utilizing an IHP that specifies what steps to take if a problem arises (e.g., cramping, gastrostomy tube is pulled out) will assist school personnel in taking the proper steps. ECPs should be in place for potential emergencies (e.g., uncontrolled seizures). Because health care procedures are often viewed as forms of self-help or independent living skills, the educational team needs to decide if the student will learn to independently perform or participate in the performance of the health care procedures and have IEP goals addressing them. Having students direct others in performing their health care procedures or increasing students' knowledge about their health care procedures are other goal options to consider. Finally, teachers need to be aware of the impact of severe and multiple disabilities on health and school performance and utilize effective teamwork strategies to address school and health needs.

REFLECTION QUESTION

You have a student who is a wheelchair user, has asthma, and receives feeding through a gastrostomy tube:

- How can you make the environment safe for this student?

- What training would need to be in place to delegate tube feeding to the teacher to perform?

- What could the student learn to do on his or her own behalf?

CHAPTER ACTIVITY

Construct some of the important components of an IHP for the student who is a wheelchair user, has asthma, and receives feeding through a gastrostomy tube, including necessary education to staff and common problems and actions to take.

REFERENCES

American Nurses Association. (2006). *Joint statement on delegation: American Nurses Association (ANA) and the National Council for State Boards of Nursing (NCSBN).* Retrieved from https://www.ncsbn.org/Delegation_joint_statement_NCSBN-ANA.pdf

Bock, S.A., Munoz-Furlong, A., & Sampson, H.A. (2007). Further fatalities caused by anaphylactic reactions to food, 2001-2006. *Journal of Allergy and Clinical Immunology, 119,* 1016–1018.

Bryant, R., & Nix, D. (2012). Developing and maintaining a pressure ulcer prevention program. In R. Bryant & D. Nix (Eds.), *Acute and chronic wounds: Current management concepts* (4th ed., pp. 137–153). New York NY: Elsevier.

Canadian Press. (2013). Ontario mom urges schools to let asthmatic kids carry puffers. Retrieved from http://www.cbc.ca/news/canada/ottawa/ontario-mom-urges-schools-to-let-asthmatic-kids-carry-puffers-1.2455861

Cedar Rapids Community School Districts v. Garrett F., 526 U.S. 66 (1999).

Centers for Disease Control and Prevention. (2006). *Common asthma triggers.* Retrieved from http://www.cdc.gov/asthma/triggers.html

Centers for Disease Control and Prevention. (2011). *Guide to infection prevention for outpatient settings: Minimum expectations for safe care.* Atlanta, GA: Author.

Chadwick, D.D., Jolliffe, J., & Goldbart, J. (2002). Career knowledge of dysphasia management strategies. *International Journal of Language and Communication Disorders, 37,* 345–357.

Cicutto, L., Julien, B., Li, N., Nguyen-Luu, N., Butler, J., Clarke, A.,. . . . & Waserman, S. (2012). Comparing school environments with and without legislation for the prevention and management of anaphylaxis. *Allergy, 67,* 131–137.

Clynes, M., & O'Connor, C. (2010). Gastrointestinal system. In I. Coyne, F. Neill, & F. Timmins (Eds.), *Clinical skills in children's nursing* (pp. 317–350). Oxford, England: Oxford University Press.

Cobussen-Boekhorst, H.J., Kuppenveld Van, J.H., Verjeij, P.P., Jong De, L.L., Gier De, R.R., Kortmann, B.B., & Feitz, W.W. (2009). Teaching children clean self-catheterization (CISC) in a group setting. *Journal of Pediatric Urology, 6,* 288–293.

Coffey, K., & Obringer, S.J. (2009). Diastat: A necessary related service. *Physical Disabilities: Education and Related Service, 27,* 7–17.

Coha, T. (2012). Skin care needs of the pediatric and neonatal patients: Part I: The pediatric patient. In R. Bryant & D. Nix (Eds.), *Acute and chronic wounds: Current management concepts* (4th ed., pp. 485–502). New York, NY: Elsevier.

Colicchio, G., Montano, N., Fuggetta, F., Papacci, F., Signorelli, F., & Meglio, M. (2012). Vagus nerve stimulation in drug-resistant epilepsies: Analysis of potential prognostic factors in a cohort of patients with long-term follow-up. *Acta Neurochirurgica, 154,* 2237–2240.

Council on School Health. (2008). The role of the school nursing providing school health services. *Pediatrics, 121,* 1052–1056.

Diggins, K.C. (2008). Treatment of mild to moderate dehydration in children with oral rehydration therapy. *Journal of the American Academy of Nurse Practitioners, 20,* 402–406.

Division for Physical, Health, and Multiple Disabilities. (2008). *Position statement on specialized health care procedures.* Retrieved from http://web.utk.edu/~dphmd/DPHD _position_health.pdf

Farmer, S.E., & James, M. (2001). Contractures in orthopaedic and neurological conditions: A review of causes and treatment. *Disability Rehabilitation, 23,* 549–558.

Gupta, R.S. (2014). Anaphylaxis in the young adult population. *American Journal of Medicine, 127*(1A), S17–S24.

Gursky, B., & Ryser, B. (2007). A training program for unlicensed assistive personnel. *Journal of School Nursing, 23,* 92–97.

Hamill, L., & Everington, C. (2002). *Teaching students with moderate to severe disabilities: An applied approach for inclusive environments.* Upper Saddle River, NJ: Merrill/Prentice Hall.

Harmes, K.M., Blackwood. A., Burrows, H.L., Cooke, J.M., Van Harrison, R., & Passamani, P.P. (2013). Otitis media: Diagnosis and treatment. *American Family Physician, 88,* 435–440.

Heller, K.W. (2004). Integrating health care and educational programs. In F.P. Orelove, D. Sobsey, & R.K. Silberman (Eds.), *Educating children with multiple disabilities: A collaborative approach* (4th ed., pp. 217–251). Baltimore, MD: Paul H. Brookes Publishing Co.

Heller, K. (2009). Learning and behavioral characteristics of students with physical, health, or multiple disabilities. In K.W. Heller, P.E. Forney, P.A. Alberto, S.J. Best, & M.N. Schwartzman (Eds.), *Understanding physical, health, and multiple disabilities* (pp. 18–34). Upper Saddle River, NJ: Pearson.

Heller, K.W., & Avant, M.J. (2011). Health care procedure considerations and individualized health care plans. *Physical Disabilities: Education and Related Services, 30,* 6–29.

Heller, K.W., Forney, P.E., Alberto, P.A., Schwartzman, M.N., & Goeckel, T. (2000). *Meeting physical and health needs of children with disabilities: Teaching student participation and management.* Belmont, CA: Wadsworth.

Heller, K.W., Fredrick, L., Dykes, M.K., Best, S., & Cohen, E. (2000). Specialized health care procedures in schools: Training and service delivery. *Exceptional Children, 66,* 173–186.

Heller, K.W., Schwartzman, M., & Fowler, L. (2009). Asthma. In K.W. Heller, P.E. Forney, P.A. Alberto, S.J. Best, & M.N. Schwartzman (Eds.), *Understanding physical, health, and multiple disabilities* (pp. 316–332). Upper Saddle River, NJ: Pearson.

Hester, L.L., Wilce, M.A., Gill, S.A., Disler, S.L., Collins, P., & Crawford, G. (2013). Roles of the state asthma program in implementing multicomponent, school-based asthma interventions. *Journal of School Health, 83,* 833–841.

Hjorne, E., & Saljo, R. (2014). Analyzing and preventing school failure: Exploring the role of multi-professionality in pupil health team meetings. *International Journal of Educational Research, 63,* 5–14.

Irving Independent School District v. Tatro, 468 U.S. 883 (1984).

Jemta, L., Fugl-Meyer, K.W., Oberg, K., & Dahl, M. (2009). Self-esteem in children and adolescents with mobility impairment: Impact on well-being and coping strategies. *Act Paediatrica, 98,* 567–572.

Kari, J., Al-Deek, B., Eikhatib, L., Salahudeen, S., Mukhtar, M., Ahman, R., . . . Raboei, E. (2013). Is Mitrofanoff a more socially accepted clean intermittent catheterization (CIC) route for children and their families? *European Journal of Pediatric Surgery, 23,* 405–410.

Katalinic, O., Harvey, L.A., & Herbert, R.D. (2011). Effectiveness of stretch for the treatment and prevention of contractures in people with neurological conditions: A systematic review. *Physical Therapy, 91,* 11–24.

Katrancha, E.D. (2008). Clean intermittent catheterization in the school setting. *Journal of School Nursing, 24,* 197–204.

Lexicomp (2013). *Drug information handbook: A comprehensive resource for all clinicians and healthcare professionals.* Hudson, OH: Wolters Kluwer.

Lippincott, Williams, & Wilkins (2012). *Lippincott's nursing procedures* (6th ed.). Philadelphia, PA: Author.

Luu, N.U., Cicutto, L., Soller, L., Joseph, L., Waserman, S., St-Pierre, Y., & Clarke, A. (2012). Management of anaphylaxis in schools: Evaluation of an epinephrine auto-injector (EpiPen) use by school personnel and comparison of two approaches of soliciting participation. *Allergy, Asthma, and Clinical Immunology, 8*(4), 1–8.

Lytle, R., & Bordin, J. (2001). Enhancing the IEP team. *Teaching Exceptional Children, 33,* 40–44.

Markova, T., & Chuvirov, D. (2007). Frequently ill children. *Advances in Experimental Medicine and Biology, 601,* 301–306.

McGowan, J.E., Fenton, T.R., Wade, A.W., Branton, J.L., & Robertson, M. (2012). An exploratory study of sodium, potassium, and fluid nutrition status of tube-fed nonambulatory children with severe cerebral palsy. *Applied Physiology, Nutrition, and Metabolism, 37,* 715–723.

McNamara, K., Rasheed, H., & Delamatre, J. (2008). A statewide study of school-based intervention teams: Characteristics, member perceptions, and outcomes. *Journal of Educational and Psychological Consultation, 18,* 5–30.

Mitts, Carol v. Hillsboro Union High School District 3-8 Jt et al., Washington County Circuit Court Case 87-1142C (1990).

Moore, K.N., Fader, M., & Getliffe, K. (2007). Long-term bladder management by intermittent catheterization in adults and children. *Cochrane Database Systematic Review 2007; 4:* CD 006008.

Moye by Moye v. Special School District No. 6, South St. Paul, Minn., 23 IDELE (LRP) 229 (D. Minn., 1995).

Murphy, J., Torkelson, R., Dowler, I., Simon, S., & Hudson, S. (2003). Vagal nerve stimulation in refractory epilepsy: The first 100 patients receiving vagal nerve stimulation at a pediatric epilepsy center. *Archives of Pediatric and Adolescent Medicine, 157,* 560–564.

Oberlander, T.F., & Symons, F.J. (Vol. Eds.). (2006). *Pain in children and adults with developmental disabilities.* Baltimore, MD: Paul H. Brookes Publishing Co.

O'Reilly, M.F. (1997). Functional analysis of episodic self-injury correlated with recurrent otitis media. *Journal of Applied Behavior Analysis, 30,* 165–167.

Pannek, J. (2011). Treatment of urinary tract infection in persons with spinal cord injury: Guidelines, evidence and clinical practice. *Journal of Spinal Cord Medicine, 34,* 11–15.

Pieper, R. (2012). Pressure ulcers: Impact, etiology, and classification. In R. Bryant & D. Nix (Eds.), *Acute and chronic wounds: Current management concepts* (4th ed., pp. 123–136). New York, NY: Elsevier.

Porter, R.S., & Kaplan, J. (2011). *The Merck manual of diagnosis and therapy.* Whitehouse Station, NJ: Merck Sharp & Dohme.

Pumphrey, R.S. (2000). Lessons for management of anaphylaxis from a study of fatal reactions. *Clinical and Experimental Allergy, 30,* 1144–1150.

Rapport, M.J. (1996). Legal guidelines for the delivery of special health care services in schools. *Exceptional Children, 62,* 537–549.

Resha, C. (2010). Delegation in the school setting: Is it a safe practice? Retrieved from http://www.nursingworld.org/Main MenuCategories/ANAMarketplace/ANA Periodicals/OJIN/TableofContents/Vol15 2010/No2May2010/Delegation-in-the-School-Setting.aspx

Richards, C., Oliver, C., Nelson, L., & Moss, J. (2012). Self-injurious behavior in individuals with autism spectrum disorder and intellectual disability. *Journal of Intellectual Disability Research, 56,* 476–489.

Schachter, S. (2006). *Vagus nerve stimulation.* Retrieved from https://www.epilepsy.com /epilepsy/vns

Schieve, L.A., Gonzalez, V., Boulet, S.L., et al, (2012) Concurrent medical conditions and health care use and needs among children with learning and behavioral developmental disabilities, National Health Interview Survey, 2006-2012. *Research in Developmental Disabilities, 33,* 467–476.

School Access to Emergency Epinephrine Act of 2013, PL 113-48, 113th Congress, Congressional Record, 159(73), H2912.

Seligman, M.E. (1975). *Helplessness: On depression, development and death.* New York, NY: W.H. Freeman.

Sem, R.H. (2013). Chapter 560: Authorizing unlicensed school employees to administer antiseizure medication to students with epilepsy. *McGeorge Law Review, 43*(3), 611–624.

Shaer, C.M. (1997). The infant and young child with spina bifida: Major medical concerns. *Infants and Young Children, 9,* 13–25.

Smith, L.R., Chambers, H.G., Subramaniam, S., & Lieber, R.L. (2012). Transcriptional abnormalities of hamstring muscle contractures in children with cerebral palsy. *PLOS ONE, 7*(8), 1–13.

Smith, S.F., Duell, D.J., & Martin, B.C. (2011). *Clinical nursing skills* (8th ed.). Upper Saddle River, NJ: Prentice Hall.

Tarnowski, K., & Drabman, R.S. (1987). Teaching intermittent self-catheterization skills to mentally retarded children. *Research in Developmental Disabilities, 8,* 521–529.

Tatum, W.O., & Helmers, S.K. (2009). Vagus nerve stimulation and magnet use: Optimizing benefits. *Epilepsy and Behavior, 15,* 299–302.

Tilton, A.H. (2006). Therapeutic interventions for tone abnormalities in cerebral palsy. *NeuroRx, 3,* 217–224.

Toole, K.P. (2013). Helping children gain asthma control: Bundled school-based interventions. *Pediatric Nursing, 39,* 115–124.

Tyrer, F., & McGrother, C. (2009). Cause-specific mortality and death certificate reporting in adults with moderate to profound intellectual disability. *Journal of Intellectual Disability Research, 53,* 898–904.

Waterson, T., Helms, P., & Ward-Platt, M. (2005). *Paediatrics: A core text on child health* (2nd ed.). Oxford, England: Radcliffe Medical Press.

Wireko, B.M. (2010). Enteral tube feeding. *Clinical Medicine, 10*(6), 616–619.

World Health Organization. (1946). *Preamble to the Constitution of the World Health Organization.* Retrieved from http://www.who.int/about/definition/en/print.html

Wound, Ostomy and Continence Nurses Society. (2012). *Guideline for prevention and management of pressure ulcers.* Glenview, IL: Author.

Wyndaele, J., Brauner, A., Geerlings, S., Bela, K., Peter, T., & Bjerklund-Johanson, T. (2012). Clean intermittent catheterization and urinary tract infection: Review and guide for future research. *BJU International, 110,* E910–E917.

Zacharski, S., Kain, C.A., Fleming, R., & Pontius, D. (2012). *Medication administration in the school setting: Position statement of the National Association of School Nurses.* Retrieved from http://www.nasn.org/PolicyAdvocacy/PositionPapersandReports/NASNPositionStatementsFullView/tabid/462/ArticleId/86/Medication-Administration-in-the-School-Setting-Amended-January-2012

Zeisel, S., & Roberts, J.E. (2003). Otitis media in young children with disabilities. *Infants and Young Children, 16,* 106–119.

7

Teaching Communication Skills

PAT MIRENDA AND JUNE DOWNING

CHAPTER OBJECTIVES

1. Learn an overview of communication and how to support its development in students with severe and multiple disabilities

2. Describe interventions to support communication for students of various age ranges and abilities

3. Become familiar with the key elements of augmentative and alternative communication (AAC)

4. Recognize the relationship between communication and problem behavior

5. Understand the importance of a collaborative approach to communication intervention

KEY TERMS

- Aided communication
- Auditory scanning
- Communication applications (apps)
- Communication dictionary/gesture dictionary
- Conversation book
- Dynamic assessment
- Ecological assessment
- Eye pointing
- Eye tracking
- Functional communication training (FCT)
- Informal assessment

- Least-to-most prompting
- Most-to-least prompting
- National Joint Committee (NJC) for the Communication Needs of Persons with Severe Disabilities
- Pull-out model
- Push-in model
- Speech-generating device (SGD)
- Symbol
- Touch-screen device
- Unaided communication
- Visual scanning

Sharitha is an outgoing teenager who loves rock music, has a winning smile, and also has a severe cognitive impairment and cerebral palsy (CP). She has limited mobility in her upper extremities but can operate a power wheelchair with her left wrist. Sharitha can say a few words (e.g., *hi*, *bye*, *yeah*, *no*) but communicates primarily by looking at pictures to make choices (i.e., eye pointing) and activating a picture-based speech-generating device (SGD) that she operates with a single switch mounted by the side of her head. She has been using this combination of techniques for the past 3 years while at the same time developing her ability to read, write, and spell. Sharitha and her family hope that before she graduates from high school she will be able to make the transition to a more flexible and powerful AAC system that will accommodate both pictorial symbols and written words. Sharitha and her educational team have worked hard to develop her communication skills, and their efforts have paid off.

Communication is a critical life skill that empowers all of us to make our needs known and establish relationships with others (Warren, 2000). Despite the challenges that individuals with severe and multiple disabilities may encounter with communication, the ability to communicate is inherent in everyone, as Mirenda noted, "Breathing is the only prerequisite that is relevant to communication" (1993, p. 4). All people are capable of communicating, even though the manner, amount, and complexity of communication may vary from individual to individual or situation to situation. Communication is particularly important for individuals who have considerable difficulty completing tasks on their own. Knowing how to request assistance when needed and how to maintain control over the type and quality of that assistance are essential skills for someone who is unable to perform an action by him- or herself.

COMPONENTS OF COMMUNICATION

Communication can be thought of as a skill set with four main components:

1. Form (a way to communicate)

2. Function (a purpose or reason to communicate)

3. Content (something to communicate about)

4. Social (someone with whom to communicate)

These components are described in the following subsections.

Form

Speech is the most common means of communication, but communication can and does occur without speech and can take different forms. A raised eyebrow, a sigh, a smile, and a high-five gesture all convey different messages. Individuals without disabilities use speech, facial expressions, body language,

Table 7.1. Types of augmentative and alternative communication (AAC)

Type of communication	Unaided	Aided
Nonsymbolic	Gesture/body movement (e.g., pointing, shaking head)	Real object (e.g., a cup to ask for a drink)
	Facial expression (e.g., wide eyes to show surprise)	
	Vocalization (e.g., squeal, laugh)	
Symbolic	Manual sign (from American Sign Language or another language system)	Partial object (e.g., a cup handle to ask for a drink)
		Textured symbol (e.g., a swatch of spandex that represents "bathing suit")
		Photographs or line drawing symbols (e.g., Picture Communication Symbols)
		Speech-generating device (e.g., a computer with voice output; an iPad or other touch-screen device with a communication application that provides speech output)

objects, vocalizations, conventional gestures (e.g., pointing), and other means to express themselves. Individuals with severe and multiple disabilities who are not able to use speech to communicate effectively will use other modes depending on their physical, sensory, and cognitive abilities (Beukelman & Mirenda, 2013; Downing, 2005). Multiple modes of AAC are desirable for someone who cannot easily use speech (Mirenda, 2005; Sigafoos & Drasgow, 2001). Some of these modalities are unaided (i.e., they do not require equipment that is external to the person's body), such as manual signs, gestures, and facial expressions. Other communication modalities are aided (i.e., they require tools or equipment in addition to the user's body), such as pictorial systems, parts of objects, and SGDs with speech output. See Table 7.1 for examples of aided and unaided AAC communication.

The advantage of unaided communication modalities is that they enable an individual to communicate at any time, anywhere, and with anyone without needing adaptive equipment—the individual always has the means of communication at his or her disposal. Unaided communication can be highly symbolic and used to convey virtually any message (e.g., speech, American Sign Language [ASL]); or it can be very concrete and used to convey more limited and contextually bound messages (e.g., nodding the head, pointing to an item). Unaided communication can also be either complex to produce (e.g., speech) or very simple (e.g., facial expressions).

In contrast, aided communication bypasses difficulties that may be encountered when producing motorically demanding forms of communication, such as speech and ASL. Aided communication requires relatively simple physical behaviors to convey messages (e.g., pointing, activating a switch) and can provide the AAC user with visual, auditory, or tactile reminders of the messages that can be produced. SGDs allow an individual to express almost any message, whereas pictorial or object-based systems usually limit the number and types of messages that are possible. The greatest disadvantage to any form of aided communication is that it requires the individual to rely on an external device of some type; thus, access and portability become critical considerations.

All of us use multiple modes of communication in our daily lives, regardless of age or ability, including speech, facial expressions, and gestures; many forms of written communication (e.g., typing on a keyboard, handwriting); and an increasing array of electronic communication modalities (e.g., text messages, e-mails). In most cases, individuals who are unable to speak also use a variety of communicative modes in all of their interactions (Beukelman & Mirenda, 2013; Cress, 2002; Mirenda, 2005). The combination of modalities used by each person will depend on factors such as physical ability, sensory limitations, cultural preferences, and demands of the environment. Whereas some students may benefit from using manual signs along with some speech and gestures, other students may not have the physical ability to produce manual signs and use facial expressions, vocalizations, and pictorial information instead.

Amelia is an 8-year-old student who uses facial expressions, some vocalizations, a few body gestures, color photographs, real objects, and a few signs such as EAT, COOKIE, and MORE for both expressive and receptive communication. Amelia whines, purses her lips, and turns her head away when she is offered something to eat that she does not want. Ameila grabs a preferred toy when she is offered choices of toys with which to play. Amelia smiles and makes a giggly sound when she is asked if she wants to continue an activity that she enjoys. Caregivers or teachers use speech paired with a color photograph of the next activity when they want to tell Amelia what activity is next. Amelia does not rely on only one form of communication; instead, she uses multiple modalities that all have meaning for her and her communication partners.

Although an individual's expressive communication is typically considered when recommending AAC, various forms of communication also are used to support comprehension. People who serve as conversation partners for students with severe and multiple disabilities should make use of several modes of communication to ensure that messages are clear and understandable. For example, before recess, a fifth grader may ask his or her classmate who has severe and multiple disabilities if he or she would like to go for a walk or read a story. The fifth grader makes his or her message easily understood by using speech and gestures as well as pointing to photographs that his or her classmate uses (e.g., someone pushing a wheelchair around the playground, two people reading a book together). This use of multiple modes of communication for receptive purposes not only clarifies the message but also models the expressive communication that is desired. Furthermore, the means of communication used for expressive purposes may differ from those used receptively. For example, Jason has severe physical and cognitive impairments and relies on speech, manual signs, facial expressions, pictures, and gestures for receptive communication. He uses facial expressions, pictures, some vocalizations, and body movements expressively, however.

Function

People communicate for different purposes or functions (Beukelman & Mirenda, 2013; Downing, 2005; Light, 1997). We might communicate to request objects and activities that we need or desire or to reject something that we do not want. We may need to confirm when something is right and protest when something is wrong. We may want to share information about others or ourselves or engage in interactions for purely social reasons, or we might need to communicate social etiquette that conveys politeness within a cultural context (e.g., saying "Please," "Thank you," "Excuse me," or "You're welcome"). It is important that communication be understood by both familiar and unfamiliar partners, regardless of the function.

The communicative forms that are available to many students with severe and multiple disabilities may limit the range of functions that can be expressed.

Sami flails his arms, whines, and shows irritation on his face when he wants to get out of his wheelchair. To a communication partner who knows Sami well, these communicative forms convey the message that Sami intends— "Get me out of this chair!" Sami's message may be misunderstood or even ignored by an unfamiliar partner, however, resulting in a communication breakdown (and a very frustrated Sami). In a situation such as this, it will be important for the educational team to provide Sami with a clearer and more conventional means to request an alternative position so that all of his communication partners (both familiar and unfamiliar) can respond accordingly.

Form and function must work together in order for communication to be successful. For example, a student might be provided with two objects or pictures in order to choose a preferred item or activity, but these same forms would not allow him or her to request attention. An SGD programmed with an attention-seeking message (e.g., "Can I play with you?") would be more appropriate for that function.

Content

Communication functions for many individuals with severe and multiple disabilities are often limited to protests and requests for desired items or activities, even when a wide range of communicative forms are available. This occurs in many cases because these students are engaged in so few activities and social interactions with other people that there is little to communicate about, beyond "I want _____" or "I don't want _____" messages. Merges, Durand, and Youngblade (2005) emphasized the importance of creating opportunities for students both with and without severe disabilities to participate together in motivating activities on a regular basis. When this occurs, students with disabilities will always have something to communicate about—the current science project, a birthday party from last weekend, the football game planned for next week, or the game everyone played at recess. Individuals with severe and multiple disabilities need to have ongoing opportunities to experience all of life's activities just as anyone would, both for the sake of their overall quality of life and to provide them with communicative content they can share with others.

Social

Communication requires at least two people—a sender and a receiver of the message. Communication partners must be especially sensitive and responsive to the efforts of individuals with severe and multiple disabilities because they often struggle to clearly convey messages. Unfortunately, communication attempts made by individuals with severe and multiple disabilities often go undetected by those around them (Chung, Carter, & Sisco, 2012b; Iacono, Carter, & Hook, 1998). Therefore, competent communication partners should be encouraged to frequently interact with individuals who have severe and multiple disabilities. Classmates without disabilities can help provide this social element of communication. Several classmates are typically available at any one point in time, and they can be taught how to be effective communication partners (Chung & Carter, 2013; Trembath, Balandin, Togher, & Stancliffe, 2009; Trottier, Kamp, & Mirenda, 2011).

ASSESSING COMMUNICATION SKILLS

Meaningful assessment of a student's communication abilities and needs is a process involving the individuals who know the student best. Family members and other long-term caregivers (e.g., respite staff) can provide critical information about how a student communicates most effectively, when and where this occurs, the frequency of social interactions, and how communication breakdowns occur. They also know the student's favorite communication topics and partners and are likely to be familiar with past communication intervention efforts and their effectiveness. Perhaps most important, they can share information about their future hopes and goals related to communication intervention. The needs and desires of family members and other significant communication partners should guide the direction of any communication intervention because these individuals will be providing the most direct and long-term support.

Informal and Dynamic Assessment

Numerous informal assessment tools and interview forms are available to assess the communication skills of children and adults with severe and multiple disabilities (see Table 7.2). Although these assessment tools may provide a general idea of a particular individual's communication skills, they do not identify the specific communication needs experienced by that individual in typical environments. To this end, several authors have described the use of a dynamic assessment process that is designed to accommodate individual needs in terms of tasks, materials, procedures, and assessors (Iacono & Caithness, 2009; Snell, 2002). Dynamic assessment captures how a student needs to communicate in a meaningful context with the guidance and support of an adult (Kublin, Wetherby, Crais, & Prizant, 1998). Unlike assessments that measure performance in out-of-context situations, dynamic assessment provides meaningful information about a student's communicative efforts in specific contexts and how to support the development of more advanced skills. Although the dynamic assessment process usually requires more time than static assessments, it also provides much richer information about an individual's communication skills, the contexts and interaction methods that are most likely to facilitate communication, and the types and amount of intervention that will be needed.

Table 7.2. Informal tools for assessing the communication skills of individuals with severe and multiple disabilities

Instrument/toolkit	Use to assess . . .	Population	Source
Communication Matrix (Rowland, 1996/2004)	Communication behaviors and functions	Individuals who use any form of communication, including presymbolic communication or augmentative and alternative communication	Design to Learn https://www.designtolearn .com
Assessing Communication and Learning in Young Children Who are Deafblind or Who Have Multiple Disabilities (Rowland, 2009)	Communication behaviors and functions	Young children who are deafblind or have multiple disabilities	Design to Learn https://www.designtolearn .com
The Triple C: Checklist of Communication Competencies– Revised (Bloomberg, West, Johnson, & Iacono, 2009)	Cognitive and early communication skills	Adolescents or adults with severe and multiple disabilities who are either presymbolic or have early symbolic skills	Spectronics http://www.spectronics .com.au
Test of Early Communication and Emerging Language (Huer & Miller, 2011)	Early communication behaviors and emerging language abilities	Infants and toddlers up to 24 months old	PRO-ED http://www.proedinc.com
Inventory of Potential Communicative Acts (Sigafoos, Arthur-Kelly, & Butterfield, 2006)	Prelinguistic communication behaviors and functions	Presymbolic communicators with developmental and/or physical disabilities	Sigafoos, Arthur-Kelly, & Butterfield (2006), Appendix A

Source: Beukelman & Mirenda (2013).

Ecological Assessment

An ecological approach to communication assessment targets the skills needed in a given environment and activity. An ecological assessment can be used to analyze the communicative requirements of the natural environment for a given student, determine what the student is currently able to communicate in this environment, and identify the skills that are lacking. This type of assessment also encourages the assessor to suggest ways to support enhanced communication skills that are appropriate for the context.

An ecological assessment involves observational data that are collected while an individual participates in a wide range of natural routines and environments. Listing the environments in which a student currently spends time and the types of communicative messages that are required in those environments is a good place to start. A holistic picture of the individual's abilities and needs can be obtained by observing how the individual with severe and multiple disabilities communicates in familiar and comfortable environments with familiar communication partners (Beukelman & Mirenda, 2013; Downing, 2005). Careful and repeated observations over time provide information about how the individual communicates (form), the purposes of communication (function), the vocabulary that is both used and required (content), and the most frequent communication partners (social context). In addition, an ecological assessment also identifies how others communicate and what their expectations are for communication (Johnston, Reichle, Feeley, & Jones, 2012). The advantage of such an assessment is that the information can be directly applied to intervention strategies. A third-grade science activity (learning about solids and liquids) has been analyzed to identify behavioral and communicative expectations for all students as well as intervention solutions for Neil, a young boy with severe and multiple disabilities (see Figure 7.1). The ecological assessment breaks down the classroom activity into individual steps and analyzes the expressive and receptive communication skills necessary for completing each of these tasks. Neil's performance is also assessed (e.g., whether he demonstrated the necessary communication skills or required prompts); the discrepancy in his communication skills is analyzed; and interventions are proposed for helping him to successfully complete the science activity.

RECOMMENDED PRACTICES FOR COMMUNICATION INTERVENTION

Considerable research exists on specific strategies that can be used to support communication of students with severe and multiple disabilities (Beukelman & Mirenda, 2013; Calculator, 2009; Chung, Carter, & Sisco, 2012a; Downing, 2005; Johnston et al., 2012; Kent-Walsh & McNaughton, 2005). Such strategies include 1) teaching within natural environments and routines, 2) providing multiple opportunities for communication, 3) offering choices, 4) ensuring the availability of responsive communication partners, and 5) providing communicative strategies for social interaction.

Student: Neil is an 8-year-old with a lot of energy, very specific likes and dislikes, a mild bilateral hearing loss, and mild cerebral palsy. He has been labeled as having a severe intellectual disability.
Activity: Science—the study of liquids and solids

Steps in activity (for classmates)	Natural cues (all children)	Student performance	Receptive (R) and expressive (E) communication required	Discrepancy analysis	Intervention plan ideas
1. Attend to teacher demonstration	Teacher instructions	Prompted	R: understand teacher	May not understand	Sit Neil close to the teacher. Teacher to use pictorial instructions and examples.
2. Respond to teacher questions	Teacher asks questions	Prompted	R: understand questions E: answer questions	May not understand Nonverbal	Teacher to ask Neil one to two simple questions, with choice of two pictures to answer.
3. Choose and sit with a partner	Teacher direction Not having a partner	No response	R: understand directions E: choose and ask partner	May not understand Nonverbal	Offer two photographs of peers from which to choose. Provide "Will you please work with me?" card to give to peer he chooses.
4. Complete worksheet on topic	Teacher direction Worksheet not completed	Prompted	R: understand teacher and peer E: comment on workshop questions	May not understand Nonverbal; does not write	Ask a functional liquid question (e.g., "Can you drink this?" "Can you take a bath/swim in this?") for each item and wait for yes/no gesture. Provide a bingo dauber so he can mark the pictures of items labeled as solids or liquids by his partner.
5. Sign name to worksheet and submit	Teacher direction Other students turning in worksheets	No response	R: understand teacher	May not understand	Provide a signature stamp for him to use. Have him collect all students' worksheets.

Figure 7.1. A third-grade science activity to identify behavioral and communicative expectations for all students as well as intervention solutions for Neil, a young boy with severe and multiple disabilities.

Teaching within Natural Environments and Routines

Teaching within natural environments is a strategy that can be applied to many types of communication interventions (Beukelman & Mirenda, 2013; Ogletree, Bruce, Finch, Fahey, & McLean, 2011). Natural environments should include a number of common characteristics—they should be highly motivating, familiar, and valued by the student and his or her family, and they should provide numerous opportunities for meaningful, sustained social-communicative interactions (Light et al., 2005). Various team members analyze the environment to identify opportunities for a student to use his or her communication skills across a wide range of functions (e.g., requesting a desired item or activity, interacting with a classmate). Then, as opportunities naturally arise that require communication interactions, a teacher or support person intervenes to support and enhance the student's communication skills. Thus, students are not required to learn important communication skills in one environment (e.g., a therapy room) and then generalize those skills to environments where they are actually required.

Providing Multiple Opportunities for Communication

Most students with severe and multiple disabilities need multiple opportunities to practice new skills. Thus, numerous communication opportunities must be made available—either naturally or by design—throughout a student's day. For example, activities of daily living can provide many opportunities for communication if teachers and caregivers structure them with this purpose in mind. Routines such as dressing, bathing, eating, toileting, and (for students with mobility challenges) changing positions occur at regular times and intervals in most homes and classrooms. If this is not the case, then these routines should be implemented as much as possible so that the student can begin to anticipate their occurrence. In addition, caregivers should perform the steps of these routines in roughly the same sequence each time so that the student can begin to anticipate what happens next. Whenever possible, caregivers should allow sufficient time to carry out each routine so that communication instruction can occur concurrently with the activity. For example, a parent might plan to extend the length of the nightly bath to allow time for a child to name each body part before it is washed or to ask for specific bath toys once washing is completed. It also is important to allow for longer response times, especially for students whose motor impairments make it difficult for them to initiate communicative behaviors. Partners need to resist the temptation to answer questions for a student or provide prompts too quickly so that the student has multiple opportunities to spontaneously initiate communication.

It may be necessary in some cases to engineer school or home environments to create additional, explicit opportunities for communication. Some simple strategies that can be used in this regard include 1) withholding an item needed to complete or engage in an activity so that the student has an opportunity to request it; 2) inserting regular, frequent opportunities for symbol

Table 7.3.   Examples of communication skills across subject areas and grades

Communicative function (purpose)	Kindergarten	Grade 4	Grade 10
Rejecting	Pushes away crayon when it is offered	Clenches teeth when disliked food is offered	Shakes head "no" when asked to start math worksheet
Commenting	Uses speech-generating device to say YOU ARE FUNNY when peer does something silly at circle time	Point to "Wow, that's cool" symbol when shown a peer's science model	Smiles and points to an actor's photograph in a magazine to tell a peer he or she liked a movie
Requesting information	Moves eyebrows together and looks at a new teacher to ask his or her name	Grabs an item in science class and looks at a peer	Signs WHAT and points to a peer's computer screen during study hall
Requesting item/action	Reaches for a cookie at snack time	Vocalizes "baaa" for ball during recess with peers	Points to one of three photographs to ask that peer to work with him or her
Confirming/denying	Smiles when asked if he or she wants to draw with a red marker	Nods his or her head when asked if a photograph in his or her conversation book is his or her dog	Looks away when asked if he or she wants help

use into classroom activities (e.g., by asking questions such as "What do we need to do?" or "Whose turn is it now?"); 3) interrupting an ongoing activity to create an opportunity for requesting or protesting; 4) providing a wrong or incomplete item in response to a request (e.g., providing part of a toy so a student has to ask for the rest); and 5) delaying assistance, thereby creating the need to ask for help (Sigafoos, 1999; Sigafoos & Mirenda, 2002; Sigafoos, O'Reilly, Drasgow, & Reichle, 2002). If such strategies are used, then it is important that they be incorporated throughout the day in naturally occurring activities and contexts. Table 7.3 includes examples of a wide range of communication opportunities and skills that might occur in classrooms from kindergarten through high school.

Offering Choices

The value of choice making to enhance communication skills has been well supported in the research literature on AAC (Beukelman & Mirenda, 2013; Downing, 2005; Sigafoos, 1999). Instead of simply giving a student an item (e.g., food, drink, toy, work), allowing the student to make a choice between two or more items creates an opportunity for him or her to communicate. Choices can be offered using speech, the items themselves, representative pictures of the items, parts of the items, or manual signs. Students can also express choices in numerous ways (e.g., by signing, looking at a desired item, pointing to or exchanging a picture of a desired item, producing a vocalization or facial expression when a desired item is offered). The choice should still be offered even if a communication partner is convinced of a student's preference (e.g., juice and not water). Preferences change, and students need to learn that they can control the outcome of communicative interactions throughout the day. Many choice-making opportunities can be embedded in high-interest, fun activities.

Tyler is a kindergartner with severe and multiple disabilities who loves animals. His teacher sets out an array of plastic animals, plastic food, and doll clothes, and then manipulates the animals for Tyler while asking him to make choices. She starts by asking "Which animal wants to eat breakfast?" while holding up a bear and a lion. After Tyler gestures toward the bear, she sits it on a toy chair in front of a toy table and asks, "What does he want to eat?" while presenting photographs of cereal and eggs. Tyler looks at eggs and she says, "He wants eggs? Does he want green eggs or blue eggs?" and holds up cards representing these two colors. Tyler and his teacher continue with this pretend play activity until several animals have eaten breakfast and selected clothes to wear to school.

This example serves as a reminder that motivation is one of the key components of successful choice making. In fact, students are unlikely to exert the effort required to make meaningful choices without a motivating context. For example, some students may not be motivated to communicate between two highly preferred items (e.g., two foods they like a lot), and it may be necessary (at least during initial instruction) to provide choices between highly preferred and unpreferred items in order to motivate choices. The following choices may be relevant across a student's day, regardless of the student's age:

- Choosing a partner to work with or sit by

- Choosing materials to use in an activity

- Choosing clothes to wear

- Choosing food or drink for snack and lunch

- Choosing a rhythm instrument for music/band

- Choosing an activity at nutrition break/recess

- Choosing a position (wheelchair, wedge, or stander)

- Choosing a book to read or have read aloud

- Choosing a software program or iPad app to use

Responsive Communication Partners

Ensuring the presence of responsive communication partners is another effective way to enhance communication opportunities (Kent-Walsh & McNaughton, 2005; Siegel & Cress, 2002; Warren, 2000). Numerous studies have unfortunately demonstrated that communication partners, even those who are experienced teachers, may miss the often subtle and unconventional communicative efforts of students with severe and multiple disabilities (Carter & Iacono, 2002; Houghton, Bronicki, & Guess, 1987; Iacono et al., 1998; Rowland, 1990).

Kyla is a high school student who has limited mobility, has low affect, and is blind. She lifts up her head and smiles slightly when she wants to make a choice; however, her teachers rarely notice her attempts to communicate. Kyla learns over time that making an effort to communicate is not likely to be met with a response, and her attempts to do so decrease substantially in frequency.

Kyla's teachers clearly require support to enhance their sensitivity and responsiveness to Kyla's unique and unconventional communicative behaviors. Fortunately, a number of evidence-based partner training programs are available to teach adults who support beginning communicators across the age range to respond contingently to both nonsymbolic and symbolic communication attempts (e.g., Bloomberg, West, Johnson, & Caithness, 2004; MacDonald, 2004; Nelson, van Dijk, Oster, & McDonnell, 2009; Sussman, 1999). The goal of contingent responding essentially is to teach an individual that his or her behavior has an impact on the behavior of others in meaningful and predictable ways. When a parent consistently responds to a child's vocalizations by approaching or when a support worker routinely responds to an adult's arm wave by moving away, the child and the adult learn that their behaviors have communicative power over the behaviors of others (Harwood, Warren, & Yoder, 2002). Providing communication dictionaries and having peers serve as models and partners are other ways to ensure that students with severe and multiple disabilities have responsive communication partners.

Communication Dictionaries   Communication or gesture dictionaries (Beukelman & Mirenda, 2013; Siegel & Wetherby, 2000) can be used to help both familiar and unfamiliar communication partners consistently recognize specific behaviors for their communicative intent. Such dictionaries usually contain descriptions of a person's gestures or other communicative behaviors, their meanings, and suggestions for appropriate responses by caregivers or others. Table 7.4 provides examples of entries in a custom communication dictionary for Kyla, the student previously described. Communication dictionaries can be constructed for individuals of any age and can be especially useful for familiarizing new caregivers with the communication patterns of students in classrooms and residential environments that have a high staff turnover.

Peers as Models and Partners   When students with severe and multiple disabilities are grouped homogeneously by ability level, interacting with one another becomes difficult because they all struggle with the same limited—and often unconventional—communication skills. Students with severe and

Table 7.4. Kyla's communication dictionary

What Kyla does	What it means	How to respond
Vocalizes loudly	She wants attention	Go to her immediately and show her how to use her BIGmack to request attention. Then offer her choices of what to do.
Cries and thrashes around	She is uncomfortable in her current position	Change her position, offering her choices of alternatives. Check for redness or sores when you move her.
Thrusts her head back hard	She does not like whatever is happening	Stop what is happening and offer alternatives, if at all possible. Follow up the activity with something she really enjoys doing.

multiple disabilities have a relatively large number of communication partners who have skills in interactive behavior, however, when they are placed with same-age peers in typical classrooms. As a result, students with significant disabilities are often more awake, active, and alert and engage in more frequent communicative interactions than students with similar disabilities in special classes (Arthur-Kelly, Foreman, Bennett, & Pascoe, 2008). For example, Foreman, Arthur-Kelly, Pascoe, and King (2004) found that students with significant disabilities in special education classrooms engaged in communicative interactions during 27% of observations, compared with 49% of interactions for students in general education classrooms. Furthermore, students in special education classrooms were engaged with their peers for only 4% of all communicative interactions, compared with 17% of all interactions in general education classrooms.

It may be necessary to teach typically developing peers specific interaction strategies to help them interact most effectively with their classmates who have severe and multiple disabilities. Peers can be taught to 1) approach their classmate at eye level; 2) wait for the classmate to initiate, or initiate an interaction themselves by saying the classmate's name or using gentle touch; 3) ask yes/no questions or simple questions about recent events; 4) use manual signs or pictures to assist with comprehension; 5) wait for a response; 6) provide help, if needed (e.g., help find a message on a communication display); and 7) respond to all communicative attempts (Chung & Carter, 2013). Peers can also be taught how to use a classmate's AAC device, ensure that the device is available to the student, and encourage the student to interact by using the device (Trottier et al., 2011). If the student with severe and multiple disabilities communicates via idiosyncratic or subtle communicative behaviors, then peers can also be taught how to use the student's communication dictionary to interpret these behaviors and respond accordingly. For example, a student may vocalize when excited or happy by emitting a high-pitched squeal that sounds as if he or she might be in pain or frightened. Teaching his or her classmates the correct meaning of this vocalization will allow them to respond appropriately and encourage him or her to interact more.

Provide Communicative Strategies for Social Interaction

Although offering choices throughout the day is recommended as a strategy to increase the number of communication interactions, limiting the student to making requests (e.g., "I want this") can make it difficult for the student to experience other reasons to communicate. Teaching the student to engage in different kinds of communication interactions increases the number of opportunities to practice critical skills and recognize the power of communicating.

Establishing social closeness is one of the most meaningful reasons to communicate (Light, 1997; Light, Parsons, & Drager, 2002). Students need to be provided with various ways to share information about themselves, tease, joke, and respond to social interactions by others.

Augie enjoys using her SGD during different activities of the day to say THAT'S COOL! because of the reaction she gets from her peers. When she makes this statement, her classmates respond by giggling, approaching her, high-fiving, and/or interacting verbally with her. This is very reinforcing for a child such as Augie, who has limited mobility and finds it difficult to initiate interactions with others. Similarly, Augie has simple knock-knock jokes programmed into her SGD so that she can initiate these social routines with her peers. First, she activates a target symbol to say KNOCK, KNOCK and waits for her classmate to respond, "Who's there?" (as most North American children know to do). She then activates the next part of the joke (e.g., COWS GO) and waits for a second response ("Cows go who?"). Finally, Augie activates the punchline: NO, COWS GO MOO! and waits for her classmates' reaction. Even if Augie does not fully understand the joke's content, she very much enjoys making her classmates laugh (or groan!) and looks forward to telling one or two new jokes each week.

Additional strategies for promoting social interactions can also be included to allow students to talk about their lives, their interests, and what they find amusing. For example, students can be provided with conversation books that contain small objects, photographs, pictures, or remnants of past events (e.g., a birthday napkin that represents going to a birthday party), with printed messages for the conversation partner to read. Hunt, Alwell, and Goetz (1991) found that providing conversation books to students with severe and multiple disabilities and teaching their classmates to support use of the books resulted in increased conversational initiations and turn taking. Figure 7.2 provides an example of a conversation book used by a fourth grader with his classmates who do not have disabilities.

SYSTEMATIC INSTRUCTION

The communication intervention strategies selected for a given student will depend on a number of variables, including the student's current ability level, communication skills being taught, social context, conversational partners, and

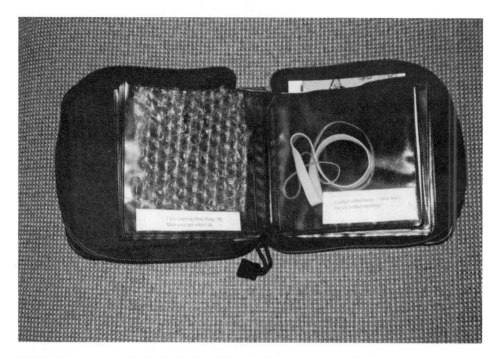

Figure 7.2. Sample conversation book with objects. Written slips in the pockets describe the items that convey personal information about the student. In this photograph, the message on the left says, "I love popping these things. My Mom goes ape when I do," and the message on the right says, "I collect rubber bands. I have tons! Do you collect anything?"

learner preferences. Beginning communicators who are provided with systematic instruction can be taught to use specific communication skills for a range of communicative purposes (Johnston et al., 2012). Systematic teaching procedures should not be overly intrusive; rather, the goal is to provide sufficient support and direction to assist a student to acquire the target behavior. For example, students with strong imitative repertoires may learn new communicative behaviors by simply observing teachers and others as they model the behavior (Solomon-Rice & Soto, 2009). A series of prompts may be required at other times. The ultimate goal is for the student to engage in spontaneous communicative behavior without instructional support.

Most-to-Least Prompting

Communicative interactions that require a discrete and immediate response (e.g., returning a greeting, indicating one's presence during a roll call) may at first require a teacher to provide full physical prompts to generate the appropriate manual sign, picture point or exchange, or SGD activation. This physical support should be faded as quickly as possible as the student begins to demonstrate the desired behavior.

When Robyn is greeted by her classmate with a high-five, her teaching assistant quickly prompts Robyn at the forearm and elbow to return the high-five. As Robyn starts to respond by moving her arm on her own, the teaching assistant offers less and less assistance by touching the back of Robyn's upper arm, then her shoulder, and finally providing only a verbal cue, "Amanda said hi to you; what can you do?" Robyn learns to independently respond to her classmates' initiations over time.

Least-to-Most Prompting

Some other types of communicative interactions, particularly those that are not time dependent, can be taught using least-to-most prompting.

When Fatemeh, a blind student with multiple disabilities, is asked by her classmates to select an activity during recess, they know that they must first wait until she has explored all of the tangible symbols on her communication display by touching them. If she makes no selection following this exploration, then the teacher taps Fatemeh's elbow and waits a few seconds (time delay) to see if that prompt is effective. If not, then the teacher asks "What do you want to do?" and moves Fatemeh's hand toward the display. If there is still no response, then the teacher reduces the number of choices and provides full physical guidance as she says, "Fatemeh, you can go on the swing (helps Fatemeh touch the symbol) or the slide (helps her touch the symbol). Which one do you want?" Finally, if Fatemeh continues to be unresponsive, then the teacher moves Fatemeh's hand to grasp one of the symbols and assists her to drop it into a classmate's hand to make a selection; they then proceed to engage in that activity. If Fatemeh continues to rely on full prompts for an extended period of time, then the teacher switches to a most-to-least prompting strategy, which can be more effective for some students (Libby, Weiss, Bancroft, & Ahearn, 2008).

ENHANCING THE SOCIAL AND PHYSICAL ENVIRONMENT

The environments where interactions occur must be carefully considered, regardless of the teaching strategy used when teaching communication skills. As previously noted, the natural environment is the preferred location for communication interventions. Teachers and caregivers must consider whether any accommodations to the natural environment are necessary for the student. Both social and physical environment accommodations can help facilitate communication skill development.

Social Environment Accommodations

Beginning communicators of any age need many opportunities within any given day to engage in and practice communication skills. Efforts should be made to place the student in physical proximity to responsive and interactive partners, including their peers without disabilities. Adults can also monitor their own positions in regard to the student and ensure that they (the adults) do not interfere with potential peer social interactions while providing support (Chung et al., 2012b). For example, instead of positioning herself between Warren and a nearby classmate, Susan (Warren's teaching assistant) deliberately sits behind both students or offers assistance from across a table or desk. Increasing the time students work in pairs or in groups can also enhance the likelihood of peer interactions; thus, opportunities should be created whenever possible to allow students with severe and multiple disabilities to work together with peers in large- or small-group contexts (Chung & Carter, 2013). Some authors, however, caution against placing students with disabilities primarily in the role of the tutee who is assisted by a peer tutor without disabilities because such unequal relationships can hinder social interactions (Hughes, Carter, Hughes, Bradford, & Copeland, 2002). Thus, if peer tutoring is employed during some activities, then students with significant disabilities should also be provided with time to interact with classmates on a more equal basis during unstructured times throughout the day (e.g., passing in the hall, eating lunch, playing at recess). Students can also be offered choices of classmates with whom to interact during these times.

Physical Environment Accommodations

Accommodations and adjustments to the physical environment can also help increase the number of opportunities for communication. For example, ensuring rich, interesting learning environments with pictures, books, and items to explore provides all students with opportunities to direct the attention of others to these items and comment on them. Books with photographs of students engaged in favorite activities at home or at school, complete with captions and questions, allow students to share important events in their lives with classmates, teachers, family members, and neighborhood friends. Books with tangible items representing a student's interests can also be used by students who are blind or visually impaired and by students who are not yet able to use pictures or other symbols to communicate.

Physical positioning must also be considered for students with severe physical and/or sensory impairments. Physical and occupational therapists can help the educational team determine the best positions for a student so that he or she can communicate more effectively and efficiently (see Chapter 3 for more information on positioning). Students must be physically supported and comfortable; must be able to see, hear, and/or touch conversational partners and the AAC symbols that are provided; and must be able to physically engage in different communicative behaviors without undue effort and fatigue. Figure 7.3 provides a checklist of important considerations to guide effective communication skills intervention.

ENSURING ACCESS TO AUGMENTATIVE AND ALTERNATIVE COMMUNICATION DEVICES

The U.S. NJC for the Communication Needs of Persons with Severe Disabilities (2003a) issued a position statement on eligibility for communication

Has the environment been arranged so that the student has opportunities to communicate for different purposes?

❑ No   ❑ Yes

Is the student in the best physical position to communicate effectively, either nonsymbolically or with an augmentative and alternative communication (AAC) device?

❑ No   ❑ Yes

Is the student at eye level and close to other students with whom to communicate?

❑ No   ❑ Yes

Is the student physically close enough to see, hear, and/or touch conversational partners?

❑ No   ❑ Yes

Does the student have easy access to his or her AAC device at all times? This is especially important if different communication devices have been obtained or developed for different social situations.

❑ No   ❑ Yes

Is the student a member of different social groups throughout the day?

❑ No   ❑ Yes

Are students encouraged to work as partners or in small groups?

❑ No   ❑ Yes

Are students encouraged to interact at lunch and recess?

❑ No   ❑ Yes

Figure 7.3. Checklist for communication skill intervention.

services and support (see http://www.asha.org/NJC/). The statement emphasized that

> Decisions regarding types, amounts, and duration of services provided, intervention
> setting, and service delivery models should be based on the individual's communica-
> tion needs and preferences. Eligibility determinations based on *a priori* criteria violate
> recommended practice principles by precluding consideration of individual needs.
> (NJC, 2003a, p. 20)

Several of the *a priori* criteria deemed inappropriate pertained to students
with severe and multiple disabilities, including 1) discrepancies between cognitive and communication functioning; 2) absence of cognitive or other skills
purported to be prerequisites; 3) failure to benefit from previous communication services and supports; and 4) restrictive interpretations of educational, vocational, and/or medical necessity. The Assistive Technology Act Amendments
of 2004 (PL 108-364) led to the dissolution of many barriers that formerly made
AAC services inaccessible to many United States citizens who needed them.
SGDs were deemed durable medical equipment in 2001, after many months of
work by a coalition of dedicated AAC professionals, and are now funded by
Medicare. Professionals, people with disabilities, and family members in many
Canadian provinces have worked with government officials to expand SGD
availability to individuals with significant disabilities. Numerous AAC systems
and devices are now available to support the communicative needs of students
with severe and multiple disabilities as a result of these efforts.

AAC devices can range from simple, low-technology communication displays with two tangible symbols to dedicated SGDs to iPads and other touch-
screen devices that are paired with various apps and also produce speech. An
individual might use one or more such devices combined with manual signs,
gestures, and vocalizations. Students across age and ability ranges can benefit
from the use of AAC devices and deserve the right to do so (Downing, 2000;
Romski, Sevcik, Hyatt, & Cheslock, 2002).

Choosing an Augmentative and Alternative Device

Decisions regarding which device(s) is appropriate for an individual student
require consideration of his or her current communication repertoire; symbolic,
language, and literacy skills; motor skills; and sensory abilities (Beukelman &
Mirenda, 2013). In addition, an individual's current and future communication
needs, interests, and preferences should determine the types of symbols used,
how they are displayed, and how they are selected to convey messages. For example, communication symbols and displays for students with visual impairments need to be clear, visually uncluttered, and with good contrast. Symbols
may need to be enlarged and/or outlined in bold, depending on the student's
abilities. Use of color to increase a symbol's resemblance to its referent should
also be considered. Symbols can range from those that closely resemble what
they represent, such as a tangible item or part of an item (e.g., a specific plate or
bib to represent snack time), or they can be more abstract (e.g., a photograph of
a swing to represent a swing). Regardless of the type of symbol or the reading

ability of the student, a written message should be paired with every symbol to make the communicative message clear to the conversational partner.

Cultural and Family Factors   Cultural and familial influences must be considered when making decisions concerning AAC device selection. Text messages may be in English as well as the family's native language, depending on such influences. In addition, families may have preferences for the types of symbols used, the vocabulary represented on the device, the outward appearance of the device, and whether voice output is provided. Symbols may be perceived differently depending on one's cultural background and experiences, making it imperative that families be involved in symbol selection (Huer, 2000). Parette, Brotherson, and Huer (2000) stressed the critical importance of involving the family in all AAC decision making, given differences in culture, values, and desired goals.

Selection Techniques   A student's motor and visual abilities largely determine how symbols are delivered to the student and selected by the student. Students with severe physical impairments who are able to look at an object or symbol and hold their gaze steady for at least a few seconds may select messages using nonelectronic eye pointing or may learn to use eye tracking on a computer (Beukelman & Mirenda, 2013). Students with good neck and head control may select symbols from a computer display using a head mouse or safe laser pointer (Beukelman & Mirenda, 2013). Students with good hand and finger control can directly select an appropriate symbol from a display by pointing to it, reaching toward it, grasping it, or handing it to a communicative partner (e.g., in the Picture Exchange Communication System [PECS]; Frost & Bondy, 2002; see Almeida, Piza, & LaMonica, 2005; Lund & Troha, 2008; and Okalidou & Malandraki, 2007 for examples of using PECS with students with severe and multiple disabilities). Alternatively, students without skills in any of these domains can use either visual or auditory scanning to select symbols or messages. Symbols are displayed or lit (on a computer device) one at a time in visual scanning, and the student uses a microswitch, vocalization, or gesture to make a selection. A person or computer voice announces message options one at a time in auditory scanning, and the student makes a selection using one of the aforementioned techniques. A student's motor and sensory abilities can be matched to one of the available selection techniques most of the time; an individualized selection option will need to be created by the educational and rehabilitation team if this is not the case.

COMMUNICATION AND PROBLEM BEHAVIOR

Many individuals who do not have an adequate communication system develop unconventional or even problematic behaviors (e.g., tantrums, self-injury) that are used to communicate wants and needs. These individuals then require systematic support and guidance to acquire conventional communication modes that are more universally recognized, socially acceptable, and efficient. Sigafoos (2000) found a strong inverse relationship between communication skills and the amount of problem behavior in 13 young children with developmental disabilities. Thus, if a child learns that banging his or her head against a wall and screaming results in adult attention, then the child may continue to use this form of communication because of its effectiveness. Or, a teenager who uses a wheelchair and is unable to speak or move without assistance may learn to rely on crying and banging on his or her wheelchair to attract assistance in order to get out of the chair or reposition his or her body.

A technique known as functional communication training (FCT) has been used widely since the 1980s in response to such behaviors. FCT requires an assessment aimed at identifying the function (i.e., communicative message) of the behavior of concern, which is then matched with one or more new, functionally equivalent communicative behaviors (Sigafoos, Arthur, & O'Reilly, 2003). The new behavior(s) must be at least as easy for the individual to produce as the problem behavior and must also be as effective in obtaining the desired outcome. Systematic teaching strategies such as prompting and fading are then used to teach the new behaviors in natural contexts (see Bopp, Brown, & Mirenda, 2004; Sigafoos et al., 2003; Tiger, Hanley, & Bruzek, 2008).

Tia bit her wrist and squealed when she became frustrated and wanted a break from schoolwork. Tia learned that biting and squealing were effective for getting what she wanted because her teacher usually gave her a short break when these behaviors occurred. These behaviors were not socially appropriate, however, and were quite disruptive in Tia's classroom, so her teacher decided to teach Tia another way to ask for a break. She provided Tia with a pictorial symbol and printed message ("I really need a break") that was affixed to a wristband that she wore most of her day on her dominant (left) arm. This solution was chosen because it was simple to use, always available, did not take up any room, and fit within the context of Tia's classroom. Careful observation of Tia in class made it clear that she usually started moving her arms before she began biting and squealing, so when Tia's educational assistant saw this early behavior, she prompted her to wave her left arm vigorously to attract the teacher's attention. Tia's teacher then approached her and offered a short break from work. Efforts were also made to offer Tia choices of which materials to use, the order in which she completed assigned tasks, and the classmates with whom she could work to increase her motivation when difficult tasks were assigned. Tia learned to wave her left arm to ask for a break within a few weeks, and her biting and squealing ceased.

Early efforts to assist children to effectively communicate using the most conventional means possible can not only prevent the development of inappropriate communication skills but can also help children meet their social needs. The challenge is to find the most effective strategies for each individual child and to support that child's receptive and expressive communication development.

A COLLABORATIVE APPROACH TO COMMUNICATION INTERVENTION

A collaborative intervention approach is recommended to ensure consistency across team members in supporting the communication skill development of students with severe and multiple disabilities. Team members readily share information, engage in role release, and cooperate in all aspects of assessment and intervention (see Chapter 1). Everyone supporting the student will need to know how the student communicates and how to build on these communication efforts because no one family member or service provider can (or should) be with a student with challenging needs all of the time. True collaborative teaming to ensure effective instruction is considered a recommended practice with students who have disabilities, regardless of where they are educated (Calculator, 2009; Giangreco, 2000; Soto, Muller, Hunt, & Goetz, 2001).

Specialists bring their expertise to students (push in) in an integrated service delivery model, rather than requiring students to leave their classrooms to gain access to expertise (pull out) (Giangreco, Suter, & Hurley, 2013; Simonsen et al., 2010). Thus, service providers contribute to a student's educational program by infusing or embedding their expertise into the ongoing activities of the classroom.

Recall Sharitha, the student introduced at the beginning of this chapter. Ms. Easton, a speech-language pathologist, provides weekly support to Sharitha in her 11th-grade drama class. Students in this class often participate in small-group activities that are ideal for addressing Sharitha's need to learn to use her AAC device. When she is in the classroom, Ms. Easton shows Sharitha's peers how to prompt her to use her device during group activities. She also checks with the drama teacher to preview the vocabulary that Sharitha will need in upcoming weeks so that she can assign an educational assistant to program the device with required vocabulary ahead of time. Ms. Easton also works with Sharitha once each week at lunchtime to support her requests for food and assistance and to facilitate her social interactions with peers through the use of a personalized conversation book. Ms. Easton is able to demonstrate to others how support is best provided by infusing her skills and knowledge into Sharitha's drama class and lunch, and, as a result, they can replicate the techniques she uses across the day (Craig, Haggart, & Hull, 1999).

CONCLUSION

Research related to strategies for supporting the functional communication and language development of people with severe and multiple disabilities has exploded since the late 1990s (e.g., Beukelman & Mirenda, 2013; Johnston et al., 2012). In particular, the AAC-RERC on Communication Enhancement (http://www.aac-rerc.com) includes a number of research and development projects that pertain directly to individuals with significant disabilities across the age range. The Pennsylvania State University AAC web site (http://aackids. psu.edu/index.php/page/show/id/1) is also a valuable resource for those working with young children with complex communication needs. The future for people who experience severe communication challenges is promising as researchers and clinicians continue to develop strategies for AAC assessment and intervention that enable these individuals to fully participate in home, school, and community life.

REFLECTION QUESTIONS

1. How are the communication needs of students with severe and multiple disabilities currently addressed in your school district?

2. Which of the practices discussed in this chapter are currently used/not used?

3. What would it take to improve communication service delivery to these students?

4. What are two actions that could be undertaken in the next 3–6 months to accomplish this?

CHAPTER ACTIVITY

Alice is a 5-year-old student with CP and severe visual impairment who does not use speech to communicate. She just entered kindergarten this year and does not have a communication system. What are 10 actions you would advise her teacher to take in the first few months of school to support Alice's ability to participate in the activities and routines of kindergarten along with her peers?

REFERENCES

Almeida, M., Piza, M., & LaMonica, D. (2005). Adaptações do sistema de comunicação por troca de figuras no contexto escolar [Adaptation of the Picture Exchange Communication System in a school context]. *Pró-Fono Revista de Atualização Científica, 17*, 233–240.

Arthur-Kelly, M., Foreman, P., Bennett, D., & Pascoe, S. (2008). Interaction, inclusion, and students with profound and multiple disabilities: Towards an agenda for research and practice. *Journal of Research in Special Educational Needs, 8*, 161–166.

Assistive Technology Act Amendments of 2004, PL 108-364, 29 U.S.C. §§ 3001 *et seq.*

Beukelman, D.R., & Mirenda, P. (2013). *Augmentative and alternative communication: Supporting children and adults with complex communication needs* (4th ed.). Baltimore, MD: Paul H. Brookes Publishing Co.

Bloomberg, K., West, D., Johnson, H., & Caithness, T. (2004). *InterAACtion: Strategies for intentional and unintentional communicators* [Videotape]. St. Kilda, Victoria, Australia: Scope Communication Resource Centre.

Bloomberg, K., West, D., Johnson, H., & Iacono, T. (2009). *The triple C: Checklist of communication competencies-revised).* St. Kilda, Victoria, Australia: Scope Communication Resource Centre.

Bopp, K., Brown, K., & Mirenda, P. (2004). Speech-language pathologists' roles in the delivery of positive behavior support for individuals with developmental disabilities. *American Journal of Speech-Language Pathology, 13*, 5–19.

Calculator, S. (2009). Augmentative and alternative communication (AAC) and inclusive education for students with the most severe disabilities. *International Journal of Inclusive Education, 13,* 93–113.

Carter, M., & Iacono, T. (2002). Professional judgments of the intentionality of communicative acts. *Augmentative and Alternative Communication, 18,* 177–191.

Chung, Y-C., & Carter, E. (2013). Promoting peer interactions in inclusive classrooms for students who use speech-generating devices. *Research and Practice for Persons with Severe Disabilities, 38,* 94–109.

Chung, Y-C., Carter, E., & Sisco, L. (2012a). A systematic review of interventions to increase peer interactions for students with complex communication challenges. *Research and Practice for Persons with Severe Disabilities, 37,* 271–287.

Chung, Y-C., Carter, E., & Sisco, L. (2012b). Social interactions of students with disabilities who use augmentative and alternative communication in inclusive classrooms. *American Journal on Intellectual and Developmental Disabilities, 117,* 349–367.

Craig, S.E., Haggart, A.G., & Hull, K.M. (1999). Integrating therapies into the educational setting: Strategies for supporting children with severe disabilities. *Physical Disabilities: Education and Related Services, XVII,* 91–109.

Cress, C.J. (2002). Expanding children's early augmented behaviors to support symbolic development. In J. Reichle, D.R. Beukelman, & J.C. Light (Eds.), *Exemplary practices for beginning communicators: Implications for AAC* (pp. 219–272). Baltimore, MD: Paul H. Brookes Publishing Co.

Downing, J.E. (2000). Augmentative communication devices: A critical aspect of assistive technology. *Journal of Special Education Technology, 15*(3), 35–40.

Downing, J.E., Hanreddy, A., & Peckham-Hardin, K.D. (2015). *Teaching communication skills to students with severe disabilities* (3rd ed.). Baltimore, MD: Paul H. Brookes Publishing Co.

Foreman, P., Arthur-Kelly, M., Pascoe, S., & King, B. (2004). Evaluating the educational experiences of students with profound and multiple disabilities in inclusive and segregated classroom settings: An Australian perspective. *Research and Practice for Persons with Severe Disabilities, 29,* 183–193.

Frost, L., & Bondy, A. (2002). *Picture Exchange Communication System training manual* (2nd ed.). Newark, DE: Pyramid Education Products.

Giangreco, M.F. (2000). Related services research for students with low-incidence disabilities: Implications for speech-language pathologists in inclusive classrooms. *Language, Speech, and Hearing in Schools, 31,* 230–239.

Giangreco, M.F., Suter, J., & Hurley, S. (2013). Revisiting personnel utilization in inclusion-oriented schools. *Journal of Special Education, 47,* 121–132.

Harwood, K., Warren, S.F., & Yoder, P. (2002). The importance of responsivity in developing contingent exchanges with beginning communicators. In J. Reichle, D.R. Beukelman, & J.C. Light (Eds.), *Exemplary practices for beginning communicators: Implications for AAC* (pp. 59–96). Baltimore, MD: Paul H. Brookes Publishing Co.

Houghton, J., Bronicki, G., & Guess, D. (1987). Opportunities to express preferences and make choices among students with severe disabilities in classroom settings. *Journal of The Association for Persons with Severe Handicaps, 12,* 18–27.

Huer, M.B. (2000). Examining perceptions of graphic symbols across cultures: Preliminary study of the impact of culture/ethnicity. *Augmentative and Alternative Communication, 16,* 180–185.

Huer, M.B., & Miller, L. (2011). *Test of early communication and emerging language (TECEL).* Austin, TX: PRO-ED.

Hughes, C., Carter, E.W., Hughes, T., Bradford, E., & Copeland, S.R. (2002). Effects of instructional versus non-instructional roles on the social interactions of high school students. *Education and Training in Mental Retardation and Developmental Disabilities, 37,* 146–162.

Hunt, P., Alwell, M., & Goetz, L. (1991). Interacting with peers through conversation turn taking with a communication book adaptation. *Augmentative and Alternative Communication, 7,* 117–126.

Iacono, T., & Caithness, T. (2009). Assessment issues. In P. Mirenda & T. Iacono (Eds.), *Autism spectrum disorders and AAC* (pp. 23–48). Baltimore, MD: Paul H. Brookes Publishing Co.

Iacono, T., Carter, M., & Hook, J. (1998). Identification of intentional communication in students with severe multiple disabilities. *Augmentative and Alternative Communication, 14,* 102–114.

Johnston, S.S., Reichle, J., Feeley, K.M., & Jones, E.A. (2012). *AAC strategies for individuals with moderate to severe disabilities.* Baltimore, MD: Paul H. Brookes Publishing Co.

Kent-Walsh, J., & McNaughton, D. (2005). Communication partner instruction in AAC: Present practices and future directions. *Augmentative and Alternative Communication, 21,* 195–204.

Kublin, K.S., Wetherby, A.M., Crais, E.R., & Prizant, B.M. (1998). Prelinguistic dynamic assessment: A transactional perspective. In A.M. Wetherby, S.F. Warren, & J. Reichle (Eds.), *Transitions in prelinguistic communication* (pp. 285–312). Baltimore, MD: Paul H. Brookes Publishing Co.

Libby, M., Weiss, J., Bancroft, S., & Ahearn, W. (2008). A comparison of most-to-least and least-to-most prompting on the acquisition of solitary play skills. *Behavior Analysis in Practice, 1*(1), 37–43.

Light, J. (1997). "Communication is the essence of human life": Reflections on communicative competence. *Augmentative and Alternative Communication, 13,* 61–70.

Light, J., Drager, K., Curran, J., Hayes, E., Kristiansen, L., Lewis, W.,... Witte, M. (2005). *AAC interventions to maximize language development for young children.* Retrieved from http://aac-rerc.psu.edu/index.php/webcasts/show/id/7

Light, J.C., Parsons, A.R., & Drager, K. (2002). "There's more to life than cookies": Developing interactions for social closeness with beginning communicators who use AAC. In J. Reichle, D.R. Beukelman, & J.C. Light (Eds.), *Exemplary practices for beginning communicators: Implications for AAC* (pp. 187–218). Baltimore, MD: Paul H. Brookes Publishing Co.

Lund, S., & Troha, J. (2008). Teaching young people who are blind and have autism to make requests using a variation of the Picture Exchange Communication System with tactile symbols: A preliminary investigation. *Journal of Autism and Developmental Disorders, 38,* 719–730.

MacDonald, J. (2004). *Communicating partners: Developmental guidelines for professionals and parents.* London, England: Jessica Kingsley Publishers.

Merges, E.M., Durand, V.M., & Youngblade, L. (2005). The role of communicative partners. In J.E. Downing (Ed.), *Teaching communication skills to students with severe disabilities* (2nd ed., pp. 175–199). Baltimore, MD: Paul H. Brookes Publishing Co.

Mirenda, P. (1993). AAC: Bonding the uncertain mosaic. *Augmentative and Alternative Communication, 9,* 3–9.

Mirenda, P. (2005). Considerations in developing and acquiring communication aids. In J.E. Downing, A. Hanreddy, & K. Peckhan-Hardin (Eds.), *Teaching communication skills to students with severe disabilities* (3rd ed., pp. 137-162). Baltimore, MD: Paul H. Brookes Publishing Co.

National Joint Committee for the Communication Needs of Persons with Severe Disabilities. (2003a). Position statement on access to communication services and supports: Concerns regarding the application of restrictive eligibility policies. *ASHA Supplement, 23,* 19–20.

National Joint Committee for the Communication Needs of Persons with Severe Disabilities. (2003b). Supporting documentation for the position statement on access to communication services and supports: Concerns regarding the application of restrictive eligibility policies. *ASHA Supplement, 23,* 73–81.

Nelson, C., van Dijk, J., Oster, T., & McDonnell, A. (2009). *Child-guided strategies: The van Dijk approach to assessment.* Louisville, KY: American Printing House for the Blind.

Ogletree, B., Bruce, S., Finch, A., Fahey, R., & McLean, L. (2011). Recommended communication-based interventions for individuals with severe intellectual disabilities. *Communication Disorders Quarterly, 32,* 164–175.

Okalidou, A., & Malandraki, G. (2007). The application of PECS in children with autism and deafness: A case study. *Focus on Autism and Other Developmental Disabilities, 22,* 23–32.

Parette, H.P., Brotherson, M.J., & Huer, M.B. (2000). Giving families a voice in augmentative and alternative communication decision-making. *Education and Training in Mental Retardation and Developmental Disabilities, 35,* 177–190.

Romski, M.A., Sevcik, R.A., Hyatt, A.M., & Cheslock, M. (2002). A continuum of AAC language intervention strategies for beginning communicators. In J. Reichle, D.R. Beukelman, & J.C. Light (Eds.), *Exemplary practices for beginning communicators: Implications for AAC* (pp. 1–23). Baltimore, MD: Paul H. Brookes Publishing Co.

Rowland, C. (1990). Communication in the classroom for children with dual sensory impairments: Studies of teacher and child behavior. *Augmentative and Alternative Communication, 6,* 262–274.

Rowland, C. (1996/2004). *Communication matrix.* Portland, OR: Design to Learn.

Rowland, C. (Ed.). (2009). *Assessing communication and learning in young children who are deafblind or who have multiple disabilities.* Portland, OR: Design to Learn.

Siegel, E., & Cress, P. (2002). Overview of the emergence of early AAC behaviors: Progression from communicative to symbolic skills. In J. Reichle, D.R. Beukelman, & J.C. Light (Eds.), *Exemplary practices for beginning communicators: Implications for AAC* (pp. 2–8). Baltimore, MD: Paul H. Brookes Publishing Co.

Siegel, E., & Wetherby, A. (2000). Nonsymbolic communication. In M. Snell & F. Brown (Eds.), *Instruction of students with severe disabilities* (5th ed., pp. 409–451). Upper Saddle River, NJ: Prentice Hall.

Sigafoos, J. (1999). Creating opportunities for augmentative and alternative communication strategies for involving people with developmental disabilities. *Augmentative and Alternative Communication, 15,* 183–190.

Sigafoos, J. (2000). Communication development and aberrant behavior in children with developmental disabilities. *Education and Training in Mental Retardation and Developmental Disabilities, 35,* 168–176.

Sigafoos, J., Arthur, M., & O'Reilly, M. (2003). *Challenging behavior and developmental disability.* Baltimore, MD: Paul H. Brookes Publishing Co.

Sigafoos, J., Arthur-Kelly, M., & Butterfield, N. (2006). *Enhancing everyday communication for children with disabilities.* Baltimore, MD: Paul H. Brookes Publishing Co.

Sigafoos, J., & Drasgow, E. (2001). Conditional use of aided and unaided AAC: A review and clinical case demonstration. *Focus on Autism and Other Developmental Disabilities, 16,* 152–161.

Sigafoos, J., & Mirenda, P. (2002). Strengthening communicative behaviors for gaining access to desired items and activities. In J. Reichle, D.R. Beukelman, & J.C. Light (Eds.), *Exemplary practices for beginning communicators: Implications for AAC* (pp. 123–156). Baltimore, MD: Paul H. Brookes Publishing Co.

Sigafoos, J., O'Reilly, M.F., Drasgow, E., & Reichle, J. (2002). Strategies to achieve socially acceptable escape and avoidance. In J. Reichle, D.R. Beukelman, & J.C. Light (Eds.), *Exemplary practices for*

beginning communicators: Implications for AAC (pp. 157–186). Baltimore, MD: Paul H. Brookes Publishing Co.

Simonsen, B., Shaw, S., Faggella-Luby, M., Sugai, G., Coyne, M., Rhein, B.,... Alfano, M. (2010). A schoolwide model for service delivery: Redefining special educators as interventionists. *Remedial and Special Education, 31,* 17–23.

Snell, M. (2002). Using dynamic assessment with learners who communicate nonsymbolically. *Augmentative and Alternative Communication, 18,* 163–176.

Solomon-Rice, P., & Soto, G. (2009). Language modeling as an efficacious early language intervention approach with young children demonstrating complex communication needs. *Perspectives on Augmentative and Alternative Communication, 18,* 21–27.

Soto, G., Muller, E., Hunt, P., & Goetz, L. (2001). Critical issues in the inclusion of students who use average and alternative communication: An educational team perspective. *Augmentative and Alternative Communication, 17,* 62–72.

Sussman, F. (1999). *More than words: Helping parents to promote communication and social skills in children with autism spectrum disorder.* Toronto, Canada: Hanen Centre.

Tiger, J., Hanley, G., & Bruzek, J. (2008). Functional communication training: A review and practical guide. *Behavior Analysis in Practice, 1*(1), 16–23.

Trembath, D., Balandin, S., Togher, L., & Stancliffe, R.J. (2009). Peer-mediated teaching and augmentative and alternative communication for preschool-aged children with autism. *Journal of Intellectual and Developmental Disability, 34,* 173–186.

Trottier, N., Kamp, L., & Mirenda, P. (2011). Effects of peer-mediated instruction to teach use of speech-generating devices to students with autism in social game routines. *Augmentative and Alternative Communication, 27,* 26–39.

Warren, S.F. (2000). The future of early communication and language intervention. *Topics in Early Childhood Special Education, 20,* 33–37.

8

Nutrition and Mealtime Considerations

CAROLE K. IVEY AND DIANNE KOONTZ LOWMAN

CHAPTER OBJECTIVES

1. Understand terms associated with mealtime

2. Describe typical development of feeding, eating, and swallowing

3. Describe the contributions of different professionals and perspectives to the feeding team

4. Understand the interrelated medical, developmental, behavioral, and psychosocial aspects of mealtime and the importance of mealtime routines

KEY TERMS

- Adaptive equipment
- Aspiration
- Dining
- Eating
- Feeding
- Food refusal
- Food selectivity

- Mealtime
- Retraction
- Rotary chewing
- Rumination
- Tongue protrusion
- Tongue thrust

A teacher has just observed Joseph's mother feeding him. Joseph is a 6-year-old child with severe spasticity due to cerebral palsy (CP). He attempts to straighten when he is placed in his Rifton seat, which forces his head into extension. His mother feeds him by using his teeth to scrape the food off the spoon. The food naturally falls down his throat because his head is extended. This method of feeding can be unsafe, however, and lead to health complications. How can we make feeding safer for Joseph? How can we collaborate with Joseph's mother about more effective and safe feeding techniques?

The staff of the vocational program has become concerned about Frank, a 15-year-old student with an intellectual disability as well as visual and auditory impairments. He has recently started ruminating (regurgitating or vomiting up food and then spitting, chewing, or reswallowing the food) daily after lunch. The staff is worried that this behavior will threaten Frank's health as well as his ability to participate in the workplace. The educational team is charged with evaluating and addressing this new behavior.

Collette is an 11th grader with CP. Collette's teacher and mother are advocating for the addition of feeding goals focused on increasing Collette's independence with self-feeding. The speech-language pathologist (SLP) and the occupational therapist (OT) on the team have serious concerns about her safety with eating, however, due to her most recent swallow study. The team must decide how to balance medical risks with teaching Collette a valued life skill.

Mealtime is an essential activity that occurs several times a day in most families, including those with and without a child with disabilities. Consider a significant family event, holiday, or rite of passage and the customs and processes associated with it. These events and milestones revolve around food in most cases. Mealtimes not only afford the sustenance that the body needs to survive, but also help build social relationships. Mealtimes are an avenue for sharing knowledge, moral perspectives, and cultural convention, and they are a social event, allowing for language development and understanding. Therefore, mealtime is a foundation of meaningful participation in everyday life and learning (Ochs & Shohet, 2006). Family mealtimes are consistently recommended for healthy families and children, and they can have an impact on decreasing obesity, improving academic achievement, and decreasing substance abuse (Cook & Dunifon, 2012). Meals provide children not only with the nutrition needed for growth and survival, but also the pleasure of enjoyable tastes and aromas, the opportunity for positive social interaction, the formation of nurturing relationships, and the chance to be independent.

In contrast, disability literature and research describe a much bleaker picture of mealtimes for children with disabilities in which the focus is almost exclusively on problems with the mechanics of eating with little consideration of the social aspects of mealtimes. Studies estimate that 33%–80% of children with developmental disabilities have problems with feeding, including 30%–40% of children with CP (Sullivan et al., 2000), 30% with intellectual disability (Matson, Cooper, Mayville, & Gonzalez, 2006), and 46%–75% with autism (Ledford & Gast, 2006). The number of children with severe motor disabilities who have feeding issues is also increasing (Andrew, Parr, & Sullivan, 2012). Furthermore, one third of children with severe disabilities are significantly undernourished, with inadequate intake due to self-feeding impairment or oral-motor dysfunction (Sullivan et al., 2000).

The types of mealtime challenges for students with severe and multiple disabilities can be many and varied. Children with CP commonly experience eating problems, inadequate food intake, and decreased appetite (Gisel, 1996; Sullivan et al., 2000). Disorders of muscle tone may make lip closure difficult, interfering with the child's ability to take food from a spoon or hold liquids in the mouth. The presence of primitive reflexes (e.g., tonic bite reflex) may make chewing difficult (Morris & Klein, 2000; Schuberth, Amirault, & Case-Smith, 2010). Structural abnormalities, such as cleft lip, can also complicate eating (Schuberth et al., 2010). Children with intellectual disabilities may have problems with inadequate food intake, food selectivity, vomiting and rumination, lack of self-feeding skills, improper pacing of food intake, and food refusal (Matson et al., 2006). In particular, children with autism may demonstrate a variety of issues with food intake and refusal, discussed in more detail later in this chapter (Marí-Bauset, Zazpe, Mari-Sanchis, Llopis-González, & Morales-Suárez-Varela, 2013).

A significant number of children with severe and multiple disabilities clearly require some form of mealtime assistance. The impact of mealtime disorders is not limited to mealtime alone, however; feeding and the resulting impact on nutrition can affect the child's quality of life, social participation, growth, general health, attention, behavior, and learning. Mealtime disorders also have an impact on the family, with increased incidence of parental stress and lost family time being reported (Andrew et al., 2012; Schwier & Stewart, 2005; Sullivan et al., 2000). Taken in this context, it is no surprise that issues related to mealtimes can have a widespread impact on children with disabilities, their caregivers, and their families.

This chapter describes many considerations associated with mealtime for students with severe and multiple disabilities, including mealtime contexts; development of mealtime skills; assessment of feeding, eating, and the mealtime process; treatment of mealtime challenges; and other specific considerations. Multiple processes and terms are involved in mealtimes, and they are so closely interrelated that they are hard to separate. The following definitions, however, are used in this chapter for greater clarity:

- *Mealtime:* This is the broadest term to encompass all that is related to eating, feeding, and dining, including associated social and contextual aspects.

- *Eating:* Eating is the process of "keeping and manipulating food [or fluid] in the mouth and swallowing it" (American Occupational Therapy Association [AOTA], 2014, p. S19). Eating includes the oral-motor processes required of the jaw, tongue, and lips. Swallowing is often considered a part of the eating process, although difficulty with swallowing or the inability to swallow is termed *dysphagia*.

- *Feeding:* Feeding is the process of "setting up, arranging, and bringing food [or fluid] from the plate or cup to the mouth" (AOTA, 2014, p. S19). This term encompasses both the process of feeding another person as well as feeding oneself, often referred to as *self-feeding*.

- *Dining:* Dining is the "meaning, activities, and context of consuming food. A shared activity rather than an act someone does to another person" (Schwier & Stewart, 2005, p. 16).

Feeding, eating, and the processes they require (e.g., swallowing) involve effective coordination among the motor, sensory, and cognitive systems. As such, intellectual, physical, and developmental disabilities largely affect feeding and eating skills. Feeding, eating, and swallowing are also strongly influenced by psychosocial, cultural, and environmental factors (AOTA, 2007). These aspects can be forgotten when the act of feeding and eating are difficult. Even when individuals are faced with considerable issues with feeding and eating, Schwier and Stewart asked for consideration of dining, which "implies something beyond the physical act of getting food into oneself or someone else" (2005, p. 15).

UNDERSTANDING FEEDING AND EATING

It is helpful to understand the typical processes associated with feeding and eating to understand feeding and eating in children with severe and multiple disabilities. This topic will be reviewed, followed by information on common issues faced by children with severe and multiple disabilities at mealtimes.

Typical Feeding, Eating, and Swallowing

Typical development of feeding, eating, and swallowing begins in utero. Fetuses are swallowing as early as 10 weeks gestational age, are suckling at 12–18 weeks, and are cupping their tongue at 28 weeks (Eicher, 2013; Lane, 2012). Typically developing newborns nurse using a pattern that allows them to breathe, suck, and swallow simultaneously. The newborn's jaw, cheeks, lips, and tongue move together as one unit, with the jaw and the front of the tongue moving up together and the tongue moving backward and forward rhythmically, a process called *suckling* (Morris & Klein, 2000; Schuberth et al., 2010). The tongue gradually shifts to an up-and-down movement with firmer lip closure (sucking) through the first 6 months, allowing for greater ability to draw soft food and liquid into the mouth. Swallowing is integrated with all of these patterns (Eicher, 2013; Morris & Klein, 2000; Schuberth et al., 2010). The next stage of eating for most children occurs when semisolid foods are introduced at 4–6 months of age (Bruns & Thompson, 2010; Eicher, 2013; Morris & Klein, 2000). The exact age varies greatly depending on caregiver expectations and cultural values. If the infant is still using the suckling pattern, then much of the food is pushed back out of the mouth by the tongue at this stage. The tongue is kept in the mouth and the lips are used to take food from the spoon as oral-motor skills gradually mature (Morris & Klein, 2000; Schuberth et al., 2010).

Children learn to bite and chew as more solid foods are introduced. Most infants exhibit munching at about 5 months of age (Eicher, 2013; Lane, 2012; Morris & Klein, 2000). Munching combines vertical jaw movements with a flattening and spreading of the tongue. Rotary chewing, which combines lateral tongue

---

Box 8.1.   Typical Development: Try It!

1. Take a drink of water from a cup. Did you pour in the liquid, or did you suck it in? What did the liquid do in your mouth? How did you swallow it? What movements did your jaw make, or was your jaw still? What movements did your tongue make? Now, take a drink of a milkshake or yogurt smoothie. What is different about this liquid from the water? What is different about your mouth movements and swallowing?

2. Take a bite of a saltine cracker. Using a munching pattern (with flat tongue and the jaw moving up and down) on the cracker. Now try this with an apple (carefully). Were you able to eat the cracker? The apple? What was the difference between the two foods?

3. Chew different types of food—chewy, soft solid, hard solid—with a partner. Pay attention to the movements of your jaw, your tongue, and the food. Notice how your tongue moves the food over to your molars to chew. Watch your partner chewing. Pay attention to his or her jaw movements. Notice how the jaw moves side to side and in a circular motion (rotary chewing) during chewing.

(Adapted from *Pre-feeding Skills* (p. 31, 35, 44, 50, 53, 56, 58), by Susan Evans Morris, Marsha Dunn Klein, 1987, Austin, TX: PRO-ED. Copyright 1987 by PRO-ED, Inc. Adapted with permission.)

---

and rotary jaw movements, replaces munching as more solid foods are increasingly presented over time. The emergence of teeth makes chewing more effective, but the basic chewing pattern is typically fully or nearly fully developed by the age of 6–9 months, well before the molars emerge. This pattern becomes increasingly smooth and well coordinated by 2–3 years of age, when the jaw movements during chewing are downward, central, and circular as the tongue moves food from side to side. Drinking from a cup is commonly introduced at 6–9 months, when the jaw has the stability to support cup drinking. Again, the child typically responds with a suckling pattern but gradually learns to control excess tongue movements and accept and hold liquids in the mouth before swallowing them (Morris & Klein, 2000; Schuberth et al., 2010). Complete the Try It exercises presented in Box 8.1 to better learn and understand these feeding processes.

Atypical Feeding in Children with Disabilities

Many children with developmental and multiple disabilities have a variety of medical, structural, neurological, developmental, gastrointenstinal, behavioral, and cardiorespiratory issues that can interfere with the mouth, nose, respiratory systems, and gastrological systems and result in feeding, eating, and swallowing issues (Andrew et al., 2012). The following subsections discuss some of the more common issues.

278 Ivey and Lowman

Atypical Reflexes   Several types of the involuntary motor patterns, called *reflexes*, can create feeding problems for children with severe or multiple disabilities (Morris & Klein, 2000; Schuberth, 2010). Primitive reflexes may persist in children with severe or multiple disabilities well beyond the time of typical integration or disappearance. For example, the asymmetrical tonic neck reflex (ATNR) creates specific problems for eating and feeding if it does not integrate or go away by 6 months of age (Schuberth et al., 2010). As the child's head rotates to one side, the arm on that side involuntarily extends, and the other arm flexes in a "fencing pose." Not only does the turning head make it difficult to put food into the mouth, but muscle contractions also generalize to the tongue and jaw, interfering with normal oral-motor control. See Figure 8.1 for a depiction of how the ATNR may affect feeding and eating, coupled with an illustration of adaptive positioning that can help with mealtime independence for children with ATNR.

In addition to primitive reflexes that are integrated within the first year of life, protective reflexes or responses persist throughout life (Bruns & Thompson, 2010; Schuberth et al., 2010). Some children with disabilities have hyposensitive reflexes (that may require higher than typical levels of stimulation) or hypersensitive reflexes (that are triggered by lower levels of stimulation). These atypical responses to stimuli may affect feeding. For example, a gag reflex is a typical

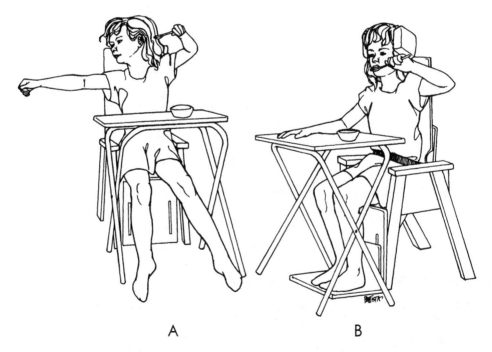

A   B

Figure 8.1.   How the use of adaptive positioning can lessen the influence of asymmetrical tonic neck reflex (ATNR) and promote independent eating: a) child attempts to feed self, but ATNR interferes with the child's ability to feed self; b) child positioned in adapted chair with external supports. The influence of the ATNR is lessened. (From Snyder, P.A., Breath, D., & DeMauro, G.J. [1999]. Positioning strategies for feeding and eating. In D.K. Lowman & S.M. Murphy (Eds.), *The educator's guide to feeding children with disabilities* [p. 74]. Baltimore: Paul H. Brookes Publishing Co.; reprinted by permission.)

response in children and adults to protect against inadvertently swallowing things that might obstruct the trachea. When hypersensitive, it may interfere with normal swallowing by producing unnecessary gagging and coughing. A hyposensitive gag reflex is also problematic because it will not protect against uncontrolled swallowing of pieces of food or foreign objects and may even allow fluids to enter the airway (Morris & Klein, 2000). Similarly, a persistent startle reflex (which usually disappears at 3–4 months of age) can increase tone throughout the body, affect self-feeding, and can cause safety issues if food is in the mouth. The control of the reflexive patterns is important for improving feeding and eating skills; consultation with an OT or physical therapist (PT) is often beneficial because those professionals work on integrating reflexes or managing reflex sensitivities.

Motor Difficulties   Feeding and eating skills are largely dependent on the structural foundation and processes of the sensory and motor systems. The balance of stability and mobility in which a stable base of support is needed to develop movement and functional skills is one of the primary components to consider with motor development (Morris & Klein, 2000; Schuberth et al., 2010). For example, before an infant can reach for, grab, and hold toys (mobility), he or she needs to learn to sit securely (stability). Similarly, oral-motor skills (mobility of the tongue and jaw) depend on stability of the neck and shoulders, which in turn depends on trunk and hip stability. Similarly, for self-feeding, arm movements to bring food from the plate to the mouth (mobility) require stability of the shoulder, trunk, and hip. Finally, the ability to manage food in the mouth depends on refined tongue and lip movements built on a stable jaw. Consideration of the balance of stability and mobility should be given in assessment and treatment of feeding and eating skills.

The influence of a child's tone on feeding and eating also needs to be considered. Muscle tone and muscle strength are different (see Chapter 3). Muscle strength is the force the muscle produces when it contracts, whereas muscle tone can be thought of as the tension inside a muscle when it is at rest. Normal muscle tone allows people to start and stop their muscles when they want. High muscle tone (also referred to as *hypertonicity* or *spasticity*) means there is too much tension inside the muscle at rest. The muscle is tight and tense when it is at rest, even though it is not doing anything or has not been purposefully activated. Controlled muscle movements normally require the contraction of one muscle while the antagonistic muscle relaxes (known as *reciprocal innervation*). For instance, when curling up an arm, one's bicep muscle contracts while the tricep muscle relaxes. Excessive tone may mean that the antagonistic muscle cannot relax, making movements difficult because the muscle pairs are working against each other. The tone can continue to pull on the muscles over time, resulting in contractures. Low muscle tone (also referred to as *hypotonicity*) means there is too little tension inside the muscle when it is at rest. The muscle is mushy and soft when it is at rest, and it requires more effort to get working when activated. Low muscle tone makes it difficult for the child to move against gravity and may result in drooping of the head, jaw, and lips, as well as weak chewing patterns. Children may have difficulty closing their lips. Hypertonicity or hypotonicity may result in the inability to maintain stability of the trunk, neck, and head, which makes control of fine oral-motor movements difficult.

Consideration needs to be given to a child's tone throughout his or her body and how tone may be influencing the child's feeding and eating. Abnormalities of muscle tone do not typically affect all muscles in the same manner or to the same extent. Most children with disorders of muscle tone exhibit uneven tone across muscle groups. Typically, patterns of extension (in which the muscles in the shoulder, arm, elbow, wrist, and fingers move together involuntarily to extend or move out from the body) or of flexion (in which the muscles flex or bend toward the joints and body) predominate because of uneven tone. This may result in the chronic retraction of lips, protrusion of the tongue, limited voluntary control, or a variety of other problems. Some children have fluctuating muscle tone that may result in involuntary movements of oral structures that make precise, coordinated movements of lips, tongue, and jaw impossible. All of these disorders of muscle tone have adverse effects on mealtime skills, and intervention to normalize tone is an important component of a mealtime intervention program.

Oral-Motor Function   Children with developmental disabilities and multiple disabilities can have limited movement patterns in and around their mouth, affecting movement needed for feeding and eating, due to developmental, neurological, or physiological issues. The most common atypical feeding patterns observed are

- *Inadequate lip closure*: The inability to keep the lips closed makes it hard to keep food inside the mouth and might increase the tendency to drool (Arvedson, 2013; Morris & Klein, 2000). This problem may be due to structural abnormalities, hypertonicity, or hypotonicity.

- *Jaw/cheek/lips/tongue retraction*: Retraction (pulling back) of the jaw, cheek, lips, or tongue may be due to strong extensor patterns, as in a child with CP. Conversely, a child with hypotonia, such as in Down syndrome, may try to adjust for low tone in the trunk by increasing the tone in the facial and oral muscles for stability, resulting in retraction (Andrew et al., 2012; Morris & Klein, 2000). Poor positioning with no place for stability, such as when the feet are dangling and the trunk is unsupported, could also result in this pattern (Redstone & West, 2004). This pattern of retraction reduces oral mobility for eating.

- *Tonic bite*: The tonic bite reflex is a forceful, involuntary, and generally prolonged clamping of the jaws in response to stimulation of the mouth (Andrew et al., 2012; Morris & Klein, 2000). This response obviously interferes with spoon-feeding and finger feeding and makes chewing extremely difficult.

Box 8.2.   Atypical Feeding Patterns: Try It!

1. Have a partner feed you pudding, water, and a cookie. Eat each food in a typi-
    cal manner, thinking about the position of your trunk, shoulders, jaw, lips, and
    tongue. Think about your jaw, lip, and tongue movements as you eat. Now pull
    your body into an extensor pattern—arch your back, pull your shoulders and
    arms back in a retracted position, pull your head back and up slightly so that
    your chin is toward the ceiling, pull your lips back in a retracted, tight position,
    and pull your tongue backward. Have your partner feed you while you are in
    this position. Think about how this extensor pattern restricts your lip, jaw, and
    tongue movements. Can you pull foods off a spoon using your upper lip? Can
    you easily take a bite of cookie? Can you drink from a cup?

2. Let your body and mouth be relaxed to experience feeding and eating with
    hypotonia. Sit in a slumped position in your chair. Let your jaw, cheeks, and
    tongue become relaxed so that your tongue hangs out. Have your partner feed
    you while you are in this position. Think about how hypotonia affects your
    lip, jaw, and tongue movements. How is eating different from the hypertonic
    extensor pattern and typical eating?

(Adapted from *Pre-feeding Skills* (p. 31, 35, 44, 50, 53, 56, 58), by Susan Evans Morris,
Marsha Dunn Klein, 1987, Austin, TX: PRO-ED. Copyright 1987 by PRO-ED, Inc. Adapted with
permission.)

- *Tongue protrusion and/or tongue thrust*: Tongue protrusion occurs when the
  tongue rests outside of the mouth, commonly seen in children with low
  tone, such as in Down syndrome. The child's tongue is bunched or forced
  out of the mouth in tongue thrust (Arvedson, 2013; Bruns & Thompson,
  2010). Both patterns push food or fluids back out of the mouth and may also
  push the teeth out of position over time.

- *Limited tongue movement*: Tongue movements are needed to move foods
  to the sides of the mouth for chewing or move food back for swallowing
  (Arvedson, 2013). Hypertonicity can result in limited tongue movements
  due to increased tension in the tongue, or hypotonicity can result in limited
  tongue movements due to decreased tension in the tongue. Delayed motor
  development may also contribute to limited tongue movement.

Complete the Try It exercises presented in Box 8.2 to better understand the
impact of these atypical feeding patterns.

Structural Abnormalities   Structural abnormalities such as cleft lip, cleft palate, micrognathia (small lower jaw often seen in children with Pierre-Robin or
Down syndrome), high-arched palate, and missing or displaced teeth may cause
or complicate eating problems (Bruns & Thompson, 2010; Morris & Klein, 2000).
Uncorrected cleft lip and cleft palate make sucking and swallowing difficult,

requiring the infant to develop abnormal patterns (e.g., increase use of the tongue to obtain milk from the nipple). The tongue often protrudes rather than resting on the floor of the mouth when the child's jaw is small. High-arched palates are also commonly observed in children with physical disabilities. Food may collect on the roof of the mouth and be impossible to reach with the tongue. Similarly, missing and/or displaced teeth can cause difficulties with spoon-feeding, cup drinking, and biting and chewing. These abnormal patterns may lead to secondary eating problems later in life (Schuberth et al., 2012).

Food Pocketing   Food pocketing (or packing) is holding food in the mouth (Morris & Klein, 2000; Patel, Piazza, Layer, Coleman, & Swartzwelder, 2005). Excessive food pocketing can result in nutritional issues, dental problems, dehydration, and aspiration. There is a limited understanding of why children pocket food, but there is an indication that some children pocket higher texture foods, such as meat (Patel et al., 2005). Packing may also be an indication of limited oral-motor skills to manage food mobility in the mouth (e.g., limited tongue lateralization to swipe food out of the cheek pocket) and decreased cheek strength (Morris & Klein, 2000), which OTs and SLPs are trained to improve.

Food Selectivity and Food Refusal   *Food selectivity* is generally defined as a child accepting only a small number of foods and may encompass unwillingness to try new foods, totally avoiding some food groups, and exhibiting strong preferences about how food is prepared and presented (Williams, Gibbons, & Schreck, 2005). Food selectivity is considered a common yet transient problem for toddlers and preschoolers, with 25%–45% of typically developing children demonstrating mild food selectivity (Davis et al., 2013; de Moor, Didden, & Korzilius, 2007; Manikam & Perman, 2000; Marí-Bauset et al., 2013; Williams et al., 2005). In contrast, 13%–80% of children with developmental delays or chronic diseases experience mild food selectivity and have a greater chance of having serious food selectivity (Manikam & Perman, 2000; Williams, Hendy, & Knecht, 2008). *Food refusal* is generally defined as a child's refusal to eat all or most foods presented, resulting in serious nutritional deficits or the need for supplemental tube feedings (Williams, Field, & Seiverling, 2010). Children with autism are more likely to have problems with food selectivity than children with other developmental disabilities; however, many children with developmental delays and medical issues also demonstrate food selectivity or refusal (Williams et al., 2005, 2010).

Very selective, problem eaters tend to eat diets high in carbohydrates and very low to no vegetables; on average, they have 13 foods or fewer in their diet (Williams et al., 2005). Behaviors may include crying, throwing food, gagging or vomiting, or spitting during meals (Williams et al., 2005, 2010). It has been hypothesized that food selectivity for some children may develop in response to other conditions. For instance, children may develop an aversion to eating foods because they associate pain and discomfort with eating due to having gastroesophageal reflux (Williams et al., 2005, 2010). Therefore, the goal should be to strike a proper balance between empowering choice and ensuring health.

Coughing, Gagging, Choking, and Aspiration   Although gagging and coughing are typical responses to clear the airway, they are also strong indicators of swallowing difficulty. It is important to note when the coughing and gagging occur during the meal because it can indicate the source of the problem (Eicher, 2013; Lane, 2012; Schwarz, 2003; Sharp, Jaquess, Morton, & Herzinger, 2010). Coughing or gagging before the meal may indicate issues with food selectivity (e.g., sensory overresponsivity to food textures or smells). Coughing or gagging during the meal may indicate issues with oral-motor management of food textures (e.g., adequately chewing food prior to swallowing, moving food to the side of the mouth for chewing). The child who coughs during drinking may have a problem controlling the flow of thin liquids. Coughing or gagging after the meal may indicate gastroesophageal reflux, which is characterized by the flowing back (reflux) of stomach contents into the esophagus (the tube in which food passes from the mouth to the stomach). Food and acid can move up into the esophagus and even into the pharynx (the area bounded by the back of the nose and mouth and top of the esophagus), which can result in a painful burning sensation. Vomiting can ensue if there is enough force behind the reflux.

Choking occurs when food becomes stuck in the pharynx. Choking can be an indicator of inadequate munching or chewing. It can also result when a child overstuffs his or her mouth. Complete airway obstruction is a life-threatening airway emergency requiring immediate assistance. Children with severe and multiple disabilities are at serious risk for airway obstruction, and staff involved in their mealtimes should be trained to identify and respond to these emergencies.

Children with sensory or motor impairments are at increased risk for aspiration (Andrew et al., 2012; Arvedson, 2013; Eicher, 2013). *Aspiration* refers to food, liquid, or any foreign substance entering the airway. Signs and symptoms of aspiration may include coughing, congestion, wheezing, blinking, eye watering, limited endurance or increased fatigue during eating, and delayed swallow reflex (Andrew et al., 2012; Arvedson, 2013; Eicher, 2013; Morris & Klein, 2000). Recurrent aspiration may lead to recurrent chest infections and chronic lung disease, so it is important to attend to a persistent wheeze or respiratory infection. Although aspiration can occur with accompanying signs and symptoms, it can also occur without any signs and symptoms, which is known as *silent aspiration*. In this case, aspiration can go undetected. Thus, it is critical that school staff assisting in feeding know the child's medical and feeding history and follow all necessary precautions to prevent aspiration in a student with severe and multiple disabilities, even in the absence of outward symptoms.

A child receiving meals by mouth should be fed in an upright position with the head flexed slightly forward to help prevent aspiration. This position encourages active swallowing and prevents food from passively running down the throat (Redstone & West, 2004). A videofluoroscopic swallow study (VFSS) is often used to detect aspiration (Arvedson, 2013; Eicher, 2013; Morris & Klein, 2000; Schwarz, 2003). VFSS is also often referred to as a *modified barium swallow study.*

It is used to analyze the anatomical and physiological functions of swallowing and identify any complications. Results of the VFSS can provide the team with useful information about optimum feeding position, rate of food presentation and intake, and appropriate textures of food and thickness of liquid (Andrew et al., 2012; Morris & Klein). See the case story of Collette for important considerations related to aspiration and swallowing

Collette

Collette is the 11th grader with CP who was introduced at the beginning of the chapter. Collette's mother and special education teacher are advocating for the development of feeding goals focused on increasing Collette's independence with self-feeding, particularly given the importance of this skill related to transition planning. Applesauce and pudding are among Collette's favorite snacks, so they are proposing to write a goal toward independently feeding and eating these foods. The SLP and OT on the team have serious concerns about this proposed goal as written, however, because Collette's most recent swallow study indicated aspiration on thick liquids and smooth solid foods.

Takeaway Points

- All people responsible for feeding a child need to thoroughly review a child's chart to determine if feeding is safe. If you are unable to understand the medical reports, then consult with a member of your team to help you decipher the results. The school nurse, SLP, or OT would be appropriate team members to assist. The parent and teacher were focused on implementing a plan that would be motivating for Collette by using her favorite foods. They did not understand that applesauce and pudding are considered thick liquids and smooth solids, however, which would be unsafe for Collette.

- Although we want to support parent goals, we have a responsibility to provide safe and ethical services. The team needs to work together to determine if feeding and eating can be safely completed. Collette's team could work together to keep this goal but rewrite it to include foods she could safely manage. Teams may not find a safe alternative, however, in other situations. The team in this case needs to discuss this together, possibly with the support of medical personnel to help all team members understand the risks of aspiration.

- All team members, particularly those intimately involved in the feeding process, need to be aware of the signs and symptoms of aspiration.

Constipation   Constipation is a frequent complaint among individuals with developmental disabilities, with reports of 74% of children with CP and more than 50% of children with severe developmental delays having chronic constipation (Bosch et al., 2002; Williams et al., 2005). Chief symptoms of constipation include decrease in appetite and increased irritability or behavior problems at meals, all of which can affect feeding (Bosch et al., 2002). Many pediatric tube feedings are milk based, which can increase the incidence of constipation for some children. Several medications, such as those used to treat seizures or reduce excessive tone, can also contribute to constipation. In addition, children who are selective or picky eaters tend to eat snack foods (which are low in fiber), drink a lot of milk, and eat no fruits and vegetables (Williams et al., 2005). This diet increases the likelihood of constipation. Caregivers and school personnel can play an important role in managing this problem by ensuring adequate hydration throughout the day. For some students, it may be important to report bowel or bladder activity that occurs at school as part of a daily communication journal because families may require this information to manage their care routines. Read more about Joseph for tips on how to manage constipation and other health issues, as well as advice on communicating with families.

Joseph

Joseph is the student with severe spasticity from CP. His muscle tone is so strong that he straightens out and becomes "hard as a board" when placed on the floor. He attempts to straighten out when seated in a Rifton corner seat that is slightly reclined, which forces his head into extension (head back, chin up). His mother feeds him in this position by scraping the food off his teeth and having the food naturally fall down his mouth and throat (sometimes called *bird feeding*). Although Joseph does not eat much, it can often take 30–45 minutes to feed him lunch. He frequently has stomach pains due to constipation.

Takeaway Points

- Children with severe spasticity are often on a variety of drugs for bladder control, tremors, spasms, and spasticity that can decrease appetite and contribute to constipation.

- CP can result in damage to the central nervous system (e.g., affecting the muscle movements and spasticity) as well as the enteric nervous system (ENS), which controls digestion-related functions, such as movement of food through the gastrointestinal tract (Andrew et al., 2012). Damage to the ENS can result in constipation, vomiting, reflux, and decreased appetite.

- Bird feeding is not safe because it can result in aspiration. In addition, this type of feeding also does not allow for the use of or development of oral-motor skills, such as tongue lateralization, lip closure, and swallowing.

- Length of feeding time is a common concern for caregivers, with estimates that caregivers typically spend 3.5 hours a day feeding a child with CP versus 50 minutes a day for feeding a typically developing child (Sullivan et al., 2000).

- Feeding and eating dysfunction is associated with poor health and nutritional status; however, nutrition continues to be a largely unmet need. In one study, approximately 40% of parents of children with moderate and severe CP considered their child malnourished, but half had never had a feeding or nutritional assessment (Sullivan et al., 2000).

- Although mom is using an unsafe technique for feeding, it is important to recognize that feeding is a major stressor for parents. Many parents report that mealtimes are stressful. The constant concern regarding adequate feeding for nutrition and weight gain can cause parents to feel a sense of failure, yet the time to learn proper techniques and strategies to promote this weight gain is limited (Sullivan et al., 2000). The team should take the time to help a parent like Joseph's mother understand safe feeding practices and learn proper techniques.

Joseph's teacher consulted with the SLP and OT on how to better feed Joseph. The entire team was able to meet and problem-solve some new, safe feeding practices. After properly positioning Joseph, the SLP and OT were able to work with mom and his feeding aide on some ways to introduce the spoon into his mouth and encourage lip closure. Mom provided valuable input on Joseph's preferences for food and pacing of eating, and the aide was able to ask questions about how to do this in a busy cafeteria environment.

Sensory Issues   Mealtime incorporates a variety of sensory experiences—smell, taste, touch, and sound. Problems with sensory processes can affect exploration of the environment, including trying new food tastes, textures, and smells. Morris and Klein (2000) described the sensory capacities in terms of 1) the ability of the sensory organs to receive sensory input, 2) the ability to process the information, and 3) the brain's ability to interpret the information. Difficulties in any of these areas can affect a child's ability to eat, drink, or participate in mealtime. Children with severe and multiple disabilities may have associated impairments, including sensory impairments such as hearing and visual impairments, that may affect mealtime abilities. It will be particularly important for the team to assess the impact of sensory impairments in relation to motor impairments on feeding and eating. For instance, visual impairment (e.g., blindness) and motor disability (e.g., hypertonicity) can affect the child's ability to use utensils to scoop or pick up food and bring it to the mouth.

Difficulties with sensory processing can fall into two categories—hypersensitivity (overresponsivity) to sensory input or hyposensitivity (underresponsivity) to sensory input. Children may have sensory processing deficits in any of their sensory areas (Davis et al., 2013; Lane, 2012). For instance, children who are overresponsive to tactile input may not want to touch foods, may not like the texture or feel of the foods in their mouth, or may become upset if any food gets on their lips or face. They may gag frequently during eating. They may soon learn what foods they do not tolerate well, and in anticipation of the feel of the foods and potential gagging during eating, they may begin gagging prior to the meal and display increased behavioral challenges before eating. Similar issues may be seen when children are overresponsive to smells or tastes. They may also be overresponsive to sounds and therefore have difficulties in noisy environments, such as school cafeterias or restaurants, due to the overwhelming stimulation to their bodies and brains.

Children who are underresponsive to sensory input are on the opposite end. They may frequently gag or choke due to a lack of sensory awareness that food is in their mouth or due to difficulty localizing the position of the food in their mouth. This may also lead to packing or stuffing their mouth with food to potentially increase the awareness of food in their mouth. They may be picky eaters. Some of these children will prefer foods that have strong tastes and textures.

In addition, children may experience a mixture of under- and overresponsivity in different sensory systems. For instance, a child may be overresponsive to noises but underresponsive to tactile input. Sensitivity to sensory input can result from a variety of reasons. Children may demonstrate oral hypersensitivity due to frequent medical interventions (e.g., intubation, nasogastric tube feeding). These procedures may impair the normal development of the sensory systems as well as teach children to become overly sensitive to oral input because of the frequent noxious stimulation that occurs. Similarly, children with early feeding problems may relate eating with feelings of discomfort and overstimulation. Some children, particularly children with developmental disabilities and autism, may experience sensory over- or underresponsivity because of problems with their sensory processing systems.

UNDERSTANDING THE CONTEXT OF MEALTIME

It is important to consider more than just the mechanics of feeding and eating (i.e., the coordination of gross and fine motor skills, oral motor skills, swallowing, and respiration) to understand mealtimes. The act of feeding and eating also needs to be put into the context of the social aspects of mealtime, routines, the feeding environment, and the family.

Social Aspects of Mealtime

Feeding and eating are only part of the mealtime process. Schwier and Stewart (2005) suggested that mealtime includes the processes of grocery shopping, preparing the meal, cooking, setting the table, washing up, serving the meal, washing dishes—and, yes, eating. Meals provide multiple opportunities for inclusive gatherings and social activities and are a critical social component of life.

"The ingredients that come to mind when we think about quality mealtimes for people with and without disabilities go far beyond the food itself. The food, really, is a good excuse to be with one another" (Schwier & Stewart, 2005, p. 21). With this is mind, we need to consider how we are including children with disabilities in mealtime. Are we just focused on providing them with the nutrition for their bodies? What about supporting their personal and social-emotional experiences? Here are some suggestions for thinking about the whole mealtime experience:

- *Show dignity and respect.* "If you are someone with a disability, having your food shoveled into you by a staff person who doesn't even sit down because she is talking to another person, you enjoy no dignity or respect" (Schwier & Stewart, 2005, p. 23). Instead, sit down, talk, and make eye contact.

- *Provide choices and respect choices.* One of the true pleasures of mealtime is having a choice about what to eat. Although some people need food monitored due to allergies or diets, choices can still be offered and respected. Asking the student for input on what color plates to use, what foods he or she wants to eat, and how to serve the food all empower the child during mealtimes. Reid and Parsons (1991) found that providing opportunities for choice lengthened mealtime by only a few minutes.

- *Include all in mealtimes.* Mealtimes can provide great opportunities for peer interactions as well as the development of feeding and eating skills. In addition, this approach supports least restrictive environment legislation mandates of the Individuals with Disabilities Education Improvement Act (IDEA) of 2004 (PL 108-446). Children with gastrostomy tubes may be fed at lunchtime (if approved to eat orally) or at least be seated at the table.

- *Provide social supports.* Matson et al. (2006) looked at the relationship between social skills training and feeding behaviors and recommended that social skills training should be a part of a multicomponent behavioral intervention targeting food refusal. This strategy may include teaching manners, such as how to pass food, how to eat only what is on one's own plate, and how to wipe one's mouth. Consider balancing this work time with the social and pleasurable aspects of feeding time as well.

The educational team will need to work together to balance nutritional needs and the physical act of eating with socialization and community integration during mealtimes. Interacting with peers in a stimulating social environment can be too distracting for some children. These distractions can make it more work for the child to eat and may even lead to unsafe eating and swallowing. The social aspect of mealtimes should not be ignored, however, and alternatives should be considered. For instance, if social interaction with a peer is important, then perhaps this can occur during a smaller snack time when calorie input is not the major emphasis or during other social opportunities during the day. It may be appropriate to set a goal of generalizing mealtime skills from an isolated to a socially inclusive environment.

Routines

Because mealtimes take place within the context of everyday life, the educational team should consider how mealtimes uniquely fit into a child's day. Some questions to ask include

- What are the child's daily mealtime routines? This may include where he or she eats at school and home, how he or she eats, what he or she eats, and with whom he or she eats. Routines are very individual. For instance, some families may eat every evening together, and some may grab food on the go. Remember that a lack of a scheduled mealtime is not a lack of routine but may just be that family's routine. Either way, knowing these routines informs the team about the family's mealtime.

- How does the routine affect the child's feeding and eating? For instance, children who have access to high-calorie snacks all day may not be hungry for a higher nutrition-laden meal. If a child is fed all night through a gastrostomy tube, then he or she may not be hungry for breakfast. Carefully examining habits and routines can provide essential insight into feeding concerns, including examining a child's expenditure of energy related to his or her caloric intake. Many children with severe and multiple disabilities may be less active than other children and therefore need fewer calories. It is important that the food children eat is meeting their nutritional needs and not providing empty calories.

- How does the child's eating and feeding affect his or her daily routine? Team members should consider whether feeding schedules are dominating the day and preventing opportunities for the child to engage in other activities. In general, a feeding session should not last longer than 30 minutes on a regular basis. Sullivan et al. (2000) reported, however, that prolonged feeding times were common in children with severe motor impairment, with 48% of children taking at least 3 hours per day to feed and three out of five of those children taking more than 6 hours per day to feed. With most school lunches limited to 30 minutes or less, this situation either results in a child not finishing lunch or missing part of his or her educational programming. A lengthy mealtime at home results in all activities being dictated by feeding in which "life becomes inexorably ruled by feeding times that cannot be relaxed even for outings or holidays" (Sleigh, 2005, p. 378). Teams need to work together to manage the reciprocal impact of feeding and routines.

Parenting Aspects and Viewpoints

Feeding difficulties that affect the child's health can be extremely upsetting for caregivers. Parents of children with feeding and eating concerns report considerable stress about mealtime. In fact, 43% of parents described feeding their child with a disability as stressful and not enjoyable (Sullivan et al., 2000). Drooling, choking, and needing help with feeding are aspects contributing to stress.

Sources of parental stress, however, were also related to the need for extra food preparation (e.g., mashing and blending of foods), extra costs, and length of feeding time. Parents also reported the physical difficulty they experience during feeding. One parent noted that feeding "is physically difficult because he's growing and [because of] the postures you have to adopt to hold him in a good position" (Sleigh, 2005, p. 378). Parents also reported stress regarding the many questions and confusion about decisions regarding tube feeding versus oral feeding (Sleigh, 2005). Overall, the psychosocial aspects of not being in control or understood were major sources of stress for parents. These feelings were largely based on interactions with and feelings of dependence on professionals (Sleigh, 2005). The premise that meeting the child's developmental growth is often viewed as a reflection of parenting skills is at the root of this stress (Kuperminc et al., 2013).

Despite the intense parental stress associated with feeding, parents also reported that feeding was a time of learning about their child and an opportunity to experience intimate time and communication with their child. Mealtime was one opportunity to provide undivided attention to their child and "led to the mother's understanding of her child" (Sleigh, 2005, p. 380). Team members who work with family members and caregivers on mealtime routines need to assess their comfort levels and work toward making mealtimes less stressful and more enjoyable.

COLLABORATIVE TEAMING TO ADDRESS MEALTIME CONCERNS

The complexity of mealtime requires planning and collaboration by a team of individuals from a variety of disciplines (Andrew et al., 2012; Bruns & Thompson, 2010; Eicher, 2013; Fayed, Berall, Dix, & Judd, 2007). Parents and other primary caregivers must be included as full members of the team as well. Parents know their child and the history of previous interventions, successes, and failures. In addition, parents generally are responsible for feeding children most of their meals. It is important for the team to discuss feeding routine(s) at home and school; they should identify who might feed the child, what is pleasurable about the feeding routine, what is difficult and needs to be changed, and any food allergies the child might have. Care should also be given to the family's cultural values and their preferences for feeding and mealtimes.

Classroom teachers can regularly provide the team with information and observations about the student because they have daily direct contact with the child. In addition, they bring expertise in teaching and instruction. Classroom assistants and other caregivers involved in daily feeding activities should be included in the planning process. They have intimate knowledge about what works because they often feed the child, and they may be unaware of specific precautions or treatment techniques if they are left out of planning.

Multiple therapists may be involved with mealtimes. SLPs often play primary roles in the evaluation and treatment of children with swallowing and feeding disorders because of their knowledge of the anatomy, physiology, and neurophysiology of the systems associated with respiration, swallowing, and speech (American Speech-Language-Hearing Association [ASHA], 2007). In addition, they are experts in communication, which is important to feeding in two primary ways: 1) the same systems are involved in speech and feeding, and 2) communication is an essential aspect of mealtime (ASHA, n.d.). OTs also play a primary role assessing areas affecting feeding, eating, and swallowing, including sensory preferences, positioning, food presentation, environmental adaptations, and adapted feeding equipment (AOTA, 2007). PTs contribute valuable information about motor skills, reflexes, positioning, and therapeutic interventions (American Physical Therapy Association, 2014; Bruns & Thompson, 2010).

Psychologists or behavior analysts may also provide important information regarding mealtime-related behaviors and can assist with the development of a behavior plan (Bruns & Thompson, 2010). Social workers may help provide information on the family's culture, routines, and community and funding supports for services. Registered dietitians or registered dietitian nutritionists have important expertise that should be included to benefit the child's health, growth, and development (Academy of Nutrition and Dietetics, n.d.). School nurses may help train staff to prevent choking and recognize signs of aspiration. In addition, nurses develop the individualized health care plan for students with health care needs (see Chapter 6), which provides the foundation for the development of clear action steps and responses to a health crisis (National Association of School Nurses, 2013). Many decisions made by these professionals and other members of the feeding team may interact with a physician's treatment decisions. In addition, the physician's role may include diagnosis of medical conditions (e.g., gastro-esophageal reflux disease) or referral for swallowing studies (Bruns & Thompson, 2010). Therefore, physicians, developmental pediatricians, and/or gastroenterologists should also be included. Similarly, dentists should play a role due to the interaction of feeding and specific oral structures as well as dental care issues associated with developmental disabilities.

Although it is not always possible to have all of these professionals attend team meetings, their input should be gathered and considered as part of comprehensive assessment and program planning (Bruns & Thompson, 2010; Fayed et al., 2007).

COMPREHENSIVE ASSESSMENT OF FEEDING, EATING, AND MEALTIME

Because feeding and eating are complex skills, the team needs to collaborate on a comprehensive assessment process in order to develop a comprehensive approach to treatment (Andrew, Parr, & Sullivan, 2012). Interviews with family members and other caregivers involved in the student's mealtimes are essential to supplement the team members' own observations of eating and feeding in order to gather as much information as possible about all aspects of feeding, eating, and the mealtime process. Assessment of eating and feeding skills requires a determination of both what the child can and cannot do and which skills are critical to improving the child's functioning in current and potential environments. Each child's assessment must be individualized, occur over a period of time, and include a variety of team members (Andrew et al., 2012; Bruns & Thompson, 2010; Eicher, 2013; Fayed, Berall, Dix, & Judd, 2007). The team can pull together the results of this assessment to develop a comprehensive feeding plan. Components of the comprehensive assessment include a medical and developmental history, feeding history, and full evaluation of current feeding skills.

Medical and Developmental History

The team needs to gather information about a child's condition, including diagnoses, severity of impairment, development, growth history, allergies (particularly food allergies), and medications (Andrew et al., 2012; Linscheid, 2006). Detailed information about current weight and growth is important, as well as any concerns regarding failure to thrive or past or current tube feeding (Eicher, 2013; Linscheid, 2006; Schwarz, 2003). Information about receptive and expressive language skills, cognition, vision and hearing, and motor ability is all pertinent to understanding the child's feeding ability and needs. Developing an understanding of past medical history, including prematurity, hospitalizations, and medications, provides an understanding of the current condition. This should result in knowledge of current diagnoses and treating physicians or therapies. The feeding team should also ensure an understanding of current medications, the reason for their use, and their possible side effects, particularly those related to appetite.

Feeding History and Current Feeding

A detailed feeding history should be gathered in collaboration with the parents. "Feeding should be placed in the context of the previous feeding history, and significant events" (Andrew et al., 2012, p. 225). Understanding feeding from prematurity, newborn, and infancy stages through the current age reveals patterns of feeding issues and behaviors. Typical nutritional intake, food preferences, quantities, consistencies, spillage, vomiting, length of time to feed, and feeding methods are all important to note. Food diaries can be used to record eating patterns, though this is sometimes burdensome to parents. Children should be observed in the settings where they typically eat—home, child care, preschool, school, and grandmother's house—to understand the mealtime environment and dynamics. Different members of the team may observe the parent or other caregiver feed a child to learn about the positions typically used for feeding, the pace of the meal, how challenges are managed, how the feeder and child communicate, and what is working and what is not (Lane, 2012; Morris & Klein, 2000; Schuberth et al., 2010). These observations should be placed within a greater context to understand the mealtime routine.

Feeding Skill Evaluation

The medical and developmental history, feeding history, and current feeding issues and concerns of the team and parents provide a broad perspective of the student's feeding skills. Further assessment may be completed by different team members to provide more detailed information to understand the child's current feeding skills and difficulties. For instance, evaluation may be completed to understand the child's learning skills and learning environment. This can be helpful to know how best to introduce new strategies for learning, find out the student's current understanding of feeding abilities, and ascertain which skills the student wants to improve. Communication skills may be assessed to determine how the child is currently communicating his or her needs during the day and at mealtime. Assessment of strength, tone, range of motion, movements, reflexes, and current positioning may inform the team on positioning needs for feeding. Observations of oral-motor skills while eating different types of food will provide information on typical and atypical oral-motor skills (e.g., retraction, tonic bite reflex). Oral-motor structures may be examined for any abnormalities. Sensory sensitivities will be assessed through interview of the student (if possible) and caregiver, along with observations. This comprehensive assessment of medical and developmental history, feeding history, current feeding skills, and assessment of related skills (e.g., oral motor, physical, sensory) can be brought to the team to develop a comprehensive treatment plan.

COMPREHENSIVE TREATMENT

Treatment for mealtime challenges will be as varied as the children themselves. Each child's history, development, personality, routine, preferences, and skills are unique, requiring treatment to be individualized. Overall, however, treatment should be comprehensive; focusing not only on feeding or eating skills but also on the development of these skills in relation to the child's communication, socialization, motor skills, food preferences, behavior, nutritional needs, and equipment needs.

Facilitating Communication and Socialization During Meals

Communication and socialization are critical components of mealtime. The feeder must read the child's cues, establish trust during the feeding session, and allow the child to be in control of the interaction as much as possible (Schwier & Stewart, 2005). Mealtimes provide great opportunities for offering meaningful choices that promote communication. Children with disabilities should be given every opportunity to make choices and indicate preferences during mealtime (Schwier & Stewart, 2005). Feeding provides opportunities for students who are fed by a staff member to establish turn-taking and coordination of movement that provide a foundation for the development of more advanced communication skills. Important guidelines for establishing this respectful interaction include the following:

- The feeder should carefully watch and listen to the child and coordinate presentation of food with the child's natural breathing and movement patterns. At the most basic level, the feeder should watch the breathing cycle and present food after an inhalation.

- The feeder should ensure appropriate lighting and positioning so that the child has a clear view of food or drink.

- The feeder should establish a smooth and predictable pace while feeding.

- A verbal or tactile ready signal from the feeder is helpful for many children. Many children will not require this signal, and some children with hypertonicity may respond with an increase in tone or perhaps a startle response.

- Children should be given the opportunity to signal (e.g., look up, move, verbalize, point) when they want the next bite of food or drink. The feeder should encourage this by waiting, observing, and reinforcing any sign of readiness.

- Distractions and interruptions (to feeder and child) need to be minimized.

The pace and cues provided by the feeder are not only important for socialization and communication but can also enhance relaxation or, conversely, increase tension in the child. The pace of feeding should be slow enough to allow for coordination of eating and drinking behavior with breathing patterns. Failure to do so will result in increased difficulty eating, at a minimum, or in life-threatening aspiration or airway obstruction, at the worst (Murphy & Lowman, 1999). Feeding is also one of the important interactive contexts for the development of attachment between children and their caregivers, and attachment is also a powerful force in the development of communication. The oral-motor skills that are refined in eating are fundamental to the development of speech (Alexander, 2001). All of these influences on the development of communication skills make mealtimes an important context for teaching early communication. Teaching more advanced communication and social skill objectives is also easily integrated into mealtime activities because these behaviors are natural elements of mealtime routines.

Positioning During Feeding and Eating

Positioning involves the use of adaptive equipment techniques or external supports to provide optimal alignment to enhance the child's functional performance and is one of the most important considerations to improve safety and performance of eating, feeding, and swallowing (Andrew et al., 2012; Eicher, 2013; Redstone & West, 2004; Schuberth et al., 2010). Postural alignment during mealtimes is needed for the preservation of an open airway to enhance breathing and decrease the risk of aspiration (Andrew et al., 2012; Redstone & West, 2004). Because there is a close relationship between body position and oral-motor skills, optimal positioning enhances specific oral-motor skills, such as lip closure on a spoon (Morris & Klein, 2000; Schuberth et al., 2010). Hastened digestion is the final benefit of positioning, which might decrease the severity of reflux. Upright sitting might enhance the management of constipation by promoting the outflow of stomach contents (Snyder, Breath, & DeMauro, 1999). Although positioning for feeding varies from child to child, the considerations provided in the positioning checklist in Figure 8.2 provide a starting point. It is important to consult with the OT and PT to meet the specific needs of each child.

Positioning Checklist

❏ Proper positioning starts at the hips. Are hips stable? The most stable position is a neutral position with the hips just under 90 degrees; check for anterior pelvic tilt (pelvis forward with an arched back) or posterior pelvic tilt (buttocks scooted forward resulting in sitting on tailbone, often causing a slumped posture). Are hips symmetrical with weight evenly distributed on both tailbones?

❏ Is the trunk stable? Symmetrical? Relaxed? If not, consider trunk side supports, armrests, or lap tray or table.

❏ Are legs and feet supported? Are knees flexed to just under 90 degrees? Dangling feet can decrease stability and increase tone in children with neuromotor disabilities. Provide a footrest for children if needed.

❏ Observe the shoulders. Are they pulled back (retracted), hiked up, or rounded forward? Determine this by placing your hands on the child's shoulders and check the position of his or her scapulae.

❏ Observe head position. The head and neck should be aligned in a neutral position, with a slight chin tuck. Does the position allow for clear eye contact with the feeder?

❏ Does the child have some movement? Although there are many parameters for a proper position, movement is also needed for feeding. If the child is strapped in with all sorts of supports, then he or she may not be able to move, limiting the mobility needed for feeding and eating.

❏ Does the position allow the child to interact and communicate with the feeder? If he or she uses an alternate means of communication (e.g., eye gaze, communication board, augmentative and alternative communication device), then is it readily available? Or is an alternative method accessible?

❏ Does the position allow the child to socially interact and communicate with others, such as family or peers?

❏ Is the feeder comfortable? Yes, the feeder's position needs to be considered too! Feeders need to watch their body mechanics. Make sure you are not reaching too far to feed a child or turning to the side. Not only will this cause tension in your arm and hand, limiting your control during feeding, but it will also put undue stress on your back muscles. Move closer to the child, have a supportive chair, and do not twist your back.

Figure 8.2. Positioning checklist. (Sources: Eicher, 2013; Morris & Klein, 2000; Redstone & West, 2004.)

Providing only the amount of support needed to ensure stability using the least amount of adaptation necessary is one of the goals of positioning. The fine motor coordination required for eating and feeding is impossible unless larger muscle groups provide a stable base. Appropriate supports might be a firm table or tray surface on which to rest the elbows and/or foot supports at the appropriate height for the child's height. Providing more support than is needed, however, can be restrictive, discourage independence, and weaken muscles that the student would otherwise use for support.

Normalizing tone is another goal of positioning. Abnormalities in muscle tone can affect trunk support and trunk/neck/head alignment necessary for proper support for jaw stability, tongue control, and lip mobility. This may affect a child's ability to retain food in the mouth, chew, swallow, and coordinate breathing and swallowing. It is therefore important to securely position a child during mealtime (and other activities). Children typically attempt to compensate with increased muscle tone in their body when they are not comfortably or securely supported in their seats. This tone will often generalize to their oral structure, interfering with the oral-motor control required for eating and feeding. For instance, if the child's feet are not secure on the ground or a stable surface, then the lack of balance and stability can result in a lack of stability for jaw and tongue movements.

Keeping the child as near to upright as possible is another goal of positioning (Eicher, 2013; Redstone & West, 2004). Most children are more successful with feeding and eating if they are seated upright with their necks slightly flexed, but the degree of flexion required must be determined individually through careful observation. Presenting the spoon from below the chin encourages the student to maintain this slightly flexed neck position, whereas presenting the spoon from above eye level encourages neck extension and may increase aspiration. Positioning should also encourage symmetry. A majority of children will eat best if their position is as symmetrical as possible. Slightly asymmetrical postures may work better for some children with unilateral reflex patterns. Again, food presentation can influence postural symmetry. For example, presenting the spoon from one side may encourage a student to turn his or her head toward the approaching spoon, which could trigger a reflex that could interfere with eating. It is important to consult with the PT and OT to determine the most appropriate position for each child.

Finally, positioning should be as normalized as possible. It is important to use positions that promote function and active participation, facilitate comfort, and ensure the safety of the child and the feeder. They should also be useful for and acceptable to the parent or caregiver. Positioning should also consider social interaction with peers; therefore, if possible, consider sitting a child at a table with other children rather than separating him or her due to using a tray table. The optimal position for eating and feeding varies from child to child. The principles previously listed are general; careful collaborative assessment and planning are key to determining the best position for each student.

Food Selection and Food Consistency

The feeding team needs to work together to create a feeding plan that meets the multiple needs of the child—oral motor, self-feeding, nutritional, and growth—when selecting foods for a student. Careful planning and coordination are required. For instance, foods that may encourage self-feeding, such as snack foods, may not promote the oral-motor, nutritional, or growth needs of the child. The nutritional aspect should not be overlooked because children with severe disabilities who have feeding difficulties often do not eat a diet with enough different foods to provide adequate nutrients needed for growth and health (Morris & Klein, 2000). The emphasis becomes more on caloric intake than on balance of nutrients when intake of food is limited.

Difficulty with the oral management and swallowing of different textures and consistencies of food is one aspect limiting food intake (Eicher, 2013; Morris & Klein, 2000; Schuberth et al., 2010). For example, some children may be able to manage smooth solid food (e.g., yogurt, pudding), but have difficulty managing lumpy solids, such as commercially available third-stage baby foods. The child may not be able to use jaw, tongue, and cheek movements to manage this lumpy, mixed food (which has some solids mixed with liquids) into a bolus (the mounded mass of food formed by chewing). Instead, the food pieces become scattered in the mouth and can slip down the throat more easily, causing choking or aspiration. These mixed foods are also harder to manage during swallowing because the patterns of food transport and swallowing initialization are different than for just liquids or solids (Saitoh et al., 2007). Other children may have difficulty managing chewy solid foods. Hypertonicity, hypotonicity, or poor oral-motor skills may make chewing difficult, resulting in the child swallowing the chewy food whole or with minimal chewing. Yet, other children are at increased risk for aspiration with pureed foods and thin liquids because they can easily run down the throat without stimulating a true swallow response. It is important for the team to work together to increase the child's ability to manage the foods or determine how to expand his or her food repertoire and nutrition intake.

Adaptive Feeding Equipment

Adaptive equipment is useful to promote independence with feeding and oral-motor skills or compensate for skills that are lacking. A variety of equipment is available, and the team should work together to determine what equipment may be useful. It is important to remember the child's perspective in selecting equipment. Does it look different than what other children use? Will he or she be embarrassed to use it? Try to use regular equipment as much as possible, adapting as needed, and use specialized eating utensils only when a clear benefit over regular utensils can be demonstrated.

Adaptive utensils are available (see Figure 8.3). Spoons with shallow, flat bowls help children with decreased lip closure to remove food more easily using the upper lip, thereby promoting oral-motor skills and feeding. A deeper

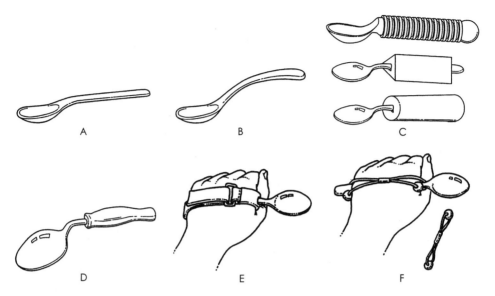

Figure 8.3. Different types of spoons and adaptations to aid in holding spoons: a) spoon with a flat bowl, b) spoon with a deep bowl, c) spoons with large handles, d) spoon with a bent handle, e) universal cuff, and f) elastic handle made from a ponytail holder. (From Lowman, D.K. [1999]. Adapted equipment for feeding. In D.K. Lowman and S.M. Murphy (Eds.), *The educator's guide to feeding children with disabilities* [p. 148]. Baltimore: Paul H. Brookes Publishing Co.; reprinted by permission.)

spoon bowl may provide more success for a self-feeder at other times because the deep bowl retains liquids easier if there are movement issues with bringing the food from the plate to the mouth. Spoons with bumps or ridges may help children with sensory issues. Consider using a rubber-coated metal spoon or one with a plastic bowl for a child who is hypersensitive to temperature because metal utensils conduct heat to or from oral structures very rapidly. Rubber-coated spoons are recommended if a child bites on the utensil or demonstrates a tonic bite. Although small, disposable plastic spoons are excellent for some children because they minimize stimulation, they are not suitable for a child who may bite down on them because they break, often leaving sharp splinters of plastic in the mouth (Alexander, 2001). Utensils with shorter handles, extended handles, and curved handles can provide independence toward self-feeding. Curved handles provide a more direct line to the mouth for children with limited mobility in the wrist and hand. Short handles are useful for children with limited coordination and motor skills, whereas longer handles are useful for children with limited strength or range of motion. Built-up handles can be added to utensils to help children grasp utensils easier. Universal cuffs, which strap around the hand, are helpful if the child has difficulty maintaining his or her grip on a utensil.

Varieties of cups are also available to help make drinking easier and safer. When opaque cups are used, feeders commonly position themselves above the child to look into the cup so they can see when the fluid is reaching the mouth, which encourages the student to extend the neck and look up. This results in the fluid passively running down the throat and into the airway instead of being actively swallowed. Clear cups will help make the liquid visible to the caregiver when assistance is provided, allowing for more active control of the fluid due to increased visibility as well as better positioning of the feeder and student. Regular glasses and cups require hyperextension of the neck; when they are tipped up enough for the contents to pour into the mouth, the rim hits the drinker's nose unless the head is tipped back. Many children with severe and multiple disabilities unfortunately choke, gag, or have other difficulties when they tip their heads back to drink. Cups with a notch cut out (called *cutaway*, *flexicup*, or *nosey cups*) are helpful in allowing the child to get liquid from the bottom of the cup when tipped so that he or she does not have to extend the head back, which could increase tone, affect postural alignment, or result in aspiration. Cups with handles may help a child with fine motor skill difficulties and decreased grip to hold a cup for self-feeding. Straws may also be a useful option for increasing liquid intake or independence. Straws come in a wide variety of heights and widths. Consider a child's suck strength, lip closure, and the thickness of a liquid when selecting the straw. For instance, a shorter straw is usually used for a beginning straw user. A longer straw may be useful for children with limited mobility to be able to reach their drink. Some straws provide a mechanism for graded control of liquid flow if the child is unable to manage a larger volume of liquid in the mouth. Some straws also prevent flow back down if the child has difficulty sustaining a suck. Flexible straws are generally recommended for children who have seizures because rigid straws can cause serious injuries to the eye or face if a seizure occurs.

Different plates and bowls are available to help with mealtime challenges. Some plates and bowls have a higher rim on one side to allow the user to scoop food onto his or her utensil. Plates and spoons with a weighted bottom are useful to prevent spilling if a child has motor incoordination. Plates with partitions may be useful for children with sensory challenges and food selectivity to keep foods in their own compartments. Even paper plates with cartoon characters may provide enough motivation to encourage eating. Adapted plates and cups are not what is needed for some children, but rather a nonskid surface to place the dishes on to prevent excess movement during scooping of food. There are specially designed products for this purpose, although shelf liner can work as well.

Addressing Mealtime Behavior

It has been estimated that as many as 50% of children with developmental disabilities have behavioral feeding problems (Kedesdy & Budd, 1998). For example, children with autism may demonstrate problematic eating and feeding behaviors due to difficulties adapting to change, resulting in behaviors such as insisting on using the same utensil or dish and having the same food prepared in the same ways (Martins, Young, & Robson, 2008; Williams et al., 2005). Children with CP may exhibit feeding behaviors such as spitting foods to avoid the difficulty with chewing and swallowing that occurs because of oral-motor impairments. Behavioral feeding problems may have serious implications for nutrition, growth, and general health. For example, long-term rumination of stomach acids can burn and damage the esophagus and teeth. Although behavioral mealtime problems are mentioned briefly here, they should be considered as part of a full functional behavioral assessment (FBA) with the team.

Mealtime behaviors, like all behaviors, are often multifaceted and require the team to hypothesize the reason for the behavior. Food refusal behaviors may begin due to physical structural impairments (e.g., cleft palate), invasive medical interventions (e.g., nasogastric tubes), or physical disorders (e.g., gastroesophageal reflux), yet they may continue well past the presence of these factors (de Moor et al., 2007). Children learn that "behaviours, such as crying, tantrums, food expulsion and/or keeping the mouth closed, result in escape from and avoidance of an aversive feeding situation" (de Moor et al., 2007, p. 670).

Behavioral challenges can be among the harder ones for the team to manage because they require a coordinated, consistent approach. Treatment of behavioral issues not only requires consistency between home, school, and among many people, but it also requires agreement about how to approach the targeted behaviors. This aspect is particularly challenging because there is not always agreement in the field (Linscheid, 2006; Morris & Klein, 2000). There is agreement, however, that behavior is a form of communication. Children express their concerns, fears, feelings, and needs through their behavior (Morris & Klein, 2000). Therefore, we need to carefully examine what the child is communicating to us (communicative intent), not only the acting-out behavior. Mealtime behaviors, such as refusal to eat, throwing food, or intentional vomiting, are ways to communicate that something is wrong. Morris and Klein noted that children "may be uncomfortable, frightened, feel out of control, have a stomachache, or feel overwhelmed by the mealtime environment" (2000, p. 266). Take the time to determine what the child is attempting to communicate through the inappropriate behavior instead of trying to eliminate it. It may be hard to decipher or treat what the child may be communicating in some cases (e.g., sensory hypersensitivities from a lifetime of invasive procedures), whereas the child may be communicating something that can be more readily addressed, such as stomach discomfort due to constipation, in other cases. A mealtime communication board, placemat with communication board included, or a mealtime book may be helpful (Morris & Klein, 2000). A mealtime communication board can be a simple board of words or pictures so the child can indicate his or her food and drink choices, pacing needs (e.g., faster, slower), and other related mealtime information (e.g., bathroom needs, conversation words) through his or her preferred communication method (e.g., pointing, eye gaze). Similarly, a placemat can have the main words on the edges for easy access on their tray. A mealtime book may have a greater number of pages and words for meal planning, visual recipes, or social words for conversation.

Treatment using behavior modification is common in the research literature on children with mealtime behavioral challenges (de Moor et al., 2007;
Ledford & Gast, 2006; Linscheid, 2006; Williams et al., 2010). Positive reinforcement is the most common intervention technique. Children are provided
with praise and/or tangible reinforcers (e.g., preferred toys, games, or foods) in
response to engaging in appropriate mealtime behavior. Ignoring inappropriate behaviors while attending to appropriate mealtime behaviors (e.g., eating,
sitting quietly, using utensils) is another common method (Ledford & Gast,
2006; Linscheid, 2006; Williams et al., 2010). Escape prevention/extinction techniques are also used (Ledford & Gast, 2006; Williams et al., 2010), including a
variety of methods to prevent learners from being able to avoid eating. These
techniques range from invasive, such as restraint and forced feeding, to less
invasive, such as returning a child to his or her chair or nonremoval of the
spoon (in which a spoon is held in front of the child's mouth until a bite is
eaten). This type of technique is most commonly used with children display-
ing severe food refusal who need the intensive services in an inpatient or day
treatment program (Williams et al., 2010). The use of such restrictive and intrusive procedures should be avoided when possible and considered by the team
only when more positive approaches have been exhausted and there is a clear
need based on the child's health and welfare. Stimulus fading is another intervention method and involves gradually changing or increasing the amount of
refused food provided, such as blending preferred foods or slowly increasing
or decreasing food textures.

Although behavioral therapists argue that behavior modification techniques are well supported through research and clinical experience, others
suggest that rigid behavior modification programs are hard to implement outside a structured hospital setting and are not compatible with a child-guided
mealtime program (Linscheid, 2006; Morris & Klein, 2000). Breaking down
steps into small changes to allow time for practice and repetition is one aspect of a child-guided mealtime program (Martins et al., 2008; Morris & Klein,
2000) and allows for repeated opportunities for taste exposure to new foods.
For example, exposure for children with autism who may demonstrate sensory sensitivities and resistance to change may start with the new food being
on the table or nearby. After repeated exposure, the next step may have the
child look at the food, then touch it or smell it. Children with autism may
eventually allow the food on their plate before tasting it. Building positive
associations and changing negative associations regarding feeding are other
aspects of a child-guided mealtime program. Consider if the child associates
a particular spoon, white medical lab coat, or food with negative experiences
of feeding. Could a different spoon be used? Could the staff member associate a spoon with a more enjoyable activity, such as sand play? Child-guided
programs tend to offer children choices and control to help them learn how to
manage their feeding. Frank's story is a real-world example of how to address
mealtime behavioral challenges.

Frank

Frank has an intellectual disability as well as visual and auditory impairments and has recently begun ruminating daily after lunch at the vocational program connected with his school. The staff was puzzled by this new
behavior. The vocational staff, the school staff, and the family observed
Frank over a period of time as part of an FBA. Based on these observations, the team brainstormed a number of hypotheses for the motivations
behind Frank's behavior, which included the desire to gain attention,
escape a task, or receive additional sensory input. They decided that if the
ruminating were sensory motivated, say, a matter of taste, they could give
Frank a wider choice of foods to select at lunch. He was given a choice of
at least three different foods prior to each lunch to test this hypothesis.
The foods that were not selected were wasted because Frank's only method of selecting food was to smell and touch it. Although wasteful, it was
the only way to give Frank more choice about what he ate. The team made
an interesting discovery. Although Frank did refuse some of the choices
presented to him, he ate two servings most days. The lunch provided by
the vocational center was not typically his favorite foods, and the quantity
was not enough for Frank. Frank was hungry and did not like some of his
lunch choices, so he was ruminating to feel fuller. He stopped ruminating
when he was given enough food to satiate his hunger.

(From Lowman, D.K., Kientz, M., & Weissman, R.A. [1999]. Behavior strategies for feeding.
In D.K. Lowman and S.M. Murphy (Eds.), *The educator's guide to feeding children with disabilities* [p. 169–170]. Baltimore: Paul H. Brookes Publishing Co.; adapted by permission.)

CONCLUSION

This chapter presented information and discussion concerning mealtime skills
and related concerns for children with severe and multiple disabilities. Mealtime skills are essential for survival, health, and a good quality of life. Ongoing
observation and assessment of respiration, physical development, oral-motor
skills, sensory issues, communication and socialization skills, and nutrition are
critical to the development of an appropriate plan of intervention. A carefully
designed feeding plan can do a lot to promote development, health, learning, and quality of life by providing instruction in eating and feeding skills,
protecting against the dangers of airway obstruction and aspiration, ensuring
good nutrition, and creating a typical and relaxed mealtime environment complete with dining experiences. Collaborative teamwork is required to assess
and continue to manage the child's current ability and needs.

REFLECTION QUESTIONS

1. This chapter has thoroughly discussed the importance of the context of
    mealtime. Thinking of a specific student (if possible), describe at least three

concrete, specific ways to enhance his or her involvement in mealtime. If you do not have access to a specific student, then consider the case studies of Frank, Collette, and Joseph.

2. Examine adaptive feeding equipment through an online catalog to determine what equipment may be useful for different feeding difficulties (look at the Atypical Feeding in Children with Disabilities section).

3. Create a list of questions to ask parents/caregivers about their child's feeding as well as a list to ask children about their feeding. What would be important topics to include? What would be the best way to phrase questions to gather the most detailed information?

4. Observe the current routines of a classroom. Consider the following observations: What is the classroom's typical lunch routine? How do students get their lunch (e.g., walk through line, get served, serve themselves, carry food on tray, bring their own lunch)? How do they open containers? Where do they sit (e.g., benches, chairs, chairs attached to tables)? How long do they have for mealtimes? Then consider these routines in relation to the case studies of Joseph, Collette, and Frank.

CHAPTER ACTIVITY

Recall the case story of Joseph from the chapter. Imagine that you are member of Joseph's educational team. Discuss and carefully consider the following questions related to treatment and assessment:

Assessment

1. What questions do you have for his parents?

2. What information do you want about his medical and developmental history?

3. What questions do you have about his feeding history?

4. What do you want to know about his current feeding?

5. Who should be involved in the feeding assessment?

Treatment

1. What are some considerations about his positioning needs?

2. What strategies will you use to facilitate socialization during mealtime?

3. What aspects will you consider with communication?

4. What other aspects might need to be considered for Joseph's mealtime?

REFERENCES

Academy of Nutrition and Dietetics. (n.d.). *What are the qualifications of a registered dietitian?* Retrieved from http://www.eatright.org

Alexander, R. (2001). Feeding and swallowing. In J.L. Bigge, S.J. Best, & K.W. Heller (Eds.), *Teaching individuals with physical, health, or multiple disabilities* (4th ed., pp. 504–535). Upper Saddle River, NJ: Merrill/ Prentice Hall.

American Occupational Therapy Association. (2007). Specialized knowledge and skills in feeding, eating, and swallowing for occupational therapy practice. *American Journal of Occupational Therapy, 61,* 686–700. doi:10.5014/ajot.61.6.686

American Occupational Therapy Association. (2014). Occupational therapy practice framework: Domain and process (3rd ed.). *American Journal of Occupational Therapy, 68,* S1–S48. doi:10.5014/ajot.2014.682006

American Physical Therapy Association. (2014). *Guidelines: Physical therapist scope of practice.* Retrieved from http://www.apta.org

American Speech-Language-Hearing Association. (2007). *Scope of practice in speech-language pathology.* Retrieved from http://www.asha.org/policy

American Speech-Language-Hearing Association. (n.d.). *Pediatric dysphagia* [Clinical topics]. Retrieved from http://www.asha.org/Practice-Portal/Clinical-Topics

Andrew, M.J., Parr, J.R., & Sullivan, P.B. (2012). Feeding difficulties in children with cerebral palsy. *Archives of Disease in Childhood: Education and Practice Edition, 97,* 222–229. doi:10.1136/archdischild-2011-300914

Arvedson, J.C. (2013). Feeding children with cerebral palsy and swallowing difficulties. *European Journal of Clinical Nutrition, 67,* S9–S12.

Bosch, J., Mraz, R., Masbruch, J., Tabor, A., Van Dyke, D., & McBrien, D. (2002). Constipation in young children with developmental disabilities. *Infants and Young Children, 15,* 66–77.

Bruns, D.A., & Thompson, S.D. (2010). Feeding challenges in young children: Toward a best practices model. *Infants and Young Children, 23,* 93–102.

Cook, E., & Dunifon, R. (2012). *Do family meals really make a difference?* Retrieved from http://www.human.cornell.edu/pam/outreach/upload/Family-Mealtimes-2.pdf

Davis, A.M., Bruce, A.S., Khasawneh, R., Schulz, T., Fox, C., & Dunn, W. (2013). Sensory processing issues in young children presenting to an outpatient feeding clinic. *Journal of Pediatric Gastroenterology and Nutrition, 56,* 156–160. doi:10.1097/MPG.0b013e3182736e19

de Moor, J., Didden, R., & Korzilius, H. (2007). Behavioural treatment of severe food refusal in five toddlers with developmental disabilities. *Child: Care, Health and Development, 33,* 670–676. doi:10.1111/j.1365-2214.2007.00734.x.

Eicher, P.S. (2013). Feeding and its disorders. In M.L. Batshaw, N.J Roizen, & G.R. Lotrecchiano (Eds.), *Children with disabilities* (7th ed., pp. 121–140). Baltimore, MD: Paul H. Brookes Publishing Co.

Fayed, N., Berall, G., Dix, L., & Judd, P. (2007). A dynamic and comprehensive model of paediatric feeding practice. *International Journal of Therapy and Rehabilitation, 14,* 7–15.

Gisel, E.G. (1996). Effects of oral sensorimotor treatment on measures of growth and efficiency of eating in the moderately eating-impaired child with cerebral palsy. *Dysphagia, 11,* 48–58.

Individuals with Disabilities Education Improvement Act (IDEA) of 2004, PL 108-446, 20 U.S.C. §§ 1400 *et seq.*

Kedesdy, J.H., & Budd, K.S. (1998). *Childhood feeding disorders: Biobehavioral assessment and intervention.* Baltimore, MD: Paul H. Brookes Publishing Co.

Kuperminc, M.N., Gottrand, F., Samson-Fang, L., Arvedson, J., Bell, K., Craig, G.M., & Sullivan, P.B. (2013). Nutritional management of children with cerebral palsy: A practical guide. *European Journal of Clinical Nutrition, 67,* S21–S23. doi:10.1038/ejcn.2013.227

Lane, S.J. (2012). Disorders of eating and feeding, and disorders following prenatal substance exposure. In S.J. Lane & A.C. Bundy (Eds.), *Kids can be kids: A childhood occupations approach* (pp. 417–436). Philadelphia, PA: F.A. Davis.

Ledford, J.R., & Gast, D.L. (2006). Feeding problems in children with autism spectrum disorders: A review. *Focus on Autism and Other Developmental Disabilities, 21,* 153–166. doi:10.1177/10883576060210030401

Linscheid, T.R. (2006). Behavioral treatments for pediatric feeding disorders. *Behavioral Modification, 30,* 6–23. doi:10.1177/0145445505282165

Lowman, D.K., Kientz, M., & Weissman, R.A. (1999). Behavior strategies for feeding. In D.K. Lowman & S.M. Murphy (Eds.), *The educator's guide to feeding children with disabilities* (pp. 155–172). Baltimore, MD: Paul H. Brookes Publishing Co.

Lowman, D.K., & Murphy, S.M. (1999). *The educator's guide to feeding children with disabilities*. Baltimore, MD: Paul H. Brookes Publishing Co.

Manikam, R., & Perman, J.A. (2000). Pediatric feeding disorders. *Journal of Clinical Gastroenterology, 30,* 34–46.

Marí-Bauset, S., Zazpe, I., Mari-Sanchis, A., Llopis-González, A., & Morales-Suárez-Varela, M. (2013). Food selectivity in autism spectrum disorders: A systematic review. *Journal of Child Neurology, 29,* 1–8. doi:10.1177/0883073813498821

Martins, Y., Young, R.L., & Robson, D.C. (2008). Feeding and eating behaviors in children with autism and typically developing children. *Journal of Autism and Developmental Disorders, 38,* 1878–1887. doi:10.1007/s10803-008-0583-5

Matson, J.L., Cooper, C.L., Mayville, S.B., & Gonzalez, M.L. (2006). The relationship between food refusal and social skills in persons with intellectual disabilities. *Journal of Intellectual and Developmental Disability, 31,* 47–52. doi:10.1080/13668250600561937

Morris, S. E., & Klein, M. D. (1987). *Pre-feeding skills*. Tucson, AZ: Therapy Skill Builders.

Morris, S.E., & Klein, M.D. (2000). *Pre-feeding skills* (2nd ed.). Tucson, AZ: Therapy Skill Builders.

Murphy, S.M., & Lowman, D.K. (1999). Communication strategies for feeding. In D.K. Lowman & S.M. Murphy (Eds.), *The educator's guide to feeding children with disabilities* (pp. 127–140). Baltimore, MD: Paul H. Brookes Publishing Co.

National Association of School Nurses. (2013). *Individualized healthcare plans: The role of the school nurse* [Position statement]. Retrieved from http://www.nasn.org/PolicyAdvocacy

Ochs, E., & Shohet, M. (2006). The cultural structuring of mealtime socialization. *New Directions for Child and Adolescent Development, 111,* 35–49. doi:10.1002/cad.153

Patel, M.R., Piazza, C.C., Layer, S.A., Coleman, R., & Swartzwelder, D.M. (2005). A systematic evaluation of food textures to decrease packing and increase oral intake in children with pediatric feeding disorders. *Journal of Applied Behavior Analysis, 38,* 89–100. doi:10.1901/jaba.2005.161-02

Redstone, F., & West, J.F. (2004). The importance of postural control for feeding. *Pediatric Nursing, 30,* 92–100.

Reid, D.H., & Parsons, M.B. (1991). Making choice a routine part of mealtimes for persons with profound mental retardation. *Behavioral Residential Treatment, 6,* 249–261.

Saitoh, E., Shibata, S., Matsuo, K., Baba, M., Fujii, W., & Palmer, J.B. (2007). Chewing and food consistency: Effects on bolus transport and swallow initiation. *Dysphagia, 22,* 100–107. doi:10.1007/s00455-006-9060-5

Schuberth, L.M., Amirault, L.M., & Case-Smith, J. (2010). Feeding intervention. In J. Case-Smith & J.C. O'Brien (Eds.), *Occupational therapy for children* (6th ed., pp. 446–473). St Louis, MO: Mosby.

Schwarz, S.M. (2003). Feeding disorders in children with developmental disabilities. *Infants and Young Children, 16,* 317–330.

Schwier, K.M., & Stewart, E.S. (2005). *Breaking bread, nourishing connections: People with and without disabilities together at mealtime*. Baltimore, MD: Paul H. Brookes Publishing Co.

Sharp, W.G., Jaquess, D.L., Morton, J.F., & Herzinger, C.V. (2010). Pediatric feeding disorders: A quantitative synthesis of treatment outcomes. *Clinical Child and Family Psychology Review, 13,* 348–365. doi:10.1007/s10567-010-0079-7

Sleigh, G. (2005). Mothers' voice: A qualitative study on feeding children with cerebral palsy. *Child: Care, Health and Development, 31,* 373–383.

Snyder, P.A., Breath, D., & DeMauro, G.J. (1999). Positioning strategies for feeding and eating. In D.K. Lowman & S.M. Murphy (Eds.), *The educator's guide to feeding children with disabilities* (pp. 65–109). Baltimore, MD: Paul H. Brookes Publishing Co.

Sullivan, P.B., Lambert, B., Rose, M., Ford-Adams, M., Johnson, A., & Griffiths, P. (2000). Prevalence and severity of feeding and nutritional problems in children with neurological impairment: Oxford feeding study. *Developmental Medicine and Child Neurology, 42,* 674–680. doi:10.1111/j.1469-8749.2000.tb00678.x

Williams, K.E., Field, D.G., & Seiverling, L. (2010). Food refusal in children: A review of the literature. *Research in Developmental Disabilities, 31,* 625–633. doi:10.1016/j.ridd.2010.01.001

Williams, K.E., Gibbons, B.G., & Schreck, K.A. (2005). Comparing selective eaters with and without developmental disabilities. *Journal of Developmental and Physical Disabilities, 17,* 299–309. doi:10.1007/s10882-005-4387-7

Williams, K.E., Hendy, H., & Knecht, S. (2008). Parent feeding practices and child variables associated with childhood feeding problems. *Journal of Developmental and Physical Disabilities, 20,* 231–242. doi:10.1007/s10882-007-9091-3

9

Designing and Adapting the Curriculum

KATHLEEN GEE

CHAPTER OBJECTIVES

1. Understand the principles for collaboratively developing educational goals that will increase quality of life

2. Learn to develop priority educational goals based on three areas—person-centered/family-centered planning, age-referenced school curriculum and age-referenced school and life activities, and capacity-specific skills

3. Understand the concepts of modification and adaptations to input and output

4. Recognize how to modify outcomes that are referenced to the core curriculum standards

5. Learn strategies for collaborating with general education team members

6. Understand how to develop participation and support plans for individuals with severe and multiple disabilities in general education classes

KEY TERMS

- Active and informed participation
- Age-referenced, academic, and ecological curriculum
- Capacity-specific information
- Collaborative teams
- Functional relevance
- Inclusive education
- Instructional matrix
- Participation and support plans

- Person-centered/family-centered approaches
- Positive behavior interventions and supports (PBIS)
- Quality of life
- Team planning between general education and special education teachers

Zoe is a spirited first grader who attends her neighborhood elementary school in a semirural community. This is her second year of being fully included in the general education program after attending a preschool program that served only children with disabilities. Zoe's team got her a hands-free KidWalk (Prime Engineering, 2014) a few months ago, and she is delighted. She is now exploring and going places. Zoe loves being around all the children and attempts to interact with them through touching and vocalizing. She also uses augmentative and alternative communication (AAC), specifically, a speech generating device (SGD), and she is working on using it to communicate with peers and adults. She is challenged with retaining the visual memory of what a symbol or word means. Zoe also comprehends some American Sign Language and can use some of these signs expressively.

Zoe has spastic cerebral palsy that affects all four of her limbs, and she also has an intellectual disability. She recently was fitted for hearing aids to augment a mild to moderate hearing loss in each ear. Although Zoe's family struggled to understand the effects of her hearing loss, everyone hopes that Zoe's verbal communication will improve after learning to wear the aids. Zoe really wants to communicate with her own voice. She is working on several modified academic goals, including emergent literacy and numeracy skills. Zoe's school adopted the Common Core State Standards (CCSS) this year, and her first-grade teacher is working hard on the language of numeracy. Zoe also has modified goals for social studies and science. In addition to communication and academics, Zoe is working on increasing her ability to take care of her personal needs in the bathroom and at lunch, finding new games that she likes to play at recess, taking turns, and improving her self-determination skills.

Jabari is a fifth grader with a great sense of humor. He likes to ride in the carrier attached to his father's bicycle and enjoys activities that give him a lot of tactile input. Jabari is in his last year at a suburban elementary school. His younger brother attends second grade at the same school. Jabari's school recently decided to desegregate their special education classes, and this will be his second year with full access to all special education supports and services while attending classes with his general education peers. Jabari is deafblind and has a minimal amount of light perception and a profound hearing loss. As a result, Jabari learns primarily through tactile and proprioceptive input. He also has spastic quadriplegia and significant intellectual challenges. He is working on increasing his symbolic communication through receptive tactile signs and objects and expressive objects and textures. Jabari has been more comfortable at school since his team and peers began consistently providing him with cues about the context of what was going on using these tactile means of communication. In addition, staff developed a communication dictionary to help themselves and peers better understand Jabari's nonsymbolic communication forms, a strategy that helped staff and peers to consistently respond to his communication behaviors.

Jabari's parents feel that fifth grade will be even better because he will be moving to a class with friends he made in the fourth grade. Jabari's special education support teacher made it a priority to facilitate friendships and help his peers learn the best way to communicate with Jabari, and to find ways to play together, and work together in class.

Brandon is a seventh-grade student at a large urban middle school. This is his first year being fully included in general education classes and the curriculum after his family moved from another community. Brandon loves to listen to the latest popular music and hang out with friends at lunch, and his English/social studies teacher is his favorite teacher. Brandon was developing typically until he incurred a massive brain trauma when he was only 14 months old. He was in the hospital for a long time after his injury. He received minimal educational services at home following his release from the hospital, but he did receive around-the-clock nursing services until he was 9 years old. Brandon's family wanted him in school, but they were not sure how school could work. They needed assurance that his specialized health care needs could be met while going to school with his typically developing peers, that people would know how to support his engaged participation in the core curriculum and other activities, and that teachers would know how to facilitate his peer relationships and communication. Brandon was finally included in general education in the seventh grade.

Determining the best possible means for Brandon to have control over his environment and communicate more effectively was a high priority for Brandon. Brandon has several challenges related to communication. He has low vision (see Chapter 4) and needs materials presented 12 inches from his eyes. He no longer has a blink reflex and wears specially designed goggles with moisturizing techniques to protect his eyes. He can shift his gaze in his left eye, but he struggles to use his right eye to shift or scan. Due to his massive trauma, the only movements under Brandon's physical control are his shift of gaze in the left eye, his ability to move his eyebrows slightly, and his breathing. His breath control allows him to take a deep breath and cause his right cheek to move. This movement is used to activate technology. Brandon's hearing is still intact. Brandon's schedule is as follows: first period—theatre; second period—English; third period—(wheel) computer technology, cooking and nutrition, and gardening; fourth period—science, lunch; fifth period—private personal needs; sixth period—social studies.

Louisa is 17 and is a happy senior in a large urban high school where she has developed some wonderful friendships over the years. Louisa has been included with her general education peers in classes and activities since the ninth grade. Louisa was not always so happy. She experienced a lot of frustration in her upper elementary, middle school, and early high school years. Her school team did not know how to support her learning and communication. As a result, she experienced fear, anger, and depression, which caused Louisa to have several behavioral challenges, including scratching and biting, which created further difficulties at school and at home.

Louisa has autism, has intellectual disabilities, and she is also blind. Louisa's school team received support and training when she was in 10th grade. Improvements in Louisa's education included the development of a communication system, instruction in orientation and mobility (O&M), meaningful access to the curriculum, systematic instruction, facilitation of friendships and peer-mediated instruction, and development of a behavior intervention plan using PBIS. Louisa now communicates using several means—she verbalizes some words and sentences, uses a speech-generating device (SGD) through tactile discrimination, and uses some tactile signs. Louisa's senior year schedule will consist of government, medical technology, South American literature, choir, physical education, and community-based work internship.

Zoe, Jabari, Brandon, and Louisa all have multiple disabilities. Their cognitive, sensory, and physical abilities are each unique. They are always learning! Their stories capture just a short moment in time during their educational and home lives. Since the time that this chapter was written, the descriptions of the four students and what they are working on in school has undoubtedly changed. What is compelling about these students is the rich ways in which they connect to the people and places in their homes, schools, and communities. It is important to know how educators and team members observe, analyze, and process the wonderfully unique ways in which each child with multiple disabilities learns. Learning and communicating are ultimately key contributors to quality of life (Beukelman & Mirenda, 2013).

Because quality school outcomes improve quality of life, it is important for teams to identify desirable outcomes for students with multiple disabilities before discussing a process to achieve these outcomes. Envisioning a desirable future for a student helps guide the individualized education program (IEP) team as it designs a meaningful educational program (O'Brien, 2014). Snell and Brown (2011) highlighted three outcomes of what effective educational programs hope to achieve—skills, membership, and relationships. The skills outcome refers to all the relevant skills that students must acquire to increase their participation in academic coursework, activities of daily living, activities of their typically developing peers at school and in nonschool environments, and activities in the community and the workplace. The membership outcome refers to belonging (Carter, 2011; Carter, Cushing, & Kennedy, 2009; Kunc, 1992). Belonging to peer groups in school and after-school activities and to groups in the community, the neighborhood, and in the workplace provides the opportunity for relationships to develop. The relationships outcome refers to the development of interactions, social relationships, and friendships. All children and youth need a variety of meaningful relationships with peers and adults, including reciprocal relationships, play relationships, companionship, intimate relationships, being a helper, being a helpee, or one of many other relationship roles.

Self-determination is another critical outcome of effective educational programs (Agran & Hughes, 2014). *Self-determination* can be defined as learning to make choices; having an effective way to communicate with others; and having a means to exercise responsible control over one's life routines, one's own behavior, and one's own relationships. When making educational decisions, the student, his or her family, and the educational team should consider with whom the student will go to school, hang out, spend leisure time, live, and work, as well as how the student will get around and access activities and services in the community. Envisioning a future for every child that includes meaningful relationships, engagement in the community, work, a choice of where and with whom to live, safety and health, and ongoing learning is an important place to start.

A FRAMEWORK FOR DEVELOPING CURRICULUM AND INSTRUCTION

This chapter discusses effective practices central to the development of high-quality curriculum and instruction for students with multiple disabilities. The discussion begins with a description of a guiding framework for program development and then moves to development of the IEP and personalized curriculum.

Research-Based Principles

The research-based framework for educational program development in this chapter is guided by the following five principles: 1) person-centered/family-centered planning; 2) age-referenced, ecological, and academic curriculum; 3) functional and social relevance; 4) individualized systematic instruction; and 5) active and informed participation. A person-centered/family-centered approach seeks input first from the family. The individual and his or her family focus the team on key priorities for the present and future through their vision of quality of life, important relationships, access, and participation (Turnbull, Turnbull, Erwin, Soodak, & Shogren, 2011). Professional team members also play an important part in this visioning and futures planning process. Teams need to understand, advocate for, and help to generate the student's desirable future through systems-change thinking that is outside of the box (O'Brien, 2014). Systems-change thinking challenges societal perceptions that often limit individuals with disabilities to lifestyles based on their intellectual or physical capacities. Understanding how individuals can participate in and be supported in desirable lifestyles helps change the system towards having higher expectations for students with severe and multiple disabilities.

An age-referenced, academic, and ecological curriculum is based on the school curriculum/standards and school- and nonschool related activities of same-age, typically developing peers. Through a process of considering the student's needs for growth across academic, functional, and basic skills, the educational team can set priorities that involve the student in the same educational activities as typically developing peers, challenge the student at his or her cognitive and academic level, and lead toward positive adult outcomes (Downing, 2010; Jackson, Ryndak, & Wehmeyer, 2008–2009; McDonnell & Hunt, 2014).

The resulting priorities should be functionally and socially relevant to the current and future contexts in which the child or youth is expected to participate and engage in learning and social activities. Functional relevance means that the curricular goals and methods of instruction are socially valid, representing areas of need that will truly have a significant impact on the student's life (Turnbull et al., 2011). Parents and team members should be able to quickly and easily answer the question, "Why are we teaching this?", and the answer should be obvious and important to all team members. Functionally relevant priorities ultimately increase the student's skills, membership and participation, relationships, and self-determination (the four outcomes identified earlier).

After determining functionally relevant priorities, the team is charged with the important task of analyzing the student's cognitive, sensory, and motor skills within the general education curriculum and other priority learning contexts in order to determine goals and define systematic instructional methods. Research conducted since the late 1990s has shown that systematic and responsive instruction achieves effective outcomes for students with multiple disabilities in inclusive schools and communities (Snell & Brown, 2011). Instruction may be geared toward academic skills such as literacy and numeracy (Browder & Spooner, 2011, 2014; Hudson, Browder, & Wood, 2013); cognitive skills such as early intentional communication skills (Beukelman & Mirenda, 2013); community access skills (McDonnell & Hardman, 2010); or functional skills such as taking care of one's personal belongings or self-care needs (Snell & Delano, 2011). Systematic yet responsive instruction means that the outcomes desired are behaviorally specific; the teaching strategies are carefully selected to match learners' needs; and instruction is consistently implemented. Errors are analyzed, and modifications are data-based (Collins, 2012). Educators need to be flexible, assess within the context of teaching, observe and adjust their teaching practices as needed, and respond to changes in communicative initiations from their students. Responsive educators both perceive and utilize critical moments for instruction to provide optimal opportunities for growth and success (Agran & Hughes, 2014; Collier, McGhie-Richmond, & Self, 2010; Gee, 2001; Rowland & Schweigert, 2004).

Active and informed participation (Gee, 1995, 2004; Gee, Alwell, Graham, & Goetz, 1995) refers to structuring both curriculum and instructional adaptations and methods to ensure that all students are not only included in school and community activities but also are truly active and informed participants within each setting or activity. This is particularly important for individuals with multiple disabilities and/or serious communication challenges. An informed participant has a means to get information about what is going on, has an understanding of the context, and has been given adequate support to be connected to both the social and task demands of the situation. An active participant is a student who has also been given a meaningful way to contribute both socially and academically to the activity or task. Teachers working within this framework analyze how each student will receive information and how best to connect the student with people, materials, and activities in the teaching context to increase anticipation and initiation of communicative and other skills (Beukelman & Mirenda, 2013; Downing, 2010). Teachers structure supports and instruction to ensure that the student's actions and initiations result in functionally relevant consequences connected to the activities and environments in which the student is engaged (Campbell, 2011; Gee, Alwell et al., 1995; Rowland & Schweigert, 2004).

Jabari's team uses these strategies to make sure that he is provided with clear tactile information about what is happening and what happens as a result of his engagement during fifth-grade activities. For example, Jabari's peers make sure that his hands are on the pulleys they are manipulating and experimenting with during the science unit on the relationship between energy and force so that he can experience both the action motion and the results of their cooperative efforts.

Systemic Supports

Achieving the valued outcomes described in this chapter through the five research-based principles is easier when school districts make systemic commitments to inclusive education, PBIS, and collaborative teaming. Although not all schools have these systemic supports in place, the literature cites these practices as being central to effective programs for students with multiple disabilities (Agran & Hughes, 2014). When these practices are not in place, it becomes the role of educational team members to work toward these systemic changes while still providing the best possible educational program within the constraints of their school environment.

Inclusive Schools The examples and processes provided in this chapter are set in inclusive classrooms and school settings because evidence suggests that students with severe and multiple disabilities benefit both academically and socially from being served in inclusive school settings (see Fisher & Meyer, 2002; Halvorsen & Neary, 2009; Jackson et al., 2008–2009; McDonnell & Hunt, 2014; Spooner, McKissick, Hudson, & Browder, 2014).

Inclusion happens when students with disabilities attend school with their peers without disabilities and receive specially designed instruction and supports to help them succeed in their education. It involves setting high standards for every learner and ensuring that they become fully participating members of the classroom community.

An inclusive school provides the support and setting within which true membership and relationships can form. Without this systemic support, teachers who serve students in special education only classes must work harder at creating opportunities for their students to spend time with their typically developing peers, participate in grade-level academic and nonacademic activities, and develop friendships. This puts an extra burden on the special education teacher to develop these opportunities (Sailor & Roger, 2005). Although skills can indeed be practiced in special education classrooms, strong evidence shows that context does matter (McDonnell & Hunt, 2014; Ryndak, Moore, Orlando, & Delano, 2008–2009; Spooner et al., 2014) and that an inclusive education environment offers opportunities for desired quality outcomes that cannot be attained in segregated educational settings (Downing, 2008; Jackson et al., 2008–2009; Turnbull et al., 2011). There is neither room in this chapter to discuss all the relevant research, nor to provide the strategies for systems change that are often required to facilitate the transition to the inclusive school organizational structure. The reader is referred to The U.S. Department of Education, Office of Special Education Programs (http://www2.ed.gov/about/offices/list/osers/osep/index.html) that provides academic and behavioral support to promote the learning and academic achievement of all students, including those with the most extensive support needs.

Positive Behavior Interventions and Supports   A schoolwide and individual commitment to using PBIS is the second critical systemic support for effective educational programs (Brown & Bambara, 2014; Carr et al., 1999; Sailor, Dunlap, Sugai, & Horner, 2009). PBIS has been developed since the mid-1980s as a result of numerous federally funded research and demonstration projects and the participation of thousands of schools across the United States. Effective and positive support of all students, especially those with the most serious challenging behaviors, can be difficult for teachers, schools, and parents. Schoolwide PBIS provides strategies for schools to develop a set of principles and practices that guide students to behave positively. These proactive strategies are focused more on teaching students positive ways to behave than on what type of consequences will ensue if students misbehave (Sailor et al., 2009). Individual PBIS plans are developed for the smaller number of students who need extra and intensive supports to learn positive ways of communicating, interacting, and having a sense of control. Because many challenging behaviors are communication-based (Beukelman & Mirenda, 2013), students with multiple disabilities are at a greater risk of developing challenging behaviors if their teams do not pay close attention to developing communication systems, predictability, a means to actively engage in their environment, and relationships that are responsive and reciprocal. The reader is encouraged to seek more information on PBIS through the *Journal of Positive Behavior Interventions*, the TASH journal (*Research and Practice for Persons with Severe Disabilities*), and by going to the PBIS web site (http://www.pbis.org) or the TASH web site (http://www.tash.org).

Collaborative Teams   Effective curriculum and instruction are also supported by a systemic belief in the power of collaborative, transdisciplinary teams. *Collaboration* is a word that has been used widely in the literature regarding students with multiple disabilities (Campbell, 2011; Downing, 2008; Giangreco, 2011; Rainforth & York-Barr, 1997; Westling & Fox, 2009). Because students with multiple disabilities have a range of challenges in their lives, professionals and family members need to combine their expertise and experience in ways that will benefit and not fragment the child's educational day and home life. This includes collaboration between general and special education teachers (Potts & Howard, 2011), occupational therapists (OTs) and physical therapists (PTs) (Campbell, 2011), speech-language pathologists (SLPs) (Beukelman & Mirenda, 2013), vision and hearing specialists, nurses and other health professionals, and, of course, families and peers.

The remainder of this chapter provides a practical, curricular, and instructional planning process that is based on the five guiding principles (person-centered/family-centered planning; age-referenced, ecological, and academic curriculum; functional and social relevance; individualized systematic instruction; and active and informed participation) and these systemic commitments to inclusive education, PBIS, and collaborative teaming.

GATHERING INFORMATION AND SETTING PRIORITIES

The team must consider multiple sources of information when determining educational priorities for the student (see Figure 9.1). The first step is to form the student's team and then enlist the support of all team members in sharing information and contributing to the collaborative decision-making process. Students' teams will vary in their makeup but should include the family, special education (support) teacher, general education teacher(s), key related services personnel (e.g., OTs, PTs, SLPs, vision specialists, nurses), close friends, and any other individuals that the family considers critical to the team. The team gathers information from four important sources—the current and future priorities from the person-centered planning meeting; the core curriculum standards for the child's age-appropriate grade level; an inventory of typical life activities of same-age peers; and capacity-specific information regarding the child's intellectual, social, communicative, physical, and sensory abilities and challenges.

Person-Centered/Family-Centered Planning

As previously stated, the student's team must agree on a vision for the student's future and a clear sense of long-term outcomes that are desired for the student. Chapters 1 and 2 provide information and methods for developing reliable alliances with families. True partnerships and collaborative problem solving with families are often enhanced through the use of processes designed to envision desirable futures and formulate priorities (Turnbull et al., 2011).

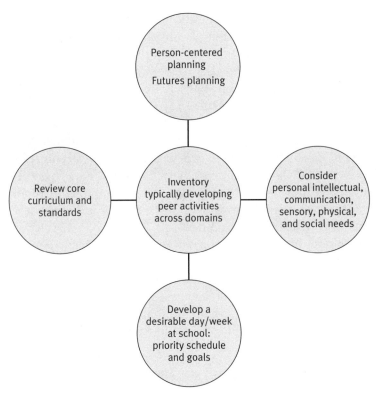

Figure 9.1. Planning and information gathering process.

Using one of many person-centered planning processes provides a framework for teams to develop a vision for a quality future for each individual with a disability (Claes, Van Hove, Vandevelde, van Loon, & Schalock, 2010; Holburn & Viest, 2002; O'Brien, 2014). Some popular person-centered planning processes include Making Action Plans (MAPS) and Planning Alternative Tomorrows with Hope (PATH) (O'Brien, Pierpoint, & Kahn, 2010), *Choosing Options and Accommodations for Children with Disabilities* (COACH; Giangreco, Cloninger, & Iverson, 2011), and person-centered thinking (Sanderson & Lewis, 2012).

The most important aspect of these processes related to establishing educational priorities is that the student and his or her parents and other family members are truly central members of the team with equal participation in all aspects of the meeting. The purpose of a person-centered/family-centered meeting, held prior to the actual IEP meeting, is to develop a personal profile of the focus student, emphasize strengths and abilities, and formulate a vision for the individual's future and plans for getting there. The team is able to address issues in the community and school and begin determining ways to work together and support each other in the implementation of the student's educational and/or transition plan. The meeting often begins with the parents and/or the special education teacher providing a short summary of previous experiences in school and any other issues that are important for setting the stage.

Participants in the meeting share their visions and concerns for the individual's near and distant future. The student's strengths and needs, preferences, and learning styles are discussed from a personal point of reference. This means that the language of the meeting is not the language of a psychological or discipline-specific assessment tool but the language of people who know the student—talking together about who the individual student is, what they want for him or her, and how they can help. Assessment tools and reports are left at the office, and people who spend the most time with an individual (at home, in school, and in the community) share and discuss their concerns and ideas about the individual's education and quality of life. Information regarding the student's previous school and community integration, social networks, and age-specific program issues are a natural part of the discussion.

The facilitator prompts the discussion by asking some key questions such as, "When we look at the dreams we have listed here on the wall, the visions we have for Jabari, what are his strengths? What are the qualities and abilities that he already has that will help him achieve his dreams/our dreams for him?" The facilitator also asks about the student's needs, "What are some of the things Jabari needs to fulfill his/our vision for the future?" Discussing learning and support from a holistic point of view is another important part of a family-centered meeting. Jabari's support (special education) teacher questioned the team as follows: "What do we know that really works for Jabari? When he has been really successful at something, what did it look like? What do we know that does not work? Let's make two lists." With some additional prompting, Jabari's team begins to talk about what they know.

Summarizing what the team has learned and making recommendations for the IEP and school program are the final step of the person-centered planning meeting. The team makes a list of priorities for the coming year and also looks at long-term planning and support ideas that may involve bringing in other resources. The results of the person-centered/family-centered planning meeting are extremely helpful for the IEP process. Finding agreement on the more specific goals and objectives, adaptations, and supports at the IEP meeting is much easier because the primary team members have already met and agreed on what they think are the most important aspects of the student's program for the coming year. The lead support teacher (the special education teacher) writes a summary of the meeting that is included in the IEP document and is read and discussed at the beginning of the IEP meeting. Sometimes the notes and chart paper from the meeting are also posted in the room where the IEP meeting takes place. This validates the family's and student's input and sets the tone for the meeting. Using person-centered planning strategies puts everyone on equal ground. It changes the way the person with disabilities is discussed and encourages common terminology. The group is focused on increasing the individual's quality of life through choices and empowerment,

creating a common bond through which the IEP process can be greatly enhanced. This group can continue to meet on a regular basis to positively influence the implementation of actions that will have a direct impact on the
individual's future (O'Brien, 2014). The results of Jabari's planning meeting
are depicted in detail in Figure 9.2. Shorter summaries of all four of our focus
students' planning meetings are included later in the chapter in Figures 9.3,
9.4, 9.5, and 9.6.

Age-Referenced Sources of Curriculum Content: The General Education Core Standards and Instructional Activities in the General Education Classroom

Important work that has been done since the late 1980s has demonstrated that
children and youth with the most significant challenges benefit from being
included in the core curricular activities of their same-age peers in general
education classrooms (Jackson et al., 2008–2009; McGregor, 2003). In addition,
highly important work has been conducted around using explicit and systematic instruction to teach complex academic skills, including literacy, numeracy, and science concepts (Bradford, Shippen, Alberto, Houchins, & Flores,
2006; Browder, Mims, Spooner, Ahlgrim-Delzell, & Lee, 2008; Carnine, Silbert,
Kame'enui, & Tarver, 2010; Hudson et al., 2013) to children and youth with significant intellectual disabilities who were previously excluded from academic
instruction (see Spooner et al., 2014, for review). Strategies for teaching children who are nonverbal to read have also been developed (Copeland & Keefe,
2007; Light & McNaughton, 2013), and the direction of literacy research has
changed as researchers have recognized the importance of integrating symbols, communication systems, and literacy for the purpose of participation in
many life activities (Copeland, Keefe, & de Valenzuela, 2014). Although some
researchers have indicated that these skills can be taught in special education
settings, the majority of authors have written that the instructional context of
the typical classroom and other natural environments provide benefits that
exceed the achievement of academic skills alone (Jackson et al., 2008–2009;
McDonnell & Hunt, 2014).

The general education curricular activities and core content can provide
the context for goals that are both functional and relevant to the student's
future. The core curriculum provides not only the opportunity of vertical learning of academic skills but also enriched horizontal learning in new vocabulary,
varied experiences, and all aspects of topics, culture, and the arts. *Vertical learning* refers to the depth of the curriculum and the scaffolded skills that students build on as they gain increasing intellectual understanding of a concept.
Horizontal learning refers to learning from the exposure to the breadth of the
core curriculum that they might not have had access to previously. Research
over several decades has shown that instruction of important basic skills (e.g.,
self-determination, early cognitive skills, communication skills, social skills,
motor skills, sensory skills) should be delivered and embedded in natural, integrated daily activities. Evidence shows that this kind of instruction allows
students to more effectively generalize skills (Beukelman & Mirenda, 2013;

People present: Jabari's parents, grandma, aunt, two cousins, younger brother, the support (special education) teacher, a friend from fourth grade and his mom, his augmentative and alternative communication (AAC) specialist, and his fifth-grade teacher.

A brief history was provided: Jabari's mom talked about the wonderful changes she had seen in Jabari since he was included at his brother's school in the fourth grade. Before fourth grade, Jabari had been riding the bus a long way to a special education class in another part of the community. The long bus ride was hard on him, and he would often get dehydrated, causing headaches. The first year at the new school had a few bumps in the road, but overall they were happy for the change. Jabari's grandma can now pick him up when she picks up Jabari's younger brother from school and walk home. There is still an issue of access, however, because they do not have a wheelchair accessible vehicle at home. This is difficult on rainy days. Jabari's nutrition and hydration have been a problem since birth, but the school team is working hard to make sure this is taken care of across the day. Jabari's aunt and cousins and his younger brother all talked about how great it is having Jabari at school with everyone else. Jabari's dad stressed how much it has helped to provide Jabari with consistent tactile and object cues for routines at home. This has also really helped at school.

Who is Jabari? Funny, gentle, obstinate, sometimes happy, sometimes frustrated and angry, a hard worker, searching, wants to know, loves bike rides with his dad

What are our dreams for Jabari? What we want to see happen for Jabari: Get better at communicating, have more ways to play with us, have ways to contribute more in school and eventually in a job, see if there is an object-based way to work with a speech-generating device, travel in the community and on trips, more friendships with other fifth graders, making sure Jabari goes to middle school with the same kids he knows from fifth grade, a good middle school team who will know how to teach and include him, gain weight, less headaches, increase his ability to use his hands effectively

What are our nightmares? What we do not want to see happen for Jabari: He would be segregated again, having teachers who do not value his contributions and potential, being sent to a middle school where he has to start over with friendships, losing weight, more health problems

What strengths does Jabari bring to meeting his goals, and what things do we know work well for Jabari? Jabari will try hard at things when he is given time and consistent ways of knowing what is going on through tactile and object cuing and appropriate means of giving him input. Jabari also likes to be active, and people should not treat him as if he will break. Jabari loves his family and his friends, and he really knows who is who by their touch and their scent. He is anticipating routines now, and sometimes he gets upset if things are not quite routine, but in many ways that is a good thing because it shows us that he is thinking and remembering. Jabari likes his object/tactile memory book and the fifth-grade teacher's room because she has rabbits in there and he has visited before.

What are Jabari's needs, and what things do we know to avoid? Communication is probably the biggest need, but also access issues for travel in the community and farther; tactile scanning and identifying capabilities; friendships; modifications and adaptations for participation in fifth-grade activities; nutrition and hydration plan for fifth-grade schedule; nonclass activities with peers at school and after-school activity ideas; playdates. Planning for middle school should start early; Jabari is growing and he will need a new seating system, which should be coordinated with the AAC system for future. We know that pushing Jabari too fast in a new activity does not work; we also know that it is harder for Jabari to learn when he is not given enough time to process and not given enough consistent input. We know that our interactions with him need to be on his terms and include as much hand-under-hand guidance as possible versus moving him through things. We also know that we should not treat him with kid gloves because he likes to play and do things that jostle him.

(continued)

Figure 9.2.   Notes from Jabari's person-centered planning meeting (based on an adapted Making Action Plans [MAPS] process).

Figure 9.2. *(continued)*

What should be our next steps for the individualized education program (IEP) and the school year? Fifth-grade teacher and support teacher collaborate to develop goals related to the content in fifth grade, continue to work on the communication system—both expressive and receptive, add to the memory book and communication dictionary, make sure kids in fifth grade, the teacher, the support teacher, and paraeducators know how to communicate with Jabari, make a plan for hydration and nutrition at school, work with the regional center on finding ways to have an accessible vehicle funded, sign up for paratransit in the community, plan to make an appointment for a new seating system, visit the middle school where Jabari's cousins and peers from class will most likely attend, begin meeting with the school district to ensure Jabari continues on with his peers, develop an instructional matrix to ensure that all the priorities get addressed

The support teacher will write up the summary and include it in the IEP. She will help Jabari develop a PowerPoint with video clips of things he did in fourth grade to share at his IEP meeting. A plan for introducing Jabari to new peers in his class was developed by the fifth-grade teacher and his support teacher within the typical beginning-of-the-year cooperative activities in which the fifth-grade class engages.

Campbell, 2011; Gee, Graham, Sailor, & Goetz, 1995; McDonnell & Hunt, 2014; Snell & Delano, 2011; Soto & Zangari, 2009).

Since the mid-2000s, a variety of authors have advocated that the same-age general education curriculum and standards should be a key source of goal development based on their own research and experience with including students with severe and multiple disabilities in general education classrooms and core curriculum (Downing, 2010; Gee, 2004; Ryndak et al., 2008–2009; Sailor, 2009; Snell & Brown, 2011). This does not mean that teams focus on isolated skills randomly grabbed from the core curriculum as some authors have suggested (Ayres, Douglas, Lowrey, & Sievers, 2011). Rather, it means determining a meaningful set of academic, basic, and relevant goals, taking into account lifelong learning and quality of life. Thus, because it is considered a basic civil right and recommended practice for children and youth from K–12th grade to attend and participate in school alongside their typically developing peers, the school, classroom, and curriculum form the ecology, or context, for instruction. Other authors have provided similar rationales for understanding a balance of the broad range of priorities for students such as Zoe, Jabari, Brandon, and Louisa (Hunt, McDonnell, & Crockett, 2012; McDonnell & Hunt, 2014).

With an understanding of the general education curriculum standards and how they are implemented in the student's general education classroom, the team can plan to determine modified goals/outcomes based on the standards within each subject area (see section on curriculum collaboration) and determine ways that other nonacademic goals can also be targeted for instruction. For example, Zoe's first-grade classroom was doing a unit on family histories related to California Social Studies Standard 1.5 (students describe the human characteristics of familiar places and the varied backgrounds of American citizens and residents in those places) while also working on the CCSS Reading Literature for first grade (RL 1–4). Within this unit, Zoe worked on communication goals for identifying and remembering new symbols (in this case man and woman, boy and girl) on her SGD and also foundational emergent reading skills related to both letter–sound recognition and early sight words.

Louisa's team enrolled her in the medical technology course for her senior year. The California science standards for grades 9–12 include Standard Set 10: Physiology (infection and immunity). Louisa's goals in this course were to understand that infection is related to being sick and to learn about how to stay healthy and how to care for herself when she is not feeling well, an important life skill as well as a content standard. In addition, getting comfortable with the various types of equipment and procedures that occur in doctors' offices (e.g., blood pressure cuffs, stethoscopes, scales) was an important functional goal for Louisa. All students in this general education classroom practiced these procedures. This was a priority for Louisa's family because going to the doctor's office was stressful for Louisa. The course also offered hands-on training and a variety of project-based learning activities within which Louisa could improve her work skills.

Life Activities of Same-Age Peers

Life activities of typically developing peers are another important source of information in the development of the IEP. From an ecological perspective, school is only one part of a person's life experience. The team must take an inventory not only of the coursework and school activities in which same-age, typically developing children and youth are engaged, but also other life activities, including personal care, caring for one's belongings, recreation, community access skills, social relationships, and skills related to employment (Ayres et al., 2011; Snell & Brown, 2011; Wehman, 2013). Teachers supporting children and youth with multiple disabilities need to keep the priorities related to quality of life and future plans for adult life generated by the person-centered plan foremost in mind, and they should link these priorities with both the general education curriculum standards and the typical activities of same-age peers.

A well-executed school inventory and typical peer inventory help the special education team connect to the typical structures, policies, and procedures for all students in the school and take note of important life activities of same-age peers. For example, an inventory at Zoe's school prompted the school inclusion team to reexamine the after-school activities to determine methods for access for all students. Jabari's elementary school teachers already worked in teams and had scheduled time on Wednesday mornings for planning. These Wednesday morning planning meetings and professional development opportunities were important for the new structures and skills being put into place because this was only the second year since the school had moved to an inclusive model. Brandon's middle school had a variety of clubs that met at lunchtime. The team determined that eating lunch with peers was a priority because of the excellent social opportunities and because attending to some of Brandon's health care procedures could occur after lunch during fifth period. An inventory at Louisa's high school revealed three different types of programs through which high school students could participate in internships both on and off campus.

There are electives and a range of coursework choices in many middle schools and in most high schools to satisfy high school graduation requirements. An understanding of the course content in science, social studies, English, and math, as well as the electives, gives the team a wide range of choices for courses that are best matched to a secondary student's short- and long-term goals. In addition, some courses may better suit the learning style of the focus student. In many ways, this makes including students in high school courses easier and more flexible. Deciding which courses to take also may be determined by peer friendships and supports.

An inventory of the student's neighborhood and what typically developing peers do after school and on weekends can yield information as to whether community settings are readily available for community-based instruction of various functional skills (e.g., traveling in the community, purchasing items, accessing various community services) or whether other arrangements will need to be made. The team can also consider the types of recreational and other community activities that are frequented by the student's same-age peers as a way to determine if any goals in these areas are a priority. Jabari is now attending the school that the other children in his neighborhood attend. Many of his neighbors walk to school, and some are driven. Getting to know where his friends live and what they like to do after school will help his team look at important recreational and social interaction goals. Zoe's family belongs to the YMCA, where Zoe swims and attends summer camps. An inventory of Brandon's community revealed that Brandon and many of his friends live quite a distance from community services in his urban area, even though the school is located near the town center. Brandon's family did not yet have adequate transportation for his wheelchair, making connections difficult. Access to friends and the community and support for the family to gain transportation became team priorities.

Capacity-Specific Information from Teachers and Related Services Providers

Capacity-specific information about the basic skills that can be taught within and across the general education curriculum and other functional activities in the school, home, and community is an additional source of information to consider. *Capacity-specific information* refers to an analysis of the student's current strengths and challenges related to cognitive/intellectual processes, sensory capacities, motor capacities, social interactions, and receptive and expressive forms of communication. This information is critical to determining priority goals. Input from all relevant team members should be synthesized for practical and functional use across contexts. Recommended practice indicates that assessments and analyses conducted by discipline-specific team members, such as PTs or OTs, should be conducted within and across the home, school, and community contexts where the student spends his or her time (Campbell, 2011; Downing, 2008). This approach ensures that skills targeted for instruction will have practical and functional application throughout the day.

For example, the PT on Zoe's team was working with all team members to increase Zoe's capacity to maneuver in and out of her wheelchair and her Kid-Walk. Zoe's team also worked with her on her communication skills throughout the entire day using both manual signs and her SGD. Staff incorporated development of Jabari's fine motor skills throughout his school activities. His SLP worked with the teacher to develop tactile object and texture cues and tactile signs, which staff incorporated throughout all the activities of his day. Jabari also needed to receive sufficient nutrition and hydration throughout the day, so his food and liquid intake were regularly monitored. Positioning and assistance protocols for both Jabari and Brandon were designed by the OTs but carried out daily by the whole team. Similarly, Brandon's specialized health care needs were provided by several team members. The school nurse instructed staff and conducted competence checks on suctioning, catheterization, tube feedings, and respiratory therapy. In addition, important early cognitive skills related to contingency awareness (the understanding of cause and effect) and communicative intent were a high priority for Brandon, so these goals were implemented throughout the day. Louisa's O&M specialist worked with the special education teacher and paraeducators to plan ways to develop Louisa's mobility skills as she traveled from class to class and in the community. The whole team approved Louisa's PBIS plan, and staff continued to incorporate her communication system as a key component of every class and activity.

It is important that instruction associated with goals related to increasing specific capacities and protocols for managing physical, sensory, and health needs be implemented within and across all of the student's activities. These skills and priorities are noncontext bound, meaning that they are basic to and underlying almost all of the academic and nonacademic activities in which the students are involved. Instruction of these skills can thus be embedded into the student's activities in the general education curriculum, the school, at home, and in the community. If children and youth with multiple disabilities are provided with an interesting, activity-based school day in which they engage with typically developing peers at school and (in older years) in the community, then the team should not have a problem finding naturally reinforcing situations in which to develop basic skill capacities. Teams using the instructional matrix (see following section) can quickly determine whether activities or schedules need to be changed in order to get more practice on important skills.

SYNTHESIZING THE PRIORITIES AND
DEVELOPING THE INSTRUCTIONAL DAY/WEEK

Our work in preparing teachers has taught us that it is helpful for teachers to create a summary sheet in which all of the priorities from all sources (families, core curriculum, typical life activities, and specific capacities) are briefly listed so that an action plan can be developed. This action plan should include three things—an activity/course-based schedule for the school day; a list of priority instructional goals; and a list of other types of considerations related to health, physical or sensory management, and equipment and technology needs.

A schedule that is activity/course-based means the chunks of time during the student's school day are defined not by narrow skills, but rather by age-appropriate activities and courses based on curriculum content and typical school and nonschool activities, depending on the age of the student. This is easy to do when students are included with their same-age peers, whether in elementary school or secondary school, because the general education bell schedule or class schedule will form the structure of the day. The team can then determine whether any goals cannot be worked on within the general education classroom (e.g., bathroom skills, community skills) and then set times during the day for those goals to receive appropriate amounts of attention. Teachers who primarily work in special education classrooms are still responsible for creating a class schedule that provides a similar age-appropriate set of coursework and activities. Their day should follow the bell schedule in secondary schools or the same classroom schedule as the typical elementary grade classrooms. Both general and special education teachers should focus on creating learning contexts that are interesting, functional, and relevant. In other words, creating contexts for learning using the principles of universal design for learning (UDL) versus simply drill and kill is crucial to all students (see Chapters 10 and 11).

The list of priority goals should include standards-based goals (modified for the learner), goals based on other age-appropriate life activities that are not related to content standards, and goals that are basic to all contexts (i.e., basic cognitive, social, communication, motor, and sensory skills). Of course, priority goals will vary for every child. Listing the equipment, technology, positioning, and other health care needs for the learner is also an important step to ensure that everything is addressed. Figures 9.3–9.6 provide a summary sheet and action plan for each of the focus students.

The next step in planning the instructional day is to develop an instructional matrix that shows when and where each of the student's goals will be addressed throughout the day and what equipment, technology, positioning, and health care issues need to be addressed during each period. The instructional and support matrix provides the whole school team and the family with a visual summary of what is happening throughout the school day/week. There may be more than one matrix, depending on the complexity of the student's schedule. Some secondary schools operate on a block schedule with a reduced number of classes but longer periods each day. Most elementary classrooms have

Student's name: Z.R.   Age/grade: 6 years, first grade

Team members: Mrs. L (first-grade teacher), inclusion support teacher, physical therapist, occupational therapist, speech-language pathologist

> **Summary of person-centered planning meeting (priorities and areas to be addressed related to quality of life/futures planning):** Friendships are highly important. Communication skills, more ways to play with brothers and sisters, learning to read, making more sounds and words, hearing aids, getting around, playdates—access issues, self-determination—letting others know when she does not want them to do something

Needs related to core curriculum and academic options at the school	Needs related to nonacademic, same-age typical life activities	Capacity-specific needs
Emergent literacy skills, both foundational reading and literary reading	Using the lunchroom	Using both her primary and portable speech-generating device (SGD)—expressive and receptive communication
Expressive and receptive communication	Playing with others at recess	
	Using the bathroom	Symbol vocabulary memory
Beginning number sense	Making friends	Transfers: chair, walker, floor, toilet
Modified social studies goal	Self-determination—letting others know when she does not want them to do something to her or for her	Wearing hearing aids
Modified science goal		Fine motor use of tools
		Walking safely using the KidWalk (hands-free walker)

Action Plan

Schedule of courses/activities	Prioritized instructional goals	Equipment, technology, health care, and so forth
Mrs. L.'s first-grade class:	Reading—foundational reading skills: letter sounds, beginning sight words, and so forth	Hearing aids
Morning meeting		Dynavox (SGD)
Language and literacy	Reading—literature: responding to questions about a story, repeated storylines, and so forth	Small portable voice output for recess, lunch
Recess	Expressive communication: use of symbols paired with words to request and to comment/share, and yes/no	Wheelchair
Restroom		Kid-Walk
Math and math workshop	Expressive communication: use of small portable device to make prepared social interactions	Adaptive utensils
Lunch	Receptive vocabulary	Adaptive scissors, pen holders, and so forth for classroom
Recess	Numeracy: beginning number sense	
Restroom	Modified science goal	
Social studies or science	Modified social studies goal	
Reader's theatre and closing	Social interactions with peers	
	Independent physical transfers	
	Using the KidWalk	
	Personal care: using the bathroom	
	Lunchroom skills	

Figure 9.3. Zoe's summary sheet for prioritizing educational needs.

Student's name: J.N.   Age/grade: 10 years, fifth grade

Team members: Mrs. R. (fifth-grade teacher), inclusion support teacher, physical therapist, occupational therapist, speech-language pathologist/augmentative and alternative communication (AAC) specialist

Summary of person-centered planning meeting (priorities and areas to be addressed related to quality of life/futures planning): Fifth-grade teacher and support teacher collaborate to develop goals related to the content in fifth grade, continue to work on the communication system—both expressive and receptive, add to the memory book and communication dictionary, make sure kids in fifth grade, the teacher, the support teacher, and paraeducators know how to communicate with Jabari, make a plan for hydration and nutrition at school, work with the regional center on finding ways to have an accessible vehicle funded, sign up for paratransit in the community, plan to make an appointment for a new seating system, visit the middle school where Jabari's cousins and peers from class will most likely attend, begin meeting with the school district to ensure Jabari continues on with his peers, develop an instructional matrix to ensure that all the priorities get addressed

Needs related to core curriculum and academic options at the school	Needs related to nonacademic, same-age typical life activities	Capacity-specific needs
Fifth-grade curriculum:	Recess	AAC—expressive and receptive
English language arts	Lunchtime activities	Use of single switch
Math	School performances	Tactile scanning and selection
Science	Assemblies	
Social studies	School fundraisers	
Visual and performing arts (incorporated into social studies and English language arts [ELA])	Playdates	
	After-school activities	
Technology (incorporated in math and science)	Sibling and cousin relationships	
	Helping around the house/chores	
Physical education	Participation at church	
Social living		

Action Plan

Schedule of courses/ activities	Prioritized instructional goals	Equipment, technology, health care, and so forth
Fifth grade:	ELA: tactile memory book for sharing stories, topical object/texture books for literature	AAC: low-tech memory book and communication dictionary, switch-activated call device and go/stop
Morning meeting		
Book share	Math: left to right and up and down patterns	
Math: half period/break for food and drink	Modified social studies goal	Wheelchair
	Modified science goal	New seating soon
Recess	Modified physical education goal	Nutrition and hydration plan
English language arts	Modified social living goal	
Lunch	Expressive communication: single switch, object and tactile signs/gestures	
Recess		
Social studies and language arts	Receptive communication	
	Friendships/social relationships	
Science and language arts	Classroom/school chores: fundraisers	
Physical education/social living	Left to right scanning	
	Object discrimination	
	Bringing items to self and pushing items away from self—finding/locating	

Figure 9.4. Jabari's summary sheet for prioritizing educational needs.

Student's name: B.R.   Age/grade: 13 years, seventh grade

Team members: Homeroom teacher, inclusion support teacher, occupational therapist, speech-language pathologist, vision specialist

---

Summary of person-centered planning meeting (priorities and areas to be addressed related to quality of life/futures planning): Highest priority need is some control over his environment through directed communication efforts, both nonsymbolic and through technology for voice output; try to teach auditory/object scanning; develop receptive and expressive communication strategies; input—best way to teach Brandon new concepts; reexamine and provide consistent opportunities throughout all age-appropriate subjects and activities; facilitation and development of friendships is a high priority; activities to do outside of school; specialized health care needs—training, planning, and support; futures planning

---

Needs related to core curriculum and academic options at the school	Needs related to nonacademic, same-age typical life activities	Capacity-specific needs
Seventh-grade requirements: English language arts Math Social studies Science Physical education Electives: The wheel: technology/cooking and nutrition/gardening Visual or performing arts: choose one all year, either choir, band, or theatre	Lunchtime clubs at school Social get-togethers: making friends Hanging out at lunch Going places in the community with friends Self-determination: directing his care through more switch access to basic communication Relationships with family	Communication system: both expressive and receptive Access to control over environment: microswitch through controlled breathing and cheek movement Object symbols Auditory/object input Visual symbol instruction

Action Plan

Schedule of courses/activities	Prioritized instructional goals	Equipment, technology, health care, and so forth
Seventh-grade homeroom schedule: First period: theatre Second period: English Third period: wheel Fourth period: science Lunch Fifth period: personal health care needs Sixth period: social studies	Receptive communication and acquisition of vocabulary: object, verbal, auditory Expressive communication: call device; power words/symbols for WANT, GO, COME, AFFIRM, DENY Environmental controls: directing others and technology Access to printed materials: in literature and media Friendships and social relationships at school and outside of school Community access Modified theatre goal Modified English goal Wheel: different goal for each subject Modified science goal Modified social studies goal	Microswitch and mount for cheek access Low-tech voice output Object/auditory schedule Software symbol programs Objects for communication Computer with him at all times Health care: suctioning, catheterization, respiratory therapy, vital signs, tube feeding

Figure 9.5.   Brandon's summary sheet for prioritizing educational needs.

Student's name: L.M.   Age/grade: 17 years, 12th grade

Team members: School counselor, inclusion support teacher, orientation and mobility instructor, speech-language pathologist

> **Summary of person-centered planning meeting (priorities and areas to be addressed related to quality of life/futures planning):** The following priorities were generated from the Planning Alternative Tomorrows with Hope (PATH) process. Louisa and her family want her to be employed, live with supportive roommates in an apartment or condo, participate in community activities, continue to learn and take classes, travel, do things with friends, and participate in taking care of her home after she leaves high school. In addition, priorities for her senior year were to continue development of an effective communication system and access to text; continue team implementation of positive behavior interventions and supports (PBIS) plan; continue to practice orientation and mobility skills in familiar and unfamiliar environments; get involved in more school activities; get internship and work experience in the community—two different experiences in a year; typical classes selected from catalog—choir, medical technology, government, South American literature, physical education—cycling (first semester), modern dance I (second semester); internship

Needs related to core curriculum and academic options at the school	Needs related to nonacademic, same-age typical life activities	Capacity-specific needs
12th grade: seven periods in the day	Clubs	Orientation and mobility skills
A variety of options exist related to the core subjects: social studies, science, English, math.	Friendships at school as well as outside of school	Communication skills: both receptive and expressive
Selections depend on the student's goals.	Community access for recreation and tasks	Text access
	Lunch—open campus: community	Auditory/texture schedule
A number of electives are also available in foreign languages, performing arts, and visual arts.	Part-time work	Use of money in the community and at school
	Taking care of and choosing one's own belongings at school and home (e.g., locker, backpack, clothing)	PBIS plan
		Means of effective exercise
		Weight management

Action Plan

Schedule of courses/ activities	Prioritized instructional goals	Equipment, technology, health care, and so forth
First period: government	Modified government goal	Voice output system
Second period: physical education	Physical education: modified cycling and modern dance goal	Auditory/tactile schedule system
Third period: literature	Modified literature goal	Objects
Fourth period: choir	Modified choir goal	Orientation and mobility cane
Fifth period: medical technology	Modified medical technology goal	
	Expressive communication	Book share
Sixth and seventh periods: internship	Receptive communication	Software for text access
	Orientation and mobility: school and community	
	Self-determination: 1) "what to do when I am frustrated" and 2) choosing types of support	
	Using locker and keeping track of personal belongings	
	Friendship, social relationships	
	Campus club participation	
	Internship: supported employment	
	Using money in the community	

Figure 9.6. Louisa's summary sheet for prioritizing educational needs.

alternative schedules for specific days/times during the week. The instructional matrix also gives the lead support teacher the opportunity to ensure that planning for instruction of every goal occurs with as much intensity and efficiency as possible. Figures 9.7 and 9.8 depict the instructional and support matrices for Zoe and Brandon. The support teacher has written a *D* in the boxes in which the student will receive planned, direct instruction on a particular goal; an *I* in the boxes in which the student will receive incidental instruction (i.e., instruction that occurs as opportunities arise within an activity/lesson) on the goal; and an *X* in boxes to indicate any necessary equipment, technology, positioning, or health care needs that are required.

COLLABORATING WITH THE GENERAL EDUCATION TEACHER TO DETERMINE GOALS RELATED TO THE CONTENT STANDARDS

The general education content standards/curriculum and the instructional activities that are designed to support it are the primary contexts within which students with multiple disabilities will receive instruction. Students with multiple disabilities may have curricular outcomes that are the same as their typically developing peers, or their outcomes may be quite different. Aligning learning outcomes with the general education content standards and modifying the expectations for individual students within the curriculum require the ability to scaffold cognitive skill development and determine underlying skills within a large subset of standards. A majority of states have adopted the CCSS for English and math (National Governors Association Center for Best Practices & Council of Chief State School Officers, 2010a, b) and the Next Generation Science Standards (NGSS Lead States, 2013) since 2013. A smaller number of states still use their own sets of standards. The CCSS were developed in an effort to try to standardize the expectations in schools across the country. Whether teachers are using the CCSS, the NGSS, or standards specific to their state, the task is the same for the collaborative team—determining how the student with multiple disabilities will learn meaningful skills within the activities of the classroom and how meaningful goals related to the standards will be developed.

Designing modifications to outcomes for students with disabilities has been discussed by numerous authors (Downing, 2010; Halvorsen & Neary, 2009; Jorgensen, Schuh, & Nisbet, 2006; Snell & Brown, 2011; see Chapters 10 and 11). McGregor (2003) made an important distinction between standards-based goals and standards-referenced goals. *Standards-based goals* refer to using the grade-level standards, which are scaffolded for increasing levels of difficulty. Goals for many students at their cognitive level can be found within the standards by looking at grade levels cognitively below the student's age. For example, there are standards in the CCSS for math related to algebraic functions, which start at a basic level in kindergarten and increase in complexity through the grade levels. *Standards-referenced goals* allow the team to cognitively scaffold even further and personalize the instruction related to the standard by using both the depth and breadth of the curriculum. For example, a standards-referenced goal

Instructional and Support Matrix

Student's initials: Z.R.   Age/grade: 6 years, first grade

Date: _____

D = Instruction on goal is planned and directly implemented in this session; I = Goal is incidentally instructed at relevant moments; X = Yes, this is needed

Column groups: columns 2–9 = Curriculum-based goals; columns 10–14 = Other goals; columns 15–22 = Technology and equipment needed.

Student's schedule	Language and literacy (RL)	Language and literacy (RF)	Expressive communication	Expressive communication	Receptive communication	Numeracy	Science	Social studies	Social interactions with peers	Independent physical transfers	Using the KidWalk	Personal care: bathroom skills	Lunchroom routine	Primary speech-generating device (SGD)	KidWalk (hands-free walker)	Hearing aids	Wheelchair	Adaptive utensils and plate	Adapted scissors	Magnetic letters and numbers	Portable SGD
Arrival, morning meeting	D		D	D	D				D	D				X		X	X				
Language and literacy	D	D	D	D	D									X		X			X	X	
Recess			D	I	I				D	D	D	D			X	X					
Math and math workshop					D	D			I					X		X			X	X	X
Lunch			D	D	D				D	D	D	D	D			X	X	X			X
Recess				I					I	D	D	D	D		X	X	X				X
Literacy and math in social studies or science	D		I	I	I	D	D	D	I					X		X			X	X	
Reader's theatre	D	D	D	D	D				I							X					

Figure 9.7. Zoe's instructional and support matrix.

Instructional and Support Matrix

Student's initials: B.R.   Age/grade: 13, seventh grade

Date: _____

D = Instruction on goal is planned and directly implemented in this session; I = Goal is incidentally instructed at relevant moments; X = Yes, this is needed

Student's schedule	Curriculum-based goals							Other goals							Technology and equipment needed								
	Theatre goal	English goal	Wheel: computer goal	Wheel: cooking and nutrition goal	Wheel: gardening goal	Science goal	Social studies goal	Receptive communication	Expresive communication	Environmental control	Access to print	Friendships: in school and outside of school	School clubs	Community access	Microswitch and cheek mount	Low-tech voice output	Visual/auditory schedule	Computer and software programs	Objects for input	Suctioning equipment	Tube feeding	Catheter equipment	Vital signs equipment
Period 1: Theatre	D		D	D	D			D	D	D	D	I		D	X	X	X		X	X			X
Period 2: Homeroom and English		D		D	D			D	D	D	D	I			X	X	X	X	X	X			X
Period 3: Wheel: currently computer technology			D					D	D	D	D	I			X	X	X	X	X	X			X
Period 4: Science						D		D	D	D	D	D			X	X	X	X	X	X			X
Lunch: Clubs, hang out								D	D	D	D	D	D	D	X	X	X		X	X			X
Period 5: Personalized health care needs								D	D	D	D		D	D		X	X		XX	X	X	X	X
Period 6: Social studies							D	D	D	D	D	D	D	D	X	X	X	X	X	X			X

Figure 9.8. Brandon's instructional and support matrix.

for Zoe in science was to use photographs and symbols to demonstrate her understanding of the vocabulary/concepts for the differences between plants and animals; the sun, moon, and the earth; and the five senses (Ref. CA NGSS Grade One: Disciplinary Core Ideas).

For definitional purposes here, *modified outcomes* refer to changes the team makes in expected academic or cognitive outcomes for individual students. For example, Louisa was working on comprehension of text modified to a second-grade level while her peers were working on 12th-grade English content standards. Specifically, one of her goals was to identify the key characters and important events in a story (modified from the literature of her peers) that was read to her or listened to through alternate audio media. Brandon was working on using his eye gaze to demonstrate his understanding of heat and cold in his science class while his peers were working on demonstrating their understanding of the physics of energy from the sun. Zoe was working on emergent literacy skills (letter sounds) while her first-grade peers were working on reading phonetically and identifying sight words. Jabari was working on how to use tactile/object memory books during his fifth-grade language arts lessons.

Adaptations and *accommodations* refer to the types of changes the team makes in the ways in which information is both provided and required. In other words, a student's outcomes may be the same as all the other students, with adaptations in either input (the ways in which the student receives information) or output (the ways in which the student produces information or lets people know what he or she knows). A student may require both modified outcomes and adaptations to benefit most from the curricular activities. Some adaptations are standard practices that teams always agree to do for a student, such as using specific seating arrangements or modifying physical equipment, providing a longer time to produce a product, or agreeing to accept spoken versus typewritten answers. Other adaptations are specific to certain subjects or particular teaching activities.

Zoe, Jabari, Brandon, and Louisa all require adaptations in the ways in which information is provided throughout all activities. Their receptive communication systems require more than just verbal input. Louisa and Jabari both use tactile object systems and some tactile signs. Louisa uses an auditory schedule as well as verbal input. Brandon and Zoe both use visual symbols and photographs, and Zoe uses visual signs and some words for input. Louisa, Brandon, Jabari, and Zoe also require adapted ways of demonstrating what they know (their output systems) within each general education activity. Louisa is working on using her words and her tactile symbol/voice output book to provide information to others. Brandon is working on using eye gaze and a switch activated by his deep breath movement to indicate choices and communicate. Jabari is working on scanning for specific objects to demonstrate his understanding, and Zoe is working on using symbols, photographs, and words to demonstrate her understanding. See Chapter 11 for more on adaptations, accommodations, and modifications.

Each student's IEP should include goals that describe the expected outcomes within each core content area, course, or subject in which the student is enrolled or participating. This approach is crucial for several reasons. First, it gives general education teachers a specific frame of reference for the expectations for the student within the class or subject area. Second, it organizes the IEP around the educational contexts selected by the team. Third, it provides a clear guide for what the student is working on and when. Teams will find it especially helpful when there are goals that indicate the purpose and outcomes related to the general curriculum content standards. Tables 9.1 and 9.2 depict modified goals for the focus students. The English language arts and mathematics goals in Table 9.1 are referenced to the CCSS. The sample, modified goals for social studies, visual and performing arts, and science in Table 9.2 are referenced to the CCSS for social studies, the California State Standards for Visual and Performing Arts (California Department of Education, 2001) and the NGSS (NGSS Lead States, 2013).

COLLABORATING WITH THE GENERAL EDUCATION TEACHER TO DEVELOP PARTICIPATION AND SUPPORT PLANS

The development of participation and support plans for each curricular period of the student's day is one of the most important phases of instructional planning. The process can have a significant influence on the student's success in the general education curriculum/classroom, whether done prior to entry in the class or shortly after the school year begins. The updated planning process for designing participation and support plans recommended in this chapter has been documented in other sources and has been used with numerous educational teams across the country (Gee, 1995, 2004; Gee, Alwell et al., 1995). Use of the process sets a tone for collaborative ownership of the curriculum, the students in the class, and the special needs of the children with disabilities. The outcomes of the process should be as follows: refined modified goals for the IEP based on the standards, an outline of how the student's modified content goals will be met within the general education activities, a description of what other goals (not based in the standards) will be implemented within the general education activities, knowledge of what specific adaptations to both input and output need to be developed, and an understanding of what additional supports are necessary.

The focus begins with the general education curricular unit (e.g., an English unit focused on a particular novel, a science unit focused on light and energy). Although all teachers are responsible for teaching to the same content standards, teachers will creatively organize the instruction, group the students, develop skills, and measure progress in a variety of ways. Various levels of this process can be utilized, depending on whether support (special education) teachers and general education teachers have previously collaborated for other students and on how well they know each other. The collaborative planning process in Box 9.1 assumes that team members are new to

Table 9.1. Sample modified goals referenced to the Common Core State Standards for English language arts (ELA) and math, for Zoe, Jabari, Brandon, and Louisa.

Zoe	Jabari	Brandon	Louisa
Modified English language arts goals Given letter sounds and use of visual scanning, Zoe will demonstrate her knowledge of letter sounds and beginning letter combinations; she will recognize at least 10 sight words. (Ref. ELA reading—foundational skills standards for grade 1: #3) Zoe will respond to comprehension questions related to stories using pictures to sequence beginning, middle, and end, characters, and so forth. (Ref. ELA reading—literature standards for grade 1: #1–3) *Modified math goals* Given objects and magnetic numbers to work with, Zoe will count out and answer questions of how many for numbers 1–10 and will order numbers 1–10 with 80% accuracy. (Ref. math standards for K: counting and cardinality) Zoe will follow a visual schedule of activities, demonstrated by her visual matching of the materials and pictures of participants to the symbols and time for each activity. (Ref. math standards for Grade 1: measurement and data: #3—telling time)	*Modified English language arts goals* Given topical object/texture books for literature stories, Jabari will be able to use the books from left to right, turning pages and touching objects on each page. (Ref. ELA reading—literature standards for grade 5: #5) Sharing stories: Given objects/artifacts from activities outside of school, Jabari will put objects in his chosen order in memory book and use to share his stories with the class. (Ref. ELA writing standards for grade 5: #3). *Modified math goal* Using a tactile tray with raised edges, Jabari will both order and find familiar objects in left to right and up and down patterns, demonstrated by tactile placement. (Ref. math standards for grade 5—operations and algebraic thinking: #3—analyze patterns and relationships).	*Modified English language arts goal—access to literature* Given the opportunity to watch the piece of literature on film, see photographs of the literature in a modified book, and hear selections from the piece, Brandon will indicate through eye gaze his recognition of which visual matches the sounds of the key words in a story. (Ref. ELA reading—literature standards for grade 7: #7) Given use of microswitch technology with computer access, Brandon will select photographs, objects, and auditory sound effects for representation of topics across units. (Ref. ELA writing standards for grade 7: #7)	*Modified literature class goals* Given a topic related to a piece of literature the class is reading, Louisa will select excerpts from at least four recorded stories of her personal events to present as indicators of her comprehension of the theme of focus and use technology to present it. (Ref. ELA speaking and listening standards for grades 11 and 12: #4a.) After listening to a piece of literature on tape and class reader's theatre and discussions, Louisa will indicate the tone of individual voices in the piece as happy, sad, and so forth with 80% accuracy. (Ref. ELA speaking and listening standards for grades 11 and 12: #1a–d.). Louisa will learn at least four new vocabulary words related to each piece of literature/instructional unit in her literature class. (Ref. ELA reading—literature standards for grades 11 and 12: #4.) *Modified math goal* When using money to make a purchase, Louisa will use the tactile shape modeling board to determine size and matched coins. (Ref. math standards for grades 9–12: geometry standards #1–3).

Shortened versions of the goals that do not include all of the measurements are provided in order to save space.

Table 9.2. Sample modified goals referenced to the Next Generation Science Standards (NGSS), the California social studies standards, and the visual and performing arts standards

Zoe	Jabari	Brandon	Louisa
Modified social studies goal Zoe will demonstrate her understanding of class and school rules and respect for others by using visual photographs and symbols to respond to questions. She will also demonstrate recognition of symbols and songs of the United States. (Ref. CA social studies standard for grade 1: 1.1 and 1.2) Zoe will demonstrate understanding of three new photographs or symbols related to each unit. (Ref. CA social studies standards for grade 1: 1.3–1.6). *Modified science goal* Using photographs and symbols, Zoe will demonstrate her understanding of the vocabulary/concepts for the differences between plants and animals; sun, moon, and earth; and the five senses. (Ref. CA NGSS for grade 1: disciplinary core ideas)	*Modified social studies goal* For each social studies unit in fifth grade, Jabari will match artifacts/objects and textures/smells related to the theme of each unit; he will provide information to the class in group presentations with objects, textures, and smells. (Ref. CA social studies standards for grade 5: 5.1–5.9). *Modified science goal* Using real plants, soil, animals, and so forth, given tactile sequences, Jabari will discriminate between plants and animals; water and earth; and rain, sun, and wind. (Ref. CA NGSS for grade 5: disciplinary core ideas)	*Modified social studies goal—world history and geography* Given photographs and objects that are relevant to each ancient and medieval history unit, Brandon will use eye gaze to match photographs and objects corresponding to the visual media and use a microswitch to use voice output technology to describe artifacts for group presentations. (Ref. CA social studies standards for grade 7: 7.1–7.11) *Modified science goal* Given photographs and simple photo/symbol sequences, Brandon will use eye gaze to select and demonstrate core concepts of each unit (e.g., sun = energy). (Ref. CA NGSS grade 7: disciplinary core ideas) *Modified theatre performing arts goal* Given prerecorded passages for parts in skits and full one act and two and three act plays, Brandon will activate his voice output device to say his lines on cue at least 80% of the time. (Ref. CA visual and performing arts: theatre standard for grade 7: creative expression 2.0)	*Modified social studies goal—government: principles of American democracy* Louisa will demonstrate her understanding of the three branches of government by giving three key defining words for each using verbal skills and auditory scanning; demonstrate her understanding of what a vote is by participation in class mock projects; and demonstrate her understanding of personal rights and responsibilities related to class and school rules. (Ref. CA social studies standards for grade 12: 12.1–12.10) *Medical technology modified goal* Given modified auditory lecture notes and tactile symbols, using technology, Louisa will demonstrate her ability to define at least five core vocabulary words for each unit and will demonstrate her ability to help implement at least five medical procedures (e.g., blood pressure) with peers and self. (Ref. CA NGSS for grades 9–12: growth and development of organisms) *Modified goal for visual and performing arts: music* Given the opportunity to listen to the choir repertoire on audio tape and participate in regular choir class rehearsals, Louisa will sing and perform on at least 75% of the choir's repertoire. (Ref. CA music proficiency standard for grades 9–12: 2.0–creative expression)

Shortened versions of the goals that do not include all of the measurements are provided in order to save space.

Box 9.1.   Collaborative Planning Process

Questions to ask in the collaborative planning process with general education partners:

1. What are the primary outcomes/expectations for the students during this up-coming curricular unit? What are the range of expectations within the class? What are the social expectations?

2. What are the main teaching activities and routines you will be using to engage students in the learning process during this unit?

3. How does each of the activities look? Tell me more about how they are organized.

4. What are the primary products or assignments for students within these activities, and how will students be evaluated?

5. Can I tell you a little about (student's name)?

The team is now ready to brainstorm:

6. What are the modified goals based on the standards? What will be the ex-pectations for the student with disabilities within each of the main activities/routines and the special projects? What other goals will the student work on during this class?

7. Are there any adaptations that need to be made in the way information is pro-vided to the student (input)? How will the team ensure that the student is an informed participant?

8. Are there any changes/adaptations that need to be made to the ways in which the student will provide information to the teachers and his or her peers (output)? How will the student be a contributing member of the class both socially and academically?

9. What other instructional or social support strategies need to be put into place?

10. I will be finishing the participation and support plan and will give you a copy. How should we regularly communicate? What works best for you?

---

working with each other and learning about the specific focus student and/or the curricular units. General education teachers who are new to including students with multiple disabilities in their classrooms will also be guided by the process.

Both the general and special education (support) teachers review the grade-level standards for the subject area prior to the meeting. The special education teacher starts by asking the general education teacher questions about how he or she organizes things for the year. It is generally easiest to start with an in-structional unit of material—or the way in which the general education teacher organizes his or her teaching. For example, some secondary English teachers may organize their course around units for each assigned novel, connecting various ongoing assignments that relate to those novels. A history teacher may organize units of material based on particular periods of history or major historical events. Elementary school teachers' units may be shorter than secondary units. For example, a science unit may revolve around a creek study or garden project. Language arts units may be organized based on particular reading curriculum units, whereas direct reading and math instruction may be ongoing and individually monitored.

The special education teacher may be a member of an existing grade-level team, making it even easier to collaborate. Some schools are more readily organized for team meetings than others. It is important to stress with the general education teachers and the principal that getting some substantive time to focus only on the curriculum and instructional outcomes and supports will save time later. A carefully organized and focused brainstorming and planning session can yield positive results that will last for a longer period of time, rather than expecting teachers to meet too often. The following focus questions and formats for participation plans have been found to be useful to numerous teams. The special education teacher should take the lead in carefully following through with the outlined planning process because it can be a valuable means for indirect in-service as well. The process will move faster and become more comfortable as the school year progresses.

Question 1: What are the primary outcomes/expectations for the students during this upcoming curricular unit? What is the range of expectations within the class? What are the social expectations? These questions prompt the general education teacher to talk generally about the class, the focus for the unit, and the social expectations. For example, Brandon's English teacher said that the class was going to be doing a unit on a novel called *A Day No Pigs Would Die* (Peck, 1972). Her overall goals were related to the language and literacy goals from the CCSS, but she also wanted the students to love to read and to share her interest in this particular novel. She indicated that she had a wide range of reading levels in the class. Some students were advanced and would probably read ahead, whereas others were behind grade level and would no doubt struggle with some of the vocabulary in this text, so she was prepared to preteach vocabulary and new words. The classroom had a set of class rules and expectations that were posted on the wall that the students helped develop at the beginning of the school year.

Question 2: What are the main teaching activities and routines you will be using to engage students in the learning process during this unit? The special education teacher listens and writes down the key teaching activities to be used in the unit to get a projection of all the different teaching activities that will be happening over the next few days or weeks and the ways in which these activities are organized. This gives the special education/support teacher a clear picture of the activities in which the student will be participating during class time.

Ideally, the support teacher and the general education teacher collaborate on ways they can co-teach or co-plan for this unit. Brandon's English teacher was quick to say that they would not be doing the same thing every day but was able to list some of the key activities that would regularly occur (e.g., journal writing, reading aloud) and describe various projects (e.g., developing a mandala and a sociogram) and the types of assignments students would be given (see Figure 9.9).

Unit/grade level: <u>Seventh grade: English/language arts—novel</u>   Student(s) name(s): <u>Brandon</u>

Individualized education program goals the student is working on within this unit: object schedule; object communication book; using microswitch competence for call device, tape recorder, and computer; picture matching; using eye gaze to trigger attention; and language arts

Primary routines and activities of the unit	Adaptations to input/ how the student will get information	Modified outcomes and adaptations to output	Support strategies
The following activities happen regularly:			
Organize for the day	Object communication book	Work on object match	Make sure object calendar is available
Read aloud/ questions	*General education teacher not only calls on Brandon but also comes to him and touches his arm	*Brandon will work on using microswitch to activate tape-recorded reading from text	*Prerecord passages from chapters and mark in teacher's book
Character sociograms	Pictures for characters with sounds paired—touch activated	*Brandon uses eye gaze shift to indicate character choices and matches to pictures	Make pictures ahead
Debates	Student partner will move Brandon back and forth	*Shift in gaze or facial expression will trigger partner move—cause and effect	Train peers ahead of time
Vocabulary words	Preload vocabulary words and pictures into computer; general education peers will need to come to Brandon for the vocabulary lists	Brandon works on using switch access for computer each time student comes to him	Adult support needed for instruction and adaptations
Chapter homework in thoughtful contextualized format for each chapter	Partner work in free time or at lunchtime; modify the questions—only one per chapter—and match the picture	*Selections on computer for visual presentation	Provide support to peer partners
Special project: Mandalas illustrating symbolism	Visuals ready to utilize	*Brandon indicates choices for placement through eye gaze and switch activation	
Group project: Write a fantasy play and act it out	*Peers provide indicator when they are leading conversation	*Brandon records dialogue and hits switch to activate his lines	*Prerecord, train peers, recorder

Any additional notes: *When read aloud and discussion is going to be for a long time, an alternative activity for Brandon is to use the computer with the switch. The teacher will tell you the agenda for each day.

Figure 9.9.   Sample participation and support plan for Brandon: English class.

Question 3: What does each learning activity look like? Tell me more about how each one is organized. Questions 2 and 3 allow the opportunity for teaming, hearing suggestions from other professionals, and getting the chance to get to know each other's strengths. It is also important to understand the formats for instruction, the instructional groupings, and types of peer-mediated learning activities that typically occur. For example, Brandon's teacher indicated that journal writing and time to start homework assignments is typically done individually, but some people work as partners. The upcoming sociogram project and playwriting are done in groups. The students have time to work together in class several times a week and can work in the teacher's room during lunchtime if they want more time. She also described the debate, which was very helpful. The students divide the room in half during the debate, and each side takes one side of the argument. As the debate ensues, students physically switch sides when they agree or disagree with a particular point, which makes the debate very active. The teacher then gave the special education teacher a sample of the chapter homework and journaling activities so she could see how these activities are constructed.

Some special and general education teachers may plan units jointly under a team or co-teaching structure, which is helpful for inclusive schooling (Jorgensen et al., 2006). These questions must still be answered, however, in order to specifically determine what the outcomes for the student with disabilities will be, when and where instruction will occur, and what types of adaptations and supports will need to be developed.

Question 4: What are the primary products or assignments for students within these activities, and how will students be evaluated? The special education teacher writes down key expectations, outcomes, or products that will be generated and how the evaluation will take place. For example, the expectation for seventh graders during debates is that they clearly state arguments, use complete sentences to articulate their positions, and respect other points of view. Grading on written assignments is done with a rubric that has been developed by the English department.

Question 5: Can I tell you a little about (student's name)? The special education teacher shares information about the student with disabilities and provides the general education teacher with a copy of the action plan or an IEP summary sheet, which gives the general education teacher an opportunity to ask questions. The support teacher specifically shares how the student best communicates and the best ways to communicate with the student, as well as particular areas of need and the other goals on which the student is working. For example, the special education teacher provided extensive information and modeling of how best to communicate with Brandon and to look for ways in which he expressively communicates. A discussion of his suctioning needs also occurred. The team is now ready to brainstorm.

Question 6: What are the modified goals based on the standards? What will be the expectations for the student with disabilities within each of the main activities/routines and the special projects? What other goals will the student work on during this class? The team members know the student's academic, cognitive, sensory, and communicative abilities and begin to brainstorm standards-based goals and other goals that are the basis for instruction within this core content period or course. These are the objectives that will require specific instructional plans. For example, visually recognizing artifacts/objects related to the text is one of Brandon's outcomes. Using an SGD to indicate a partner for shared reading is one of Zoe's outcomes during reading and language arts. It may be difficult for general education teachers or other team members to generate ideas in the beginning because they are less experienced or do not know the student as well. This usually changes over the year.

Question 7: Are there any adaptations that need to be made in the way information is provided to the student (input)? How will the team ensure that the student is an informed participant? Will there need to be visual supports, modified text, or peer support? Preteaching? These questions are important considerations for each individual student with severe and multiple disabilities. Jabari received input through tactile symbols and physical gestures as well as an object system. Peers and/or adults took responsibility for letting him know what was happening and gave new information to him. Teachers and peers utilized Zoe's picture/word communication system for input in addition to verbal instructions.

Question 8: Do any changes/adaptations need to be made in the ways that the student will provide information to the teachers and his or her peers (output)? How will the student be a contributing member of the class both socially and academically? A variety of adaptations may be required in order for the student to actively participate in the general education classroom. All of the focus students provide information and demonstrate knowledge in adapted ways. Zoe uses a variety of means, including her SGD; Jabari uses objects, textures, and tactile signs; Brandon uses his eye gaze and switch access; and Louisa uses her voice, auditory scanning, and object manipulation.

Question 9: What other instructional or social support strategies need to be put into place for this student? The team should ask a variety of questions related to supports. What materials need to be made ahead of time? Does any peer training need to be done? Is any preteaching or follow-up teaching needed? Does the student need extra supports from another person during all or part of the period? If so, will this be done by the general education teacher, the special education teacher, peers, a paraeducator, or a volunteer? If direct teaching will be done during this unit, then will it be done by peers, the general educator, the support teacher, or a paraeducator? What types of actual support are necessary, and does there need to be preteaching? What is the most effective and efficient use of staff time to generate support?

Question 10: I will be finishing the participation and support plan and give you a copy. How should we regularly communicate? What works best for you? Scheduling collaborative teaching time may be easier at some schools than others, depending on the teaching structures at the school. The integration of the special education teacher, working closely with the general education teacher and/or paraprofessionals, has been shown to be highly connected to positive results in inclusive classrooms (Downing, 2010). A significant amount of the special education teacher's time should be spent in providing direct, small-, and large-group instruction in the general education classrooms versus simply managing people. It may not be necessary to ask all of the previous questions after the general education and special education teachers have been working with each other within this framework and planning methods for a while, and teams may be able to move directly to the support plans. The key questions become natural to the problem-solving process once the team has practiced addressing each question over a couple of curricular units.

The special education support teacher develops one-page participation and support plans that are easy to read and follow after the brainstorming session, and they are distributed to everyone. These plans depict the key activities and routines of the upcoming unit, the adaptations to input for the student, the output adaptations and modified outcomes, and the additional supports that need to be provided and by whom. Indicating which instructional goals are the focus and who will be implementing that instruction is another key component in the support plan. The summary participation plan that was developed after the meeting with Brandon's seventh-grade English teacher is included in Figure 9.9, and Figure 9.10 provides a summary participation plan for Louisa's government class.

COLLABORATING TO WRITE GOALS FOR NONACADEMIC PRIORITIES AND PLANNING FOR THEIR INSTRUCTION

Contextual goals related to life activities that are nonacademic in nature and goals related to basic self-determination, cognitive, communicative, social, sensory, and motor skills are the two other types of goals that should be included in the educational plan. Some goals for same-age life activities may be context specific. For example, goals to learn how to gain access to the community or goals related to employment experience require instruction to occur in the community or places of work. Personal care goals may require opportunities for instruction in the bathroom or the locker room. Nonacademic goals related to participation in nonacademic school activities, such as clubs or sports, may also be instructed outside of the classroom. It is preferable that these goals be taught alongside typically developing peers if at all possible. The process for developing supports and services within other educational contexts (e.g. the locker room, the cafeteria, the library, community settings, work settings) is similar to what was described for classroom activities, except that the special education

Unit/grade level: <u>12th grade: Government class (project-based learning) unit: three branches of government</u>

Student(s) name(s): <u>Louisa</u>

Individualized education program goals the student is working on within this unit: Three key vocabulary words/concepts related to each of the three branches of government; expressive communication; receptive communication; social interactions with peers; self-determination goals

Primary routines and activities of the unit	Adaptations to input/ how the student will get information	Modified outcomes and adaptations to output	Support strategies
Students sit in their respective branches and call meetings to order in the three groups and plan agendas for the day	Auditory schedule: peer puts agenda for the class period into auditory schedule; Louisa listens several times	Louisa acknowledges agenda by verbally repeating it	Make sure peers know how to operate the auditory output agenda tool
Teacher meets with each of the three groups, and they lay out their plan for research	Suggestions will be taken for Louisa's role in what needs to be done for the day; each person says his or her name before speaking; job/task options are orally provided to Louisa for her choice of what and with whom to work	Research: computer software for reading text; Louisa selects excerpts from DVDs of the public recordings of the three branches Sound/word output with excerpts—practice matching	Intermittent support from special education teacher for peers to provide coaching; materials developed ahead of time with librarian and uploaded into computer
Project development	Provide verbal, sound, and touch cues	Make copies for class, staple	Peer supports to provide Louisa with computer and headphones for auditory review
Presentations	Left to right organization of low-tech sound/word output	Organize excerpts in order with peer support	Special education staff support as needed
Test	Provide auditory/sound scanning test for three vocabulary match concepts for each branch of government	Sound and media controller; follow left to right sequence; three main concepts or vocabulary—play for class Louisa makes selections based on auditory scanning	Special education teachers provide test

Figure 9.10. Sample participation and support plan for Louisa in government class.

support teacher has the responsibility of designing the activities. The special education teacher analyzes the context in which the activities will occur and determines what primary teaching activities will take place during the period of time the student spends there. A similar instructional analysis is completed in which the special education teacher determines input and output strategies, and the team writes the goals and develops the instructional plans.

Louisa receives instruction on a variety of objectives during her internship hours at the veteran's hospital. The job specifications have been modified for her, and she is learning to do a variety of office tasks; but she is also working on her communication skills, orientation and mobility skills, and social skills on her break. She is working on community mobility skills on her way to and from work, and she is learning to use her money in a vending machine when she takes a break. Zoe is learning mobility skills with her KidWalk and working on riding an adapted bicycle at recess. She is also working on communication skills with friends and learning how to participate in some of the games her friends play on the playground. The focus is on developing her friendships. Jabari and two of his fifth-grade peers are the ice cream salespeople for the fifth-grade fundraiser at lunch recess. He is also working on using his tactile object/voice output device to communicate with friends and learning how to handle making the transition from one place to the next. Examples of nonacademic, life activity goals for Zoe, Jabari, Brandon, and Louisa are included in Table 9.3.

Although some goals require specific natural environments for instruction, goals related to the most basic cognitive, sensory, social-communication, motor, and self-determination skills can and should be taught within and across multiple academic and nonacademic activities in the student's day. These skills are not context specific. It is important to stress the contexts for instruction when writing goals for these basic skills. Because children and youth with multiple disabilities will have numerous priorities related to basic capacity skills, writing goals in this contextualized format ensures that the student's day does not become a series of fragmented skills instruction. Rather, the course and activity-based schedule of instruction described in this chapter provides the contexts for these skills to be taught.

Many general education activities provide excellent, motivating instructional opportunities for basic communication, sensory, motor, cognitive, and social skills. Research has shown that students with severe and multiple disabilities not only can learn these basic skills within the same activities of their general education peers, but these instructional situations are also motivating and highly effective (Gee, Graham et al., 1995; Hunt, Farron-Davis, Beckstead, Curtis, & Goetz, 1994; Jackson et al., 2008–2009; McDonnell & Hunt, 2014; McGregor & Vogelsberg, 1998; Snell & Brown, 2011). Zoe is working on physically transferring herself between positions and equipment during the transitions that her first-grade class makes from carpet to tables, to the door, and so forth. Jabari is working on his tactile communication symbols during the morning meeting with his fifth-grade peers. During debates in his social studies class, Brandon is working on intentionality when communicating by operating a switch with his deep breath so that his friends will zip him over to the other side of the room/debate. Louisa has particular social interaction goals that she works on during all activities, but especially during lab times and project-based activities in her government class. She works on several skills related to her PBIS plan throughout the day, including following an auditory schedule, learning how to indicate "no" using her words, and learning how to use her tactile conversation book. Louisa also works on carrying and finding her materials in her backpack and on organizing lab materials.

Understanding how to create goals that utilize natural cues and reinforcement in collaboration with related services professionals is an important skill for the educator to develop. Writing goals that are maximally comprehensive, yet measurable, can be challenging for many teams.

Table 9.3. Sample of some activity and basic skill goals for Zoe, Jabari, Brandon, and Louisa

Zoe	Jabari	Brandon	Louisa
Expressive communication: Throughout her school day, when Zoe is asked a question or when she desires to ask a question or share, Zoe will be able to use her Dynavox to make two- and three-word combinations in order to request and comment/share on at least 90% of the opportunities sustained over a 3-week period.	*Expressive communication:* Across all activities of the day, given a tactile object grid of eight items representing desired activities and actions, Jabari will be able to scan left to right and find the desired item, then hold it long enough for a clear choice with 80% accuracy maintained over a 3-week period.	*Expressive communication:* Throughout his school day, given a microswitch mounted close to his left cheek, Brandon will be able to activate the switch to use as a call device to get others' attention and activate other environmental controls for the computer, games, and lights with 80% accuracy maintained over 4 weeks.	*Mobility:* Given her cane with marshmallow tip, Louisa will be able to walk next to a support person using her cane in a constant surface diagonal position on her routes throughout the school day accurately at least 80% of the time.
Expressive communication: When Zoe is on the playground, in the lunchroom, and in class, she will initiate the use of her wrist talker to get a peer or adult's attention and use four different prepared social interactions on at least 4 out of 5 opportunities maintained over a 4-week period.	*Receptive communication:* Throughout his daily schedule, and during all activities, given tactile signs/cues, Jabari will demonstrate recognition of the information through his anticipatory actions on 90% of the opportunities maintained over a 3-week period.	*Expressive communication:* With the object, photograph, and word presented, Brandon will make selections using his eye gaze from a field of two with 90% accuracy.	*Self-determination:* Given use of her communication system and peer support, when Louisa still gets frustrated by something, she will clap her hands and say "nope," then wait for someone to provide her with options and problem-solve what to do next.
Mobility: Throughout the school day in class, in the lunchroom, and on the playground, Zoe will be able to transfer herself from her wheelchair to the floor, from the floor to a chair, and from the chair to her KidWalk independently.	*Friendships:* Through a circle of friends group and peer training, Jabari will develop social relationships that extend outside of school, demonstrated by a social report card provided by his parents each month.	*Receptive communication:* Throughout his school day, given consistent input through paired object/photo/auditory vocabulary, Brandon will demonstrate recognition of familiar vocabulary through eye gaze matching on 80% of the opportunities over a 3-week period.	*Self-determination:* Throughout the school day and at work, when Louisa is involved in learning something new or needs assistance, she will use her small voice output device to indicate whether she would like to FOLLOW SOMEONE ELSE'S HANDS or HAVE GENTLE GUIDANCE ON HER OWN HANDS in order to continue the activity or task.
	Class fundraisers: Given the fifth-grade fundraising team's choices of activities throughout the year, Jabari will assist in these endeavors by using his grasp to place items in and out of containers and accept money and place in containers with at least 80% accuracy, supported by peers.	*Access to print and other visual/sound media:* At lunchtime and during appropriate class times, given the opportunity to gain access to social media, auditory books/software, movies, and YouTube, Brandon will indicate his preferences by making eye gaze selections.	*Internship:* During her senior year, Louisa will have the opportunity to work in two different internships through the school's community partnerships program. The jobs will be customized/modified for Louisa.

Friendships and Relationships as Part of the Curriculum and the Individualized Education Program

This section stresses the importance of social relationships and friendships as part of the school day and part of the curriculum/IEP. Developing friendships is an important IEP goal (Carter et al., 2009; Turnbull et al., 2011). Membership and belonging lead to relationships, which ultimately are one of the keys to quality of life. Children and youth with multiple disabilities, like all children and youth, benefit from healthy social relationships and friendships. School teams must prioritize the facilitation of social relationships because many children and youth with multiple disabilities have significant challenges related to communication, mobility, and social interaction (Carter, 2011). Active facilitation and support for peer interaction and relationship building are important parts of the instructional day (Carter, 2011; Gee, Alwell et al., 1995).

Each of the focus students had goals geared to their relationships with peer partners and friends. Zoe enjoys playing with others on the playground but needed to find ways to let her friends know when she did not want their help because they sometimes wanted to help too much. Her mother also needed some support to find ways for Zoe to get together for playdates outside of school hours. Jabari's inclusion support teacher organized a circle of friends who could learn how best to communicate with Jabari so he could have some special individuals he could get to know through tactile sign and other interactions. Consistent facilitation of interactions is an ongoing aspect of his instructional day, but especially with his peers. Now that Jabari attends his neighborhood school, his parents can more easily organize play dates and gain access to other after-school activities. The inclusion support teacher asked Jabari's parents to use a social report card once a month to let the teacher know of any social get-togethers with Jabari and his friends. Tactile memory books for playdates were developed to share with others.

Brandon's special education/inclusion support teacher also developed a circle of friends for him. This group of students not only provided companionship at lunchtimes but also regularly created ways for Brandon to participate in classes and other activities. These seventh graders took an active role in ensuring that Brandon was included in all aspects of school life. Brandon used a voice output conversation book and worked on activating prepared messages about photographs of him doing fun things with his friends at school using the microswitch attached near his cheek. Louisa's friends were coached on her PBIS plan as well as recommended ways to support her in classes and during other activities. They served as a great resource on senior class activities and ways that Louisa could be involved. These friends have been sustained through the high school years and often get together with Louisa outside of school hours. Louisa is working on ways to connect with her friends using both her voice and other technology.

CONCLUSION

Although each of them has multiple disabilities, Zoe, Jabari, Brandon, and Louisa are four different individuals. By not letting their disabilities become the focus of their lives, their families, teachers, and peers can participate with these children in their learning and living. Children and youth with multiple learning and health challenges are often at risk for being segregated and having their school day focus on therapies, procedures, and isolated skills instruction. This chapter emphasizes the creation of active and informed learning through access to the general education curriculum and the activities of typically developing peers. The students' specific needs related to their sensory, motor, cognitive, and social capacities are threaded throughout the student's educational day with multiple opportunities for instruction and development. The process of developing an educational plan that is described in this chapter is intended to create a desirable school day/week that leads to a desirable future.

REFLECTION QUESTIONS

1. Think about a student who has multiple disabilities that you know from your experiences. Look at the CCSS for a particular subject area (e.g., social studies, science) for that student's grade level. How might you modify the outcomes for your focus student using both depth and breadth?

2. What are the five principles that guide our choice of goals? Explain them in your own words and give examples.

3. What is meant by person-centered/family-centered planning, and why is it so important to have someone with a vision for what is possible at the meetings?

4. Why is it so important to develop a participation and support plan when students with multiple disabilities are in general education classes and curricular activities?

CHAPTER ACTIVITY

Use the summary sheet format shown in Figures 9.3–9.6 and complete it for one of your students with multiple disabilities. Then arrange to meet with a general education teacher to utilize the process for developing a participation and support plan for an upcoming unit of instruction he or she will be doing in the classroom. If your student is included in the class already, then this process will be helpful for collaborating and planning for the student. If your student is not included in the general education class yet, and this is being done hypothetically as a learning activity, then this could open the door by helping the general education teacher understand how and why this is done. If you are a credential-seeking student preparing to be a special educator and not currently student teaching, then partner with a general education credential student using one of the units they have developed and work through the process hypothetically.

REFERENCES

Agran, M., & Hughes, C. (2014). Promoting self-determination and self-directed learning. In M. Agran, F. Brown, C. Hughes, C. Quirk, & D.L. Ryndak (Eds.), *Equity and full participation for individuals with severe disabilities: A vision for the future* (pp. 75–98). Baltimore, MD: Paul H. Brookes Publishing Co.

Ayres, K.M., Douglas, K.H., Lowrey, K.A., & Sievers, C. (2011). I can identify Saturn, but I can't brush my teeth: What happens when the curricular focus for students with severe disabilities shifts. *Education and Training in Autism and Developmental Disabilities, 46,* 11–21.

Beukelman, D.R., & Mirenda, P. (2013). *Augmentative and alternative communication: Supporting children and adults with complex communication needs* (4th ed.). Baltimore, MD: Paul H. Brookes Publishing Co.

Bradford, S., Shippen, M.E., Alberto, P., Houchins, D.E., & Flores, M. (2006). Using systematic instruction to teach decoding skills to middle school students with moderate intellectual disabilities. *Education and Training in Developmental Disabilities, 41,* 333–343.

Browder, D., Mims, P.J., Spooner, F., Ahlgrim-Delzell, L., & Lee, A. (2008). Teaching elementary students with multiple disabilities to participate in shared stories. *Research and Practice for Persons with Severe Disabilities, 33,* 3–12.

Browder, D.M., & Spooner, F. (2011). *Teaching students with moderate and severe disabilities.* New York, NY: Guilford Press.

Browder, D.M., & Spooner, F. (2014). *More language arts, math, and science for students with severe disabilities.* Baltimore, MD: Paul H. Brookes Publishing Co.

Brown, F., & Bambara, L.M. (2014). Providing respectful behavior supports. In M. Agran, F. Brown, C. Hughes, C. Quirk, & D.L. Ryndak (Eds.), *Equity and full participation for individuals with severe disabilities: A vision for the future* (pp. 99–130). Baltimore, MD: Paul H. Brookes Publishing Co.

California Department of Education. (2001). *Visual and performing arts content standards for California public schools: Pre-kindergarten through grade 12.* Sacramento, CA: Author.

Campbell, P. (2011). Addressing motor disabilities. In M.E. Snell & F. Brown (Eds.), *Instruction of students with severe disabilities* (7th ed., pp. 340–376). Upper Saddle River, NJ: Pearson.

Carnine, D., Silbert, J., Kame'enui, E., & Tarver, S.G. (2010). *Direct instruction reading* (5th ed.). Upper Saddle River, NJ: Pearson.

Carr, E.G., Horner, R.H., Turnbull, A.P., McLaughlin, D.M., McAtee, M.L., Smith, C.E. . . .Doolabh, A. (1999). *Positive behavior support for people with developmental disabilities: A research synthesis.* Washington, DC: American Association on Mental Retardation.

Carter, E.W. (2011). Supporting peer relationships. In M.E. Snell & F. Brown (Eds.), *Instruction of students with severe disabilities* (7th ed., pp. 431–460). Upper Saddle River, NJ: Pearson.

Carter, E.W., Cushing, L.S., & Kennedy, C.H. (2009). *Peer support strategies for improving all students' social lives and learning.* Baltimore, MD: Paul H. Brookes Publishing Co.

Claes, C., Van Hove, G., Vandevelde, S., van Loon, J., & Schalock, R. (2010). Person-centered planning: Analysis of research and effectiveness. *Intellectual and Developmental Disabilities, 48,* 422–453.

Collier, B., McGhie-Richmond, D., & Self, H. (2010). Exploring communication assistants as an option for increasing communication access to communities for people who use augmentative and alternative communication. *Augmentative and Alternative Communication, 26,* 48–59.

Collins, B. (2012). *Systematic instruction.* Thousand Oaks, CA: Sage Publications.

Copeland, S.R., & Keefe, E.B. (2007). *Effective literacy instruction for students with moderate or severe disabilities.* Baltimore, MD: Paul H. Brookes Publishing Co.

Copeland, S., Keefe, E., & de Valenzuela, J.S. (2014). Literacy and communication. In M. Agran, F. Brown, C. Hughes, C. Quirk, & D.L. Ryndak (Eds.), *Equity and full participation for individuals with severe disabilities: A vision for the future* (pp. 177–196). Baltimore, MD: Paul H. Brookes Publishing Co.

Downing, J.E. (2008). *Including students with severe and multiple disabilities in typical classrooms: Practical strategies for teachers* (3rd ed.). Baltimore, MD: Paul H. Brookes Publishing Co.

Downing, J.E. (2010). *Academic instruction for students with moderate and severe intellectual disabilities in inclusive classrooms.* Thousand Oaks, CA: Corwin.

Fisher, M., & Meyer, L.H. (2002). Development and social competence after two years for students enrolled in inclusive and self-contained educational programs. *Research and Practice for Persons with Severe Disabilities, 27,* 165–174.

Gee, K. (1995). Facilitating active and informed learning in inclusive settings. In N. Haring & L. Romer (Eds.), *Welcoming students who are deaf-blind into typical classrooms: Facilitating school participation, learning, and friendships* (pp. 369–404). Baltimore, MD: Paul H. Brookes Publishing Co.

Gee, K. (2001). Looking closely at instructional approaches which honor and challenge all children and youth in inclusive schools. In W. Sailor (Ed.), *Whole-school success and inclusive education: Building partnerships for learning, achievement, and accountability* (pp. 123–141). New York, NY: Teachers College Press.

Gee, K. (2004). Developing curriculum and instruction. In F.P. Orelove, D. Sobsey, & R.K. Silberman (Eds.), *Educating children with multiple disabilities: A collaborative approach* (4th ed., pp. 67–114). Baltimore, MD: Paul H. Brookes Publishing Co.

Gee, K., Alwell, M., Graham, N., & Goetz, L. (1995). *Inclusive instructional design: Facilitating informed and active learning for individuals with deaf-blindness in inclusive schools.* San Francisco, CA: California Research Institute (CRI), San Francisco State University.

Gee, K., Graham, N., & Sailor, W., & Goetz, L. (1995). Use of integrated regular school and community settings as primary contexts for skill instruction of students with severe multiple disabilities. *Behavior Modification, 19*(1), 33–58.

Giangreco, M.F. (2011). Foundational concepts and practices for educating students with severe disabilities. In M.E. Snell & F. Brown (Eds.), *Instruction of students with severe disabilities* (7th ed., pp. 1–30). Upper Saddle River, NJ: Pearson.

Giangreco, M.F., Cloninger, C.J., & Iverson, V.S. (2011). *Choosing outcomes and accommodations for children (COACH): A guide to educational planning for students with disabilities* (3rd ed.). Baltimore, MD: Paul H. Brookes Publishing Co.

Halvorsen, A.T., & Neary, T. (2009). *Building inclusive schools: Tools and strategies for success* (2nd ed.). Upper Saddle River, NJ: Pearson.

Holburn, S., & Viest, P. (2002). *Person-centered planning: Research, practice and future directions.* Baltimore, MD: Paul H. Brookes Publishing Co.

Hudson, M., Browder, D., & Wood, L.A. (2013). Review of experimental research on academic learning by students with moderate and severe intellectual disabilities in general education. *Research and Practice for Persons with Severe Disabilities, 38*(1), 17–29.

Hunt, P., Farron-Davis, F., Beckstead, S., Curtis, D., & Goetz, L. (1994). Evaluating the effects of placement of students with severe disabilities in regular education versus special classes. *Journal of The Association for Persons with Severe Handicaps, 19,* 200–214.

Hunt, P., McDonnell, J., & Crockett, M. (2012). Reconciling an ecological curricular framework focusing on quality of life outcomes with the development and instruction of standards-based academic goals. *Research and Practice for Persons with Severe Disabilities, 37*(3), 139–152.

Jackson, L., Ryndak, D., & Wehmeyer, M. (2008–2009). The dynamic relationship between context, curriculum, and student learning: A case for inclusive education as a research-based practice. *Research and Practice for Persons with Severe Disabilities, 33–34*(4-1), 175–195.

Jorgensen, C.M., Schuh, M.C., & Nisbet, J. (2006). *The inclusion facilitator's guide.* Baltimore, MD: Paul H. Brookes Publishing Co.

Kunc, N. (1992). The need to belong: Rediscovering Maslow's hierarchy of needs. In R. Villa, J. Thousand, W. Stainback, & S. Stainback (Eds.), *Restructuring for caring and effective education* (pp. 25–42). Baltimore, MD: Paul H. Brookes Publishing Co.

Light, J.C., & McNaughton, D.B. (2013). Literacy intervention for individuals with complex communication needs. In D.R. Beukelman & P. Mirenda (Eds.), *Augmentative and alternative communication: Supporting children and adults with complex communication needs* (4th ed., pp. 309–351). Baltimore, MD: Paul H. Brookes Publishing Co.

McDonnell, J., & Hardman, M.L. (2010). *Successful transition programs: Pathways for students with intellectual and developmental disabilities.* Thousand Oaks, CA: Sage Publications.

McDonnell, J., & Hunt, P. (2014). Inclusive education and meaningful school outcomes. In M. Agran, F. Brown, C. Hughes, C. Quirk, & D.L. Ryndak (Eds.), *Equity and full participation for individuals with severe disabilities: A vision for the future* (pp. 155–176). Baltimore, MD: Paul H. Brookes Publishing Co.

McGregor, G. (2003). Access to general education and state standards. In D.L. Ryndak & S. Alper (Eds.), *Curriculum and instruction for students with significant disabilities in inclusive settings* (2nd ed., pp. 32–50). Boston, MA: Allyn & Bacon.

McGregor, G., & Vogelsberg, R.T. (1998). *Inclusive schooling practices: Pedagogical and research foundations.* Baltimore, MD: Paul H. Brookes Publishing Co.

National Governors Association Center for Best Practices & Council of Chief State School Officers. (2010a). *Common Core State Standards for English language arts and literacy in history/social studies, science, and technical subjects.* Washington, DC: Author.

National Governors Association Center for Best Practices & Council of Chief State School Officers. (2010b). *Common Core State Standards for mathematics.* Washington, DC: Author.

Next Generation Science Standards Lead States. (2013). *Next Generation Science Standards: For states, by states.* Washington, DC: National Academies Press.

O'Brien, J. (2014). Person-centered planning and the quest for systems change. In M. Agran, F. Brown, C. Hughes, C. Quirk, & D.L. Ryndak. (Eds.), *Equity and full participation for individuals with severe disabilities: A vision for the future* (pp. 57–74). Baltimore, MD: Paul H. Brookes Publishing Co.

O'Brien, J., Pierpoint, J., & Kahn, L. (2010). *The PATH and MAPS handbook: Person-centered ways to build community.* Toronto, Ontario, Canada: Inclusion Press.

Potts, E.A., & Howard, L.A. (2011). *How to co-teach: A guide for general and special educators.* Baltimore, MD: Paul H. Brookes Publishing Co.

Peck, R.N. (1972). *A day no pigs would die.* New York, NY: Knopf.

Prime Engineering. (2014). *KidWalk: Dynamic mobility system.* Retrieved from http://www.primeengineering.com/product_pages/kidwalk.html

Rainforth, B., & York-Barr, J. (1997). *Collaborative teams for students with severe disabilities: Integrating therapy and educational services.* Baltimore, MD: Paul H. Brookes Publishing Co..

Rowland, C., & Schweigert, P. (2004). *First things first: Early communication for the pre-symbolic child with severe disabilities.* Portland, OR: Design to Learn.

Ryndak, D.L., Moore, M., Orlando, A., & Delano, M. (2008–2009). Access to the general curriculum: The mandate and the role of context in research-based practice for students with extensive support needs. *Research and Practice for Persons with Severe Disabilities, 33-34*(4-1), 199–213.

Sailor, W. (2009). *Making RTI work: How smart schools are reforming education through schoolwide response-to-intervention.* San Francisco, CA: Jossey-Bass.

Sailor, W., Dunlap, G., Sugai, G., & Horner, R. (Eds.). (2009). *Handbook of positive behavior support.* New York, NY: Springer.

Sailor, W., & Roger, B. (2005). Rethinking inclusion: Schoolwide applications. *Phi Delta Kappan, 86*(7), 503–509.

Sanderson, H., & Lewis, J. (2012). *A practical guide to delivering personalization: Person-centered practice in health and social care.* London, England: Jessica Kingsley Publishers.

Snell, M.E., & Brown, F. (2011). *Instruction of students with severe disabilities* (7th ed.). Upper Saddle River, NJ: Pearson.

Snell, M., & Delano, M. (2011). Teaching self-care skills. In M.E. Snell & F. Brown (Eds.), *Instruction of students with severe disabilities* (7th ed., pp. 377–430). Upper Saddle River, NJ: Pearson.

Soto, G., & Zangari, C. (2009). *Practically speaking: Language, literacy, and academic development of students with AAC needs.* Baltimore, MD: Paul H. Brookes Publishing Co.

Spooner, F., McKissick, B.R., Hudson, M.E., & Browder, D.M. (2014). Access to the general curriculum in general education classes. In M. Agran, F. Brown, C. Hughes, C. Quirk, & D.L. Ryndak (Eds.), *Equity and full participation for individuals with severe disabilities: A vision for the future* (pp. 217–234). Baltimore, MD: Paul H. Brookes Publishing Co.

Turnbull, A., Turnbull, R., Erwin, E.J., Soodak, L.C., & Shogren, K.A. (2011). *Families, professionals, and exceptionality: Positive outcomes through partnerships and trust* (6th ed.). Upper Saddle River, NJ: Pearson.

Wehman, P. (2013). *Life beyond the classroom: Transition strategies for young people with disabilities* (5th ed.). Baltimore, MD: Paul H. Brookes Publishing Co.

Westling, D.L., & Fox, L. (2009). *Teaching students with severe disabilities* (4th ed.). Upper Saddle River, NJ: Pearson.

10

Instructing Students with Severe and Multiple Disabilities in Inclusive Classrooms

ALICE UDVARI-SOLNER, KATHERINE AHLGREN BOUCHARD, AND KIEL HARELL

CHAPTER OBJECTIVES

1. Become familiar with the state of instruction for students with severe and multiple disabilities, including how universal design for learning (UDL), differentiated instruction, and culturally responsive teaching can guide inclusive instruction

2. Understand the importance of teacher collaboration in the codesign of instruction for students with severe and multiple disabilities and the effects of inadequate collaboration

3. Describe the universal design process as a means for collaborative instructional planning

4. Recognize critical principles, tenets, and methods of instruction for students with severe and multiple disabilities, including the least dangerous assumption, principle of partial participation, and systematic and embedded methods of instruction

5. Identify how active and collaborative instructional methods, community-referenced instruction, and service learning can facilitate inclusive academic programming for students with severe and multiple disabilities

This chapter is dedicated to Mary Beth Udvari, who has lived a life of conscious compassion. She worked as an occupational therapist and stood beside individuals with significant disabilities in advocacy for more than 5 decades. Today she is experiencing the last stages of Parkinson's disease and needs the same compassion that she gave so unconditionally to all others she encountered. She has negotiated this arduous journey with the utmost tenacity and grace. Her spirit may live on in the work we do to fight for quality inclusive lives in partnership with individuals who experience severe and multiple disabilities. She reminds us that we may, by some unforeseen circumstance, find ourselves in a less than desirable future dictated by the nature of our institutions and societal norms. Consequently, we must stand ready to act as change agents and advocates for others and perhaps, in the future, for ourselves.

KEY TERMS

- Active learning
- Advocacy service learning
- Affective networks
- All or nothing hypothesis
- Applied behavior analysis
- Collaborative learning
- Common Core State Standards (CCSS)
- Community-referenced instruction
- Cues
- Culturally responsive teaching
- Developmental age hypothesis
- Differentiated instruction
- Direct service learning
- Embedded systematic instruction
- Fading
- Funds of knowledge
- Inclusive education
- Indirect service learning
- Legitimate peripheral participation
- Partial participation
- Presuming competence
- Principle of the least dangerous assumption
- Prompts
- Recognition networks
- Research service learning
- Research teams
- Retrofitting
- Service learning
- Stages of learning
- Strategic networks
- Systematic instruction
- UDL
- Understanding by design
- Universal design process

Emma is greeted by two of her first-grade classmates as she arrives at school and the lift lowers her wheelchair to the sidewalk. This week the three girls have leadership roles in facilitating the class morning meeting. The girls greet Emma excitedly, touch her hand, and make sure they move in close to her face, giving her a few moments to focus her gaze. Emma's partners know they must wait after greeting her to give her time to initiate touching her voice output switch. Today Emma responds GOOD MORNING! LET'S GET TO CLASS! Once in the classroom, the girls prepare for their roles in the class meeting by immediately checking the morning message written on the whiteboard by their teachers. Emma's partners draw her chair up close to the board and read the message aloud. After one read through, the girls read in unison while recording the message on Emma's iPad. Emma has started to intentionally vocalize when she hears others reading aloud. Emma will lead the entire class in a choral reading of the message with the support of her two classmates when the morning meeting begins.

Several members of the fourth-grade Green Team stand assembled, ready to give their public service announcement on the school's in-house live news channel. Azahr has autism and cerebral palsy (CP) and is one of the team's 15 members. The Green Team meets throughout the week to plan and carry out projects to inform their school and community about ways to reuse, reduce, and recycle waste. Today the team is showcasing three instruments made from plastic bottles and cardboard and is performing a rap. Azahr and a teammate have used the MadPad app to record sounds from their instruments and have created a repetitive beat to which the group will rap their public service message.

Writing workshop is taking place in Charlie's eighth-grade classroom. The general and special educators have just finished their mini-lesson on creating stories about *Small Moments* (Calkins & Oxenhorn, 2003) as one form of personal narrative writing. Charlie is asked during the mini-lesson to share his Instagram photograph showing him eating an ice cream cone amid friends at a local ice cream shop to illustrate how authors use rich detail to write about and embellish small moments in life. The teachers use a variety of picture and verbal cues to prompt Charlie to use his limited sign language and answer simple yes/no questions about what he is doing and how he feels in that moment. Students then begin writing their own small moments stories while the teachers conference with individuals. A small group of students, including Charlie, cluster at the writing center table. The students at the center were part of the weekly writing team that had ventured into the community to take photographs of their own small moment experience for the writing assignment. The team shares the experience of enjoying ice cream together, and each person has a different photograph to document the event. The small group has access to either a computer with a PowerPoint program or the Pictello app installed on an iPad. Both applications allow users to combine picture slides with written and audio narration. The students use the same strategies they saw modeled by their teachers to solicit information from Charlie about the experience. The context of the event also provides an opportunity to generate and practice related sign language vocabulary. A short narrative statement is written by a peer to accompany the pictures. Charlie chooses the order of the pictures to create a logical story while a peer records the narration. These electronic texts, which are constructed each week featuring a new experience, become Charlie's books to read during reading workshop, take home and share with family, and read to younger learners during cross-age shared reading time.

These vignettes represent a positive end-state for all of the learners in these general education classrooms. Although Emma, Azahr, and Charlie are students with severe and multiple disabilities whose learning differences and needs pose substantial challenges, the vignettes illustrate how access to and meaningful participation in general education can be designed in ways that are creative, responsive to the common core curriculum, and beneficial for students with and without disabilities. Reaching that desired end-state and preferred future for all of children requires teachers to operationalize key instructional beliefs and approaches.

This chapter presents instructional methodologies for supporting students with severe and multiple disabilities in inclusive classrooms and complements the content in Chapters 9 and 11. Effective instruction and the decisions surrounding how we teach do not happen in isolation. Therefore, instruction and instructional approaches should be situated in the current educational context and within a broader process for designing differentiated curriculum, instruction, and assessment that is shared by general and special educators. Foundational tenets and methods of instruction for students with severe disabilities will be articulated and further illustrated in the three case examples of Emma, Azahr, and Charlie.

   Inclusive educators must ask some essential questions to frame and transform traditional instructional inquiry. These questions prompt divergent and expansive thinking and encourage educators to plan lessons that compel students to become thoughtful, engaged producers of their own knowledge as opposed to idle recipients of their educators' teachings (McTighe & Wiggins, 2013). The following essential questions structure the chapter contents, provoke reader reflection, and invite discussion on how to provide instruction in inclusive classrooms:

- How might current frameworks for instruction, including UDL, differentiated instruction, culturally responsive teaching, and teacher collaboration, guide methodologies for instructing students with severe and multiple disabilities?

- How might I integrate critical principles, tenets, and methods of instruction for students with severe and multiple disabilities into my teaching? How will doing so facilitate inclusive outcomes?

- Which instructional practices for students with severe and multiple disabilities are worth advocating (and agitating) for?

THE STATE OF INSTRUCTION FOR STUDENTS WITH SEVERE AND MULTIPLE DISABILITIES

Today's educational landscape has a direct impact on the instruction of students with severe and multiple disabilities. The state of the educational system has been shaped by educational reforms that include the development of innovative frameworks for teaching all learners and a call for collaboration in designing instruction. The following subsections describe critical intersections between the current educational landscape and instruction for students with severe and multiple disabilities. The subsections also address the first essential question for educators instructing children with severe and multiple disabilities: How might current frameworks for instruction guide methodologies for instructing students with severe and multiple disabilities?

Educational Reforms and the Current Educational Landscape for Students with Severe and Multiple Disabilities

Increasing rigor and relevance is an enduring, critically important endeavor for educators of students with severe and multiple disabilities. Historical critiques of special education from within the field have persistently questioned the benefit of instructional strategies that emphasize narrow, disconnected splinter skills (Brown et al., 1977). Examples of splinter skills may include practicing sitting on a rug, matching like objects, or repeatedly writing one's name and address. When taken out of context, these skills represent meaningless prerequisites that serve as unnecessary barriers to enter general education environments. Other scholarly appraisals have indicated that low expectations (Gold, 1980), weak or nonexistent entry points for diverse learners to gain access to content (Udvari-Solner, 1996), and lack of contextually based, peer-referenced instruction (Falvey & Givner, 2005) have all contributed to inequitable access to meaningful, relevant curriculum and typically developing peers.

In response to critiques of special education, scholars promote inclusive instructional design to increase challenge, relevance, and universal access for all students, while emphasizing equity for students with severe and multiple disabilities. Udvari-Solner maintained inclusive schooling

> Promotes a critique of contemporary school culture, encouraging practitioners to reinvent what can be and should be to realize more humane, just, and democratic learning communities. Inequities in treatment and educational opportunity are brought to the forefront, thereby fostering attention to human rights, respect for difference and value of diversity (1997, p. 142).

Thus, inclusive education has a purpose, an origin, and implications that affect all educational contexts, yet are visible in instructional methodologies shared in this chapter. As we write from the tradition of inclusive education, the approaches presented should be considered inclusive in nature.

Students with severe and multiple disabilities are part of larger educational reforms as never before (Courtade, Spooner, Browder, & Jimenez, 2012; Lazarus, Cormier, & Thurlow, 2011; Thompson, Johnstone, Thurlow, & Altman, 2005), so it is important and timely to discuss legal and political imperatives that call educators to focus on instructional delivery for students with severe and multiple disabilities. Increased accountability measures for students with severe and multiple disabilities have been dictated by the guidelines of the Individuals with Disabilities Education Improvement Act (IDEA) of 2004 (PL 108-446) and the No Child Left Behind Act (NCLB) of 2001 (PL 107-110) (Courtade et al., 2012). These measures have developed from simple participation in assessment, to publicized achievement of adequate yearly progress in content areas, to current expectations that alternative assessments of achievement for students with severe and multiple disabilities show gains that clearly link to grade-level content standards.

Among specific accountability measures, the CCSS call states to define a common core of knowledge and skills that students should develop in K–12 education and has import for instructing students with severe and multiple disabilities. Deeming the CCSS a historic opportunity for students with disabilities to gain access to demanding content standards, proponents of this initiative specifically advocate for UDL, curriculum differentiation, and the integration of supports and specialized services for students with disabilities within the context of a general education classroom (CCSS Initiative, 2014). Thurlow (2011) highlighted the initiative's promise for instructing students with disabilities, citing that the CCSS brings to an end 4 decades of special education practices often characterized by remedial programming and individualization at the expense of rigor.

Supporters of the CCSS view UDL as a mechanism for providing students with disabilities access to rigorous content, a further impetus for educators to explore and carefully consider instruction. As the basis of standards-driven instruction, the CCSS also offer new possibilities for vibrant connections among schools, school districts, and state accountability systems for children with disabilities. Finally, this initiative provides students receiving special education services the opportunity to fully participate in school accountability measures and serves as a vehicle for equity and transformative social justice (Sailor & Roger, 2005).

Existing Innovative Frameworks for Teaching All Students

The growing diversity of learners in public schools has provided impetus in the field of general education to anticipate, better understand, and ultimately plan for student differences. Several important frameworks for teaching and learning have been established to better serve all students. The following subsections present an overview of UDL, differentiated instruction, and culturally responsive teaching. Each approach alone can promote dramatic changes in instructional design, but they are not mutually exclusive and should be used in combination. Educators must not only be aware of these frameworks but also be conversant with their associated language and concepts to effectively collaborate in the design and delivery of instruction.

Universal Design for Learning UDL considers how to reduce barriers to instruction and maximize learning for all students, particularly those with disabilities (Rose & Meyer, 2002). UDL is an instructional and curricular innovation that has its roots in architectural principles that were established to comply with accessibility regulations from the Americans with Disabilities Act (ADA) of 1990 (PL 101-336). As existing buildings and physical structures were altered for accessibility, these retrofitted additions noticeably lacked unity, grace, and utility. In response, architects considered particular populations and their specialized needs at the inception of designing their projects rather than as an afterthought, which ultimately resulted in more imaginative and functional spaces. Rose and Meyer simultaneously noticed that educators inside the school building were grappling with essentially the same fundamental problem of practice; that is, how might we use flexible practices and tools to design a standards-based environment that meets the needs of everyone? By utilizing flexible instructional methods and materials at the beginning and throughout lesson planning and implementation, teachers using UDL offer their students what architects bestow on their building and structures—coherence, utility, and access for all. Lessons are more carefully thought out and preplanned so specialized instruction for students with severe and multiple disabilities can be integrated from the start.

Furthermore, although UDL prioritizes the needs of those learners at the margins, every student benefits from a well-planned learning environment designed for all—a goal similar to the architectural inspiration of creating functional and useful spaces for every person. The Higher Education Opportunity Act of 2008 (PL 110-315) offers a definition of UDL:

> The term *Universal Design for Learning* means a scientifically valid framework for guiding educational practice that:
>
> (a) provides flexibility in the ways information is presented, in the ways students respond or demonstrate knowledge and skills, and in the ways students are engaged; and
>
> (b) reduces barriers in instruction, provides appropriate accommodations, supports, and challenges, and maintains high achievement expectations for all students, including students with disabilities and students who are limited English proficient (p. 12).

   Three main principles guide the implementation of UDL and involve three distinctive, yet interrelated, learning networks in the brain (Hall, Strangman, & Meyer, 2009). Recognition networks analyze and receive information— the "what" of learning. Strategic networks relate to how the brain plans and performs actions—the "how" of learning. Affective networks regulate the "why" of learning and involve the development of preferences and interests and the setting of priorities (Coyne, Pisha, Dalton, Zeph, & Smith, 2012; Rose & Meyer, 2002). Operationalizing these principles, The Center for Applied Special Technology (http://www.cast.org) offers three sets of broad teaching methodologies that support the three learning networks in the brain: 1) multiple methods of presentation and representation; 2) multiple methods of action, expression, and goal setting; and 3) multiple options for engagement. The principles are as follows:

- Principle 1 supports recognition learning and provides multiple methods of presentation and representation. For example, teaching strategies in this area can include providing instruction and expectations in various visual, written, and auditory formats and multimedia at different levels of complexity; presenting a range of examples; highlighting the most critical features of instruction; and establishing a context when background knowledge is limited.

- Principle 2 advances strategic learning and provides multiple methods of action, expression, and goal setting. Accompanying teaching strategies might include authentic experiences to demonstrate skills, such as planning and planting a garden as opposed to writing a paragraph about the process. Also, teachers provide opportunities to practice skills with graduated instructional support. Students may visit a variety of community gardens and map their size and plot plan in preparation for their own garden. Teachers support goal setting by making learning targets and benchmarks clear and visible for students and providing ongoing, descriptive feedback on student performance toward the targets.

- Principle 3 honors affective learning and encourages multiple options for engagement. Teachers can arouse interest, curiosity, and attention by engineering choices for students, which include deciding on the level of challenge, using different materials for learning, and selecting the context in which to learn (e.g., reading at a desk versus an open area where more movement is allowed) (National Center on Accessible Instructional Materials: http://aem.cast.org/).

Thus, the UDL framework guides the development of curricula and approaches that maximize every student's access to and participation and progress in all three essential facets of learning, leading to universal gain at no learner's expense.

Differentiated Instruction   The practice of differentiated instruction represents another framework that can guide decision making for students with significant disabilities. Ravitch offered that differentiated instruction seeks to

> Maximize each student's growth by recognizing that students have different ways of learning, different interests, and different ways of responding to instruction. In practice, it involves offering several different learning experiences in response to students' varied needs. Educators may vary learning activities and materials by difficulty, so as to challenge students at different readiness levels; by topic, in response to students' interests; and by students' preferred ways of learning or expressing themselves (2007, p. 75).

Tomlinson (2003) identified three elements of the curriculum available for differentiation in her early work on differentiated instruction. Teachers can make changes to and choices about 1) content ("What should I teach?"), 2) process ("How should I support students in making sense of what they have learned?") and 3) products ("How will I know the students have learned?"). Effective differentiation comprises 1) high-quality curriculum, 2) data-based instructional decision making, 3) respectful learner tasks (i.e., tasks that allow all children to learn new things at an appropriate level of challenge and promote growth in their abilities), 4) high expectations for all learners, and 5) supportive learning environments (Santangelo, Knotts, Clemmer, & Mitchell, 2008). Teachers utilizing differentiation thus assume and plan for learner differences in a methodical and concerted way. Anticipating and framing student difference as a strength and a curricular opportunity are hallmarks of differentiated instruction and afford students with severe and multiple disabilities a path to inclusive instruction.

Tomlinson married her work on curriculum differentiation with McTighe's understanding by design (Tomlinson & McTighe, 2006). Understanding by design complements curriculum differentiation by emphasizing what we teach and what evidence we collect to determine mastery of concepts. Furthermore, understanding by design requires teachers to cultivate enduring understandings in their students and address essential questions related to learning. Teachers should consider what content is worth understanding, what specific overarching ideas all students should encounter, and how educators and students will know when learning has been achieved. The complementary models of UDL, differentiated instruction, and understanding by design ensure that we no longer view the student as the object of remediation as we design instruction for students with significant disabilities. Rather, it is our materials, goals, teaching procedures, and forms of assessment that must change in order to provide these students access to the general education curriculum. These instructional design reforms originated in the field of general education as a proactive response to diversity, creating opportunities to avoid old models of post hoc modifications by special educators just to meet the needs of some students receiving specialized support services.

Culturally Responsive Teaching   Culturally responsive teaching is a framework and a pedagogy that appreciates the necessity of integrating students' cultural backgrounds in all teaching decisions (Ladson-Billings, 1995). Culturally responsive teaching includes a set of knowledge, beliefs, and practices that depend on these essential teacher competencies: 1) facilitating differentiated instruction that supports culturally and linguistically diverse students' achievement across environments; 2) using knowledge of cultural identities of students and their families to design and implement instruction; 3) continuously examining patterns of power (and teachers' own deeply held values and beliefs) that may serve to marginalize historically marginalized students who are culturally and linguistically diverse, often identified with disabilities, in schools; and 4) developing high expectations and seeing capacity in every student (Blanchett, 2006; Delpit, 2006; Gay, 2002; Ladson-Billings, 1995). Teachers thus work from a place of inquiry as they consider students' various learning profiles, interactional styles, and heritage, as well as their own, to connect learners to the curriculum.

Teachers implementing culturally responsive teaching inherently utilize UDL and differentiation principles, including flexible means of representing content, expressing strategies, and recruiting and sustaining engagement. Culturally responsive teaching compels educators to consider multiple and varied options for what students will learn, how they will make sense of what they learn, and how they will demonstrate mastery. Educators who use culturally responsive teaching focus on rejecting instructional content and methodologies that reproduce social injustices while promoting culturally responsive classroom climates and instructional strategies that support learners who are culturally and linguistically diverse (Bal, 2012; Gay, 2002).

Culturally responsive classroom climates include caring personnel who demonstrate authentic concern for individual students through the use of multicultural content, diverse instructional strategies, and rich and varied materials. Students in culturally responsive environments experience "the images, sounds, and symbols of their ethnic and cultural diversity" (Gay, 2002, p. 621) as teachers create assessments and make instructional decisions that are informed by their students' identities (Harmon, Kasa-Hendrickson, & Neal, 2009; Klingner et al., 2005; Shealey & Callins, 2007). For example, teachers may instruct thematically, meeting interdisciplinary standards by exploring social issues that have resonance for their students, such as war, disease, conflict, and oppression (Banks & McGee Banks, 2001; Gay, 2002). Educators working for cultural responsiveness throughout instruction gain access to and cultivate students' sociocultural funds of knowledge (i.e., political, historical, and personal knowledge students obtain from their families and cultural backgrounds) (González, Moll, & Amanti, 2005). Educators recognize that students' households offer a rich store of cultural knowledge and experiences that should be acknowledged, honored, and intentionally utilized in the classroom. Furthermore, specific culturally congruent instructional approaches include providing entry points for students to engage in inductive reasoning, facilitating performance assessments (e.g., engaging in a science experiment, performing skits illustrating conversational Spanish, buying school supplies at a school store with the correct amount of money) to show mastery of concepts and storytelling. These methods allow students to authentically engage in instruction and go beyond traditional teacher-led formats and designs (Santos, Fowler, Corso, & Bruns, 2000). Salend and Duhaney (2005) suggested peer support committees and class meetings, which provide opportunities for group problem solving and student-led instructional formats that are empowering and antidiscriminatory, to build classroom communities necessary for culturally responsive instruction.

Culturally responsive teaching has particular relevance when considering the education of students with disabilities. Educators are legally required to consider the use of supplementary aids and services to support the participation of students with disabilities in integrated classrooms and should ensure that these services are conceived, designed, and implemented with the student's culture in mind. (Harmon et al., 2009). To illustrate, a student with autism may use assistive technology (AT) for communication that reflects his or her home language, specifies family member's names, considers food preferences when shopping, or uses neighborhood signifiers. Similarly, a student with severe and multiple disabilities may engage in community-referenced instruction in neighborhoods he or she regularly gains access to instead of the neighborhood near the school, which may have little relevance to the student's daily life.

The Call for Collaboration in Designing Instruction

Collaboration is a key tenet to educating students with severe and multiple disabilities. Friend and her colleagues (Cook & Friend, 1993; Friend & Bursuck, 2002) defined *collaboration* as how people work together when they are trying to accomplish a shared goal. This goes beyond simply doing work alongside each other in various school-based teams or functioning together in the classroom as co-teachers. Friend and Bursuck wrote, "Only on teams where all members feel their contributions are valued and the goal is clear, where they share decision making, and where they sense they are respected, does true collaboration exist" (2002, p. 75). Garmston and Wellman (1999) expanded on this definition, indicating that collaboration requires developing a sense of mutual support and responsibility while sharing expertise on teaching and learning to codesign curriculum and instruction. Consequently, collaboration in the design and delivery of instruction for students with severe and multiple disabilities requires that educators not only share a common vision of the student's participation in the classroom, but also engage in an agreed-on instructional planning process that promotes equitable input and honors each educator's expertise.

Effects of Inadequate Collaboration in Instructional Design   Collaboration among educators can be inadequate for several reasons—lack of time or commitment, opposing philosophies in instructional approaches, or conflicting views of power and authority in which the ownership for planning instruction is viewed as the sole responsibility of one educator. Retrofitting of lessons is much more likely to occur in any of these instances. Retrofitting is a process by which something is remodeled after the fact in order to make it more accessible to people with different needs (King-Sears, 2009). This occurs in education when changes must be made to a lesson that was designed in isolation of team input and without adequate consideration of the unique learning needs of all the students in the classroom. It is typically the special educator or paraprofessional who notices or is made aware of the incongruity between lesson expectations and the student's abilities and who needs to make changes for a student with disabilities. These changes often happen right before the lesson starts or after instruction has begun, leading to poor or unpredictable outcomes.

Retrofitting as a stopgap approach to including students in general education settings has many negative consequences that undermine the promises of inclusive school reform (Udvari-Solner, Villa, & Thousand, 2002). This approach is reactive, one that is based on a student failing before an intervention is provided, as opposed to a proactive approach that builds in different instructional methods at the ground level of lesson planning. Retrofitting is used only to make surface-level changes to a lesson that is already in motion. If even one student is struggling to participate or be engaged, then it is likely there are deeper structural problems with the lesson that are affecting more learners. It is likely that fixing or doctoring aspects of instruction in the moment will be inadequate in addressing these global problems.

Retrofitting requires the special educator to solve one issue at a time (reactive) instead of taking a step back to address more fundamental instructional problems through a universal design process in collaboration with general educators (proactive). In addition, retrofitting is a stressful way to teach and can be costly in terms of human resources because it requires someone to be present to adapt the lesson on the spot. The goals of inclusive schooling are not met when special educators are artificially attached to students with disabilities, standing at the ready for when instruction goes wrong. This practice reinforces the divide between general and special education and undercuts reforms that aim to include every student so that no child is isolated or denied access to quality instruction (Giangreco, Edelman, Evans Luiselli, & MacFarland, 1997). To summarize, retrofitted lessons are less rigorous, more resource intensive, and often stigmatizing for students with disabilities.

A Collaborative Instructional Planning Process   Although retrofitting will always occur to some degree because of unforeseen circumstances, a collaborative approach to lesson design limits these instances and distributes the responsibility of instructional design among the instructional team members. A truly collaborative approach to inclusive education for students with severe and multiple disabilities depends on a shared process for making decisions about curriculum and instruction that brings together all relevant professionals well in advance of instruction. It is also essential that planning for a student with severe and multiple disabilities does not take place as an isolated discussion, but instead is integral to a broader instructional planning process that ensures the lesson will be designed appropriately for any student who enters the classroom.

The universal design process is one method for collaboratively designing instruction (Udvari-Solner, 1996; Udvari-Solner et al., 2002; Udvari-Solner, Villa, & Thousand, 2005). The universal design process is offered here because it assembles the best practices and intersecting principles of UDL, differentiated instruction, and culturally responsive teaching. The universal design process is a framework and planning template for developing differentiated instruction that requires dialogue between general educators and special educators using shared academic language and concepts for decision making (see Figure 10.1).

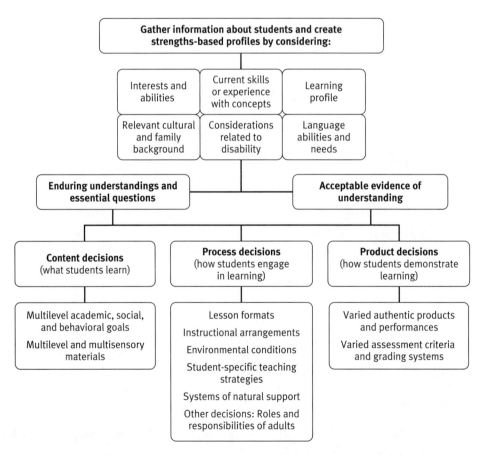

Figure 10.1.   The universal design process for instructional planning (flow chart).

General and special educators engage in this process by sharing information about all learners in their classroom while keeping any learner who has unique learning characteristics (e.g., students who are English language learners, students who exhibit advanced academic skills, students with behavioral challenges, students with disabilities) in the forefront of their minds. Team members define enduring understandings (e.g., the big ideas behind a lesson that are critical for students to know), core curricular standards to be addressed in the unit and associated lessons, and acceptable evidence of student understanding that will be used for assessment. Discrete decisions are then made about content, processes, and products to ensure multiple entry points to the lesson for students with diverse abilities. Outlining the roles, responsibilities, and co-teaching options for adults finalizes the process. Figure 10.2 provides a planning template to facilitate collaborative instructional planning using the universal design process. A daily plan resulting from this process highlights the instructional program for morning meeting for Emma, our student in the first vignette, in the section on systematic and embedded instruction.

PRINCIPLES, TENETS, AND KEY METHODS OF INSTRUCTION

This section addresses the second essential question that frames this chapter: How might I integrate critical principles, tenets, and methods of instruction for students with severe and multiple disabilities into my teaching? How will doing so facilitate inclusive outcomes? Although special educators might be familiar with philosophies emphasizing the strengths and capabilities of students with disabilities and the importance of their participation in the general education classroom, these ideas might be new and influential to general educators being trained in inclusive practices for the first time. Just as there is a need for general and special educators to share a tangible and agreed-on process for instructional design, it is also vital that they are versed in and abide by a common set of instructional tenets and methodologies.

The following subsections present important instructional tenets for educating students with severe and multiple disabilities so that they can be mutually adopted and implemented by all members of an instructional team. These tenets will be illustrated whenever possible through the three student case examples introduced at the beginning of the chapter.

Principle of the Least Dangerous Assumption: Presuming Competence

The opening vignette introduced Emma, a first grader who has a leadership role in morning meeting. We alluded to Emma's disabilities but did not explicitly state them. The following are some ways that Emma has been described in her formal evaluations:

- Shows delays across all areas of development

- Has no reliable communication system and is a presymbolic communicator

- Language development is estimated at a 6- to 8-month-old level

Content area of focus: _____ Team members: _____

Unit of study: _____

Time frame for implementation: _____

I. Information about learners

Identify students who represent the range of learners in class and must be considered in the forefront when designing curriculum and instruction. Consider these learning characteristics:

- Interests, abilities, and learning profile
- Current skills or experience with concepts
- Relevant cultural and family background
- Unique considerations related to disability
- Language ability or language proficiency level

Notes: _____

_____

_____

_____

II. Define the enduring understandings that guide this unit

- What Common Core, district, or state curriculum standards are addressed?
- What are the big ideas worthy of understanding in this unit and daily lessons?
- What do we want all students to know and be able to do?
  - Knowledge: facts, concepts, principles
  - Skills: processes, strategies, methods

Notes: _____

_____

_____

_____

III. Determine acceptable evidence of student understanding

A. Product decisions: How students will demonstrate their learning

What forms of assessment will be used?

_____

_____

_____

_____

(continued)

Figure 10.2. The universal design process for instructional planning.

Figure 10.2. *(continued)*

What are the varied authentic products, performance tasks, or projects that students will produce?

_____

_____

_____

_____

Are there multilevel criteria in assessment such as effort or improvement? Will different levels of mastery be accepted? Are changes in grading appropriate? Will individualized rubrics be designed?

_____

_____

_____

_____

IV. Develop differentiated curriculum and instruction

A. Content decisions: What students will learn

Multilevel academic, social, and behavioral goals. Describe the objectives for all class members as well as specific instructional objectives for students with unique learning needs. Consider the district standards, students' learning profiles, educational priorities, and critical individualized education program (IEP) goals to formulate the objectives.

_____

_____

_____

_____

Multilevel and multisensory materials that best convey concepts and content to each student. Describe the range of materials that will be available to students and unique considerations for specific students in terms of alternative texts, adaptive devices, assistive technology, and visual or tangible materials. Will the materials used for reading, writing, mathematics, notetaking, or test taking need to be changed to ensure students can gain access to information and express knowledge?

_____

_____

_____

_____

(continued)

Figure 10.2. *(continued)*

B. Process decisions: How students will engage in learning

Learning activities and lesson formats. What kind of instructional activities will promote student learning? What type or combinations of formats best suit the instructional purpose and offer the greatest benefit for the range of learners? Consider the use of

❏ Mini-lectures
❏ Teacher demonstration
❏ Whole-class question and answer or whole-class discussion
❏ Active, collaborative, or cooperative learning
❏ Community-referenced, experiential, or service learning
❏ Station/center learning
❏ Peer dialogues or critiques
❏ Role plays, games, or simulations
❏ Computer-assisted learning
❏ Self-directed study
❏ Other

Instructional arrangements. How will students be grouped during lessons? Will partnerships, teacher- or student-directed small groups, or cross-age pairings be used? Is it appropriate in this lesson for students to have options for working individually or in groups?

_____

_____

_____

_____

Environmental conditions. Are changes in the physical set up of the room, instructional positioning, or arrangement of materials necessary? Are there changes in the sociocultural rules of the classroom (e.g., amount of talking or noise allowed, rules to stay seated, rules to raise hands)?

_____

_____

_____

_____

Student-specific teaching strategies. What specific strategies will be used by the teacher to facilitate student learning? Are there specific presentation or questioning techniques, prompts, cues, or instructional or behavioral strategies that are needed for specific students?

_____

_____

_____

_____

Systems of support and supervision. What natural supports from instructors or peers will be provided to specific students? Determine if others beyond the general educator and peers will be needed to provide support: What will support look like, and how frequently will it be provided? If a peer provides support, then what information is needed for him or her to be an

(continued)

Figure 10.2. *(continued)*

effective partner? How have you ensured that providing assistance does not interfere with the achievement of the peer acting in a supportive role?

_____

_____

_____

_____

Other decisions: Roles and responsibilities of adults. How will adults be configured to support one another and learners with diverse needs? Consider what co-teaching models might be appropriate.

_____

_____

_____

_____

- Cries, bites her hand, or turns away to show protest, distress, or discomfort

- Uses a wheelchair but has no independent method of mobility

- Diagnosed with a rare chromosomal disorder that causes a range of seizures

- Qualifies for special education services under the labels of other health impaired, speech and language disorder, and visual impairment

- Has a cortical visual impairment causing legal blindness in both eyes

- Can sit unassisted only for 20 seconds without support

Like the written records of so many students with significant disabilities, assessments often read as a collection of deficits. It is difficult to ascertain what Emma knows or what her potential is for learning due to her complicated learning characteristics. Educators have two possible paths. They might assume that Emma is not and never will be an academic learner based on the skills assessed. Or, they can make the least dangerous assumption—she is complex, competent, and has the capacity to learn in both typical and alternative ways.

Donnellan defined the *concept of the least dangerous assumption* and proposed that the adequacy of instruction and curriculum should be critically examined first before assuming a student is incapable.

> The criterion of least dangerous assumption holds, that in the absence of conclusive data, educational decisions ought to be based on assumptions which, *if incorrect*, will have the least dangerous effect on the likelihood that students will be able to function independently as adults. (1984, p. 142).

In other words, in the absence of absolute evidence about a student's capacities, it is best to make decisions that will have the least dangerous outcomes or consequences for the individual. Donnellan (2000) and others (Gardner, 1983; Gould, 1981; Jorgensen, 2005) also ask us to question the validity and accuracy of the tests we use to secure evidence of intelligence in students with significant disabilities and whether intelligence can ever be reliably measured when students cannot communicate and/or receive information in conventional ways. Consequently, it is least dangerous to presume that all students are competent and have the ability to learn.

Presuming competence challenges developmental models that have influenced the instructional programs of students with significant disabilities for decades. Students' abilities are assessed under these models in the areas of cognitive, motor, and language acquisition using normative standards and developmental skill sequences. Normative standards are the skills that can be expected of a typically developing child at a certain age. For example, Piaget proposed four stages of normal intellectual development that map changes in cognition from infancy through adulthood. These four stages are sensorimotor, preoperational, concrete, and formal operational. Children in the age range of 18–24 months to 7 years old are expected to develop the preoperational skills to think symbolically, imagine, and use memory to distinguish between past, present, and future (Wadsworth, 1996). Theoretically, the acquisition of each more complex skill in this type of development skill sequence or learning hierarchy is dependent on achieving the prerequisite or prior skill (Gagné, 1968). Discrepancies in a student's performance along these normative guidelines are equated to scores associated with a mental age. We still derive and report some assessment scores representing a perceived developmental level, just as Emma's language was described as being that of a "6- to 8-month-old infant." Although these scores do provide normative comparisons, teachers who use these as a primary indicator of the student's abilities and educational needs often design limiting and age-inappropriate instructional programs. Baumgart et al. described this thinking as the "developmental age hypothesis" (1982, p. 18), frequently resulting in curriculum and instruction being arrested at a hypothesized developmental level. Students are often relegated to repeated skill practice on nonfunctional tasks for the sake of prescribed developmental sequences. For example, a 15-year-old student assigned a mental age of 2 may be required to sort nuts and bolts to distinguish shapes or zip an artificial zipper to practice motor skills at his or her developmental level. Baumgart and her colleagues pointed out that students with severe and multiple disabilities rarely, if ever, progress at reasonable rates through the same developmental sequences as children without disabilities. In addition, some skills may never be acquired due to complex physical limitations, which makes strict adherence to typical norms of development also problematic, as well as socially undesirable.

Jorgensen (2005, 2006) expanded on the educational impact of the least dangerous assumption. She proposed that the decision to abide or not abide by the principle profoundly influences educational goals, the environments in which the student will learn, how we interact with the individual, the support and resources we provide to teach methods of communication, what is engineered socially, and ultimately our vision for a person's future. She explained that we might do the following if we assume a child is not able, can learn only a few skills, and will not get anything out of general education:

- Not include the student in general education or do so only for socialization purposes because precious instructional time might be wasted on skills he or she will never learn

- Create individualized education program (IEP) goals that focus only on functional, communication, movement, self-regulation, and work skills

- Use materials for instruction that are not related to those used by peers of the same age

- Treat and speak to the student as though he or she were at a younger age than his or her chronological age

Jorgensen (2005, 2006) noted that if our original assumptions about a student's abilities were wrong and he or she did have greater capacity to learn, then the result would likely be fewer educational opportunities, inferior academic instruction, and a more segregated education. Our perceived level of the student's competence drives opportunities we provide; these limited opportunities lead to results that influence perceived levels of competence and keep us from seeing the student's full capabilities—and the cycle continues.

Emma's educational team chose to presume competence. Consequently, they looked for every opportunity to expose her to and engage her in rich general education curriculum that includes literacy, mathematics, problem solving, and high levels of interaction with peers. They used the typical routines of the first grade to determine her communication requirements and supported her in using an augmentative and alternative communication (AAC) device in the context of academic instruction. They continually sought ways to uncover and discover her abilities rather than assuming that what you see is what you get.

Presuming competence promotes the mindset that every child has intellectual ability and an inherent desire to learn, to contribute, and be engaged in relationships with others. It pushes educators to maintain high expectations while providing opportunities to advance and actualize their students' abilities (Downing & McFarland, 2010).

Principle of Partial Participation

Partial participation is a foundational practice at the heart of the inclusive instruction shared in the vignettes at the opening of this chapter. Students with severe and multiple disabilities are included in classroom instruction in each of the three school scenarios by encouraging them to meaningfully participate in activities to the greatest degree possible. Partial participation "suggests that though a student with severe disabilities may not be able to fully participate in an activity, he or she may be able to partially participate, thus allowing the student to be included" (Frattura & Capper, 2007, p. 141). In other words, inclusion in school, community, and work environments should not depend on a student's ability to fully perform or reach independence in a given activity before instruction begins.

The principle of partial participation challenges traditional views of disability that have served to exclude students from chronologically age-appropriate classrooms. Baumgart et al. (1982) argued against many hypotheses about learning that have historically denied children with severe and multiple disabilities an equal education, advocating for supporting these students' participation in the classroom as much as possible as a safeguard against these exclusionary ideas. In particular, partial participation opposes the all or nothing hypothesis, which states that there must be "reasonable assurances that a student can acquire all the skills in an activity before instruction is initiated" (Baumgart et al., 1982, p. 18). By setting the standard for participation in classroom instruction at this unreasonably high level, the vast majority of students with severe and multiple disabilities are relegated to few academic experiences. Educators operating under the all or nothing hypothesis will usually either not teach the given skill, complete the task for the student who is unable to fully participate, or prescribe a simplified version or an alternative activity designed for much younger students. These practices undermine educational and social opportunities, whereas partial participation minimizes performance discrepancies between typically developing students and students with severe and multiple disabilities through continued practice at learning in the general education classroom.

As an instructional tenet, partial participation also has important connections with learning theories not directly related to the education of people with disabilities. In their influential work on communities of practice, Lave and Wenger (1991) put forward a theory of legitimate peripheral participation that closely parallels the ideas behind partial participation (Lawthon & Chataika, 2012). Legitimate peripheral participation is the process by which new participants in a formal or informal community, such as a classroom, become experts and gain full membership into the community. New members of these communities initially participate in simple tasks that are often low risk and supported by others. These initial tasks are nonetheless necessary ones that must be completed in order for the project, activity, or job to move forward. New members begin to increase the types of tasks they complete over time and with experience as they move on a continuum toward becoming a mature expert in the community. This view recognizes that learning is situated in a social context and depends on collaboration among members of a group.

Legitimate peripheral participation is presented as universal to all communities of practice; however, it has important parallels to partial participation as a strategy for including students in inclusive classrooms. Students with severe and multiple disabilities are included instructionally, regardless of their ability to fully participate in all classroom activities. Their instruction is carefully designed to ensure they are able to partially participate in meaningful ways based on their interests, strengths, current abilities, and identified goals. Their participation level during their experience in the classroom can increase or change based on their emerging abilities. Much like the newcomers in a community of practice, students with severe and multiple disabilities are not performing useless or irrelevant tasks, but they are contributing to the social process in a way that is appropriate and geared toward growth.

Systematic and Embedded Methods of Instruction

Systematic instruction is an essential element of providing high-quality instruction for students with significant and multiple disabilities. The basic belief behind this key tenet is that all students are able to learn if provided appropriate instruction. When students are failing to learn or make progress toward their goals, "there is nothing to gain by lowering our expectations. Failure to learn indicates the need for a more powerful instructional approach" (Halvorsen & Neary, 2008, p. 120). Systematic instruction is a carefully planned approach to prompting and correcting students while collecting data on progress, with the goal of fading assistance and facilitating skill acquisition. Stated another way,

A systematic instructional approach consists of a well laid out plan of teaching that involves targeting and evaluating what students can learn given meaningful

opportunities to practice their skills. Such instruction involves specific procedures
for identifying, prompting and reinforcing targeted behaviors, within typical age-
appropriate environments. (Downing & MacFarland, 2010, p. 4).

Systematic instruction has its roots in the field of applied behavior analysis
(Alberto & Troutman, 2012; Cooper, Heron, & Heward, 2007). Applied behavior analysis is a data-based approach to teaching that focuses on promoting skill
acquisition by systematically cuing, prompting, and providing reinforcement to
support the development of discrete skills. This work involves a set of rules for
making decisions about instruction and careful measurement designed to indicate
whether a given procedure is effective for an individual student. For example,
using an individual performance goal as a target, a student's ability to independently activate a switch may be charted across multiple days of instruction. If skill
acquisition did not meet expected rates, then educators would collaboratively
determine next instructional steps and methodologies. Although early work in
applied behavior analysis was most often seen in separate special education classrooms and clinical settings, it has become an important aspect of inclusive education for students with severe and multiple disabilities (Davis, Boon, Cihak, &
Fore, 2010). Systematic instruction borrows its terminology from applied behavior
analysis and is an application of this approach in general education settings.

Students with severe and multiple disabilities often had many structured
(and sometimes contrived) opportunities to practice skills in repeated succession
throughout their day during earlier attempts at providing systematic instruction;
however, they were segregated from their typically developing peers. Systematic instruction has become less prevalent in many general education classrooms
because inclusive education has disrupted categorical separation. In fact, some
scholars claim it has simply become a lost art, which may be due in part to the emphasis on social inclusion that occurred in the early stages of establishing inclusive
practice (Halvorsen & Neary, 2008). Although students with severe and multiple
disabilities deserve to be included in the general education setting, their inclusion
need not come at the cost of instructional tools designed to teach critical skills.
Systematic instruction can most certainly be compatible with the principles of inclusive education, and it can have tremendous impact on the progress of students
with severe and multiple disabilities toward their academic, social, and functional
goals. Systematic instruction can be an effective tool for educating any student, especially for students with severe and multiple disabilities because educators must
use data-based evidence to identify instructional targets, plan teaching strategies,
and fade instruction to facilitate independence, which leads to skill acquisition.

Educators should pay attention to common phases of learning when
developing an individualized systematic instructional plan for students with
severe and multiple disabilities. Learning progresses through the same phases
of acquisition, fluency, generalization, and maintenance, regardless of disability
(Collins, 2012; Ghere, York-Barr, & Sommerness, 2002; Halvorsen & Neary,
2008). During the acquisition phase, a student is introduced to a new behavior
that he or she previously could not perform. Because it is a new behavior, this
phase focuses on improving accuracy and reaching a level in which the student

can complete the task with minimal support from the teacher. Next, the fluency phase focuses on building speed while maintaining the accuracy achieved in the previous learning phase. The maintenance phase refers to the ability of the student to be able to perform the same behavior over time while maintaining accuracy and speed. Finally, the generalization phase focuses on improving the student's ability to transfer his or her new skills to different settings and novel situations (Haring, Lovitt, Eaton, & Hansen, 1978).

Although students with severe and multiple disabilities travel through the same sequence en route to being able to perform a skill with reliability, progressing through the phases of learning may take longer and often requires uniquely designed instructional sequences. Systematic instruction requires educators to develop individualized instructional plans that are appropriate to the stage of learning and the setting in which the instruction is taking place. For instance, a student working on a task in the fluency phase may require direct repetition of a skill while receiving continual feedback on speed and accuracy. Yet, a student working on a task in the generalization phase may be expected to perform a task across multiple settings during his or her day instead of focusing on repeated drills. Systematic instruction must occur on a regular basis throughout the day because students with severe and multiple disabilities require additional opportunities to practice new skills. Long periods between practicing a skill should be avoided because it will likely mean the student will be starting the learning process over each time.

Before going deeper into a discussion of the components of systematic instruction, it is important to note that analytic work must be completed to inform the design of systematic instruction for an individual student. A task analysis in which the targeted task for instruction is broken down into its individual components is the first stage in this process. This is followed by a discrepancy analysis wherein the student's current abilities are gauged against the findings in the task analysis. This process provides information to guide the development of an instructional plan by pointing out the individual components of the task that the student is unable to complete independently. Instructors employ four possible responses to the discrepancies: 1) teach the skill as it is performed by others, 2) employ instructional adaptations that modify the requirements of the task, 3) use adaptive materials or devices to support or circumvent the skill, or 4) omit minor activities/skills within the instructional sequence (See Chapter 11 for a detailed description and example of the discrepancy analysis process.)

Systematic instruction is designed to promote continual student progress; therefore, it requires ongoing collection of objective assessment data (Halvorsen & Neary, 2008). The baseline data collected in the discrepancy analysis is the starting point in systematic instruction. This is followed by the collection of formative assessment data (data collected during the learning process in order to modify instruction to improve student performance). In addition to collecting baseline data before instruction begins, Collins (2012) stressed the importance of graphing formative assessment data and conducting visual analyses of data that reveal trends in responses or behavior. Although eager educators may feel pressure to bypass these steps in order to jump into providing instruction or intervention, doing so diminishes the power of systematic instruction because it prevents educators from seeing, analyzing, and verifying the results of the individualized program. Systematic instruction is revised according to whether students are progressing through the stages of learning and so requires refined systems of data collection and analysis.

Natural Cues and Consequences, Prompts, and Fading Assistance A systematic plan for instruction requires the mindful integration of natural cues, consequences, prompts, and fading sequences. Natural cues are the information that we gather from observing what is happening in a classroom or any environment and are universally used to figure out what to do and how to act in a situation. Natural cues in general education classrooms are subtle, brief, and numerous, and they are often simultaneously and unsystematically presented to an entire class of students. For instance, the ringing of a bell at the beginning of a class period in many secondary classrooms serves as a natural cue to all students that it is time to take their seats and prepare for instruction to begin. This is but one of many natural cues that students in a general education setting are expected to understand. Students with severe and multiple disabilities often have difficulty recognizing natural cues and understanding their meaning in these circumstances. Similarly, the natural consequences of an action provide valuable information about whether a given action is appropriate. The student who fails to comply with the expectations of the bell at the beginning of class experiences a natural consequence in the form of being listed as tardy or absent in the teacher's attendance record.

These important yet sometimes subtle feedback mechanisms can be easily missed or misinterpreted, particularly by students with severe and multiple disabilities. For these reasons, students must be explicitly taught how to respond appropriately to natural cues and to natural consequences, which are important elements of systematic instruction. By making natural cues and natural consequences more salient or obvious, students learn to recognize them and act accordingly. Assistance is faded over time as students begin to rely more on their own ability to recognize these classroom features. Put simply, when students are taught to recognize and respond to natural cues and natural consequences, they learn "why things happened and to adapt their behavior next time" (Ghere et al., 2002, p.57).

Prompting is instruction that is given either before or during an educational activity. Although it is present in all instruction, prompting holds a distinct place in systematic instruction and must be carefully designed to ensure the prompts evoke appropriate responses from students. The goal of prompting is to create a situation in which the student is able to experience errorless learning, defined by making errors less than 20% of the time during a given instructional session (Collins, 2012). In this situation, the learner experiences less frustration and is able to experience success, which can be reinforced by the instructor. "If a learner does not know how to perform a behavior, then the instructor should prompt the learner to perform it correctly rather than allow the learner to become frustrated, practice incorrect responses or make guesses"

(Collins, 2012, p. 7). Prompting requires careful attention to a given student's reaction because a prompt should only be as intense as is required to elicit a desired response. Overprompting students may result in learned helplessness, whereas underprompting may fail to prevent errors.

Different types of prompts can be employed based on students' learning profiles as well as the level of assistance needed. Because systematic instructional programs are based on a student's individual learning style, prompts can be visual, verbal, or tactile and should reflect personal strengths, needs, and preferences (Downing & MacFarland, 2010). There are physical prompts, gestural prompts, modeling prompts, and verbal prompts (Collins, 2012; Ghere et al., 2002; Halvorsen & Neary, 2008). This list ranges from the most intrusive form (physical prompting) to the least intrusive form (verbal prompting). An intrusive physical prompt may take the form of manually moving a student's hands to complete a desired behavior, such as placing them on a computer keyboard and performing keystrokes with them. A gestural prompt may involve a teacher pointing or gesturing toward materials or activities to prompt the student to begin the task. Modeling prompts often take the form of a teacher or fellow student demonstrating the correct completion of a task in order to prompt the student with a disability to imitate their behavior. Finally, verbal prompts may involve single words, commands, or questions spoken by a teacher in order to direct a student toward a desired response. In any case, it is common for different types of prompts to be used together simultaneously.

Regardless of the type of prompting, the ultimate goal of instruction is independent completion of the task without any prompting. Careful attention needs to be given to systematically fading the assistance because prompts are not meant to continue indefinitely.

> Once we introduce a prompt, we must consider how we're going to ultimately remove it. This removal process must be done in a manner that continues to allow for student success. Continually and systematically fading the intensity of our assistance or the amount of information provided allows a student to approach natural performance criteria. It is also very important to remember that a prompt must not detract from the natural stimulus, but rather highlight it. (Halvorsen & Neary, 2008, p. 133)

Different prompting will occur depending on the phase of learning, and the fading of assistance should not begin before the student moves into practicing fluency and onto maintenance of the skill. Just as the goal of providing specific attentional cues is to fade assistance as the student begins to respond to natural cues, the goal of fading prompts is to eventually have the student respond to a natural stimulus. The goal of systematic instruction is to reduce the discrepancy between the number of artificial supports provided to students with severe and multiple disabilities and those provided to their peers in the inclusive classroom.

The first-grade morning meeting provided ample opportunities for Emma to receive multiple trials and systematic instruction in using switch-activated AT. The universal design process was used to plan for Emma's instruction and create a responsive morning meeting for all students. Figure 10.3 provides the resulting lesson plan for the morning meeting that highlights Emma's role as leader and participant as well as specific elements of differentiation. Figure 10.4

illustrates Emma's systematic instructional plan that incorporates data collection for decision making. The plan shows her instructional objective, the types of instructional prompts, and the actions she is expected to initiate. Emma is not yet able to reliably perform the task in response to natural cues (i.e., the typical flow of actions and interactions that happen among students and teachers as part of the morning meeting routine) because she is in the acquisition stage of learning. The plan outlines the instructional prompts that match her sensory and physical needs that are provided by either the teacher or peer. Data show that Emma was able to activate her voice output device or electronic spinner by the third day by consistently touching the switch on at least 75% of the opportunities. She must now maintain that level of performance across six consecutive morning meetings, however, to reach the target criterion. Looking closely at the daily data, during three sessions, she had particular difficulty with the step to play the prerecorded sentence frame (e.g., I'M FEELING _____ BECAUSE_____) to cue classmates to share their feelings. Consequently, these data prompted instructors to pay close attention to this step and determine if a more intensive level of prompting was needed or if the sequence should be further modified.

Embedded Systematic Instruction: The Integration of Academic, Social, and Functional Skills Embedded systematic instruction is a process in which teachers integrate learning opportunities within the routines of general education instruction using systematic instruction to arrange for skills to be practiced and demonstrated in inclusive environments (McDonnell, Johnson, & McQuivey, 2008). Educators who embed instructional trials in the inclusive classroom support generalization of skills through the use of real materials, authentic contexts, and interaction with peers who are diverse (Jimenez & Kamei, 2013). Systematic instruction remains specific and measurable in embedded instruction. Embedded systematic instruction is best implemented when general and special educators design curriculum and instruction together so that there are explicit instructional targets for the student with severe and multiple disabilities throughout a lesson sequence.

To illustrate embedded systematic instruction, an instructional program to develop a communication skill designed for a student with severe and multiple disabilities could be presented throughout his or her day during core academic subjects as well as elective courses, transition times, and extracurricular activities. Embedding learning opportunities and systematic instruction throughout the day provides students with severe and multiple disabilities with many trials, in multiple settings, involving a variety of cues, to make progress toward their goals under natural conditions. Extending the logic of embedding instruction, educators may collaborate with the students' family members to determine opportunities for the students to demonstrate skills learned in school during nonschool days and times. Advocates emphasize that students are better able to generalize and maintain information because embedded instruction is deliberate and concerted and explicit teaching occurs in authentic environments (Jimenez & Kamei, 2013; Spooner, Knight, Browder, & Smith, 2012).

Curriculum area: English language arts (ELA)

Name of lesson: Morning meeting

Time frame: 20–25 minutes

Grade level: 1

I. Enduring understandings

Note: These understandings are ongoing in the context of morning meeting

- We increase our capacity to effectively communicate when we use a discussion structure with agreed-on roles and responsibilities.

- We are all leaders and participants in our community.

- I am using self-knowledge when I reflect on my progress and feelings.

- We have many choices of words to describe the world and ourselves.

Standards addressed in this lesson: Common Core, state, or district standards

- Comprehension and collaboration

  CCSS.ELA-LITERACY.SL.1.1
  - Participate in collaborative conversations with diverse partners about grade 1 topics and texts with peers and adults in small and large groups.

  CCSS.ELA-LITERACY.SL.1.1.A

  - Follow agreed-on rules for discussions (e.g., listening to others with care, speaking one at a time about the topics and texts under discussion).

  CCSS.ELA-LITERACY.SL.1.1.B

  - Build on others' talk in conversations by responding to the comments of others through multiple exchanges.

  CCSS.ELA-LITERACY.SL.1.1.C

  - Ask questions to clear up any confusion about the topics and texts under discussion.

  - Presentation of knowledge and ideas

  CCSS.ELA-LITERACY.SL.1.4

  - Describe people, places, things, and events with relevant details, clearly expressing ideas and feelings.

II. Evidence of understanding (product decision)

Formative performance assessment

Evidence will be gathered by teacher observation and student self-assessment

- Each student will lead morning meeting and follow a protocol to engage others in reading the morning message, giving a greeting, and producing a self-reflection using descriptive synonyms.

- Each student will participate in morning meeting by chorally reading the morning message, engaging in a greeting, and responding to a self-reflection prompt using descriptive synonyms.

III. Multilevel academic, social, and behavioral goals (content decision)

- Each student will demonstrate leadership and knowledge of the structure of morning meeting by leading the class at least once per month in the morning message, greeting, and

(continued)

Figure 10.3. Morning meeting lesson plan. (The Common Core State Standards are © Copyright 2010. National Governors Association Center for Best Practices and Council of Chief State School Officers. All rights reserved.)

Figure 10.3. *(continued)*

self-reflection. Each component will be named, directions will be given or demonstrated, and members of the group will be enlisted for responses.

- Given a review of word wall synonyms for feelings, a self-reflection prompt, and a sentence frame, each student will act as participant in morning meeting by choosing an appropriate synonym and responding in a complete sentence to the prompt: "Using words from the word wall, tell us how you feel today and why. You can say: I am feeling _____ because_____."

- When leading or participating in morning meeting, and given an indirect physical prompt at the elbow by a peer or teacher that is paired with the natural cue, Emma will activate her voice output device or electronic spinner by consistently touching the switch on at least 75% of the opportunities across six consecutive meeting sessions.

- Using the iPad and an online American Sign Language (ASL) dictionary, Andrea will search for the ASL sign of a feeling word, show the class the video, and demonstrate the sign in a sentence voiced by the teacher or peer of choice: "I feel __(sign)__today."

IV. Multilevel and multisensory materials (content decision)

- Sequence of morning meeting on the whiteboard or chart paper with words and picture symbols

- Word wall synonyms for feelings (e.g., joyful, glad, pleased, cheerful)

- iPad, electronic spinner, and switch interface for Emma

- iPad for Andrea to find additional synonyms and ASL sign for a feeling word.

- Spinner overlays with pictures of classmates and greeting options (the snake, chicken shake, spider web).

V. Learning activities, lesson formats, and instructional sequence (process decisions)

- *Lesson formats:* Whole-class discussion, peer interchange for greeting, and Think-Pair-Share for self-reflection.

- *Environmental considerations:* All students will gather chairs in a circle to be at the same height as Emma.

- *Student-specific teaching strategies:* Emma is scheduled to lead morning meeting three times per week to ensure she has sufficient trials to achieve her instructional goal. Teachers will model how to provide prompts to Emma that reference the natural cue in the meeting. For example, a natural cue for Emma to express how she feels using her iPad will be a peer asking her during morning meeting, "Emma, how do you feel today?" Teachers will also demonstrate the latency time needed to allow Emma to respond. If Emma becomes agitated and cries, then teachers will make a best guess about the communicative function of the behavior in a way that peers can understand. For example, "Emma, you look and sound unhappy. Maybe you are uncomfortable; let's take a break from sitting in your chair."

- *Systems of support and supervision:* The general and special educator will switch roles each day supporting the triad responsible for leading the meeting. The adult's role will be to model interactions with Emma, remind the team of the meeting sequence, and intervene if additional classroom management is needed.

- *Instructional sequence (also see systematic instructional plan and data sheet for Emma)*

1. Before class starts, the general education teacher meets with the triad leading the morning meeting to review the meeting sequence and assist in recording the morning

(continued)

Figure 10.3.   *(continued)*

message on Emma's iPad. Emma's partners will inform her that they will read the message and she will record it. When message is recorded, the teacher models for Emma and partners how to activate the switch and then asks Emma to practice the process with the prompt: "We are going to read the morning message together. Emma, please play the morning message." The teacher provides an indirect physical prompt to Emma at the elbow.

2. The teacher also helps set up Emma's self-reflection that will be recorded on her iPad to prompt others and to participate in the meeting herself. At the request of her teachers, Emma's parents have sent information in her communication notebook about how she is feeling today and why. The teacher asks Emma to pick one of her partners to be her voice for the recording by looking at one of the girls.

3. Leaders call the class to rug at 7:45 A.M. and ask them to put chairs in a circle. One leader reviews meeting agenda that is written on the whiteboard.

4. The meeting begins by reading the morning message. The peer leader prompts Emma to start the choral reading: "We are going to read the morning message together. Emma, please read the morning message." Peer provides indirect physical prompt.

5. One peer leader asks three students for suggestions for the greeting. Pictures of each greeting option are placed on the electronic spinner for Emma to make a random choice. Peer leader prompts Emma by saying, "Emma, which morning greeting should we use?" Peer provides indirect physical prompt. Students engage in the selected greeting.

6. One of the leaders guides a self-reflection by describing how sharing will proceed in partners using Think-Pair-Share. Leader reviews word wall and reads synonyms for feelings, letting students know they will choose a word to describe how they are feeling and asks Emma to provide the sentence frame to the group. "Today I am feeling _____ because _____."

7. A leader asks Andrea to find a synonym for the word *happy* on an ASL web site and demonstrate it for the group so people can choose to use the sign in their response.

8. In partnerships, each student takes turns sharing his or her self-reflection. Emma's partner asks, "Emma, how do you feel today?" and provides an indirect physical prompt to prompt her to share the recorded message: I FEEL HAPPY TODAY BECAUSE I GOT TO PLAY WITH MY COUSINS THIS WEEKEND.

9. Group share: Emma uses the electronic spinner and template of classmates' pictures and activates the switch three times to pick three students who will share their self-reflections with the whole class. The peer leader provides the prompt, "Emma, pick a student to share" paired with an indirect physical prompt.

10. The peer leader closes the meeting by thanking participants and asking them to quietly move their chairs. Students will self-assess their participation with a simple rubric once per week.

11. The teacher assists the class to make the transition to the next instructional activity.

Student: Emma
Activity or routine: Leading and participating in morning meeting
Objective: When leading or participating in morning meeting, and given an indirect physical prompt at the elbow by a peer or teacher that is paired with the natural cue, Emma will activate her voice output device or electronic spinner by consistently touching the switch at least 75% of the opportunities across six consecutive meeting sessions.
Stage of learning: *Acquisition*—Using the iPad to provide directions and comments is a new skill for Emma. She has used the electronic spinner in recreational games, but using it in morning meeting is a new application. She is not yet able to reliably perform the task in response to the natural cue. She has received direct physical prompts to learn how to activate the switch at the correct time. She is beginning to activate the switch in response to the natural cue paired with an indirect physical prompt at her elbow. Gestural prompts are ineffective due to her limited vision. Direct verbal prompts (e.g., "touch the switch") are avoided so that the natural cue stands out as the stimulus.

Instructional sequence	What teacher or peer does	What Emma does	9/2	9/4	9/5	9/8	9/10	9/12	9/15	9/17
Prior to morning meeting: The message is reviewed and activating switch is practiced with the teacher and peers.	After the teacher models playing the morning message, the natural cue is given: "We are going to read the morning message together. Emma, please read the morning message." Indirect physical prompt at the elbow is given.	Emma activates the switch to play the morning message.	-	-	+					
During morning meeting: The morning message is played.	Peer says, "We are going to read the morning message together. Emma, please read the morning message." Indirect physical prompt at the elbow is given.	Emma activates the switch to play the morning message.	-	+	+					
Morning greeting is selected.	Peer says, "It is time for our greeting, Emma. Which greeting should we use?" Indirect physical prompt at the elbow is given.	Emma activates electronic spinner to select a morning greeting.	+	-	+					
Sentence frame for self-reflection is given.	Peer says, "Using the word wall, tell us how you feel today and why. Emma, please play the sentence." Indirect physical prompt at the elbow is given.	Emma activates the switch to play the prerecorded sentence frame (e.g., I am feeling ___ because ___).	-	-	+					

Partners take turns sharing self-reflection.	Peer asks, "Emma, how do you feel today?" Indirect physical prompt at the elbow is given. *Note:* Self-reflection prompt may vary each meeting.	Emma activates the switch to play her prerecorded self-reflection.	+	+	-
Three students are selected to share self-reflections with the class.	Peer says, "Who wants to share? Emma, please pick a student to share." Indirect physical prompt at the elbow is given. (This cue is used for each of the three trials.)	Emma activates electronic spinner to select a student (three times)	+	-	+
			+	+	+
			-	-	+
Percent of trials achieved during each morning meeting **Target:** 75% of opportunities in each morning meeting across six consecutive meeting sessions			50%	38%	75%

Figure 10.4. Instructional plan and data sheet for Emma in morning meeting.

General educators, special educators, and paraprofessionals have been responsible for carrying out embedded instruction. There has been promising research, however, on the practice of engaging students without disabilities as partners in delivering embedded instruction to their same-age peers (Jameson, McDonnell, Polychronis, & Riesen, 2008; Jimenez, Browder, Spooner, & DiBiase, 2012). Educators have peers deliver embedded instruction partially to address the logistical challenges of providing the frequent trials sometimes needed in explicit instruction for students with significant disabilities, which can be more difficult (although with far more efficacious outcomes) to achieve in integrated environments. Peers who deliver instruction have more frequent, authentic, and spontaneous opportunities to offer instructional trials and deliver natural cues, thus further increasing the likelihood that the student with severe and multiple disabilities will be able to generalize and maintain targeted skills.

Although much of the literature on embedded instruction is related to teaching academic skills, embedded instruction for social and behavior skills is another important pedagogical consideration. Since the 1970s, researchers have been advocating for students with severe and multiple disabilities to have opportunities to practice functional and adaptive skills across multiple environments (Guess et al., 1978). Inclusive educators believe that supporting prosocial behavior and enhancing social skills for students with significant disabilities are key skills for living, working, and playing in integrated environments. Integrated environments found in schools—inclusive classrooms—provide the most productive, inexpensive, and genuine context for teaching and practicing social skills. The most relevant opportunities for embedding instruction for students with severe and multiple disabilities may occur during lesson formats with consistent structures, such as morning meeting or reading and writing workshops. These activities have inherently predictable sequences, yet still offer novel opportunities for students' participation and success (Atwell, 1998). For example, if students are typically expected to exchange ideas with classmates in reading workshop, then peers or educators can anticipate opportunities to prompt students to demonstrate communication skills in spontaneous conversations with peers. In addition, when a student with severe and multiple disabilities does not adhere to class rules, peers can model how to act appropriately in the moment and thereby promote desired behaviors (Fenty, Miller, & Lampi, 2008). The student with severe and multiple disabilities would not always be receiving peer support in an authentic classroom community but, likewise, would be encouraged to provide cues or feedback to a classmate without a disability who is learning to follow classroom agreements.

In conclusion, students with severe and multiple disabilities are better able to generalize skills when instruction on academics and social skills is embedded in authentic environments that include peers without disabilities than when instruction is provided in a contrived or segregated environment. For instance, from the moment that Emma (our first grader from the introductory vignette) arrives at school, she is engaged in lively, reciprocal interactions with her peers, who model for her and engage her in procedural, social, and academic tasks.

Peers gradually share responsibility with Emma as they model and scaffold activities for her and then collaboratively lead the morning message. The instructional methods described in the following section support the principle of systematic, embedded instruction as well as the other tenets of instruction essential to an inclusive education for students with severe and multiple disabilities.

EFFECTIVE INSTRUCTIONAL PRACTICES FOR STUDENTS WITH SEVERE AND MULTIPLE DISABILITIES

Which instructional practices for students with severe and multiple disabilities are worth advocating (and agitating) for? The following subsections address this third and final essential question for planning and transforming instruction for students with significant support needs, delving into the best instructional methods for including and educating students with severe and multiple disabilities so that they become engaged and active learners.

Active and Collaborative Instructional Methods

> Learning is not a spectator sport. Students do not learn much just by sitting in class listening to teachers, memorizing prepackaged assignments, and spitting out answers. They must talk about what they are learning, write about it, relate it to past experiences, apply it to their daily lives. They must make what they learn part of themselves. (Chickering & Gamson, 1987, p. 4)

Active and collaborative instructional strategies are powerful tools to promote engagement in learning for a wide range of students from early childhood to higher education (Beichner, 2014; Bonwell & Eison, 1991; Brophy, 1987; Hohmann, Epstein, & Wiekart, 2008; Udvari-Solner & Kluth, 2007). The quote by Chickering and Gamson (1987) captures the importance of making learning dynamic and interactive. Active and collaborative lesson formats offer alternatives to traditional teaching approaches that rely on whole-class and teacher-directed instruction. These strategies affect the process of learning and offer multiple means of expression and engagement in the UDL and differentiated instruction frameworks.

Students with and without disabilities too often spend significant portions of their instructional day sitting passively while being taught in a large-group format. We have little or no evidence of many students' thoughts or their understanding of the content while instruction is taking place in these settings. The belief that all students are able to process information in the same way and at the same rate is the underlying assumption in using traditional teaching formats. In addition, after students have received the information, we assume they can inherently synthesize, elaborate on, and apply the new knowledge as they work independently. These expectations and outcomes are doubtful when we consider typical learners. They are even more unlikely when we consider the learning characteristics of students with severe and multiple disabilities. Consequently, opportunities to include students with significant disabilities in core instruction diminish when teachers spend a significant amount of classroom time in large-group, whole-class, and lecture-based formats. Alternatively, active and collaborative strategies offer many more entry points for students with significant disabilities to meaningfully participate in general education and can be designed to incorporate individualized instructional goals (Udvari-Solner & Kluth, 2007). A variety of active and collaborative instructional strategies should be integrated when planning curricular units and daily lessons.

The following subsections briefly define the characteristics of active and collaborative learning and then outline specific instructional strategies and their benefits for students with severe and multiple disabilities, concluding with a case example featuring Azahr, the fourth grader introduced at the beginning of the chapter.

Characteristics of Active and Collaborative Learning   Active learning approaches put students directly and immediately at the center of the educational process. Learning is structured so that students must apply, solve, create, question, experiment, and interact (Udvari-Solner & Kluth, 2007). Active learning is experiential because students directly engage with objects, curricular materials, ideas, events, and people. Students are encouraged to be active agents in their own learning and may feel intrinsic engagement because personally meaningful experiences and outcomes can be created. Paulson and Faust (2010) noted that active learning can be simple or multifaceted and can include a wide range of practices, from listening techniques or short writing tasks to "complex group exercises in which students apply course material to 'real life' situations and/or to new problems" (para 2).

Collaborative learning is a subset of active learning. Whereas many active strategies can be independently performed, all collaborative learning is inherently active because it requires individuals to interact in organized ways with others to problem-solve, practice skills, or produce work together in some way (Keyser, 2000; Roschelle & Teasley, 1995). Collaborative learning is a broad category referring to a set of small-group educational approaches that share common characteristics. Forms of collaborative learning by other names include reciprocal learning, team learning, study groups or circles, peer teaching, and the most well known—cooperative learning (Johnson & Johnson, 2005; Udvari-Solner, 2012a).

Collaborative learning is arranged in partnerships or small groups with no more than six members. Groups are intentionally configured for heterogeneity, with members who vary along the dimensions of ability, race, class, gender, sexual identity, ethnicity, and religion. True collaboration can happen only when groups are monitored and taught how to share leadership, input, and responsibilities. Students should also be taught the social and communication requirements for working well in groups, such as learning to share materials, paraphrasing a classmate's statement, or expressing an opinion. Active and collaborative learning strategies are explicit approaches or step-by-step procedures to guide the process of learning; shape academic and social interactions in the classroom; and teach students how to work in pairs, teams, or as an entire class. Most strategies are content-free procedures that can be used across subjects, grades, and age levels with variations in complexity and academic purpose (Kagan & Kagan, 2009; Udvari-Solner, 2012b) Table 10.1 describes

Table 10.1.   Examples of active and collaborative strategies and methods to differentiate

Strategy description	Methods to differentiate
Three-Step Interview (Bennett & Rolheiser, 2001)	

Teams of three students rotate the roles of interviewer, interviewee, and recorder to ask questions, share their thinking, and take notes. Some uses of this strategy are

- To conduct a prewriting exercise to capture students' ideas
- To determine a student's background knowledge on a topic or concept
- To review concepts at the end of a unit or lesson
- To conduct an opinion survey

Steps

1. Place students into groups of three.
2. Assign each student a letter and a role.
3. A = interviewer, B = interviewee, C = recorder/reporter
4. Rotate roles after each interview.
5. At the end of the session, have students share the information they recorded when they were the recorder in a round robin manner.
6. Group-to-group sharing can also be arranged.

Students are encouraged to compare similarities and differences in responses.

When a student is the interviewee, ask questions in a yes/no format; provide multiple-choice answers using picture or word cues.

Group members record all of the interview questions on a voice output device, and each interviewer uses the device to conduct the interview.

Place questions on a customizable game spinner available as an app or online that can be activated by touch or by switch (e.g., Decide Now! app, imageSpinner app, Wheeldecide.com).

Allow the reporter to use an iPod, iPad, or digital voice recorder to capture responses.

Act Like It (Udvari-Solner & Kluth, 2007)

Students work in small teams to become words, concepts, ideas, or things that are relevant to the curriculum and can help them demonstrate their knowledge. For example, a group may be asked to act like the water cycle after the teacher provides a mini-lecture on the topic.

- Different concepts are assigned to each group, or every group illustrates the same concept.
- Everyone in the room might know the assigned concept, or each group might have a secret identity that observing groups must guess.
- After the prompt is given verbally or in writing, groups are given a short period of time to generate ideas for an on-the-spot performance or are given greater time to plan with more specific criteria for the demonstration.

Provide some groups with more concrete, familiar, or common terms, whereas others are given more abstract concepts.

Rather than on-the-spot performances, allow more planning time with the expectation that the group must create a meaningful role for everyone in the group.

Provide a box of costumes and props for students to use in their acts. Offer items such as scrap paper, blankets, paper towels, ribbons, paper plates, and school supplies and ask them to create props on the spot.

Some team members can be responsible to provide narration or select and play music, a learning song, or sound effects related to the concept.

Ask students to make impromptu revisions of each scene. Put key students into groups who have various jobs related to improving the short skits. One student might be asked to fact check and another might suggest helpful visuals. Still another might work on sound (e.g., suggest dialogue or certain types of music) to extend the meaning of the scene.

(continued)

Table 10.1. *(Continued)*

Strategy description	Methods to differentiate
Save the Last Word for Me (Buehl, 1995)	
This literacy strategy helps students reflect on what they have read, elicit different opinions, and hear multiple interpretations.	Including illustrated books or poems, web sites, songs, and video clips varies the materials used for analysis of a topic so that a student who is an emerging or nonreader is more likely to express a preference to share a portion of the material. For example, if a middle school class is reading the novel *Hatchet* by Gary Paulsen (1987), an adapted version with photographs and very simplified text is available online at Tar Heel Reader (http://tarheelreader.org), allowing a student to share one photograph or one piece of text.
Steps	
1. Provide the same story, short text, or passage to students.	
2. Students read individually and find and mark five statements that interest them or to which they would like to react. Selected statements might be something they agree with, disagree with, have heard before, found interesting, or want to say something about.	
3. Students write the actual statements on the front of separate index cards or sticky notes.	Reduce the rounds of statements from five to only one round.
4. Students write comments they would like to share with the group about each statement on the back of each card.	Allow students to work in partnerships to express their selection and provide prompts about ways to solicit a choice from their peer. For example, provide question stems, such as
5. In small groups of four or five, one person begins by reading one statement to the group and helps them locate it in the text. The reader is not allowed to make any comment.	
6. All other group members react to the statement and make comments.	"Do you want to talk about _____ or _____?"
7. When everyone is done commenting, the student who wrote the statement gets the last word.	"Which illustration do you want to share?"
8. A second group member is selected, and the process is repeated until all cards are shared.	
Numbered Heads Together (Kagan & Kagan, 2009)	
This strategy provides time for a small group to respond to a problem or question and jointly agree on an answer. Only one member of each group is called on to answer, thus holding each person accountable for the material.	Call on two students to answer together ("I want 2s and 4s to collaboratively give a response").
Steps	If a student finds it difficult to share in a large-group format, then have the team write a collective response on paper or whiteboard and have that student hold it up or hand it to the teacher.
1. Arrange students in equal-numbered teams, then assign each individual a number.	
2. Pose a question, an idea to brainstorm, or a task to complete.	
3. Monitor the groups to encourage everyone to participate and contribute. Give the groups a set time to answer the question and make sure that everyone in the group can answer the question. Explicitly explain that all students are responsible for the learning of all others.	If a class member is nonverbal, then allow sufficient time for the group to record the answer on the student's augmentative and alternative communication system.
4. Ask the question again after sufficient time and call out a student number (e.g., "Tell me what you already know about the country of Mexico. I want to hear answers from all of the 4s").	When a number is called, any student in the group, including the learner who is nonverbal, uses the device to respond to the question (Udvari-Solner & Kluth, 2007).
5. The student with that particular number in each group stands and reports an answer for the group.	Include some students as number callers using online spinners previously mentioned or real or electronic dice (e.g., virtual dice available at http://www.bgfl.org/virtualdice).
6. If the answer needs clarifying, then ask another student number (all of the 3s) to expand on the answer.	

(continued)

Table 10.1. *(Continued)*

Strategy description	Methods to differentiate

Team Word Webbing (Kagan & Kagan, 2009)

This team brainstorming strategy helps expand vocabulary, increase the use of academic language, and helps students see how ideas are connected or expanded. Accountability is built in because each student contributes to the web with a different color marker. This strategy can be used to review concepts, as a method to generate descriptive language before writing, and as a method to check students' prior knowledge.

Steps

1. Give each student or each group a different colored pen or marker.

2. Have students write the topic, core concept, or idea in a rectangle in the center of a large poster-size paper.

3. In the first round, each student adds one main concept related to the core concept to the web.

4. Group members then begin to freely add to the web. Indicate whether students should be adding main concepts, supporting elements, or pictures to illustrate concepts.

5. At some point, students should freely add ideas of their choice as they see connections—main concepts, minor concepts, bridges, or connectors between items to fill in the web.

6. Posters can also be passed from group to group, and teams must add ideas to the new web.

Provide one student with a series of pictures or single words that have been preselected and are main concepts related to the core topic. As each main concept is taped to the word web, the rest of the group must draw supporting elements or make further connections. For example, if sources of light is the core topic, then the student in charge of main topics would hold words or images of the sun, a candle, a flashlight, the moon, car headlights, and a glowworm that would be progressively offered to the team word web.

When a group is stuck, assign a student to access an online visual thesaurus that generates related word webs (e.g., Visuwords, available at http://www.visuwords.com; Thinkmap Visual Thesaurus, available at https://www.visualthesaurus.com).

One student might provide a word in American Sign Language (ASL) or a different language, and the group must represent it on the web and determine how it relates to the concept. A student could also act as the translator and look up the words or concepts using an ASL online dictionary or online translator to teach the group (e.g., Signing Saavy, available at http://www.signingsavvy.com).

Assign one student in each group as the core concept captain, using picture symbol cards or a voice output device to call out the items the group must map (e.g., bridge, main concept, supporting elements).

Say Something (Short, Harste, & Burke, 1996)

This shared reading strategy promotes comprehension and construction of meaning from text. Students read a piece of text together and then stop at key points and exchange thoughts about what has been read. Learners are encouraged to look for relationships between new information and their existing knowledge.

Steps

1. Select a piece of text that ranges in length from a few sentences to a few pages.

2. Place students in pairs or triads, and give each learner the reading selection.

This strategy can be used with nontext material. In partners, one examines a text and the other examines visual media (e.g., photographs, pictures, video excerpts). At an agreed-on time (e.g., 3 minutes), students stop and say something. The student with nontext material may point to something relevant for discussion.

Pair students with readings on the same topic, but who are at different reading levels. Students share something gained from their own reading at the stopping points. *Note:* even the best readers in class should be given nontext material and different levels of reading to reinforce that information can be gained from many sources.

(continued)

Table 10.1. *(Continued)*

Strategy description	Methods to differentiate

3. Tell students they will be reading the text as a team. Direct them to skim the text and determine a place they will stop and say something to one another. They may choose what they say or can be directed to
 	
  • Ask a question
  • Make a prediction
  • Make a key point
  • Connect the information to personal experience
  • Note something that was particularly interesting
  • Make an argument
  • Paraphrase what was read
 	
4. Partners begin reading again, repeating the process of stopping, sharing, and starting until they finish the selection.
 	
5. A whole-group discussion can be facilitated after all pairs have completed the selection.
	One person in the partnership (or a teacher in a small group) can read aloud, stop, and then partners say something to each other.
	
	When students read at different paces, whoever completes the reading first can write down his or her response while his or her partner completes the reading.
	
	When a student uses a communication board, pictures, or symbols to communicate, he or she can select a response to share with his or her partner to make a comment or pose a question (e.g., "That was interesting." "I did not understand that." "Can you put that in your own words?").
	
	To teach and reinforce a partner's communication system, the peer can be encouraged to use the system as well. (Udvari-Solner & Kluth, 2007)
	
	One student acts as the moderator of the conversations by tossing a "Say Something Cube" to cue group members of their response. On each side of a paper or foam cube, write six types of responses. These can be single statements or provide sentence starters for the responders. For example:
	
	Make a Prediction:
	I predict that . . .
	I bet that . . .
	I think that . . .
	Since this happened (fill in detail) . . .
	Then I bet the next thing that is going to happen is . . .
	Reading this part makes me think that this (fill in detail) is about to happen
	I wonder if . . .
	
	A customizable cube creator is available from ReadWriteThink at http://www.readwritethink.org/classroom-resources/student-interactives/cube-creator-30850.html

several active and collaborative learning strategies, with suggestions for differentiating the strategy for students with significant disabilities.

Benefits of Active and Collaborative Strategies for Students with Severe and Multiple Disabilities   Active and collaborative learning strategies that are appropriately planned can have many benefits for students with severe and multiple disabilities. First, there are multiple ways to incorporate student-specific academic, language, and communication goals within the lesson because active and collaborative strategies commonly include reading, talking, writing, describing, touching, interacting, listening, and reflecting. An expectation that students should interact with one another while learning provides spontaneous opportunities for interactions between students with and without disabilities. Instructors can precisely plan for social and academic interchanges to occur at key points throughout an activity. Natural supports from peers in the form of prompts and cues can also be engineered as explicit steps in the activity.

Extremely quiet and sedentary classrooms often are inhospitable for some students with significant disabilities. For students who struggle to sit or remain quiet for long periods of time, many collaborative and active instructional strategies create a livelier classroom climate in which talking, thinking aloud, and physically moving occur more often. In addition, instructors may be more able to take on the role of facilitator to guide interactions among students, model teaching techniques, and provide necessary instructional prompts to students with significant support needs because they are not the central source of information at these times.

Example in Practice: Using a Collaborative Learning Strategy with Azahr Udvari-Solner and Kluth (2007) developed the Classify, Categorize, and Organize collaborative learning strategy that can be used for small groups or an entire class. The approach is a good match for promoting problem solving and learning by discovery when information is given to students that can be grouped by similarities, properties, or function. The steps in the process are

1. The instructor creates notecards, strips of paper, or pictures or provides actual items related to grade-appropriate concepts that can be classified, categorized, or ordered in two or more groups (e.g., different species of animals, words that are different parts of grammar, numbers and mathematical operations that when combined make various equations and solutions).

2. Each student receives one card or item that will fit into at least one category or group. Students must actively move around the room viewing every class member's item to find others with related concepts.

3. When students believe they have correctly classified themselves, the group is given a short amount of time to determine the connections among the different pieces of information each person holds. Each group is asked to report its findings to the class. The group members may also add new or related information they know about the concept that is not represented on their cards.

4. The instructor is able to listen to and observe the students' interactions while they are problem solving, assessing learners' background knowledge, conceptual understanding, and use of academic language. Only after each group presents its findings does the instructor provide input by asking questions, correcting misunderstandings, and reinforcing or elaborating on key concepts. Watching students as they engage in this process can provide important information about gaps in students' understanding or inform the instructor that students have a solid grasp on content and are ready for deeper or different applications (Udvari-Solner, 2012b; Udvari-Solner & Kluth, 2007).

The Classify, Categorize, and Organize strategy was used in an integrated science and social studies unit on environmental citizenship for Azahr. The service learning Green Team in which Azahr participates was a natural outgrowth of this unit. The teachers used Classify, Categorize, and Organize as a unit introduction to assess what their students already knew about conservation. The general and special educator planned together in advance and prepared a variety of pictures and actual items representing materials, products, or energy sources that could be sorted into the "three R's" of environmental conservation—reduce, reuse, and recycle. The pictures or actual items included products such as paper, grocery bags, junk mail, cans, plastic bottles, paint containers, toys, styrofoam, and energy sources such as electricity and fuel. Initially, the teachers simply asked the students to categorize themselves in some way that made sense. Students logically grouped themselves by "like items" (i.e., paper products, items made of glass, energy sources each clustered in separate groups) in this first sort. The teachers then asked students to reconfigure based on whether their item could be reduced, reused, or recycled, thus making the task more challenging because many items fit in more than one category. Students could deliberate until they felt satisfied with their sort and could justify their decisions. The activity was followed by students working in small groups to look up local guidelines for recycling or national statistics on environmental waste.

Although the academic goal for most students was to compare and contrast the properties of various objects and determine which products could be reduced, reused, or recycled, Azahr's participation in this activity targeted language, communication, and literacy goals. Azahr was given a picture of a milk container paired with the word *milk*. His objective was to identify the picture of milk, repeat the word out loud, and approach others to compare pictures or actual items to find a match. One classmate had the same image as Azahr, and another classmate had an actual milk carton. Based on similar materials, these classmates also were actively seeking Azahr during the process of categorization to make comparisons, ask questions, and initiate interactions such as, "Azahr, what is on your card? Is it the same as mine? I think you are part of our group." Azahr's item was selected in advance because it was already a familiar picture symbol in his AAC system and a favorite beverage choice for lunch.

The general and special educator worked equitably together to lead and guide instruction during the process of Classify, Categorize, and Organize. The special educator introduced the activity. The general and special educator modeled together how students would engage in the activity. Although students categorized themselves, the general educator supported Azahr to use language to express his assigned item and find his group. At the same time, the special educator supported multiple groups to find associations among products that could be reduced, reused, or recycled.

This activity created a shared experience with classmates during which the concepts, academic language, and actions of conservation were previewed and made more concrete. This lesson set the foundation for the vocabulary, materials, and activities that would later be integral to Azahr's participation with the Green Team as they tackled schoolwide recycling efforts.

Community-Referenced Instruction and Service Learning for All Students

Community-referenced or community-based instruction is characterized by learners gaining access to nonschool settings to apply skills that have relevance now and in their future and has a long and important history in the education of students with severe and multiple disabilities (Falvey, 1989; Ford et al., 1989; Kluth, 2000). Community-referenced instruction was initiated in the mid-1970s in response to the limits of existing developmental approaches taking place in segregated schools and self-contained classrooms (Spooner & Browder, 2012). Pioneers in this practice began moving out of segregated instructional settings into the community to teach functional skills that were chronologically age appropriate (Brown, Nietupski, & Hamre-Nietupski, 1976; Brown et al., 1983; Hamre-Nietupski, Nietupski, Bates, & Maurer, 1982). Central goals were to enhance quality of life by teaching students to function as independently as possible as adults in authentic community, domestic, recreation, and work environments, as well as to promote their rightful place as visible and capable members of society. Teaching directly in current and anticipated environments addressed issues of skill transfer and generalization that were characteristically difficult for learners with significant disabilities. In addition, the arena of the real world provided interactions with community members without disabilities that were lacking or absent in segregated school environments. Early and ongoing research demonstrated that students with significant disabilities could live and work with far more independence than previously realized, thereby establishing the efficacy of community-referenced instruction (Browder & Grasso, 1999; Walker, Uphold, Richter, & Test, 2010).

In part, the gains made in community settings set the stage for higher expectations in the realm of academic learning. Access to general education classrooms and curriculum for reasons beyond mere presence and socialization became the next frontier. Many who were responsible for defining recommended practices in community-referenced instruction became the innovators of inclusive practice (Browder, 1987; Brown et al., 1989; Downing, 2008; Snell & Brown, 2011). This paradigm shift to inclusive education has prompted some educators, families, and scholars in the field to question if it is acceptable to remove students from general education classrooms during the day to engage in community-referenced instruction that is unrelated to the school life of their peers (Tashie & Schuh, 1993). Because community-referenced instruction remains a vital factor in adequately preparing students for transition to postschool environments, others are grappling with how to balance implementing both inclusive and community-referenced instruction while questioning when or if one practice should have precedence over the other (Ayres, Lowrey, Douglas, & Sievers, 2011; Frattura & Capper, 2007).

Integrating Community-Referenced Instruction with Academic Learning

School-age students, families, and educators should not have to choose between academic and community-referenced learning. It is important to reinvent how academic instruction and community-referenced instruction, two seemingly disparate practices, can intersect in ways that are beneficial for both students with and without disabilities. Methods of inclusive community-referenced instruction have been developed and continue to emerge as the field acknowledges that all relevant, critical, and enriching skills cannot be solely taught in the confines of a classroom (Kluth, 2000; Udvari-Solner & Thousand, 1995). Community-referenced instruction jointly planned by general and special educators can promote learning experiences for all students that are both pragmatic and academically challenging. By bringing students to authentic situations, they learn by doing, making instruction come alive. Academics are reinforced and deepened by engaging with real-life issues and problems. More chances are available to embed functional academic and lifelong skills for students with severe and multiple disabilities when community-referenced instruction is regularly incorporated into courses, units of study, and weekly lessons. Several examples of inclusive community-referenced instruction follow, highlighting the instructional programs of our featured students, Charlie and Azahr.

Community as a Source of Curriculum and Instruction   Charlie, our eighth-grade student, is an integral member of Reading and Writing Workshop (Calkins, 2011). Charlie has Down syndrome and experiences a significant seizure disorder affecting his attention and endurance. He is nonverbal but is gaining a vocabulary of sign language, gestures, and vocalizations. Charlie's general and special educator had to think creatively about his participation in literacy block while integrating his IEP goals related to literacy and communication. Given his middle school status, his parents also wanted Charlie to increase his access to the community and gain independence in skills such as crossing the street and making purchases in local venues like his typically developing peers.

Both teachers encouraged and expected all students to tap into their personal experiences and interests for units on narrative, persuasive, informational, and poetry writing. Reading and Writing Workshop (Calkins, 2011) is student centered by nature and uses mini-lessons, conferencing with students, independent reading or writing time, and daily student-to-student sharing, thereby providing flexibility for Charlie's academic instruction (Atwell, 1998; Rief & Heimburge, 2007). Regularly scheduled community-referenced instruction was integrated into the lesson to ensure Charlie had personal, tangible, and immediate experiences from which to write. The opening vignette described that Charlie and a team of students gained access to the community to engage in a simple shared experience together, which served as the foundation for narrative writing about small life moments. In this instance, students, including Charlie, took Instagram photographs of their trek to a local ice cream shop, which were later used to construct alternative picture-based texts. Table 10.2 shows the eighth-grade CCSS in writing and variations in goals for Charlie that guided instruction.

This approach was replicated weekly while incorporating subsequent CCSS in other writing genres. During the informational writing unit in which students had to explain and demonstrate a procedure or process, the writing group generated a range of topics requiring community access to create "how to" essays. Topics such as "How to buy and prepare nutritional low-cost snacks," "How to ride the Metro system," "How to ask a friend out for lunch," or "How to get help when you are lost" were ideas that had challenging, yet practical, applications for Charlie and his peers. Although the purposes and products of Charlie's writing could function as guided recipes (nutritional snacks), social stories (asking a friend to lunch), or a step-by-step instructional sequence (riding the Metro), his classmates were able to take the same subjects and create multiple paragraph essays using well-researched factual information and supporting details while using precise domain-specific vocabulary to explain the topic. The students returned to some of the same high-priority community environments during the poetry unit. These environments served as a rich source of descriptive language to create acrostic poems and as a basis of new sign language vocabulary for Charlie. Charlie and members of the writing

Table 10.2. Common Core State Standards (CCSS) guiding community-referenced writing team

Eighth-grade CCSS	Differentiated CCSS for Charlie
Write narratives to develop real or imagined experiences or events using effective technique, relevant descriptive details, and well-structured event sequences.	Write about events or personal experiences.
a. Engage and orient the reader by establishing a context and point of view and introducing a narrator and/or characters; organize an event sequence that naturally and logically unfolds.	a. Write a narrative about a real or imagined experience using a picture sequence that has at least one character and contains two or more elements/scenes of the event.
b. Use narrative techniques, such as dialogue, pacing, description, and reflection, to develop experiences, events, and/or characters.	b. Sequence pictures to signal order or the temporal concepts of first, then, and next.
c. Use a variety of transition words, phrases, and clauses to convey sequence, signal shifts from one time frame or setting to another, and show the relationships among experiences and events.	c. Use words that describe the feelings of characters or provide other sensory information about the setting, experiences, or events.
d. Use precise words and phrases, relevant descriptive details, and sensory language to capture the action and convey experiences and events.	
e. Provide a conclusion that follows from and reflects on the narrated experiences or events.	

team created the digital acrostic poem for *ice cream* that was signed and spoken in short video clips:

I is for *I love* ice cream

C is for *cold*

E is for *excited* to eat

C is for *chocolate* chunk

R is for *really* good!

E is for *empty* bowl

A is for feeling *awesome*

M is for *me* eating ice cream with friends

The following parameters directed implementation of each community-referenced session:

- Every student in the eighth-grade class participated in the writing team on a rotating basis, whereas Charlie's membership was ongoing.

- The selection of community locations took into account student interests and relevance to the curriculum and reflected priority environments for instruction identified by Charlie's family.

- Functional skills were intentionally integrated and consistently practiced in the context of the community expedition (e.g., street-crossing skills, purchasing goods and services, using local transportation systems).

- The purpose of instruction was driven by academic standards and Charlie's IEP goals.

- Instruction was conducted under the close supervision of a general educator or special educator.

- A systematic instructional plan and sequence was employed that included explicit goals, levels of prompting, and data collection.

Using research teams (Kluth, 2000; Udvari-Solner, 1992, 1996), which are deliberately formed and linked with curricular units of instruction, is another application of community-referenced learning. Small, heterogeneous groups of students with and without disabilities gather information from community sources that will inform and enhance the study of particular subjects or concepts. Inquiries naturally arise during any unit of instruction that can best be answered by gaining access to environments and resources outside of the classroom. Research teams generate their own questions of interest or can be assigned a question of relevance to the curriculum for investigation. The team gathers pertinent data and returns to share its findings and integrate data into the work of the classroom. This instructional format allows students to gather materials or artifacts, interview local people with expertise, and observe real events and

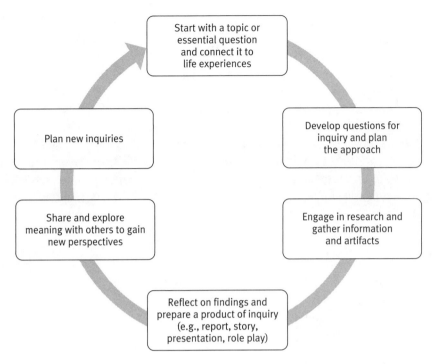

Figure 10.5   An inquiry cycle for research teams. (Adapted from *Creating Classrooms for Authors and Inquirers, 2/e,* by Kathy G. Short and Jerome C. Harste with Carolyn Burke. Copyright ©1996 by Kathy G. Short and Jerome C. Harste. Published by Heinemann, Portsmouth, NH. Reprinted by permission of the Publisher. All rights reserved.)

phenomena. Students are encouraged to use their world to transform the learning process into something relevant to them. The use of such teams provides direct and authentic ways to enact the following CCSS priorities for all students:

- Conduct short research projects to answer a question (including a self-generated question), drawing on several sources and generating additional related, focused questions that allow for multiple avenues of exploration.

- Report on a topic or text or present an opinion, logically sequencing ideas and using appropriate facts and relevant, descriptive details to support main ideas or themes (National Governors Association Center for Best Practices & Council of Chief State School Officers, 2010).

Research teams also align with recommended practices in inquiry and problem-based learning (Larmer & Mergendoller, 2010). An inquiry cycle adapted from Short, Harste, and Burke (1996) that provides systematic guidance for the work of research teams is shown in Figure 10.5. This process provided the instructional framework for the three examples that follow.

Charlie's eighth-grade teachers in language arts and social studies teamed up for a cross-curricular unit addressing standards in persuasive writing and political science in which students were required to "(a) locate, organize, and use relevant information to understand an issue of public concern, take a position, and advocate the position in a debate; and (b) identify ways in which advocates participate in public policy debates" (Wisconsin Department of Public Instruction, n.d., para 1). A research team, which included Charlie, was formed to investigate a current local issue concerning whether the city should offer free public Wi-Fi in low-income neighborhoods. This would be the classwide persuasive essay topic. This issue was particularly relevant to Charlie and several other team members because they lived in one of the neighborhoods that would benefit from the passage of the proposal. The research team developed interview questions for a number of stakeholders, including the mayor, neighborhood residents, and individuals in opposition. Charlie was able to have an active role initiating the interviews because he had questions recorded on an iPad. He helped document the sequence of events in photographs that the team later assembled in a PowerPoint to ac-company their report of findings to the class. In this situation, Charlie had the opportunity to learn about the streets of his own neighborhood, had multiple communication opportunities with team members and the public, used AT, and added new vocabulary to his repertoire in picture symbols and sign language that represented the experience.

A mathematics teacher often heard this rant from students: "When are we ever going to use this?" That question became the perfect charge for research teams to investigate where math exists in our daily lives and how people use math in their professions. During class time set aside for review and independent practice, alternating student groups went into the com-munity on a weekly basis to interview people such as architects, farmers, construction contractors, artists, engineers, landscapers, restaurateurs, medical personnel, and accountants. The class first viewed the testimoni-als and examples put together by Brigham Young University on their web site (http://www.weusemath.org) and then captured short video vignettes of community members describing their work. In the style of short TedTalks (https://www.ted.com) or a Kahn Academy tutorial (https://www .khanacademy.org), interviewees were also asked to demonstrate how to solve a math problem that was part of the students' upcoming curriculum. These video vignettes were presented to the class by the research team at the beginning of the week to motivate and spark interest. Partnerships between the community and the class were developed, resulting in monthly math circles where they worked together to solve interesting math problems.

A third-grade class decided to establish a school store and community snack cache because they were troubled by the fact that many students came to school with no daily snacks and inadequate supplies for learning. "What daily supplies do we need as a classroom community to support our learning?" was the research question that emerged for the class. While brainstorming needs with the whole class, students discovered that a class-mate with autism also benefitted from different fidget toys to remain calm and attentive. Equipped with an initial budget of $30.00, the research team gained access to the local discount store to price out needed items, take digital images of products that would be used for choice making in the classroom, and prioritize items for purchase based on their budget. The student with autism who was on the research team was able to use a picture list to help purchase personal and classroom items. Managing the classroom store and snack supply became a weekly classroom job requiring regular community trips to restock needed items. As one outcome of this instructional sequence, authentic functional mathematics could be applied daily for the student with disabilities and his classmates.

Engaging with the Community Through Service Learning Service learning is another form of community-referenced instruction that has gained attention in education and holds promise for the participation of students with severe and multiple disabilities. The National Service Learning Clearinghouse defines *service learning* as "a teaching and learning strategy that integrates meaningful community service with instruction and reflection to enrich the learning experience, teach civic responsibility, and strengthen communities" (Seifer & Connors, 2007, p. 5). Civic action and community service are valued at all educational levels, including the very early grades, and evidence of participation in community service is increasingly considered in university admissions and high school graduation requirements (Lake & Jones, 2012; Melaville, Berg, & Blank, 2006; Spring, Grimm, & Dietz, 2009). A growing body of research indicates that students involved in service learning are more likely to stay in school, be more engaged with subject matter, perform better academically, and be more civic minded (David, 2009).

   The outcome of service learning is not simply doing good for the world and others. It deliberately enables students to achieve learning goals, engages them actively, integrates curricula and standards with practice, and deepens understanding of the complex causes of social problems (National Center for Learning and Civic Engagement, n.d.). Service learning projects can be classified by four different approaches (Kaye, 2010):

1. *Direct service:* Person-to-person projects in which the service has a direct impact on recipients

2. *Indirect service:* Projects that provide benefits to the community by having students work on broad issues or environmental and community development projects; however, students may not meet the recipients of the service in person

3. *Research:* Projects that find, gather, and present information on areas of public interest or need

4. *Advocacy:* Service that helps create awareness, educates others, or promotes public action about topics of public concern.

The environmental Green Team developed by Azahr's fourth-grade class is an example of a multiyear project that integrated direct, research, and advocacy service learning. The integrated science and social studies unit on environmental citizenship linked important standards from each discipline—engage in credible research methods, investigate environmental questions, and communicate understanding to others. This ongoing curricular project served two larger social purposes—address the need for a school recycling program and increase ways for Azahr, the class member with autism and CP, to have sustained, meaningful participation in general education.

Azahr is learning to use a Picture Exchange Communication System (PECS) and walk with greater independence. His need to be active, his fascination with banging or drumming items to make noise, and the significant vocalizations he makes have made it challenging for him to participate in the general education classroom for the duration of every class. The fourth-grade team thought outside of the box and designed ways to integrate Green Team activities across subject areas within each instructional day so that Azahr could have more frequent and meaningful participation. Following is a partial list of Green Team activities/events, noting curricular areas of relevance:

- Document results of a school community survey before and after the environmental campaign to determine how people recycle at school and at home (mathematics).

- Write letters to organizations and companies to secure funding and recycling containers for the school (English language arts, social studies).

- Create a reduction campaign after studying the amount of trash that ends up each day in classroom garbage cans. Extend to other aspects of the community by examining the waste that ends up in local lakes and landfills (English language arts, mathematics, social studies).

- Create school and community posters to inform and advocate for change (art/English language arts).

- Design Green Team logos and T-shirts for the team and school sales (art, mathematics).

- Pick up and sort recycling from classrooms daily that is weighed, categorized, graphed, and reported back to the school in their campaign to reduce (mathematics, social studies, English language arts).

- Publish weekly "Eco-News Letter," highlighting an environmental challenge for the classroom, school, or community. Eco-letters are sent electronically and delivered to classrooms to be read aloud (English language arts).

- Pose a weekly reuse challenge that engages students to take a discarded item and repurpose it (social studies and science).

- Create a showcase and demonstration of items that can be reused or repurposed at the school, local library, and community center. Create instruments out of recycled items (social studies, art, music).

- Use technology (e.g, Madpad App) to create music from environmental sounds and invented instruments that complement live and digital public service announcements for the school and community (music, social studies, English language arts, drama).

- Create terrariums from liter soda bottles for the study of the water cycle (science).

- Construct simple composters from wood pallets and chicken wire for sale and donation to community gardens (science, mathematics, social studies)

- Organize a school community bring an item/take an item garage sale exchange (social studies, mathematics).

Given this rich list of hands-on activities, Azahr had daily or weekly contexts to use technology; interact via his PECS system; and use functional mathematics to count, sort, measure, and purchase supplies in the community. Azahr used an adaptive cart and gained further independence walking while delivering newsletters and collecting recyclables. In addition, Azahr's fascination with drumming was shaped and given purpose with an age-appropriate outlet of rhythm and music making associated with Green Team activities.

Options for inclusive service learning are innumerable and are limited only by the creativity of educators and their students. The National Youth Leadership Council (https://gsn.nylc.org/projects/all) provides a list of projects by topic that offers excellent ideas and promise for inclusive practice. All students, including those with disabilities, can be involved in and benefit from service learning, particularly when care is taken to incorporate priority goals from the general education curriculum and the IEP that promote desired adult outcomes (Dymond, Renzaglia, & Slagor, 2011). Vandercook and Montie (2010) noted that service learning is an ideal format to foster teamwork, community building, leadership, communication, problem solving, and advocacy skills for every participant. Furthermore, when the needs of students with disabilities are considered:

> Service Learning provides the opportunity for learners with disabilities to be seen by classmates and community members in a different light, to be seen learning and contributing to others, rather than only receiving service. Learners with disabilities have all too often been expected to be in passive, receiving roles. How a person is seen or viewed by others has everything to do with the attitudes expressed about the individual, the behaviors that are expected or not expected, and ultimately the behavior and expectations that the person has about him- or herself. This curriculum

intends to change opinions about who can contribute and to learn, ultimately, that each person can contribute and we are all enriched when everyone is supported to do so. (Vandercook & Montie, 2010, p.1)

CONCLUSION

We are well into the 21st century, yet we continue to see students with severe and multiple disabilities unnecessarily segregated for portions of their day or minimally involved in general education settings. We see educational reforms and innovative curricular frameworks designed to increase rigor, full of potential and promise, yet failing to meaningfully address how students with disabilities can purposefully participate. We acknowledge key tenets and methodologies that best prepare students who are most vulnerable for integrated lives, full of choices and opportunities, yet notice structural and institutional barriers continue to stand in the way of realization. We see teachers struggle alone and with one another to find a set of beliefs to guide their instructional decisions. We notice the gap between our current reality and preferred future. Therefore, we must consciously engineer our students' learning opportunities, even when they are not readily apparent or are not currently in place. We can leverage our dissatisfaction with our willingness to advocate for change. This chapter presents a sketch for how educators may begin or continue the essential work of generating worthy outcomes for students with severe and multiple disabilities. We see ourselves as fellow agitators on the road. Partner with us.

REFLECTION QUESTIONS

1. How might current frameworks for instruction—UDL, differentiated instruction, culturally responsive teaching, and teacher collaboration—guide methodologies for instructing students with severe and multiple disabilities?

2. How might I integrate critical principles, tenets, and methods of instruction for students with severe and multiple disabilities into my teaching? How will doing so facilitate inclusive outcomes?

3. Which instructional practices for students with severe and multiple disabilities still need to be advocated in our local school communities? How might I initiate and engage in this advocacy?

CHAPTER ACTIVITY

Select one of the major concepts presented in the chapter and articulate its potential to improve outcomes for a student with severe and multiple disabilities to your colleagues.

1. Briefly describe the student's attributes.

2. Name and define the concept.

3. Describe how the concept might come alive in an inclusive K–12 environment. What will the student with severe and multiple disabilities learn and be able to do? What will other students learn and be able to do?

REFERENCES

Alberto, P.A., & Troutman, A.C. (2012). *Applied behavior analysis for teachers* (9th ed.). Columbus, OH: Charles E. Merrill.

Americans with Disabilities Act (ADA) of 1986, PL 101-336, 42 U.S.C. §§ 12101 *et seq.*

Atwell, N. (1998). *In the middle: New understandings about writing, reading, and learning* (2nd ed.). Portsmouth, NH: Boynton/Cook.

Ayres, K.M., Lowrey, K.A., Douglas, K.H., & Sievers, C. (2011). I can identify Saturn but I can't brush my teeth: What happens when the curricular focus for students with severe disabilities shifts. *Education and Training in Autism and Developmental Disabilities, 46,* 11–21.

Bal, A. (2012). Participatory social justice for all. In L.G. Denti & P.A. Whang (Eds.), *Rattling chains: Exploring social justice in education* (pp. 99–110). Boston, MA: Sense Publishers.

Banks, J.A., & McGee Banks, C.A. (Eds.). (2001). *Multicultural education: Issues and perspectives* (4th ed.). New York, NY: Wiley.

Baumgart, D., Brown, L., Pumpian, I., Nisbet, J., Ford, A., Sweet, M., . . . Schroeder, J. (1982). Principle of partial participation and individualized adaptations in educational programs for severely handicapped students. *Journal of The Association for the Severely Handicapped, 7*(2), 17–27.

Beichner, R. (2014). History and evolution of active learning spaces. *New Directions for Teaching and Learning (Special Issue: Active Learning Spaces), 137,* 9–16.

Bennett, B., & Rolheiser, C. (2001). *Beyond Monet: The artful science of instructional integration.* Toronto, Ontario, Canada: Bookation.

Blanchett, W. (2006). Disproportionate representation of African American students in special education: Acknowledging the role of white privilege and racism. *Educational Researcher, 35*(6), 24–28.

Bonwell, C., & Eison, J. (1991, September). *Active learning: Creating excitement in the classroom.* Washington, DC: George Washington University Clearinghouse on Higher Education.

Brophy, J. (1987). Synthesis of research on strategies for motivating students to learn. *Educational Leadership, 45,* 40–48.

Browder, D.M. (1987). *Assessment of individuals with severe handicaps: An applied behavior approach to life skills assessment.* Baltimore, MD: Paul H. Brookes Publishing Co.

Browder, D.M., & Grasso, E. (1999). Teaching money skills to individuals with mental retardation: A research review with practical applications. *Remedial and Special Education, 20,* 297–308.

Brown, L., Long, E., Udvari-Solner, A., Davis, L., VanDeventer, P., & Ahlgren, C. (1989). The home school: Why students with severe intellectual disabilities must attend the schools of their brothers, sisters, friends and neighbors. *Journal of The Association for Persons with Severe Handicaps, 8*(3), 71–77.

Brown, L., Nietupski, J., & Hamre-Nietupski, S. (1976). Criterion of ultimate functioning. In M.A. Thomas (Ed.), *Hey, don't forget about me! Education's investment in the severely, profoundly and multiply handicapped* (pp. 2–15). Reston, VA: Council for Exceptional Children.

Brown, L., Nisbet, J., Ford, A., Sweet, M., Shiraga, B., York, J., & Loomis, R. (1983). The critical need for nonschool instruction in educational programs for severely handicapped students. *Journal of The Association for Persons with Severe Handicaps, 8,* 71–77.

Brown, L., Wilcox, B., Sontag, E., Vincent, B., Dodd, N., & Gruenewald, L. (1977). Toward the realization of the least restrictive educational environments for severely handicapped students. *The American Association for the Education of the Severely/Profoundly Handicapped Review, 2*(4), 195–201.

Buehl, D. (1995). *Classroom strategies for interactive learning.* Schofield, WI: Wisconsin State Reading Association.

Calkins, L. (2011). *A curricular plan for the writing workshop.* Portsmouth, NH: Heinemann Publishing.

Calkins, L., & Oxenhorn, A. (2003). *Small moments: Personal narrative writing.* Portsmouth, NH: Heinemann Publishing.

Chickering, A., & Gamson, Z.F. (1987). Seven principles for good practice. *American Association for Higher Education Bulletin, 39,* 3–7.

Collins, B.C. (2012). *Systematic instruction for students with moderate and severe disabilities.* Baltimore, MD: Paul H. Brookes Publishing Co.

Cook, L., & Friend, M. (1993). Educational leadership for teacher collaboration. In B. Billingsley (Ed.), *Program leadership for serving students with disabilities* (pp. 421–444). Richmond, VA: Virginia Department of Education.

Cooper, J.O., Heron, T.E., & Heward, W.L. (2007). *Applied behavior analysis* (2nd ed.). Upper Saddle River, NJ: Pearson.

Courtade, G., Spooner, F., Browder, D., & Jimenez, B. (2012). Seven reasons to promote standards-based instruction for students with severe disabilities: A reply to Ayres, Lowrey, Douglas, & Sievers (2011). *Education and Training in Autism and Developmental Disabilities, 47*(1), 3–13.

Coyne, P., Pisha, B., Dalton, B., Zeph, L.A., & Smith, N. (2012). Literacy by design: A universal design for learning approach for students with significant intellectual disabilities. *Remedial and Special Education, 33*(3), 162–172.

David, J. (2009). What research says about service learning and civic participation. *Educational Leadership, 66*(8), 83–84.

Davis, K.M., Boon, R.T., Cihak, D.F., & Fore III, C. (2010). Power cards to improve conversational skills in adolescents with Asperger syndrome. *Focus on Autism and Other Developmental Disabilities, 25,* 12–22.

Delpit, L. (2006). Lessons from teachers. *Journal of Teacher Education, 57*(3), 220–231.

Donnellan, A. (1984). The criterion of the least dangerous assumption. *Behavioral Disorders, 9,* 141–150.

Donnellan, A. (2000, May). Absence of evidence: Myths about autism and mental retardation. *TASH Newsletter,* 26–32.

Downing, J.E. (2008). *Including students with severe and multiple disabilities in typical classrooms: Practical strategies for teachers* (3rd ed.). Baltimore, MD: Paul H. Brookes Publishing Co.

Downing J.E., & MacFarland, S. (2010). *Severe disabilities (Education and individuals with severe disabilities: Promising practices).* Retrieved from http://cirrie.buffalo.edu/encyclopedia/en/article/114

Dymond, S., Renzaglia, A., & Slagor, M. (2011). Trends in the use of service learning with students with disabilities. *Remedial and Special Education, 32*(3), 19–26.

Falvey, M. (1989). *Community-based curriculum: Instructional strategies for students with severe handicaps* (2nd ed.). Baltimore, MD: Paul H. Brookes Publishing Co.

Falvey, M.A., & Givner, C.C. (2005). What is an inclusive school? In R. Villa & J. Thousand (Eds.), *Creating an inclusive school* (pp. 1–26). Alexandria VA: Association for Supervision and Curriculum Development.

Fenty, N.S., Miller, M.A., & Lampi, A. (2008). Embed social skills instruction in inclusive settings. *Intervention in School and Clinic, 43*(3), 186–192.

Ford, A., Schnorr, R., Meyer, L.H., Davern, L.A., Black, J., & Dempsey, P. (1989). *The Syracuse community-referenced curriculum guide for students with moderate and severe disabilities.* Baltimore, MD: Paul H. Brookes Publishing Co.

Frattura, E.M., & Capper, C.A. (2007). *Leading for social justice: Transforming schools for all learners.* Thousand Oaks, CA: Corwin Press.

Friend, M., & Bursuck, W.D. (2002). *Including students with special needs: A practical guide for classroom teachers.* Boston, MA: Allyn & Bacon.

Gagné, R.M. (1968). Learning hierarchies. *Educational Psychologist, 6,* 1–9.

Gardner, H. (1983). *Frames of mind: The theory of multiple intelligences.* New York, NY: Basic Books.

Garmston, R.J, & Wellman, B.M. (1999). *The adaptive school: A sourcebook for developing collaborative groups.* Norwood, MA: Christopher-Gordon Publishers.

Gay, G. (2002). Culturally responsive teaching in special education for ethnically diverse students: Setting the stage. *Journal of Qualitative Studies in Education, 15*(6), 613–629.

Ghere, G., York-Barr, J., & Sommerness, J. (2002). *Supporting students with disabilities in inclusive schools: A curriculum for job embedded paraprofessional development.* Minneapolis, MN: Institute for Community Integration and Department of Educational Policy and Administration.

Giangreco, M., Edelman, S., Evans Luiselli, T., & MacFarland, S. (1997). Helping or hovering? Effects of instructional assistant proximity on students with disabilities. *Exceptional Children, 64*(1), 7–18.

Gold, M. (1980). *Try another way.* Champaign, IL: Research Press.

González, N., Moll, L., & Amanti, C. (2005). *Funds of knowledge: Theorizing practices in households, communities, and classrooms.* Mahwah, NJ: Lawrence Erlbaum Associates.

Gould, S. (1981). *The mismeasure of man.* New York, NY: W.W. Norton.

Guess, D., Horner, R., Utley, B., Holvoet, J., Maxon, D., Tucker, D., & Warren, S. (1978). A functional curriculum sequencing model for teaching the severely handicapped. *American Association for the Education of the Severely/Profoundly Handicapped Review, 3*(4), 202–215.

Hall, T., Strangman, N., & Meyer, A. (2009). *Differentiated instruction and implications for UDL implementation.* Retrieved from http://www.cast.org/udlcourse/DifferInstruct.doc

Halvorsen, A.T., & Neary, T. (2008). *Building inclusive schools: Tools and strategies for success.* Upper Saddle River, NJ: Pearson.

Hamre-Nietupski, S., Nietupski, J., Bates, P., & Maurer, S. (1982). Implementing a community-referenced educational model for moderately/severely handicapped students: Common problems and suggested solutions. *Journal of The Association for Persons with Severe Handicaps, 7,* 38–43.

Haring, N.G., Lovitt, T.C., Eaton, M.D., & Hansen, C.L. (1978). *The fourth R: Research in the classroom.* Columbus, OH: Charles E. Merrill.

Harmon, C., Kasa-Hendrickson, C., & Neal, L.I. (2009). Promoting cultural competencies for teachers of students with significant disabilities. *Research and Practice for Persons with Severe Disabilities, 34,* 137–144.

Higher Education Opportunity Act of 2008, PL 110-315, U.S.C. §§ 101-1122.

Hohmann, M., Epstein, A., & Wiekart, A. (2008). *Educating young children: Active learning practices for preschool and child care programs* (3rd ed.). Ypsilanti, MI: High/Scope Educational Research Foundation.

Jameson, J.M., McDonnell, J., Polychronis, S., & Riesen, T. (2008). Embedded constant time delay instruction by peers without disabilities in general education classrooms. *Intellectual and Developmental Disabilities, 46*(5), 346–363.

Jimenez, B.A., Browder, D.M., Spooner, F., & DiBiase, W. (2012). Inclusive science inquiry using peer-mediated embedded instruction for students with moderate intellectual disabilities. *Exceptional Children, 78,* 301–317.

Jimenez, B.A., & Kamei, A. (2013). *Embedded instruction: An evidence based practice to support academic achievement in inclusive core academics.* Manuscript submitted for publication.

Johnson, D., & Johnson, R. (2005). New developments in social independence theory. *Genetic, Social, and General Psychology Monographs, 131*(4), 285–358.

Jorgensen, C. (2005). The least dangerous assumption: The challenge to create a new paradigm. *Disability Solutions, 6*(3), 1, 5–9, 15.

Jorgensen, C.M. (2006). Ten promising practices in inclusive education: The inclusion facilitator's guide for action. In M.C. Schuh & J. Nisbet (Eds.), *The inclusion facilitator's guide* (pp. 25–64). Baltimore, MD: Paul H. Brookes Publishing Co.

Kagan, S., & Kagan, M. (2009). *Kagan cooperative learning.* San Clemente, CA: Kagan Publishing.

Kaye, C. (2010). *The completed guide to service learning: Proven, practical ways to engage students in civic responsibility, academic curriculum and social action.* Minneapolis, MN: Free Spirit Publishing.

Keyser, M. (2000). Active learning and cooperative learning: Understanding the difference and using both styles effectively. *Research Strategies, 17*(1), 35–44.

King-Sears, M. (2009). Universal design for learning: Technology and pedagogy. *Learning Disability Quarterly, 32,* 199–201.

Klingner, J.K., Artiles, A.J., Kozleski, E., Harry, B., Zion, S., Tate, W., . . . Riley, D. (2005). Addressing the disproportionate representation of culturally and linguistically diverse students in special education through culturally responsive educational systems. *Education Policy Analysis Archives, 13*(38), 1–43.

Kluth, P. (2000). Community-referenced learning and the inclusive classroom. *Remedial and Special Education, 21,* 19–26.

Ladson-Billings, G. (1995). Toward a theory of culturally relevant pedagogy. *American Educational Research Journal, 32,* 465–491.

Lake, V., & Jones, I. (2012). *Service learning in the PreK–3 classroom.* Minneapolis, MN: Free Spirit Publishing.

Larmer, J., & Mergendoller, J. (2010). 7 essentials for project-based learning. *Educational Leadership, 68*(1), 34–37.

Lave, J., & Wenger, E. (1991). *Situated learning: Legitimate peripheral participation.* Cambridge, United Kingdom: Cambridge University Press.

Lawthon, R., & Chataika, T. (2012). Lave and Wenger: Communities of practice and disability studies. In D. Goodley, B. Hughes, & L. Davis (Eds.), *Disability and social theory: New developments and directions* (pp. 233–251). New York, NY: Palgrave Macmillan

Lazarus, S.S., Cormier, D.C., & Thurlow, M.L. (2011). The relationship between states' accommodations policies and the development of alternate assessments based on modified achievement standards (AA-MAS): A discriminant analysis. *Remedial and Special Education, 32*(4), 301–308.

McDonnell, J., Johnson, J.W., & McQuivey, C. (2008). *Embedded instruction for students with developmental disabilities in general education classrooms.* Arlington, VA: Division on Developmental Disabilities of the Council for Exceptional Children.

McTighe, J., & Wiggins, G.P. (2013). *Essential questions: Opening doors to student understanding.* Alexandria, VA: Association of Supervision and Curriculum Development.

Melaville, A., Berg, A., & Blank, M. (2006). *Community-based learning: Engaging students for success and citizenship.* New York, NY: Coalition for Community Schools.

National Center for Learning and Civic Engagement. (n.d.). http://www.ecs.org/initiatives/national-center-for-learning-civic-engagement/

National Governors Association Center for Best Practices & Council of Chief State School Officers. (2010). *Common Core State Standards.* Washington, DC: Author.

National Youth Leadership Council. (n.d.). *Project examples.* Retrieved from https://gsn.nylc.org/projects/all

Paulson, P., & Faust, J. (2010). *Active learning for the college classroom.* Retrieved from http://web.calstatela.edu/dept/chem/chem2/Active/index.htm

Ravitch, D. (2007). *EdSpeak: A glossary of education terms, phrases, buzzwords, and jargon.* Alexandria, VA: Association for Supervision and Curriculum Development.

Rief, S., & Heimburge, J. (2007). *How to teach and reach all children through balanced literacy, grades 3-8: User-friendly strategies, tools, activities, and ready-to-use materials.* San Francisco, CA: Jossey-Bass.

Roschelle, J., & Teasley, S.D. (1995). The construction of shared knowledge in collaborative problem solving. In C. O'Malley (Ed.), *Computer supported collaborative learning* (pp. 69–97). New York, NY: Springer.

Rose, D., & Meyer, A., (2002). *Teaching every student in the digital age: Universal design for learning.* Alexandria, VA: Association for Supervision and Curriculum Development.

Sailor, W., & Roger, B. (2005). Rethinking inclusion: Schoolwide applications. *Phi Delta Kappan, 86*(7), 503–509.

Salend, S.J., & Duhaney, L.M. (2005). Understanding and addressing the disproportionate representation of students of color in special education. *Intervention in School and Clinic, 40*(4), 213–221.

Santangelo, T., Knotts, G., Clemmer, K., & Mitchell, M. (2008). Differentiated instruction: Legislative support and classroom practices. In T. Jimenez & V. Graf (Eds.), *Education for all: Critical issues in the education of children and youth with disabilities* (pp. 195–240). New York, NY: Wiley.

Santos, R.M., Fowler, S.A., Corso, R.M., & Bruns, D. (2000). Acceptance, acknowledgement, and adaptability: Selecting culturally and linguistically appropriate early childhood materials. *Teaching Exceptional Children, 32*(3), 30–37.

Seifer, S., & Connors, K. (2007). *Faculty toolkit for service learning in higher education.* Scotts Valley, CA: National Service-Learning Clearinghouse.

Shealey, M.W., & Callins, T. (2007). Creating culturally responsive literacy programs in inclusive classrooms. *Intervention in School and Clinic, 42,* 195–197.

Short, K.G., Harste, J., & Burke, C. (1996). *Creating classrooms for authors and inquirers* (2nd ed.). Portsmouth, NH: Heinemann Publishing.

Skrtic, W., Sailor, W., & Gee, K. (1996). Voice, collaboration, and inclusion. *Remedial and Special Education, 17*(4), 142–157.

Snell, M.E., & Brown, F. (2011). *Instruction of students with severe disabilities* (7th ed.). Upper Saddle River, NJ: Pearson.

Spooner, F., & Browder, D. (2012). How we arrived at the Common Core State Standards and the promise it holds for students with severe disabilities. *TASH Connections, 38*(3), 26–28.

Spooner, F., Knight, V.F., Browder, D.M., & Smith, B.R. (2012). Evidence-based practices for teaching academic skills to students with severe developmental disabilities. *Remedial and Special Education, 33*(6), 374–387.

Spring, K., Grimm, R., & Dietz, N. (2009). *Community service and service-learning in America's schools.* Washington, DC: Corporation for National and Community Service, Office of Research and Policy Development.

Tashie, C., & Schuh, M. (1993). Why not community-based instruction? High school students with disabilities belong with their peers. *Equity and Excellence, 1,* 15–17.

Thompson, S.J., Johnstone, C.J., Thurlow, M.L., & Altman, J.R. (2005). *2005 state special education outcomes: Steps forward in a decade of change.* Minneapolis, MN:

University of Minnesota, National Center on Educational Outcomes.

Thurlow, M. (2011). *Common Core State Standards: Implications for students with disabilities.* Retrieved from http://www.ncscpartners.org/Media/Default/PDFs/Resources/Thurlow-CCSS-SWD-8-2011.pdf

Tomlinson, C.A. (2003) *Differentiation in practice: A resource guide for differentiating curriculum, grades K–5.* Alexandria, VA: Association for Supervision and Curriculum Development.

Tomlinson, C.A., & McTighe, J. (2006). *Integrating differentiated instruction and understanding by design: Connecting content and kids.* Alexandria, VA: Association for Supervision and Curriculum Development.

Udvari-Solner, A. (1992). *Curricular adaptations: Accommodating the instructional needs of diverse learners in the context of general education* (Monograph). Topeka, KS: Kansas State Board of Education, Services for Children and Youth with Deaf-Blindness Project.

Udvari-Solner, A. (1996). Examining teacher thinking: Constructing a process to design curricular adaptations. *Remedial and Special Education, 17*(4), 245–254.

Udvari-Solner, A. (1997). Inclusive education. In C. Grant & G. Ladson-Billings (Eds.), *The dictionary of multi-cultural education* (pp. 142–143). Phoenix, AZ: Oryx Press.

Udvari-Solner, A. (2012a). Collaborative learning. In N.M. Seel (Ed.), *Encyclopedia of the sciences of learning* (pp.631–634). New York, NY: Springer.

Udvari-Solner, A. (2012b). Collaborative learning strategies. In N.M. Seel (Ed.), *Encyclopedia of the sciences of learning* (pp. 636–639). New York, NY: Springer.

Udvari-Solner, A., & Kluth, P. (2007). *Joyful learning: Active and collaborative learning in inclusive classrooms.* Thousand Oaks, CA: Corwin Press.

Udvari-Solner, A., & Thousand, J. (1995). Promising practices that foster inclusive education. In R. Villa & J. Thousand (Eds.), *Creating inclusive schools* (pp. 87–109). Alexandria, VA: Association for Supervision and Curriculum Development.

Udvari-Solner, A., Villa, R., & Thousand, J. (2002). Access to the general education curriculum for all: The universal design process. In J. Thousand, R. Villa, & A. Nevin (Eds.), *Creativity and collaboration: A practical guide to empowering students and teachers* (pp. 85–103). Baltimore, MD: Paul H. Brookes Publishing Co.

Udvari-Solner, A., Villa, R., & Thousand, J. (2005). Access to the general education curriculum for all: The universal design process. In R. Villa & J. Thousand (Eds.), *Creating an inclusive school* (2nd ed., pp. 134–155). Alexandria, VA: Association for Supervision and Curriculum Development.

Vandercook, T., & Montie, J. (2010). *Together we make a difference: An inclusive service learning curriculum for elementary learners with and without disabilities.* Minneapolis, MN: National Inclusion Project and the Institute on Community Integration, University of Minnesota.

Walker, A., Uphold, N., Richter, S., & Test, D. (2010). Review of literature of community-based instruction across grade levels. *Education and Training in Autism and Developmental Disabilities, 45*(2), 242–267.

Wadsworth, B. (1996). *Piaget's theory of cognitive and affective development: Foundations of constructivism* (5th ed.). New York, NY: Longman Publishing.

Wisconsin Department of Public Instruction. (n.d.). *Wisconsin model standards. Social studies standard C: Political science and citizenship performance standards—Grade 8.* Retrieved from http://standards.dpi.wi.gov/stn_ssc8

11

Creating Educational Adaptations, Accommodations, and Modifications

JULIE CAUSTON, ALICE UDVARI-SOLNER, AND KATE M. MACLEOD

CHAPTER OBJECTIVES

1. Become familiar with the key elements of adaptations, accommodations, and modifications used to support students in their school communities

2. Recognize the need for developing individualized adaptations for students with severe and multiple disabilities to support their inclusive academic involvement and membership in their school community

3. Learn the four-step process to developing and implementing adaptations for students with severe and multiple disabilities in general education settings

4. Discover how specific adaptations for Jack, a sixth-grade student, promote independence and interdependence and allow for meaningful participation with his classmates and with the academic curriculum

5. Understand 10 key considerations when creating adaptations for students with severe and multiple disabilities

KEY TERMS

- Accommodations
- Adaptations
- Assistive technology (AT)
- Discrepancy analysis
- Modifications

Portions of this chapter appearing in the third edition of this book were rewritten and updated by Alice Udvari-Solner and Julie Causton-Theoharis. Earlier versions contained critical elements that remain pertinent and were therefore preserved. We thank the original authors, Jennifer York-Barr, Beverly Rainforth, and Peggy Locke, for their significant contributions. This chapter is dedicated to Sam Theoharis, who was born during the writing of the first edition of this chapter and is now Jack's classmate.

Jack is an 11-year-old boy with physical and intellectual disabilities who requires extensive supports. He is involved in all social and academic aspects of sixth grade through adaptations, accommodations, and modifications. When you see Jack move through the hallways in between classes in his middle school, you hear many of the students acknowledge, "Hey Jack" and "What's up?" Jack has his iPad set up with phrases such as what's going on? great to see you! and hey! as he passes in his wheelchair. Several students slow down to wait for his response to their greeting, and many of his friends stop and wait for a fist bump.

Jack, like so many other students with severe and multiple disabilities, uses a variety of adaptations to support his academic involvement and membership in his school community. Accommodations and modifications are adaptations to instruction, the environment, or materials that help someone accomplish a task more effectively. *Accommodations* are changes in how a student gains access to information and demonstrates learning that do not substantially change the instructional level, content, or performance criteria. For example, Jack does not have the motor capabilities required for speech. Consequently, his iPad speaks his greetings as he moves through the hallways. In addition, he requires peer support for notetaking and tape recordings of lectures. In contrast, *modifications* are changes in what a student is expected to learn in order to provide meaningful and productive participation (Causton-Theoharis, 2009). For example, instead of writing an essay about the arc of plot and character development in the novel *Esperanza Rising* (Ryan, 2002), Jack may be expected to create a digital story highlighting character reactions to a series of episodes in the novel.

The need for adaptations is significantly intensified as Jack and other students with severe and multiple disabilities are more frequently included in general education environments. Research shows that the appropriate use of adaptations can increase student academic-related responses and student engagement (Lee, Wehmeyer, Soukup, & Palmer, 2010) and result in improved learning and fuller participation (Kurth & Keegan, 2012). Educators and other professionals therefore must be able to identify the need for, develop, and implement educational adaptations or AT devices.

This can initially seem like a formidable task to educators and others with little experience in creating adaptations for students with significant disabilities. A student's competence and intelligence sometimes may be called into question, and educators may wonder what the student is learning or gaining. This situation likely occurs because many students with significant disabilities often have difficulties with communicating and, consequently, educators are presented with unique challenges in assessing what is being learned. Presuming competence, however, is an important principle in educating students with severe and multiple disabilities and is based on Donnellan's (1984) initial idea of making the least dangerous assumption about a student's ability to learn (see Chapter 10). Biklen and Burke (2006) reiterated the importance of presuming competence, explaining that outside observers (e.g., therapists, teachers, parents) have a choice in how they see a child with disabilities. It is always better and far less dangerous to assume that students can learn than to expect that they cannot. It is important to recognize that no one can definitively know another person's thinking unless the other person (accurately) reveals it. Educators have been repeatedly surprised about what students can communicate, learn, share, and do when given the opportunity. This chapter presents a process to assist educators in developing and implementing adaptations to increase the participation of people with significant disabilities in school environments. The following sections provide examples of how this strategy was used to create adaptations for Jack, the middle school student introduced at the beginning of this chapter. The process for creating adaptations is applied to various aspects of Jack's educational programming. Jack's experiences illustrate how creative use of adaptations can increase meaningful participation, provide access to the Common Core State Standards (CCSS) (National Governors Association Center for Best Practices & Council of Chief State School Officers, 2010), and promote friendships in general education environments. This chapter highlights recommended practices and current ATs, provides reproducible templates and charts, and concludes with a discussion of considerations related to the effective use of adaptations.

PROCESS OF DEVELOPING INDIVIDUALIZED ADAPTATIONS

The four-step process for developing adaptations is grounded in an ecological approach and draws from foundational concepts formulated by researchers in the field (Baumgart et al., 1982; Brown et al., 1979, 1980; Brown, Shiraga, York, Zanella, & Rogan, 1984a, 1984b; Downing, 2010; Falvey, 1995; Ferguson & Baumgart, 1991; Piuma & Udvari-Solner, 1993a, 1993b; Udvari-Solner, 1995, 1996). The process provides a series of questions that guide observation and provide a framework for identifying student needs and developing adaptations (see Figure 11.1). They are designed to facilitate dialogue, problem solving, and decision making among team members, resulting in adaptations and support that promote active participation and skill development for students with disabilities. Research shows that this type of collaboration process among team members is essential for the successful inclusion of students with disabilities (Bauer, Iyer, Boon, & Fore, 2010; Carter, Prater, Jackson, & Marchant, 2009; Causton-Theoharis, 2009; Hernandez, 2013). Identifying the abilities, strengths, needs, and overarching educational goals of the student and the inclusive environments in which these goals can be achieved is the first step in the process. These identified educational goals and environments will serve as an essential guide for determining the student's needed accommodations, adaptations, and modifications. Gathering information about the student's abilities, strengths, and needs allows the educational team to develop a more complete student profile, which is essential when

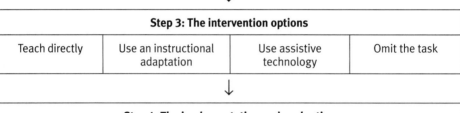

Step 1: The learner and environment
What are the student's strengths, abilities, needs, and priority goals?   What are the specific inclusive environments in which these goals can be achieved?

↓

Step 2: The discrepancy analysis
What are the required activities and skills in the environment?   How does the student perform in the environment?   What are the student's performance discrepancies, and what might be the source of these discrepancies?   What are the priority instructional goals for the student in the environment?

↓

Step 3: The intervention options			
Teach directly	Use an instructional adaptation	Use assistive technology	Omit the task

↓

Step 4: The implementation and evaluation
After use, how will the adaptation be changed, modified, or faded to advance student performance and increase independence?

Figure 11.1.   A four-step process for developing individualized adaptations. (*Source*: Udvari-Solner, Causton-Theoharis, & York-Barr [2004]).

determining strategies and supports for effective teaching. Determining the activities and skills necessary to participate in the environment and observing how the student engages in these activities and skills is the second step. This step provides the opportunity to identify and analyze the student's areas of difficulty, referred to as performance discrepancies, and hypothesize why these discrepancies exist. Understanding the potential intellectual, motor, sensory, and behavior characteristics attributed to performance discrepancies is essential for targeting a student's priority instructional goals and designing effective interventions (Piuma & Udvari-Solner, 1993b).

Educators can choose from four interventions to address performance discrepancies in the third step. One is to teach the student to perform the skill in the same way that a person without a disability would perform it. For example, a student who is unable to carry his or her science lab materials to the lab table might be taught to do so in a way identical to how his or her classmates without disabilities perform the skill. If a student is unlikely to learn essential intellectual, motor, or sensory requirements for performing a skill in a typical manner, then an adaptation is one way to accommodate the difficulties. Employing instructional adaptations that modify the requirements of the task is the second option for intervention. For example, the student might be taught to carry each lab item individually. The third option involves using adaptive materials or devices. For instance, a student carries lab items in a basket attached to his or her walker. The fourth option is to omit minor activities or skills if the student is already meeting his or her priority instructional goals and fully participating with peers.

Implementing and evaluating the intervention strategy is the final step of the process and encourages educators to provide systematic instruction and engage in ongoing evaluation and progress monitoring of performance (Piuma & Udvari-Solner, 1993b). Evaluations should emphasize whether the adaptation is increasing access to skills, peer interaction, and independence.

The following sections explain the actions to take when completing each of the four steps presented in Figure 11.1 and provide an example of the process at work as Jack gives a presentation about Mount Vesuvius in his sixth-grade physical systems of the environment (science) class.

Step 1: The Learner and the Environment

Educators begin to develop effective and appropriate adaptations by extensively learning about their students. Gathering information that results in a profile of the student's social and academic abilities, strengths, and learning concerns is an essential first step. These facts help establish a shared vision of the student's active involvement for the team and can reveal pertinent strategies for effective teaching (Causton & Tracy-Bronson, 2015; Udvari-Solner, Villa, & Thousand, 2002, 2005).

What Are the Student's Strengths, Abilities, Needs, and Priority Goals? Knowledge of the student's preferences and learning style, past instruction, and reliable physical and motor movements (especially for a student with severe and multiple disabilities) will affect the selection of adaptations. Information gathering and sharing must be collaborative and include the learner, the family, past and current teachers, peers, and others close to the student.

Jack's challenges or disabilities can be described as follows. Jack has significant and multiple disabilities that necessitate the use of a variety of supports and assistance. Jack has muscular dystrophy, which considerably limits his gross and fine motor abilities. He also has a metabolic disorder that causes him to have varying energy levels. He needs frequent breaks and snacks to give him the energy needed to function throughout each school day. He has a significant intellectual disability that affects his ability to respond to questions or engage in academic tasks. He does not use verbal speech but uses eye pointing or hand selecting to communicate choice. He also communicates through facial expressions and body movements. He requires a wheelchair for mobility and uses a nonelectric wheelchair because he is unable to drive it independently. Jack is able to move his arms and hands and grasp objects independently but has difficulty reaching for items. These abilities vary considerably day to day based on his physical status. Figure 11.2 provides a student profile of Jack and describes

Student Profile

Name: Jack Wyatt   **Grade:** 6   **School:** Pawnee Middle School
Age: 11   **Gender:** Male

General information Jack lives at home with his parents and his one brother. His sister is away at college. He has been included with his peers since kindergarten.	*Learning style* Jack benefits from visual and auditory directions. He works best with familiar people. He understands both verbal and visual information.
Strengths and interests Jack is very social and enthusiastic about learning. He loves to be surrounded by friends. He enjoys technology and is a Hoosier fan. He also is a fan of Bruno Mars and the Avett Brothers. He enjoys adaptive skiing.	*Academic information* Jack has not demonstrated an ability to decode. Therefore, the preferred mode of access is through listening. He does respond consistently to yes/no questions, and he has demonstrated the ability to recognize numbers.
Communication style Jack responds using eye gaze and hand selection for choices. He also communicates through facial expression and body movements, and he can select choices on his iPad.	*Behavioral information* We are not concerned about Jack's behavior. He is cooperative and patient. If he is unable to respond, then fatigue is typically the reason. We are working on getting Jack to express preferences and advocate for himself more fully.
Social information Jack works best with partners and in small groups. He has a circle of friends that meets weekly to eat lunch and plan social times. Jack has three friends that he likes to hang out with on the weekend and text often.	*Other information* He needs frequent breaks and snacks to help him maintain the energy required for learning.

Figure 11.2.   A positive student profile of Jack Wyatt.

his skills and abilities for the purposes of designing appropriate adaptations. Jack's parents and educational team identified the following educational priorities:

- Increasing self-initiated communication with peers, general educators, and the public, which includes expressing his preferences and needs, making requests, and responding to questions

- Increasing comprehension of vocabulary associated with instructional units/topics in sixth grade and synthesizing information into 5–10 big ideas for each curricular topic

- Increasing his access to and use of a computer-generated voice output device

- Reaching and grasping, assisting in movements guided by others, and moving his legs purposefully

- Using eye gaze to consistently select and make choices

Background information about the student and the student's priority educational goals should guide the next step of selecting relevant environments for instruction.

What Are the Specific Inclusive Environments in Which These Goals Can Be Achieved?   Selecting the environments in which the student's educational goals can be accomplished is the second phase of Step 1 in the process of developing adaptations. These environments should promote access to and participation in general education curriculum and instruction, a priority for a school-age student. In addition, home, community, and work environments for older students should be identified in which the students are functioning or will be expected to function in the future. Environments are determined individually for each student with inclusive age-appropriate criteria in mind.

Core sixth-grade classes (e.g., social studies, language arts, science), exploratories (e.g., art, physical education, music), and extracurricular clubs are critical environments for Jack. The mall, local restaurants, the neighborhood pool, and the YMCA are other environments of importance to Jack. The sixth-grade general education classroom will be selected as the inclusive environment of choice in the four-step process used to develop adaptations for Jack because it is where Jack's typically developing sixth-grade peers are educated, and it is the best location for learning the content. This decision is clearly supported under the least restrictive environment clause in the Individuals with Disabilities Education Improvement Act (IDEA) of 2004 (PL 108-446). In addition, it meets Jack's preferences and his family's desire that he be included in all academic subject areas and given access to standards-based curriculum.

Step 2: The Discrepancy Analysis

Important questions to address when determining a student's performance discrepancies are presented in the following subsections.

What Are the Required Activities and Skills in the Environment?   First, the expected activities and skills (referred to as the activity sequence in Figure 11.3) within the environment are identified. This outline of sequential skills and the assessment that follows has been referred to as a discrepancy analysis (Brown et al., 1984b; Downing, 2010; Falvey, 1995; Kurth, 2013). This sequence serves as a guide for assessing the performance of the target student. It is important to note, however, that there are multiple ways to accomplish any activity; there is not necessarily a right way, a wrong way, or a universal standard. The team should try to select the most logical and efficient method to carry out the task as the outline of skills is generated. An activity sequence required to complete a sixth-grade science project on Mount Vesuvius is detailed in the first column of Figure 11.3.

Discrepancy Analysis Report

Name: Jack Wyatt   **Class:** Physical systems of the environment   **Grade:** 6th
Activity: Mount Vesuvius research project

Activity sequence	Jack's activity sequence	Potential reasons for discrepancy	Intervention options
(What are the expected activities and skills in the environment?)	(How does the student perform in the environment?)	(What are the factors preventing a target student from performing the expected tasks?)	(What should the teacher do to support the student and mitigate the discrepancy?)
To begin the Mount Vesuvius project, students are asked to select partners.	Jack listens to the teacher's directions. He makes eye contact with a peer of his choice. He is able to power his wheelchair over to the peer without difficulty. Jack is unable to ask the student to be partners.	Student learning factors	*Assistive technology* Jack uses his switch to activate his iPad voice output app to ask a prerecorded message: do you want to be my partner?
Students read about Mount Vesuvius in a common text.	Jack is unable to read the text independently.	Student learning factors	*Instructional adaptation* Jack's partner reads the text aloud.
Students research additional information on Mount Vesuvius from at least three different sources.	Jack is unable to independently research additional sources on his iPad.	Student learning factors Physical, sensory, or motor factors	*Omit the task* Jack's partner will research additional information and jot down main ideas and supporting details.
Students create a PowerPoint that includes several main points about Mount Vesuvius and 9–12 supporting details and/or examples.	Jack is unable to verbally communicate main points or supporting details. Jack is unable to manipulate the iPad or computer to independently create the PowerPoint.	Student learning factors Physical, sensory, or motor factors	*Instructional adaptation* Give Jack's partner instruction about asking Jack for input using yes/no prompts. *Instructional adaptation* Jack's partner reads suggested main points aloud and asks for Jack's preference using yes or no prompts. *Assistive technology* Jack eye-points yes or no using the Proloquo2Go app on his iPad to communicate his selections.

(continued)

Figure 11.3.   A discrepancy analysis of a research project and presentation in a general education science class.

Figure 11.3. *(continued)*

Students choose visual elements to include in their PowerPoint presentation.	Jack is unable to Google images independently. Jack is unable to verbally communicate his choices.	Student learning factors Physical, sensory, or motor factors	*Assistive technology* Jack eye-points yes or no using the Proloquo2Go app on his iPad to communicate his selections.
Students socialize during partner work.	Jack is unable to respond to spontaneous conversation with his partner.	Student learning factors	*Instructional adaptation* Give Jack's partner instruction about asking Jack yes/no questions about familiar topics. *Assistive technology* Jack eye-points yes or no using the Proloquo2Go app on his iPad to communicate his selections Jack activates prerecorded conversational questions on his iPad using his switch.
Students present PowerPoint to the class.	Jack is able to sit next to his partner in the front of the class. Jack is unable to present information verbally or request questions from the class. Jack is unable to manipulate the computer to change the PowerPoint slides.	Student learning factors Physical, sensory, or motor factors	*Instructional adaptation* Give peers some instruction on how to record short messages on Jack's iPad voice output app. *Assistive technology* Jack activates his switch to 1) change PowerPoint slides projected on the SmartBoard and 2) activate recorded messages on his iPad to present information and request questions.
For homework, students create a labeled diagram of Mount Vesuvius using 5–10 vocabulary words.	Jack is unable to independently illustrate or label a diagram.	Student learning factors Physical, sensory, or motor factors	Omit the task

How Does the Student Perform in the Environment? Next, the team as-
sesses how the student with disabilities performs the activity sequence. This
step requires observing the student in the specific environment and recording
his or her step-by-step performance. It is important to record both what the
student is able to do and what the student is not able to do. Assessment information for Jack's performance in his science class during the Mount Vesuvius
project activity sequence is provided in the second column of Figure 11.3. Jack
is able to listen to the teacher's directions, establish eye contact with a peer
he wants to work with, and power his wheelchair over to the peer. During
the presentation, Jack is able to sit next to his partner in the front of the class
and hear the cue to begin. His performance of all other skills required peer or
teacher assistance.

Some teachers, paraprofessionals, and other specialists unfortunately
might stop problem solving once they recognize that Jack is able to perform
such a limited number of skills. Educators often decide that the majority of the
activity will be done for the student, resulting in the student passively observing others or being physically manipulated through an experience. Therefore,
the following guiding questions in the process are intended to stimulate more
complex problem solving. If a student cannot complete an activity or skill in
the sequence, then team members must ask why in order to better develop
systems that will teach, compensate for, or circumvent unsuccessful aspects
of performance. For adaptations to be successful, team members must believe
that all students can learn and the team must share the responsibility for student success (Causton & Tracy-Bronson, 2015, Choate, 2004; Kurth & Keegan,
2012).

***What Are the Student's Performance Discrepancies and What Might Be the
Source of These Discrepancies?*** After the assessment is conducted in the actual environment, student performance discrepancies or problem areas are
identified in relation to the expected activities or skills (i.e., information from
Column 2 is compared with the sequence in Column 1 in Figure 11.3). In this
way, specific activities and skills in which the student requires instruction or
intervention can be identified. The activities and skills for which Jack required
assistance are recorded in Column 2 of Figure 11.3. Jack's key areas of difficulty include the ability to read independently, make independent selections
of important information about Mount Vesuvius to include in his presentation,
communicate with his partner about his decisions for their presentation, manipulate the computer/iPad to create the presentation, and verbally present information or request questions from the class.

Educators must question why these performance discrepancies exist.
Piuma and Udvari-Solner found that professionals who were skilled at developing adaptations "engaged in a complex discourse of discriminating questions, in a sense theorizing, making educated guesses about the source of the
discrepancy" (1993b, p. 16). These educators used their hunches to engage in a
process of elimination and ultimately acted on educated guesses to determine

the origin of the discrepancy. Five categories were identified that could lead to the systematic selection of adaptations:

1. *Student learning factors* pertain to the unique learning characteristics, rate of skill acquisition, preferences, and established patterns of behavior of the student.

2. *Instructional factors* refer to the selection; pacing; and delivery of prompts, cues, and teaching strategies used during the activity.

3. *Physical, sensory, or motor factors* include aspects that relate to the student's physical status, fine and gross motor abilities, vision, hearing, information processing, and mobility.

4. *Motivation factors* are concerned with the instructional elements that affect the student's behavior; what is reinforcing; or whether the student is expressing lack of interest, frustration, boredom, or fear.

5. *Environmental factors* include the general physical conditions of the environment, the atmosphere, and organization or use of materials.

Table 11.1 provides an adapted list of questions suggested by Piuma and Udvari-Solner (1993b) that educators should consider to understand the source of the discrepancy. A best guess as to the reason for the discrepancy can be proposed after considering these questions. One or more factors often will surface that will direct the nature of the intervention(s). The third column in Figure 11.3 shows the potential reasons for Jack's discrepancies. In his case, answers to these guiding questions pointed to learning factors and physical/motor issues.

What Are the Priority Instructional Goals for the Student in the Environment? Educators can analyze the identified discrepancies and write instructional goals. Information gathered during the performance discrepancy assessment allows the team to further refine the broad educational goals created in the first step of this process. This information is also helpful in connecting priority goals to standards-based curriculum. When selecting priorities, team members typically consider enhancing participation in current and future integrated environments, increasing inclusion and interactions with peers, providing the student frequent and multiple opportunities to practice skills across environments and activities, and honoring the student's or family's preferences for maintaining health and vitality (Janney & Snell, 2013; Rainforth & York-Barr, 1997).

Jack's assessment indicated several instructional priorities, including 1) having a means to engage with the reading, 2) communicating his preferences about what to include in the presentation, 3) participating in the creation of the PowerPoint, 4) presenting to the class with a partner, and 5) communicating with classmates in class. Jack's broad communication and physical/motor goals, previously identified in Step 1, are now embedded within and more specific to the science classroom environment.

Table 11.1. Sample questions to determine reasons for performance discrepancies related to various factors

Factor affecting performance	Guiding questions
Student learning factors	Has the student been observed performing the same or similar activity sequence in other contexts (e.g., at home, in the community, in the classroom)?
	Does past experience with learning rate, style, and abilities indicate that it is feasible for the student to learn the task as expected?
	Do the student's unique learning characteristics preclude him or her from engaging in specific steps (e.g., the student has a very brief short-term memory and is unable to remember more than one direction at a time)?
Instructional factors	Has the instructional sequence been communicated to the student in ways that match his or her primary modalities (e.g., picture sequence, written or verbal directions)?
	Will the student benefit from more intensive instruction?
	Does the instructional sequence need to be modified (e.g., Are there too many steps or too few? Do the steps need to be rearranged?)?
	Is the pacing of instruction correct for the student (e.g., Does the student need more time between steps?)?
	Is the level and type of teacher assistance correct?
Physical, sensory, or motor factors	If the activity requires the use of specific physical movements, does the student have the necessary fine or gross motor movements to complete the task?
	If the student has the necessary basic motor movements and responses, but they are weak, without intention, or disorganized, does the student have the potential to build and strengthen these responses through instruction, practice, and/or therapy services?
	What are the student's preferred movements? Is it possible to select a way to do the activity that builds on these movements?
	What is the student's endurance level? Can the endurance be increased through practice, position, or better physical arrangements (e.g., standing versus sitting)?
	Does the student experience any sensory difficulties? Does the nature of these difficulties preclude the student from performing any parts of the task? Specifically, does the task have inherent tactile, visual, or auditory cues that must be followed?
Motivation factors	Is the environment and activity motivating? If not, is there another location that would be more motivating?
	Would the student be more motivated by working with a peer than with the selected instructor?
	Does the student fall asleep during the task? Is the sleepiness caused by the environment, avoidance, or physical/health reasons?
	Are inappropriate behaviors interfering with performance or required skills (e.g., falling asleep, self-stimulation)?
	Have proactive behavioral strategies been employed within the context of the environment and task?
	Does the student have opportunities to express preferences and choices through the work day, and are communication attempts (verbal and nonverbal) acknowledged by instructor or peers?
Environmental factors	Does the student have easy access to the environment and necessary materials?
	Is the immediate work area too confining or cluttered for the student to perform?
	If the student uses a wheelchair and needs to be taken out of the chair during instruction, is there a location where this can be done without bringing undue attention, or can alternative seating be arranged for continued participation in the activity?
	Is the lighting sufficient?
	Is the noise level of the environment tolerated or agreeable to the student?

Source: Piuma & Udvari-Solner (1993b).

Step 3: Four Intervention Options

Next, team members must decide how the discrepancies and the priority skills will be addressed. Teams must use their knowledge of the student, their inferences as to the cause of the discrepancy, and their collective expertise to select from four intervention options. The decision is then made whether to teach the skill directly (i.e., the way the skill is typically expected to be performed), employ an instructional adaptation, use AT that will enable greater and more independent participation, or omit a minor skill or activity if the student fully participates with peers and has already met his or her priority goals.

Teach Directly   The decision to teach directly is made only when it is feasible for the student to learn and perform the skill as would a peer without a disability. Given Jack's performance discrepancies in science class, the team decided his needs would be best addressed through the use of instructional adaptations and AT. The following sections describe these adaptations and provide examples specific to Jack. The fourth column in Figure 11.3 summarizes the interventions determined for Jack.

Instructional Adaptations   Four types of instructional adaptations are considered when teaching skills to students with significant and multiple disabilities: 1) modify skills or activities; 2) modify the physical environment; 3) modify rules, policies, or procedures; and 4) provide personal assistance. These forms of adaptation give educators the option to alter aspects of instruction, conditions in the environment, or the way in which people exchange support.

Modify Skills or Activities   This type of adaptation involves changing typical skill sequences or the way the task is completed. Ways of learning and performance expectations may be tweaked, revised or completely changed. Jack cannot independently read the information on Mount Vesuvius or verbally make his choices about what important information to include in the presentation. Rather than having Jack read, his peer partner can read the information aloud and jot down main points. The peer can be given instruction on how to pose yes/no questions to Jack and use this prompt to assist him in selecting key points to be included in their presentation. The need for Jack to verbally state his choice is eliminated and replaced with another pertinent communication skill. Along a similar vein, peers could be taught to read Jack's eye pointing or facial expressions so that he could indicate his preferences about what images, colors, or graphics to use in the creation of his group's PowerPoint presentation.

Another instructional adaptation that modifies the skills required in completing a task is employed during Jack's conversation with his peer partner. While working on in-class projects, partners typically have a spontaneous conversation in which they ask and answer a jumble of open-ended questions. Jack's communication difficulties do not allow him to express complex responses on the spot. Consequently, the skills required are modified by teaching his peers to ask a range of yes/no questions about familiar topics. Jack can then affirm or negate these questions with facial expressions or eye-point to the yes/ no options on his Proloquo2Go iPad app.

In order to participate in the presentation portion of the activity, Jack's partner was easily taught to program Jack's iPad with the information Jack selected to share using the simple voice output app. The specific use of AT is discussed in greater detail in the AT section.

Modify the Physical Environment   Making adjustments to the physical surroundings or environmental conditions is the second type of instructional adaptation. Accommodations that facilitate accessibility, such as creating curb cuts, ramping entryways to buildings, rearranging furniture to create space for maneuvering a wheelchair, and modifying public transportation vehicles with lifts are the most common examples.

Environmental modifications also relate to conditions such as lighting, noise level, visual and auditory input, and location of materials. Elements of the environment may need to be consciously engineered for students who experience sensory impairments, physical disabilities, information processing difficulties, or communication difficulties. Accommodations in this category are required by the Americans with Disabilities Amendments Act (ADA) of 2008 (PL 110-325).

Jack did not face environmental barriers in the science classroom. There was sufficient room to maneuver his wheelchair to work with a partner and to present at the front of the classroom. Yet, moving a futon couch into the student commons area—a place used by all students to gather and socialize during free periods—is an example of a significant environmental adaptation for Jack. The futon offered a location for Jack to get out of his wheelchair and sit or recline in a relaxed position. This age-appropriate environment offered Jack an alternative to an isolated physical therapy room when he needed breaks from his wheelchair.

Modify Rules, Policies, or Procedures   Changing the usual patterns, practices, or customs of a particular environment is the third type of instructional adaptation. The informal or formal guidelines for typical conduct are relaxed or somehow altered. For example, an implicit rule in most high school classrooms is that students sit at their desks while listening to a lecture or while completing an assignment. Yet, consider a student with autism who finds it impossible to sit for any length of time. In response, the typical rules of conduct could be loosened so that the student would be allowed to move around the classroom during lecture and write standing up using a music stand. These types of modified rules and policies can benefit all students, providing environments where learning continues for all while also accounting for multiple intelligences and needs (Gardner, 1999).

"No food or drink" is a general rule in Jack's sixth-grade classes; however, Jack's metabolic condition necessitates that he have periodic snack and juice breaks to boost his blood sugar. Jack is allowed to eat and drink while still engaging in instruction, rather than leaving the class and fragmenting his understanding of the curriculum. It is important to consider the explicit and implicit social rules that have been constructed in all environments and determine if any elements require change to promote a better student/environmental match.

Provide Personal Assistance Providing personal assistance to the student is a fourth instructional adaptation. Promoting positive interdependence among classmates is a central tenet in inclusive education. Reciprocal (i.e., mutually beneficial) social and academic interactions must be fostered between students with and without disabilities. As a student with disabilities enters the adult world, school relationships translate to connections with employers and co-workers who typically do not have disabilities. These individuals are the natural support systems in school and community environments and can provide unobtrusive personal assistance to students and adults with disabilities. Personal assistance may be needed on a temporary or ongoing basis in order for some students to learn skills that they are unlikely to learn using direct instruction or other adaptations. For example, a student who has been unsuccessful learning to independently move between high school classes may require the assistance of a peer on a long-term basis. Peers in Jack's science class were easily taught how to include Jack in selecting key points for their presentation on Mount Vesuvius, how to interpret his eye-point responses or facial expressions, and how to program his iPad so that Jack could utilize simple voice output during the presentation to share information and request questions from the class. The team should clarify the roles of students with and without disabilities when considering the use of personal assistance so that excessive or inappropriate help does not occur.

Use Assistive Technology Teaching directly or using instructional adaptations may be insufficient during the problem-solving process to address a student's performance discrepancies. Using AT, which is the third intervention option, may be necessary. This category includes portable objects, equipment, tangible devices, or instructional materials individually designed for the student. These types of adaptations, either commercial or teacher made, can help students compensate for intellectual or physical challenges and encourage students with significant disabilities to more effectively participate in activities (Lancioni, Sigafoos, O'Reilly, & Singh, 2012; Langone, Malone, & Kinsley, 1999; Mistrett, Lane, & Ruffino, 2005).

Two categories of AT are particularly useful for students with significant disabilities. Low-tech AT includes picture boards, communication boards, and switches. High-tech AT includes computers, tablets, touchscreens, alternative keyboards, and augmentative and alternative communication (AAC). AAC may be the only way for some students to talk and interact with their typically developing peers and therefore may be the most important adaptations for students with significant communication disabilities. Box 11.1 provides a list of popular and effective AT to help students with significant disabilities gain access to information and achieve goals. In addition, Figure 11.4 provides a checklist that the collaborative team can use to consider and select adaptations for students with severe and multiple disabilities.

Box 11.1. Assistive Technology

Picture communicators can be electronic boards and buttons comprised of pictures in which each button verbally communicates a preprogrammed message.

iPads have incredible assistive technology (AT) capabilities and can be accessed on their own or with a switch. Several iPad applications that benefit students with severe and multiple disabilities include, but are not limited to, simple voice output, communications and feature matching, visual schedules, self-regulation and organization skills, and audio recordings. Several useful iPad app examples follow:

- *Symbol Support*—adds symbols or speech to text to help develop vocabulary and word recognition and improve reading comprehension. Also great for teaching social stories and step-by-step directions.

- *Proloquo2go*—symbol-supported communication that allows the student to speak by tapping buttons with words or phrases. An excellent way to support a student who has difficulty with verbal communication.

- *Me Moves*—plays music and provides changing geometric shapes for the student to trace with his or her fingers. Assists with self-regulation, focus, and calming.

- *iThoughts*—a mind-mapping visual organizer that can assist with understanding classroom concepts, brainstorming, and goal planning.

Switches are beneficial for students with limited body movement. Switches are physically activated devices that connect the student with a piece of electronic AT. An actual switch usually allows the student to look at pictures, words, and so forth until the one he or she wants is found. Selecting the desired piece of data, such as Jack's selection of recorded messages on his iPad, is another way to use the switch.

Alternative keyboards simplify a keyboard for students with severe disabilities who may have difficulty remembering order of keys or are overwhelmed by the amount of keys. Alternative keyboards can be useful to assist students with severe disabilities when using the computer and accessing the Internet.

Hotkey overlays allow students with disabilities to enter numbers, words, and phrases by pressing one key on the keyboard.

Touchscreens are used by students with severe disabilities to help them use and gain access to information on computers. Touchscreens can either be accessible directly on the monitor of the computer device or can be a supplementary device, such as an iPad. They can be assigned to work with pressure or by simply sensing a student's finger on the screen.

General computer/mobile access
❏ Keyboard using accessibility options
❏ Word prediction
❏ Hotkeys/shortcuts
❏ Text to speech
❏ Voice recognition software
❏ Keyguard
❏ Arm support
❏ Track ball/track pad/joystick with on-screen keyboard
❏ Alternate keyboard
❏ Mouth stick/head mouse with on-screen keyboard
❏ Switch
❏ Other:

Communication
❏ Communication board/book with pictures/objects/letters/words
❏ Eye gaze board/frame
❏ Simple voice output device (e.g., iPad, BIGmack, Cheap Talk, PictureFrame)
❏ Voice output device w/icon sequencing (e.g., SymbolSupport, AlphaTalker II)
❏ Voice output device with dynamic display (Speaking Dynamically with laptop computer)
❏ Device with speech synthesis for typing (e.g., Cannon Communicator)
❏ Other:

Writing
❏ Word cards/word book/word wall
❏ Pocket dictionary/thesaurus
❏ Writing templates
❏ Electronic/talking electronic dictionary/thesaurus/spell checker
❏ Word processing with spell checker/grammar checker
❏ Talking word processing
❏ Abbreviation/expansion
❏ Word processing with writing supports
❏ Multimedia software
❏ Voice recognition software
❏ Other:

Reading, studying, and math
Reading
❏ Standard text
❏ Predictable books
❏ Changes in text size, spacing, color, background color
❏ Book adapted for page turning (e.g. page fluffers, three-ring binder)
❏ Use of pictures/symbols with text
❏ Talking electronic device/software
❏ Single-word scanners
❏ Scanner w/optical character recognition (OCR) and text-to-speech software
❏ Software to read web sites and e-mails
❏ Other:

(continued)

Figure 11.4. Assistive technology checklist the collaborative team can use to consider and select adaptations for students with severe and multiple disabilities. The checklist can be included in the student's individualized education program. (From Gierach, J.E. [Ed.] [2009]. *Assessing students' needs for assistive technology (ASNAT): A Resource Manual for School District Teams* [5th ed.]. WI: IDEA Discretionary Grant number 9906-23. AT Checklist. Retrieved 3/11/2016 from http://www.wati. org/content/supports/free/pdf/ASNAT5thEditionJun09.pdf; http://www.wati.org; reprinted by permission.

Figure 11.4. *(continued)*

Learning/studying
❑ Print or picture schedule
❑ Low-tech aids to find materials (e.g., index tabs, color-coded folders)
❑ Highlight text (e.g., markers, highlight tape, ruler)
❑ Recorded material (e.g., books on tape, taped lectures with number coded index)
❑ Voice output reminders for assignments, steps of task, and so forth
❑ Electronic organizers
❑ Pagers/electronic reminders
❑ Single-word scanners
❑ Handheld scanners
❑ Software for concept development/manipulation of objects—may use alternate input
   device (e.g., switch)
❑ Touch window
❑ Software for organization of ideas and studying
❑ Palm computers
❑ Other:

Math
❑ Abacus/math line
❑ Enlarged math worksheets
❑ Low-tech alternatives for answering
❑ Math smart chart
❑ Visual manipulatives
❑ Money calculator and coinulator
❑ Tactile/voice output measuring devices
❑ Talking watches/clocks
❑ Calculator/calculator with printout
❑ Calculator with large keys and/or large display
❑ Talking calculator
❑ Calculator with special features (e.g., fraction translation)
❑ On-screen/scanning calculator
❑ Alternative keyboard
❑ Software with cuing for math computation (may use adapted input methods)
❑ Voice recognition software

Recreation and leisure
❑ Toys adapted with Velcro, magnets, handles, etc.
❑ Toys adapted for single switch operation
❑ Adaptive sporting equipment (e.g. lighted or beeping ball)
❑ Universal cuff/strap to hold crayons, markers, etc.
❑ Modified utensils (e.g. rubber stamps, brushes, etc.) arm support for drawing/painting
❑ Electronic aids to control/operate computers/TV/DVD player, etc.
❑ Software
❑ Completion of art activities
❑ Games on the computer/mobile device
❑ Other:

Activities of daily living
❑ Nonslip materials to hold things in place
❑ Universal cuff/strap to hold items in hand
❑ Color-coded items for easier locating and identifying

(continued)

Figure 11.4. *(continued)*

❏ Adaptive eating utensils (e.g., foam handles, deep sides)
❏ Adaptive drinking devices (e.g., cup with cut-out rim)
❏ Adaptive dressing equipment (e.g., button hook, elastic shoelaces, velcro instead of buttons)
❏ Adaptive devices for hygiene (e.g., adapted toothbrush, raised toilet seat)
❏ Adaptive bathing devices
❏ Adaptive equipment for cooking
❏ Other:

Mobility
❏ Walker
❏ Grab bars and rails
❏ Manual wheelchair including sports chair
❏ Powered mobility toy (e.g., Cooper Car, GoBot)
❏ Powered scooter or cart
❏ Powered wheelchair with joystick or other control
❏ Adapted vehicle for driving
❏ Other:

Positioning and seating
❏ Nonslip surface on chair to prevent slipping (e.g., Dycem)
❏ Bolster, rolled towel, blocks for feet
❏ Adapted/alternate chair, sidelyer, stander
❏ Custom fitted wheelchair or insert
❏ Other:

Vision
❏ Eyeglasses
❏ Optical aids
❏ Large-print materials
❏ Auditory materials
❏ Dictation software (voice input)
❏ CCTV (closed circuit television)
❏ Screen magnifier (mounted over screen)
❏ Screen magnification software
❏ Screen color contrast
❏ Screen reader, text reader
❏ Braille notetaker
❏ Braille translation software
❏ Braille embosser
❏ Enlarged or braille/tactile labels for keyboard
❏ Alternate keyboard
❏ Other:

Hearing
❏ Pen and paper
❏ Computer/portable word processor
❏ TDD for telephone access with or without relay
❏ Signaling device (e.g., flashing light, vibrating pager)
❏ Closed captioning
❏ Real-time captioning

(continued)

Figure 11.4. *(continued)*

❏ Computer-aided notetaking
❏ Screen flash for alert signals on computer
❏ Telephone amplifier
❏ Personal amplification system/hearing aid
❏ FM or loop system
❏ Infrared system
❏ Other:

Control of the environment
❏ Light switch extension
❏ Use of interface and switch to activate electronic appliances or battery-operated devices (e.g., radio, fan, blender)
❏ Radio/ultrasound to remotely control appliances
❏ Use of electronic aid to control environment in connection with an augmentative and alternative communication device
❏ Other:

Comments:

Jack's iPad interfaced to his switch was the most important AT for the science environment. He was able to use his iPad voice output app to ask a peer to be his partner, socialize and present information to the class, and request questions after the presentation. Multiple messages totaling 75 seconds in length were programmed by a peer partner Jack selected and recorded in a young man's voice. These messages included social comments or questions he could activate during in-class work time, such as, "Did you have a good weekend?" or "I agree!" Jack also worked on one of his broad priority goals—increasing self-initiated communication with peers—by using his switch and iPad to initiate conversation rather than waiting for his partner to pose a yes/no question.

After Jack and his partner had created their presentation, his partner also programmed the information Jack wanted to share with the class into the iPad. Sequentially, Jack could use his switch to communicate his part of the presentation and ask the class, "Do you have any questions?"

Omit Minor Skill or Activity   The decision to omit a minor skill or activity is made only if the student continues to fully participate and has already met or continues to work toward his or her priority goals. For example, Jack used his iPad in math to view the electronic version of the class math modules. His peers were expected to use a standard algorithm to divide multidigit numbers, but Jack's team decided they would omit this skill and he would instead use his adapted calculator on the iPad, which speaks the operations aloud to him in order to perform the operations. Jack therefore worked toward the CCSS of fluently computing with multidigit numbers as well as his priority goal of increasing his use of a computer-generated voice output device.

Step 4: Implementation and Evaluation

Direct instruction is necessary and setting meaningful goals is essential whether teaching skills directly or using instructional or device adaptations. Use of an adaptive device serves only to simplify the task or make the task accessible—it does not teach the student. In fact, some have criticized the common practice of substituting adaptive devices for skill development, which sometimes causes passive involvement (Ferguson & Baumgart, 1991). Therefore, instructional programs that delineate systematic cuing and fading strategies should be designed, implemented, and evaluated. Systematic instruction programs provide the entire team with a plan for exactly what to do when teaching a particular skill, what type of prompting to use (e.g., gestural, verbal, model, physical), and a time line to follow for when and how to fade out these prompts so the student can independently complete the skill or task (Browder, 2001; Westling & Fox, 2009). For example, when Jack learned to respond to yes/no questions using the app Proloquo2Go, his team utilized specific verbal and gestural prompts to teach him to eye-point. They then taught Jack's peers to use these same prompts to facilitate his interdependence with peers. They monitored his progress and created a plan to fade the frequency of these peer prompts with the ultimate goal that Jack will no longer require a peer prompt to use eye-point to express his preferences.

Evaluation criteria for determining the effectiveness of adaptive devices should determine whether the adaptation 1) performs its intended functions, 2) is integrated into the instructional sequence, 3) is accompanied by sufficient instruction to learn the adaptation, 4) facilitates independence or interdependence with same-age peers, 5) results in the least intrusive assistance, 6) is attractive and safe, 7) fits in the specific context, 8) results in acceptable rate and quality of performance, and 9) does not interfere with interactions.

A DAY OF ADAPTATIONS FOR JACK

Jack spends his entire day with his peers without disabilities in general education environments, and multiple forms of adaptations support him during each sixth-grade class period. Several examples are provided to demonstrate how these adaptations promote independence and interdependence and allow Jack meaningful participation with his classmates and with the academic curriculum. Because students like Jack are increasingly expected to gain access to and make progress in the general education curriculum (Browder & Spooner, 2006; Vaughn & Swanson, 2015; Wehmeyer, 2006), our examples for developing and implementing adaptations for Jack will also address CCSS (National Governors Association Center for Best Practices & Council of Chief State School Officers, 2010).

Social Studies

A 15-minute student-led activity opens Jack's sixth-grade social studies class daily. Individuals or pairs of students are assigned to present a current news event from written or electronic media sources. The student(s) presenting the current event must read the article and provide a three-point summary of the primary content. This synopsis then launches an open discussion among class members. Jack uses some of the same instructional adaptations and high-tech devices in this school environment as those identified in his science class. Jack and a partner prepare for their presentation of a current event in the following ways. Jack's partner reads the article aloud while periodically jotting down main points. The peer then poses yes/no questions to Jack to select the key points to be included in their summary. Three to four statements are recorded on his iPad so that Jack can lead the presentation of the summary. His partner has also selected several points to communicate. Class members are then free to react to the topic, and an informal discussion takes place facilitated by the social studies teacher. When Jack is expected to present alone, the same preparation sequence occurs the night before class at home with his parents. This activity allows Jack to meaningfully engage with his peers and adhere to the sixth-grade CCSS for history and social studies requiring that students "determine the central ideas or information of a primary or secondary source" (National Governors Association Center

A   B

Figure 11.5. Examples of adapted devices used by Jack in sixth-grade general education classes: a) Big Red Switch; b) NEW Blue2™ Switch. Images © AbleNet, Inc. (2016). Reprinted by permission. All rights reserved

for Best Practices & Council of Chief State School Officers, 2010). Examples of the two assistive technology switches that Jack uses are depicted in Figure 11.5.

Language Arts

Jack's language arts class is reading the novel *The Hunger Games* (Collins, 2008) and using social media (e.g., Twitter, Facebook, Pinterest) as a platform to engage with the text. Jack reads an entirely adapted version of the story online, which uses Mayer-Johnson picture symbols paired with adapted text to tell the story.

Students work in pairs for this activity and are given the option to post tweets, create a Facebook page, or build a Pinterest board to share a particular character's thoughts and feelings as the story progresses. Jack and his partner have chosen to create a Pinterest board. After each chapter, they brainstorm new images and captions that represent their chosen character's feelings and thoughts. Jack always initiates the partnered work by activating a prerecorded message on his iPad, let's get started! His partner jots down ideas about their character and then reads each aloud, pausing to allow Jack to provide a yes or no facial response or eye-point a yes/no response on his iPad. Once they decide on their images, they work together to Google the best versions and write brief captions for these images before uploading them to their character's Pinterest board.

This activity allows Jack to meaningfully interact with the reading process and his peers, and it also directly addresses the ELA RL6.3 common core standard "Describe how a particular story's or drama's plot unfolds in a series of episodes as well as how the characters respond or change as the plot moves toward a resolution" (National Governors Association Center for Best Practices & Council of Chief State School Officers, 2010).

Math

The publisher of the math series provided an electronic version of the math modules that can be viewed on Jack's iPad. All of the assignments are then easily modified. Most of the changes require reducing the number of practice problems and allowing multiple-choice options with a scrolling choice format. Jack uses the adapted calculator on the iPad, which speaks its operations. After figuring out the problem, Jack uses his switch to select the correct answer.

Choir

Jack is in the sixth-grade choir with his peers without disabilities. This choir performs quarterly for the entire school and one evening for parents. They also sing for various community organizations around the city. Much time is spent in class preparing for such performances. One of Jack's many roles in the choir class involves helping the choir review and assess their performance in preparation for various presentations. Jack's switch is interfaced with his iPad, and his iPad is connected to speakers. Jack is situated with a peer in the front of the class. The students watch him to determine when to begin singing. He then records the entire musical piece on the Voice Recorder app and operates his switch again to play the song back for the choir to hear. Students listen to their performance and fill out a card for the purposes of assessing their sound. The students determine the musical aspects of the song that need improvement (e.g., diction, pitch, rhythmic accuracy, blend, dynamics). Students work to perfect their sound, and this activity is repeated for each musical piece. Jack is not a passive member during this activity; instead, he is a central participant responsible for facilitating the rehearsal.

Art

Students are learning about 20th-century abstract painters and are assigned to small groups to create a mural in the tradition of a famous artist such as Klee, Miro, or Kandinsky. The painter Jackson Pollock served as the inspiration for Jack's group. Equipped with quarts of paint, paint balls, and paint guns, the group was ready to create. Jack was fitted with a light pointer that could be attached to a hat on his head, wrist, or foot. Jack was one of the group's designers and directed the location of the paint splashes and paint bombs with the light streaks or pinpoints created by his volitional movements.

Physical Education

Automatic ball pitchers are available at most discount stores for a reasonable cost. These devices are battery powered and switch operated and discharge balls for slow-pitch games. Jack consistently acted as the pitcher during games and batting practice during physical education. The built-in switch of the pitching device was replaced with a larger microswitch called the Big Red, available through AbleNet. The switch was mounted in various locations so that Jack could activate it with his head, hands, or feet, encouraging him to use more active physical movements. Figure 11.5a shows the Big Red switch.

10 THINGS TO REMEMBER WHEN CONSIDERING ADAPTATIONS

Keep the following key considerations in mind when developing and implementing adaptations for students with severe and multiple disabilities.

1. *Teach the skill:* Is an adaptation necessary at all? If a student can learn to engage in an activity without using an adaptation, then the student should be taught to directly engage in that activity.

2. *Consider student strengths:* Focus on what the student can do and what you would like the student to achieve. Always presume competence and hold high expectations for the student.

3. *Determine student preference:* Student preference is an essential consideration for increasing successful implementation of adaptations (Foley & Ferri, 2012; Sax, 2001). Consider what the student enjoys or finds interesting. Would a particular adaptation allow a student to engage in those activities or preferences? Would a particular adaptation allow the student to participate in activities highly valued by family members or peers?

4. *Utilize family input:* Parents and families can offer positive and unique views about their child's skills, strengths, and talents. Teams should regularly meet with families to problem-solve and create effective adaptations and education plans. In addition, families of students without disabilities can assist their children in learning effective ways of interacting and communicating with students with significant disabilities. For example, families can teach their child to pose yes/no questions or record messages on an iPad.

5. *Create adaptations:* Be creative! There are no right or wrong ways to create adaptations, but it is important to determine who is responsible for creating the adaptation and how and when all the team members will learn how to implement and evaluate the adaptation. Keep in mind that simple is often better. Complex adaptations have a greater likelihood of breakdown and abandonment, which can lead to delays in teaching students the skills that will enhance their participation in school, home, and community environments.

6. *Increase active participation:* Adaptations should increase a student's participation in an activity, minimize adult assistance, and increase a student's opportunity to interact with classmates. Adults assigned to support students in general education classrooms sometimes unintentionally inhibit interactions between the student and peers or even between the student and the classroom teacher (Causton-Theoharis, 2009; Causton-Theoharis & Malmgren, 2005; Giangreco, Broer, & Edelman, 1999; Giangreco & Doyle, 2002).

7. *Consider longevity of use:* Consider whether the adaptation will be used in future as well as current environments and whether it will remain age

appropriate. For example, programming Jack's iPad with conversational messages likely will benefit him in school and community settings for years. The team must also be sure to regularly reevaluate the iPad messages, however, so that they remain age appropriate and on trend.

8. *Teach adaptation:* It is important to utilize systematic instruction when teaching students to learn appropriate use of adaptations (Downing, 2008; Snell & Brown, 2006; Westling & Fox, 2009). For example, Jack was not simply handed an iPad when he was learning to communicate his preferences using yes/no options on Proloquo2Go. It was necessary to directly teach him to eye-point and activate different apps using his switch.

9. *Use peer support:* Utilizing peers is one of the best ways to support students with disabilities. Peers can be partners, tutors, role models, and friends. They can best assist students with disabilities to develop age-appropriate social-communication skills as well as academic skills (Carter & Kennedy, 2006; Downing & Peckham-Hardin, 2007). In addition, everyone benefits when peers support peers. For example, when a partner supported Jack during the Mount Vesuvius science project, she was learning the valuable skills of summarizing information, restating questions in a yes/no fashion, communicating with someone who communicates differently than she does, and learning the basics of how to support someone with dignity.

10. *Evaluate adaptation:* Adaptations must be modified, replaced, or eliminated based on changes in student abilities and/or task requirements. A first attempt at an adaptation is often not the perfect match to address a performance discrepancy. It is necessary to continuously monitor and document whether the adaptation is increasing access to skills, peer interaction, and independence.

CONCLUSION

As it becomes more common for students with severe and multiple disabilities to take their rightful place in schools, communities, and recreation alongside their peers without disabilities, educational teams must work to increase their independence and ease in actively participating in these environments. Instructional adaptations can be the key to minimizing students' disabilities and maximizing opportunities for interaction, participation, and contribution. Selecting and using the right adaptations can be a complex and delicate endeavor. No formula exists when making such decisions, but a process does exist for developing individual adaptations, with an emphasis on student strengths, knowledge of student goals, and selection of student interventions. This process should be used when selecting and using individualized adaptations. After considering the multitude of preexisting adaptations, teams of professionals may have to design or fashion the adaptive device, taking care to avoid potential negative and unintentional problems. Adaptations should allow students to learn, discover, contribute to society, and lead more fulfilling lives. Useful adaptations are a result of a thoughtful and dedicated team. Remember that student potential is limited only by the bounds of the team's collective creativity.

REFLECTION QUESTIONS

1. What ideologies and beliefs might teachers need to adopt in order to best implement the four-step process for developing and implementing adaptations?

2. What type of collaboration is necessary to implement this adaptation creation process?

3. In what ways did Jack benefit from the adaptations throughout his day?

4. In what ways did Jack's peers benefit?

CHAPTER ACTIVITY

1. With a partner or group, consider a target student.

2. Using the student profile and discrepancy analysis templates to guide you, work through the four-step process together to determine effective adaptations for your target student.

3. When finished, reflect on the 10 things to remember in relation to your adaptation decisions.

REFERENCES

Americans with Disabilities Act Amendments Act (ADA) of 2008, PL 110-325, 42 U.S.C. §§ 201 et seq.

Bauer, K.L., Iyer, S.N., Boon, R.T., & Fore, C. (2010). 20 ways for classroom teachers to collaborate with speech-language pathologists. *Intervention in School and Clinic, 45*(5), 333–337.

Baumgart, D., Brown, L., Pumpian, I., Nisbet, J., Ford, A., Sweet, M. . . .Schroeder, J. (1982). Principle of partial participation and individualized adaptations in educational programs for severely handicapped students. *Journal of the Association for the Severely Handicapped, 7*(2), 17–27.

Biklen, D., & Burke, J. (2006). Presuming competence. *Equity and Excellence in Education, 39*(2), 166–175.

Browder, D.M. (2001). *Curriculum and assessment for students with moderate and severe disabilities.* New York, NY: Guilford Press.

Browder, D.M., & Spooner, F. (Eds.). (2006). *Teaching language arts, math, and science to students with significant cognitive disabilities.* Baltimore, MD: Paul H. Brookes Publishing Co.

Brown, L., Branston-McLean, M., Baumgart, D., Vincent, L., Falvey, M., & Schroeder, J. (1979). Utilizing the characteristics of current and subsequent least restrictive environments as factors in the development of curricular content for severely handicapped students. *AAESPH Review, 4*(4), 407–424.

Brown, L., Falvey, M., Vincent, L., Kaye, N., Johnson, F., Ferrara-Parrish, P., & Gruenewald, L. (1980). Strategies for generating comprehensive, longitudinal, and chronological age appropriate individualized education programs for adolescent and young adult severely handicapped students. *Journal of Special Education, 14*(2), 199–215.

Brown, L., Shiraga, B., York, J., Zanella, K., & Rogan, P. (1984a). Ecological inventory strategies for students with severe handicaps. In L. Brown, M. Sweet, B. Shiraga, J. York, K. Zanella, P. Rogan, & R. Loomis (Eds.), *Educational programs for students with severe handicaps* (Vol. XIV, pp. 33–41). Madison, WI: Madison Metropolitan School District.

Brown, L., Shiraga, B., York, J., Zanella, K., & Rogan, P. (1984b). The discrepancy analysis technique in programs for students with severe handicaps. In L. Brown, M. Sweet, B. Shiraga, J. York, K. Zanella, P. Rogan, & R. Loomis (Eds.), *Educational programs for students with severe handicaps* (Vol. XIV, pp. 43–47). Madison, WI: Madison Metropolitan School District.

Carter, E.W., & Kennedy, C.H. (2006). Promoting access to the general curriculum using peer support strategies. *Research and Practice for Persons with Severe Disabilities, 31*(4), 284–292.

Carter, N., Prater, M.A., Jackson, A., & Marchant, M. (2009). Educators' perceptions of collaborative planning processes for students with disabilities. *Preventing School Failure: Alternative Education for Children and Youth, 54*(1), 60–70.

Causton, J., & Tracy-Bronson, C.P. (2015). *The educator's handbook for inclusive school practices*. Baltimore, MD: Paul H. Brookes Publishing Co.

Causton-Theoharis, J. (2009). *The paraprofessional's handbook for effective support in inclusive classrooms*. Baltimore, MD: Paul H. Brookes Publishing Co.

Causton-Theoharis, J., & Malmgren, K. (2005). Building bridges: Strategies to help paraprofessionals promote peer interactions. *Teaching Exceptional Children, 37*(6), 18–24.

Choate, J.S. (2004). *Successful inclusive teaching: Proven ways to detect and correct special needs* (4th ed.). Boston, MA: Pearson Education.

Collins, S. (2008). *The hunger games*. New York, NY: Scholastic Press.

Donnellan, A.M. (1984). The criterion of the least dangerous assumption. *Behavioral Disorders, 9*(2), 141–150.

Downing, J.E. (2008). *Including students with severe and multiple disabilities in typical classrooms: Practical strategies for teachers* (3rd ed.). Baltimore, MD: Paul H. Brookes Publishing Co.

Downing, J.E. (2010). *Academic instruction for students with moderate and severe intellectual disabilities in inclusive classrooms*. Thousand Oaks, CA: Corwin.

Downing, J.E., & Peckham-Hardin, K.D. (2007). Inclusive education: What makes it a good education for students with moderate to severe disabilities? *Research and Practice for Persons with Severe Disabilities, 32*(1), 16–30.

Falvey, M.A. (Ed.). (1995). *Inclusive and heterogeneous schooling: Assessment, curriculum, and instruction*. Baltimore, MD: Paul H. Brookes Publishing Co.

Ferguson, D.L., & Baumgart, D. (1991). Partial participation revisited. *Journal of The Association for Persons with Severe Handicaps, 16*(4), 218–227.

Foley, A., & Ferri, B.A. (2012). Technology for people, not disabilities: Ensuring access and inclusion. *Journal of Research in Special Educational Needs, 12*(4), 192–200.

Gardner, H. (1999). *Intelligence reframed: Multiple intelligences for the 21st century*. New York, NY: Basic Books.

Giangreco, M.F., Broer, S.M., & Edelman, S.W. (1999). The tip of the iceberg: Determining whether paraprofessional support is needed for students with disabilities in general education environments. *Journal of The Association for Persons with Severe Handicaps, 24*(4), 281–291.

Giangreco, M.F., & Doyle, M.B. (2002). Students with disabilities and paraprofessional supports: Benefits, balance, and band-aids. *Focus on Exceptional Children, 34*(7), 1–12.

Hernandez, S.J. (2013). Collaboration in special education: Its history, evolution, and critical factors necessary for successful implementation. *Online Submission, 3*(6), 480–498.

Individuals with Disabilities Education Improvement Act (IDEA) of 2004, PL 108-446, 20 U.S.C. §§ 1400 et seq.)

Janney, R., & Snell, M.E. (2013). *Modifying schoolwork: Teachers' guides to inclusive practices* (3rd ed.). Baltimore, MD: Paul H. Brookes Publishing Co.

Kurth, J.A. (2013). A unit-based approach to adaptations in inclusive classrooms. *Teaching Exceptional Children, 46*(2), 34–43.

Kurth, J.A., & Keegan, L. (2012, November 30). Development and use of curricular adaptations for students receiving special education services. *Journal of Special Education, 48(3)*, 191-203.

Lancioni, G.E., Sigafoos, J., O'Reilly, M.F., & Singh, N.N. (2012). *Assistive technology: Interventions for individuals with severe/profound and multiple disabilities*. New York, NY: Springer Science and Business Media.

Langone, J., Malone, M., & Kinsley, T. (1999). Technology solutions for young children with developmental concerns. *Infants and Young Children, 11*(4), 65–78.

Lee, S.H., Wehmeyer, M.L., Soukup, J.H., & Palmer, S.B. (2010). Impact of curriculum modifications on access to the general education curriculum for students with disabilities. *Exceptional Children, 76,* 213–233.

Mistrett, S.G., Lane, S.J., & Ruffino, A.G. (2005). Growing and learning through technology: Birth to five. In D. Edyburn, K. Higgins, & R. Boone (Eds.), *Handbook of special education technology research and practice* (pp. 273–307). Whitefish Bay, WI: Knowledge by Design.

National Governors Association Center for Best Practices & Council of Chief State School Officers. (2010).*Common core state standards.* Washington, DC: Authors.

Paul V. Sherlock Center on Disabilities (n.d.). *Adapted version of The Hunger Games.* Retrieved from http://www.ric.edu/sherlock-center/textonly/wwslist1.html

Piuma, C., & Udvari-Solner, A. (1993a). *A catalog of vocational assistive devices for individuals with severe intellectual disabilities.* Madison, WI: Madison Metropolitan School District and University of Wisconsin–Madison.

Piuma, C., & Udvari-Solner, A. (1993b). *Materials and processes for developing low cost vocational adaptations for individuals with severe disabilities.* Unpublished manuscript, Madison Metropolitan School District and University of Wisconsin–Madison.

Rainforth, B., & York-Barr, J. (1997). *Collaborative teams for students with severe disabilities: Integrating therapy and educational services* (2nd ed.). Baltimore, MD: Paul H. Brookes Publishing Co.

Reed, P., & Walker, P. (2009). *Wisconsin Assistive Technology Initiative: Assistive technology checklist.* Retrieved from http://www.wati.org/content/supports/free/pdf/ASNAT5thEditionJun09.pdf

Ryan, P. M. (2002). Esperanza rising. New York, NY: Scholastic Inc.

Sax, C. (2001). Using technology to support belonging and achievement. In C. Kennedy & D. Fisher (Eds.), *Inclusive middle schools* (pp. 89–103). Baltimore, MD: Paul H. Brookes Publishing Co.

Snell, M.E., & Brown, F. (2006). *Instruction of students with severe disabilities* (6th ed.). Upper Saddle River, NJ: Pearson.

Udvari-Solner, A. (1995). A process for adapting curriculum in inclusive classrooms. In R. Villa & J. Thousand (Eds.), *Creating an inclusive school* (pp. 110–124). Alexandria, VA: Association for Supervision and Curriculum Development.

Udvari-Solner, A. (1996). Examining teacher thinking: Constructing a process to design curricular adaptations. *Remedial and Special Education, 17*(4), 245–254.

Udvari-Solner, A., Causton-Theoharis, J., & York-Barr, J. (2004). Developing adaptations to promote participation in inclusive settings. In F.P. Orelove, D. Sobsey, & R.K. Silberman (Eds.), *Educating children with multiple disabilities: A collaborative approach* (4th ed., pp. 151–192). Baltimore, MD: Paul H. Brookes Publishing Co.

Udvari-Solner, A., Villa, R.A., & Thousand, J.S. (2002). Access to the general education curriculum for all: The universal design process. In J.S. Thousand, R.A. Villa, & A.I. Nevin (Eds.), *Creativity and collaborative learning: The practical guide to empowering students, teachers, and families* (2nd ed., pp. 85–103). Baltimore, MD: Paul H. Brookes Publishing Co.

Udvari-Solner, A., Villa, R., & Thousand, J. (2005). Access to the general education curriculum for all: The universal design process. In R. Villa & J. Thousand (Eds.), *Creating an inclusive school* (2nd ed., pp. 134–155). Alexandria, VA: Association for Supervision and Curriculum Development.

Vaughn, S., & Swanson, E.A. (2015). Special education research advances knowledge in education. *Exceptional Children, 82*(1), 11–24.

Wehmeyer, M.L. (2006). Beyond access: Ensuring progress in the general education curriculum for students with severe disabilities. *Research and Practice for Persons with Severe Disabilities, 31*(4), 322–326.

Westling, D.L., & Fox, L. (2009). *Teaching students with severe disabilities* (4th ed.). Upper Saddle River, NJ: Merrill/Pearson.

12

Alternate Assessments for Students with Severe and Multiple Disabilities

HAROLD L. KLEINERT AND JACQUELINE F. KEARNS

CHAPTER OBJECTIVES

1. Describe the role of alternate assessments in measuring learning for students with severe and multiple disabilities

2. Understand the importance of communication competence as a foundation for learning for all students

3. Understand the role of formative assessment in aligning instruction with assessment

4. Be aware of other elements of college and career readiness not captured by alternate assessments

KEY TERMS

- Alternate achievement standards
- Alternate assessments
- College and career readiness
- Common Core State Standards (CCSS)
- Communicative competence
- Community-based instruction
- Dynamic Learning Maps (DLM)

- Expressive communication:
  - Presymbolic
  - Emerging symbolic
  - Symbolic
- Formative assessment
- Grade-level content standards
- National Center and State Collaborative (NCSC)

This manuscript was supported in part by the U.S. Department of Education Office of Special Education and Rehabilitative Services (Grant No. H324D990044). The opinions expressed, however, do not necessarily reflect the position or policy of the U.S. Department of Education, and no official endorsement should be inferred.

- Self-determination
- Significant cognitive disabilities
- Tactile enhancements

- Tactile graphics
- Teacher effectiveness
- Universal design for learning (UDL)

Gavin is a kindergarten student who has communication and motor challenges. He is emerging in his use of symbols (he uses a small set of words paired with pictures) to communicate using a device with a dynamic screen—he touches the screen to select the word and picture. His instructional team includes his kindergarten teacher, a speech-language pathologist (SLP), physical therapist (PT), occupational therapist (OT), a special educator, and Gavin's parents. The team knows that communication and language development is a high priority because Gavin needs to use his communication skills to learn new knowledge and skills. Although the team does not have to worry about accountability assessments until Gavin is in the third grade, it is not too early to start building competence in communication, use of augmentative and alternative communication (AAC), and early literacy skills. The team has decided that Gavin's communication targets should include requesting, asking questions, and commenting. He is already good at selecting or refusing choices. The team also wants to build Gavin's vocabulary and begin early literacy and reading. They decide to continue the use of pictures and words. The PT and OT are working on correct positioning in his chair as well as mounting the AAC device to facilitate easy access. The SLP and teacher are working on how to organize the options on the device to make it easy for Gavin to use it for communicating core vocabulary related to what the class is studying. Gavin's team plans for transition to the next school and grade by collecting video clip samples of his literacy skills and his use of his AAC device to share with new teachers. In addition to teaching Gavin to use his device, the team decides it is important to teach peers to also use the device so that they can communicate with Gavin.

A LOOK AHEAD: GAVIN IN THIRD GRADE

Gavin is proficient in using his device to request, refuse, ask questions, and comment by third grade. He can also answer basic questions about text if the answers are available on the device. He is learning to type words and create sentences on the device. Gavin will need to select the correct answer from two or three options during the accountability assessment, which is presented on a computer. He will need to practice using the computer to view the screen, listen to the passages and question items as they are read, and select his answer. The use of the dynamic screen device actually has helped Gavin because he is used to using a screen and selecting responses. The team is continuing to increase the complexity of Gavin's literacy skills and have begun to build a reading vocabulary that is readily available on the device.

Content standards for third grade include identifying the main character and two details from a literary passage. Gavin's class practiced reading
passages and identifying the main character and two details about the story.
Similarly, Gavin responded to passages and assessment items designed to
mirror this content standard in the assessment. The passage(s) were read
aloud, and Gavin was presented with question and answer selections based
on the main character and story details. Each answer choice included an illustration and a word depicting the responses. He selected the answer choice
that aligned with the question. Additional examples of instructional and
assessment items for Gavin taken from another core content area (i.e., social
studies) are provided later in the chapter (see Figures 12.5 and 12.6).

Throughout his primary years, Gavin's team has instructed him on using
his AAC device, which has grown along with Gavin's increasing communication
skills. Gavin was competent at using a screened device and had many communication skills by the time of the accountability assessment in third grade.
This team understood that communication is a natural pathway to literacy and
took advantage of early learning to focus on these fundamental skills.

Teaching students with severe and multiple disabilities presents exacting challenges and enduring rewards. Among those rewards is the sense that one has
enabled a student to accomplish a valued life skill, become more independent
in daily routines, have a greater sense of self-efficacy and control over his or her
environment, experience a deeper sense of membership with his or her same-
age peers, and master elements of the general curriculum deemed to be an essential part of the education for all children.

As has been noted throughout this book, all students, including students with
the most significant disabilities, have the right to participate and progress in the
general education curriculum according to the Individuals with Disabilities Education Improvement Act (IDEA) of 2004 (PL 108-446). Moreover, the No Child Left
Behind Act (NCLB) of 2001 (PL 107-110) mandates that all students are to be assessed
annually on grade-level content standards in math and reading in grades 3–8 and
once in high school. Students must be assessed in science once in grades 3–8 and
once in high school. This chapter is about how we measure that learning, including
participation in state alternate assessments on alternate achievement standards
(AA-AAS) specifically developed for students who are considered to have "the
most significant cognitive disabilities" (U.S. Department of Education, 2004, p.15).

Students with the most significant cognitive disabilities make up an estimated 1% or less of all students (U.S. Department of Education, 2004). Federal
regulations define *students with the most significant cognitive disabilities* simply
as those students for whom regular educational assessments—even with accommodations and modifications—are not appropriate for their full participation in measures of school accountability. *Most significant cognitive disabilities* is
a noncategorical term; students with significant cognitive disabilities typically
include students with moderate and severe intellectual disabilities as well as
many students who are labeled as having autism, multiple disabilities, and

deafblindness (Towles-Reeves, Kleinert, & Muhomba, 2009). Not all students with these categorical labels will need an alternate assessment, however, and students with other categorical labels (e.g., orthopedic disability) may also qualify to participate in their respective state's AA-AAS. In short, we decide whether a student meets the criteria for having a most significant cognitive disability based on individual student needs. The decision about whether a student qualifies to participate in the AA-AAS rests with the individualized education program (IEP) team and should be based on the specific eligibility criteria that each state sets for its AA-AAS. Students with severe and multiple disabilities typically (but not always) participate in state educational assessment and accountability systems through their respective state AA-AAS.

Alternate achievement standards, on which alternate assessments for students with the most significant cognitive disabilities are based, are described as reflecting reduced complexity within academic content, but these alternate achievement standards still must be aligned to the content standards for all students, and they must reflect best professional judgment about what students with the most significant cognitive disabilities can learn (U.S. Department of Education, 2003). It is important to note here that achievement standards are an estimation of how the intended population will perform on an assessment instrument, whereas *content standards* refer to the specific knowledge and skills that frame both curriculum and instruction. These two terms are often incorrectly used interchangeably. IDEA 2004 notes that "it is important to reiterate that states shall provide for alternate assessments that are aligned with each state's challenging academic content standards and challenging student academic achievement standards" (Sec. 612 [a][16][C][ii][I]). Most specifically, alternate achievement standards must be linked to the grade-level curriculum for all students (U.S. Department of Education, 2004). This chapter discusses the implications of this policy decision delineating the relationship of alternate assessments to IEPs and to college and career readiness.

WHAT IS ALTERNATE ASSESSMENT INTENDED TO MEASURE?

The alternate assessment is intended to measure concepts and skills that are chronologically age/grade appropriate as reflected in a school or district curriculum, but it is not intended to measure everything of importance to a student's individualized goals on the IEP. The IEP represents a subset of concept knowledge and skills that the IEP team deems most important and appropriate for an individual student, as well as essential accommodations, modifications, and strategies for supporting curriculum access for that student. These skills should be readily embedded within existing curriculum activities across the student's school day. In some cases, skills may be included on the IEP that are not referenced in the grade-level curriculum. For example, a high school student may have vocational skills included in his or her IEP that require a specific array of services. These skills are clearly important indicators of college, career, and community readiness (see Kleinert, Kearns, Quenemoen, & Thurlow, 2013), but these skills are not explicitly included in the CCSS nor are they assessed by the alternate assessment. In addition, skills necessary for gaining access to the curriculum may be included in the IEP. For example, students with significant cognitive and visual (or dual) sensory disabilities often use highly individualized tactile symbols (Rowland & Schweigert, 1996), like those described later in this chapter. Tactile graphics, symbols, or braille are not likely outlined in the general curriculum, but they are necessary for students to participate and understand that curriculum.

A COLLABORATIVE APPROACH TO ALTERNATE ASSESSMENT

Running through this text is the broad theme as well as the essential elements of a collaborative approach to the education of students with severe and multiple disabilities. Alternate assessments must likewise reflect the basic assumptions that lie at the heart of a collaborative approach (see Chapter 1):

- *Services are coordinated rather than isolated and fragmented.* This principle is at the heart of the inclusive assessment requirements of IDEA 2004, which requires that we must find a way to measure and report the learning of every student, either through participation in the regular assessment with appropriate accommodations or modifications or through the use of an AA-AAS. The point of alternate assessments is that we measure the important achievements of students with multiple disabilities in ways that connect to the general curriculum. An accurate measure of these achievements must involve a collaborative approach.

- *All team members share a framework for team functioning.* The basic assumption of this text is that the collaborative team (including special and general educators, the parents and student, related services providers, and administrators) is essential in the design and implementation of the student's educational program. As a matter of law, this same team is also required to determine how the student will participate in large-scale educational assessments under IDEA 2004, as well as how the student will participate in the general education curriculum. How the student will be assessed in state or district assessments and how the student will participate in the general curriculum are challenges that can be effectively addressed only by the whole team working in a collaborative and integrated fashion. Successful participation in the general curriculum and documentation of educational results are possible only in the context of shared educational goals and role release across disciplines so that students have the needed supports throughout the school day and across all critical environments. The next section touches on the essential roles of each of the team members.

CHANGING LANDSCAPE OF ALTERNATE ASSESSMENTS

Ysseldyke and Olsen (1999) originally suggested a range of formats that alternate assessments can take, including observations of student performance, structured interviews and checklists, performance records (instructional data, graphs, anecdotal records), and performance tests on specified tasks. The most widely used assessment formats to date include (Towles-Reeves, Kleinert, & Muhomba, 2009)

- A portfolio or body of evidence approach. Portfolios are systematic collections of student work (often referred to as *entries*) that are scored against predetermined criteria for accountability purposes. Portfolio approaches vary in the kinds of evidence required and in how much input teachers and students have in selecting targeted skills to illustrate specific grade-level standards.

- A checklist approach, which requires that teachers identify whether students are able to perform certain skills, tasks, or activities. Evidence for performance can come from direct observation, interviews, and/or examples of student work samples.

- A performance assessment or performance event approach. This is a direct measure of a skill under controlled assessment conditions (e.g., the student responding to questions about an adapted grade-level story that he or she has just read).

Two significant developments, however, are rapidly changing how state alternate assessments will be administered in the future. The first is the development of the CCSS (http://www.corestandards.org), released in 2010. Although not without controversy, the CCSS had been adopted by 42 states and the District of Columbia as of Fall 2015. As states adopt a common set of content standards, the possibility of having common alternate assessments, administered across states, is much more likely. Second, the U.S Department of Education subsequently funded two large-scale state consortia—the National Center and State Collaborative (NCSC; http://www.ncscpartners.org) and Dynamic Learning Maps (DLM; http://www.dynamic learningmaps.org). Both of these consortia have developed item-based assessments linked to the CCSS that will be delivered primarily through technology systems.

The NCSC included 24 states and U.S. territories (14 core states and 10 Tier II states) as of late 2015, focused on building an AA-AAS for students with the most significant cognitive disabilities. The goal of the NCSC project "is to ensure that students with the most significant cognitive disabilities achieve higher academic outcomes. All students should aim to leave high school ready for college and/or careers" (NCSC, 2014, p. 3).

The DLM project is also guided by the core beliefs that the assessment should "provide links between the general education content standards and grade-specific expectations" (DLM, n.d., p. 2). Embedding assessment tasks in ongoing or daily instruction is a primary aspect of the DLM approach. Like NCSC, the DLM project has also developed an end-of-the-year assessment that functions as a summative assessment for NCLB accountability requirements. As of 2015, 17 states were participating in the DLM assessment.

Both the NCSC and DLM assessments have completed their initial administrations across a portion of their participating states as of Spring of 2015. Both assessments feature online delivery systems, and both assessments have been specifically designed to connect with good instruction on academic content linked to grade-level standards and not as simple stand-alone tests.

The NCSC alternate assessment is a summative assessment (e.g., a single snapshot in time) (Kearns, Kleinert, Thurlow, Quenemoen, & Gong, 2015). It is not designed as a formative or ongoing assessment, although it has embedded formative assessment tools within its curricular materials (https://wiki .ncscpartners.org). The DLM alternate assessment, however, does include optional formative assessment tasks that can be embedded throughout the year, in addition to the year-end summative assessment.

All states will have the option of using either the NCSC or the DLM assessment in the future now that the full-scale implementation of these state consortia assessments are complete. The implementation of these assessments will allow states to compare their students' performance with other states using the same assessment.

Changing Roles of Special and General Education Teachers, Related Services Personnel, and Parents

The early history of alternate assessments is largely one of special educators trying to determine how students with significant disabilities could participate in their respective state educational assessments (Kleinert, Kearns, & Kennedy, 1997). Alternate assessment was thus seen primarily as a special education concern to be addressed in conjunction with state education assessment and accountability offices. With the required link to grade-level content standards, general educators have now become critical in 1) helping to define that link between alternative assessment and grade-level content standards and 2) providing instruction in the context of grade-level inclusive classrooms.

Moreover, the importance of related services personnel, including SLPs, is highlighted in several studies (Kearns et al., 2015; Kearns, Towles-Reeves, Kleinert, Kleinert, & Thomas, 2011; Towles-Reeves, Kearns, Kleinert, & Kleinert, 2009). Approximately 30% of students in state alternate assessments do not yet have a symbolic mode of communication (e.g., verbal language, AAC, American Sign Language), and approximately 10% of students in the AA-AAS are still functioning at a presymbolic level (i.e., without the formal use of symbolic communication) at the secondary level (Kleinert et al., 2015). Because academic content is by definition symbolic content, students' movement toward symbolic communication is essential to academic achievement, and SLPs are thus essential partners in ensuring access to the general curriculum aligned to appropriate alternate assessments.

The importance of other related services personnel (e.g., PTs, OTs, assistive technology [AT] experts) in both instruction and assessment is illustrated by an 18-state study of students participating in their respective state alternate assessments ($N = 49,669$); at least 17% of participating students in that study required adaptations as a result of motor or physical disabilities (Towles-Reeves et al., 2012). These related services personnel may also be playing essential roles, along with SLPS and teachers, in the development of formal communication systems.

Parents also have a vital role in shaping expectations for their son's or daughter's education (Doren, Gau, & Lindstrom, 2012). In an earlier study of parents whose students participated in a state alternate assessment, Roach (2006) found that although most parents believed it was important for their child to learn academic content, parent perceptions were less positive as students entered the higher grades and as the percentage of life skill objectives (as opposed to strictly academic content objectives) increased on their child's IEP. The relationship of alternate assessments to broader determinants of life outcomes and their role as a measure of college and career readiness for high school level students are important considerations for policy makers, teachers, and parents.

Finally, the role of the student is important when considering alternate assessment. As states move away from portfolio assessments constructed by teachers and students, students will have less of a role in determining what goes into their individual assessments. Yet, students will need to take an active role in using self-monitoring, self-evaluation, and problem-solving skills as alternate assessments increasingly link to grade-level content standards and emphasize critical thinking skills. Self-monitoring, self-evaluation, and problem solving (Agran, King-Sears, Wehmeyer, & Copeland, 2003) are all essential elements of self-determination, a critical factor in enhancing life outcomes (Shogren, Wehmeyer, Palmer, Rifenbark, & Little, 2015; Wehmeyer & Palmer, 2003). Self-determination is discussed in greater detail in Chapter 13.

A COMPREHENSIVE SYSTEM OF CURRICULUM, INSTRUCTION, AND ASSESSMENT

Any effective approach to alternate assessment has to be built on two underlying principles: 1) the fundamental importance of communicative competence and 2) the alignment of curriculum, instruction, and assessment.

Communicative Competence

The ability to communicate is at the heart of all learning. Yet, research has clearly indicated the unmet communication needs of a significant percentage of students who are eligible for the alternate assessment (Kearns, Towles-Reeves et al., 2011; Kleinert et al., 2015; Towles-Reeves, Kearns et al., 2009; Towles-Reeves et al., 2012). Of course, the issue of communicative competence goes far beyond simple access to the general curriculum and participation in alternate assessments. Life outcomes—at least as we have traditionally measured them—are uniformly poor without communicative competence (Kleinert et al., 2002). Several large-scale, multistate studies provide what we know about communicative competence for students with significant cognitive disabilities participating in their state's respective alternate assessments.

In a three-state study of students eligible for the AA-AAS in those states, Towles-Reeves, Kearns et al. (2009) found the largest percent of students (approximately 70%) communicated expressively using symbolic language (generally oral speech) to express a variety of intents. As the authors noted,

> To communicate expressively, most students in each state used verbal or written words, signs, Braille, or language-based augmentative systems to request, initiate, and respond to questions; describe things or events; and express refusal (71%, 63%, and 74% respectively in States 1, 2, and 3). (p. 245)

An additional 17%–26% represented emerging symbolic language users. These were students who may have used pictures, objects, or regularized gestures (e.g., pointing to preferred objects) to communicate a variety of intents. Finally, 8%–11% of students were communicating at a presymbolic level for expressive communication, meaning that they used facial expressions and/or body movements to communicate basic intentions (Towles-Reeves, Kearns et al. 2009). Students at a presymbolic level thus had no consistently interpretable mode of communication, whereas emerging symbolic communicators were just beginning to use regularized modes to communicate intents.

In a larger study involving more than 12,000 students, Kearns, Towles-Reeves et al. (2011) examined the learner characteristics of students in the AA-AAS across seven states. Kearns et al. noted similar percentages to those of Towles-Reeves, Kearns et al. (2009) for those students who were symbolic language users (an average of 72% across all seven states), for those who were emerging in their use of symbolic language (17.3% across the seven states), and for those who were presymbolic (no formal model of communication) (10.3% across all seven states). The relative lack of change in the percentage of students communicating at a pre-symbolic level across the grade spans from elementary to high school was perhaps the most significant finding in the Kearns et al. study. Although this study was not a longitudinal study of the same students over time, it is reasonable to expect that substantially fewer high school students would be at a presymbolic level in the secondary grades than in the elementary years. Yet, overall, whereas 12.6% of students in the alternate assessment in these states were rated by their teachers as presymbolic communicators in the elementary years, that percentage had decreased only slightly—to 9.5% in the high school grades. A small, but significant percentage of students in state alternate assessments were clearly completing their schooling without a formal communication system.

In the largest data set of students participating in AA-AAS collected to date, Towles-Reeves et al. (2012) studied the learner characteristics of 49,669 students who participated in their respective state alternate assessments during the 2010–2011 or 2011–2012 academic year across 18 states. The participating states were partners of the NCSC project described earlier in this chapter. Learner characteristics data were collected on 49,669 students across the 18 states. The percentage of students at each level of communication was again very similar to the earlier Towles-Reeves, Kearns et al. (2009) and Kearns, Towles-Reeves et al. (2011) studies. Teachers across all 18 states reported that the majority of students (69%) used symbolic language to communicate; 18% of students were emerging symbolic communicators; and 10% were presymbolic. Towles-Reeves et al. also considered whether students identified by their teachers as either emerging symbolic or pre-symbolic communicators had access to AAC systems. As these authors described:

> Further, for the 10% of students identified by their teachers as *presymbolic* (i.e., communicating primarily through cries, facial expressions, but who have no clear use of gestures, pictures, signs, etc.), only 40% use AAC; and of the 18% of students identified by their teachers as *emerging symbolic* (using only a limited number of gestures, signs, pictures, etc.) only 39% use AAC. (p. 43)

Although this largest study did not examine the percentage of students at each communication level across grade spans (elementary, middle, and high school), certainly if students without formal communication modes are not given opportunities to use AAC, then we cannot expect that increased communicative competence will automatically increase for students as a function of their years in school. The lack of availability of AAC for many students with limited communicative competence (i.e., those students functioning at an emerging or presymbolic level of communication) is a cause of great concern for our field and is, of course, a fundamental prerequisite to both access to the general curriculum and participation in large-scale assessments based on that curriculum. Recall how important and beneficial it was to develop Gavin's communication system very early in his educational career. His increasing competence with his AAC device and growing literacy skills were instrumental in his participation in the general education curriculum and accountability assessment.

The NCSC Communication Tool Kit (https://wiki.ncscpartners.org), developed by researchers and practitioners with expertise in communicative competence for students with the most significant disabilities in collaboration with NCSC partner states, is a key resource for addressing communicative status and the lack of AAC for students who most need that access. The Communication Tool Kit is a set of online modules designed to provide educators with information on 1) identifying a student's communication level (e.g., presymbolic, emerging symbolic), 2) identifying factors that impeded communication, 3) selecting communication targets (key communication goals for students), 4) embedding communication targets into the academic curriculum, 5) types of AAC, 6) evidence-based strategies to improve expressive communication, and 7) monitoring progress on key student communication goals.

Alignment of Curriculum, Instruction, and Assessment

Alternate assessment should never be designed or used in isolation, but rather must be viewed within the broader framework of rigorous and relevant curriculum and instruction. Assessing students without first ensuring ongoing, carefully structured opportunities for learning within the grade-level curriculum can hardly be expected to result in meaningful changes in student outcomes. A key reason for ensuring access to rigorous and relevant grade-level curriculum is that students should also have access to inclusive environments and shared instructional experiences with peers of the same chronological age. Instructional practices based on a rigorous curriculum provide a shared instructional narrative in which students participate in common literature, mathematics, social studies, and science experiences. These experiences become sources for new communication opportunities, new vocabulary, and conceptual connections to a broader array of topics. For example, sixth-grade students learning about types of government and economic examples (e.g., mining, logging, fishing) make connections to important things in their own community. These connections make the learning rigorous, the content relevant, and the subject meaningful and not just an exercise in memorizing vocabulary. This section explains the alignment of curriculum, instruction, and assessment as it has been developed by the NCSC—one of the two large state consortia discussed earlier.

In keeping with the notion of shared curriculum, the NCSC consortium chose to use learning progression frameworks (Hess & Kearns, 2011). Learning progression frameworks identify a common set of knowledge and skill priorities sequenced across grades—essentially, a learning map. Given that coherent curriculum sequences for students with significant cognitive disabilities rarely exist, coupled with the absence of data about how students in this population progress in academic domains (Hess, 2011), learning progression frameworks are designed to consolidate essential knowledge and skills and outline a sequential path of appropriate instructional targets. A learning progression framework simply highlights a predictable sequence of curriculum content that is designed to enable students to achieve increasingly more complex skills. Application of those skills to real-world settings (a very important instructional element for students with significant disabilities) is generally included as an integral part of the standards themselves.

Core content connectors (CCCs) within the NCSC model have been used to prioritize the academic content within the learning frameworks. CCCs identify the most important content while retaining the grade-level content focus and the learning targets of the learning progression frameworks. The CCCs also inform the development of assessment items aligned to the CCSS at each grade. This approach provides a curriculum sequence across grades that leads to important knowledge and skills required to be prepared for postschool environments—college, career, and community. Figure 12.1 illustrates this alignment of curriculum, instruction, and assessment—undergirded by the essential element of communicative competence. Alternate assessment in this model is simply one

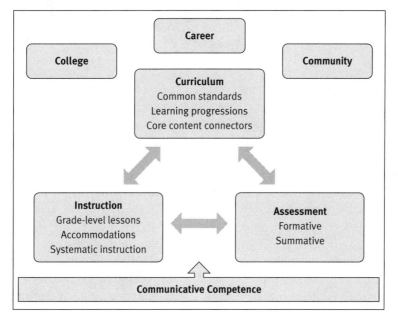

Figure 12.1. The foundational principles of the National Center and State Collaborative alternate assessment. (From Kearns, J. Thurlow, M., Quenemoen, R., & Kleinert, H. [2014]. The NCSC model for a comprehensive system of curriculum, instruction, and assessment. National Center on Educational Outcomes, National Center and State Collaborative; reprinted by permission.)

element in a continuous process of enabling students with significant disabilities to fully engage, learn, and demonstrate their understanding of academic content alongside their peers. Kleinert et al. noted this approach considers not just the role of assessment but "the broader framework of rigorous and relevant curriculum and instruction" (2013, p. 2).

Effective instruction includes the use of systematic, evidence-based instructional procedures (i.e., frequent opportunities for student responses, systematic prompting procedures, immediate student feedback, ongoing data collection), individualized adaptations that enable the student to gain access to the material, and structured lesson plans that embed grade-level content. Assessment within the NSCS model does not only refer to one-time summative assessments (typically a year-end assessment, which is the format of many, if not most, alternate assessments) but also ongoing, regular formative assessments designed to give specific feedback to the teacher and student on progress on learning targets throughout the year. The reader is referred to the NCSC Wiki (https://wiki.ncsc partners.org) for examples of curricular materials linked to grade-level content standards and adapted for students with the most significant disabilities for how curricular materials, instruction, and ongoing assessment can be clearly aligned.

Finally, this model incorporates the importance of postschool outcomes and college and career readiness. The model recognizes academic learning as one of the essential elements in preparation for adult life, specifically in its focus on the "the essential knowledge and skills that allow students to build competence in academic domains most likely to lead to enhanced college, career, and community outcomes" (Kleinert et al., 2013, p. 3). Formative assessment and college and career readiness are described more fully in the following sections.

THE ROLE OF FORMATIVE ASSESSMENT

Formative assessment is the collection of ongoing student progress data on key student learning targets. Formative assessment, whether it is part of a state's formal alternate assessment, is nevertheless a critical part in ensuring that curriculum, instruction, and assessment are aligned and that each of these elements reinforces the other two elements of this learning triangle. Summative assessments administered annually can provide only a tiny snapshot of what a student knows and can do, whereas formative assessment strategies and techniques are essential for monitoring a student's ongoing progress in a timely manner.

The use of errorless, systematic instructional procedures, along with ongoing assessment of progress, are evidence-based practices for students with severe and multiple disabilities (McDonnell, Jameson, Riesen, & Polychronis, 2014). Using these strategies with appropriate data collection and analysis procedures provides the instructional team with weekly or even daily data to inform instructional decisions. The key instructional questions or decision points include

• Are the student's correct, independent responses increasing?

• Has the target been met, and if so, what is the next target?

- If independent responses are not increasing, then where are the sources of error, and what procedures are needed to correct those errors?

In addition, instructional procedures must include a fluency building and a generalization phase. Generalization (the ability to respond correctly across a broad array of novel situations) has long been noted as an essential element in skill acquisition for students with severe and multiple disabilities (Kleinert, Browder, & Towles-Reeves, 2009). Fluency (the ability to respond at a rapid and accurate rate) is not as well documented for academic skill progression for this population of students. Kearns, Towles-Reeves et al. (2011) found that the majority of students participating in alternate assessments read at the sight word level and used a calculator to compute math problems; moreover, the percentage of students at these skill levels did not appreciably change across elementary, middle, and high school. The problem may be a lack of opportunities to acquire and demonstrate fluency in reading and math. Progress monitoring tools, including those that measure reading and math fluency, are essential for sequenced skill acquisition across grades (Fuchs, Fuchs, & Vaughn, 2014; Lemons, Kearns, & Davidson, 2014).

Formative assessment tools and strategies utilizing regular data-based decision making provide the essential information needed for enhancing skill acquisition, fluency, generalization, and maintenance in ways that summative assessments administered annually can never accomplish. The integration of these tools into ongoing instruction is essential for maximizing achievement, both throughout the school year and on the summative assessment itself. As noted earlier, the NCSC Wiki is an example of a searchable, online curricular tool that has embedded formative assessment tools within its curricular materials.

Formative Assessments: Examples in Practice

Progress monitoring, also known as *curriculum-based measurement,* is useful for collecting data on student performance. These data then help to improve instruction by guiding instructional decisions (National Center on Student Progress Monitoring, n.d.). By providing systematic instruction, recording student data, charting the data, and conducting an analysis based on that data, teachers can determine if students have demonstrated skill acquisition and when to move on to build fluency.

GAVIN

Gavin, the student introduced in the beginning of this chapter, is a third-grade student who has learned to request items using an AAC device. His teacher collected and charted his independence in using his device to make requests of teachers and other adults at school. Figure 12.2 illustrates his results. It is clear that while there is some day-to-day variation, his overall performance indicated by the trend line shows that he has indeed mastered this skill and is independent in 80% of the opportunities. This is a good

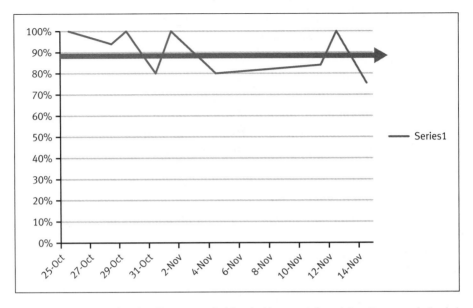

Figure 12.2.   Gavin's independence in making requests of adults using his augmentative and alternative communication device.

example of using progress monitoring to answer the second instructional decision point question of whether the instructional target has been met. If so, the team must decide on the student's next instructional target.

The team decided that Gavin really needed to learn how to make requests of peers as well, especially in the context of general education activities and other school activities (e.g., lunch, library time). The team ensured that the peers in his third-grade class understood how Gavin's AAC system operates and recognized the importance of Gavin requesting assistance with his system whenever he needed help to complete a class activity. The SLP also instructed peers in how to prompt Gavin to use his AAC if he clearly needed something to complete an assignment. Figure 12.3 shows Gavin's progress in making independent requests of peers in instructional and other school activities. The instructional data (percentage of opportunities in which he independently used his AAC system to make a request) was collected by a classroom paraprofessional and indicates that Gavin independently initiated requests of peers in at least 80% of observed opportunities for the last 3 days in both the general education classroom and other school activities.

JEFF

Jeff is a middle school student and is working on fluency in multi-digit subtraction using a calculator. He completes five problems every day with multiple digits. The target is to increase the number of correctly subtracted digits across problems. His teacher administers a probe, or a quick set of instructional items or tasks, once per week. Jeff uses his calculator during

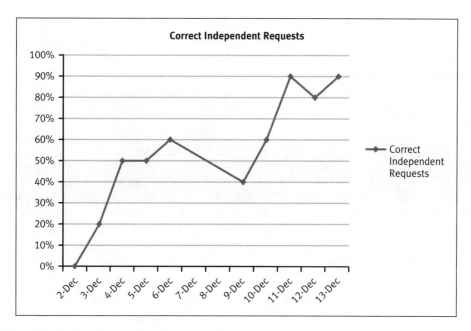

Figure 12.3. Gavin's independence in making requests of peers in instructional and other activities.

the probe to subtract as many digits correctly in as many problems as he can solve in 3 minutes. Figure 12.4 illustrates his results. Jeff's chart shows that his performance has significantly increased in weekly probes, indicating that he is making steady progress in using a calculator to solve multi-digit subtraction problems.

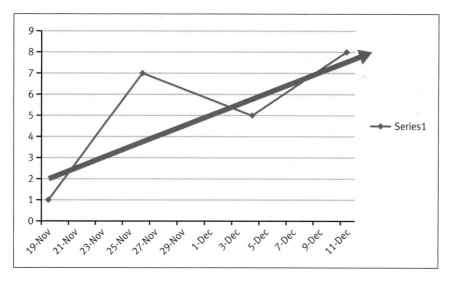

Figure 12.4. Number of digits subtracted correctly with a calculator in weekly probes.

The use of progress monitoring provides the formative instructional data needed to make important decisions in a timely manner. Indeed, high-quality formative instructional data provide a rich source of information when used in conjunction with summative assessment data. It is important to note that high-quality formative data will be a better indicator of student progress than summative assessment results, particularly for students with significant cognitive disabilities.

UNIVERSAL DESIGN AND ASSESSMENT ACCESSIBILITY

The principles of UDL are critical in making both the content of the general curriculum and the alternate assessments linked to that curriculum accessible to the broadest range of students (see Chapter 10) (Ryndak, Jackson, & White, 2013). These principles present some unique challenges when applied to assessments because the need for standardization of the assessment instrument must be balanced with the flexibility required for maximum participation (Gong & Marion, 2006). Evidence-centered design is one promising practice to enhance universal features in assessments (Cameto, Haertel DeBarger, & Morrison, 2010; Mislevy, Steinberg, & Almond, 1999). Cameto et al. described procedures for developing alternate assessments that consider universal features during the initial design of alternate assessments. Two important components are critical elements of the evidence-centered design process for alternate assessments. The first is the input of content domain experts (e.g., reading, math, science). These experts must work in close collaboration with professionals highly knowledgeable about students in the assessment population, including students with significant intellectual disabilities, sensory and multiple disabilities, and those students who rely extensively on AT (the second part of the design equation). The goal is to design an assessment that presents the same items for all learners but with the flexibility to customize the items for individual student needs by applying accommodations such as pictures, auditory supports, or tactile graphics.

Figure 12.5 represents the key points from an adapted third-grade information passage about hamsters. The content standard to be assessed focuses on identifying the main idea and recalling details from the text. The text is read aloud to the student, perhaps by a peer, and images/illustrations are provided to support the student's understanding of the text. Gavin is reading this story with his third-grade classmates. Figure 12.6 represents the response options for two comprehension questions about the story (the first question is on the main topic of the story, and the second question is on a supporting detail). The response options for the two questions are programmed into Gavin's AAC system. Note that these questions are linked to the grade-level content but presented in his communication mode. They are appropriate for both in-class instruction and formative assessment, or they could also be part of a state summative alternate assessment for his grade level.

Even as elements of UDL (e.g., picture supports, simplified text or format) are considered in creating both instructional materials and alternate assessment items, some students will require even further, highly specialized features such

This story is about a popular family pet, where he lives, and what he likes to eat.

Read the story and point to the illustration or provide the tactile symbol for the student to explore as supported by the text.

      i. Hamsters are a popular family pet.
      ii. They are furry and gentle.
      iii. They live in a cage.
      iv. Hamsters need plenty of water and special food. They eat grain, seeds, and corn.
      v. Hamsters are called *pocket pets* because they fit in your pocket.

Figure 1: Illustrations supporting an informational passage.

The questions following the passage are presented in Figure 12.6.

Figure 12.5.   Instruction and assessment example.

as tactile graphics, systematic presentation, and sign language interpretation protocols. The literature about using highly specialized accommodations in alternate assessments is limited (Zebehazy, Zigmond, & Zimmerman, 2012). Furthermore, many tactile symbols used by students in this population are highly individualized, making their use problematic under assessment conditions. The example in the following section illustrates the challenges in ensuring access to both instruction and assessment.

Assessment Items and Accessibility Options

Accessibility of academic content for students with sensory, motor, and multiple disabilities requires the student to use symbols or symbolic representations. For example, if the informational story about hamsters was an actual alternate assessment item, then the images provided to most students participating in the test would be the following: an image of a hamster, an image of a cage, and an image of corn. The diversity of the population of students in the alternate assessment, however, requires that more than one accessibility option be available. For example, some students with visual impairments may simply be able to listen to the text without the images. The addition of images for these students may actually increase the complexity of the item. They simply listen for their answer choice and use oral speech to make their selection.

For other students with more complex sensory disabilities, providing the images with tactile enhancements or representation symbols may engage the

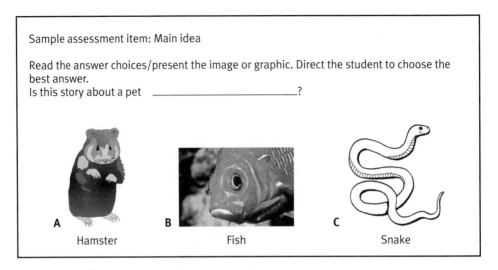

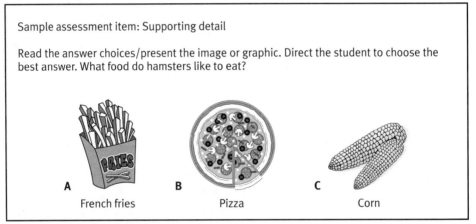

Figure 12.6.   Sample assessment items using picture supports.

students and provide more concrete information to respond to the item. The use of these types of symbols is generally highly individualized for the student by individual teachers. Although there are some standardized versions of tactile symbols (Texas School for the Blind, n.d.), most are oriented to daily living activities and not specifically to academic content. These symbols may look like those in Figure 12.7. As we have noted, one problem with these types of

Figure 12.7.   Examples of tactile symbols that could support an informational passage.

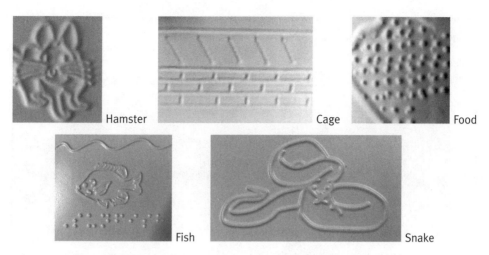

Figure 12.8. Examples of tactile graphics that could support an informational passage.

tactile symbols is that they are often idiosyncratic. They are very appropriate for instruction but may become problematic with the need for standardization in summative assessments.

The use of tactile graphics is a promising option to address the requirement for greater standardization in summative assessments. Tactile graphics are used more extensively by people with visual impairments participating in general assessments. These embossed or thermographed graphics, which mirror the illustrations and images that are more typical, are a bit more complex to learn and use. The examples in Figure 12.8 illustrate embossed or thermographed tactile graphics as an additional way of presenting the same information. Tactile graphics can also be paired with the words in braille to enhance print literacy.

Returning to our example of Gavin and the informational passage about hamsters, if Gavin also had a significant visual impairment, then his communication system may have used tactile representations as in Figure 12.9. The teacher would have provided Gavin with prior instruction on how to use tactile graphics such as these and would have incorporated the tactile graphics into the actual story itself. Gavin's teacher could then have used these graphics to test his understanding of the main topic of the story.

Including students with severe and multiple disabilities, as well as students with additional visual and dual sensory impairments, in alternate assessments based on grade-level content standards requires creativity, an understanding of the grade-level content, and a clear knowledge of the student's mode of communication. We have a lot to learn about how to do this; yet, in providing opportunities for students with severe and multiple disabilities to learn grade-level content with their same-age peers, we are not only providing access to new and rigorous academic content but are also enabling our students to enter into a broader community of learners, with opportunities to practice all of the critical social-communication skills that are part of being a member of that community.

Sample assessment item: Main idea

Read the answer choices and present the image or graphic. Direct the student to choose the best answer.

This story is about a pet _____.

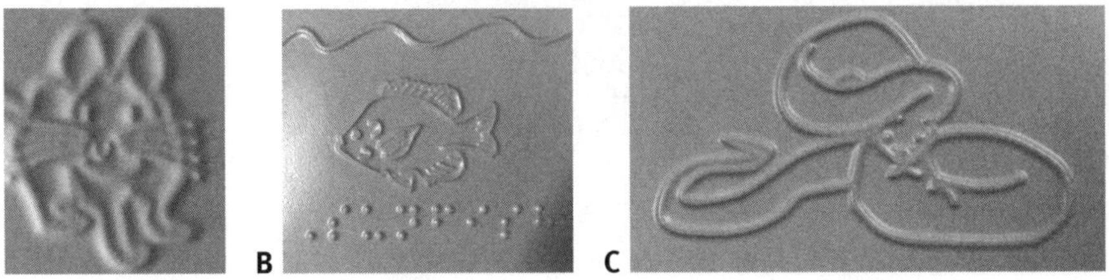

A   Hamster   B   Fish   C   Snake

Figure 12.9. Sample instruction and assessment item using tactile graphics.

ALTERNATE ASSESSMENTS AND COLLEGE AND CAREER READINESS

Alternate assessments for students with significant disabilities have been developed to measure academic achievement linked to grade-level content standards. Yet, we know that students with significant disabilities need a broad range of skills to achieve independence and community inclusion in adult life (Hunt, McDonnell, & Crockett, 2012). As states increasingly make large-scale assessment results part of their equation for determining college and career readiness, teachers and parents are rightfully asking to what extent alternate assessments can measure college and career readiness for students with significant cognitive disabilities (Kearns, Kleinert et al., 2011). Although it is true that important life outcomes can never fully be predicted by a single test result for any student, "success in one's career and life is more than just having a strong mastery of academic content" (Kleinert et al., 2013, p. 5). In a paper for the NCSC, we have identified eight elements crucial for successful transition to adult life that alternate assessments simply are not designed to measure (Kleinert et al., 2013).

1. *Self-determination:* Self-determination, the ability to make one's own decisions and life plans, has long been correlated with enhanced postschool outcomes (e.g., employment, community independence) (see Wehmeyer & Palmer, 2003; Wehmeyer & Schwartz, 1998). Wehmeyer and colleagues have shown a clear causal link between students' level of self-determination and their subsequent postschool lives (Shogren et al., 2015; Wehmeyer, Palmer, Shogren, Williams-Diehm, & Soukup, 2013). Self-determination is a broad rubric for students' ability to set their own goals, make plans to achieve their goals, and evaluate their progress in achieving those goals. We often miss opportunities to teach those skills

(Carter, Owens, Trainor, Sun, & Swedeen, 2009), but those opportunities are present daily in the lives of our students. The essential skills within the broad rubric of self-determination clearly lie outside the domain of what alternate assessment can directly measure.

2. *Student involvement in the IEP planning process:* Actively participating in the development of their IEPs is one of the ways in which students can develop self-determination (Test et al., 2004; Thoma & Wehman, 2010). Students can help summarize their yearly achievements, identify their career and life interests, create their own goals, assist in identifying needed supports and modifications, and subsequently monitor their progress on their IEP goals and objectives. Although mere presence at one's IEP meeting is not indicative of enhanced self-determination, taking an active role in one's IEP is (Shogren, 2013).

3. *Community-based vocational training and paid employment while in school:* The best way to learn about a job is to experience a job, and paid employment during school is the best predictor of actual employment after high school for students with significant disabilities (Carter, Austin, & Trainor, 2012). IEP teams need to identify how students can obtain these experiences through a combination of in-school, after-school, and, perhaps, summer opportunities (Carter et al., 2010).

4. *Community-based instruction:* We have long recognized that students with significant cognitive disabilities have difficulties in generalizing their knowledge and skills to new situations, settings, people or activities (Kleinert et al., 2009). Community-based instruction can be an important supplement to academic instruction, especially for older students. Moreover, community-based instruction does not have to take students away from the general curriculum. It can be conducted in collaboration with peers without disabilities and can focus on life skills that can often readily be related to other content students are learning in school.

5. *Inclusion in general education:* Participation in general education is a strong predictor of postschool outcomes for students with disabilities, including both employment and participation in postsecondary education (Test, 2012). Yet, studies have found that across 15 states, only 7% of all students participating in their respective state alternate assessments are being served in either primarily general education or resource room placements (Kleinert et al., 2015). The vast majority of students in alternate assessments are served primarily in separate classrooms in regular schools (nearly 80% of all students in alternate assessments) or in separate schools altogether (nearly 12%). More than just access to the general curriculum, we need to ensure that students with significant cognitive disabilities have access to peers without disabilities and to the social interactions, communication opportunities, and friendships that can arise from that access. All of these have tremendous implications for the future lives of our students.

6. *Social interaction skills and networking opportunities with peers:* Carter and associates (Carter, Austin, & Trainor, 2012; Carter, Swedeen, & Moss, 2012) documented the importance of peer interactions, friendships, and social skills in not only academic learning, but also in participation in extracurricular activities and inclusive service learning activities. These opportunities ultimately extend to broader postschool outcomes (Carter, Austin, & Trainor, 2012). Again, these skills lie outside the domain of any alternate assessment.

7. *Knowledge of one's own support needs:* Knowing one's own support needs and being able to advocate for those supports are important elements of self-determination as well as preparation for adult life. Being able to appropriately request assistance is an important life skill that we all need.

8. *Interagency transition collaboration:* Interagency transition is a mandated part of transition planning under IDEA 2004, but there is ample evidence that this often does not happen (Cameto, Levine, & Wagner, 2004). Employment outcomes are enhanced when vocational rehabilitation and adult agencies (supported employment, postsecondary education, and so forth) are systematically included at the policy and fiscal levels (Winsor, Butterworth, & Boone, 2011). These supports may need to be lifelong in nature for students with significant cognitive disabilities, and they must be coordinated across agencies.

All of these dimensions are critical to the lives of students with severe and multiple disabilities, and all are important parts of students' educational programming.

PREPARING STUDENTS FOR THE ALTERNATE ASSESSMENT: RECOMMENDATIONS FOR PRACTITIONERS

The following recommendations emerge as we begin to better understand the purposes of alternate assessments used as summative assessments:

- Ensure all students have a way to communicate needs and information as well as express thoughts, opinions, and ideas.

- Work in close coordination with related services providers to implement a collaborative related services model.

- Work collaboratively with general education teachers to develop chronologically age-appropriate instructional activities aligned with grade-level curriculum.

- Use evidence-based formative assessment tools and strategies, including ongoing progress monitoring, to inform instructional decisions and facilitate learning progression across grades.

- Work at the building level to develop and implement opportunities for students to develop social relationships with peers as a context for both learning age-appropriate content and communicating and applying that content across settings.

THE FUTURE OF ALTERNATE ASSESSMENTS

One element of alternate assessment that states will need to address is its role as one possible measure of teacher effectiveness, an issue that has increasingly come to the forefront as states request flexibility under NCLB requirements through the waiver process made available by the U.S. Department of Education (2012). Although it is difficult to predict how much of a role alternate assessments will play as a measure of teacher and school effectiveness in the next decade, we argue that alternate assessments are at best one measure (and certainly not the most important measure) of teacher effectiveness (Kearns et al., 2015). Alternate assessments were not designed as measures of teacher effectiveness, and they should not serve as the primary variable for measuring teacher effectiveness because there are inherent measurement issues (including very small numbers of students at each grade in an alternate assessment in a particular school and individual teachers having responsibilities for students across multiple grades) in alternate assessments (see Steinbrecher, Selig, Cosbey, & Thorstensen, 2014). Rather, multiple measures should be considered in teacher evaluations. These measures include the use of valid, reliable classroom observation tools that measure the degree to which teachers implement evidence-based teaching practices across settings (including general and special education settings, community-based instruction, and, as appropriate, other school settings) (see Kearns et al., 2015) and the use of progress monitoring on prioritized instructional targets (see the section on formative assessments earlier in this chapter). Evidence of teacher leadership in broader school activities and success in working with families are other potential indicators of teacher effectiveness. Indeed as this chapter goes to press, the US Congress has passed, and the President has signed, the *Every Student Succeeds Act* (ESSA, S. 1177), which is the new reauthorization of the Elementary and Secondary Education Act (formerly referred to as *No Child Left Behind*). The new legislation removes the federal requirement for student assessment data as a part of teacher evaluation.

A second issue of importance for both practice and policy is what relationship, if any, exists between alternate assessment scores and student postschool outcomes. Students with severe and multiple disabilities have the poorest postschool outcomes of any group of students (see Wagner, Newman, Cameto, Levine, & Garza, 2006). We would hope, but have yet to confirm, that improved academic competence will translate to better postschool outcomes. Although postschool success is contingent on many factors, including the quality of student transition planning and services and the capacity of the adult service system to provide individualized supports (Antosh et al., 2013), we should expect that increased academic competence, achieved in the context of inclusive learning experiences, will promote a successful future for students with severe and multiple disabilities.

We do not yet know what students with severe and multiple disabilities can learn with explicit, carefully designed, and longitudinal instruction in core academic content until we have first ensured that all students are equipped with a mode of communication to demonstrate their learning. Hopefully this next decade will enable teachers, related services personnel, families, and others to discover what is possible—while striking a curricular balance that ensures that instruction for students with severe and multiple disabilities is relevant to their own lives and their goals for their future.

CONCLUSION

This chapter presented an overview of alternate assessments for students with significant disabilities in the United States. The requirements that alternate assessments link to grade-level content standards (and through the work of two federally funded, multistate consortia to the CCSS) reflect the idea that students with severe and multiple disabilities should have access to both inclusive school experiences and to the academic content that all other students are learning. Alternate assessments are not intended to measure everything of importance to a student's individualized goals. Rather, IEPs are the broader educational tool intended to address the other needs that arise from a student's disability; that is, those life skills that may lie outside the context of the general curriculum.

Furthermore, we have reviewed what we know about the communicative competence of students with significant cognitive disabilities because communication is the foundation not only for accurate assessment of core academic domains but also as a basis for all learning. It is clear that our field still has a long way to go to ensure that all students, including students with the most severe disabilities, have achieved this most fundamental of all educational outcomes. And it is also clear that only a transdisciplinary approach to communication, including the systematic application of the principles of AAC, can improve the communicative status of students with the most significant disabilities.

We also presented a model that emphasized the interconnectedness of assessment, curriculum, and instruction in helping students with severe and multiple disabilities to learn in inclusive classrooms, gain access to the general education curriculum, and demonstrate understanding of academic content. Learning progressions are an essential part of that model and are implemented so that students with significant disabilities do not learn an isolated collection of academic skills or concepts as they move through the grades, but rather obtain a deepening and more sophisticated ability to apply what they are learning in core academic subjects to what is relevant in their lives. We highlighted the importance of formative assessment and progress monitoring in helping teachers make ongoing instructional decisions and illustrated how the principles of

UDL enable increased access to the general curriculum for students with the most severe disabilities. The principles of UDL also need to be part of the design of AA-AAS.

As of late 2015, we are still learning whether large-scale alternate assessments, delivered through online platforms, can fully address the needs of the extremely heterogeneous population of students that qualify to participate in alternate assessments. Although alternate assessments relate to college and career readiness for students with significant cognitive disabilities, teachers and families should view these assessments as just one marker of that readiness for the next step in their students' lives. The final chapter of this book discusses how to plan a successful future and transition to adulthood for students with severe and multiple disabilities.

REFLECTION QUESTIONS

1. Is it fair to include all students in measures of school accountability under the Every Student Succeeds Act (formerly No Child Left Behind)?

2. Should alternate assessments be linked to grade-level content learning and/or to some other indicator(s) of student achievement for students with severe and multiple disabilities? If so, what indicators?

CHAPTER ACTIVITY (SMALL GROUP)

Sara is a 14-year-old ninth grader with a significant cognitive disability participating in her state's alternate assessment. She had proficient scores in both reading and math, and her IEP team is pleased with her academic progress. In considering transition planning, what other factors are important to ensure that Sara is prepared for a career or further postsecondary education upon graduation?

REFERENCES

Agran, M., King-Sears, M., Wehmeyer, M., & Copeland, S. (2003). *Student-directed learning: Teachers' guide to inclusive practices.* Baltimore, MD: Paul H. Brookes Publishing Co.

Antosh, A., Blair, M., Edwards, K., Goode, T., Hewitt, A., Izzo, M., & Wehmeyer, M. (2013). *A collaborative interagency, interdisciplinary approach to transition from adolescence to adulthood.* Silver Spring, MD: Association of University Centers on Disabilities.

Cameto, R., Haertel, G., DeBarger, A.H., & Morrison, K. (2010). *Applying evidence-centered design to alternate assessments in mathematics for students with significant cognitive disabilities: Alternate assessment design.* Menlo Park, CA: SRI International.

Cameto, R., Levine, P., & Wagner, M. (2004). *Transition planning for students with disabilities: A special topic report of findings from the National Longitudinal Transition Study-2 (NLTS-2).* Menlo Park, CA: SRI International.

Carter, E., Austin, D., & Trainor, A. (2012). Predictors of postschool employment outcomes for young adults with severe disabilities. *Journal of Disability Policy Studies, 23,* 50–63. doi:10.1177/1044207311414680

Carter, E., Ditchman, N., Sun, Y., Trainor, A., Swedeen, B., & Owens, L. (2010). Summer employment and community experiences of transition-age youth with severe disabilities. *Exceptional Children, 76,* 194–212.

Carter, E., Owens, L., Trainor, A., Sun, Y., & Swedeen, B. (2009). Self-determination skills and opportunities of adolescents with severe intellectual and developmental disabilities. *American Journal of Intellectual and Developmental Disabilities, 114*, 179–192.

Carter, E., Swedeen, B., & Moss, C. (2012). Engaging youth with and without significant disabilities in inclusive service learning. *Teaching Exceptional Children, 44*(5), 46–55.

Doren, B., Gau, J., & Lindstrom, L. (2012). The relationship between parent expectations and postschool outcomes of adolescents with disabilities. *Exceptional Children, 79*, 7–24.

Dynamic Learning Maps (undated). *Our parent brochure*. Retrieved from: http://dynamiclearningmaps.org/sites/default/files/documents/dlm_parent_brochure.pdf

Every Student Succeeds Act, S.1177. Retrieved from: https://www.congress.gov/bill/114th-congress/senate-bill/1177/text

Fuchs, D., Fuchs, L.S., & Vaughn, S. (2014). What is intensive instruction and why is it so important? *Teaching Exceptional Children, 46*(4), 13–19.

Gong, B., & Marion, S. (2006). *Dealing with flexibility in assessments for students with significant cognitive disabilities*. Dover, NH: National Center for the Improvement of Educational Assessment.

Hess, K. (2011). *E-x-p-a-n-d-e-d learning progressions frameworks for K–12 mathematics: A companion document to the learning progressions frameworks designed for use with the common core state standards in mathematics K–12*. Lexington, KY: University of Kentucky, National Alternate Assessment Center.

Hess, K., & Kearns, J. (2011). *Learning progressions frameworks designed for use with the common core state standards in English language arts and literacy K–12*. Lexington, KY: University of Kentucky, National Alternate Assessment Center.

Hunt, P., McDonnell, J., & Crockett, M. (2012). Reconciling an ecological curricular framework focusing on quality of life with the development and instruction of standards-based academic goals. *Research and Practice in Severe Disabilities, 37*(3), 139–152.

Individuals with Disabilities Education Act Amendments (IDEA)of 1997, PL 105-17, 20 U.S.C. §§ 1400 *et seq.*

Individuals with Disabilities Education Improvement Act (IDEA) of 2004, PL 108-446, 20 U.S.C. §§ 1400 *et seq.*

Kearns, J., Kleinert, H., Harrison, B., Sheppard-Jones, K., Hall, M., & Jones, M. (2011). *What does 'college and career ready' mean for students with significant cognitive disabilities?* Lexington, KY: University of Kentucky, National Alternate Assessment Center.

Kearns, J., Kleinert, H., Thurlow, M., Quenemoen, R., & Gong, B. (2015). Alternate assessments as one measure of teacher effectiveness: Implications for our field. *Research and Practice in Severe Disabilities, 40*(1), 20–35.

Kearns, J., Towles-Reeves, E., Kleinert, H., Kleinert, J., & Thomas, M. (2011). Characteristics of and implications for students participating in alternate assessments based on alternate academic achievement standards. *Journal of Special Education, 45*(1), 3–14.

Kleinert, H., Browder, D., & Towles-Reeves, E. (2009). Models of cognition for students with significant cognitive disabilities: Implications for assessment. *Review of Educational Research, 79*(1), 301–326.

Kleinert, H., Garrett, B., Towles, E., Garrett, M., Nowak-Drabik, K., Waddell, C., & Kearns, J. (2002). Alternate assessment scores and life outcomes for students with significant disabilities: Are they related? *Assessment for Effective Intervention, 28*(1), 19–30.

Kleinert, H., Kearns, J., & Kennedy, S. (1997). Accountability for all students: Kentucky's alternate portfolio system for students with moderate and severe cognitive disabilities. *Journal of The Association for Persons with Severe Handicaps, 22*(2), 88–101.

Kleinert, H., Kearns, J., Quenemoen, R., & Thurlow, M. (2013). *NCSC GSEG policy paper: Alternate assessments based on Common Core State Standards: How do they relate to college and career readiness?* Minneapolis, MN: University of Minnesota, National Center and State Collaborative.

Kleinert, H., Towles-Reeves, E., Quenemoen, R., Thurlow, M., Fluegge, L., Weseman, L., & Kerbel, A. (2015). Where students with the most significant cognitive disabilities are taught: Implications for general curriculum access. *Exceptional Children, 81*, 312–329.

Lemons, C., Kearns, D., & Davidson, K. (2014). Data-based individualization in reading: Intensifying interventions for students with significant reading disabilities. *Teaching Exceptional Children, 46*(4), 20–30.

McDonnell, J., Jameson, J.M., Riesen, T., & Polychronis, S. (2014). Embedded instruction in inclusive settings. In D.M. Browder & F. Spooner (Eds.), *More language arts, math, and science for students with severe disabilities.* Baltimore, MD: Paul H. Brookes Publishing Co.

Mislevy, R., Steinberg, L., & Almond, R. (1999). *Evidence-centered assessment design.* Retrieved from http://www.education.umd.edu/EDMS/mislevy/papers/ECD_overview.html

National Center and State Collaborative. (n.d.). *The NCSC model for a comprehensive system of curriculum, instruction, and assessment.* Retrieved from http://www.ncscpartners.org/resources

National Center and State Collaborative. (2014). *National Center and State Collaborative project summary.* Retrieved from http://www.ncscpartners.org/resources

National Center on Student Progress Monitoring. (n.d.). *Common questions for progress monitoring.* Retrieved from http://www.studentprogress.org/progresmon.asp#2

No Child Left Behind Act of 2001, PL 107–110, 115 Stat. 1425, 20 U.S.C. §§ 6301 *et seq.*

Roach, A. (2006). Influences on parent perceptions of an alternate assessment for students with severe cognitive disabilities. *Research and Practice for Persons with Severe Handicaps, 31,* 267–274.

Rowland, C., & Schweigert, P. (1996). *Tangible symbol systems.* Retrieved from http://www.ohsu.edu/xd/research/centers-institutes/institute-on-development-and-disability/design-to-learn/completed-projects/tangible-symbol-systems.cfm

Ryndak, D., Jackson, L., & White, J. (2013). Involvement and progress in the general curriculum for students with extensive support needs: K–12 inclusive-education research and implications for the future. *Inclusion, 1*(1), 28–49.

Shogren, K. (2013). A social-ecological analysis of the self-determination literature. *Intellectual and Developmental Disabilities, 51,* 496–511. doi:10.1352/1934-9556-51.6.496

Shogren, K., Wehmeyer, M., Palmer, S., Rifenbark, G., & Little, T. (2015). Relationships between self-determination and postschool outcomes for youth with disabilities. *Journal of Special Education, 48,* 256–267.

Steinbrecher, T., Selig, J., Cosbey, J., & Thorstensen, B. (2014). Evaluating special educator effectiveness: Addressing issues inherent to value-added modeling. *Exceptional Children, 80,* 323–336.

Test, D.W. (2012). *Evidence-based instructional strategies for transition.* Baltimore, MD: Paul H. Brookes Publishing Co.

Test, D., Mason, C., Hughes, C., Konrad, M., Neal, M., & Wood, W. (2004). Student involvement in individualized education program meetings. *Exceptional Children, 70,* 391–412.

Texas School for the Blind and Visually Impaired. (n.d.). *Tactile symbols directory to standard tactile symbols list.* Retrieved from http://www.tsbvi.edu/tactile-symbols

Thoma, C.A., & Wehman, P. (2010). *Getting the most out of IEPs: An educator's guide to the student-directed approach.* Baltimore, MD: Paul H. Brookes Publishing Co.

Towles-Reeves, E., Kearns, J., Flowers, C., Hart, L., Kerbel, A., Kleinert, H . . . . Thurlow, M. (2012). *Learner characteristics inventory project report (A product of the NCSC validity evaluation).* Minneapolis, MN: University of Minnesota, National Center and State Collaborative.

Towles-Reeves, E., Kearns, J., Kleinert, H., & Kleinert, J. (2009). Knowing what students know: Defining the student population taking alternate assessments based on alternate achievement standards. *Journal of Special Education, 42,* 241–254.

Towles-Reeves, E., Kleinert, H., & Muhomba, M. (2009). Alternate assessment: Have we learned anything new? *Exceptional Children, 75,* 233–252.

U.S. Department of Education. (2003, December 9). Improving the academic achievement of the disadvantaged. *Federal Register, 66*(236), 68698–68708.

U.S. Department of Education. (2004). *Standards and assessment peer review guidance.* Washington, DC: Author.

U.S. Department of Education. (2012). *ESEA flexibility: Review guidance.* Washington: DC: Author.

Wagner, M., Newman, L., Cameto, R., Levine, P., & Garza, N. (2006). *An overview of findings from Wave 2 of the National Longitudinal Transition Study-2 (NLTS-2).* Menlo Park, CA: SRI International.

Wehmeyer, M., & Palmer, S. (2003). Adult outcomes for students with cognitive disabilities three-years after high school: The impact of self-determination. *Education and Training in Developmental Disabilities, 38*(2), 131–144.

Wehmeyer, M.L., Palmer, S.B., Shogren, K., Williams-Diehm, K., & Soukup, J. (2013). Establishing a causal relationship between intervention to promote self-determination and enhanced student self-determination. *Journal of Special Education, 146*(4), 195–210.

Wehmeyer, M., & Schwartz, M. (1998). The relationship between self-determination and quality of life for adults with mental retardation. *Education and Training in Mental Retardation and Developmental Disabilities, 33*(1), 3–12.

Winsor, J., Butterworth, J., & Boone, J. (2011). Jobs by 21 Partnership Project: Impact of cross-system collaboration on employment outcomes of young adults with developmental disabilities. *Intellectual and Developmental Disabilities, 49*, 274–284.

Ysseldyke, J., & Olsen, K. (1999). Putting alternate assessments into practice: What to measure and possible sources of data. *Exceptional Children, 65*, 175–186.

Zebehazy, K., Zigmond, N., & Zimmerman, G. (2012). Performance measurement and accommodations: Students with visual accommodations in Pennsylvania's alternate assessment. *Journal of Visual Impairments and Blindness, 106*(1), 17–30.

13

Transition to Adulthood for Youth with Severe and Multiple Disabilities

MARY E. MORNINGSTAR

CHAPTER OBJECTIVES

1. Use a student's strengths, preferences, and interests to guide transition planning

2. Understand legal requirements for transition planning

3. Define adult life engagement for students with severe and multiple disabilities

4. Identify evidence-based practices for student-focused transition planning

5. Understand concepts related to supported self-determination

6. Learn methods for ensuring students achieve inclusive adult outcomes of employment, independent living, and community participation

KEY TERMS

- Customized and supported employment
- Evidence-based transition practices
- Interagency collaboration
- Measurable postsecondary goals
- Person-centered transition planning
- Postschool outcomes
- Postsecondary education and training
- School- and work-based learning
- Supported self-determination
- Transition services
- Transition to adulthood

Cassie is a 16-year-old sophomore in high school who has multiple disabilities. She gets around school by driving an electronic wheelchair, and everyone knows when she is late for her next class—she sometimes yells, "Get out of the way!" using her augmentative and alternative communication (AAC) device. She is considered to have a significant intellectual disability as well as cerebral palsy and some vision limitations. She spends time in both general education classes and a special education classroom. Her course enrollment was carefully considered to account for the transition-related goals and skills needed to help her succeed in adulthood, including targeting skills such as strengthening her communication skills to convey information, initiating and sustaining social interactions, and making choices related to her desires and her needs. She is also working on common core expanded standards aligned with the alternate assessment for literacy (e.g., listening to a story and answering questions using her communication device) and numeracy (e.g., developing increased understanding of quantities). For the most part, her general education classes, such as language arts, social studies, home economics, choir, and introduction to technology, are the best places to work on these skills. In addition, she is enrolled in a career development class through the special education department.

Cassie lives in a rural community; her dad is a farmer and her mom works at a local grocery store. Her sister is a senior in high school, and her two brothers are in elementary and middle schools. She participates in family chores at home. Luckily, her grandfather and dad are excellent carpenters, and they have modified the family home to make it as accessible as possible. Her family is very concerned about her future adult life. They attended their first transition planning meeting when Cassie was 15, when the special education teacher started talking about transition. It was shocking for them, as they really hadn't started to think through Cassie's future, and, quite honestly, they don't remember a whole lot of the new terms and forms associated with this meeting. They have heard from other families that there aren't a whole lot of services for adults with severe and multiple disabilities. They have a lot of questions and concerns and are not sure where to go for information.

Transition to adulthood is typically marked by the high school graduation ceremony, a ritual that takes place for hundreds of thousands of youth across the country each spring. These young adults leave high school and enter postsecondary educational settings, go straight to work, or perhaps take some time off before they decide which direction their life will take. For youth with severe and multiple disabilities, however, the transition from school to adult life often looks very different. When compared with other students with disabilities, youth with severe and multiple disabilities continue to experience the least successful adult outcomes (Sanford et al., 2011). Too often, it is considered appropriate for these young adults to transition to segregated work and residential settings that are devoid of real opportunities for inclusion in the community. Given the prevalence of segregated services for this group of young adults, the trend toward innovative ways to support most adults with disabilities in attaining a quality adult life is still unobtainable for most (Braddock et al., 2013), even when models of positive and inclusive transitions exist (Certo et al., 2006).

In special education, transition was historically seen as a bridge between the security of school and home to the risks and opportunities of adult life (Will, 1984). One common denominator among adolescents with severe and multiple disabilities making the transition from school to adult life is that these individuals have complex support needs, especially when it comes to finding and sustaining inclusive employment, community engagement, and ongoing education. However, a critical shift in the way planning and services are provided has taken place, with secondary special educators focusing upon the student's and family's desired post-school outcomes as the guiding force of transition planning. Accomplishing this shift can occur by concentrating on the student's strengths, preferences, and interests; and then developing transition plans that address the unique support needs leading to inclusive adult lives.

This chapter describes the legal requirements for transition planning and services, shares an approach to defining adult life engagement, and presents evidence-based practices for supporting a student-focused approach to transition planning. Concepts related to supported self-determination, along with strategies for acknowledging and teaching this skill, are shared. Finally, this chapter describes methods for ensuring that students with severe and multiple disabilities achieve critical adulthood outcomes of supported and customized employment, supported living, and supported community membership.

IDEA DEFINITION AND REQUIREMENTS FOR TRANSITION

In the United States, transition planning and services were first mandated under the reauthorization of the Individuals with Disabilities Education Act (IDEA) of 1990, PL 101-476. More recently, other countries have acknowledged the importance of transition through laws and regulatory policies that mirror the US mandates; therefore IDEA will be used as the prime example. Understanding the compliance requirements of the transition Individualized Education Program (IEP) is important, but it is even more important to support students to achieve positive adult outcomes by using effective strategies for student-focused transition planning. Equally relevant is for educators to ensure that they implement effective interventions and practices for preparing youth for adulthood. Assisting students and their families to connect with services both within and outside of the school system is a cornerstone of transition.

From the early research on post-school outcomes, it was evident that the first generation of students with disabilities who had received special education services were not making successful transitions to adulthood. This was especially true for students with the most significant support needs (Will, 1984). Fast-forwarding 30 years from when Madeleine Will, then Assistant Secretary of the Department of Education, first introduced the concept of transition to adulthood as a federal policy, we know that students with disabilities have been making steady progress toward achieving more positive adult outcomes (Sanford et al., 2011). Unfortunately, substantially fewer outcomes exist for students with severe and multiple disabilities when compared to their peers with and without disabilities, and inclusive adult outcomes are even less likely to be obtained (Carter, Austin, & Trainor, 2012; Newman, Wagner, Cameto, Knokey, & Shaver, 2010). The urgency to improve both planning and transition services for this group of students is undeniable and can be felt by advocates, families, researchers, and practitioners.

The 2004 reauthorization of IDEA mandates that transition planning must begin by the time the student turns 16 years old. In some states, the regulations for transition planning begin even younger, with many starting by age 14. Of course, for students with severe and multiple disabilities and their families, beginning the transition planning process should occur as early as possible, to allow substantial time to create opportunities that will lead to inclusive adult outcomes. We can consider the IEP as a road map for reaching the final destination: the student's and family's vision for a future adult life. Therefore, it is critical that a sufficient amount of time and energy be given to developing the IEP and ensuring that it is guided by quality transition planning.

IDEA mandates that when the purpose of an IEP team meeting is to consider a student's postsecondary goals, then the student must be invited to attend the meeting as a team member. Because the IEP is based upon a student's needs, strengths, preferences, and interests, it makes sense for the student to be present and actively engaged during transition meetings. The law makes it clear that parents are to be active members of IEP teams. Unfortunately, as was the case with Cassie, her first meeting to discuss transition met the compliance requirements of IDEA, but her family was not prepared for the discussion about transition. Teachers and other school district personnel can prepare families for transition planning by providing trainings where families can learn about transition; and by developing and distributing brochures and other types of information about transition, including videos and web sites.

Transition planning entails reviewing students' postsecondary goals, educational services, and transition activities with the focus on supporting the interests, preferences, and strengths of the student. It is important for teachers and related service providers to facilitate and support the student to reach his or her goals, or what IDEA calls *measurable postsecondary goals* (MPGs). IEP teams must develop and specify measurable postsecondary goals (MPGs) in the areas of employment, education and/or training, and, where appropriate, independent living. This requires IEP teams to focus on long-term goals that are measurable, meaning the team can demonstrate how they facilitated the student to achieve his or her postsecondary goals. Identifying independent living goals is an essential element of transition planning for students with severe and multiple disabilities.

> Because Cassie has significant support needs, her family and IEP Team completed the Independent Living IEP Team checklist that included several areas to target for transition planning. A measurable postsecondary goal for supported living was included in her IEP: "Upon graduation from high school, Cassie will live in an apartment with roommates of her choosing with the supports and services required to maintain her supported living arrangements." Annual IEP goals that addressed skills specific to her measurable postsecondary goal, such as using a switch to cook food in the microwave, making choices on her AAC device for clothing, and communicating her personal needs, were included for the year.

Measurable postsecondary goals are not set in stone. In fact, they may change each year, especially when working with a younger student, or with someone who hasn't had an opportunity to experience any employment or postsecondary educational settings, as is often the case for students with severe and multiple disabilities. IDEA is very clear one must *facilitate the movement toward* the student's measurable postsecondary goals in employment, education/training and independent living when developing a transition plan. This is why transition IEP teams must first develop the postsecondary goals, so that the rest of the IEP will relate to the student's future goals.

Transition services are used to help the student achieve his or her desired postsecondary goals. The transition services that must be considered by the IEP team include:

- **Instruction:** The services and activities that are a part of the teaching and learning process, and are generally provided by school systems in classrooms. However, instruction can take place in other settings, such as the community, and with a variety of people.

- **Community experiences:** Activities provided in community settings by family members, schools, employers, and other agencies (e.g., independent living centers, vocational rehabilitation, intellectual and developmental disabilities organizations). Community experiences may include activities such as school-sponsored field trips, participation in community organizations and clubs, and community work experiences.

- **Related services:** These must now be considered for each student as a possible way to meet transition outcomes. Rehabilitation counseling was added as a related service under IDEA 2004, allowing schools to provide or contract with outside agencies to provide rehabilitation counseling to meet transition outcomes.

- **Employment:** Includes experiences and activities that lead to a job or career plan that can be provided by the school or other community entities. Schools can provide classes or community experiences that address career and job awareness, exploration, and work training experiences.

- **Other post-school adult living outcomes:** These incorporate adult living skills and access to community services (e.g., government services, transportation, specialized services, health care) and general community activities (e.g., church, volunteer activities).

- **Daily living skills:** Activities that adults do every day or on a regular basis (e.g., preparing meals, budgeting, maintaining a home, paying bills, caring for clothes, and grooming).

- **Functional vocational evaluation:** An assessment process that provides information about job or career interests, aptitudes, and skills as well as work habits and work attitudes. It may be compiled through situational assessments, observations, and standardized measures.

When identifying transition services for students, the educational team should be able to answer YES to the following three questions:

1. Are the transition services focused on improving the student's academic and functional achievement?

2. Do the transition services facilitate the student's movement from school to postsecondary settings?

3. Are the transition services listed appropriate for helping the student meet his or her postsecondary goal(s)?

Transition services identified by Cassie's IEP team related to her measurable postsecondary goal to live in an apartment with roommates included several supports and services that were going to be completed by several different IEP team members, including: (a) specific community-based experiences for accessing community services; (b) family responsibility to apply for independent living skills classes through the local center for independent living; and (c) Cassie's in-home personal care attendant, who provided explicit instruction for daily living skills.

As is evident, transition services are much broader than annual IEP educational goals and services, and are included in transition plans to ensure that schools provide relevant experiences leading to improved postsecondary outcomes. In addition, parents, students and other outside agencies can be listed as partners in providing transition services.

Because parents are active members of IEP teams, during transition, they must be notified of upcoming transition meetings, which helps give them more information about transition prior to the meeting. Providing a simple brochure, such as the one found in Figure 13.1, can go a long way to helping families know more about the process. Parental notification of an IEP meeting must indicate that the student will be invited, inform the parents of any agencies that will be represented, and inform parents that they may invite other people to participate on the IEP team. Of course, involving families in transition planning requires more than just having them at the IEP meeting. Communicating with families so that they are up to date on current issues about transition is something to be done on a regular basis.

Cassie's high school special education and related services staff recently attended a workshop where they learned about supporting families and students during transition. One idea they really liked, and plan to implement in the spring, is to hold a PIE (Parent Information Exchange) Night. This will be tied into another school activity, so the most parents can attend. At a PIE night, parents and students learn about transition-related issues such as guardianship, supplemental security income, vocational rehabilitation services, and planning for the future for their sons and daughters. Often, adults and family members of older students who have successfully made the transition to adulthood will share their stories. For Cassie's family, this will help them to see what the possibilities are for Cassie's future.

Once a student's transition IEP is developed, then the real work begins for the educational team. What skills students learn and what experiences they gain through their secondary school years are significant contributors to their success as adults. For students with severe and multiple disabilities, this means participating in real-life and inclusive experiences such as work-based learning, preparation for independent living, and participating in the general curriculum and community activities. Deciding which skills and experiences to target must be based upon the individual student's postsecondary goals and will not look the same for every student. Developing inclusive educational and adult life goals means holding high expectations for students with severe and multiple disabilities. The team will also need to provide examples and role models to share with families if transition planning is to focus on inclusive adult life engagement. Strategies to do this will be shared next. Figure 13.2 illustrates the essential elements of transition outlined in Cassie's IEP.

Cassie's teacher shared a video that highlighted successful young adults with multiple disabilities who were leading inclusive adult lives. This helped her family develop a vision for Cassie's future in which she would make meaningful and reciprocal contributions and be a true member of her community.

There's a world of
opportunity out there...
if you dream and prepare!

What path
will your child take *after*
High School?

Students and families are vital
to the transition planning process

•••

For information about transition in
your school:

Transition
Planning

can help you

with the answers...

(continued)

Figure 13.1. Transition Brochure to Share with Families. From The Transition Coalition (2015). Transition planning brochure. Retrieved from http://transitioncoalition.org/blog/tc-materials/transition-planning/. The University of Kansas: Lawrence, KS; adapted by permission.

Figure 13.1. *(continued)* Transition Brochure to Share with Families. From The Transition Coalition (2015). Transition planning brochure. Retrieved from http://transitioncoalition.org/blog/tc-materials/transition-planning/. The University of Kansas: Lawrence, KS; adapted by permission.

Do you have questions about how your child will learn, work, have friends and a good life after high school?

Transition services help students and families establish a vision for the future about where students will live and work, and how they will participate in their community

Transition planning focuses on:

- Future Education & Training
- Future Careers & Employment
- Community Involvement
- Connections with Agencies & Services

Students, families, schools, and agencies work as a team to support the student's plans for the future.

(continued)

Figure 13.1. *(continued)* Transition Brochure to Share with Families. From The Transition Coalition (2015). Transition planning brochure. Retrieved from http://transitioncoalition.org/blog/tc-materials/transition-planning/. The University of Kansas: Lawrence, KS; adapted by permission.

Transition Planning consists of... curriculum, services and supports to help students move successfully to life after high school.

- Transition planning must begin by the IEP in effect when a student turns 16.

- Transition planning can begin earlier, if needed.

- Some states start transition planning when the student turns 14.

- ALL students with IEPs must receive transition planning and services.

- Each year, the student and IEP team identify what the student wants to do after high school for employment, education/training, and independent living.

- The IEP must include coursework, annual goals and transition services to work toward the student's future plans.

You and your son or daughter will help identify:

- A vision for the future

- High School courses to take

- College and other future learning & training options

- Employment options and experiences

- Extracurricular activities to participate in

- Community experiences, and

- Agencies or services

It's never too early to start preparing for a successful future.

1. Present Level of Academic Achievement and Functional Performance

How the child's disability affects his or her involvement and progress in the general education curriculum; or for preschool children, participation in age-appropriate activities. (For students with transition plans, consider how the child's disability will affect the child's ability to reach his or her postsecondary goals— what the child will do after high school.)

Cassie has an educational identification of multiple disabilities. The combination of her intellectual disability and orthopedic impairment results in significant educational needs. She requires specialized instruction in all core curricular courses due to the intense need to build skills for reading, math, and written language. She is able to participate with her peers without disabilities in some courses for the purpose of increasing socialization skills.

The strengths of the child. (For students with transition plans, consider how the strengths of the child relate to the child's postsecondary goals.)

Cassie enjoys being around others and being able to communicate with them, particularly as a sport is being played. She is able to communicate her wants and needs appropriately to familiar peers and adults around her. She can conduct simple office tasks such as sorting and making copies. She is able to follow a checklist to stay focused and complete a task that has been assigned to her; this will be very beneficial to her being able to work on her independent living skills.

Concerns of the parent/guardian for enhancing the education of the child. (For students with transition plans, consider the parent/guardian's expectations for the child after the child leaves high school.)

Cassie's mother is concerned about her ability to survive the real world. She would like to see her receive on-the-job training so she is able to work productively. She would also like for her to continue to receive guidance on self-help skills regarding her independent living skills; she is still having trouble with her self-care skills. She plans on having her continue to live with her after she graduates and has a job, continues her education, or partakes in appropriate daytime activities. Cassie and her parents will start looking at supported living apartments in the community in 2 years.

Changes in current functioning of the child since the initial or prior individualized education program (IEP). (For students with transition plans, consider how changes in the child's current functioning will affect the child's ability to reach his or her postsecondary goal.)

Cassie now works several hours a week in the school café. She is learning how to use the cash register. She is also working on her social-communication skills. Cassie works in the front office as a volunteer office assistant—making copies and distributing information to teachers via a mailbox system. She uses a checklist system to keep her systematic and on task. There are plans in place to help Cassie learn to staple and file information within the next year. In learning these skills, Cassie will be able to transition her learning opportunities to jobs she has interest in pursuing. Cassie continues to expand her verbal vocabulary. In the past year, she increased her expressive language using an augmentative and alternative communication (AAC) device to 50 pictures and phrases. She uses her AAC device to further her communication with others, increasing her vocabulary. She is expanding her social skills with unfamiliar individuals.

A summary of the most recent evaluation/reevaluation results.

Cassie's last diagnostic testing was on 02/05/14. Her full scale IQ score obtained using the Stanford-Binet Intelligence Scales, Fifth Edition (SB-5) was 50, indicating intellectual disabilities. The Vineland Adaptive Behavior Scale scores were as follows: communication, 40; daily living, 55; and socialization, 50; ab quotient was 48. Her highest areas were in receptive communication, play and leisure time, and gross motor skills. The areas she scored lowest on were socialization, expressive communication, community living skills, and fine motor skills. Cassie continues with the medical diagnosis of cerebral palsy, and with the combination of intellectual disabilities, Cassie continues to meet the eligibility criteria of multiple disabilities. Cassie scored proficient on the alternative assessment. Cassie is able to manipulate her electric wheelchair semi-independently. She has difficulty maneuvering through tight spaces including classroom and shopping store aisles.

Formal or informal age-appropriate transition assessments.

Cassie has been assessed using formal and informal assessments that address training, education, employment, and independent living, as needed. She was assessed using a student interview and the Picture Interest Career Survey given in October 2014. Cassie's main interest areas were information technology (investigative) and scientific research, engineering, and math (investigative). On the Vineland Adaptive Behavior Scale, Cassie's highest scores were in the areas of receptive communication, play and leisure time, and gross motor skills. Her lowest scores were in the areas of expressive and written communication, community living skills, and fine motor skills. In an interview with Cassie and her parents, she would like a career in office clerical. She also indicated that she wants to live in her own place, hang out with friends, and attend art and cultural events.

(continued)

Figure 13.2. Cassie's individualized education program for transition. Source: The Transition Coalition [2014].

Figure 13.2. *(continued)*

Name: Cassie	Projected date of graduation: 06/2016	Date of initial transition program Previous: 04-02-2014 Update: 04-01-2015

Measurable postsecondary goals (these goals are to be achieved after graduation, and there must be a goal for education/training, employment, and independent living as needed)

Education/training: Cassie will enroll in adult education classes in her community and will receive on-the-job training.

Employment: Cassie will work in an office clerical position with the supports needed to maintain her position.

Independent living (as appropriate): Cassie will live in an apartment with a roommate and the supports needed to live in the community.

Transition Services

Based on age-appropriate transition assessments, identify transition services appropriate for the child's postsecondary goals in the following spaces.

Services may include: Instruction, related services, community experiences, the development of employment and other postschool adult living objectives, acquisition of daily living skills or provision of a functional vocational assessment

Education/Training

Measurable postsecondary goal	Transition services	Person/agency involved	Date of completion/ achieved outcome
Cassie will enroll in adult education classes in her community and will receive on- the- job training when she completes high school and the community-based transition program for 18- to 21-year-old individuals.	School will assist in setting up an appointment with community college or program counselor to explore course options.	Little Town High School (guidance counselor)	9/2015
	Speech-language pathologist (SLP) will support communication skills in Cassie's high school arts and cooking classes.	Little Town High School (SLP)	5/2016
	Complete an assistive technology (AT) evaluation to see if additional AT will be needed in community adult education classes.	Little Town High School (AT specialist)	11/2015
	Collect information about enrolling in art and cooking classes at the community center.	Tricia and Scott (parents)	5/2016

Employment

Measurable postsecondary goal	Transition services	Person/agency involved	Date of completion/ achieved outcome
Cassie will work in an office clerical position with the supports needed to maintain her position when she completes high school and the community-based transition program for 18- to 21-year-old individuals.	School will identify three different office clerical work experiences for Cassie to assess her preferences and capabilities and increase her job-related behaviors (e.g., communicating, initiating social interactions, working with a team).	Special education teacher Work-based learning coordinator	5/2016
	School will complete the discovery assessment process to identify Cassie's individualized preferences related to employment.	Work-based learning coordinator	12/2015
	Cassie's parents will apply for rehabilitation service.	Tricia and Scott (parents) Rehabilitation services	11/2015
	An assessment of Cassie's positioning and AT needs on the job will be completed before the end of the school year.	School occupational therapist and AT specialist	

(continued)

Figure 13.2.   *(continued)*

Independent Living			
Measurable postsecondary goal	**Transition services**	**Person/agency involved**	**Date of completion/ achieved outcome**
Cassie will live in an apartment with a roommate and the supports needed to live in the community when she completes high school and the community-based transition program for 18- to 21-year-old individuals.	Provide instruction in consumer purchasing and shopping for groceries.	Personal finance teacher and special education teacher	5/2016
	Teach about making choices about recreational/leisure activities using her communication device.	SLP, special education teachers, paraprofessional	5/2016
	Support communication skills and initiating social interactions throughout her day.	Cassie, Tricia and Scott (parents)	5/2016
	Encourage Cassie to participate in meal preparation and to cook one meal each week.		5/2016

TRANSFER OF RIGHTS (Required by age 17): _____ was informed on _____

                                                                        Name   Date

of his or her rights, if any, that will transfer at age 18.

RIGHTS WERE TRANSFERRED (Required by age 18): _____ was informed on _____

                                                                              Name   Date

of his or her rights.

Four-year course of study

Ninth grade	10th grade	11th grade	12th grade
English I	English II	English III	Life skills
Life skills	Life skills	Life skills	Personal finance 2
Physical science	Elective (Foods 2)	Elective (Art)	Biology
Elective (Foods 1)	Elective (Weight training)	Elective (Health and wellness)	Elective (Art)
Elective (Art)	Civics	Personal finance 1	Elective (Career explorations/ Foods 1)
Physical education	Work-based learning experiences	Work-based learning experiences	Work-based learning experiences
Careers class	Work-based learning experiences	Work-based learning experiences	Work-based learning experiences

(continued)

Figure 13.2. *(continued)*

(Sample of one IEP goal)

Annual IEP Goals

Annual Measurable IEP Goals
Note: There must be at least one measurable annual transition IEP goal to help the child reach each of the desired measurable postsecondary goals.

Annual Goal 1: Independent living

Cassie will use the dollar-up strategy with 100% accuracy when grocery shopping.

For students with postsecondary transition plans, please indicate which goal domain(s) their annual goal will support:

☐ Postsecondary education/training   ☐ Employment   ☒ Independent living

Progress toward the goal will be measured by: **(check all that apply)**

☐ **Work samples**	☐ **Curriculum-based tests**	☒ **Portfolios**	☐ **Checklists**
☒ **Scoring guides**	☐ **Observation chart**	☐ **Reading record**	☒ **Other:** Informal assessments and discussion with teacher

Comments:

Cassie learned this skill in middle school but has not yet generalized to community setting. The goal is to generalize in the grocery store.

Annual Goal 2: Employment

Cassie will participate in three career exploration work-based learning sites to identify her preferences for working in an office clerical position.

For students with postsecondary transition plans, please indicate which goal domain(s) their annual goal will support:

☐ Postsecondary education/training   ☒ Employment   ☐ Independent living

Progress toward the goal will be measured by: **(check all that apply)**

☒ **Work samples**	☐ **Curriculum-based tests**	☐ **Portfolios**	☐ **Checklists**
☐ **Scoring guides**	☐ **Observation chart**	☒ **Reading record**	☐ **Other:**

Comments:

Cassie job sampled during the 10th grade and seems to enjoy office-type positions in which there are a lot of opportunities to engage with co-workers.

ADULT LIFE ENGAGEMENT: BROADENING
THE FOCUS OF SUPPORTED ADULTHOOD

In discussing their son Ian's transition from school to adult life, Diane and Phil Ferguson described a framework of adulthood that combines theories of chronological development with societal perceptions of adulthood: autonomy, membership, and change (Ferguson & Ferguson, 2006). Table 13.1 defines and outlines these three dimensions. Autonomy refers to having the freedom, independence, and self-sufficiency to make important life choices; whereas membership denotes belonging, connection, and collaboration with others in the community.

To address the specific life circumstances of youth with severe and multiple disabilities, they expanded the traditional notions of adulthood by articulating a model of supported adulthood emphasizing the "dual sense of independence and belonging as the most basic benefits of social support programs" (Ferguson & Ferguson, 2006, p. 626). Components of supported adulthood require: (a) promoting inclusion in the natural context; (b) blending informal and formal supports within natural settings; (c) ensuring services meet the unique preferences of the individual and his or her family; and (d) maintaining a community-focused point of view.

As teams work with students with multiple disabilities and their families, the planning and services offered should align with the skills, experiences, and supports needed to help learners make the transition from school to a supported adult life (Buntinx & Schalock, 2010). Predominantly, schools consider adult success from an overly simplistic perspective (employed/unemployed;

Table 13.1. Dimensions of adulthood

Autonomy	Being your own person, expressed through symbols such as
	• *Self-sufficiency:* having resources to take care of yourself (e.g., working, living on your own, participating in community); includes emotional self-sufficiency
	• *Self-determination:* individuality, independence, maturity, personal freedom to make life choices, responsibility for one's actions
	• *Completeness:* possessing confidence about capabilities and how to act in a variety of situations
Membership	Community connections, collaboration, and sacrifice expressed through
	• *Affiliation:* voluntary associations and fellowships in both organized groups (e.g., service organizations, church membership) and individual interpersonal relationships
	• *Citizenship:* responsibilities to one's community and to others; most directly played out in activities of collective governance (e.g., voting, signing up for the draft, volunteering for a political candidate, recycling)
Change	Adulthood is viewed a continual process of growth.
	• Change occurs across all aspects of adult life (e.g., employment, living, friendships, relationships)
	• Realization of accomplishments and place in life
	• Leads to a sense of wholeness and striving for order and meaning

living independently/living at home); yet, what constitutes a quality life for individual students and their families may not be considered. Halpern (1993) introduced planning for the transition to a quality adult life that encompassed three domains: (a) physical and material well-being, (b) performance of adult roles (e.g., employment/career, relationships/social networks, education, citizenship), and (c) personal fulfillment. Teams typically spend considerable time identifying and planning for the individualized supports needed to fulfill students' desired adult lives. One can use an individualized supports approach to bring together practices such as person-centered planning, community inclusion, and personal growth and empowerment (Schalock et al., 2010)—all of which are critical elements of supported adult life engagement. Each of these is described in Table 13.2 and is discussed throughout the rest of this chapter, with examples of models and practices that promote and facilitate supported adulthood for youth with severe and multiple disabilities.

The transition to supported adulthood for students with severe and multiple disabilities requires new ways to plan and prepare for quality adult outcomes. Unfortunately, educational and adult service delivery systems often operate in ways that deny the full participation of adulthood for students, and that perpetuate "unfinished transitions by encouraging dependency, social isolation and personal chronicity" (Ferguson & Ferguson, 2006, p. 625).

Fortunately, innovative professionals, family members, and self-advocates have begun to operationalize the new paradigm of supported adulthood. The good news is that models of inclusive supported adulthood have been developed and taken root in many communities; however, gaps in replicating systems of support still exist. Such new and innovative means for supporting young adults with severe disabilities will be described in the remaining sections of this chapter.

Table 13.2. Defining supported adulthood

Supported employment	Competitive work in integrated employment settings for people with the most severe disabilities for whom competitive employment has not traditionally occurred. It is designed for those who need intensive support services in order to find and maintain work because of the severity of their disability (Wehman & Brooke, 2013).
Supported living	An individual with severe and multiple disabilities lives in a home or apartment of his or her choice, shared with roommates he or she has selected, that is not owned or operated by an agency. Supports are provided to the individual based on his or her preferences and needs (Klein, Wilson, & Nelson, 2000).
Supported membership in the community	Providing support so that individuals with severe and multiple disabilities can participate in community activities and organizations that meet their individual preferences and interests. Supports are designed to facilitate a wide variety of relationships, including acquaintances, being a regular customer, having a sense of belonging in a group or organization, and developing friendships (Amado, 2013).
Supported self-determination	Supported self-determination assists students with severe and multiple disabilities to experience a quality life consistent with their values, preferences, strengths, and needs. Through supported self-determination, the individual can actualize a quality future through daily routines and relationships (McDougall, Evans, & Baldwin, 2010).

EVIDENCE-BASED PRACTICES TO PREPARE FOR THE
TRANSITION TO SUPPORTED ADULTHOOD: AN OVERVIEW

The most current innovations in transition are the results of an increase in the research and implementation of evidence-based practices (Test, Fowler et al., 2009). Kohler (1996) examined published literature, research studies, and model transition programs and created the Taxonomy for Transition Programming Framework comprising five domains: student-focused planning, student development, interagency collaboration, family involvement, and program structures. The Taxonomy conceptually organized a diverse set of practices for delivering transition-focused education and services (Kohler & Field, 2003). Subsequently, researchers have launched rigorous research studies to identify a body of evidence that supports the range of transition practices.

Evidence-based Transition Planning

As part of the *What Works in Transition Research Synthesis*, Cobb and Alwell examined both studies that met the definition of *transition planning/coordinating interventions* to identify approaches that successfully "facilitate the child's movement from school to post-school activities" (2007, p. 11). Only a limited number of rigorous research studies were found to include student-focused planning; however, sufficient evidence was found that providing student-centered transition planning holds great promise for leading to positive postsecondary outcomes. The most effective methods of transition planning include involving students during transition IEP meetings and supporting them to be highly engaged during the planning process by having a valued place on the team. In addition, several of the qualitative studies supported the notion that adding transition to an already full IEP meeting is not sufficient; transition planning requires enough time and space to be implemented well. Finally, Cobb and Alwell found that focusing specifically on person-centered planning approaches leads to more positive experiences for all involved in transition planning.

More recently, Test, Mazzotti et al. (2009) completed a systematic review of transition research for the *National Secondary Transition Technical Assistance Center* (www.nsttac.org). They identified specific practices with moderate to high evidence of success, including: (a) teaching students to be actively involved in transition IEP meetings (Test et al., 2004); (b) utilizing evidence-based self-advocacy strategies and skills (Van Reusen & Bos, 1994); (c) teaching students strategies for a self-directed IEP meeting (Martin et al., 2006); and (d) promoting self-determination skills that are more likely to lead to improved postsecondary outcomes in employment and independent living (Shogren, Wehmeyer, Palmer, Rifenbark, & Little, 2013; Wehmeyer & Palmer, 2003).

Transition plans will be more individualized, comprehensive, and collaborative when students and families are placed at the center of planning and a strengths-based approach is used, (Keyes & Owen-Johnson, 2003). Person-centered planning is a strategy one can embed within transition planning that focuses on students' strengths and empowers families, thereby establishing collaborative relationships (Michaels & Ferrara, 2005). By illuminating the students' preferences, connecting them to formal and informal supports in the community, and involving family and community members, one can provide students with inclusive experiences (Kincaid & Fox, 2002; Rasheed et al., 2006).

Implementing Person-Centered Transition Planning

Using person-centered approaches specifically to plan for the transition to adulthood has been discussed for some time (Stineman, Morningstar, Bishop, & Turnbull, 1993). Furney (1993) created an approach that embedded person-centered planning into transition by adapting *Making Action Plans* (MAPs; O'Brien & Forest, 1989). The adaptation, *Making Dreams Happen* (Furney, 1993), begins by having a team respond to five questions:

1. Who is the student?

2. What is the student's history?

3. What are the student's dreams?

4. What are the student's fears for the future?

5. What is needed to make the student's dreams a reality?

Team members can include family members, peers, and friends/neighbors, as well as teachers and other support staff. The team spends about an hour developing the student's and family's vision for the future, as well as generating strategies for how to realize his or her dreams. The responses to the five questions are illustrated and displayed on large sheets of paper, which is typically done in MAPs meetings.

The team is then guided to complete specific transition planning for the IEP. Because this approach does not adhere to traditional planning methods, and uses colorful graphics to record the planning, it easily accommodates students with a range of communication and intellectual supports, and it is much more appealing and accessible to students and other team members. The information generated from the MAP meeting often "sparks new ideas and creative ways to overcome barriers that have previously stood in the way of reaching a student's dreams for the future" (Furney, 1993, p. 6). The following four steps must be completed to develop a person-centered transition plan:

1. Hold a MAP meeting and summarize information from the MAP into charts.

2. Organize results of the MAP meeting into four quadrants to consider possible postsecondary goals: employment, community participation, education, and community living.

3. Complete the following steps during the IEP meeting:

    • Include results from the MAP in the transition assessments section of the IEP.

    • Develop measurable postsecondary goals for the IEP based on the dreams for the future generated during MAP and organized in the quadrants.

- Consider which annual IEP goals are to be developed and implemented to facilitate progress toward the measurable postsecondary goals.

- Identify specific transition services needed (e.g., instruction, community experiences).

- Include interagency linkages and services from outside agencies who are or may be involved in providing services.

4. Implement the IEP, track student progress toward goals and services provided, and reconvene the IEP team if needed.

The end result of the first meeting, the completed person-centered plan, can then be used as a basis for developing the transition plan. The final step is to develop measurable postsecondary goals, develop annual IEP goals, and identify specific transition services for the student, all of which are included in the IEP.

Implementing person-centered planning takes more time than the traditional IEP meeting; therefore it is most appropriate before a major change takes place, or when progress toward achieving a goal has been halted or stalled, as a way to breathe life back into the process and get it moving again. If there have been recent changes in a student's life or if there is great uncertainly about future outcomes and services, a person-centered process can support the transition planning efforts.

SUPPORTED SELF-DETERMINATION AND STUDENT INVOLVEMENT IN TRANSITION

Over the decades, a combination of policies and research has established not only the basic right of individuals to make decisions affecting their lives, but has promoted a consistent body of evidence of how important it is toward achieving quality adult lives (Agran & Hughes, 2014). We now know that self-determination is associated with improved adult outcomes for individuals with intellectual disabilities such as employment and living (Shogren, Lopez, Wehmeyer, Little, & Pressgrove, 2006; Wehmeyer & Palmer, 2003). In addition, the realization of self-determination has been shown to improve access to the general education curriculum and increase academic skills (Fowler, Konrad, Walker, Test, & Wood, 2007; Shogren, Palmer, Wehmeyer, Williams-Diehm, & Little, 2012). Self-determination has been defined as consisting of six components: "the ability to make choices, solve problems, set goals, evaluate options, take initiative to reach one's goals, and accept consequences of one's actions" (Rowe et al., 2013, p. 8). Therefore, educators must be prepared to teach individual students the skills associated with the six elements, which include self-advocacy, goal-setting, choice-making, and problem solving.

Since the passage of the transition requirements of IDEA, certain curricula and interventions for teaching and supporting self-determination have been identified as leading to improved postsecondary outcomes (Test, Fowler et al., 2009). Unfortunately, the more extensive the support needs of students, the less likely teachers are to consider teaching self-determination skills to be important (Wehmeyer,

Agran, & Hughes, 2000). Furthermore, when teachers are interested in supporting self-determination, they often do not have knowledge of evidence-based curricula, materials and strategies (Thoma, Nathanson, Baker, & Tamura, 2002).

Supported Self-determination

Unfortunately, most of the self-determination curricula and interventions do not specifically address the communication and response needs of students with multiple disabilities. Therefore, how to support students to be self-determined requires thinking outside the box. Furthermore, Wehmeyer (2005) argued that self-determination should not be considered a set of skills because of the limitations this approach imposes on students with significant disabilities, particularly if their performance repertoire is highly limited, as is common. Supported self-determination specifically addresses how students with severe and multiple disabilities express their needs and affect their worlds.

Because students often are unable to communicate their desires verbally, supported self-determination requires that teachers interpret the meaning and intentions of students' choices and decisions (Brown, Gothelf, Guess, & Lehr, 1998; Wehmeyer, 2005). Supported self-determination is a means for experiencing quality of life consistent with the values, preferences, strengths, and needs of the student and to actualize this life through daily routines and relationships (McDougall, Evans, & Baldwin, 2010; Turnbull & Turnbull, 2000).

Cassie's path toward supported self-determination includes first and foremost making sure that the people in her life fully understand her communication abilities. For those who know her well, it's easy to interpret her pre-symbolic behaviors (e.g., facial expressions, vocalizations, body language), but for others, having some guidance on what certain behaviors mean is critical to ensuring that others are really listening to her. In addition, she needs many opportunities across the day to express herself and to learn to make choices. Finally, the more opportunities for her to be included in general education classes and surrounded by peers without disabilities, the more likely she is to have the much needed opportunities to practice her skills and to pay attention to her peer models. At home, it's equally important that her family doesn't do everything for her, but that they give her opportunities to express her choices and take the time to wait for her to express herself.

Evidence tells us that students with severe and multiple disabilities can participate in elements of complex tasks such as decision-making or problem solving. Indeed, they can clearly act with intention, often with support from others (Wehmeyer, 2005). In addition, students with severe disabilities can become more self-determined, even if they are not fully independent. In one study (Agran, Blanchard, & Wehmeyer, 2000), teachers learned how to support their students to set and reach transition-related goals. The teachers provided supports and adaptations that led to increased student participation in individual goal setting.

Although many of the students were non-verbal, they were still able to express responses to goal-setting tasks because the teachers developed activities promoting active student involvement. For example, teachers helped students identify personal preferences in transition (work, living, recreation) using pictures, videos and interviews with others. The teachers also used the principle of partial participation (Baumgart et al., 1982; Browder et al., 2007) to support student engagement in choice making, whereby students participated in certain aspects of an activity such as using a switch to turn on the computer or using eye gaze to identify a choice.

The Path to Supported Self-Determination for Students with Severe and Multiple Disabilities

Having the ability to communicate is essential to supported self-determination by providing students with ever expanding control and autonomy in their daily lives (Downing, 2005). Students who are able to access methods of communication can improve their quality of life by obtaining basic needs, engaging in desired activities, seeking information, and developing social closeness with others (Lund & Light, 2007). Given the communication challenges of students with multiple disabilities, their ability to control their world (i.e., supported self-determination) is highly dependent on our ability to interpret meaning from unconventional methods (Brown et al., 1998). This requires that educators be able to identify and interpret the functions of their students' unique, idiosyncratic, inconsistent and unconventional communication styles, and respond accordingly.

In order to facilitate supported self-determination successfully, students must be offered many different opportunities to express their choices and preferences using a variety of means (e.g., body language, eye gaze, AAC device). Unfortunately, many students with multiple disabilities have limited opportunities to participate in inclusive settings, meaning limited opportunities to learn to communicate with or to make choices known to competent peers. To compensate for these circumstances, the team needs to use targeted and direct instruction to teach transition-focused communication skills (Alwell & Cobb, 2007). Other students with severe dsabilities do not express their preferences though conventional means and, thus, may require alternative means to assess their personal preferences. Hughes, Pitkin, and Lorden (1998) identified several strategies for identifying student preferences, including:

- Pay attention to a student's behavior as he or she responds to situations in which choices are presented or occur naturally to determine his or her preferences and choices.

- Use AT, including switches, AAC, and computers, to increase students' ability to indicate preferences.

- Consider the wide range of verbal, gestural, and other presymbolic communication behaviors as a means to determine preference.

- Gather information from those who know the student best, particularly the family, who will have considerable knowledge regarding preferences and interests.

Students with severe and multiple disabilities are capable of becoming self-determined; however, it may look different from what we typically think of as self-determination. In addition, supporting students to participate to the highest degree possible in all activities in school, at home and in the community is essential for increasing supported self-determination.

PREPARING FOR THE TRANSITION TO
SUPPORTED AND CUSTOMIZED EMPLOYMENT

Supported employment and, more recently, the emergence of customized employment, are primarily intended for individuals with disabilities who need ongoing and intensive supports because of the severity of their disability in order to gain access to and maintain integrated community employment (Wehman & Brooke, 2013). These models were developed because of dissatisfaction with traditional segregated work options such as sheltered workshops and adult day centers. First legislated through the Rehabilitation Act Amendments of 1986 (PL 99-506), the number of individuals with severe disabilities participating in supported employment has increased over the past several decades (Cimera & Cowan, 2009). Unfortunately, young adults with severe and multiple disabilities are among those least likely to access services (Butterworth et al., 2013).

Additionally, the number of individuals with disabilities who are entering supported employment has remained stagnant over the past ten years, remaining at less than 15% of all working adults during the 2011-12 reporting year; with any gains offset by the continued expansion of segregated work placements (Human Services Research Institute, 2014). Several reasons account for young adults with severe disabilities not having access to supported and customized employment, including: (a) the lack of work-based learning (WBL) programs available in secondary schools (Guy, Sitlington, Larsen, & Frank, 2009); (b) limited or low expectations of students while they are still in school (Hetherington et al., 2010); and (c) the lack of quality adult services to provide supports post-school (Bose, 2010). These issues run counter to research supporting the relationship between work experiences in high school and improved post-school employment (Carter, Austin, & Trainor, 2012). Fortunately, emerging school- and work-based models that bridge these gaps are gaining momentum.

Customized Employment for Students with Severe and Multiple Disabilities

The advent of customized employment evolved out of creative efforts associated with supported employment. However, customized employment is considered a distinct departure from past, more market-driven models of supported employment in which individuals with disabilities were placed into existing job openings (Griffin, Hammis, Geary, & Sullivan, 2008). The Office of Disability Employment Policy defined customized employment as:

> A flexible process designed to personalize the employment relationship between a job candidate and an employer in a way that meets the needs of both. It is based

on an individualized match between the strengths, conditions, and interests of a job candidate and the identified business needs of an employer. Customized Employment utilizes an individualized approach to employment planning and job development—one person at a time . . . one employer at a time. ("What is Customized Employment?" para. 1).

Certain essential characteristics of customized employment include: (a) the employer voluntarily negotiates the specific job duties of the candidate; (b) the duties are based upon the unique contributions of the individual; and (c) the potential contributions of the candidate are considered in direct response to employer needs, thereby allowing for customized matches (Callahan, 2002). Essential steps to follow for successful customized employment include:

1. *Discovery:* Use a person-centered approach to determine the job seeker's interests, skills, and preferences. The end result is an individualized career profile that identifies specific types of jobs and environments compatible with the individual's unique attributes.

2. *Job search planning:* Use the information from the career profile to create a plan for finding meaningful employment that matches the unique characteristics of the job seeker, with specific environmental factors that might lead to a more successful job match.

3. *Job development and negotiation:* Work collaboratively with the student and the employer to negotiate a customized job. This may take considerable time, and it is not expected that every teacher contributes this level of effort. Most often, district-level personnel coordinate these work-based learning activities.

4. *Postemployment support:* Once a set of job duties has been negotiated, assist with providing ongoing supports and monitoring of the employment relationship to ensure satisfaction of both the student and employer. Even staff who are not responsible for supporting the student on the job or supervising school job coaches can still share considerable knowledge about their students' communication, behavior/social, and work-readiness skills and provide insights into the most effective school-based interventions that can be translated into job settings.

Self-employment is an emergent area of customized employment that is proving to be highly effective for individuals with severe disabilities. This customized option supports individuals to create a micro-enterprise based on the strengths and contributions of the individual and the unmet needs of a local market (Griffin, Hammis, Keeton, & Sullivan, 2014). The *Road to Self-Sufficiency* developed by the National Collaborative on Workforce & Disability for Youth (NCWD; Kauffman & Stuart, 2007) is an excellent guide for schools to develop entrepreneurship programs for youth with disabilities.

Creating self-employment might be a great option for Cassie and her family. Because of her strong interests in animal care and her love of the outdoor farm life, figuring out a "home grown" business that matches her skills, with the support of her family and support providers, would be awesome. She might like to take care of bees and sell her honey at the farmers markets near her community, or perhaps design and sell the home-made dog biscuits her family makes for their farm dogs. Using a person-centered planning approach is a great way to launch this idea. Those who know her well can help brainstorm marketable ideas. The team might also include the small business association and the agricultural extension agency in her region, which might be excellent resources for knowing more about the market. Her sister can help her set up a website to sell her products, and her brothers might want to partner with her to earn extra money.

School-Sponsored Work-Based Learning Focused on Integrated Employment

Preparing students with severe disabilities for supported and customized employment requires careful planning while they are in school. One can make clear connections between school-sponsored planning and preparation and employment success, particularly for students with severe disabilities (Carter et al., 2012; Test et al., 2009). The emergent research identified work-based learning (WBL) experiences as a significant predictor of employment success for students with severe disabilities, especially if students have had a paid work experience prior to exiting high school. Other important influences include competencies in self-care and household skills, social and communication skills, and parental expectations that their son or daughter will work.

Developing systematic programs of career development leading to post-school employment is a primary responsibility of schools. A collaborative team's primary role will be to support and enhance the WBL programs available to the students. Given the complexities of developing relationships with employers and ensuring successful work-based experiences, most districts support staff responsible for WBL programs (sometimes called WBL, vocational or transition/career coordinators). Educators/advocates in school districts that lack such programs might take an active role in creating work-based experiences that meet students' and families' future employment aspirations. Figure 13.3 provides an overview of the critical components of school-sponsored career readiness programs for students with significant disabilities (Morningstar, 2004). This model contains five essential elements: (a) career assessment, (b) school-based learning, (c) work-based learning, (d) onsite supports and training, and (e) school-business partnerships.

Career Assessment Students with severe disabilities must be assessed across several areas including career awareness, career exploration, and career experiences. Because of the unique learning characteristics of these students,

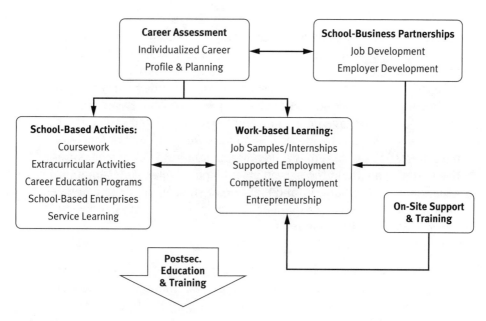

Figure 13.3. Effective career preparation models: Developing quality school and work-based learning. (From Morningstar, M.E. [2004]. *Models of work-based learning programs.* Unpublished manuscript, University of Kansas, Lawrence, KS; adapted by permission.)

typical assessment methods such as paper and pencil or computer-based interest inventories may be ineffective. School personnel should work closely with families and others who know the student best to create person-centered career assessment profiles. An individualized career profile that is based on the *Discovery* approach (Griffin, Hammis, & Geary, 2007) can identify students' preferences, interests, and contributions that ultimately will lead to good job matches. These profiles take many forms, but most often are easy-to-follow summaries of the information gathered during the person-centered process that accomplish at least three functions:

1. Provide an overview of the job-seeking student, including where he or she lives; his or her neighborhood and community; and his or her educational history, career development experiences, and employment history.

2. Offer a comprehensive description of the important domains of the student's life, including positive interventions and strategies to support the student, particular interests and preferences for an ideal job, unique personality characteristics, and job-related skills and experiences.

3. Summarize the information in a way that leads to a customized plan for employment that includes possible functions of jobs that motivate the student and that he or she is capable of performing, necessary supportive work environments, and possible employers and businesses known to team members who can make the initial employment contact (Callahan, n.d.).

Cassie and her family and neighbors could brainstorm about possible farm-related activities she could try out. Also, her mother's connections in the local business community are other areas to explore. Because career assessment is an ongoing process, Cassie was afforded a few opportunities during 9th and 10th grade, mostly during her school-based learning experiences, to engage in unpaid career exploration and career assessments, which have expanded her career profile. She and her teachers have started to put together a visual-resume [photographs and narrative information about the person including his or her skills, abilities, experiences, contributions, and tasks he or she can do for an employer, Condon, nd.] of her work experiences, similar to those created by students in other rural communities.

School-Based Learning Students with severe disabilities must have school-based learning opportunities to prepare them for community work sites. School-based learning most often is associated with a specific class students are enrolled in, such as a career and technical education class, or a career exploration class. For students with multiple disabilities, learning about careers requires systematic opportunities for hands-on learning.

Cassie participated in a career class for hands-on experiences and opportunities to increase her career awareness and exploration during her freshman and sophomore years. She had tried school-based jobs, including working as an office aide as well as working in the school-based enterprise—the Jayhawk Café. It was clear from systematic observations of Cassie's behavior and demeanor on the job that she did not like the food handling aspects of the café, but she did enjoy being involved in record keeping and inventory duties that she completed with modifications and supports. Based on her individualized career profile, Cassie sampled three types of occupations in the office/clerical field during her sophomore year. The data from the situational assessments completed by the work-based learning coordinator, as well as feedback from the employer who reviewed her behaviors on the job, led the team to determine that indoor clerical positions with many natural opportunities to engage with co-workers were an excellent fit for Cassie.

Most often, individual teachers and paraprofessionals develop these unique school-based learning experiences and can more specifically tie learning specific to career awareness and exploration to ongoing learning throughout the school day. For example, in a school that operates a school-based enterprise such as a school store, staff not only will be working with students during the store hours, but can be reinforcing skills such as counting change, budgeting, ordering supplies, and communicating effectively with customers throughout the school day.

Work-Based Learning   School sponsored, supervised programs of community work experiences should be more than a series of individual job samples or unpaid training experiences. In implementing WBL, team members link the student's experiences on the worksite to school-related planning, the student's program of study, and the career assessment process. Work experiences range in intensity and in structure and scope, depending upon the career development path of the student. WBL helps students to gain workplace skills such as communication skills, teamwork, problem-solving, networking and maintaining positive attitudes (Office of Disability Policy, 2007).

For Cassie, the opportunities she will have during her junior and senior years to complete internships in several different office/clerical positions will provide her and her support network with a clear sense of careers she most enjoys and for which she is best suited. Then, during an innovative community-based transition program (discussed later in this chapter) at a community college in her town, she will have several intensive work-related training experiences in a paid internship program to hone her job-specific aptitudes, communication, and socialization skills using her AAC device and increase her workplace skills.

On-Site Supports and Training   Providing on-the-job supports, such as systematic instruction and data collection, allows students with severe and multiple disabilities to participate successfully in work experiences. This effort is another area in which teachers will collaborate with staff involved in work experiences.

Cassie's WBL coordinator identified the natural supports available on the job before Cassie started working. Her teacher assisted by providing information about Cassie's preferences and capabilities. This helped the WBL coordinator to carefully analyze both specific job duties as well as soft skills (e.g., communication, teamwork, problem-solving, networking and positive attitudes). The WBL coordinator, job coach, and a work-site mentor (a co-worker) helped Cassie orient to the job and provided initial training and skill acquisition. As Cassie became more proficient on the job, and as the workplace mentor learned more about the best way to support Cassie, school supervision was faded.

Keep in mind that supporting students on the job is most often the responsibility of teachers and paraprofessionals, with the WBL coordinator supervising and supporting staff. This means that the teacher plays a role in sharing essential information with the job coach/paraprofessionals, who will then support and facilitate co-workers to gradually provide more of the on-the-job supports. Throughout all of these experiences, staff may share data collection methods(s) such as the *Student Job History Form* (Hughes & Carter, 2012) to collect and summarize essential job-related skills and experiences. (See Figure 13.4.)

FORM 8.3

Student Job History Form

Student: Amanda Jocz

		Dates: 8/10 to 12/10	Dates: 1/11 to 5/11	Dates: 8/11 to 12/11
Basic information	Worksite	Community Blood Bank	Heimer, Lief, & Ali Law Offices	Varner's Family Restaurant
	General job types or positions experienced	Receptionist, front desk, courier	Janitor, copy person	Wait staff, bus staff, cashier
	Job tasks experienced	Answering telephones, filing, customer service, deliveries	Mopping, painting, photocopying, filing	Washing dishes, food prep, cashier, customer service
	Location and transportation	1 ② 3 N/A	1 ② 3 N/A	① 2 3 N/A
Task characteristics	Job task requirements	1 ② 3 N/A	1 2 ③ N/A	① 2 3 N/A
	General mobility	① 2 3 N/A	1 ② 3 N/A	1 ② 3 N/A
	Gross motor demands	① 2 3 N/A	1 ② 3 N/A	① 2 3 N/A
	Fine motor demands	1 ② 3 N/A	1 2 ③ N/A	① 2 3 N/A
	Length of work tasks	1 ② 3 N/A	1 2 ③ N/A	① 2 3 N/A
	Variability of daily job tasks	① 2 3 N/A	1 2 ③ N/A	1 ② 3 N/A
	Problem-solving requirements	① 2 3 N/A	1 ② 3 N/A	1 ② 3 N/A
	Production rate	① 2 3 N/A	1 2 ③ N/A	① 2 3 N/A
	Work product quality	1 ② 3 N/A	1 2 ③ N/A	① 2 3 N/A
	Continuous working requirements	① 2 3 N/A	1 2 ③ N/A	① 2 3 N/A
Task-related characteristics	Co-worker presence	① 2 3 N/A	1 2 3 ⓃⒶ	① 2 3 N/A
	Nontask social contacts	1 2 ③ N/A	1 2 ③ N/A	① 2 3 N/A
	Social atmosphere of worksite	1 ② 3 N/A	1 2 ③ N/A	① 2 3 N/A
	Interaction with customers	1 2 ③ N/A	1 2 ③ N/A	① 2 3 N/A
	Supervisory contact	1 2 ③ N/A	1 2 ③ N/A	① 2 3 N/A
Environmental characteristics	Distraction level	1 ② 3 N/A	1 ② 3 N/A	1 ② 3 N/A
	Comfort factors	1 ② 3 N/A	1 ② 3 N/A	1 ② 3 N/A
	Equipment/tool use	① 2 3 N/A	1 ② 3 N/A	① 2 3 N/A
Natural supports	Environmental support	① 2 3 N/A	1 ② 3 N/A	① 2 3 N/A
	Supervisor/co-worker support	1 ② 3 N/A	1 2 ③ N/A	① 2 3 N/A

Key: 1 = excellent job match; 2 = fair job match; 3 = poor job match; N/A = not applicable.

Figure 13.4. Job History Form. (From Renzaglia A., and Hutchins, M. [1995]. A model for longitudinal vocational programming for students with moderate and severe disabilities. Grant funded by the U.S. Department of Education, Office of Special Education and Rehabilitation Services; adapted by permission).

School–Business Partnerships The most successful work experiences involve partnerships with local business owners and managers who agree to serve as part of both unpaid work-based learning sites and paid internships. Typically, the WBL coordinator takes responsibility for developing and facilitating business involvement by making new business contacts and building on existing relationships. Schools use a variety of ways to find and engage with employers, including online research, attending community and employer organizations (e.g., the chamber of commerce), and working within school and colleagues' employer networks (Carter et al., 2009). Most programs have materials such as brochures that explain their program and the benefits to the business community for engaging in the partnership. Involving parents on the program's advisory committee and helping to build on their personal business network are other strategies for connecting with employers (Certo et al., 2008). Of course, building an extensive network of businesses to participate takes time, and often begins with less intensive commitment such as serving as a guest speaker for a careers class, and then, as the business gets to know the program and students, the school can expand its relationship to include serving as a work-based learning site. Figure 13.5 provides examples of different types of ways businesses can be involved.

Bridging Gaps Between School and Community Employment

Supported and customized employment have, as their ultimate goal, real work for real pay (Wehman, Inge, Revell, & Brooke, 2007). With this in mind, the most successful models establish collaborative partnerships between schools and community agencies so that a seamless transition occurs between school-sponsored work-based learning and workplace supports and services (Certo et al., 2008). Two highly innovative models – Project SEARCH and Seamless Transitions - will be described next.

Project SEARCH: Work-Based Learning Leading to Success Project SEARCH presents a model of a school-to-work program that has had a positive impact on youth with disabilities across the U.S. It is a work-based intervention for high school students with significant disabilities whose main post-school goal is integrated employment. The program combines real-life work experiences with training in employability, soft skills and independent living skills. The

Figure 13.5. Examples of ways businesses can be involved in work-based learning. (From Morningstar [2004]. Models of work-based learning programs. Unpublished manuscript. University of Kansas: Lawrence, KS; reprinted by permission).

hallmark of this model is that, although it is school-sponsored, the program itself is implemented within a specific worksite, thereby facilitating smoother transitions to employment through tightly integrated classroom and work-based learning and supports (Rutkowski, Daston, Van Kuiken, & Riehle, 2010).

In addition, Project SEARCH offers several internship rotations for an entire school year to ensure that students receive career exploration, assessment, and specific work-related experiences and training. When students are ready to exit school, work placement supports are provided through the highly collaborative relationships developed among the school district, vocational rehabilitation services, other disability specific organizations providing long-term supports to students post-school (e.g., community supported employment agencies, community organizations supporting students with intellectual disabilities), and the business community (Wehman et al., 2012).

When Cassie turns 18, and through to her 21st year, her district might develop a Project SEARCH site at the regional hospital in her town or perhaps at the nearby Community College. By using large industries, students can try out multiple jobs within a single location. For example, Cassie might work in the medical records department, the cafeteria, and the gift shop. When not scheduled to work on her jobs, Cassie would report to the "home base," usually a large office or setting within the building, to work on independent living skills, community access, and other transition-related skills identified within her IEP.

Seamless Community Transition Programs: Service Integration Leading to Employment   The seamless community transition model embraces a service integration delivery model, in which transition services for students with significant disabilities who are entering their final years of support under IDEA (i.e., between 18-21 years old) shift from the schools as the sole provider to include multiple community systems (Certo et al., 2008; Owens, Johnson et al., 2002). Specifically, a service integration model is one in which schools partner with community and adult agencies that support young adults post-school (e.g., vocational rehabilitation, agencies serving individuals with intellectual and developmental disabilities, supplemental security income, centers for independent living). In addition, non-disability community supports and networks such as generic employment agencies, public transportation, co-workers, friends, and neighbors come into play.

A second critical element of a transition service integration model is the shift in a school-centered locus of services to one that is fully immersed in the community (Luecking & Certo, 2003). This approach is often referred to as an "18–21 year old transition program" or "community transition program" (Gaumer, Morningstar, & Clark, 2004). Traditionally, secondary school experiences for students with severe disabilities consisted of intensive community-based instruction and vocational experiences from within a "home base" of the high school setting (Morningstar & Lattin, 2004). However, when older students who typically receive special education services until age 21 are taught in a community or postsecondary setting, learning more age-appropriate adult roles is possible. Community transition programs improve student outcomes by differentiating the secondary school experiences offered in a typical high school (for students 14–18 years old) from a transition-focused community-based program offered to older students (aged 18–21 years old) (Fisher, Sax, & Pumpian, 1999).

Community transition programs are designed to continue to support students with severe disabilities who have met their high school requirements (diploma or exit certificate), but who have unmet transition needs and goals in their IEP (Grigal, Neubert, & Moon, 2002). The result offers students with severe disabilities the best of both worlds—inclusive education during the traditional high school years and a comprehensive and inclusive community-based program after high school—but while the students continue to receive special education services (Morningstar & Lattin, 2004).

A third key component of seamless transition programs is the focus on coordinated oversight in which all key stakeholders involved in the program meet on a regular basis to review student progress on the goals and to ensure adherence to quality program indicators. Another activity of this group is to secure cross-agency agreements that lead to sharing staff and to funding support program operation. This collaborative group ensures long-term supports and services for students exiting the program. The end result is a seamless transition from special education services to supported and customized employment and inclusive community living and full participation (Certo & Lueking, 2006).

In terms of success, one specific program, the *transition service integration model* (TSIM), has documented positive outcomes for students with severe disabilities. Over a five-year period, TSIM successfully exited 89% of over 290 students with significant disabilities into supported employment. In addition, 71% were still employed up to three years after program exit (Certo et al., 2008). The postsecondary employment results of the TSIM are well above averages reported from a secondary analysis of the National Longitudinal, a sample of students with severe and multiple disabilities (Carter et al., 2012).

POSTSECONDARY EDUCATION FOR STUDENTS WITH SEVERE AND MULTIPLE DISABILITIES

Increased interest in students with intellectual disabilities attending college, vocational technical schools, or some form of postsecondary education (PSE) has emerged as a result of some community transition programs existing on postsecondary campuses. Percentages of students with intellectual disabilities receiving education and training on postsecondary campuses has increased from 8% in 1990 to 28% in 2005 (Newman et al., 2010). Postsecondary education (PSE) is a natural transition for a large proportion of young adults graduating from high school, in general; with PSE leading to improved employment outcomes for all students, including those with disabilities (Thoma et al., 2011).

Therefore, it is not surprising that parents express a desire for this option for students with significant intellectual disabilities (Grigal, Hart, & Migliore, 2011). Given the innovation surrounding PSE for students with severe disabilities, it is also not surprising that schools may not have sufficient information or resources about PSE. In one study, parents believed extending education in postsecondary settings would significantly benefit their children with intellectual disabilities. However, the barrier most often reported by parents was the lack of knowledge and guidance from teachers and other school staff, including guidance counselors (Griffin, McMillan, & Hodapp, 2010).

The Higher Education Opportunity Act of 2008 (PL 110-315) included provisions to facilitate the enrollment of students with intellectual disabilities in PSE. With increased federal investments, PSE programs are expanding. Grigal, Hart, and Weir (2012) surveyed approximately 150 programs, and about half reported enrolling students into regular non-credit and credit-bearing classes. However, an equal number of programs (45%) indicated that students with disabilities received the majority of their instruction only with others with intellectual disabilities. The high level of variability among programs in terms of focus and levels of inclusion is of concern. Certainly more work is needed to understand better the critical elements of postsecondary programs that most likely improve adult outcomes and to ensure that those elements are included in all programs.

PREPARING FOR THE TRANSITION TO
SUPPORTED LIVING AND COMMUNITY PARTICIPATION

> Once Cassie exits school services at age 21 years old, she should have experienced the range of services and supports to prepare her to live an inclusive and meaningful life, including: a) supports from her network of formal services including those that are time-limited such as vocational rehabilitation services, and b) long-term supports including Home and Community-based Services (HCBS) through Medicaid and her Supplemental Security Income (SSI).

Over the past two decades, we have seen a shift from traditional congregate care settings such as large group homes to individualized supports in the community (Rogan & Walker, 2007). For students with severe disabilities, strategies and methods to support living in the community are a necessary focus. From this perspective, teachers will be supporting students and their families to be prepared to live with the supports needed to maintain a fully inclusive quality life.

Supporting students to live in the community, rather than in congregate care settings such as group homes, continues to fall outside of prevailing models of adult living options offered by many state and local agencies. In the traditional model, the individual with disabilities and his or her family either accept existing services (e.g., living in a group home) or they are not served by the community services agency. In some cases, group home providers have not admitted individuals with significant medical and cognitive disabilities because they require too intensive a level of support and care (Morningstar et al., 2001). Ironically, it was families who had been rejected from traditional service systems who first created comprehensive and inclusive lifestyles (e.g., supported living) for their adult children with severe disabilities (Turnbull & Turnbull, 2000).

Supported living means living in a home chosen by the individual with disabilities, shared with roommates determined by the individual, and in a home or apartment not owned or operated by an agency (Klein, Wilson, & Nelson, 2000). This model requires agencies and services to operate from a set of values predicated on the belief that individuals with severe disabilities should control the front door:

- Supporting and listening to what individuals with severe disabilities are telling us by ensuring they have access to a means of communication

- Ensuring each individual's control over personal supports by developing a plan for self-directed care and services as well as involving informal supports from within his or her personal network

- Supporting and facilitating friendships by ensuring students are a part of their community and engaging in activities that are of interest to them and others

- Offering flexible services and supports so that students and families can determine which supports are best for them, rather than accepting an all-or-nothing approach

- Ensuring that AT is available across all areas of adult life, including communication, employment, and community living and participation

- Valuing the role and contributions of students with severe and multiple disabilities who are engaging in their community as fully participating citizens (Klein & Strully, 2000)

Preparing Youth with Severe and Multiple Disabilities for Supported Living

Teaching skills to prepare students for participating in home and community has undergone scrutiny, particularly related to the increased emphasis on access to the general education curriculum. While concerns have been raised that increased access to general education may dilute a focus on functional skills instruction (Ayres, Lowery, Douglas, & Sievers, 2011; Bouck, 2009), it is now apparent that curriculum decisions are not an either/or proposition. Students can participate in inclusive academic curricula while achieving functional and community-referenced skills (Wehmeyer, Field, Doren, Jones, & Mason, 2004). Unfortunately, teachers often perceive that inclusion in general education classes limits opportunities to learn life skills (Ruppar & Gaffney, 2011), even though functional life skills and access to general education can be mutually beneficial (McDonnell, Hunt, Jackson, & Ryndak, in press). We know that critical skills needed for successful adult lives—communication, self-determination, team-work, and problem-solving—all are best learned in inclusive settings rather than in separate, special education functional/life skills classrooms. In fact, the movement within education to focus on college and career readiness skills supports the movement toward inclusive education for students with severe disabilities.

Educators can support students with severe disabilities to gain the skills needed to prepare for living and participating in the community in several ways. Bambara, Koger, and Bartholomew (2011) describe several steps: a) Person-centered planning is used to create a vision for the student; b) Teachers partner with students and families to coordinate instruction; c) Student self-determination is considered as a critical domain of instruction; d) School personnel examine the range of settings in which to teach home and community skills (e.g., general educational environments, school, home and community); and e) Transition planning targets home and community skills that should be considered. Table 13.3 offers a range of examples of how these guidelines can be actualized as part of the day-to-day teaching and learning process for students, families, and educators.

In summary, planning for the transition to community supported living for young adults with severe disabilities involves more than finding an agency that provides residential services. An inherent principle of supported living is promoting full community inclusion through individualized supports and services. Despite examples of remarkable outcomes, there remain limited opportunities for individuals with severe disabilities to live on their own with the supports they want and need. We should no longer be promoting a continuum mindset, but instead focus on supported living, supported adulthood, and the funding structures to support this model. The educational team must prepare students and families to develop a vision of supported living and to inform them of the new and innovative resources, funding structures, and policies that exemplify these values.

Transition to Supported Membership, Friendships, and Community Inclusion

As described earlier, families, educators and many service providers now consider the importance of offering individual supports for sustained community inclusion. Yet, traditional services often only offer sheltered and segregated settings. Not surprisingly, social isolation is often a top concern of families with young adults with severe disabilities in that they recognize the importance of having friends and a social network outside of the family (Kraemer & Blacher, 2001; Targett & Wehman, 2013). Ferguson and Ferguson (2006) describe the importance of supported membership for their son, Ian, in this way:

> The more hands that are there to catch him when he falls the better. We firmly believe that the more deeply embedded Ian is in the life of his neighborhood, workplace, and the city in general, the more people there will be who will notice if he is not there and who will work to keep him there as a member of his community (2006, p. 615).

Table 13.3. Guidelines and instructional strategies for teaching supported living and community participation skills

Guidelines	Instructional strategy	Description
Use person-centered planning strategies to create vision for supported living and community participation	Person-centered planning strategies	Use methods such as personal futures planning (Mount, 2000), Making Action Plans (MAPs; Forest & Pearpoint, 1992), *Making Dreams Happen* (Furney, 1993), choosing outcomes and accommodations for children (COACH; Giangreco, Cloninger, & Iverson, 2011), and Planning Alternative Tomorrows with Hope (PATH; Pearpoint, O'Brien, & Forest, 2003) to collaboratively plan with students, families, and others so that instruction fits within desired postschool vision for supported adult living.
Plan instruction in partnership with students and families	Collaborative planning to target critical skills for home instruction	Teams come together to solve problems around a specific issue, focusing on the goals and preferences of the student and family. Include community and home support staff if available. Consider increasing participation in family routines and activities, decreasing challenging behaviors, being more involved with peers at school and in the community, increasing community access and participation, and finding ways that teachers and family members can work together to support students' needs. Support families to use the adaptations and assistive technology (e.g., video modeling, picture activity schedules) at home.
	Share information with families	
Choose instruction that blends with general education contexts and encourages peer interaction	Choose inclusive instructional settings first and foremost	Consider the following questions: What settings will be used for instruction, and are they similar to those students without disabilities would use? Can the skills be embedded in typical school activities (e.g., learning cooking skills in a home economics class)? If not, then how can you schedule instruction in the settings where the skills are typically used (e.g., going out to lunch with high school peers without disabilities)?
	Plan for generalization of skills	Teachers can maximize instructional time by carefully planning for the generalization of skills by 1) identifying relevant instructional settings (e.g., grocery stores student might access), 2) writing a generic task analysis for purchasing groceries, 3) selecting stores to train the skills and considering how cues and response options vary among the grocery stores (e.g., electric doors, push doors, pull doors), 4) teaching the skills in the variety of store settings selected, and 5) testing for generalization at new stores not used for training.
	Use effective and efficient instruction	
	Use peer mentors to support skills in natural settings	Use systematic instruction such as 1) observational learning—direct instruction; prompting and reinforcing other students to observe and follow instructions, 2) instructive feedback to include additional information to teacher prompts (e.g., "Use a mitt because the food may be hot and could burn you"), 3) involve peers without disabilities to support students in school settings that reinforce skills (e.g., putting on makeup after gym class, reading the menu in the cafeteria).
Home and community skills gain importance as students become older	Use transition planning to target community-based instructional needs	Younger students can complete small household chores, but community access (e.g., shopping, eating at restaurants) is done primarily with family members. Adolescents and young adults complete complex household tasks (e.g., laundry) and prepare meals. They are going places in the community on their own (e.g., getting dropped off at the movies). Community-referenced skills and activities are selected using a person-centered approach to enhance dignity and inclusion in community settings.
	Emphasize skills and instruction in 18- to 21-year-olds in their community-based programs	By age 18, students should not remain in high school by the time they are 18 years old, but they should be participating in community-based transition programs located in community settings or on a postsecondary campus. The focus of the program is community access, employment/career development, and ongoing adult learning.

Source: Bambara, Koger, & Bartholomew (2011).

Developing social connections in their communities to enrich their lives is a critical goal for adolescents with severe disabilities. Unfortunately, individuals with severe disabilities rarely have the opportunities to develop social relationships outside of traditional approaches that most often involve only others with disabilities. Rather than being a mere presence at school, at home, and in the community, students with severe disabilities should experience a sense of community belonging (Hunt, Soto, Maier, & Doering, 2003).

Teachers who are developing a community inclusive approach can identify both individual (e.g., personal friends) and organized social opportunities for their students (e.g., participation in clubs and activities). There is no doubt that a first step one can take is to develop a plan to increase social networks and community memberships. Table 13.4 describes four steps that can be used by school and community staff to begin the development of social networks and community memberships.

Remember, building relationships involves more than teaching social skills, and requires professionals to facilitate and support students in getting to know and be known by many different people in school and the community. Expanding the student's social network and maximizing a variety of relationships are important goals.

Table 13.4.   Steps to planning for community membership

Step	Explanation	Example
Assess	Identify the interests, gifts, strengths, and contributions of the individual.	Hold a person-centered meeting with same-age peers as a way to identify strengths and interests of students this age and develop a circle of friends for the student.
Explore and plan	Brainstorm possible community activities and connections based on student interests. This step will involve exploring the community and identifying local community liaisons who can support access to specific organizations/activities.	Spend time visiting different places in the community; meet people in public places and at organizations. Review school clubs and organization directories to see what kinds of clubs and activities are available in the school.
Make introductions	Provide personal introductions, which include shared interests, focusing on reciprocity, not what someone can do for the student with disabilities.	"Nancy, this is Carol. I know you love to watch Kansas Jayhawks basketball, and Carol is a huge fan too." Not, "Nancy, would you like to be Carol's friend?"
Support, evaluate, and maintain	Provide support and assistance; share tips for best ways to communicate with student. Identify when to fade out so that the supports and friendship progress naturally.	Share ways to support the student that are respectful and maintain the dignity of the person. Be sure to emphasize the personality of the student rather than the disability. Problem-solve specific supports for behavior, health, communication, and so forth when needed.

Cassie has been fortunate to have a special education teacher and a social worker in her high school who understand her desire to connect with her peers. They have used a variety of structured strategies for facilitating friendships and social connections. When Cassie first moved to the high school, they formed a circle of friends with her, consisting of both academic and social leaders in the school as well as students with similar interests as Cassie (e.g., music, dancing, being outside). The circle of friends identified the ways Cassie was able to be included in classes, clubs, and after-school events. They also provided "ability awareness" training when Cassie first joined the Band and Choir classes. This helped others to get to know Cassie, and to be supported to get to know her as an individual and friend. The teachers also assisted this effort. They helped both students and teachers learn how to communicate with Cassie and the best ways to respectfully support her.

Building intentional communities or circles of friends is an effective strategy to increase student membership in the school (Forest & Pearpoint, 1992). Circles of friends began as a strategy to support inclusion for elementary students with severe disabilities, and are less commonly found in secondary schools. Secondary schools that use the circles approach often do so in conjunction with extracurricular clubs and sports teams as a better way to meet the structure and climate of the secondary school setting.

Another method to build community connections for students is to introduce them to a new setting that meets a strong preference or interest (e.g., high school poetry club), connect them to supportive members of the group, and continue to support them in building and sustaining new relationships (Walker, 2007). Taking advantage of volunteer and service opportunities can connect students with a broader community group, both within high school and in the community. It is important to remember to provide students with opportunities to make contributions, which helps to create a sense of belonging and builds opportunities to learn, which in turn generates respect from others (Miller, Hinterlong, & Greene, 2010).

In summary, in order to successfully build inclusive communities for students with severe and multiple disabilities, it is often helpful to develop social support networks. An essential element of creating support networks is to encourage social relationships with peers without disabilities while the students are in school (Jorgensen, McSheehan, & Sonnenmeier, 2007). In other words, we must all make the shift from viewing students with severe disabilities as merely participating in activities in school and the community to one in which they are actively contributing to community groups and associations. Teachers and other team members can provide students with severe disabilities with opportunities to meet people with whom they can develop lasting and meaningful friendships. Students can be supported through giving them opportunities to volunteer, to provide assistance to others, and to make contributions to their community at large. Friendships do not evolve overnight, but rather require opportunities, support, and ongoing nurture. The method of providing transition services should not hinder this vital part of the human experience.

SUMMARY

What will Cassie's life, and the lives of all students, look like as they are successfully prepared for the transition to adulthood? If transition planning is implemented according to both the letter and spirit of IDEA, we can envision that students with severe disabilities will be supported to be contributing members of their transition planning teams, and planning will use strengths-based approaches, such as person-centered planning. Students will be included in general education classes that meet their long-term, post-school goals by offering opportunities to improve skills and to develop a network of formal and informal supports. Families will be informed and engaged during transition planning and will be supported by school personnel to develop a long-term vision for their child's future. In addition, team members will help coordinate the family's access to long-term services needed to ensure a quality of life for students.

Schools have the capacity to utilize evidence-based interventions and models of transition that lead to positive outcomes for students with severe disabilities, including methods that provide experience and skill development toward college and career readiness. The most effective school-based programs are those that integrate and collaborate with community members, including employers, adult service providers, and informal networks of community supports. Students like Cassie should be graduating from high school along with their same-aged peers without disabilities at 18 years old. During their young adult years, while they are still being served under IDEA, they can continue to achieve postsecondary goals in postsecondary and community settings, while developing the experiences and skills to achieve supported adulthood. During this period of time, it is essential that students be exposed to the risks of normal adulthood, while there is still a strong safety net of school, family and agency supports. Implementing a transition service integration model such as the ones described in this chapter can provide students and families intensive employment and community experiences, leading to a network to support every student during the transition to adulthood.

Cassie can become a contributing member of her community, and it could be that she will be hired by a business in her rural community where she will be supported to work a real job for real pay. This might be a customized job that has been carved out for her based on the collaborative partnership across the employer, service agencies, Cassie, and her family. Or, it might be that Cassie chooses to develop her own micro-enterprise and sell her goods and services directly to community members. Having found the promise of work, Cassie, her family, and her support network can begin to develop a vision for inclusion in her community where she is supported as a contributing member with an expanding circle of friends and supports.

Cassie's future is full of potential—as is the future of every student with severe and multiple disabilities. Through the collaborative efforts of dedicated professionals, their families, and all the people that love and care for them, these children can receive a meaningful education, form powerful social relationships, and become fully included in their communities as they make the transition to adulthood.

REFLECTION QUESTIONS

1. What are ways you can have your students actively involved in their own IEP meeting or support them in self-directing their IEPs?

2. How might you approach an employer who is reluctant to begin engaging in supported employment for individuals with disabilities?

3. What are some key steps you would need to take as a student looks to move into supported living?

CHAPTER ACTIVITIES

1. In small groups, hold a mini-MAP meeting for one of the group members. Organize the ideas and conversations in the quadrant format described in the chapter.

2. Pick a general education subject (e.g., science, math, reading) and write a lesson plan that incorporates functional living skills and transition skills into the general education curriculum. Make the lesson plan appropriate for a high school classroom.

REFERENCES

Agran, M., Blanchard, C., & Wehmeyer, M.L. (2000). Promoting transition goals and self-determination through student self-directed learning: The self-determined learning model of instruction. *Education and Training in Mental Retardation and Developmental Disabilities, 35*(4), 351–364.

Agran, M., & Hughes, C. (2014). Promoting self-determination and self-directed learning. In M. Agran, F. Brown, C. Hughes, C. Quirk, & D.L. Ryndak (Eds.), *Equity and full participation for individuals with severe disabilities: A vision for the future* (pp. 75–98). Baltimore. MD: Paul H. Brookes Publishing Co.

Allen, S.K., Smith, A.C., Test, D.W., Flowers, C., & Wood, W.M. (2001). The effects of self-directed IEP on student participation in IEP meetings. *Career Development for Exceptional Individuals, 24*(2), 107–120.

Alwell, M., & Cobb, B. (2007). *Social/communication interventions and transition outcomes for youth with disabilities: A systematic review.* Charlotte, NC: National Secondary Transition Technical Assistance Center.

Ayres, K.M., Lowrey, K., Douglas, K.H., & Sievers, C. (2011). I can identify Saturn but I can't brush my teeth: What happens when the curricular focus for students with severe disabilities shifts. *Education and Training in Autism and Developmental Disabilities, 46*(1), 11–21.

Bambara, L.M., Koger, F., & Bartholomew, A. (2011). Building skills for home and community. In M.E. Snell & F. Brown (Eds.), *Instruction of students with severe disabilities* (7th ed., pp. 529–568). Boston, MA: Pearson.

Baumgart, D., Brown, L., Pumpian, I., Nisbet, J., Ford, A., Sweet, M.,...Schroeder, J. (1982).

The principle of partial participation and individualized adaptations in educational programs for severely handicapped students. *Journal of The Association for the Severely Handicapped, 7*(2), 17–27.

Bose, J. (2010, November). Supporting employment choices: Lessons learned—Part I. *Job Training and Placement Report, 34*(11).

Bouck, E.C. (2009). No Child Left Behind, the Individuals with Disabilities Education Act and functional curricula: A conflict of interest? *Education and Training in Developmental Disabilities, 44*(1), 3–13.

Braddock, D., Hemp, R., Rizzolo, M.C., Tanis, E.S., Haffer, L., Lulinski-Norris, A., & Wu, J. (2013). *The state of the states in developmental disabilities* (8th ed.). Washington, DC: American Association on Intellectual and Developmental Disabilities.

Browder, D.M., Wakeman, S.Y., Flowers, C., Rickelman, R.J., Pugalee, D., & Karvonen, M. (2007). Creating access to the general curriculum with links to grade-level content for students with significant cognitive disabilities: An explication of the concept. *Journal of Special Education, 41*(1), 2–16.

Brown, F., Gothelf, C.R., Guess, D., & Lehr, D.H. (1998). Self-determination for individuals with the most severe disabilities: Moving beyond chimera. *Research and Practice for Persons with Severe Disabilities, 23*(1), 17–26.

Buntinx, W.H.E., & Schalock, R.L. (2010). Models of disability, quality of life, and individualized supports: Implications for professional practice in intellectual disability. *Journal of Policy and Practice in Intellectual Disabilities, 7*(4), 283–294.

Butterworth, J., Hall, A.C., Smith, F.A., Migliore, A., Winsor, J., Domin, D., & Sulewski, J. (2013). *State data: The national report on employment services and outcomes.* Boston, MA: University of Massachusetts Boston, Institute for Community Inclusion.

Callahan, M. (n.d.). *Using alternatives to traditional vocational assessment: The why and how of exploration strategies such as discovery.* Gautier, MS: Marc Gold and Associates.

Callahan, M. (2002, Sept./Oct.). Employment: From competitive to customized. *TASH Connections Newsletter, 28*(9), 16–19.

Carter, E.W., Austin, D., & Trainor, A.A. (2012). Predictors of postsecondary employment outcomes for young adults with severe disabilities. *Journal of Disability Policy Studies, 23*(1), 50–63.

Carter, E.W., Trainor, A.A., Cakiroglu, O., Cole, O., Swedeen, B., Ditchman, N., & Owens, L.

(2009). Exploring school–employer partnerships to expand career development and early work experiences for youth with disabilities. *Career Development for Exceptional Individuals, 32*(3), 145–159.

Certo, N.J., & Luecking, R.G. (2006). Service integration and school to work transition: Customized employment as an outcome for youth with significant disabilities. *Journal of Applied Rehabilitation Counseling, 37*(4), 29–35.

Certo, N.J., Luecking, R.G., Murphy, S., Brown, L., Courey, S., & Belanger, D. (2008). Seamless transition and long-term support for individuals with severe intellectual disabilities. *Research and Practice for Persons with Severe Disabilities, 33*(3), 85–95.

Cimera, R.E., & Cowan, R.J. (2009). The costs of services and employment outcomes achieved by adults with autism in the U.S. *Autism, 13*(3), 285–302.

Cobb, B., & Alwell, M. (2007). *Transition planning/coordinating interventions for youth with disabilities: A systematic review.* Retrieved from http://www.nsttac.org/sites/default/files/assets/pdf/pdf/what_works/2c_full_text.pdf

Condon, E. (n.d.). *Using a visual resume for job development.* Gautier, MS: Marc Gold and Associates.

Downing, J.E., & Hanreddy, A. (2015). *Teaching communication skills to students with severe disabilities* (3rd ed.). Baltimore, MD: Paul H. Brookes Publishing Co.

Erickson, A.G. (2007). *Independent living checklist.* Lawrence, KS: Transition Coalition, University of Kansas.

Ferguson, D.L., & Ferguson, P.M. (2006). The promise of adulthood. In M.E. Snell & F. Brown (Eds.), *Instruction of students with severe disabilities* (6th ed., pp. 614–637). Boston, MA: Pearson.

Ferguson, D.L., & Ferguson, P.M. (2011). The promise of adulthood. In M.E. Snell & F. Brown (Eds.), *Instruction of students with severe disabilities* (7th ed., pp. 612–641). Boston, MA: Pearson.

Fisher, D., Sax, C., & Pumpian, I. (1999). *Inclusive high schools: Learning from contemporary classrooms.* Baltimore, MD: Paul H. Brookes Publishing Co.

Forest, M., & Pearpoint, J.C. (1992). Putting all kids on the MAP. *Educational Leadership, 50*(2), 26–31.

Fowler, C.H., Konrad, M., Walker, A.R., Test, D.W., & Wood, W.M. (2007). Self-determination interventions' effects on the academic performance of students with developmental disabilities. *Education and Training in Developmental Disabilities, 42*(3), 270–285.

Furney, K.S. (1993). *Making dreams happen: How to facilitate the MAPs process.* Burlington, VT: Vermont's Transition Systems Change Project.

Gaumer, A.S., Morningstar, M.E., & Clark, G.M. (2004). Status of community-based transition programs: A national database. *Career Development for Exceptional Individuals, 27*(2), 131–149.

Giangreco, M.F., Cloninger, C.J., & Iverson, V.S. (2011). *Choosing outcomes and accommodations for children (COACH): A guide to educational planning for students with disabilities* (3rd ed.). Baltimore, MD: Paul H. Brookes Publishing Co.

Griffin, C., Hammis, D., & Geary, T. (2007). *The job developer's handbook: Practical tactics for customized employment.* Baltimore, MD: Paul H. Brookes Publishing Co.

Griffin, C., Hammis, D., Geary, T., & Sullivan, M. (2008). Customized employment: Where we are; where we're headed. *Journal of Vocational Rehabilitation, 28*(3), 135–139.

Griffin, C., Hammis, D., Keeton, B., & Sullivan, M. (2014). *Making self-employment work for people with disabilities* (2nd ed). Baltimore, MD: Paul H. Brookes Publishing Co.

Griffin, M.M., McMillan, E.D., & Hodapp, R.M. (2010). Family perspectives on postsecondary education for students with intellectual disabilities. *Journal of Pediatric, Maternal and Family Health-Chiropractic, 45*(3), 339–346.

Grigal, M., Hart, D., & Migliore, A. (2011). Comparing the transition planning, postsecondary education, and employment outcomes of students with intellectual and other disabilities. *Career Development for Exceptional Individuals, 34*(1), 4–17.

Grigal, M., Hart, D., Smith, F.A., Domin, D., Sulewski, J., & Weir, C. (2015). *Think College National Coordinating Center: Annual report on the transition and postsecondary programs for students with intellectual disabilities (2013–2014).* Boston, MA: University of Massachusetts Boston, Institute for Community Inclusion.

Grigal, M., Hart, D., & Weir, C. (2012). A survey of postsecondary education programs for students with intellectual disabilities in the United States. *Journal of Policy and Practice in Intellectual Disabilities, 9*(4), 223–233.

Grigal, M., Neubert, D.A., & Moon, M.S. (2002). Postsecondary options for students with significant disabilities. *Teaching Exceptional Children, 35*(2), 68–73.

Guy, B.A., Sitlington, P.L., Larsen, M.D., & Frank, A.R. (2009). What are high schools offering as preparation for employment? *Career Development for Exceptional Individuals, 32*(1), 30–41.

Halpern, A.S. (1993). Quality of life as a conceptual framework for evaluating transition outcomes. *Exceptional Children, 59*(6), 486–498.

Hetherington, S.A., Durant-Jones, L., Johnson, K., Nolan, K., Smith, E., Taylor-Brown, S., & Tuttle, J. (2010). The lived experiences of adolescents with disabilities and their parents in transition planning. *Focus on Autism and Other Developmental Disabilities, 25*(3), 163–172.

Higher Education Opportunity Act of 2008, PL 110-315.

Hughes, C., & Carter, E.W. (2012). *The new transition handbook: Strategies high school teachers use that work!* Baltimore, MD: Paul H. Brookes Publishing Co.

Hughes, C., Pitkin, S.E., & Lorden, S.W. (1998). Assessing preferences and choices of persons with severe and profound mental retardation. *Education and Training in Mental Retardation and Developmental Disabilities, 33*(4), 299–316.

Human Services Research Institute. (2014). *Working in the community: The status and outcomes of people with intellectual and developmental disabilities in integrated employment—an update.* Cambridge, MA: Author.

Hunt, P., Soto, G., Maier, J., & Doering, K. (2003). Collaborative teaming to support students at risk and students with severe disabilities in general education classrooms. *Exceptional Children, 69*(3), 315–332.

Individuals with Disabilities Education Act (IDEA) of 1990, PL 101-476, 20 U.S.C. §§ 1400 *et seq.*

Individuals with Disabilities Education Improvement Act (IDEA) of 2004, PL 108-446, 20 U.S.C. §§ 1400 *et seq.*

Jorgensen, C.M., McSheehan, M., & Sonnenmeier, R.M. (2007). Presumed competence reflected in the educational programs of students with IDD before and after the beyond access professional development intervention. *Journal of Intellectual and Developmental Disability, 32*(4), 248–262.

Kaufmann, B., & Stuart, C. (2007). *Road to self-sufficiency: A guide to entrepreneurship for youth with disabilities.* Washington, DC: National Collaborative on Workforce and Disability for Youth, Institute for Educational Leadership.

Keyes, M.W., & Owens-Johnson, L. (2003). Developing person-centered IEPs. *Intervention in School and Clinic, 38*(3), 145–152.

Kincaid, D., & Fox, L. (2002). Person-centered planning and positive behavior support. In S. Holburn & V.M. Vietze (Eds.), *Person-centered planning: Research, practice, and future directions* (pp. 29–49). Baltimore, MD: Paul H. Brookes Publishing Co.

Klein, J., & Strully, J.L. (2000). From unit D to the community: A dream fulfilled. In M.L. Wehmeyer & J.R. Patton (Eds.), *Mental retardation in the 21st century* (pp. 165–178). Austin, TX: PRO-ED.

Klein, J., Wilson, B., & Nelson, D. (2000). Postcards on the refrigerator: Changing the power dynamic in housing and assistance. In J. Nisbet & D. Hagner (Eds.), *Part of the community: Strategies for including everyone* (pp. 117–202). Baltimore, MD: Paul H. Brookes Publishing Co.

Kohler, P.D. (1996). *Taxonomy for transition planning.* Champaign, IL: University of Illinois.

Kohler, P.D., & Field, S. (2003). Transition-focused education foundation for the future. *Journal of Special Education, 37*(3), 174–183.

Kraemer, B.R., & Blacher, J. (2001). Transition for young adults with severe mental retardation: School preparation, parent expectations, and family involvement. *American Journal on Mental Retardation, 106*(2), 173–188.

Luecking, R.G., & Certo, N.J. (2003). Integrating service systems at the point of transition for youth with significant support needs: A model that works. *American Rehabilitation, 27*(1), 2–9.

Lund, S.K., & Light, J. (2007). Long-term outcomes for individuals who use augmentative and alternative communication: Part III—contributing factors. *Augmentative and Alternative Communication, 23*(4), 323–335.

Martin, J.E., Dycke, J.L.V., Christensen, W.R., Greene, B.A., Gardner, J.E., & Lovett, D.L. (2006). Increasing student participation in IEP meetings: Establishing the self-directed IEP as an evidenced-based practice. *Exceptional Children, 72*(3), 299–316.

McDonnell, J., Hunt, P., Jackson, L., & Ryndak, D. (in press). Educational standards for students with significant intellectual disabilities: A response to Lou Brown. *Connections,* Washington, DC: TASH.

McDougall, J., Evans, J., & Baldwin, P. (2010). The importance of self-determination to perceived quality of life for youth and young adults with chronic conditions and disabilities. *Remedial and Special Education, 31*(4), 252–260.

Michaels, C.A., & Ferrara, D.L. (2005). Promoting post-school success for all: The role of collaboration in person-centered transition planning. *Journal of Educational and Psychological Consultation, 16*(4), 287–313.

Miller, C.R., Hinterlong, J., & Green, A.D. (2010). Perspectives on inclusive service-learning from a state-wide model program. *School Social Work, 34*(2), 71–89.

Morningstar, M.E. (2004). *Models of work-based learning programs.* Unpublished manuscript, University of Kansas, Lawrence, KS.

Morningstar, M.E., & Lattin, D.L. (2004). Transition to the community. In C. Kennedy & E. Horn (Eds.), *Including students with significant disabilities: Putting research into practice* (pp. 282–309). Boston, MA: Allyn & Bacon.

Morningstar, M.E., Turnbull, H.R., Lattin, D.L., Umbarger, G., Reichard, A., & Moberly, R. (2001). Students supported by medical technology making the transition from school to adult life. *Journal of Developmental and Physical Disabilities, 13*(3), 229–259.

Mount, B. (2000). *Person-centered planning: A sourcebook of values, ideas, and methods to encourage person-centered development.* New York, NY: Graphic Futures.

Newman, L., Wagner, M., Cameto, R., Knokey, A.M., & Shaver, D. (2010). *Comparisons across time of the outcomes of youth with disabilities up to 4 years after high school. A report of findings from the National Longitudinal Transition Study (NLTS) and the National Longitudinal Transition Study–2 (NLTS–2).* National Center for Special Education Research.

O'Brien, J., & Forest, M. (1989). *Action for inclusion.* Toronto, Ontario, Canada: Inclusion Press.

Pearpoint, J., O'Brien, J., & Forest, M. (1993). *PATH: A workbook for planning positive possible futures and planning alternative tomorrows with hope for schools, organizations, businesses, and families* (2nd ed.). Toronto, Ontario, Canada: Inclusion Press.

Rasheed, S.A., Fore III, C., & Miller, S. (2006). Person-centered planning: Practices, promises, and provisos. *Journal for Vocational Special Needs Education, 28*(3), 47–9.

Rehabilitation Act Amendments of 1986, PL 99-506, 20 U.S.C. §§ 701 et seq.

Rogan, P., & Walker, P.M. (2007). Toward meaningful daytimes for adults with significant disabilities. In P.M. Walker & P.M.

Rogan (Eds.), *Make the day matter! Promoting typical lifestyles for adults with significant disabilities* (pp. 1–14.) Baltimore, MD: Paul H. Brookes Publishing Co.

Rowe, D.A., Alverson, C.Y., Unruh, D., Fowler, C., Kellems, R., & Test, D.W. (2013). *Operationalizing evidence-based predictors in secondary transition: A Delphi study.* Manuscript in preparation.

Ruppar, A.L., & Gaffney, J.S. (2011). Individualized education program team decisions: A preliminary study of conversations, negotiations, and power. *Research and Practice for Persons with Severe Disabilities, 36*(1),11–22.

Rutkowski, S., Daston, M., Van Kuiken, D., & Riehle, E. (2010). Project SEARCH: A demand-side model of high school transition, *Journal of Vocational Rehabilitation, 25,* 85–96.

Sanford, C., Newman, L., Wagner, M., Cameto, R., Knokey, A.-M., & Shaver, D. (2011). *The post-high school outcomes of young adults with disabilities up to 6 years after high school: Key findings from the National Longitudinal Transition Study–2 (NLTS–2).* Menlo Park, CA: SRI International.

Schalock, R.L., Borthwick-Duffy, S.A., Bradley, V.J., Buntinx, W.H., Coulter, D.L., Craig, E.M., . . . Yeager, M.H. (2010). *Intellectual disability: Definition, classification, and systems of supports* (Vol. 26). Washington, DC: American Association on Intellectual and Developmental Disabilities.

Shogren, K.A., Lopez, S.J., Wehmeyer, M.L., Little, T.D., & Pressgrove, C.L. (2006). The role of positive psychology constructs in predicting life satisfaction in adolescents with and without cognitive disabilities: An exploratory study. *Journal of Positive Psychology, 1*(1), 37–52.

Shogren, K.A., Palmer, S.B., Wehmeyer, M.L., Williams-Diehm, K., & Little, T.D. (2012). Effect of intervention with the self-determined learning model of instruction on access and goal attainment. *Remedial and Special Education, 33*(5), 320–330.

Shogren, K.A., Wehmeyer, M.L., Palmer, S.B., Rifenbark, G.G., & Little, T.D. (2013). Relationships between self-determination and postsecondary outcomes for youth with disabilities. *Journal of Special Education,* Advance online publication. doi:10.1177/0022466913489733

Stineman, R.M., Morningstar, M.E., Bishop, B., & Turnbull, R. (1993). Role of families in transition planning for young adults with disabilities: Toward a method of person-centered planning. *Journal of Vocational Rehabilitation, 3*(2), 52–61.

Targett, P., & Wehman, P. (2013). Families and young people with disabilities: Listening to their voices. In P. Wehman (Ed.), *Life beyond the classroom: Transition strategies for young people with disabilities* (5th ed., pp. 69–92). Baltimore, MD: Paul H. Brookes Publishing Co.

Test, D.W., Fowler, C.H., Richter, S.M., White, J., Mazzotti, V., Walker, A.R., . . . Kortering, L. (2009). Evidence-based practices in secondary transition. *Career Development for Exceptional Individuals, 32*(2), 115–128.

Test, D.W., Mason, C., Hughes, C., Konrad, M., Neale, M., & Wood, W.M. (2004). Student involvement in individualized education program meetings. *Exceptional Children, 70*(4), 391–412.

Test, D.W., Mazzotti, V.L., Mustian, A.L., Fowler, C.H., Kortering, L., & Kohler, P. (2009). Evidence-based secondary transition predictors for improving postsecondary outcomes for students with disabilities. *Career Development for Exceptional Individuals, 32*(3), 160–181.

Thoma, C.A., Lakin, K.C., Carlson, D., Domzal, C., Austin, K., & Boyd, K. (2011). Participation in postsecondary education for students with intellectual disabilities: A review of the literature 2001-2010. *Journal of Postsecondary Education and Disability, 24*(3), 175–191.

Thoma, C.A., Nathanson, R., Baker, S.R., & Tamura, R. (2002). Self-determination: What do special educators know and where do they learn it? *Remedial and Special Education, 23*(4), 242–247.

Turnbull, A., & Turnbull, R. (2000). Self-determination for individuals with significant cognitive disabilities and their families. *Research and Practice for Persons with Severe Disabilities, 26*(1), 56–62.

U.S. Department of Labor. (2014). *What is customized employment?* Retrieved January 20, 2014, from http://www.dol.gov/odep/categories/workforce/CustomizedEmployment/what/index.htm

Van Reusen, A.K., & Bos, C.S. (1994). Facilitating student participation in individualized education programs through motivation strategy instruction. *Exceptional Children, 60*(5), 466–475.

Walker, P.M. (2007). Promoting meaningful leisure and social connections: More than just work. In P.M. Walker & P.M. Rogan (Eds.), *Make the day matter! Promoting typical lifestyles for adults with significant disabilities* (pp. 75–90). Baltimore, MD: Paul H. Brookes Publishing Co.

Wehman, P., & Brooke, V. (2013). Vocational internships, placements, and careers: Working in the community. In P. Wehman (Ed.), *Life beyond the classroom: Transition strategies for young people with disabilities* (5th ed., pp. 309–337). Baltimore, MD: Paul H. Brookes Publishing Co.

Wehman, P., Inge, K.J., Revell, W.G., & Brooke, V.A. (2007). *Real work for real pay: Inclusive employment for people with disabilities*. Baltimore, MD: Paul H. Brookes Publishing Co.

Wehman, P., Schall, C., McDonough, J., Molinelli, A., Riechle, E., Ham W., & Thiss, W.R. (2012). Project SEARCH for youth with autism spectrum disorders: Increasing competitive employment on transition from high school. *Journal of Positive Behavior Interventions, 15*(3), 144–155.

Wehmeyer, M.L. (2005). Self-determination and individuals with severe disabilities: Re-examining meanings and misinterpretations. *Research and Practice for Persons with Severe Disabilities, 30*(3), 113–120.

Wehmeyer, M.L., Agran, M., & Hughes, C. (2000). A national survey of teachers' promotion of self-determination and student-directed learning. *Journal of Special Education, 34*(2), 58–68.

Wehmeyer, M.L., Field, S., Doren, B., Jones, B., & Mason, C. (2004). Self-determination and student involvement in standards-based reform. *Exceptional Children, 70*(4), 413–425.

Wehmeyer, M.L., & Palmer, S.B. (2003). Adult outcomes for students with cognitive disabilities three years after high school: The impact of self-determination. *Education and Training in Developmental Disabilities, 38*(2), 131–144.

Wehmeyer, M.L., Palmer, S.B., Soukup, J.H., Garner, N.W., & Lawrence, M. (2007). Self-determination and student transition planning knowledge and skills: Predicting involvement. *Exceptionality, 15*(1), 31–44.

Will, M. (1984). *OSERS programming for the transition of youth with disabilities: Bridges from school to working life*. Washington, DC: U.S. Department of Education, Office of Special Education and Rehabilitative Services.

Index

Experiential deficits, 235–236
Expression, multiple methods of, 113, 357
Expressive communication
  emerging symbolic, 444–446
  presymbolic, 445–446
  in students with sensory disabilities,
      121–122, 121t, 123t
  symbolic, 443–446
Extended level of team membership, 8
Extracurricular activities, for students with
      physical disabilities, 82–84
Eye
  anatomy of, 102, 102f
  see also Visual impairments
Eye pointing, 265
Eye tracking, 265

Face-to-face interactions, 9
Fading, 374
Families, 27–60
  in AAC device selection, 265
  abuse in, 46–47
  adaptation in, 37–39, 42–43
  in adaptations, development of, 431
  in alternate assessments, 443–444
  as collaborative team members, 12
  common characteristics of, 31–32
  communication with, 44–45, 52–56, 55t
  cultural diversity of, 44–46
  in curriculum design, 315–318
  definitions of, 31
  educators as partners of, 29–30
  encouraging involvement of, 41–42
  expectations of, 39–41
  extended, 43–44
  feeding and eating difficulties in,
      289–290
  getting acquainted with, 48–49, 48t
  laws and guidelines on roles of, 29
  meetings with, 50–52, 53t
  in program planning, 49–50
  resolving disputes with, 52, 54t
  and seizure disorders, 190
  siblings in, 35–36, 56–57
  stress and challenges in, 32–36, 289–290
  in transition planning, 468, 471,
      472f–475f
Family-centered planning
  in curriculum design, 311, 315–318
  definition of, 47–48
Family-friendly education, 47–48
Fatigue, 235
FCT, see Functional communication
    training
Feeding and eating, 273–305
  adaptive equipment for, 294, 297–299, 298f
  assessment of, 291–293

atypical patterns in, 277–287, 281b
behavior problems during, 299–302
common problems with, 275
cultural diversity and, 44
definition of, 275
positioning for, 278, 278f, 283–284,
    294–296, 295f
prevalence of problems with, 274
social aspects of, 274, 287–290, 293–294
among students with physical disabilities,
    88
team members needed to address, 290–291
treatment for problems with, 293–302
typical development of, 276–277, 277b
see also Tube feeding
Fencing pose, 278
Fine motor skills, promoting, 87
First aid training, 160–161
  see also Emergencies
Flu vaccines, 170, 171
Fluency phase of learning, 372–373, 449
Food, see Feeding and eating
Food allergies, prevalence of, 143–144
Food pocketing, 282
Food refusal, 282
Food selectivity, 282
Foreign body airway obstruction, 161–163
Formative assessment, 448–452
Foster care, 31, 32
Friends, circles of, 502
Friendships, see Social relationships
Functional communication training (FCT),
    266
Functional relevance, 311, 312
Functional skills, embedded systematic
    instruction of, 376–383
Functional vision, 103
Functional vocational evaluation, 470
Funds, of knowledge, 360

Gag reflex, 278–279
Gagging, 283–284
Gastroesophageal reflux, 282, 283
Gastrostomy tubes, 220–221, 221f
GCD, see Goals of care designation
General education core curriculum,
    318–321, 329
General education teachers
  in alternate assessments, 443
  as collaborative team members, 13
  in determining goals related to content
      standards, 329–333
  in developing participation and support
      plans, 333–341, 336b
Generalization phase of learning, 372–373,
    449
Generalized seizures, 178t, 180–181, 187, 187t